FOURTH EDITION

CRIMINOLOGY

Theory, Research, and Policy

Gennaro F. Vito, PhD
University of Louisville

Jeffrey R. Maahs, PhD
University of Minnesota Duluth

JONES & BARTLETT
LEARNING

World Headquarters
Jones & Bartlett Learning
5 Wall Street
Burlington, MA 01803
978-443-5000
info@jblearning.com
www.jblearning.com

Jones & Bartlett Learning books and products are available through most bookstores and online booksellers. To contact Jones & Bartlett Learning directly, call 800-832-0034, fax 978-443-8000, or visit our website, www.jblearning.com.

Substantial discounts on bulk quantities of Jones & Bartlett Learning publications are available to corporations, professional associations, and other qualified organizations. For details and specific discount information, contact the special sales department at Jones & Bartlett Learning via the above contact information or send an email to specialsales@jblearning.com.

10546-9

Production Credits

Executive Publisher: Kimberly Brophy
Executive Editor: William Larkin
Associate Acquisitions Editor: Marisa Hines
Associate Production Editor: Rebekah Linga
Marketing Manager: Lindsay White
Manufacturing and Inventory Control Supervisor: Amy Bacus
Composition: S4Carlisle Publishing Services
Rights & Media Research Assistant: Robert Boder

Cover and Title Page Images: Texture: © Malchev/ Shutterstock; Shooter: © Malchev/Shutterstock; Puzzle Piece: © Photodisc; Police Tape: © SkillUp/Shutterstock; Splatter: © Igor Kolos/Dreamstime.com: Title Texture: © EKy Chan/Shutterstock
Printing and Binding: RR Donnelley
Cover Printing: RR Donnelley

Library of Congress Cataloging-in-Publication Data
Vito, Gennaro F., author.
    Criminology : theory, research, and policy/Gennaro Vito and Jeffrey Maahs.—Fourth edition.
        pages cm
    Includes bibliographical references and index.
    ISBN 978-1-284-09092-5 (paper.)
    1. Criminology. I. Maahs, Jeffrey R., author. II. Title.
    HV6025.V57 2015
    364—dc23
    2015030636

6048

Printed in the United States of America
19 18 17 16 15   10 9 8 7 6 5 4 3 2 1

Gennaro F. Vito dedicates
this book to Harry E. Allen.

Jeffrey R. Maahs dedicates
this book to his family.

Brief Contents

Texture: © Malchev/Shutterstock; Puzzle Piece: © Photodisc

Texture © Maldov/Shutterstock; Puzzle Piece: © Photodisk

Contents

CHAPTER 3

Neoclassical Criminology 43

CHAPTER 4

Biology and Crime 67

CHAPTER 5

Psychology and Crime 93

Texture © Maldivi/Shutterstock; Puzzle Piece: © Photodisc

Texture: © Malchev/Shutterstock; Puzzle Piece: © Photodisc

Acknowledgments

Contributors

Special thanks to the following people for their contributions to the text:

George E. Higgins
University of Louisville
Louisville, Kentucky
Chapter 14: Cybercrime

George E. Richards
Edinboro University of Pennsylvania
Edinboro, Pennsylvania
Chapter 13: Terrorism

Reviewers

B. Keith Crew
University of Northern Iowa
Cedar Falls, Iowa

Jennifer Myers
Fairmont State University
Fairmont, West Virginia

Ed Croissant
Ybor City Campus
Tampa, Florida

Andrea J. Nichols
St. Louis Community College at Forest Park
St. Louis, Missouri

Christopher H. Hale
Southern Connecticut State University
Torrington, Connecticut

Bill W. Shaw
Northwestern State University
Natchitoches, Louisiana

Jerry Hoover
Feather River College
Quincy, California

Beth Warriner
Naugatuck Valley Community College
Rockfall, Connecticut

J. Scott Lewis
Pennsylvania State Harrisburg
Middletown, Pennsylvania

Kurt Ward
Elms College
Chicopee, Massachusetts

About the Authors

Gennaro F. Vito is Professor and Chair of the Department of Criminal Justice at the University of Louisville. He also serves as a faculty member in the Administrative Officer's Course at the Southern Police Institute and Vice Chair of degree programs. He holds a PhD in Public Administration from The Ohio State University. Active in professional organizations, he is a past President, Fellow, and was awarded the Bruce Smith Award from the Academy of Criminal Justice Sciences. He is also the recipient of the Educator of the Year Award from the Southern Criminal Justice Association (1991) and the Dean's Outstanding Performance Award for Research and Scholarly Activities from the former College of Urban and Public Affairs at University of Louisville (1990), the Dean's Award for Outstanding Research from the College of Arts and Sciences, and the President's Distinguished Faculty Award for Excellence in Research (2002). He is the author of over 100 professional, refereed journal articles (in such journals as *Criminology*, *The Journal of Criminal Law and Criminology*, *Justice Quarterly*, *Police Quarterly*, and *The Prison Journal*) and over 40 technical research reports. He has published on such topics as: capital sentencing, police consolidation, police traffic stops, policing strategies for drug problems in public housing, attitudes toward capital punishment, and the effectiveness of criminal justice programs, such as drug elimination programs, drug courts, and drug testing of probationers and parolees. He has made over 90 presentations at professional meetings, including the American Correctional Association, the International Community Corrections Association, and the Kentucky Bar Association.

Jeffrey R. Maahs is an Associate Professor in the Department of Sociology and Anthropology at the University of Minnesota Duluth. He received his BA in psychology from the University of Wisconsin-Eau Claire in 1993, an MA in criminal justice from Sam Houston State University in 1997, and a PhD in criminal justice from the University of Cincinnati in 2001. His research interests include corrections (probation outcomes, drug courts, prison privatization) and criminological theory, and he has authored numerous articles, book chapters, and agency reports in these areas.

Crime and the fear of crime have permeated the fabric of American life.

—**Warren E. Burger,** Chief Justice, U.S. Supreme Court[1]

We don't seem to be able to check crime, so why not legalize it and then tax it out of business?

—**Will Rogers**[2]

CHAPTER 1

Crime and Criminology

Objectives

- Define criminology and understand how this field of study relates to other social science disciplines. Pg. 4

- Understand the meaning of scientific theory and its relationship to research and policy. Pg. 8

- Recognize a "good" theory of crime, based on criteria such as empirical support, scope, and parsimony. Pg. 10

- Know the criteria for establishing causation and identify the attributes of good research. Pgs. 9–10

- Understand the politics of criminology and the importance of social context. Pgs. 19–20

- Define criminal law and understand the conflict and consensus perspectives on the law. Pg. 5

- Describe the various schools of criminological theory and the explanations that they provide. Pgs. 9–14

Crime is a social phenomenon that commands the attention and energy of the American public. When crime statistics are announced or a particular crime makes national headlines, the public demands that "something be done." American citizens are concerned about their own safety and that of their families and their possessions. In 2011, 48 percent of respondents felt that there was more crime than there was a year ago or less.[3] Because of the public's concern about the safety of their communities, crime is a perennial political issue that candidates for political office are compelled to address.

Dealing with crime commands a substantial portion of the country's tax dollars. In fiscal year 2011, the criminal justice system operations (police, courts, corrections) cost taxpayers over $131.8 billion—down from a peak expenditure of $138.4 billion in 2009.[4] This decline is due in part to the fact that governments and citizens have become more sensitive to the great cost of incarceration. Revision of the drug laws and their sentences have fed this decline. From 2007 to 2012, the overall state imprisonment rate fell from 447 sentenced prisoners per 100,000 population to 413 per 100,000.[5] Over the same period, the federal imprisonment rate edged higher, from 59 to 62 sentenced prisoners per 100,000.[6]

As these statistics indicate, crime is an important social issue. Further, *how* policymakers deal with crime (via crime policy) can have enormous social and financial implications. A basic tenant of this text is that a combination of theory and research can help provide direction to crime policy. The chapters in this book attempt to organize ideas in order to explain criminal behavior. This includes the factors that contribute to crime and the social reactions (including proposed and actual policies) to crime. In short, this book explores the discipline of criminology.

> ... how *policymakers deal with crime (via crime policy) can have enormous social and financial implications.*

Deviance is behavior that violates social norms.

© Cora Reed/ShutterStock, Inc.

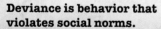

Simply put, criminology is the scientific study of crime. More broadly, Edwin Sutherland identified criminology as the study of lawmaking, law-breaking, and the response to law-breaking.[7] Some scholars further distinguish criminal justice from criminology. Here, Sutherland's definition is subdivided into two related fields, where criminology focuses on law-breaking (i.e., the nature, extent, and causes of crime), and criminal justice focuses on the response (i.e., policing, courts, and corrections) to criminal behavior. Scholars interested in criminal justice, for example, may study the causes and consequences of prison crowding or the effectiveness of different policing models. Of course, there is a relationship between criminology and criminal justice. The response to crime depends largely on one's view of the causes of crime. For this reason, many criminologists work in both of these areas.

Another discipline related to criminology is the study of *deviance*. A "deviant" is anyone who violates social norms. *Norms* are guidelines that define for members of a society the types of behaviors that are appropriate or inappropriate in certain situations. Norms are classified as folkways, mores, and laws, based largely on the response to their violation.[8] Folkways are norms against actions that may evoke a snicker or some teasing as a response (e.g., nose picking). Violations of a society's *mores* evoke a more serious response from others (e.g., teen pregnancy). *Laws* are norms that have been codified, and the response to violations comes from formal government agencies. Therefore, although some deviant behavior is criminal, deviance can also include acts (e.g., cross-dressing, membership in a motorcycle gang) that are not defined as crimes. Deviance scholars are often interested in how deviant behaviors come to be criminalized; that is, they focus on the "lawmaking" aspect of Sutherland's definition.

Criminology and Academics

Until recently, people with an academic interest in criminal behavior sought degrees in social science disciplines such as anthropology, psychology, economics, law, political science, ethics, and sociology; thus, a student might earn a degree in sociology with an emphasis on deviance and crime. Although some people still study crime through other disciplines, most universities now offer degrees in criminology or criminal justice. Moreover, many universities have separate criminology departments, divisions, or schools. In that sense, criminology has recently emerged as a distinct social science discipline.

This emergence has been partial, however, and a bit awkward. In part, this is because unlike other social science disciplines, criminology is organized around a class of behaviors (crime) rather than a particular way of understanding these behaviors. Social science disciplines tend to be organized around common assumptions, guiding insights, and specific research methodologies.[9] For example, psychologists generally seek to understand the mental processes that explain human behavior, while sociologists emphasize the role of social institutions and processes. Within any social science discipline, "crime" is only one type of human behavior that attracts interest. A psychologist might also be interested in intelligence, a political scientist in voting behavior, and a sociologist in explaining social movements. One might expect, therefore, that criminology would be multidisciplinary in nature. This is indeed the case—many disciplines have made contributions to the scientific study of crime. Some of the earliest scientific theories of crime came from biologists and psychologists. Few would dispute the fact, though, that sociology has had the largest impact on the study of crime.

Throughout most of the 20th century, sociologists were prominent in social scientific discourse about criminal behavior. The roots of this contribution can be traced to members of the sociology department at the University of Chicago. Ernest W. Burgess, W. I. Thomas, and a host of other sociologists created a body of research methodology, research findings, and theory related to crime that came to be called simply the "Chicago School of Crime."[10] During the 1930s, Edwin Sutherland, a student of the Chicago School sociologists, became the dominant advocate of criminology with his theories of differential association and white-collar crime. At about the same time, Robert K. Merton, a Columbia University sociologist, developed the sociological theory of *anomie* to explain crime. This theory has been utilized to study different forms of crime, from street crime to organized crime.

Sociological theories have provided one basis for the discipline of criminology. However, criminology is now recognized as interdisciplinary. Scholars from many disciplines, such as political science, psychology, social work, public policy, and law, and those with advanced degrees in criminal justice and criminology all contribute to criminology.

A Brief History of the Criminal Law

The criminal law has a long history, dating back over 3500 years. The first acknowledged set of laws (dated 1792 BC), the Code of Hammurabi, established the precept that the punishment should fit the crime. This code was adopted from Babylonian and Hebrew laws that existed as early as 2000 BC. The Mosaic Code of the Israelites (1200 BC) developed the laws of the Old Testament, which include the Ten Commandments.[11]

The root of American law is English common law. Common law developed from English "circuit" courts, where judges traveled from community to community hearing cases. Judges kept written records of their court decisions and initially decided cases based on prevailing community standards. Over time, these judges began to unify and standardize the legal code across different communities. To accomplish this, they used past decisions as precedents (regardless of community) for new legal disputes. Eventually, this web of legal decisions evolved into a national unified set of codes or common law.[12]

The English colonies followed common law, and after the revolution, the new federal and state governments of the United States adopted many of these laws by passing specific legislation called statutes. For this reason, most of the U.S. criminal code is considered **statutory law**. Even here, judges must interpret laws and apply them to specific circumstances; this creates **case law**. Also, where laws do not cover a particular circumstance, U.S. courts still rely on common law. Finally, the federal government and each state have separate, written constitutions that define the general organization and the powers (or limits of power) of the government. **Constitutional law** is expressed within these documents and is the supreme law of the land—the U.S. Constitution for the country and state constitutions for their respective states.[13]

Defining the Criminal Law

The substantive criminal law consists of prohibited behaviors and the possible sanctions for these behaviors. As noted previously, each state has its own criminal code, as does the federal government. Federal and state codes (as well as constitutions) are accessible on the Internet. The Legal Information Institute at Cornell Law School maintains a site that features links to all federal and state statutes.[14]

Crimes are defined by two components: the specific act (*actus reas*) and the criminal intent (*mens rea*). *Actus reas* includes the act and the circumstances under which the act occurs (e.g., the common law crime of burglary includes the breaking and entering of another's dwelling, at night, without consent). *Mens rea* refers to a person's mental state. There are different levels of criminal intent, defined by the elements of purpose, knowledge, negligence, and recklessness:[15]

- A person purposely commits a criminal act when they desire to engage in criminal conduct to cause a particular criminal result.
- To knowingly commit a criminal act, a person must know, believe, or suspect that an action is criminal.
- Criminal negligence occurs when a person grossly deviates from a standard that a reasonable person would use under the same circumstances—the

person is accused of taking a substantial and fore-seeable risk that resulted in harm.

- Criminal recklessness is the conscious disregard of a substantial risk—a person accused of recklessness is viewed as more blameworthy than someone accused of negligence.

Some offenses (e.g., traffic offenses) do not require criminal intent. These are considered strict liability offenses. Criminal behavior carries a variety of formal punishments, including imprisonment, death, fine, or probation.

There are various ways to classify crimes within the criminal law. Among the oldest is the distinction between crimes that are *mala in se* and *mala prohibita*. Mala in se crimes, considered "evil in themselves," encompass the core of the criminal code, including acts such as homicide and robbery. Mala prohibita crimes are "wrong because they are prohibited." These crimes represent a particular society's attempt to regulate behavior, such as drug abuse, gambling, and prostitution, that offends their moral senses. *Mala prohibita* offenses are likely to vary over time and across jurisdictions. For example, casino gambling is legal in several states, and many states have state-sanctioned lotteries. Similarly, the use of alcohol has shifted from legal to illegal and back to legal over time in the United States.

Another common way to classify crimes is according to the seriousness of the offense. On a general level, jurisdictions distinguish between felonies (serious crime) and misdemeanors (petty crimes). Criminal codes further categorize felonies according to degree (e.g., first-, second-, or third-degree felony offenses).

In addition to the substantive criminal law, procedural law dictates what actions actors within the criminal justice system may legally take. Procedural law dictates, for example, how police may interact with citizens (e.g., search-and-seizure law) and how criminal trials proceed (e.g., the admissibility of evidence).

The criminal law can also be distinguished from civil law. Civil law includes (among other things) contract law, property law, and tort law.[16] Among the various forms of civil law, tort law bears the strongest resemblance to the criminal law. In a tort case, an individual or group seeks compensation to redress some wrongdoing or harm. Violations of the criminal law can result in both a criminal and tort trial. For example, a person can be tried in criminal court for homicide and also in civil court for wrongful death, regardless of how the criminal trial turns out.[17]

Laws are dynamic and greatly influenced by current events, politics, economics, and numerous other external factors. Criminal law continues to change, as judges have to interpret situations associated with the emergence of new technology (e.g., computers) and new threats (e.g., terrorism). For example, the September 11, 2001, terrorist attack in the United States had a substantial impact on the law. The USA Patriot Act was passed on October 24, 2001, just 6 weeks after the events of 9/11. Although the Patriot Act amended numerous laws, the primary intent of the act was to relax the procedural laws that restrict law enforcement investigation and surveillance powers.

The U.S. Department of Justice hails the Patriot Act as an effective tool for counterterrorism efforts.[18] Critics contend that the law grants sweeping search and surveillance powers to domestic law enforcement without proper judicial oversight.[19] One of the most controversial provisions of the law is the "sneak-and-peek" search warrant, which authorizes law enforcement officers to enter private premises without the occupant's permission or knowledge and without informing the occupant that such a search was conducted.[20] The act also expanded the government's ability to view records on an individual's activities that are held by third parties (e.g., libraries, doctors, Internet service providers). Key provisions of the Patriot Act were set to expire on December 31, 2009. Amid debate about whether the act sacrifices too many civil liberties, President Barack Obama approved a 1-year extension of the act on March 1, 2010, without any alterations in its provisions.[21]

Perspectives on the Criminal Law

Criminal law serves several functions in society. First, criminal law discourages revenge, because the government, rather than the victim, is responsible for punishing law violators. Second, the law serves to express public opinion and morality; this is especially apparent for *mala prohibita* offenses. Third, punishment meted out according to criminal law serves as a warning to other citizens who may be thinking of committing the same crime.[22]

Typically, criminal law also attempts to make the punishment fit the crime. The aim is to match the severity of the punishment to the severity of the offense and the harm that it creates; thus, the punishment balances the damage caused by the crime. However, the punishment does not always fit the harm of the crime. For example, white-collar offenses often involve large sums of money and affect great numbers of people but typically result in shorter (if any) prison sentences than robbery or burglary. Another area to consider is illicit drugs relative to alcohol. By most measures, alcohol is more dangerous or harmful than marijuana. Despite this fact, marijuana is illegal while alcohol is legal. If criminal laws and the punishments for law violators do not directly reflect the harm caused to society, then what determines how a crime is punished? How do some acts come to be criminalized while others do not? Criminologists approach such questions within the framework of two general perspectives.

The consensus perspective illustrates the belief that laws are set in place to keep people from engaging in behaviors that the majority of society believes to be harmful to others and society as a whole. Consensus is defined as a general agreement, and thus, this perspective sees society as having classified specific behaviors as wrong or immoral. This consensus comes from a society's culture, which includes its beliefs, values, attitudes, and behaviors. From this perspective, criminologists would argue that laws are in place to be fair to all members of society.

In contrast to the consensus view, the **conflict perspective** portrays the law as the result of a continuous competition or "conflict" among members of society. Here, the law reflects the interests, values, and beliefs of whatever group has power. Power can come from a variety of sources, such as group size or wealth. For example, Karl Marx portrayed capitalist societies as riddled with constant competition that breeds continued conflict among its members. In Marx's analysis, conflict stems from a system of inequality that allows the wealthy elite to rule or control all other members of society. On a smaller scale, the conflict perspective sheds light on how political interest groups try to shape laws (e.g., gun control, abortion) in a way that is consistent with their beliefs and values. The preceding discussion of the controversy surrounding the USA Patriot Act also illustrates the conflict perspective in action.

> *The relationship between the victim and the offender also affects the severity of punishment as does the distance between a citizen and the law.*

These general perspectives on the law influence the research questions that criminologists ask and also help determine how they go about answering such questions. Following the consensus model generally leads criminologists to ask, "Why do some in society violate laws that exist to benefit all members of society?" The conflict perspective generally leads to questions regarding the content and enforcement of the law, such as, "Why is marijuana illegal, and how did it come to be criminalized?" Each of these perspectives appears to have some credence within a specific realm of behavior. Laws against *mala in se* offenses, such as homicide and robbery, are backed by widespread consensus. *Mala prohibita* offenses, such as gambling, prostitution, and illicit drug use, are more relevant to the conflict perspective.

Donald Black's esteemed treatise, *The Behavior of Law* (2010), lists several propositions about how the criminal justice system, specifically arrest, conviction, and sentencing, operate. To Black, law is governmental social control that is affected by social considerations: "It varies with who complains about whom, who the legal official is, and who the other parties are."[23] It varies inversely with other forms of social control. For example, a policeman is more likely to arrest a juvenile who lives with his single mother and it is probable that that same juvenile will receive a more severe sentence from a judge.

The behavior of the law also affects how individuals utilize and are treated by the criminal justice system. Among persons of different social status, a higher ranking victim is more likely to call the police when the offender has a lower rank.[24] An offender of higher rank who is convicted and sentenced, is more likely to be pardoned or paroled.[25] An investigation of a crime as well as subsequent arrest, prosecution, conviction, and punishment is more likely among wealthy victims.[26] Likewise, poor people are more likely to be arrested, prosecuted, convicted, and sentenced to prison.[27]

The relationship between the victim and the offender also affects the severity of punishment as does the distance between a citizen and the law. Black asserts that capital punishment has generally been reserved for homicides among strangers.[28] A police officer is more likely to be lenient toward someone known (friend, relative, neighbor, or fellow officer). Black's work on the behavior of law is also one on the behavior of actors in the criminal justice system.

However, studies that test Black's theory have produced mixed results. For example, studies on the police decision to arrest have partially supported Black's hypotheses. Smith found that police decision making was influenced by victim attributes. He found that the police were less likely to mobilize the law by making arrests in violent incidents involving black or female victims.[29] Regarding the decision to call the police, one study found that the poor relied on the police more than did middle-class people, and women used the law more often than men—directions not supported by Black's theory.[30]

In terms of sentencing for cocaine offenses, it was found that both blacks and Hispanics were shown to be significantly more likely to be sent to prison and charged with a felony rather than being released (compared to whites) while controlling for type of drug. This finding supports the black hypothesis that less conventional individuals will be subjected to more law than more conventional offenders. Black and Hispanic cocaine offenders were more likely to be charged with felonies and sentenced to prison than their white counterparts. However, the study also found that cocaine offenders with more prior arrests were less likely to be charged with a felony compared to being released but that those with more prior arrests were more likely to be sent to prison than released, a finding that offers mixed support for Black's theory.[31]

 ## Theories of Crime

Theory represents the foundation on which all discussion of crime is built. Unfortunately, students of criminology often struggle to understand the various theories of crime or simply find them to be boring, useless, and confusing.

The premise of this section is that when properly understood, theory can be exciting, thought provoking, and useful. This section covers basic information on theory that will allow students to understand and evaluate the discussions on crime that follow in later chapters.

Defining a Scientific Theory

There is no shortage of opinions regarding the roots of criminal behavior; news articles, movie dialogue, politicians, relatives, and friends all offer opinions on the causes of crime. Often these sources point to a single factor: drugs, violent movies, poor parenting, or bad companions. Such theories are often based on speculation or "hunches." Scientific theories of crime include many of these common-sense explanations, yet unlike a hunch, a theory of crime must explain in a logical and clear manner how such factors relate to crime.

A theory is nothing more than a set of principles or statements that attempts to explain how concepts are related. In the case of crime theory, these statements typically explain how one or more factors lead to criminal behavior. A scientific theory must also be testable, meaning that it must be stated in such a way that other scientists can go out into the real world, collect information, and test the theory's validity. If a theory is too vague or if the central concepts cannot be measured, it is essentially useless to science.

Consider, for example, the following statement: "Little green creatures that live inside peoples' brains cause them to engage in crime." Furthermore, suppose that one argues that science is unable to detect little green creatures through brain scans or other technology and that people are generally unaware of their existence. How could one test this theory? Of course, the little green creature theory is rather absurd. However, what if the words "little green creatures" were changed to "a lack of conscience," and the theory becomes

that a lack of conscience causes crime? Unless researchers devise a way to measure conscience, this will remain a theory with no scientific value, even though it may sound credible.

A theory may also be impossible to test if it is based on circular reasoning. Scientists refer to this kind of reasoning as *tautological*. Literally, a tautological theory of crime would argue that "crime causes crime." Of course, tautological statements are usually not as obvious as that and can therefore be more difficult to detect. Let us stick with the example of "a lack of conscience" as the cause of crime and think about how one might test that theory. One could argue that people who do bad things must not have a conscience. In doing so, however, one is engaging in circular reasoning: People who do "bad things" engage in criminal behavior (bad things), which is like arguing that crime causes crime.

In order for a theory to be useful then, one must be able to subject it to empirical tests. Assuming that a theory meets this minimal standard (and most do), what next? What makes one scientific theory better than another?

Evaluating Theory

A number of useful criteria are presented here for evaluating theory. An important fact to keep in mind, however, is that not all criteria are equally important. FIGURE 1-1 illustrates how different criteria relate to one another. Testability has already been covered; the remaining criteria include empirical support, scope, and parsimony.

Empirical Evidence

After a theory is determined to be testable, the next step in the evaluation process is establishing whether those tests support the theory. In other words, when this theory is applied to the real world, does it work? Does the research support this theory? The importance of this criterion cannot be overstated; if tests fail to support a theory, that theory is incorrect. It makes little sense to look at other aspects of the theory if it fails to work in the real world.

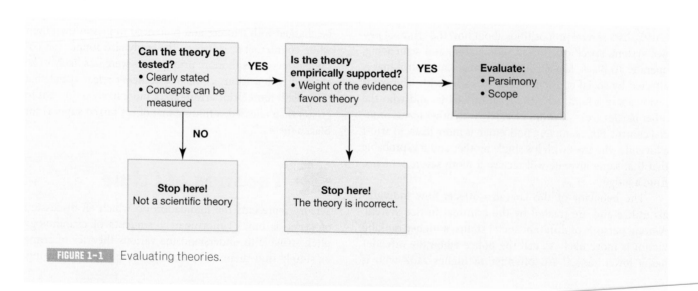

FIGURE 1-1 Evaluating theories.

Unfortunately, most theories of crime are never completely supported or refuted. Some empirical tests may support the theory, others might offer partial support, and still others may refute the theory. It may also be necessary to compare different theories against each other and consider:[32]

- The amount of empirical support (confirming evidence)
- The scope of coverage (breadth of explanation offered)
- The weight of statistical evidence

The final question suggests that not all empirical tests are the same. How much weight to put on an individual study depends on how confident the researcher is in the research design. Some research designs are better than others at demonstrating cause-and-effect relationships.

Demonstrating Cause and Effect

A number of methods are available to test theories of crime. Because most theories predict cause-and-effect relationships (e.g., poverty causes crime), a good empirical test tries to establish that certain factors have a causal relationship with crime. To clarify this point, an example may be useful. Start with a simple theory: Hanging around with criminal friends causes criminal behavior. To establish causation, a test needs to demonstrate three things:

1. Having criminal friends is related to criminal behavior.
2. Having criminal friends happens before engaging in criminal behavior.
3. The relationship between criminal friends and criminal behavior is not spurious.

The first point would be rather easy to demonstrate. Ask a group of people to report how many of their closest friends have been arrested for a crime. Also ask them to report their own criminal behavior. If those with criminal friends are more likely to engage in crime themselves, a relationship was established (mathematically, this is called a correlation). The second point, called time ordering, is a little more difficult to verify. The researcher must demonstrate that these individuals had criminal friends before they engaged in crime (i.e., the factor that does the causing must happen before the effect). Demonstrating this is important because the relationship between criminal friends and criminal behavior might be the result of criminals wanting to hang out together. In other words, engaging in criminal behavior might cause people to seek out other criminals. One way to demonstrate time ordering is to conduct a longitudinal study. The researcher could measure criminal friends at one point in time and then measure criminal behavior 6 months later and then further on in time. Assuming that the researcher can establish time ordering, they can move to the third point.

A relationship is considered spurious when, even though two things are related, one does not cause the other. For example, suppose that a survey of residents in a city revealed that "time spent in the past week riding a bicycle" was correlated (related) to engaging in vandalism. People who reported riding a bicycle were more likely to have also engaged in vandalism. Does this mean that the act of riding a bicycle caused people to vandalize property? A more plausible explanation is that younger people were more likely to ride bikes (because they do not yet have a driver's license) and vandalize property. Isolating causes of crime (and excluding spuriousness) is the most difficult challenge of doing research in criminology. How spuriousness is dealt with depends largely on research methods.

Experimental Designs

Experimental research designs are the most efficient way to establish cause-and-effect relationships and exclude spuriousness. Although there are many variations, the basic experimental design is illustrated in **FIGURE 1-2**. The key to the experimental method is the random assignment of subjects to control and experimental groups. If the sample

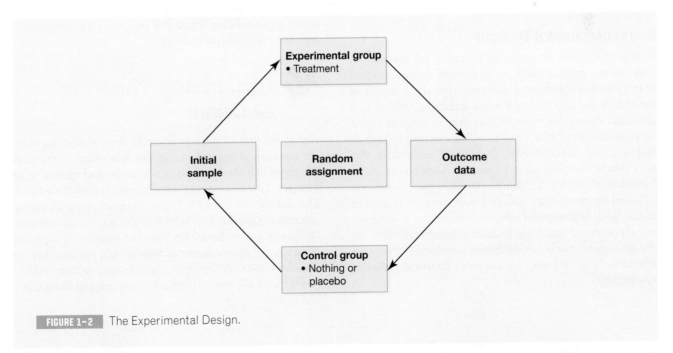

FIGURE 1-2 The Experimental Design.

is large enough, random assignment leads to groups that are equivalent on all factors, measured or not. For example, one would expect roughly the same number of males, overweight individuals, people with high IQs, and so forth in each group. The experimental group receives some form of treatment, whereas the other group, known as the control, does not.

In drug studies, participants in the control group are often given a placebo (typically a sugar pill) to exclude the possibility that subjects would report improvement simply because they received some treatment. The power of the experimental design is that the only thing that could cause differences between the two groups is the experimental treatment. Thus, if a pill designed to reduce headaches does so in the experimental group, and there is no improvement in the control group, this is very persuasive evidence that the pill works. Unfortunately, many of the factors of interest to criminologists cannot be assessed through experiments. A criminologist cannot, for example, randomly assign children to "poverty" and "no poverty" conditions and assess their criminality.

Nevertheless, some criminologists do use experimental methods to study crime. One way to test a theory is to follow its policy implications and see whether the counteracting policy that was developed actually reduces crime. For example, many sociological and psychological theories of crime identify "targets" (e.g., pro-criminal attitudes, delinquent friends) for rehabilitation programs. If changing these targets reduces crime, the theory behind the target is supported. Researchers can randomly assign offenders to either a rehabilitation program or a control group and see whether the rehabilitation program reduces future criminal behavior, or **recidivism**. Criminologists have also manipulated policing practices, using random assignment to dictate how police respond to a domestic violence dispute or how they patrol cities. Finally, researchers sometimes capitalize on natural experiments, where conditions in the environment naturally allow comparisons between two similar groups.

Nonexperimental Designs

Despite the many examples of experimental research in criminology, most research on theories of crime continues to involve nonexperimental methods. Typically, a sample of individuals are surveyed and asked questions relevant to a particular theory. For example, they may be asked to report on their attitudes, behaviors (including criminal behavior), and/or social circumstances. Sometimes researchers also have people complete tasks to measure such constructs as "impulsivity" or IQ. Criminologists also use information collected by government agencies, such as arrest records or census data. Regardless of how the information is obtained, nonexperimental methods share a common problem: although they are useful in establishing whether two things are related (correlation), they are not very efficient at excluding spuriousness.

To demonstrate cause-and-effect relationships in a nonexperimental design, the researcher must (1) identify and measure those factors that might render a relationship spurious and then (2) control for those factors in a mathematical model. For example, recall the hypothetical relationship between bicycling and vandalism. A criminologist could statistically control the effects of age. If the relationship between vandalism and bicycling disappears after this control, the relationship is spurious. The major limitation of this approach is that the researcher must identify, measure, and control for many factors that might make a relationship spurious. This limitation often leaves an empirical study open for criticism because someone can point to an important factor that was statistically controlled.

However, nonexperimental research is still worthy of consideration. Indeed, as pointed out earlier, many theoretical concepts simply cannot be studied experimentally. Furthermore, to the extent that many empirical studies (controlling each for different factors) find non-spurious relationships, one can gain confidence that the studies have identified a true cause-and-effect relationship.

Scope and Parsimony

Assuming that a theory has generated sufficient empirical support, other criteria can be applied to identify "good" theories. The related concepts of parsimony and scope are two such criteria.[33] A theory that uses only a few concepts to explain crime is better than a theory that uses many concepts. This is the principle of parsimony: the more concise explanation is preferable. Scope refers to what a particular theory can explain. A theory that explains "criminal behavior" is better than a theory that explains only "burglary committed by youth gangs." This is the principle of scope. **Grand theories** (wide scope) strive to explain all types of criminal behavior. For example, Gottfredson and Hirschi argue that their general theory of crime explains all forms of criminal behavior, in addition to similar behaviors (adultery, cigarette smoking) that are noncriminal. Combining scope and parsimony, a good theory is one that explains a lot (scope) with very few concepts (parsimony).

Organizing Theories of Crime

A student's first exposure to scientific theories of crime is often less than pleasant. Some of this frustration stems from the sense that there is evidence both for and against most theories. As seen, however, not all research studies are equal. Throughout the theory chapters, those studies with strong research designs are highlighted to give a sense of where the "weight of the evidence" lies. Another maddening aspect of theory is the sheer number of theories and authors. To help students cope with this issue, the following sections outline several ways to classify theories into meaningful categories.

Theories of "Lawmaking, Law-breaking, and Reaction to Law-breaking"

As noted earlier, Edwin Sutherland identified criminology as the study of lawmaking, law-breaking, and the response to law-breaking.[34] This definition of criminology is also a useful way to categorize the theories covered in this text. Theories of "law-breaking" are the most common and obvious. These theories seek to answer questions such as, "Why do people commit crimes?" or "What makes some countries more prone to crime than others?" Theories of lawmaking attempt to explain why some acts are outlawed whereas others are not or why legal acts become illegal over time. Theories of the response to law violations concern the criminal justice system's reaction to crime. Many "critical" theories focus on these latter two issues. Such theories might question why police arrest certain offenders and not others or why certain laws are enforced more stringently than others.

Macro- and Micro-Level Explanations

Theories can also be classified by their level of analysis. Some theories operate at the individual, or micro, level. A micro-level theory explains why some individuals engage in crime and others do not. In contrast, a macro-level theory attempts to explain differences in groups. For example, a macro-level theory might offer an explanation for why some neighborhoods have higher crime rates than others or why some countries have higher crime rates than others. A simple trick to identify whether a theory is macro or micro level is to look at what the theory predicts. If crime is expressed in "rates," then it is a macro-level theory (only a group has a rate). Most theories of crime (especially those in biology

Does having friends who are smokers cause youth to smoke or do youth who are smokers hang out together? What kind of study is necessary to answer such a question?

© BananaStock/age fotostock

and psychology) operate at the micro level, focusing on the individual offender.

Theoretical Traditions in Criminology

In some disciplines (particularly sociology), theories develop as a tradition. The basic thrust of the theory remains the same, but different authors update, revise, and change the particulars of a theory. For example, the work of Robert Merton spawned several related "strain" theories that revised or changed some of his original ideas but maintained the same core theme. These theoretical traditions are another important tool for organizing theories of crime—where relevant, how these traditions unfold is highlighted. Of course, the academic disciplines themselves offer a useful way to classify theories; for example, Chapters 4 and 5 in this text are organized around the specific disciplines of psychology and biology. On a much broader scale, students can locate theories of crime in two historical theoretical traditions: the classical and positivist schools of crime.

The Origins of Criminological Theory

When did humans first begin to devise theories to explain criminal behavior? The answer depends greatly on what qualifies as a theory. **TABLE 1-1** illustrates the major schools of thought regarding the causes of crime. Throughout much of Western history, the "demonic perspective" dominated thinking about crime and punishment.[35] Although the specifics differed according to the particular society and time, the gist of this perspective is that supernatural forces cause criminal behavior. Quite literally, people believed that the devil (or other demons) made people commit crimes. In primitive societies, crimes were viewed as acts against the gods, aided and abetted by evil spirits.[36] In that context, punishment was often designed to placate the gods.

Throughout the Middle Ages (1200–1600) in Europe, people who engaged in deviant, sinful, or criminal behavior (especially if they were women) were labeled "witches" and burned at the stake.[37] Brutal methods were often used to determine guilt or innocence. Trial by ordeal involved subjecting the accused to some form of painful torture—only God's intervention could demonstrate their innocence. For example, the suspected witch would be tied up and thrown into a body of water. If God allowed the individual to float, he or she was innocent; if not, the unfortunate person was presumed guilty and allowed to drown.[38]

Corporal punishments (e.g., gibbeting, ear clipping, drawing and

TABLE 1-1

Major Schools of Thought in Criminology

School of Thought	Cause of Crime	Implication for Criminals
Demonic perspective	Demonic possession, God's will, or other supernatural forces cause crime.	Brutal corporal punishments designed to placate the gods, cleanse the community, and identify individuals as deviant.
Classical school	Crime is the result of a rational decision based on a calculation of costs and benefits.	Swift, certain, severe punishment within the framework of a rational legal system will deter criminal behavior; Punishment should fit the crime.
Positivist school	Criminal behavior is determined by biological, social, or psychological factors outside of a person's control.	Advocate a medical model (and reject the importance of punishment). Individuals are "treated" based on the set of factors that caused them to engage in crime. The punishment (rehabilitation) should fit the individual.

quartering, dismembering, blinding, burning, and branding) were frequently used in Europe and America as late as 1700. Powerless members of society (e.g., slaves, women, and children) were often the targets of corporal punishment.[39] Mutilation and branding identified offenders and sent a message to others. The punishments also were designed to purge the body of the offender of evil and restore the community to its proper relationship with God.[40] Again, the idea here is that crime was caused largely by demonic influence. Although the "devil made me do it" is certainly an explanation of criminal behavior, it is not a scientific theory. Supernatural forces cannot be observed, and the demonic perspective (like our "little green creature" example) is therefore not testable. Toward the end of the 1700s, the demonic perspective was challenged by a group of philosophers who came to be called classical school criminologists.

The Classical School of Crime

The Age of Enlightenment burned hot in Europe during much of the 18th century. Enlightenment thinkers such as John Locke and Jean-Jacques Rousseau challenged the prevailing belief that God (or demons) directly determined human behavior. Rather, they believed that God instilled in humans the capacity to exercise free will and the ability to choose a course of behavior through reason. Scholars such as Cesare Beccaria used this general platform to argue for legal reform. In doing so, these penal reformers also articulated a scientific theory of criminal behavior.[41]

To appreciate the importance of the legal reforms advocated by Beccaria, one first needs to understand the state of the legal system at the time in which he wrote. Laws were vague, and judges often interpreted them to suit their own interests. Those accused of crimes had few legal protections. The state provided neither legal assistance nor access to family and friends and commonly used torture to obtain confessions.

Witnesses testified against the accused in secret proceedings. Punishments for those found guilty included whipping, branding, mutilation, and death by various means.[42,43]

Rebelling against the brutal and arbitrary nature of the legal system, Beccaria argued that the function of law was to promote justice.[44] In his 1764 essay "On Crimes and Punishments," he formulated the following principles, which represented a dramatic departure from the way in which criminal law had previously been conceived:[45,46]

- Prevention of crime is more important than punishment for the crime committed. Punishment is desirable only as it helps to prevent crime and does not conflict with the ends of justice.
- The purpose of punishment is to deter persons from the commission of crime, not to give society an opportunity for revenge.
- Desirable criminal procedure calls for the open publication of all laws, speedy trials, humane treatment of the accused, and the abolishment of secret accusations and torture. Moreover, the accused must have every right and facility to bring forward evidence.
- The criminal code should be written with all offenses and punishments defined in advance.
- The criminal law should be restricted in its scope because it can result in the curtailment of freedoms.
- The presumption of innocence should be the guiding principle at all stages of the justice process; individual rights must be protected.

Beccaria deserves much credit for "pulling together many of the most powerful 18th century ideas of democratic liberalism" and connecting them to issues of criminal justice.[47] His ideas directly influenced the American Bill of Rights as well as the Declaration of the Rights of Man and Citizen, the precursor to the French Constitution of 1791.[48] The linchpin that holds together all of Beccaria's legal reforms was the argument that a properly designed legal system had the potential to prevent or deter criminal behavior. Beccaria believed that because humans were rational, they would consider the consequences of their behavior before acting. Swift, certain, and sufficiently harsh punishment should therefore deter a rational actor from engaging in crime. Beccaria argued that punishment should only be severe enough to deter crime and denounced the use of the death penalty.49

Another influential scholar and reformer of the classical school of criminology was Jeremy Bentham, who embraced Beccaria's ideas and made contributions to his deterrence theory. Specifically, Bentham described human decision making as a **hedonistic calculus**. In other words, people will act in ways that maximize positive outcomes and minimize negative ones. Naturally, a person commits a crime because of the perception that the benefits of the act are greater than the costs of punishment. The corollary to this is that punishment should be painful enough to outweigh the pleasure of the criminal act.

Like Beccaria, Bentham believed that the purpose of punishment should be crime prevention and that punishment must be proportional to the severity of the crime to have a deterrent effect. Moreover, the severity of punishment should be directly proportionate to the number of persons injured by the crime. Although some of their ideas are taken for granted today, classical theorists were liberal reformers who sought to restate the definitions of crime and to reformulate punishments. Their proposed legal reforms were revolutionary—a complete break with customary practices. As a theory of crime, the classical school idea of deterrence is relatively simple: People will refrain from crime if punishment is swift, certain, and sufficiently severe. Because empirical tests of this proposition are possible, it represented a dramatic departure from the demonic perspective. Classical school theory dominated criminological thought into the late 1800s, until it was challenged by a new group of theorists.

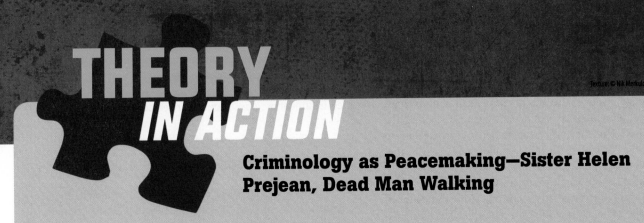

THEORY IN ACTION

Texture: © Nik Merkulov/Shutterstock, Inc.

Criminology as Peacemaking—Sister Helen Prejean, Dead Man Walking

The death penalty is the ultimate weapon in the war on crime—it personifies the violent response of the criminal justice system to crime. Sister Helen Prejean, a Roman Catholic nun in Louisiana, has committed herself to stand against the death penalty. Her actions demonstrate the commitment that criminology as peacemaking requires—service to both offenders and victims—and serve as a classic example of applied criminology. Her work as a spiritual advisor to condemned men was documented in her book, *Dead Man Walking,* and in an Academy Award–nominated movie by the same name. It was also the basis for an opera. The book was on the *New York Times* Best Seller List for 31 weeks and was nominated for a Pulitzer Prize. Over the span of 15 years, she has witnessed five executions and accompanied three men to the electric chair. One received a life sentence on appeal.

Her personal journey has encouraged many people to rethink their position on the death penalty. To Sister Helen, the death penalty embodies "the three deepest wounds of our society: racism, poverty, and violence." It led her to consider not only the plight of the death row inmate but also that of the families of their victims. She recognized that the families of the victims and the inmates shared one element— they were abandoned by friends and family. As a result, she

founded Survive, a victim's advocacy group, and works closely with other groups such as Murder Victims' Families for Reconciliation.

She has received two of the highest honors bestowed on American Catholics—the Vision 2000 Award from Catholic Charities USA and the Laetare Medal from the University of Notre Dame for illustrating the ideals of the church—as well as eight other peace awards. She has also been nominated for the Nobel Peace Prize. Her second book, *The Death of Innocents*, analyzes how flaws in the death penalty system allow innocent people to be executed.

Sources: Helen Prejean official website. Retrieved May 17, 2014, from http://www.sisterhelen.org/; Prejean, H. (1994). *Dead man walking.* New York: Vintage; Prejean, H. Would Jesus pull the switch? Retrieved March 11, 2010, from http://salt.claretianpubs.org/issues/deathp/prejean.html; Prejean, H. (2004). *The death of innocents.* New York: Random House. *See also;* Bingham, A., Cochran, J. K., Boots, D. P., & Heide, K. M. (2011). Public support for preventive/corrective remedies against miscarriages of justice in capital cases. *Justice Quarterly, 30,* 4, 594–618.

The Positivist School of Crime

The influence of the classical school of criminology began to wane in the late 1800s. One reason for this decline was that changes in the legal system based on classical theory failed to reduce crime (i.e., crime rates continued to increase).[50] More importantly, the underlying assumption of the classical school—that behavior was the result of rational calculation—was criticized for being too simplistic. Throughout the 1700s, scientists such as Galileo and Newton made great discoveries about the workings of the physical world. These demonstrations of cause-and-effect relationships were made through careful observation and analysis of natural events. It was not long before scholars applied this scientific method beyond the physical world to the social world. In criminology, the use of the scientific method to study the causes of crime was known as positivism.[51]

The history of scientific inquiry into criminal behavior is uneven—several pioneers in scientific criminology predate Auguste Comte's positivism. For example, Benjamin Rush (United States) and Philippe Pinel (France), writing in the late 1700s, argued that serious, repeat criminal behavior was caused by "moral insanity," a mental disease.[52] Despite these early efforts to scientifically study crime, positivism did not gain wide acceptance until the mid-1800s. During this time, for example, Charles Darwin's *Origin of Species* (1859) outlined the theory of evolution.

Influenced by Darwin's theory of evolution, the first widely acknowledged positivist theories of crime focused on biology. For example, phrenologists like Franz Joseph Gall studied the pattern of bumps on the skull and attempted to correlate them to criminal behavior. Cesare Lombroso, building off Darwin's theory of evolution, argued that some criminals were evolutionary throwbacks to a more primitive species. Over time, biology gave way to a psychology/psychiatry focus on "feeble-mindedness" and mental disease. During the 20th century, sociological positivism dominated criminology and found causes of crime in social factors such as learning experience and poverty.

Regardless of the particular discipline or historical time frame, positivist theories share some commonality. Positivists are committed to the use of the scientific method to study the causes of crime. They emphasize methodological issues such as proper data collection, statistical sampling, and the validity and reliability of measurement.[53] Criminologist C. Ray Jeffery outlined several other precepts of positivist criminology and contrasted them with the classical school. According to Jeffery, the positivist school advocated the following:[54]

- A rejection of punishment and its replacement with treatment based on the medical (rehabilitation) model.
- A rejection of free will and its replacement with scientific determinism.
- A rejection of the study of criminal law and its replacement with a study of the individual offender and his or her medical, psychological, and social characteristics.

The positivist school of crime, like the classical school, had a great deal of influence on the operation of the criminal justice system. In the United States, rehabilitation (the medical model) emerged as a primary goal of the justice system during the early 1900s. The underlying assumption of the medical model is that the factors that make a criminal can be identified and treatment plans can be formulated and administered to rehabilitate them. In the medical model, the offender is viewed as a patient to be treated, not an evildoer to be punished. The "rehabilitative ideal" involved isolating and correcting, within each individual, the specific deficits that led to his or her criminal behavior. In that sense, the punishment must fit the offender, rather than the offense.[55]

Although rehabilitation remained the dominant goal of corrections throughout much of the 1900s, the medical model was never fully realized. The seriousness of the crime (and not the nature of the criminal), for example, remained the primary determinant of the punishment. In other words, the punishment still tended to "fit the offense." Still, the rise of rehabilitation produced a number of innovations that remain part of the current criminal justice system. For example, many states embraced indeterminate sentencing, where offenders were incarcerated without a firm release date (e.g., 20 years to life). Parole boards emerged as a way to judge when offenders, based on their treatment progress, should be released.

The Classical and Positivist Schools—Where Do We Stand Now?

The positivist school of criminology has dominated theorizing since it replaced the classical school. Classical school theorizing, however, made a comeback in the 1970s. A number of theories derived from the classical school (called neoclassical theories) now compete with positivist theories for acceptance.

 Crime Policy

A tenet of this book is that theory and policy are intimately related. To be sure, criminology is an "applied" social science. In other words, criminologists investigate crime in order to generate practical solutions to the problem. Theory and research on the causes of crime and criminal behavior can provide information that can be used either to prevent crime from occurring or to lessen its impact on society.

The applied nature of criminology is illustrated by the research questions that are

> *In other words, criminologists investigate crime in order to generate practical solutions to the problem.*

addressed in criminological research. Gibbs identified four major questions that criminologists traditionally attempt to answer:[56]

1. Why does the crime rate vary?
2. Why do certain individuals and not others commit crimes?
3. Why is there variation in reactions to alleged criminality?
4. What are the possible means of controlling criminality?

The fourth question specifically deals with crime policy. Note, though, that the answer to the fourth question depends largely on responses to the first two questions. In other words, if one knows what causes crime, one is better able to develop effective policies.

Similarly, Canton and Yates contend that criminology can inform criminal justice policy and practice by answering three key questions:[57]

1. What is to be done with offenders?
2. What is to be done about crime?
3. What is to be done for (or on behalf of) victims of crime?

Theory, coupled with sound research, should help guide policymaking throughout the criminal justice system. Empirically supported theory can provide clues for the passage of legislation and the sound operation of social programs. To proceed without theoretical guidance is to take a shot in the dark—there is no logical basis to assume that a particular program will work. Policy prescriptions based on theories that are not supported empirically are also unlikely to work. Unfortunately, crime policy often violates these principles; programs with little theoretical guidance emerge time and again. Thus, students need to be prepared with a firm grounding in theoretical criminology and an understanding of how these theories can be applied to policy and practice in criminal justice.[58]

Policy Without Theory—The Case of Intensive Supervision

To illustrate the need to link theory with policy, consider the highly praised intensive supervision programs (ISPs). These programs reflect the belief that probation/parole officers can do a better job of monitoring and supervising high-risk offenders if the officers' caseloads are smaller. ISPs emerged in the 1980s as a potential solution to the crowding problem in U.S. jails and prisons. One attractive feature of intensive supervision is that it pleases people with conflicting views. ISPs promise to increase surveillance (protect society), provide more treatment, and reduce the size of jail and prison populations—yet, the emergence of intensive supervision took place in "the absence of any true theory that more supervision will lead to lower recidivism rates."[59]

Research on intensive supervision initially found that it led to higher rates of probation revocation and had little influence on recidivism.[60] In fact, had ISP supporters reviewed research from the 1960s, they would have discovered that lowering probation caseloads did not reduce recidivism.[61] Although research on ISPs was largely negative, it did provide information that suggested conditions under which these programs might be more successful. In particular, the rehabilitative aspects of the program (providing better services and referrals) have proven effective.[62] ISPs that implemented the suggested changes achieved reductions in recidivism rates.[63,64]

Theoretically Informed Policy: The Case of Multisystemic Therapy

In contrast to ISPs, multisystemic therapy (MST) is based explicitly on well-known and empirically supported theories of crime. Developed by psychologist Scott Henggeler and his associates, MST is a community-based treatment program that targets many known causes of delinquency and crime. The targets of MST are drawn from several empirically supported theories of crime, including social learning theory, social control theory, and cognitive theory. Examples of treatment targets include parental supervision and discipline, antisocial attitudes, association with delinquent peers, and the mix of rewards and punishments for antisocial behavior.[65] MST has accumulated a track record of success, reducing crime substantially among serious/chronic offenders, including inner-city juvenile delinquents, adolescent sex offenders, and abusive parents. This track record has led some scholars to conclude that MST is perhaps the best treatment option available to reduce recidivism.[66]

How has MST achieved this success? Part of the answer lies in the structure of the program: MST therapists receive extensive training and support and are held accountable for the progress (or lack thereof) of offenders. Also, treatment plans are individualized to the needs/problems of each offender, and each treatment has multiple targets for change. A central reason for success, however, is that MST identifies known (from theory and empirical research) causes of delinquency and targets these factors for change. For example, parental discipline is a key factor in several theories of crime, and empirical research consistently demonstrates that lax supervision and harsh/inconsistent punishment promote delinquency. Therefore, theory dictates that improving the disciplining skills of the parents of delinquents should lead to a reduction in recidivism.

Limitations of Criminological Research

One purpose of research is to validate or test the accuracy of theories, yet the most common conclusion of criminological research is that more information on a given subject is needed before any definite conclusions can be drawn. There are at least three reasons for this.

First, criminology is a part of the research tradition in sociology. One norm of sociological research, established primarily by German sociologist Max Weber (1864–1920) is that the research and its results should be value free. Weber contended that if researchers sought definite conclusions, their work could be biased by their desire to achieve certain results. The primary aim of sociological research was to generate accurate, unbiased, and objective data—not to draw conclusions. As a result, some criminological studies do not contain policy recommendations on crime.

Second, most criminological studies are based on limited data. Because all statistical analyses of a given sample reflect probabilities, a small sample increases the chance of drawing erroneous conclusions. The possibility always exists that the conclusions based on a single study are wrong and that the patterns found in the sample being studied may not truly exist in the general population. The possibility of inaccurate findings causes criminologists to be cautious.

Third, criminological studies are not always methodologically sound. For example, Robert Martinson reviewed studies and research reports published between 1945 and 1967 on the effectiveness of correctional treatment. He included only those studies that met the following methodological criteria: "[They] had to employ an independent measure of the improvement secured by that method, and [they] had to use some control group, some untreated individuals with whom the treated ones could be compared."[67] Reviewing over 20 years of research, Martinson found only 231 studies that met these basic standards of research. Based on this information, the "Martinson report" reached this now-famous conclusion: "With few and isolated exceptions, the rehabilitative efforts that have been reported so far have had no appreciable effect upon recidivism."[68]

A related research problem is **overgeneralization**, which relates to the scope of the applicability of the research findings.[69] Martinson's own pessimistic conclusion on offender rehabilitation ("Nothing works!") is an example of an overgeneralization—one that he later recanted.[70–72] Reviews of rehabilitation programs have shown success in the treatment of offenders.[73–75] Latessa asserts that correctional programs have become more evidence based and that correctional research can be used to implement change and improve programs while holding both offenders and administrators accountable for performance.[76] Unfortunately, overgeneralization is far from uncommon—two additional examples include research on felony probation and domestic violence.

Studies of Felony Probation

Another example of overgeneralization is the study by Rand Corporation researchers of felony probation in California.[77] They reached the widely publicized conclusion that these offenders represented a threat to public safety. Rand reported that 65 percent of felony probationers (offenders placed on probation based on a felony-level offense) were rearrested within 2 years of their release. What the media neglected to report was that the sample under study was not representative of the overall California felony offender population. Moreover, the California results could not reflect felony probation recidivism rates across the nation. Indeed, replications of this study reported much lower rearrest rates, ranging from 22 to 43 percent.[78–83] Replication of research can determine whether findings and their policy implications are stable over time and place. Despite these conflicting replications, the Rand study was used to justify the creation of intensive supervision programs.

Experiments on the Impact of Mandatory Arrest in Domestic Violence Cases

A third example of overgeneralization occurred with domestic violence experiments. Lawrence Sherman has conducted several studies on the impact of arrest in domestic violence cases. In the first study, suspects in Minneapolis were randomly assigned to one of three potential responses by the police: (1) arrest, (2) threat of arrest (with the suspect leaving the home), and (3) a "talking to" by the police (with the suspect left at the scene).[84] The results supported the use of arrest in domestic violence cases as a way to protect the victim. The suspects who were arrested had the lowest rate of recidivism.[85,86]

This literature on the effectiveness of arrest in domestic violence incidents has also been questioned.[87] The findings of the studies may have differed due to the fact that the definition of a domestic violence relationship and the type of police response differed in each study[88] and failed to show the effects of arrest on prosecution and conviction.[89]

Nevertheless, the Sherman study had a dramatic impact on policing in domestic violence cases. Although the authors were careful to recommend against the passage of mandatory arrest laws until further research was conducted, the results of the Minneapolis experiment contributed to the passage of such laws in 15 states by 1991.[90] The study was replicated (repeated with the same method in a different location) in Omaha,[91] Charlotte,[92] and Milwaukee[93,94] with dissimilar results. Arresting domestic violence suspects in both Omaha and Charlotte was no more effective than other methods of handling the case (e.g., citation or advisement).

In Milwaukee, Sherman and his colleagues specifically examined the impact of arrest on domestic violence cases in poverty-stricken inner-city areas. The authors concluded that short-term arrest might even cause harm by increasing anger at society without increasing the fear of rearrest.[95]

Sherman and Berk have been severely criticized for the impact of their studies on public policy in domestic violence cases. Critics have chastised the researchers for failing to acknowledge that the use of arrest in domestic violence cases failed to achieve the desired result upon replication. They also note that the Minneapolis study resulted in a "dramatic change in public policy with potentially substantial negative effects on many people and an unwarranted large expenditure of public monies."[96] Sherman[97] and Berk[98] countered these objections by noting that three of the six experiments provided some evidence of deterrence and that they always fully listed the policy limitations of the findings of the studies.

As these examples suggest, criminological studies must be interpreted with caution. Sound policy should only follow accurate research. Research should be replicated in other locations to be certain that results generated in one area apply to others. The value of replication is underscored by Sherman and Harris' 23-year follow-up of the Milwaukee domestic violence experiment. They found that arrested suspects in the experiment were almost three times more likely to have died as the result of homicide than the suspects originally assigned to a warning. There was no evidence that these suspects died at the hands of their former victims, but the findings illustrate that long-term replications of such policies may be in order.[99] For these reasons, criminologists are often reluctant to reach definite conclusions based on their studies.

> As these examples suggest, criminological studies must be interpreted with caution.

Theory Versus Streetwise Criminology

Students are often frustrated by the failure of criminology to provide certain and clear-cut answers to the crime problem. This frustration also promotes the view that theory is both illogical and impractical. Jeffery has accurately portrayed this attitude:[100]

Theoretical courses are characterized as useless. "I want some course material that is relevant," is the usual student response to the curriculum. When one asks, "What is relevance?" it turns out to be vocational training in being a police [officer] or a corrections officer.

Clearly, these students are saying that "street smarts" are more valuable than "book knowledge" of criminal behavior. One exemplar of this type of thinking is the student who has worked or is working in the criminal justice system and who believes that the only legitimate source of knowledge is experience. Carter summarizes the argument:[101]

Nothing personal, but most professors don't know what they are talking about. They sit on campus putting out all this good shit about rehabilitation and causes of crime. Most of them haven't ever been on the street and if you want to know what's happening, you have to be on the street. Instead of telling us about crime, we ought to be telling them. If they would spend a couple of days with us, they might find out what's happening. No, they don't want to do that. It might upset all their theories.

Indeed, this belief is not limited to students. In academia, one of its most vocal and visible adherents is George Kirkham. His experience as "the professor who became a cop" led him to first gently admonish his colleagues to observe firsthand the problems of police officers before criticizing them.[102] He later turgidly stated that a "criminologist would not know a criminal if one bit him on the ass."[103]

Another source of the street-smarts bias stems from what Carter calls the Dick Tracy Mentality. This mindset is characterized by several beliefs:[104]

- The crime fighter is no mere mortal but, rather, a super crime fighter.
- The criminal is distinctive, unique, readily identifiable, and different (from a "normal" person).
- There are two kinds of people in society—good guys and bad guys.

A corollary view holds that theoretical statements represent attempts to provide a defense for criminals. The reality, however, is that criminological theory attempts to explain—rather than excuse—criminal behavior.

Still another version of this mentality can be bluntly called the "asshole theory" of crime, by which police officers guide their actions in specific situations. "Assholes" commit crimes that are motiveless, completely senseless, or otherwise irrational. Carter relates this statement by a police officer/student:[105]

I've heard all the theories of crime. Let me tell you, crime is caused by assholes. That's the asshole theory. If you want to check that, come out on the street. See it like it is.

Readers of this text, however, will discover that theory does not always clash with street knowledge. In fact, theory is often verified by experience. In fact, other studies of the police view of crime causation demonstrate that they often view their experiences through the lens of criminological theory. For example, Wesley's examination of police opinions found that they tended to view offenders as: (1) victims of their deprived environment, (2) morally weak or deficient, (3) biologically deficient, or (4) shrewed and intelligent operatives.[106] Similarly, a study of college police officers reported that they tended to view campus crime as the result of a combination of an environment that presents attractive criminal opportunities and an absence of social control among the students.[107] Thus, the library attracts thieves because students fail to protect their laptops and other property when in that location.[108] Students engage in subtance abuse and underage drinking because they want to have fun and have escaped the control of their parents.[109] In this case, the officers' observations are a reflection of theories of rational choice and social control that are presented later in this text (see Chapters 3 and 7).

The Utility of Criminological Theory

Yet, a good deal of frustration exists over the apparent inability of criminology to solve the crime problem. Indeed, serious questions about the utility of criminological theory have arisen. Mary Tuck asserts the following:[110]

Many argue that criminological theories have changed so wildly over the years—that criminologists have often provided "the wrong" advice about policies now claimed to be "right." They have argued for rehabilitative custody and against it, for longer sentences and against them; criminology both created the treatment model and destroyed it. As for "the causes of crime"—you are as aware as I am that "you pay your money and you take your choice." Even on supposedly narrow practical questions . . . criminologists speak with no single voice.

As Austin indicates, when Congress and state legislatures consider crime legislation, their first question is not: "What do the criminologists think?"[111] However, Tuck also suggests that policies cannot proceed directly from any one criminological theory. They emerge from debate—"the gradual working out of disagreement and contradiction."[112]

Similarly, Joan Petersilia believes that this problem stems from the development of criminology into an academic discipline. As academics, she argues, criminologists have lost touch as they pursue theories rather than deal with day-to-day realities. As a result, they often lose sight of the value of practical applications. Like Tuck, Petersilia asserts that research can be an unimpeachable guide to policy. She argues that criminologists should strive for "research [that] is more likely to influence the way policymakers think about problems than to provide solutions 'off the shelf.'"[113] Furthermore, she urges criminologists to make clear the policy implications of their research findings. As noted throughout this text, this is not an easy task, but it is certainly essential if criminology is to stay relevant.

Criminology must also abandon the pretense of value-free research and state how findings can be best applied in real-world situations. There is a rich tradition to draw from in this regard. From Beccaria and Bentham, Shaw and McKay, to Cloward and Ohlin, criminologists have developed theories to meet the problems of the day and have sought to apply them. As James Gilsinan has aptly noted, "criminological theory has never been confined to the ivory tower."[114] Policy and criminology have a symbiotic relationship that forms a significant link with research. Clearly, each cannot function effectively in isolation. Theory organizes thoughts about crime and its causes; research tests the validity of theory. Policy is fed by both theory and research.

Tonry[115] presents the history of the relationship between criminal justice policy and research evidence. Although the President's Crime Commission promoted the development of criminal justice education and produced several reports on the operations of the criminal justice system, resulting criminal justice policies have not always been evidence based. As in the case of other disciplines, Tonry[116] notes, "research evidence seldom influences policy or practice directly." When it does, the adoption of research evidence into policy is due to "windows of opportunity."[117] These windows of opportunity are dependent upon: (1) the filter of prevailing paradigms and ways of thinking, (2) prevailing ideology, (3) short-term political considerations, and (4) short-term bureaucratic considerations and inertia.[118] Thus, the deaths of basketball player Len Bias, Megan Kanka, and Polly Klaas led to the implementation of harsh penalties for cocaine violations, sex offenders, and career criminals.

Gibbs declares that criminologists must take up the question of crime control and prevention:[119]

> *No scientific enterprise will be supported indefinitely unless it benefits someone other than the scientists, and perhaps much of criminology's support stems from a concern with crime prevention. There is simply no justification for the indifference of theorists to attempt to prevent criminality, including delinquency.*

Criminology must return to its roots as an applied social science. The complex nature of the crime problem demands that policy implications be developed through criminology.

The Demise of the Criminological Imagination?

Frank Williams has decried the "demise of the criminological imagination." He cites three major reasons for this decline. First, there is a lack of critical analysis of both issues and actions; for example, a theory that explains homicide may not apply to serial or mass murder. How can social learning theory provide an explanation for such disparate crimes as computer theft, insider stock trading, and domestic violence? Is it possible that the nature of crime is changing so rapidly that some criminological theories are no longer applicable without modification or even replacement?[120]

Second, Williams criticizes the overconcentration of criminology on empiricism—quantitative, multivariate analyses of large data sets. The recent trend of training criminologists to emphasize quantitative skills "has raised methodology and large data sets above theory development."[121] Intuitive skills—the very skills needed to determine the policy implications of any given research findings—are thus not developed. One

> **Criminology must also abandon the pretense of value-free research and state how findings can be best applied in real-world situations.**

wonders how well the work of Sutherland, Sykes, Matza, and other qualitative analysts would be accepted today. Is quantitative analysis the only route to scientific validity?

Like Petersilia, Williams blames the demise of criminological theory on the emergence of criminal justice as an academic discipline. Williams claims that the discipline emphasizes how the criminal justice system responds to crime—therefore, it ignores the behavior of criminals. Naturally, one can take exception to this characterization. Academicians in criminal justice programs may be more concerned with questions of management (efficiency and effectiveness of policies and programs), but many of them are or were practitioners or have their academic training in applied areas (e.g., public administration).[122]

Similarly, L. Edward Wells notes that research and policy seem to "control the development of limited theories chosen to suit practical contingencies."[123] New models that promote deterrence and incapacitation have not been supported by research, but they are still favored because they "are closer to political sensibilities and more consistent with what people feel should be true."[124]

Politics: The "Left" and "Right" of Criminal Justice Policy

Although scientists often attempt to offer "value-neutral" theories and research, the reality is that science occurs within the political landscape of a society. Crime has been a major campaign issue in almost every presidential election since 1964, and most victors have made criminal justice policy a central theme in their administrations. For example, consistent with his aim of creating a "Great Society" through civil rights legislation and a war on poverty, President Lyndon Johnson made fighting crime an integral part of his programs. Democrats Johnson, and later Jimmy Carter, were guided by the promise of distributive justice: that increased economic opportunity is the best defense against crime. President Bill Clinton emphasized community policing—an approach that attempts to foster closer relationships between police and citizens. In contrast to this liberal tradition, Republicans such as Richard Nixon, Gerald Ford, Ronald Reagan, and George H. W. Bush generally took the more conservative law and order stance against crime, emphasizing individual responsibility, deterrence, and retribution.[125]

Each president was aware of the political capital that could be generated by addressing the crime problem, and each dealt with the issue in ways that reflected his own political ideologies. For example, as part of his campaign to promote a new federalism, Nixon cut the strings attached to the Law Enforcement Assistance Administration funds, allowing state and local governments to decide spending priorities. Ford established career criminal prosecution programs. In accord with his populist views, Carter stepped up federal efforts to apprehend and prosecute white-collar criminals. Reagan denounced liberal spending programs as destructive to individual values and made the fight against violent crime a priority of his administration. President George H. W. Bush derailed Democratic nominee Michael Dukakis' bid for the presidency with his infamous Willie Horton ads that painted Dukakis as a liberal who was more concerned with the rights of criminals than their victims. Horton was a convicted murderer who committed a violent rape and murder while on furlough from a Massachusetts prison. During his presidency, George H. W. Bush continued the Reagan administration's war on drugs. After the September 11, 2001, tragedies, President George W. Bush made terrorism his crime priority through the creation of the Department of Homeland Security.

For all of the rhetoric, however, crime policy is not a distinct entity. Criminal justice policy does not drive any administration's programs; rather, it follows the same themes as other social policies—it fits within a political ideology.[126] Ideology is a set of relatively unquestioned assumptions about how the world works. Walter Miller outlined the "crusading issues and general assumptions" of both conservatives and liberals regarding crime.[127] Conservative politicians tend to view crime as a "bad choice" made freely by an offender. Conservatives therefore view the criminal as directly responsible for his or her own behavior. Their ideology is consistent with the classical school of crime.

Furthermore, traditional conservative values include discipline and respect for authority. Therefore, they see the following as the most important causes of crime:[128]

- Excessive leniency toward lawbreakers
- Emphasis on the welfare and rights of lawbreakers at the expense of the welfare and rights of victims, law enforcement officials, and law-abiding citizens
- Erosion of discipline and respect for authority
- Excessive permissiveness in society

In contrast, liberals are generally dissatisfied with the present social order and emphasize dysfunctional elements of the criminal justice system such as the following:[129]

- Overcriminalization
- Labeling and stigmatization
- Overinstitutionalization
- Overcentralization of authority
- Discriminatory bias, especially racism and sexism

The schism between left and right is reflected not only among politicians but among criminologists as well. On the right, the neoclassical school has a common interest in dealing with predatory crimes and substantially less interest in the "root causes" of crime that have entertained the more liberal social determinists for so long. The neoconservatives are concerned more with dealing with the symptoms and intermediate correlates of social problems than in affecting major changes in the social fabric of society.[130]

As noted previously, the neoclassical school has influenced criminal justice policy in several areas, particularly with respect to career criminal laws and incapacitation. One leading advocate of this point of view is James Q. Wilson. In the provocative book *Thinking About Crime*, Wilson argues that the typical causal analysis of sociologists has nothing to do with policy analysis:[131]

Causal analysis attempts to find the source of human activity in those factors which themselves are not caused, which are, in the language of sociologists, "independent variables." Ultimate causes cannot be the object of policy efforts precisely because, being ultimate, they cannot be changed.

Policy analysis considers only the condition that the government wishes to create. Its focus is on current circumstances, and its purpose is identifying the forces the government can marshal to bring the desired state into being.

In fact, Wilson declares that there is no reason for criminologists to be policy analysts.[132] He believes the policy analyst should ignore the study of the causes of crime and instead focus on the manipulation of objective conditions because "the only instruments society has by which to alter behavior in the short run require it to assume that people act in response to the costs and benefits of alternative courses of action."[133] Thus, Wilson advocates such policies as the incapacitation of career criminals, a return to foot patrols by police, and the continued criminalization of drugs.

Left-leaning criminologists identify with the positivist school of crime and seek the root causes of criminal behavior. Liberal criminologists also attempt to debunk the assumptions that inform the conservative law and order ideology in the United States.[134-136] A leading critic of conservative criminology is Elliot Currie. He considers crime a symptom of such social problems as child poverty and abuse/neglect, inadequate public services, and economic inequality. As a result, Currie calls for the following reforms:[137]

- We should move to reduce inequality and poverty.
- We should move toward crime prevention rather than incapacitation. Prevention priorities include preventing child abuse, enhancing children's intellectual and social development, and providing support to vulnerable adolescents.
- We should work toward a genuinely supportive national family policy.
- We should begin assuming greater responsibility for the economic and social stability of local communities.
- We need to learn more about how to create comprehensive strategies for high-risk communities and understand why some societies have lower crime rates than others.[138-140]

Clearly, politics cannot be divorced from policymaking. Ideas from the left and the right will always shape criminology research, theories of crime, and crime policy. The value of science, however, is that theories of crime from both the left and the right are subject to the same empirical scrutiny. There is much to be learned, however, about how policy is made and implemented within a political context.[141]

 # The Influence of Social Context: The "Martinson Report" as a Case Study

As the preceding discussion of ideology and politics makes clear, science does not operate in a completely objective, value-neutral environment. Social context shapes scientific research, theory, policy, and the law. The previously discussed "Martinson report" provides an illustration of how social context can shape the interpretation of research results. As noted, Martinson concluded that few, if any, rehabilitation programs appeared to work. Many credit this report with ending rehabilitation as a goal of corrections and ushering in a conservative, get-tough approach to crime. Did the Martinson report, through a scientific review of the literature, persuade lawmakers and scholars to abandon rehabilitation? A careful analysis suggests otherwise.

First, Martinson was not the first scholar to review the rehabilitation literature and conclude that rehabilitation programs appeared to be ineffective. Between 1950 and 1966, several scholars reached equally pessimistic conclusions about scientific evaluations of rehabilitation programs. The response, however, was a call to find better programs, conduct better research, and enhance funding for rehabilitation. Also, few people are even aware that Martinson recanted his original statements. If the Martinson report led to the demise of rehabilitation, then why didn't his recantation have a similar influence? Finally, positive findings in reviews of rehabilitation efforts in the 1980s and 1990s have been met with a great deal of skepticism.[142]

Why did the Martinson report generate such interest, and why was it interpreted as the death knell of rehabilitation? The answer lies largely in the social context of the late 1960s and early 1970s. This was a period of great social change in America—events such as the Vietnam War, the Watergate scandal, civil rights protests, the Kent State University shootings, and the Attica prison riot shaped the social context. For liberals, government responses to civil rights marchers and the Watergate scandal signified that the government could not be trusted at any task, including rehabilitation. To conservatives, the "hippie movement" was evidence of a growing social disorder that a "get-tough approach" might correct. Thus, by the time the Martinson report appeared, many criminologists and other commentators had already concluded that rehabilitation was a failed endeavor.[143]

Apart from corrections policy, social context impacts which theories of crime gain popularity, how research findings are interpreted, and what areas within criminology are deemed important enough to study. For this reason, readers are encouraged to keep in mind the social context of research and theory; social context is discussed explicitly on a number of occasions throughout the remaining chapters.

Crime as a Normal Phenomenon

A common belief is that crime is something that can and must be eliminated from society. President Lyndon Johnson's War on Crime in the 1960s and, more recently, President George H. W. Bush's War on Drugs represent large-scale efforts to reduce crime. These much-trumpeted campaigns notwithstanding, one needs to consider what French sociologist Emile Durkheim (1858–1917) wrote about crime through the course of history:[144]

> Crime is present not only in most societies of one particular species but in societies of all types. There is no society that is not confronted with the problem of criminality. What is normal is the existence of crime. Crime is normal because a society exempt from it is utterly impossible. Even a community of saints will create sinners.

Clearly, Durkheim did not mean that it was desirable or even acceptable to kill one's neighbor. Rather, he was pointing out that wherever there is conformity, there is also deviance—and some deviance will inevitably be deemed criminal.

Durkheim also noted that deviance is a prerequisite for social change. Without deviance, a society stagnates. Cohen followed up on this observation by outlining seven ways the deviant may make positive contributions to the success and vitality of societies:[145]

1. *Deviance cuts through "red tape."* The deviant rebels against the categorical and stereotypical nature of rules, often violating the rules to accomplish organizational tasks.
2. *Deviance acts as a "safety valve" for societal pressures.* The deviant prevents the excessive accumulation of discontent and reduces strain on the legitimate order.
3. *Deviance clarifies the "rules."* The deviant enables other members of society to learn what deviance is and how far one may safely venture.
4. *Deviance unites the group against the deviant.* The deviant provides society with a common enemy.
5. *Deviance unites the group for the deviant.* The deviant gives society an opportunity to save and reclaim or rehabilitate the deviant.
6. *Deviance accents conformity.* The deviant serves as a reference point against which conformity can be measured and gives others a feeling of self-satisfaction for adhering to the rules.
7. *Deviance acts as a "warning signal."* The deviant alerts others to the defects in an organization or society.

Of course, there is a point at which crime becomes dysfunctional. If a high level of crime becomes "normalized" or is considered inevitable, the consequences can be devastating for a community,[146] yet crime and deviance are not always threatening. Although Durkheim and Cohen were writing about deviant behaviors such as political protest and not murder, the message is that the elimination of crime cannot be accomplished.

How to Study Crime

Knowledge about crime stems from several sources, including personal experience and studies by others. Each source, however, has its own problems and limitations. Common-sense observations about crime may be limited to an individual's own experience and not reflect broader trends. Such a limited perspective impedes one's ability to understand the nature of crime. As noted previously, scientific studies may have problems with generalizability, and interpretations of findings are always subject to the influence of social context. However, the construction of theory, the development of **hypotheses**, and empirical testing provide the best promise of understanding the crime problem. Such careful study both generates and organizes data in a meaningful way.

Where do these limitations leave the student? This text offers several suggestions on how the reader should approach criminology. First, keep an open mind. One student probably will enthusiastically agree with certain theories about the nature of criminal behavior and the causes of crime; another may violently disagree with others. (This is ideology at work.) Keep in mind, however, that the reader's task is to learn the components of each theory no matter what his or her personal feelings may be. Only then can the student compare and contrast theories, see how they interact, and synthesize them. Remember, too, that each theory is a product of and is influenced by its social, intellectual, and historical context.[147]

Second, students are cautioned against discounting a theory based on the "exceptional case." Students often cite the one instance, example, or individual that the theory fails to explain. There are always exceptions to the rule, but they are just that—exceptions beyond the average. For example, many people know a person who smoked cigarettes their whole life and did not die of cancer. Does this mean that cigarettes do not cause cancer? Try to examine the strengths and weaknesses of each theory in its own context. In other words, apply another of Max Weber's sociological concepts, *verstehen,* or empathetic understanding. To examine a theory properly, the student must understand it on its own terms.

Third, learn not to expect easy answers, and do not accept them without reservation. Finckenauer cautions against settling for simple solutions to the delinquency problem, but his words apply to any aspect of criminology:[148]

> The highway of delinquency prevention history is paved with punctured **panaceas** [emphasis added]. First, a certain approach is posed as a cure-all or becomes viewed and promoted as a cure-all—as an intervention that will have universal efficacy and thus be appropriate for nearly all kids. Unfortunately, the approach, no matter what it is, almost always fails to

deliver; fails to live up to the frequently unrealistic or unsound expectations raised by the sales pitch.

If easy answers were readily available, criminologists would have delivered them long ago, and the crime problem would not exist today.

Criminological theory often cannot provide literal answers to the crime problem. Nevertheless, when studying a social problem like crime, researchers are trying to explain it and figure out its causes. Explanations do more than describe what has happened. They give reasons for what has occurred—the "how" and the "why." To be of practical value, explanations should improve the ability to predict events more accurately than through the use of common sense alone. As noted, each criminological theory provides a set of causes.

Good theory should be linked to reality through research: The empirical testing of theory confers relevance—and criminological theory is no exception. This text presents the latest research on the various theories and reviews the policy implications of this research, but it will become clear that the "doctors don't always have the cure." In other words, physicians can often find the causes of an illness (e.g., AIDS), but they cannot develop a cure. This is also frequently the case in criminology. Knowledge of the nature of the problem is no guarantee that a solution will be found. Unfortunately, such knowledge is no consolation to the victims of crime.

> *Good theory should be linked to reality through research...*

Approaches to the crime problem, however, should have a firm foundation—one provided by both theory and research, not guesswork.

 ## Conclusion

Crime should be viewed not as a single phenomenon but as one in which many kinds of behavior occur in different situations and under different conditions. No single theory can provide all the explanations for—let alone answers to—the crime problem. Again, criminological theory attempts to explain the causes of criminal behavior, not to excuse crimes or the people who commit them.

The next several chapters discuss theories of crime across several disciplines, including biology, psychology, and sociology. The reader is encouraged to organize them in some meaningful way as they are encountered. This chapter provided a number of ways to accomplish this task. Theories can focus on law-breaking (crime) or the criminal justice system's response to crime. They can operate at the micro or macro levels; they are generally part of an academic discipline, and they are often part of a specific theoretical tradition within a discipline. Although virtually all of the theories encountered are positivistic, a few theories are grounded firmly in the classical school of crime.

Texture: © Malchev/Shutterstock; Police Tape: © SkillUp/Shutterstock

- Edwin Sutherland defined criminology as the study of lawmaking, law-breaking, and the response to law-breaking. Modern scholars often distinguish criminology (the study of law-breaking) from criminal justice (the study of responses to law-breaking). The study of deviance also overlaps with criminology.

- Within academia, criminology is currently in a state of flux. Some consider criminology an independent discipline, while others view it as a general field open to all social science disciplines. Historically, sociology has had the largest impact on the study of crime, and sociologists tend to view criminology as a subdiscipline of sociology.

- The substantive criminal law is a codification of prohibited behaviors and the possible sanctions for these behaviors. The definition of a criminal act has two components: the *mens rea* (criminal mind) and the *actus reas* (criminal act).

- Criminal laws can be classified in a number of ways. *Mala in se* (evil in themselves) crimes, including homicide, robbery, rape, and burglary, make up the core of the legal code. *Mala prohibita* (wrong because they are prohibited) crimes, such as gambling and illicit drug use, tend to vary across societies and over time.

- Two general perspectives on the law exist. The consensus perspective views the law as the result of widespread societal agreement about what acts should be illegal. The conflict perspective suggests that the legal code is the end result of a power struggle among competing interest groups.

- A scientific theory is a set of principles or statements that attempt to explain how concepts are related. In the case of crime theory, these statements typically explain how one or more factors lead to criminal behavior. A scientific theory must also be testable, meaning that it must be stated in such a way that other scientists can go out into the real world, collect information, and test the theory's validity.

- A good theory of crime is supported by empirical tests. In other words, it appears to "work" in the real world. Aside from empirical support, a good theory is also parsimonious (concise) and wide in scope (explains a wide range of phenomena).

- Historically, the first explanations of criminal behavior invoked spirits and gods to explain crime. The scientific study of crime is dated to the classical school of crime. Classical school theorists argued that humans were rational, hedonistic beings—they choose criminal actions because of the benefits of crime. Accordingly, humans could be deterred from crime if the legal system was properly structured. The positivist school of crime suggests that criminal behavior is determined by factors that are partially or completely outside the control of individuals. Different social science disciplines (e.g., psychology, sociology, biology) highlight different factors that cause criminal behavior.

- Criminology is an applied science. Theory, coupled with sound research, should help guide policymaking throughout the criminal justice system. To proceed without theoretical guidance is to take a shot in the dark—there is no logical basis to assume that a particular program will work. Intensive supervision programs (ISPs) are an example of a policy implemented with little theoretical guidance, while multisystemic therapy (MST) is theoretically grounded.

- Although science generally strives to be "value free," criminology is heavily influenced by ideology. Liberal (left) criminologists tend to associate with the positivist school of crime and to focus on social causes of crime. Conservative (right) criminologists lean toward the classical school of crime and tend to focus on deterrence.

PUTTING IT ALL TOGETHER

1. What is "criminology"? How does criminology relate to other social science disciplines?
2. What is a scientific theory? How can you tell whether or not a theory is good?
3. What is the substantive criminal law? Describe the two main perspectives on the criminal law, and give an example of a crime that is consistent with each perspective.
4. Describe the history of theorizing about crime. How does the classical school of crime differ from the positivist school of crime?
5. Discuss the linkage between theory and policy.
6. What does it mean to be a "liberal" or "conservative" criminologist? How does ideology impact the study of crime?

KEY TERMS

case law Law that is created when judges interpret constitutional provisions, statutes, or regulations created by administrative agencies.

conflict perspective View that criminal law is the result of constant clashes between groups with different levels of power. Those groups that win the clashes define the legal code in a manner consistent with their values.

consensus perspective View that criminal law is the result of widespread agreement among members of society as to what should be legal and illegal.

constitutional law The law as expressed in the U.S. Constitution, as well as the constitutions of individual states. Constitutions are the supreme law of the land.

distributive justice Campaign theme of liberal Democrats that contends that increased economic opportunity is the best defense against crime.

grand theories Sweeping theories that attempt to explain all types of criminal behavior.

hedonistic calculus Jeremy Bentham used this term to describe human nature—humans seek pleasure (hedonism) in a rational, calculating manner.

hypotheses Testable statements about the relationship between variables in a scientific study.

intensive supervision Practice based on the assumption that probation/parole officers with reduced caseloads can more effectively monitor and supervise high-risk offenders. This practice also has been touted as a potential solution to jail- and prison-crowding problems.

law and order Campaign theme of conservative Republicans that a "hard line" is the best defense.

mala in se Crimes that are considered as "evil in themselves" (e.g., homicide).

mala prohibita Crimes that are forbidden by laws that attempt to regulate behavior (e.g., drug abuse, gambling, prostitution).

overgeneralization Jumping to sweeping conclusions based on the results of a single study.

panaceas Cure-alls. Applied to criminology, the term refers to the search for simple solutions to the crime problem.

policy analysis Focuses on the condition the government wishes to create rather than on the root causes of crime.

procedural law The portion of the criminal law that dictates the type of behaviors in which criminal justice actors can legally engage.

recidivism Repeat offending.

statutory law Criminal code created by legislatures and governing bodies.

value free The belief that researchers should keep their personal views out of their study and the interpretation of its findings. Objectivity is the goal.

If we knew more about the character of both offenders and victims, the nature of their relationships and the circumstances that create a high probability of crime conduct, it seems likely that crime prevention programs could be made much more effective.

—The President's Commission on Law Enforcement and the Administration of Justice (1967)[1]

CHAPTER 2

The Incidence of Crime

Objectives

Shooter: © Matchev/Shutterstock; Puzzle Piece: © Photodisc; Police Tape: © Skililip/Shutterstock

- Define the elements of the Uniform Crime Report (UCR) and identify its strengths and weaknesses as a crime data source. Pg. 29

- Define the elements of the National Crime Victimization Survey (NCVS) and identify its strengths and weaknesses as a crime data source. Pg. 33

- Define the elements of the National Incident-Based Reporting System. Pg. 32

- Understand what patterns are present in the UCR and the NCVS and what they reveal about crime. Pg. 32

- Summarize what data sources tell about the criminal justice system. Pgs. 36–38

🧩 Introduction

Like many other human activities, crime is difficult to measure. The total amount of crime in the United States is unknown. Typically, we depend on official figures and statistics that document the activities of the agencies of the criminal justice system to indicate the volume of crime in the United States. Each of these information sources has its strengths and weaknesses. In this chapter, several sources of crime data are reviewed and a number of findings presented. While wading through the sea of data in this chapter, keep in mind that it is more important to remember the conclusions based on the statistics than the numbers themselves.

Crime statistics are viewed as one indicator of societal health. A high crime rate causes alarm, while a low crime rate spurs feelings of security. For example, each year CQ Press calculates rankings for "America's Safest (and Most Dangerous) Cities." **TABLE 2-1** includes the list of the top 10 safest and most dangerous cities in the United States for 2012.[2] Information such as this affects the life choices that citizens make. There is some evidence that reductions in the crime rate of New York City were related to that city's real estate boom in the mid-1990s.[3] It was also reported that crime rates had no direct effect on housing prices in Jacksonville,

Florida, but homes were highly discounted in high crime areas.[4] Crime rates (especially violent crime) also had an impact on mortgage default rates.[5]

It is also important to collect accurate crime statistics for operational purposes. How can the police, courts, and correctional system handle the crime problem if the statistics about crime are inaccurate? How does a person know where crimes are committed, the methods used to carry them out, and just how great the problem actually is? Without valid crime data, it is impossible to address these questions.

Many problems relate to the collection of crime data. For starters, it is difficult to determine just how much crime there is in a society because not all crimes are reported to the police. Perhaps the victim feels that the police will do nothing about the crime because it is not very serious, just a theft of property of little value, or that the offender is a powerful person beyond the reach of the law. Victims may be embarrassed by their victimization—that they fell for an Internet fraud or other scam; were "dumb" enough to leave the door to the house unlocked or their car unsecured; or were attacked by a friend, family member, or date. Companies are often reluctant to report embezzlement and fraud because the negative publicity could harm their business. Victims of violent crime such as assault and rape may not report the crime because they fear retaliation by the offender or because the offender is a friend or relative.

Other crimes seem "invisible" because the evidence of the crime has been thoroughly concealed. This applies not only to violent crimes such as homicide but also to white-collar crimes such as embezzlement and computer crime, where the crime scene is not out in the open and may be under the control of the offender.

TABLE 2-1			
CQ Press: 2012 City Crime Rate Rankings			
Rank	Safest 10 Cities	Rank	Most Dangerous 10 Cities
1	Fishers, IN	1	Camden, NJ
2	Johns Creek, GA	2	Detroit, MI
3	O'Fallon, MD	3	Flint, MI
4	Carmel, IN	4	St. Louis, MO
5	Newton, MA	5	Oakland, CA
6	Mission Viejo, CA	6	Cleveland, OH
7	Ramapo, NY	7	Gary, IN
8	Naperville, IL	8	Birmingham, AL
9	Amherst, NY	9	New Orleans, LA
10	Irvine, CA	10	Newark, NJ

Source: O'Leary, K., & Morgan, S. (2005). *City crime rankings: Crime in metropolitan American, 12.* Washington, DC: CQ Press, a division of SAGE Publications.

'I think I'd rather go back to being mugged!'

Cost of White-Collar Crime
© CartoonStock.com

Crimes such as drug abuse are unlikely to be reported because there is no obvious victim. Drug abusers harm only themselves, unless of course their drug use leads to other crimes. For instance, drug addicts may commit a crime to obtain funds to buy drugs, or the drugs may spark violent behavior and lead to assault or other violent offenses.

Other crimes seem "invisible" because the evidence of the crime has been thoroughly concealed.

Sources of Crime Statistics

To study the incidence of crime, it is helpful to compare the findings from two data sources: the **Uniform Crime Report (UCR)**, which lists crimes reported to the police, and the **National Crime Victimization Survey (NCVS)**, which documents the extent of victimization. The public is often concerned with whether crime is up or down, but the main point regarding these data sources is that they are intended to measure different aspects of crime.[6] The problem is that most crime is not directly observable: "No one measure is capable of providing all the information about the extent and characteristics of crime."[7]

In 1929, the International Association of Chiefs of Police (IACP) called for the development of a uniform crime reporting program. In 1930, the Federal Bureau of Investigation (FBI) began to compile nationwide crime statistics. The FBI's famous director, J. Edgar Hoover, recognized the potential of such a program to generate positive publicity for his agency as the leader in the fight against crime.

The Uniform Crime Report

The UCR, based on the number of crimes reported to the police, is the major source of crime information in this country, and it is completely voluntary. Typically, police agencies report the number of crimes uncovered within their jurisdiction over the previous year to a centralized state clearinghouse (e.g., the state police), which passes the data on to the FBI. Thus, the annual report, entitled "Crime in the United States," consists of both crimes reported to the police by complainants or victims and those uncovered by the police as a result of investigation. Because the UCR contains information from most jurisdictions, it is the major source of nationwide crime data. This makes it possible to examine the crime rate for a particular area, as well as to compare crime rates across regions.

The UCR format features standardized definitions of crime; thus, the term uniform really is a synonym for standardized. If legal codes were used, the difference between legal definitions across the states would lead to confusion, with similar events counted and classified as different crimes. "Crime in the United States" highlights the most serious crimes, which are called Part I or **index offenses**: murder, rape, assault, burglary, larceny-theft, motor vehicle theft, and arson. These crimes were selected because their seriousness made them more likely to be reported to the police.[8] Thus, the crime index is an indicator of the level of serious crime in the United States. The UCR crime definitions are presented in **TABLE 2-2**.

Violent crimes

One murder every 34.30 minutes

One forcible rape every 6.0 minutes

One robbery every 1.20 minutes

One aggravated assault every 39.10 seconds

Property crimes

One burglary every 14.30 seconds

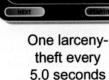

One larceny-theft every 5.0 seconds

One motor vehicle theft every 39.70 seconds

UCR Crime Clock

TABLE 2-2

Crime Definitions in the Uniform Crime Report

Crime	Definition
Murder	The willful (non-negligent) killing of one human being by another.
Forcible rape	The carnal knowledge of a female forcibly and against her will. Attempts or assaults to commit rape by force or threat of force are also included.
Robbery	The taking or attempting to take anything of value from the care, custody, or control of a person or persons by force or threat of force or violence and/or by putting the victim in fear.
Aggravated assault	An unlawful attack by one person upon another for the purpose of inflicting severe or aggravated bodily injury. The UCR program further specifies that this type of assault is usually accompanied by the use of a weapon or by other means likely to produce death or great bodily harm. Attempted aggravated assault that involves the display of—or threat to use—a gun, knife, or other weapon is included in this crime category because serious personal injury would likely result if the assault were completed. When aggravated assault and larceny-theft occur together, the offense falls under the category of robbery.
Burglary	The unlawful entry into a structure to commit a felony or theft. To classify an offense as a burglary, the use of force to gain entry need not have occurred. The UCR program has three sub-classifications for burglary: forcible entry, unlawful entry where no force is used, and attempted forcible entry. The UCR definition of "structure" includes apartment, barn, house trailer or houseboat when used as a permanent dwelling, office, railroad car (but not automobile), stable, and vessel (i.e., ship).
Larceny-theft	The unlawful taking, carrying, leading, or riding away of property from the possession or constructive possession of another. Examples are thefts of bicycles, motor vehicle parts and accessories, shoplifting, pocket-picking, or the stealing of any property or article that is not taken by force and violence or by fraud.
Motor vehicle theft	The theft or attempted theft of a motor vehicle. In the UCR program, a motor vehicle is a self-propelled vehicle that runs on land surfaces and not on rails. Examples of motor vehicles include sport utility vehicles, automobiles, trucks, buses, motorcycles, motor scooters, all-terrain vehicles, and snowmobiles. Motor vehicle theft does not include farm equipment, bulldozers, airplanes, construction equipment, or water craft such as motorboats, sailboats, houseboats, or jet skis. The taking of a motor vehicle for temporary use by persons having lawful access is excluded from this definition.
Arson	Any willful or malicious burning or attempting to burn, with or without intent to defraud, a dwelling house, public building, motor vehicle or aircraft, personal property of another, etc.

Data from Federal Bureau of Investigation, Crime in the United States, 2008 http://www2.fbi.gov/ucr/cius2008/offenses/violent_crime/index.html; http://www2.fbi.gov/ucr/cius2008/offenses/property_crime/index.html Accessed June 30, 2010

TABLE 2-3 lists crimes that are common to both the UCR and the NCVS. The UCR totals reflect the number of crimes reported to law enforcement officials. Note that property crimes such as larceny-theft, burglary, and motor vehicle theft are most common, while violent crimes such as assault, robbery, and rape occur less often. Rape, however, presents a particular problem because the seemingly low rate may actually reflect a reluctance to report the crime. Rape victims are traumatized by the offense and often feel that reporting the crime only extends their victimization, causing them to relive the event.

The change in the violent crime rate has been the subject of some controversy among criminologists who are attempting to determine the reasons for it. They consider such variables as police programs, changes in drug abuse rates, the availability of firearms, stricter sentencing, changes in the age of the population, family structure, the economy, the political system, and religious makeup.[9,10] Determining the factors that influence the crime rate is a standard function of criminology.

Limitations of the UCR

As with all crime statistics, UCR crime figures must be carefully considered. Typically, the following four factors affect the accuracy of UCR figures:[11]

1. **UCR figures reflect only the volume of crime reported to the police**. A number of reasons exist for why victims would not report a crime. For example, victims may feel that the crime is not serious or may be embarrassed by their victimization (e.g., a man robbed by a prostitute). Rape victims may not report the crime because they

TABLE 2-3

Comparison of the UCR and NCVS

	UCR	NCVS
Basic counting unit	The offense	The victimization: "A specific criminal act that affects a single victim, whether a person or a household."
Offenses measured	Murder Rape Robbery (personal and commercial) Assault (aggravated) Burglary (commercial and household) Larceny (commercial and household) Motor vehicle theft Arson	Rape Robbery (personal) Assault (aggravated and simple) Burglary (personal) Larceny (personal and household) Motor vehicle theft
Scope	Crimes reported to the police in most jurisdictions; considerable flexibility in developing small-area data.	Crimes reported and not reported to the police; all data are for the nation as a whole; some data are available for large geographic areas.
Collection methods	Police department reports to the FBI. The program is voluntary.	Survey interviews; periodically measures the total number of crimes committed by asking a national sample of 60,000 households representing 135,000 persons over the age of 12 about their experience as victims of crime during a specified period.
Kinds of information	In addition to offense counts, provides information on crime clearances, persons arrested, persons charged, law enforcement officers killed and assaulted, and characteristics of victims.	Provides details about victims (such as age, race, sex, education, income, and relationship to perpetrator) and about crimes (such as time and place of occurrence, reported or unreported, use of weapons, occurrence of injury, and economic consequences).
Sponsor	Department of Justice, Federal Bureau of Investigation	Department of Justice, Bureau of Justice Statistics

Data from Bureau of Justice Statistics, Report to the Nation on Crime and Justice: The Data (Washington, DC: U.S. Department of Justice, 1983): 6; Michael R. Rand and Callie M. Rennison, "Yes Crime Stories? Accounting for Differences in Our National Crime Indicators," Chance 15 (2002):48–49.

know the offender (e.g., incest or date rape) or because they fear the consequences of reporting (e.g., testifying in court if an arrest is made).

2. **UCR figures are affected by the recording practices of the police.** For instance, the police may report crimes in a manner that presents the police and the community in the best light. Consider the crime figures for the safest and most dangerous cities. Would law enforcers want their city to be known as the "most crime-ridden" city in the country?

3. **The UCR emphasizes street crime.** These crime figures represent only part of the crime problem. The focus on street crime obscures the

> **The UCR is the major source of crime statistics in this country dating back to 1930.**

impact of crimes of the powerful, those known as organized and white-collar crimes.

4. **Crimes reported to the police mainly reflect the results of their style of work.** The major problem in crime measurement is the source of the information. Official statistics reflect the actions of the criminal justice system itself. For example, when the police "crack down" on a certain type of crime, like prostitution, the crime figures for prostitution will certainly rise.

For these reasons, UCR figures are not representative of the actual level of crime in the United States. Still, the UCR has some obvious strengths. The UCR is the major source of crime statistics in this country dating back to 1930. It has tradition and prestige that is enhanced by the FBI's involvement in the data collection and reporting process. It presents data from every region of the country. If someone wants to know about crime in a particular city, town, or state, the UCR is the best source of information.

The National Incident-Based Reporting System

In 1991, the UCR program began to change its data collection system to generate more detailed information that would facilitate crime analysis. This system is known as the National Incident-Based Reporting System (NIBRS). NIBRS is designed to collect information that is not included in UCR data, such as where and when the offense occurred and victim information (on the harm caused by the crime). If arrests are made, it also includes data on the offenders. NIBRS will eventually replace the UCR as the official source of crime information from police departments as reported to the FBI.

NIBRS contains information on 46 Group A offenses that represent 22 categories, rather than just concentrating on the eight index offenses from the UCR. Unlike the UCR, NIBRS does the following:

- Makes a distinction between attempted and completed crimes
- Provides more inclusive definitions of crime (i.e., the definition of rape has been expanded to include male victims)

- Counts all offenses that occur during an incident rather than concentrating only on the most serious crimes. For example, if an offender held up a liquor store and shot and killed the person working there, the UCR would count the homicide but not the robbery. In the NIBRS, both offenses will be tallied.

The major distinction between the two reports is the focus on the crime incident itself.[12] A list of the differences between the UCR and the NIBRS is presented in **TABLE 2-4**. The following are highlights from NIBRS data in 2012:[13-14]

- In 2012, a total of 6,115 law enforcement agencies in the nation, representing coverage for over 90 million inhabitants, submitted NIBRS data. This coverage represents 33.4 percent of all law enforcement agencies that participate in the UCR program. More than half of these reporting agencies (51.9 percent) were located in cities with fewer than 10,000 inhabitants.
- Participating NIBRS agencies reported 5,001,060 incidents that involved 5,734,653 offenses, 6,050,049 victims, and 4,556,183 known offenders in 2012. Of the reported offenses, 64.9 percent involved crimes against property, 23.2 percent involved crimes against persons, and 12.0 percent included crimes against society (i.e., typically "victimless crimes" that represent society's prohibition against engaging in certain types of activity, such as prostitution or gambling).
- Among individual victims: 48.3 percent were male and 50.9 percent were female (sex was unknown

TABLE 2-4

Differences Between UCR and NIBRS

UCR	NIBRS
Consists of monthly aggregate crime counts for eight index crimes	Consists of individual incident records for the eight index crimes and 38 other offenses with details on: offense, offender, victim, and property
Records one offense per incident as determined by the hierarchy rule (counts only the most serious offense). Hierarchy rule suppresses counts of lesser offenses in multiple-offense incidents.	Records each offense occurring in the incident
Does not distinguish between attempted and completed crimes	Distinguishes between attempted and completed crimes
Records rape of females only	Records rape of males and females Restructures definition of assault
Collects weapon information for murder, robbery, and aggravated assault	Collects weapon information for all violent offenses
Provides counts on arrests for the eight index crimes and 21 other offenses	Provides details on arrests for the eight index crimes and 49 other offenses

Data from Ramona R. Rantala, *Effects of NIBRS on Crime Statistics* (Washington, DC: Bureau of Justice Statistics, 2002): 1.

for 0.8 percent). The majority of victims were white (72.7 percent), 21.0 percent were black, 1.2 percent were Asian/Pacific Islander, and 0.5 percent were American Indian/Alaskan Native. Race was unknown for 4.7 percent of victims. More than 24 percent (24.1) of victims were between the ages of 21 and 30 years of age.

- There were 3,971,642 known offenders of offenses reported via the NIBRS. Nearly 33 percent (32.9) of known offenders were between the ages of 16 and 25 years of age. Of all known offenders, 63.0 percent were male, 24.7 percent were female, and gender was unknown for 12.3 percent. The majority of known offenders were white (55.4 percent); 28.1 percent were black, and 1.5 percent were of other races.
- Location of the offense: The majority of crimes against persons (63.0 percent) occurred in residences/homes, 11.9 percent happened on highways/roads/alleys or streets, 4.3 percent happened in schools or colleges, 4.0 percent happened in parking lots or garages, and 2.1 percent took place at bars or nightclubs.
- Time of day: Most of the crimes against persons occurred between midnight and 12:59 a.m. The time of day most reported for incidents involving crimes against property was between noon and 12:59 p.m.
- Use of drug/narcotics was present in 9.0 percent of weapon law violations, 5.8 percent of gambling offenses, 5.4 percent of stolen property offenses, 5.3 percent of prostitution offenses, and 4.4 percent of homicide offenses. Alcohol use was involved in 12.9 percent of assault offenses, 11.1 percent of bribery offenses, 10.9 percent of kidnapping/abduction offenses, and 9.9 percent of weapon law violations.

In this manner, NIBRS presents more of the facets of crime and the relationships between them than the UCR.[15] These are the types of data that can fuel crime analysis and problem solving, such as in the determination of hot spots. A hot spot is defined as a small geographic location where the rate of crimes per square foot is higher than that of the areas surrounding it. Thus a hot spot is a useful way to determine where police patrols should focus their efforts to solve a crime problem. Crime hot spots are also examined to determine the days of the week and hours when crime calls are concentrated.[16]

National Crime Victimization Survey

Another source of crime information is the National Crime Victimization Survey (NCVS) that has been conducted by the Bureau of Justice Statistics since 1972. The purpose of the survey is to enlighten the "dark figure of crime"—uncover crime that has not been reported and thus learn the actual level of crime in the country. If the victim does not report a crime, and if it goes unseen or undetected by the police or others, it will not be reported and thus will not show up in the UCR. The NCVS attempts to solve this problem by going directly to the victim. The survey is based on the premise that citizens may report crimes to the NCVS that they did not report to the police.

The NCVS is a scientifically designed annual survey of a representative sample of some 60,000 U.S. households. Information in this report is also presented as a population rate: the number of victims per 1,000 households. As an estimate of the risk of crime victimization, the NCVS is an improvement over the UCR for two reasons. First, it presents information taken directly from victims whether or not they report a crime to the police. Second, it collects background information on victims, making it possible to decide which demographic groups have the highest rates of victimization for particular types of crime. By contrast, the data from the UCR may lead a person to incorrectly assume that every individual has an equal chance of becoming a crime victim.

There are some other substantial differences between the UCR and the NCVS:[17]

- The UCR includes homicide, arson, and commercial crimes, while the NCVS excludes these crime types.
- The UCR excludes simple assault and sexual assault, which are included in the NCVS.
- The NCVS excludes crimes against children age 11 or younger, persons in institutions (e.g., nursing homes and correctional institutions), and may exclude highly mobile populations and the homeless; however, victimizations against these persons may be included in the UCR.

TABLE 2-5 shows that the NCVS does uncover more crime than is reported in the UCR. In 2008, approximately 7 million more crimes were uncovered by the NCVS. The difference was apparent for almost every crime classification. The greatest difference was for larceny-theft and was

TABLE 2-5

UCR and NCVS Crime Rate FIGs, 2012

Type of Crime	UCR	NCVS	Difference
Rape	84,376	346,830	262,454
Robbery	354,520	741,760	387,240
Assault	760,739	996,110	235,371
Burglary	2,185,140	3,764,540	1,579,400
Larceny-theft	6,151,095	15,224,700	9,073,605
Motor vehicle theft	716,508	633,740	82,768
Total	10,252,378	21,707,680	

Data from Federal Bureau of Investigation, Crime in the United States, 2008 http://www.fbi.gov/ucr/cius2008/data/TAB_01.html Michael R. Rand, Criminal Victimization 2008 (Washington, D.C.: U.S. Department of Justice, 2008). http://bjs.ojp.usdoj.gov/content/pub/pdf/cv08.pdf Accessed May 7, 2010.

smallest was for assault. Motor vehicle theft was the only crime for which the UCR had a higher figure than the NCVS.

Although the UCR measures only the crimes reported to the police and the NCVS captures both reported and unreported crime, several studies have noted a high level of correspondence between UCR and NCVS crime rates.[18-20] The NCVS victimization rates for the period between 1993 and 2003 also note the steep decline in violent crime that occurred during the 1990s. Property crime rates apparently peaked in 1994 and then leveled off. In fact, since 1972, changes in the violent crime rate from both the UCR and the NCVS have moved in the same direction 60 percent of the time, and property crime rates moved in the same direction about 75 percent of the time.[21]

Attributes of Victimization Patterns, 2012

The NCVS gives specific information about crime by focusing on the attributes of the victim. Thus, criminologists can examine who is likely to be the victim of a particular type of crime. The following findings on victimization rates by victim attributes were reported for 2012:[22]

Sex: In 2012, males had higher rates of violent and serious violent victimization than females.

Race: The rate of serious violence in 2012 for blacks (11.3 per 1,000) was higher than the rate for whites (6.8 per 1,000).

Age: From 2011 to 2012, violent victimization rates increased for persons ages 35 to 49, from 21.9 to 29.1 per 1,000. Persons ages 12 to 17 and 25 to 34 experienced a slight increase in violence in this same period, while the rates of violent victimization for all other age groups remained flat.

Marital Status: Married persons generally had the lowest rates of violence compared to persons never married, divorced, or separated, and this was also observed in 2012. Married persons experienced 13.5 victimizations per 1,000 persons in 2012, compared to 37.0 for divorced, 40.7 for never married, and 83.1 for separated persons.

Urban Areas: In 2012, the rate of violent victimization was 32.4 per 1,000 in urban areas, 23.8 per 1,000 in suburban areas, and 20.9 per 1,000 in rural areas.

In 2012, the NCVS did not measure a statistically significant change in either the overall number of victimizations or the number of victimizations reported to police for other crime types.

Categories of Victims and Victimization

The NCVS has generated data that has led to special analyses of crime victimization by type of crime. Summaries of several of these studies follow.

> *The NCVS gives specific information about crime by focusing on the attributes of the victim.*

Intimate Partner Violence, 1993–2010

Intimate partner violence (i.e., victimizations committed by current or former spouses, intimate partners, boyfriends, or girlfriends of victims) is a significant category of crime victimization. Between 1993 and 2010, the following patterns emerged for this type of crime:[23]

- The rate of intimate partner violence has declined 64 percent from 9.8 to 3.6 victimizations per 1,000 persons age 12 and older.
- Intimate partner violence has declined more than 60 percent for both males and females during this time period.
- About four out of five victims of intimate partner violence were female.
- Females ages 18 to 24 and 25 to 34 had the highest rates of intimate partner violence.
- Females living in households comprised of one female adult with children experienced intimate partner violence at a rate more than 10 times higher than households with married adults with children and 6 times higher than households with one female only.
- Intimate partner violence declined for females of all marital statuses.

Given the recent laws and programs devoted to the prevention of domestic violence and increased public awareness of this type of crime, the decline in intimate partner victimization is encouraging.

Victims of Identity Theft, 2012

In 2012, the NCVS contained an Identity Theft supplement that collected data from victims of this crime. The results determined the following patterns about identity theft victims:[24]

- Of all victims, 85 percent reported that their most recent victimization involved unauthorized use of an existing account.
- Typically, persons from higher income households were targeted.
- Victims were also unlikely to have any form of credit-related problems.
- Victims were typically informed about the crime by a financial institution who contacted them about suspicious activity.
- In the majority of cases, victims were unaware of how the offender obtained their personal information.
- Nine out of 10 victims did not know anything about their offender.
- Overall, identity theft victims experienced an average financial loss of $1,769 (median loss = $300).
- Identity theft losses totaled $24.7 billion in 2012.

- The majority of victims spent one day or less to resolve problems caused by identity theft.
- Of the NCVS respondents, 14 percent had experienced identity theft at some point in their lives.
- Fewer than 1 in 10 identity theft victims reported the incident to the police.

Identity theft has the potential to become a widespread and common form of property crime. Identity theft and other forms of cybercrime are analyzed and discussed in Chapter 12.

School Crime and Safety

What are the patterns of victimization in schools, from elementary to high school? The NCVS has long provided direct information on this subject. Again, the aim of presenting this information is to determine who is at risk and how to prevent crime from occurring. Here are some selected findings on school crime victimization:[25]

- Of the 31 student, staff, and nonstudent school-associated violent deaths occurring between July 1, 2010, and June 30, 2011, 25 were homicides and 6 were suicides.
- From July 1, 2010, through June 30, 2011, there were 11 homicides and 3 suicides of school-age youth (ages 5 to 18) at school.
- In 2011, students ages 12 to 18 were victims of about 1,246,000 nonfatal victimizations at school, including 648,600 thefts and 597,500 violent victimizations. This was more than the number of nonfatal victimizations that occurred at school in 2010.
- During the 2009–2010 school year, 85 percent of public schools recorded that one or more crime incidents had taken place at school, amounting to an estimated 1.9 million crimes (a rate of 40 crimes per 1,000 public school students enrolled in 2009–2010).
- During the same year, 60 percent of public schools reported a crime incident that occurred at school to the police, amounting to 689,000 crimes (15 crimes per 1,000 public school students enrolled).
- During the 2009–2010 school year, 39 percent of public schools took at least one serious disciplinary action against a student for specific offenses.
- Of the 433,800 serious disciplinary actions taken during the 2009–2010 school year, 74 percent were suspensions for 5 days or more, 20 percent were transfers to specialized schools, and 6 percent were removals with no services for the remainder of the school year.

Thus, it appears schools are not immune from crime and safety problems. This report is another example of how the NCVS illuminates the level of crime in a specialized location.

Violence in the Workplace, 1993–2009

Workplace violence attracts a great idea of media attention. Yearly examinations by the NCVS have made long-term analysis of workplace victimization possible. The following patterns have emerged on this issue between 1993 and 2009:[26]

- From 2002 to 2009, the rate of nonfatal workplace violence has declined by 35 percent, following a 62 percent decline in the rate from 1993 to 2002.
- The average annual rate of workplace violence between 2005 and 2009 (5 violent crimes per 1,000 employed persons age 16 or older) was about one-third the rate of non-workplace violence (16 violent crimes per 1,000 employed persons age 16 or older) and violence against persons not employed (17 violent crimes per 1,000 persons age 16 or older).
- Between 2005 and 2009, law enforcement officers, security guards, and bartenders had the highest rates of nonfatal workplace violence.
- Strangers committed the greatest proportion of nonfatal workplace violence against males (53%) and females (41%) between 2005 and 2009.
- Among workplace homicides that occurred between 2005 and 2009, about 28 percent involved victims in sales and related occupations and about 17 percent involved victims in protective service occupations.
- About 70 percent of workplace homicides were committed by robbers and other assailants while

The impact of workplace violence.
© Euro Color Creative/Shutterstock, Inc.

about 21 percent were committed by work associates between 2005 and 2009.

- Between 2005 and 2009, while firearms were used in 5 percent of nonfatal workplace violence, shootings accounted for 80 percent of workplace homicides.

Therefore, according to these figures, the rate of violent crime in the workplace is not increasing.

In addition, the authors of the study examined NCVS workplace data from 2005 to 2009 for violent workplace victimization by demographic group. Men were more likely to be victims of workplace violence. Whites had a higher rate of workplace violence than blacks—a pattern that was directly opposite of that in society in general. Persons ages 20 to 34 and individuals from low-income households had the highest rates of workplace violence victimization. Workplace violence was less likely to involve drugs, alcohol, and firearms than violence in society.

Overall, these analyses reveal the tremendous information potential generated by the NCVS. Such specific analyses would not be possible if this survey were not routinely conducted. The NCVS provides valuable crime information that is not available from other sources.

Limitations of the NCVS

Although data for the NCVS is obtained directly from victims, there are some problems with the data of which criminologists must be aware. In sum, five factors can affect the accuracy of NCVS data:[27]

1. **Respondents are not always reliable**. Because the NCVS asks respondents to recall events from a specific time period, forgetting and telescoping (moving a crime event from the past forward or pushing a victimization backward to be included) is a problem.[28]
2. **Respondents may not be truthful**. People may conceal victimization because of embarrassment or report crimes to please the interviewer. In addition, they may report trivial incidents as crimes.
3. **The NCVS asks questions about rape in an indirect fashion**. Respondents are never asked whether they have been the victims of an attempted or completed rape. Rather, after the other crime victimizations are addressed, they are asked whether they have been attacked "in some other way."[29]
4. **There are problems administering the survey or coding the data**. The accuracy of any survey depends on the way it is conducted. If the questions are unclear or if sample members are not reached, the validity of the results is compromised. If responses are not recorded accurately, the results will be imprecise.
5. **The survey does not contain specific information on particular areas**. There are breakdowns by geographic

region, but the UCR remains the sole source of detailed regional crime information. In addition, the NCVS concentrates on large cities and may not adequately represent victimization patterns in other areas.

To some extent, these problems occur with any type of survey. In short, the truthfulness of the respondent and the skill of the survey researcher affect the quality of the data. Despite these weaknesses, the NCVS provides vital, detailed information about crime victimization—and because it collects information from victims, it can be used to direct crime prevention efforts.

Criminal Justice System Statistics

Another crime indicator is the size of the population being served by the different parts of the criminal justice system. These figures provide long-term trends about how the system operates, but this does not always mean that the results are clear indicators of the nature of crime. They are indicators of how the system operates and what type of enforcement has been a priority. For example, if the police and courts decide to crack down or go after methamphetamine dealers, this crime will "increase" in the crime statistics and thus will be noted in the UCR. In addition, if rural whites are more likely to be arrested and convicted for this crime, these statistics would lead to the conclusion that they are more involved in this offense. However, one cannot be sure of that. Whites in rural areas may be more likely to be caught, while others are not apprehended, arrested, and convicted.

Therefore, criminal justice system statistics specifically reflect who is in the system. They do not necessarily demonstrate what is going on in society regarding a particular type of offense. They are simply production figures and reflect who is processed by the criminal justice system for various crimes. Like the NCVS, these reports are conducted and maintained by the Bureau of Justice Statistics.

Jail Population

A survey of the nation's jails is conducted annually. Jails are local facilities that primarily hold inmates sentenced to short terms (generally under 1 year); receive individuals pending arraignment; hold persons awaiting trial, conviction, or sentencing; and house inmates for federal, state, or other authorities because of crowding in those facilities. Jail population figures can help to determine how to manage jail space and avoid overcrowding. At midyear 2012,

> *Workplace violence was less likely to involve drugs, alcohol, and firearms than violence in society.*

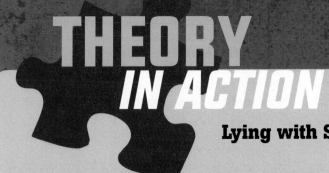

Lying with Statistics—Police Style

Crime statistics are often used to assess the quality of police performance. This gives rise to the temptation to manipulate the data to ensure that performance levels are met or exceeded.

In New Orleans, five police officers, including a district commander, were terminated and a sixth demoted to patrol when the police department's Public Integrity Bureau (PIB) discovered that they had downgraded the classification of felonies (meaning they made the reported offenses appear less serious; for instance, turning a burglary into a larceny-theft). The officers made the changes so that their district would win the coveted crime reduction award from the chief. All the officers were assigned to the city's First District, the district that had received the crime reduction award in the previous year.

PIB investigators examined 700 of the district's reports filed between January 2002 and June 2003. They determined that 42 percent of the violent crimes (such as shootings, carjackings, and stabbings) were downgraded to "miscellaneous incidents" or other lesser crimes. The investigators felt that the downgrades were questionable in another 17 percent of the cases examined.

The fired officers maintain that any downgrading that occurred was based on their professional judgment. They have appealed their firings to the civil service department in the city of New Orleans.

The Compstat method features meetings between police supervisors and their superiors to review crime problems in particular areas and determine appropriate responses to deal with them. Thus, supervisors are held accountable for crime in their area. Eterno and Silverman (2006) believe that NYPD's Compstat process fell prey to the same pressures. They state that Compstat's focus on crime reduction can lead police to ignore their "most fundamental goal"—protecting legal principles and democratic rights. This focus promotes the misperception that Compstat was a numbers game and that fear led supervisors to lying with statistics. Berated by high level NYPD command officers, commanders feared presenting their crime information at Compstat meetings and "would do almost anything to escape the embarrassment of crime statistics going up." Commanders drive their subordinates to make arrests and generate other statistics to reflect crime reduction. The rank and file officers came to view Compstat as a "numbers game" where they were required to make more arrests and issue more summonses to make commanders look good.

Eterno and Silverman also examined whether the Compstat process exuded pressure upon officers to record crime statistics in favorable ways—specifically, pressure to downgrade index crimes. Retirees who were police officers during the Compstat era reported that they felt significant pressure to decrease index crime. They also noted that the demand for integrity in crime statistics was significantly less at that time, and that promotions were more likely to be related to demonstrated decreases in the crime rate. Thus, pressure and fear can lead subordinates to cheat on statistics, rather than develop inventive ways to reach performance targets.

This problem is not limited to the United States. Detectives in Britain's Nottinghamshire police force were accused of manipulating crime statistics to influence news reporting. In particular, they allegedly failed to record gun crimes and downgraded armed robberies in an attempt to promote the appearance of safety in their territory.

Identify the weaknesses in the UCR classification system that could have contributed to this problem. How would such police manipulation influence the accuracy of UCR statistics for the city?

Sources: Sometimes the numbers crunch back. (2005, January). *Law Enforcement News XXXI,* 628, 1, 4; Foggo, D., & Fellstrom, C. (2005, April 17). Police officers manipulate the statistics to meet robbery and burglary targets. Telegraph .co.uk. Retrieved March 11, 2010, from http://www.telegraph .co.uk/news/uknews/1487992/Police-officers-manipulate-the-statistics-to-meet-robbery-and-burglary-targets. html; Eterno, J. A., & Silverman, E. B. (2006). The New York City Police Department's Compstat: Dream or nightmare? *International Journal of Police Science & Management, 8,* 218–231; Eterno, J. A., & Silverman, E. B. (2010). The NYPD's Compstat: Compare statistics or compose statistics? *International Journal of Police Science & Management, 12,* 426–449. *See also:* Eterno, J. A., & Silverman, E. B. (2012). *The crime numbers game: Management by manipulation.* Boca Raton, FL: CRC Press.

the following patterns were revealed in the analysis of the national jail population:[30]

- After 3 consecutive years of decline in the jail inmate population, the number of persons confined in county and city jails (744,524) increased by 1.2 percent (8,923 inmates) between midyear 2011 and midyear 2012.
- Rated capacity in jails reached 886,947 beds at midyear 2012, an increase of 0.8 percent (7,225 beds) from 879,722 beds in midyear 2011.
- Local jails admitted an estimated 11.6 million persons during the 12-month period ending June 30, 2012, which was similar to 2011 (11.8 million) and down from 13.6 million in 2008.
- From midyear 2000 to midyear 2012, the number of adult females in local jails increased by 38.9 percent compared to 17.4 percent in adult males.
- Between midyear 2000 and midyear 2012, the number of whites in jail increased by 30.9 percent whiles the number of blacks in jail increased by 7.1 percent.
- Increase in new bed space between 2011 and 2012 was nearly one-third of the average annual increase since 2000 while the percentage of capacity occupied held steady.

Prison Population

Of course, jail figures represent only one aspect of incarceration figures for the country. Prisoners held in federal and state adult correctional institutions are another part of the picture. Between 1991 and 2012, the following patterns were present in the prison inmate population:[31]

- In 2012, the number of admissions to state and federal prison in the United States was 609,800 offenders, the lowest number since 1999.
- The number of releases from U.S. prisons in 2012 (637,400) exceeded that of admissions for the fourth consecutive year, contributing to the decline in the total U.S. prison population.
- In 2011, the majority of state prisoners (53%) were serving time for violent offenses.
- New court commitments made up 82 percent of state admissions in 1978, 57 percent in 2000, and 71 percent in 2012.
- New court commitments to state prisons for drug offenders decreased 22 percent between 2006 and 2011, while parole violation admissions decreased 31 percent.
- Among new court commitments to state prison, more than one-third of both black and Hispanic offenders and one-quarter of white offenders were convicted of a violent offense.

These figures indicate that prison crowding is declining. Realization of the high cost of incarceration and a de-emphasis on imprisoning drug offenders seems to be having an effect on the size of the prison population.

Probation and Parole Figures

The final piece of the adult correctional system picture is probation and parole. Probation is an alternative sentence that is served in place of incarceration. Parole is a form of early conditional release from incarceration. If the conditions of probation or parole are violated, the offender can be sent to prison to complete the remainder of the sentence.

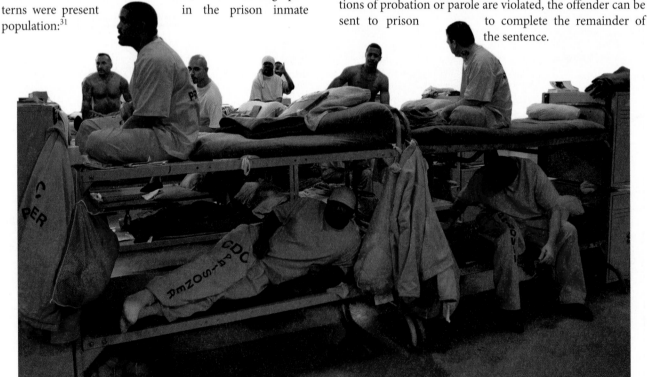

Overcrowding in prisons can lead to behavior problems among inmates and is a threat to institutional safety.
© Spencer Weiner/AP Photos

At yearend 2011, the following patterns were present in the probation and parole population:[32]

Probation statistics:

- The number of adults under community supervision declined by about 71,300 during 2011, down to 4,814,200 at yearend.
- The probation population declined by 2 percent. For the first time since 2002, the probation population fell below 4 million persons.
- The rate of incarceration among probationers at risk for violating their conditions of supervision in 2011 (5.5%) was consistent with the rate in 2000 (5.5%).

Parole statistics:

- About 853,900 adults were on parole since yearend 2011. The state parole population increased by 1.1 percent while the federal parole population grew by 5.1 percent.
- Of the parolees, 52 percent completed their term of supervision or were discharged early in 2011.
- Of the parolees who violated their terms of supervision, 12 percent were reincarcerated in 2011—a decrease from the 15 percent level in 2006.

Overall, these figures demonstrate that the offender population is on the decline.

Again, it must be emphasized that these figures represent who is processed by the system, not necessarily who commits crime or how much crime is present in society. However, they are important indicators of how the system handles the crime process. They demonstrate the volume of people present in the criminal justice system and for what types of crimes. In summary, it is important management information that can inform the operation of the various parts of the criminal justice system.

Conclusion

The actual volume of crime is difficult to estimate. Not all crimes are reported to or uncovered by the police. The reporting behavior of victims is affected by several considerations. Similarly, the figures collected from criminal justice agencies are more accurate reflections of their own operations than of the true rate of crime in society. Nevertheless, the figures presented in this chapter collectively indicate the incidence of crime in America in recent years.

WRAP-UP

CHAPTER SPOTLIGHT

Texture: © Malchev/Shutterstock; Police Tape: © SkillUp/Shutterstock

- Crime statistics are key indicators of societal health and provide information for the operation of the criminal justice system to prevent crime and victimization and to provide justice. Therefore, the quality and accuracy of crime statistics are important.
- It is difficult to estimate the amount of crime committed in America. For various reasons, not all crimes get reported to the police. The victims may feel that nothing will be done about the crime, or they may be reluctant to call the police because the offender is someone they know and they fear retaliation. They may also be embarrassed by their victimization. Other crimes go unreported because they are victimless or hidden from public view.
- There are several sources of crime information:

- The Uniform Crime Report, compiled and published by the Federal Bureau of Investigation, consists of crimes reported to the police. It is the primary source of information on national, state, and local crime rates.
- The National Crime Victimization Survey, conducted by the U.S. Bureau of Justice Statistics, surveys the public about their crime experiences regardless of whether they have reported the incident to the police. It also provides information about certain types of crime and special categories of victims.
- Several other sources of information exist that present the number of persons processed by the criminal justice system, including jail and prison populations and probation and parole figures.

PUTTING IT ALL TOGETHER

Police Tape: © SkillUp/Shutterstock

1. What is the level of crime in this country? How can this question be answered?
2. What do the crime figures tell about the level of crime in the United States? What conclusions can be drawn from this data?
3. What conclusions can be drawn from the NCVS results and the special topic reports?
4. Do the figures on the criminal justice system show that the United States is "soft on crime"?
5. Can the statistics cited in this chapter be used to make the case that crime is worse than ever?
6. Go on the World Wide Web and find current data from the UCR and the NCVS. Have crime patterns changed compared with those presented in this chapter? If so, how?

40   *Criminology: Theory, Research, and Policy, Fourth Edition*

index offenses The most serious crimes in the Uniform Crime Report: murder, rape, assault, burglary, larceny-theft, motor vehicle theft, and arson.

National Crime Victimization Survey (NCVS) A survey conducted since 1972 by the U.S. Bureau of Justice Statistics that attempts to uncover unreported crime by surveying victims. The NCVS is a representative sample drawn of about 60,000 U.S. households that is renewed every year.

National Incident-Based Reporting System (NIBRS) A system designed to collect a greater number of details than the UCR about crimes reported to the police. The NIBRS will contain information on both reported crime and arrests. It will eventually replace the UCR as the official source of crime information from police departments as reported to the FBI. NIBRS will contain information on 46 Group A offenses that represent 22 categories, rather than concentrate on the eight index offenses from the UCR. Unlike the UCR, NIBRS will make a distinction between attempted and completed crimes, provide more inclusive definitions of crime (i.e., the definition of rape has been expanded to include male victims), and will count all offenses that occur during an incident rather than concentrating on only the most serious crime.

Uniform Crime Report (UCR) An annual report, published by the FBI since 1930, consisting of crimes reported to and uncovered by the police. Currently, the UCR is the major source of nationwide crime data, containing information from most U.S. jurisdictions.

If you want to know why crime proliferates in this nation, don't look at statistics on income and wealth; look at statistics on arrests, prosecutions, convictions, and prison populations. . . The primary problem is in a criminal justice system that seems to have lost much of its capacity to determine the truth, prosecute and punish the guilty, and protect society.

—Ronald Reagan, 1975[1]

Crime has tripled in two decades because crime pays. It is the nation's growth industry because it is an exciting, enjoyable profession where the criminal element runs little risk of being forced to pay an unacceptable price. In a decade, tens of thousands of men, women, and children have been murdered. In retaliation, our defender, the state, has executed exactly one killer.

—Pat Buchanan, 1977[2]

CHAPTER 3

Neoclassical Criminology

Texture: © Malchev/Shutterstock; Shooter: © Malchev/Shutterstock; Puzzle Piece: © PhotoDisc; Police Tape: © SkillUp/Shutterstock

Objectives

- Understand the social context of neoclassical theories and their rise to prominence in America during the 1970s. Pg. 44

- Grasp the central concepts in deterrence theory, including specific, general, marginal, and focused deterrence. Pg. 45

- Understand what the various empirical tests indicate about the empirical status of deterrence theory. Pg. 46

- Know the central concepts in the routine activities and lifestyle approaches to criminal behavior. Pg. 57

- Understand rational choice theory and its relation to deterrence. Pg. 55

- Understand the policy implications of rational choice theory, including criminal justice policies and situational crime prevention. Pg. 59

Introduction

The preceding quotations illustrate the fact that toward the latter part of the 1970s, politicians, commentators, and scholars started to revive criminology's classical school ideas. As rehabilitation came under attack as the dominant goal of corrections, so too did the sociological and psychological theories of crime that supported this model. Throughout the 1980s and 1990s, the federal government and individual states increased penalties for crime. Some states returned to the use of the death penalty, while others passed legislation (e.g., truth in sentencing, "three strikes" laws) designed to deter people from criminal behavior by increasing prison sentences. One result of this effort has been a massive increase in the number of prisoners held in jails and prisons, but have these laws and prison expansions reduced crime? Do stricter legal penalties deter offenders from engaging in future crimes? Does capital punishment deter homicide?

As the name suggests, neoclassical theory builds on the work of classical school theorists. The emphasis is therefore often on the role of the criminal justice system in preventing crime. In this chapter, two complementary theories that place emphasis on punishment are discussed: Deterrence theory suggests that swift, certain, and severe punishment reduces crime, while the rational choice perspective holds that human beings calculate both the costs and benefits of criminal behavior before they decide whether to engage in crime. Additionally, routine activities theory is discussed in this chapter because it also assumes that criminals behave in a rational manner. Before introducing the individual theories, it is important to understand how and why neoclassical theory emerged.

The Rise of Neoclassical Theory

As noted in Chapter 1, the popularity of the classical school of crime diminished toward the end of the 1800s, and the positivist school gained popularity. Throughout most of the 1900s then, sociological, biological, and psychological theories of crime dominated the landscape. Because positivist theories identify potential causes of criminal behavior (e.g., poverty, personality, delinquent peers), they naturally fit with the corrections goal of rehabilitation. In essence, such theories provide the "targets" of rehabilitation efforts. During the early 1970s, however, the corrections goal of rehabilitation was attacked and labeled as a failure by both liberal and conservative commentators.[3] When rehabilitation faltered as a goal of corrections, many scholars called for a return to the use of prisons to punish and deter, rather than rehabilitate, offenders. These commentators recommended punishments such as lengthy prison terms, corporal punishment,[4] and the death penalty.[5]

The so-called "get-tough" movement also included calls to make prison itself more painful. Indeed, some jurisdictions reinstituted "chain gang crews" and old-time striped uniforms. Perhaps nobody has taken this trend further than Sheriff Joe Arpaio of Maricopa County, Arizona. Arpaio has cultivated a reputation as the "toughest sheriff in the country" through his management of the county jail. The following are some of the sheriff's policies:[6,7]

- Inmates are issued pink underwear and striped uniforms.
- Cigarettes and coffee are prohibited.
- Inmates are housed in tents outside of the jail. (The jail is located in a desert.)
- Inmates are allowed no recreation.
- Television is generally limited; those allowed to watch television can choose from CSPAN, the Disney Channel, and cooking shows.
- Inmates in chain gangs pick up garbage on city streets.
- Camera-equipped dogs roam the jail.
- Inmates are served only two cold meals per day. Each meal costs between 15 and 40 cents per inmate.

The "get-tough movement" brought together several different perspectives that emphasized the importance of punishment, including retribution, just deserts, incapacitation, and deterrence. The concept of **just deserts** suggests that punishment rightfully reflects the pain caused and is thus earned by the criminal. Punishment also serves as a collective expression of society's disapproval for criminal acts.[8]

Sherriff Joe Arpiao, the self-proclaimed "toughest sheriff in the country." Sheriff Joe believes that features such as chain gangs, pink underwear, and camera equipped dogs will make the prison experience so miserable that inmates will refrain from future criminal behavior.

© Paul Connors/AP Photos

The goal of punishment, then, is sentencing that is commensurate with the seriousness of the crime, the extent to which it adversely affects society, and the culpability of the offender. Moreover, persons who commit the same type of crime should receive the same sentence.

Retribution is similar to just deserts and implies that criminals deserve to be punished because they have violated a legal system from which everyone benefits.[9] They have taken unfair advantage of the law-abiding citizens in society. Punishing offenders restores the social balance and reaffirms social bonds; it sends a message that crime will not be tolerated. According to Earnest van den Haag, "Retribution must be paid because it is owed, because it has been threatened, and a threat is a (negative) promise."[10]

The idea of incapacitation is simple—someone who is incapacitated (through death, prison, or some other method) can no longer commit crimes against the public. Thus, the goal of incapacitation is to prevent crime by locking up criminal offenders. Like retribution and just deserts, incapacitation is a theory of punishment that does not rest on any particular theory of crime. Unlike them, however, incapacitation is designed to reduce future criminal behavior. A substantial body of literature addresses whether and how incapacitation affects crime rates (see **Theory in Action: Lock 'Em Up—Incapacitation as Goal of Corrections** for more information).

In addition to retribution, incapacitation, and just deserts, some scholars emphasize the deterrent value of punishment; that is, punishment has the potential to reduce criminal behavior by sending a message to both the offender and society that crime "doesn't pay." It is this link that clearly ties the get-tough movement with the classical school. In this case, a deterrence theory of punishment rests on an explicit theory of criminal behavior.

Deterrence Theory

Drawing on the work of classical school theorists such as Beccaria and Bentham, deterrence theorists portray humans as rational, pleasure-seeking, pain-avoiding creatures. This assumption leads to a relatively simple theory of crime: People will engage in criminal behavior when it brings them pleasure (generates rewards) and carries little risk of pain.

Consequently, formal punishment has the potential to reduce crime in two ways. One objective of punishment is to send "a message addressed to the public at large. The punishment of an offender deters others by telling them: 'This will happen to you if you violate the law.'"[11] In other words, punishing offenders broadcasts to society that there is a substantial amount of "pain" associated with criminal behavior. The idea that punishing offenders will deter the rest of society is termed general deterrence. Of course, punishing offenders might also have an effect on the offenders themselves; that is, offenders who feel the pain of punishment should be less likely to reoffend in the future. This is the principle of specific deterrence. A summary of the elements of deterrence theory is provided in **TABLE 3-1**.

Deterrence theorists, again drawing from the classical school, point out that punishment is most effective when it is swift, certain, and severe enough to outweigh the potential rewards of criminal behavior. In essence, neoclassical theorists restated and refined classical school statements about deterrence rather than making any major changes. The main contribution of deterrence theorists was to generate empirical tests of deterrence theory.

> *Punishing offenders restores the social balance and reaffirms social bonds; it sends a message that crime will not be tolerated.*

Empirical Tests of Deterrence Theory

The basis of deterrence theory—that formal punishment reduces criminal behavior—is very straightforward. Testing deterrence theory, however, is more complex. Researchers have studied both specific and general deterrence. Further, they have tried to gauge the relative importance of the certainty and severity of punishment (very few look at swiftness). To help organize this research, the different tests of both general and specific deterrence discussed are outlined in **TABLE 3-2**. Prior to discussing this research, it is important to distinguish between absolute and marginal deterrence. Absolute deterrence is the notion that having a formal system of punishments deters criminal behavior. Indeed, few would argue that a complete absence of police and prisons would have no effect on crime. As an example, some (but not all) types of crime increase when police departments go on strike.[12,13] Marginal deterrence addresses whether incremental (marginal) increases in punishment produce decreases in crime. For example, does doubling the prison sentence for robbery lead to reductions in that particular crime? Almost all empirical tests of deterrence theory test marginal deterrence rather than absolute deterrence.

General Deterrence

General deterrence is the proposition that increases in the certainty, severity, or swiftness of punishment produce decreases in criminal behavior for the population at large. Most researchers test either the certainty or severity of punishment. The severity of punishment is relatively easy to measure. One could look, for example, at the average prison sentence for crimes in different jurisdictions. Studies on capital punishment (the ultimate in severity), though, are by far the most common tests of this aspect of deterrence theory.[14] Obviously, those who are executed will never commit another crime (this is incapacitation rather than deterrence).

TABLE 3-1

Key Elements of Deterrence Theory

Element	Definition
Assumptions	Deterrence theory assumes that humans are rational and hedonistic.
Levels of deterrence	Deterrence can take place on two levels that differ in the purpose of the punishment: • Specific deterrence focuses on the individual offender. It seeks to teach criminals a lesson so that they will learn from experience and "go straight" in the future. • General deterrence is concerned with society as a whole. Here, individual punishment is aimed at sending a message to everyone—the punishment demonstrates what will happen to them if they violate the law.
Effective punishment	Deterrence theorists argue that effective punishment is swift, certain, and severe.
	Deterrence may also be conditional; that is, legal threats deter only persons who have a stake in conformity and are tied to conventional society in such a way that they will suffer from the stigma of punishment. Finally, deterrence may be marginal, which refers to the inhibiting effect of one punishment compared with another.

TABLE 3-2

Empirical Tests of Deterrence Theory

Specific Measures/Tests	Findings
General Deterrence	
Death penalty research (severity)	Most studies find that the death penalty has no effect on homicide rates. A small minority of studies find a brutalization effect, a deterrent effect, or both.
Clearance rate (certainty)	Most studies find that the clearance rate has no effect on crime. A minority of studies find that a deterrent effect emerges when the clearance rate reaches a certain tipping point.
Police experiments	The Kansas City Preventive Patrol experiment found that doubling police patrols had no effect on crime. Later experiments with directed patrol and focused deterrence are more promising.
Perceptions research (certainty and severity)	Those who believe that the punishment for crime is severe and that their likelihood of apprehension is high are less likely to engage in crime. However, this is mostly because offenders, over time, lower their estimates of severity and certainty (the experiential effect).
Specific Deterrence	
Police arrest experiments	An initial experiment found that arresting domestic violence perpetrators reduced later calls for service more than other options (e.g., warning, separating). Later studies suggest that this finding applies only to those who have conventional ties to society (e.g., employment).
Comparison of probation versus intensive programs	Intermediate sanctions (e.g., intensive probation, shock probation, boot camps) do not appear to reduce recidivism more than regular probation. The "swift, certain, fair" model used in Project HOPE is more promising.
Scared straight	Numerous experiments indicate that scared straight programs have no positive effect on criminal behavior. The weight of the evidence suggests that they actually increase crime.

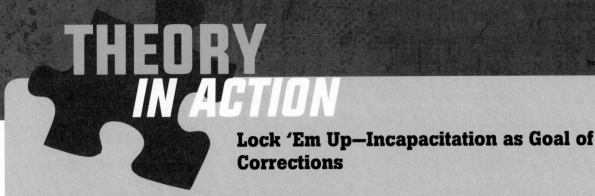

Lock 'Em Up—Incapacitation as Goal of Corrections

The basic premise of incapacitation, that "a thug in prison cannot mug your sister," is simple to grasp. When offenders are in prison, they no longer have the opportunity to engage in crime. If society locks up enough offenders, crime should decline. Scholars identify two types of incapacitation. Collective incapacitation refers to the reduction in crime achieved through a change in sentencing (e.g., mandatory minimum sentences) that affects a large proportion of offenders. Selective incapacitation attempts to control crime by sentencing individual offenders. Here, offenders who are thought to pose the greatest risk of future crime receive longer sentences. This policy provides for the identification and removal of chronic offenders from society so that crime can be controlled.

Incapacitation came to be a primary goal of corrections (especially prisons) in the 1980s largely by default. Rehabilitation was attacked as a failure, and evidence emerged that neither specific nor general deterrence was likely to have a great impact on crime. During this period, scholars began to argue that incapacitation, if done ruthlessly, could have a substantial impact. The promise of selective incapacitation, in particular, was seductive. James Q. Wilson argued that if much serious crime is committed by repeaters, isolating these repeaters from society would produce major reductions in crime rates.

Over the past 30 years, the United States has in many ways conducted an experiment in incapacitation. According to the U.S. Department of Justice, the number of individuals in secure confinement increased from under 200,000 in 1980 to a peak of almost 2.4 million in 2008, before declining moderately over the past few years. During that same time, the incarceration rate increased from roughly 150 prisoners per 100,000 citizens to over 500 prisoners per 100,000 citizens. To more clearly understand the extent to which America relies on incarceration, consider the following two facts. First, the first revealed that 1 in 100 adult Americans are incarcerated. Second, despite having only 1 percent of the world's population, the U.S. houses 25 percent of the world's prisoners. What has been the effect of such massive increases in the use of prison and jail? Has incapacitation worked?

Evaluations of Incapacitation

Critics of incapacitation often point out that throughout the 1980s and early 1990s, when many states were dramatically increasing their prison populations, crime rates continued to rise. Incapacitation supporters contend that crime rates would have risen even higher without the increased use of prisons, and they point to the recent decline in crime as evidence that incapacitation works. Researchers have tackled this issue in a number of ways, including:

- Surveying inmates as they enter prison to assess how much crime they committed in the past year. This is then used as an estimate of how many crimes they would commit in the future if they were not incarcerated.
- Comparing states that dramatically increased their prison population with states that did not during the same time period.
- Using statistical models to estimate "crime saved" through incapacitation in a single state.
- Studying the crimes committed by offenders who were released from prison early due to court-imposed prison population caps.
- Studying offenders who were sentenced to death, but had their sentence commuted, and were eventually released.

Although different studies reach somewhat different estimates of the incapacitation effect, a common theme runs through the research; large increases in prison population produce moderate decreases in some forms of criminal activity. For example, a study by researchers Thomas Marvell and Carlisle Moody, Jr., sought to assess the impact of state increases in prison population in the 1970s and 1980s on serious crimes. The researchers found that the increases had little or no impact on the crimes of rape, murder, or assault. There were moderate positive effects, however, for robbery, larceny, and burglary. Adding roughly 400,000 inmates (doubling the prison population at that time) over the course of the 1980s, for example, decreased robbery by about 18 percent.

Frank Zimring and his associates examined the effects of California's huge prison population increase in the 1980s. They first estimated what the crime rate would have been without any prison increase and then compared these figures with the actual crime rate to get an estimate of the incapacitation effect. They found that each "person year" (incarcerating one person for a year) of prison prevented roughly 3.5 crimes per year. Virtually all (93%) of the reduction, however, was due to reductions in burglary, robbery, and larceny.

The general finding is that huge increases in the use of prison produced moderate reductions in offenses such as robbery, larceny, and burglary but had little impact on assault, homicide, or rape. This finding makes sense because the former crimes tend to be high-rate offenses, while the latter do not. An individual might commit many burglaries or robberies over the course of a year. A crime like homicide, however, is extraordinarily rare; very few individuals ever commit more than one in their lifetime.

For example, several studies have traced the recidivism rates of former death row inmates who had their sentences commuted because of the 1972 *Furman v. Georgia* ruling. Because many of these offenders were eventually paroled, these studies test the argument that the death penalty, through incapacitation, prevents future murders. A study that followed the entire cohort (478) learned that only one committed murder following release from prison.

Criticisms of Incapacitation

Although this evidence offers some support for incapacitation, the massive increase in prison rates in the United States did not produce the type of crime reductions anticipated by supporters of this theory. Several factors may impede the incapacitation effect:

- By the time some offenders are incarcerated for a lengthy period, they may already be aging out of criminal activity.
- Selective incapacitation has proved elusive because one cannot predict who will be a "chronic offender" with the necessary accuracy.
- Locking up drug offenders, because they are readily replaced in society, yields no reduction in drug crime.

Further, even those who support incapacitation recognize that additional increases in imprisonment will generate even smaller reductions in crime. As states lock up a greater proportion of offenders, the remaining pool of offenders is inevitably a less serious and chronic group. Thus, while doubling the prison population might initially produce a 15 to 20 percent reduction in some crimes, doubling it again will not have the same effect. For this reason, even John Dilulio, a noted and vocal supporter of incapacitation, conceded that the country has "maxed out" on the benefits of prison.

Elliot Currie points out an even greater flaw in the incapacitation literature: The question "Does incapacitation work?" is not a very good question. The better question is "How well does incapacitation work compared with other strategies?" Reframing this issue recognizes that building and maintaining prisons generates huge costs. Could the money spent on prisons have created more crime reduction if spent elsewhere? Cost–benefit analyses suggest that is the case. One study compared early prevention programs with an incapacitation program (California's three-strikes law) and found that prevention generated similar crime reductions at a fraction of the cost. Those who support prevention and early intervention programs point out that while a thug in prison can't shoot your sister, he already shot somebody's sister to wind up in prison.

More recently, criminologists such as Todd Clear and Travis Pratt have outlined ways in which mass incarceration may actually increase crime. Clear highlights how incarcerating a high percentage of adults from already disadvantaged neighborhoods can further destabilize these areas. Similarly, Pratt highlights the social costs of incarceration, including the difficulty of reintegrating ex-inmates back into society.

The End of an Era?

Over the past decade, American enthusiasm for incarceration has waned. Many states face historically high budget deficits, worsened by the worldwide economic crisis of 2008. At the same time, the substantial drop in crime over the past 20 years has weakened the "get tough" rhetoric. In many states, legislators have closed prisons, delayed the opening of new prisons, and/or reduced sentences for some criminal acts. Accordingly, incarceration levels have declined over the past 4 years. Even the nature of the ideological battle over incarceration has shifted. Conservative politicians and thinkers who once championed incarceration have now come to believe that the corrections system is too onerous and costly. The organization Right on Crime champions reforms that move America away from an "overreliance" on prisons. These changes led Todd Clear and Natasha Frost to argue that we have reached an end to the era of mass incarceration.

Sources: Visher, C. A. (1987). Incapacitation and crime control: Does a 'lock 'em up' strategy reduce crime? *Justice Quarterly, 3,* 513–533; Greenwood, P. W. (1982). *Selective incapacitation.* Santa Monica, CA: Rand; Wilson, J. Q. (1975). *Thinking about crime.* New York: Random House; Sabol, W. J., West, H. C., & Cooper, M. (2009). Prisoners in 2008. *Bureau of Justice Statistics Bulletin.* Washington, DC: U.S. Department of Justice; Glaze, L. E., & Herberman, E. J. (2013). Correctional populations in the United States, 2012. *Bureau of Justice Statistics Bulletin.* Washington, DC: U.S. Department of Justice; Walmsley, R. (2003). *World Prison Population List* (4th ed.). London: Home Office; Piehl, A. M., & Dilulio, J. J., Jr. Does prison pay? Revisited. *Brookings Review, 13,* 20–25; Levitt, S. D. (1996). The effect of prison population size on crime rates: Evidence from prison overcrowding litigation. *Quarterly Journal of Economics, 3,* 319–351; Marquart, J. W., & Sorensen, J. R. (1988). Institutional and postrelease behavior of Furman-commuted inmates in Texas. *Criminology, 26,* 677–693; Marvell, T. B., & Moody, C. E., Jr. (1993). Prison population growth and crime reduction. *Journal of Quantitative Criminology, 10,* 109–130; Liptak, A. (2008, February 28). 1 in 100 U.S. adults behind bars, new study says. *New York Times.* Retrieved October 27, 2010, from http://www.nytimes.com/2008/02/28/us/28cnd-prison.html; Dilulio, J. J., Jr. (1999, March 12). Two million prisoners are enough. *The Wall Street Journal,* p. A14; Currie, E. (1998). *Crime and punishment in America: Why the solutions to America's most stubborn social crisis have not worked and what will.* New York: Henry Holt, p. 65; Clear, T. (2007). *Imprisoning communities.* New York: Oxford University Press; Pratt, T. C. (2009). *Addicted to incarceration.* Thousand Oaks, CA: Sage; Greenwood, P. W., Rydell, C., & Chiesa, J. (1996). *Diverting children from a life of crime: Measuring costs and benefits.* Santa Monica, CA: Rand; Butterfield, F. (2002, January 22). Tight budgets force states to reconsider crime and penalties. *New York Times,* p. A1. Clear, T. R., & Frost, N. A. (2014). *The punishment imperative: The rise and fall of mass incarceration in America.* New York: NYU Press.

The issue is whether the death penalty serves as a general deterrent against homicide. Concerning the death penalty, the most common research strategies focus on a comparison of homicide rates (1) between states that have the death penalty and those that do not and (2) executions and homicide over time within the same jurisdiction.

Among studies of the first type, the vast majority find that there is little difference in homicide rates between states that have or do not have the death penalty.[15] One study used a matching technique to compare the murder rates of death penalty states with non–death penalty states for the years 1920 to 1955 and 1920 to 1962.[16] The research discovered no difference between the two; executions appeared to have had no effect on homicide rates. A constant theme in this kind of research is the difficulty of untangling cause and effect and of controlling for differences among states.

Over time, researchers have used more complex "econometric" statistical techniques. Unfortunately, when these models are applied to homicides and executions (which are relatively rare events), they are very sensitive to particular specifications of researchers. Thus, there have been a number of recent econometric studies examining national execution/homicide data that report finding deterrent effects.[17] Using the same data, however, others have found no effect.[18] Statistician Richard Berk, commenting on these studies and their methodology, believes that given the limits of homicide data, we simply "can't tell" whether a deterrent effect exists.[19]

Many of the studies looking at the same jurisdiction over time also fail to find a relationship between executions and homicide rates. These studies usually take advantage of the moratorium on capital punishment that resulted from the 1972 Supreme Court *Furman v. Georgia* ruling. This decision stated that the capital sentencing system was arbitrary and discriminatory and that it violated the defendant's right to due process of law. McFarland examined the pattern of homicide rates in the United States following the first four executions after the death penalty was reinstated in 1976.[20] He failed to find significant evidence, nationally or locally, of a deterrent effect for executions.

Two pieces of research examined the results of Oklahoma's 1990 return to the use of capital punishment after a 25-year moratorium.[21,22] In each study, using different methodologies, weekly homicide figures were tracked for 1 year before and after the execution. Little or no evidence of deterrence emerged from these studies. Both studies, however, found that certain types of homicides actually increased following the execution—a **brutalization effect**. Scholars suggest that the state's execution legitimizes the use of violence, demonstrating that it is appropriate to kill people who have gravely offended.[23]

An analysis of California's resumption of executions (again, after a lengthy moratorium) revealed a more complex pattern.[24] The authors categorized homicides as stranger/nonstranger and felony/nonfelony. Felony murders occur when an offender commits homicide to further another felony (e.g., an armed robbery that results in homicide). Because the underlying felony is rationally planned, the offenders might be deterred by the existence of the death penalty. The analysis revealed a small but significant deterrent effect for

A hospital TAB used in lethal injection executions at the Osborne Correctional Institution in Somers, Connecticut. In May 2005, the state of Connecticut executed its first inmate in 45 years.

© Bob Child/AP Photos

felony murder, but only when it involved nonstrangers. This effect, however, was overshadowed by a much larger brutalization effect for homicides resulting from arguments among strangers. Muddying the waters even further, researchers studying homicides in Texas between 1994 and 2007 got results that were the reverse of those found in California. In Texas, a short-term (lasting 1 month) modest deterrent effect emerged for nonfelony homicides, while a smaller brutalization effect was found for felony homicides.[25]

What can be learned from decades of death penalty research? First, readers should bear in mind that most studies of the death penalty find that it has no effect on homicides. Second, the brutalization and deterrent effects discovered in recent studies are small and very sensitive changes in calculation methods. The conservative conclusion is that there is no strong empirical evidence that the death penalty deters homicides. Research on the deterrent effect of nonlethal penalties (e.g., length of prison terms) is no more encouraging to deterrence advocates. Again, the most common finding for these studies is that the length of prison terms has no effect on crime rates.[26]

Evidence regarding the deterrent effect of the certainty of punishment is more promising. Clearance rate, the proportion of total crimes cleared by arrest, is a common measure of certainty. A high clearance rate means that offenders' odds of getting caught are also high. Deterrence theory predicts that crime should be lower when the clearance rate is high. Like death penalty studies, researchers compare different jurisdictions to see whether clearance rates predict arrest rates. Although some early studies found that high clearance rates were associated with lower crime rates, more recent studies (using better methodology) failed to replicate these findings. The typical finding among these studies is that clearance rates are not related to crime rates.[27]

Several studies, however, appear to have identified an exception to the general finding that clearance rates do not predict crime. A study of Florida cities discovered that when the clearance rates reached a certain "tipping point" (roughly 30%), a modest deterrent effect emerged.[28] A later study of Pennsylvania cities documented the same pattern, but with a higher tipping point (about 40%).[29] In both studies, however, the deterrent effect was limited to small cities. Unfortunately, small cities with high clearance rates are rare—limiting the importance of the tipping point finding.

Researchers have also tested whether the certainty of punishment reduces crime by experimentally manipulating policing practices. Evidence that increased police presence (which increases the certainty of detection) reduces crime would support deterrence theory. The most famous study in this realm is the **Kansas City Preventive Patrol Study**.

> **A high clearance rate means that offenders' odds of getting caught are also high.**

In this experiment, conducted in the early 1970s, police beats were randomly assigned to one of three conditions.[30] In the reactive beats, police only entered the area to respond to calls for service. In the second group, police doubled or tripled the normal level of patrol. The final group of beats was patrolled as usual. The researchers discovered that neither increasing nor reducing police presence had any effect on the crime rate. Some have criticized the study, however, primarily because police cars left the normal or preventive beats to answer calls for service in the other beat.[31]

The effect of certainty is more apparent in studies of directed patrols. This research suggests that increasing police presence in high crime areas can lower crime. Cities tend to have a few hot spots of criminal activity, which generate most of the calls for police service. Directed patrols focus police attention toward these areas during times when criminal activity is highest (typically at night). For example, in an experiment in Minneapolis, patrol was doubled for 55 hot spots by taking patrols away from low crime areas. Normal patrol levels were continued in an additional 55 hot spots. Analyses of crime-related calls for police service revealed that the additional patrols produced a moderate reduction in crime.[32] A recent study of foot patrols deployed in violent crime hot spots by Philadelphia police also found deterrent effects.[33]

Saturation patrols, zero tolerance policing, and other forms of police crackdowns raise police presence further. Typically, police target certain offenses (drunk driving, drug dealing) in certain geographical areas and saturate these areas with police. For example, directed patrols using a heavy police presence in high crime police beats in Houston, Texas, yielded moderate crime reductions.[34] The idea of zero tolerance policing is that in addition to simply patrolling, police aggressively pursue even small infractions (e.g., loitering, panhandling, traffic violations). Zero tolerance policing is based on the theory that disorder, if unchallenged by police, breeds more serious crime. Wilson and Kelling call this the "broken windows" thesis. The idea is that buildings with broken windows send the message that crime and disorder are tolerated in the neighborhood.[35]

Policing crackdowns and zero tolerance policing have had some success in lowering certain offenses. Indeed the decline in violent crime experienced in New York City during the 1990s is often attributed to aggressive order maintenance. A recent study found that these strategies did play a minor role in the reduction of homicide and robbery, accounting for between 1 to 5 percent of the robbery decline and 7 to 12 percent of the homicide decline.[36] Critics of aggressive policing point out that the deterrent effect of crackdowns tends to be

Police restrain suspect.
© Shutterstock, Inc.

short-lived and may sometimes shift crime to neighboring areas. Zero tolerance policing and other aggressive policing strategies might also produce some negative consequences. In particular, massive increases in arrests for minor offenses may alienate residents, lower police legitimacy, and inflame racial tensions. The 2014 death of Eric Garner at the hands of New York City police officers illustrates many of these concerns. Garner was confronted by police for selling loose cigarettes. Videos from bystanders show that when he resisted arrest, police used physical force (including a chokehold) to subdue him. The videos and the subsequent decision of a grand jury not to pursue a criminal case led to waves of protest.[37]

Specific Deterrence

Specific deterrence, also called special deterrence, refers to the effect that punishment has on the offender. Deterrence theory predicts that offenders who are punished swiftly and severely will be less likely to engage in future crime. The available empirical evidence mostly concerns the effect of severity. One simplistic way to look at specific deterrence is to ask how often those who are imprisoned commit new offenses upon release. Follow-up studies of those released from prison consistently indicate that 60 to 75 percent are rearrested within 3 years—hardly comforting to advocates of specific deterrence.[38]

A more sophisticated approach would be to compare groups of similar offenders who are punished differently. The emergence of intermediate sanctions in the 1980s allowed researchers to conduct just such an experiment. Intermediate sanctions are designed to be more painful than traditional probation but less severe than prison. The two most popular types of intermediate sanctions are **intensive supervision probation (ISP)** and correctional boot camps. ISP, which includes increased contact with the probation officer, curfews, drug testing, and other enhancements, was designed to "turn up the heat on probationers."[39] However, in a very rigorous experiment (random assignment of subjects, multiple program sites), researchers discovered that ISP programs did not reduce arrests for new offenses when compared with traditional probation.[40-42]

Boot Camps promised to reduce juvenile crime.

© Bruce Parker/AP Photos

The most recent deterrence program for probation focuses on the swiftness and certainty of punishment rather than the severity. The new **swift-certain-fair (SCF) model** has enjoyed some success reducing crime among drug and alcohol offenders. In Hawaii's Opportunity Probation Enforcement (HOPE) program, offenders are explicitly warned that failing any drug test will result in immediate punishment. Individuals who fail a drug test are swiftly arrested and jailed for short period (typically a few days which can be served over weekends). A recent randomized trial found that HOPE participants were much less likely to be arrested or use illicit drugs that those in the control group.[43] These results are promising and have led many other jurisdictions to adopt the SCF model. Because HOPE and similar programs rely on the results of drug tests, it may be difficult to extend this program to non-drug offenders.

Correctional boot camps, sometimes called shock incarceration, are also designed to be more painful than traditional sanctions. Following the military boot camp model, these programs emphasize physical training and military drills. As with ISP programs, research on correctional boot camps is largely negative. A recent meta-analysis examined 44 comparisons between boot camps and control groups from published research studies. The researchers found that overall, there was no difference in recidivism.[44]

In a review of intermediate sanctions (including boot camps, ISPs, and other sanctions), Francis Cullen and his associates note that although these programs are perceived by offenders as more "painful" than regular probation, they are no more effective at reducing crime.[45]

Even Sheriff Joe Arpaio's jails, discussed earlier, appeared to have little effect on inmates' behavior after they were released. In a study commissioned and paid for by Arpaio comparing jail inmates under his tenure with inmates who served time prior to his arrival, researchers found no differences in recidivism rates. In other words, wearing pink underwear and sleeping out in the desert heat was no more of a deterrent than the normal jail experience.[46]

As with studies of general deterrence, researchers have examined and manipulated police behaviors to test the principle of specific deterrence. In particular, they have examined the consequences of police officers' decisions to arrest. Arrest can be considered punishment because it leads to booking and in most cases to at least some short-term incarceration. Indeed, Lawrence Sherman refers to arrest as "the aspirin of criminal justice, the most widely dispensed incarceration 'drug' in the United States."[47] Important here is the fact that police have a great deal of discretion in choosing whether or not to arrest an offender. Deterrence theory would predict that those who are arrested would be less likely to engage in future crime than those whom the police choose not to arrest.

A series of experiments focusing on police response to domestic violence shed some light on the effect of arrest. In the first study, suspects in Minneapolis were randomly assigned to one of three potential responses by the police: (1) arrest, (2) threat of arrest (with the suspect leaving the home), and (3) a "talking to" by the police (with the suspect left at the scene). The results supported the use of arrest in domestic violence cases as a way to protect the victim; the suspects who were arrested had the lowest rate of recidivism. Arrest appeared to have a specific deterrent effect upon domestic violence.[48,49]

This study had a dramatic impact on policing in domestic violence cases. Although the authors were careful to recommend against the passage of mandatory arrest laws until further research was conducted, the results of the Minneapolis experiment contributed to the passage of such laws in 15 states by 1991.[50] The study was replicated (repeated with the same methodology in a different location) in several other cities with dissimilar results.

Sherman and his colleagues specifically examined the impact of arrest on domestic violence cases in inner-city, crime-ridden neighborhoods in Milwaukee, Wisconsin. Suspects were randomly assigned the same potential police responses as in the Minneapolis experiment. Although interviews with victims in such cases revealed that arrest had a short-term deterrent effect, analysis of calls to police revealed no difference among the three sanctions. The authors concluded that short-term arrest may even cause harm by increasing anger at society without increasing the fear of re-arrest. Thus, "a little jail time can be worse than none."[51]

A subsequent analysis of the Milwaukee experiment suggested that suspects without a stake in conformity were less likely to be deterred by arrest. Unmarried, unemployed, and black subjects were more likely to become involved in domestic violence again. The researchers believe that the results confirm that the effectiveness of legal sanctions (e.g., arrest) is dependent on informal controls (e.g., employment, marriage).[52] Similar findings were obtained in Colorado Springs, Colorado, and Dade County, Florida. A synthesis of these four experiments found that overall, arrest appeared to do little to either increase or decrease the likelihood of repeat offending in domestic violence cases. In all four locations, however, arrest seemed to have a deterrent effect on employed suspects, but arrest increased the risk of future violence by the unemployed.[53] The researchers caution not to take these findings too literally. For example, employment may be a measure of exposure—an employed subject is less likely to be at home and thus have less interaction with the victim.

The experiments raise the possibility, however, that formal sanctions may "kick off" these social controls. Williams and Hawkins make this exact argument and outline three indirect "costs" of arrest:[54]

1. **Commitment costs:** Arrests may have an adverse effect on future opportunities (e.g., employment or education).
2. **Attachment costs:** Arrests can result in harm to or loss of personal relationships.
3. **Stigma:** Arrests can cause a loss of reputation.

Focused Deterrence

Over the past 15 years, scholars and police administrators have teamed to create several innovative programs that fall under the new concept of **focused deterrence**. David Kennedy and his colleagues have been at the forefront of this movement. They have helped police departments in Boston, Cincinnati, and other cities create and evaluate programs geared to reduce specific criminal activity (e.g., gang violence, drug markets) with a combination of specific and general deterrence. In his 2009 book, *Deterrence and Crime Prevention*, Kennedy discusses some of these programs in detail. The book also breathes some new life into the central concepts of deterrence theory.[55]

Kennedy's central insight is that many deterrence strategies fail because officials rely upon their actions (e.g., increased patrols, tougher penalties for certain crimes) to speak for themselves. Instead, he believes the potential offenders need to be explicitly told that the risk of being sanctioned has increased. In one program, drug dealers were actually sent letters by the police chief informing them that police had collected evidence and that specific sanctions would be forthcoming if their behavior continued.[56] In Boston and Cincinnati, gang members were brought to "call-ins" where they were informed by the police and community representatives that future gang violence would result in quick and severe sanctions.[57]

In order to be effective, such threats must be credible and narrowly tailored to specific offenders and offenses. In Boston, "Operation Ceasefire" targeted handgun violence being perpetrated by a small percentage of gang members. Gang members were informed that future violence would be met with severe sanctions for *all members* of any gang that used handguns. As with Al Capone (convicted of tax evasion rather than his more serious offenses), individuals would be punished through any means legally possible. In this "**pulling levers**" approach, police and prosecutors pull any legal lever to apply pressure. All members of the first gang to engage in gun violence were prosecuted for crimes unrelated to the violence or punished through revocation of probation or parole. Because these threats are very narrow (gun violence rather than crime generally), authorities have the resources to make the threat credible. This serves as a general deterrent for other gangs. In Boston, police and prosecutor response to initial (and subsequent) handgun violence among gang members was by all accounts swift and severe. A subsequent research report suggested that youth homicides decreased rapidly (in part) as a result of this intervention.[58]

In Cincinnati, Ohio, where racial tension between police and African Americans erupted into 3 days of rioting in 2001, police also targeted gang violence. University of Cincinnati researchers helped police identify "impact" gang members and map out gang activities, rivalries, and alliances. These individuals averaged over 35 prior charges and 10 prior felonies.[59] All told, researchers discovered that these people were associated (as victims, offenders, or both) with 75 percent of Cincinnati's homicides. As part of the Cincinnati Initiative to Reduce Violence (CIRV), offenders attended a "call in" and were told, face to face, that gun violence would be met with swift and severe sanctions. A program evaluation by University of Cincinnati researchers found that this initiative reduced gang-member-involved homicides by roughly 40 percent.[60]

A major advantage of focused deterrence programs is the potential to avoid the collateral damage that can be caused by heavy handed policing strategies. In contrast to the zero tolerance "broken windows" model, focused deterrence

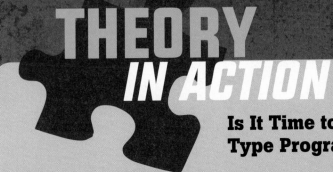

THEORY IN ACTION

Is It Time to Move Beyond "*Scared Straight!*" Type Programs?

In 1978, the Academy Award for best documentary film went to *Scared Straight!*, a film that followed a group of 17 juveniles through the Juvenile Awareness Program. In the movie, juveniles are confronted by the "lifers," a group of inmates serving lengthy sentences at the maximum security Rahway Prison in New Jersey. The inmates described prison life in graphic detail (e.g., rapes, murders) and physically confronted the youth. The theory of deterrence is clearly the rationale for this program. It is an attempt to increase juveniles' fear of punishment by emphasizing the nastiness of prison life. In the documentary, the program is described as extremely successful, having a success rate of 80 percent for the more than 8,000 youth who attended the program.

Given the social context of the late 1970s (the attack on rehabilitation and the start of the get-tough movement), this film, which aired on television in 1979, captured the imagination of the public and policymakers alike. Not surprisingly, similar programs spread across the United States and the rest of the world, and the phrase "scared straight" is now used to describe them generically. Unfortunately, scientific research on these programs indicates that they do not reduce criminal behavior. Instead, these programs likely *increase* delinquency. Anthony Petrosino, Corly Turpin-Petrosino, and James Finckenauer reviewed seven of the most methodologically sound evaluations of scared straight programs. The programs under evaluation varied on the level of inmate confrontation (from very aggressive to an educational-type approach), whether females participated, and the average age of participants. Despite these differences, a consistent finding emerged: In none of the seven studies did the scared straight group do better than a control group. Instead, these programs under study actually increased delinquency anywhere from 1 to 30 percent. A 2013 reanalysis of this data reached similar conclusions.

Because these studies were all conducted between 1967 and 1992, one might think that the scared straight programs would have vanished from the earth. While enthusiasm for such programs did wane, many of them are still operating. In August 2003, the governor of Illinois signed into law a bill that required the Chicago public school system to create a program called "Choices." This program identifies children at risk for committing crime and gives them tours of a state prison. Chicago Mayor Richard M. Daley supported the measure, saying, "As a freshman at De La Salle, they brought us down to Stateville. It shows you how harsh life is." Internet searches for "prison awareness" or "youth prison tours" reveal that other jurisdictions continue to bring youth into prisons in attempts to scare them straight. The Web page for the Monmouth (New Jersey) County Sherriff's Office advertises a "Prison Awareness Program" available for junior high and high school students.

Why do scared straight programs continue to draw support and funding from policymakers in the face of evidence indicating they actually increase delinquency? Part of the problem is that the negative scientific evidence may get drowned out by positive media portrayals. The original *Scared Straight!* documentary shows smirking, cocky kids boasting about their crime, only to have the smirk wiped off their face by prison inmates. This media formula has been repeated with great success. In 1999, "Scared Straight: 20 Years Later" aired in the United States. Hosted by Danny Glover, the program followed up on the 17 kids from the original documentary and claimed that only one had become a serious criminal. Many of them proclaim that it was the Scared Straight program that changed their lives.

In 2011, A&E Network launched "Beyond Scared Straight." Created by Arnold Shapiro, the producer of the original *Scared Straight!* documentary, the program is the highest rated show in A&E's history. Mr. Shapiro, who also produced the reality program "Big Brother," is unapologetic regarding the negative research findings for the inmate confrontation program. In an interview, he argued that such scientific research is dated and that the only accurate studies of modern programs were his shows. While it is true that the scientific evidence is now over 20 years old, the burden would seem to be on new programs to show that they are indeed not harming children. This burden cannot be met using television programs as "studies," because they lack the basic elements (e.g, a control group, random assignment, careful measurement) of scientific study. As Petrosino and his colleagues ask: Would you want a doctor to prescribe a treatment for your child that has the same track record of research results?

Aside from positive media portrayals, there are a number of reasons these programs survive. Chief among them is the belief that, as Mayor Daley put it, "If you save one child, it's worth it." The problem with this statement is that it ignores the fact that on balance, scared straight programs are doing more harm than good. A good analogy would be producing a new seat belt that, when activated during crashes, killed more people than it saved. If the new seat belt saved just one life (but ended more lives than it saved), would anyone want it installed in his or her car? Petrosino and his colleagues identify a number of other reasons that contribute to the staying power of scared straight programs, including:

Public appeal. The program does make intuitive sense. Many in the public respond to the film by saying, "Well, it scared the hell out of me." This is a powerful incentive for policymakers to support the program.

Institutional staying power. Once a program is started, it sometimes takes on a life of its own and becomes difficult to dismantle.

"It's good for the inmates." Some defenders of scared straight point out that although it may not benefit the juveniles, it may benefit the inmates by giving them something positive to work toward.

The "true believers." Some people believe so strongly in the program that they are simply not persuaded by scientific evidence of failure. Indeed, the policy response to findings from one experiment was to end the evaluation of the program rather than the program itself.

Sources: Shapiro, A. (1978). *Scared straight!* Santa Monica, CA: Pyramid Films; Petrosino, A., Turpin-Petrosino, C., & Finckenauer, J. (2000). Well-meaning programs can have harmful effects! Lessons from experiments of programs such as Scared Straight. *Crime and Delinquency, 36,* 353–379; Petrosino, A., Turpin-Petrosino, C., Hollis-Peel, M. E., & Lavenberg, J. G. (2012). Scared Straight and other juvenile awareness programs for preventing juvenile delinquency: A systematic review. *The Campbell Collaboration.* Retrieved July 20, 2014, from http://www.campbellcollaboration.org/lib/project/3/; Swanson, A. (2003). Scared straight. United Press International. Retrieved August 23, 2003, from http://newsmax.com/archives/articles/2003/8/22/225025.shtml; Monmouth County Sheriff's Office. Prison awareness. Retrieved October 26, 2010, from http://www.monmouthsheriff.org/Sections-read-23.html; Denhart, A. (2011). Beyond Scared Straight's real life controversy. *The Daily Beast.* Retrieved August 1, 2014, from http://www.thedailybeast.com/articles/2011/02/23/beyond-scared-straights-real-life-controversy.html

fits closely with the concept of "problem oriented policing." This theory of policing emphasizes the creative use of police resources to solve specific problems that are directly related to crime.[61] Because enforcement is focused on high rate offenders, the police avoid alienating law abiding residents of the neighborhood. For example, while previous crackdowns in Cincinnati had resulted in a backlash from law-abiding residents who felt harassed by police, the targeted crackdown was praised by community members.

Focused deterrence programs make it clear that if the threat of sanctions is made to a specific group, narrowly targeted toward a specific problem, and made credible by the actions of law enforcement, reductions in serious crimes are possible. A recent meta-analysis of focused deterrence programs found that 10 of the 11 studies reviewed reported significant crime reductions.[62] Of course, such programs should not be viewed as a magic solution to crime. Indeed, one weakness of this approach is that it may be difficult to maintain over long periods of time. In Boston, for example, the program disbanded (due to conflicts among team members) after 4 years, and youth homicides increased dramatically.[63]

Perceptual Deterrence

The focused deterrence approach stems in part from research on perceptual deterrence. Perceptual deterrence researchers raise the issue of whether the average citizen (or criminal) can identify with any accuracy the clearance rate or specific punishment for a particular crime. In that sense, people's perceptions about the severity and certainty of punishment are more important than the actual levels. People are asked survey questions such as "If you committed auto theft on 10 different days, on how many of those days do you think you would be caught?" Similarly, to gauge estimates of severity, one might ask a question such as "What punishment do you think you would receive if you got caught stealing an automobile?"

These "perceptual" measures of deterrence yield findings that are fairly consistent with research using objective measures. First, the studies suggest that perceptions of certainty are better predictors of crime than perceptions of severity. Second, even the effects of certainty perceptions on crime are modest.[64] The focused deterrence approach, where offenders are explicitly told that sanctions will become more certain and severe, lends support to this idea.

The relationship between perceptions and criminal behavior may not entirely reflect deterrence, though. Instead, individuals who engage in more crime may become likely to lower their estimate of the certainty or severity of the punishment. Because experience with crime causes people to change their perceptions (and not the reverse, as deterrence theory suggests), researchers have dubbed this an experiential effect.[65]

Some programs attempt to increase delinquents' perceptions of the severity of prison. The most widely recognized example is *Scared Straight!*, a program featured in multiple television shows, one of which won an Academy Award. In this type of program, youth are brought into a prison where inmates aggressively confront them and graphically describe the horrors of prison life. Although the programs are portrayed in most media as successful, scientific evaluations consistently show that, at best, the programs have no effect on criminal behavior. In fact, there is substantial evidence that scared straight programs actually *increase* criminal behavior.[66] (A more detailed analysis of the scared straight phenomenon is presented in **Theory in Action: Is it Time to Move Beyond "Scared Straight!" Type Programs?**).

Celerity

Celerity, or the swiftness of punishment, is the least studied aspect of deterrence theory. Psychological studies with animals suggest (and anyone who has successfully trained a dog understands) that swift punishments are more effective at reducing unwanted behavior than delayed punishments. The few available studies on offenders suggest, however, that immediate punishment does not decrease recidivism any more than delayed punishment. Nagin and Pogarsky note that unlike other animals, humans have the cognitive ability to connect an offense with punishment regardless of whether or not that punishment is swift. They also point out that throughout criminal justice processing, offenders are reminded repeatedly of their offense.[67]

Summary of Deterrence Theory

Deterrence theory predicts that swift, certain, and severe punishment will reduce crime, both among the general public (general deterrence) and for those being punished (specific deterrence). Deterrence theory, because it is derived from classical school theorists, focuses on formal punishment (arrest, prison) rather than informal controls. Although the empirical evidence regarding these predictions is mixed, it seems fair to make two generalizations. First, if any ingredient in the punishment mix is potent, it appears to be certainty rather than swiftness or severity. Studies of focused deterrence, clearance rates, directed patrols, and probation enforcement (recall the MUSTER program) all support the idea that crime declines when the certainty of getting punished increases. This body of research suggests that increases in certainty must be explicit and/or large enough that would-be offenders take notice. Second, even where deterrent effects emerge, they tend to be modest. In other words, official sanctions sometimes predict offending, but often not as well as measures from other theories of crime.[68]

There are several possible explanations for this limited support:

- Deterrence theory may rest on a faulty assumption; that is, people may not be as rational as they are portrayed in this theory (see the following rational choice theory).
- Almost all empirical tests focus on *marginal* increases in certainty and severity rather than on the absolute effect of deterrence.
- The capabilities of the criminal justice system are somewhat limited in a democratic society. For example, a society in which secret police assassinate suspected offenders on the spot might have lower crime rates, but few people want to live in such a society.

 Rational Choice Theory

Deterrence theory hinges in large part on the assumption that humans are rational beings; however, this assumption is tested only indirectly by looking at the effect of punishment on behavior. If people are rational and want to avoid pain and punishment, they should be deterred by formal sanctions. Rational choice theory explicitly examines the reasoning process followed by offenders. The main propositions in rational choice theory are that individuals will (1) weigh the costs or consequences of crime against the benefits of crime prior to engaging in criminal behavior and (2) choose criminal behavior when the rewards outweigh the costs.

Rational choice theorists allow for both formal (e.g., arrest, prison) and informal (e.g., shame, loss of job) sanctions. Furthermore, the benefits of crime can be tangible (e.g., money, property) or intangible (e.g., psychological thrill, respect of peers). In this sense, rational choice theory is much broader than deterrence theory; offenders consider multiple costs and rewards prior to making decisions about crime. Few rational choice theorists, however, portray criminals as purely rational.[69] Rather, the rationality of the decision process is constrained, or "bounded," by such factors as time, cognitive ability, and moral values.

Cornish and Clarke's Rational Choice Theory

Derek Cornish and Ronald Clarke's rational choice theory distinguishes between two types of decision making.[70] **Criminal involvement** decisions involve whether to engage in crime in general, as opposed to satisfying needs and wants with noncriminal alternatives. Cornish and Clarke portray this as a multistage process that unfolds over a long period of time. Rationality (a pure cost–benefit analysis of whether to engage in crime) is constrained by a host of factors. The **criminal event** involves decision making about the how, where, and when of a particular crime. In other words, a person has decided that he or she is ready to engage in crime but still considers a host of situational factors before choosing to follow through with (or refrain from) criminal activity.

Cornish and Clarke argue that separate theoretical models are necessary for particular types of crime. The decision process leading to the use of illicit drugs, for example, is different from the decision process for burglary. Also, separate models are required to explain initial involvement, the criminal event, and the decision to persist in or desist from criminal activity.

A Rational Choice Model for Burglary

As an example, consider Cornish and Clarke's explanation of burglary in a middle-class neighborhood. As just noted, decisions about whether to engage in crime (criminal involvement) tend to be multistage and unfold over an extended period of time. Both background factors and previous learning experiences constrain a purely rational assessment of costs and benefits. For example, someone with a strong conscience, strong moral values, and a cautious temperament might choose a legitimate solution (e.g., work) to fulfill a need, even when a criminal solution would have a better payoff and carry little risk of detection or punishment. Indeed, such a person might never think to consider crime as an alternative. The model presented here is a simplified version of Cornish and Clarke's explanation of criminal involvement for the crime of burglary.

- Background factors: Temperament, intelligence, cognitive style, broken home, parental crime, gender, class, education, neighborhood

  ↓

- Previous learning experience: Direct and observational experience with crime, contact with law enforcement agencies, conscience and moral code, self-perception

  ↓

- Generalized needs: Money, sex, friendship, status, excitement

  ↓

- Evaluation of solutions: Degree of effort, amount and immediacy of reward, likelihood and severity of punishment, moral costs

  ↓

- Solutions: Legitimate (work, gambling, marriage); illegitimate (burglary)

The criminal event model for burglary is a bit simpler and has few constraints on pure rational decision making. Again, this model pertains to individuals who have already decided to engage in burglary. In selecting both the area to engage in crime and the particular house to burglarize, offenders consider many situational factors that impact the rewards of the crime and the probability of detection.

- Selection of area
  - Select: Easily accessible, few police patrols, low security housing, larger gardens
  - Reject: Unfamiliar, distant, neighborhood watch, no public transportation
- Selection of home
  - Burglarized: No one at home, especially affluent, detached home, patio doors, bushes and other cover present, corner site
  - Not burglarized: Nosey neighbors, burglar alarm, no rear access, visible from street, window locks, dog

Criticisms of Rational Choice Theory

Critics identify two related problems in rational choice theory. First, empirical tests find little evidence of pure rational decision making. If one were to ask, "Do individuals choose to begin engaging in crime after a thorough comparison of all costs and benefits associated with that crime to other noncriminal alternatives?" the answer appears to be "No." For example, interviews with 3,300 adult offenders, drug addicts, and high school dropouts found that the respondents were motivated by the reward aspect of rational choice theory (i.e., the benefits of the crime), but the respondents underestimated the cost or deterrent effect (i.e., the risk of punishment).[71] In other words, offenders

are likely to be irrational regarding the threat of apprehension, which contradicts a fundamental premise of rational choice theory.

An interview with offenders imprisoned for property crimes revealed that the thought of punishment is rarely part of the crime selection process.[72] The offenders considered thoughts about the risk of punishment a distraction and focused instead on the benefits of the crime. Their experience with the criminal justice system also led them to discount the negative aspects of a prison sentence. A recent study of 34 federal inmates who had been "heavily involved" drug smugglers supports the limited role of crime risks. Though there was evidence that offenders considered the risk, many had no idea what the likely prison sentence was for their specific crime. "In the end, doubts were quelled with reference to the volume of reward awaiting them on successful completion of a drug smuggling event."[73]

A similar study with burglars revealed a discrepancy between what offenders said about planning a burglary in general and the actual burglaries they committed:

Most of our burglar informants could design a text-book burglary . . . [T]hey often described their past burglaries as though they were rationally conceived and executed. Yet, upon closer inspection, when their previous burglaries were reconstructed, textbook procedures frequently gave way to opportunity and situational factors.[74]

Of course, most rational choice theories do not portray humans as purely rational. Cornish and Clarke include a host of background and learning experience factors in their criminal involvement model. Indeed, the impulsivity and moral ambiguity cited in the study just noted are concepts within their criminal involvement model. This brings one to the second major criticism of rational choice theory. The problem with including concepts like "impulsivity," "moral values," and "temperament" is that they are all borrowed from competing theories (e.g., social learning theory, psychological theory) of crime. Further, many of these factors serve to constrain or limit a purely rational decision-making process. For example, very impulsive people might not take the time to weigh the costs and benefits of their actions; their actions may be irrational. Similarly, someone with a strong moral code might never consider a criminal response to most circumstances and therefore never weigh the risks and rewards of crime.

Rational choice theorists often portray themselves as the only theorists who allow for human choice and free will. Ronald Akers points out, however, that virtually all theories of crime allow for some rational choice, but some theories of crime emphasize the factors that limit or constrain that free will. For example, a social learning theorist would argue that delinquent peers and a person's own moral code (learned from parents and others) influence the decision to commit crimes. In that sense, rational choice theories are not as different as some may think. Indeed, some view rational choice models not as independent theories, but rather as an attempt to integrate many theories into a single explanation of crime.[75]

Despite this criticism, rational choice theory maintains an important place in criminology because it focuses attention on situational factors that may influence specific criminal events.

There is much evidence, for example, that criminals rationally plan to avoid detection by their selection of general areas and/or specific targets. One study of professional burglars found that burglars often called ahead or rang the doorbell when they arrived to make sure no one was home. If someone answered the door, they simply claimed that they were looking for a friend and had the wrong address. Further, the authors of the study discovered that burglars will avoid households with dogs or doors with deadbolt locks.[76] High-level drug smugglers paint a similar picture of the drug trade. Smugglers avoided detection through the use of high-end electronics, research on government interdiction techniques, and well-designed secret compartments. Those who broker the smuggling take into account the risk of losing a load in their pricing. As with legitimate postal services, many offered optional insurance with their shipping.[77]

Understanding what makes a good target for crime leads to very concrete policy implications, which are described later in this chapter. First discussed, however, are the routine activities and lifestyle approaches to crime because these perspectives fit very well with rational choice theorists' focus on the criminal event.

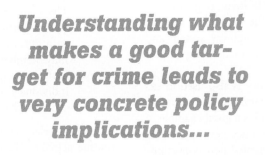

Understanding what makes a good target for crime leads to very concrete policy implications...

Thus, criminal events stem from the "routine activities" of both offenders and ordinary citizens.

Although routine activities theory identifies three elements necessary for crime FIGURE 3-1, most of the discussion and empirical testing involves target suitability and guardianship. The availability of motivated offenders is typically taken for granted. Guardianship could include police, but according to Felson and Boba, the most significant guardian in society is "not usually someone who brandishes a gun or threatens an offender with quick punishment, but rather someone whose mere presence serves as a gentle reminder that someone is looking."[80] Guardians discourage offenders from committing the crime in the first place.

Felson identifies a number of factors that influence the suitability of a target:[81]

- Value: Sometimes, value (money) is nearly universal; other times, it depends almost entirely on what is popular in the offender's world (e.g., specific CDs, sneakers, or jackets).
- Inertia: Some valuable property (e.g., large appliances) is simply too difficult to move; other property (cars, bicycles) provides its own getaway.
- Visibility: This might include valuables left in plain sight or the target living on a busy street.
- Access: Targets with easy access, such as being within walking distance of a shopping mall (which

Routine Activities Theory and the Lifestyle Approach

Routine activities theory and the "lifestyle approach" share some similarities with deterrence and rational choice theory perspectives. Like deterrence and rational choice theories, both of these perspectives assume that offenders make rational assessments about crime targets. Yet, unlike rational choice theory, they shift attention away from offenders and toward the victims of crime.

Routine Activities Theory

Routine activities theory was originally developed by Lawrence Cohen and Marcus Felson to explain "direct contact predatory crimes where at least one offender comes into direct physical contact with at least one victim."[78] Marcus Felson, now writing with Rachel Boba, has extended the theory to include illegal use and sale of drugs and white-collar crime.[79] The theory postulates that for any crime to occur, three elements must converge: (1) a motivated offender, (2) a suitable target, and (3) the absence of a capable guardian.

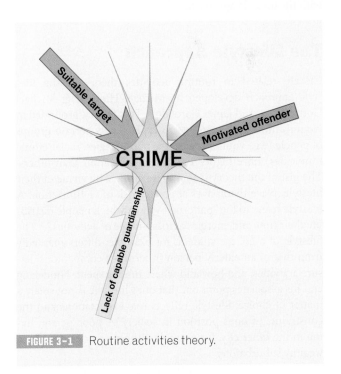

FIGURE 3-1 Routine activities theory.

attracts motivated offenders) or living on a street with exits on both sides as opposed to a cul-de-sac, are more suitable.

Similarly, the acronym CRAVED (Concealable, Removable, Available, Valuable, Enjoyable, Disposable) was coined by Ronald Clarke to describe aspects of targets that offenders crave.[82]

Cohen and Felson applied routine activities to explain why crime rates in most Western countries increased substantially between the 1950s and the 1970s.[83] They argued that while traditional theories that focus on the motivation of offenders could not explain the rising crime rate, a routine activities approach held promise. For example, during this time period, women became more likely to work outside of the home (and men no more likely to stay home). Thus, guardianship over homes during the daytime diminished. Advances in technology produced an enormous variety of lightweight, valuable items (e.g., stereos, televisions, VCRs), thus increasing the number of suitable targets. The advent of the interstate highway system and general improvement of roadways also made many targets more accessible.

Of course, routine activities theory is also used to explain current criminal behavior. In fact, the rise of online commerce and communication provides a good example of how broad changes in society can produce new opportunities for offending. The Internet has created new opportunities for Internet-perpetrated crime such as fraud and identity theft. Using survey data from Florida, Travis Pratt and his colleagues found that routine activities related to the Internet (e.g., time spent online, online purchasing practices) were related to the odds of being targeted for some form of Internet fraud.[84] Empirical tests of routine activities theory such as this often focus on victimization and overlap to some extent with the lifestyle approach.

The Lifestyle Approach

Closely related to routine activities theory is the lifestyle approach developed by Michael Hindelang, Michael Gottfredson, and James Garofalo.[85] This theory, grounded in victimization data, attempts to explain why certain groups of people (e.g., youths, males, the poor, singles, racial/ethnic minorities) have higher rates of victimization than others. The gist of the theory is that these groups, by virtue of their lifestyle, place themselves at greater risk of victimization. A lifestyle refers to the "patterned way in which people distribute their time and energies across a range of activities."[86] The lifestyle of a college student, for example, differs markedly from that of an elderly person in terms of companions, leisure activities, and how and where time is spent. Hindelang and his associates point out that one's lifestyle is not solely a matter of choice; lifestyle reflects role expectations and the constraints of one's position in society. A poor person living in the inner city, for example, cannot just decide to be a wealthy suburbanite.

Lifestyle theory includes several propositions that summarize the link between lifestyle and known correlates of victimization:[87]

- The more time that individuals spend in public places (especially at night), the more likely they are to be victimized.
- Following certain lifestyles makes individuals more likely to frequent public places.
- The interaction that individuals maintain tends to be with persons who share their lifestyles.
- The probability that individuals will be victims increases according to the extent to which victims and offenders belong to the same demographic categories.
- The proportion of time individuals spend in places where there are large numbers of nonfamily members varies according to lifestyle.
- The chances that individuals will be victims of crime (particularly theft) increase in conjunction with the amount of time they spend among nonfamily members.
- Differences in lifestyles are related to the ability of individuals to isolate themselves from those with offender characteristics.

The overlap between these lifestyle propositions and routine activities theory should be apparent. For example, time spent in public places at night (the first proposition) is a risk factor because there is less guardianship present in public places, especially at night, and a greater number of motivated offenders. Individuals who spend more time away from home have higher risk of victimization; due to their increased visibility and accessibility, they are more likely to become a target. In addition, their homes and property may be more at risk due to their absence (i.e., their decreased guardianship). For example, Cohen and Felson show that dispersion of activities away from the home is related to increased rates of homicide, rape, assault, burglary, and larceny.[88] The point here is that lifestyles predict victimization because they are often related to guardianship and target attractiveness.

Chapter 2 noted the high rates of violent crime victimization among blacks. A routine activities/lifestyle perspective can help to explain this finding. For example, blacks are more likely to live in segregated, public housing and spend their time in contact with motivated offenders. There may be an absence of capable guardians (e.g., neighbors who watch the area). Residents of public housing may tend to "mind their own business" and be reluctant to get involved because of fear of reprisal. Thus, a higher victimization rate for inner-city blacks is partly a function of an environment that increases the probability of crime.

As this example makes clear, many aspects of lifestyle cannot easily be altered. A person cannot simply choose to move to a house in a nice area of the city. Are there aspects of lifestyle that individuals might change to reduce their risk of victimization? An examination of data from 3 years of the U.S. National Crime Survey sought to answer this question.[89]

The researchers found that persons with greater daytime and nighttime activity outside the home (greater target visibility or exposure to motivated offenders) and who had a reduction in the number of household members (reduced guardianship) had higher rates of both personal and property crime victimization. Persons who maintained high levels of nighttime activity outside the household were also more likely to remain victims across the time periods covered by the surveys. The most perplexing finding, however, was that persons who took extra precautions did not reduce their risk of victimization.

A similar study from Canada, based on survey results from the Canadian Urban Victimization Study,[90] examined the same research question: What makes people prone to victimization? The results suggested that aging and getting married reduced victimization by reducing time spent in risky settings. For example, males who spent time in bars had an increased risk of victimization. In sum, risky settings were more likely to produce dangerous results.

In addition, the effect of personal lifestyle characteristics may depend on a person's neighborhood. A survey conducted in Seattle, Washington, revealed that lower levels of guardianship and high target attractiveness strongly increased the risk of burglary for residents of more affluent areas.[91] However, these variables were unrelated to the risk of burglary among residents of more socially disorganized areas. A more recent study found that the effect of individual-level target hardening (safety precautions taken by residents) depended upon neighborhood levels of guardianship. Safety precautions were most effective in neighborhoods with greater overall guardianship.[92]

The lifestyles of adolescents have also attracted some attention under this theory. With data from the National Youth Survey, a study investigated the relationship between routine activities and the risk of assault and robbery victimization among adolescents. Certain adolescent activities were related to the risk of violence. The most dangerous activities were delinquent behaviors. Delinquents were approximately two to three times more likely to be victimized by assault and robbery than nondelinquents. Engagement in conventional activities had little effect on risk after demographic characteristics and delinquent involvement were considered.[93] Further analysis by the researchers found a strong relationship between delinquent lifestyles and increased risk of both personal and property victimization.[94] Recent studies of gang involvement reveal a similar pattern: Gang membership greatly increased the likelihood of victimization. Gang members were more likely to be victimized because of the lifestyle associated with gang membership.[95,96]

A routine activities/lifestyle approach has even been used to explain the victimization of inmates within prison. A study of inmates within three different prisons revealed that inmates who spent more time in structured, supervised activities (e.g., education, working) were less likely to be victims of a violent offense. This reflects the increased guardianship associated with such activities. Participation in unsupervised recreation actually made violent victimization more likely. Unfortunately, time spent in supervised activities increased the likelihood of theft victimization, presumably because the inmates' property was left unguarded in their cells.[97]

Policy Implications: Situational Crime Prevention

Rational choice theory, routine activities theory, and the lifestyle approach share a focus on the situational factors (e.g., guardianship, target suitability) that affect whether victimization occurs. For this reason, they are sometimes grouped together under the title of opportunity theories (i.e., a focus on structure of opportunities for engaging in crime). The policy implications among these theories are therefore similar but vastly different from other theories of crime. Most crime prevention efforts, including rehabilitation and deterrence, focus on offenders because the theories from which they are derived focus on properties of offenders (e.g., personality, learning history). The exception to this rule is incapacitation, where the opportunity for crime is removed simply by segregating the offender from society. Like incapacitation, the policy implications of opportunity theories are to reduce the opportunity for offending. Rather than target specific offenders, however, these theories focus attention on the context of crime.[98] In other words, opportunity theories lead one to ask, "Can the environment be changed in a manner that reduces the opportunity for crime?"

One of the first criminologists to focus on this question was C. Ray Jeffery, who coined the phrase **crime prevention through environmental design (CPTED)**.[99] The basic premise of CPTED is that the way an environment is designed can promote or prevent crime. The term environment can mean something as broad as a community or as narrow as a convenience store. Around the same time (1972), an architect named Oscar Newman wrote *Defensible Space*, a book geared toward designing safe public housing (as opposed to high-rise projects). Newman's main idea was to create as much private space in housing developments as possible so that people maintain more guardianship over themselves and their property.[100]

From these initial contributions, a large body of literature has emerged. Some scholars and policymakers continue to use the term CPTED to describe this work, although others prefer terms such as environmental criminology or situational crime prevention. Regardless of the terminology, the literature provides numerous methods or principles for

> *The most dangerous activities were delinquent behaviors.*

crime prevention. Felson and Boba organize these methods into three groups:[101]

1. **Natural strategies:** Security results from the design and layout of space. Both human and capital costs are low.
2. **Organized strategies:** Security guards or police play the central role. These strategies are labor intensive and expensive.
3. **Mechanical strategies:** Alarms, cameras, and other hardware are employed to control access and provide surveillance. These strategies may require additional employees to watch monitors or respond to alarms. The equipment may be expensive.

One of the more prevalent mechanical strategies is the use of closed-circuit television (CCTV) cameras to monitor street corners, parking lots, and other high-crime areas. A recent review of 44 studies suggested that overall CCTV schemes led to a 16 percent decrease in crime. Most of the decrease was produced by the use of cameras in carports; CCTV in other public settings was less effective.[102] Despite the success of some mechanical strategies, most situational crime prevention advocates focus on natural strategies. They argue that crime can most often be prevented by following nature as closely as possible. This means avoiding, so far as one can, the use of the criminal justice system, armed guards, violence, and threats. Instead, it is preferable to set up situations and environments in which acting legally feels like the comfortable thing to do. Natural crime prevention should occur as a consequence of everyday life. For example, Felson and Boba offer the following tips for preventing crime in college and university parking areas:[103]

> *...situational crime prevention is more popular in other countries than in the United States.*

- Arrange for nighttime students and workers to have parking near building doors, but not so close that they block the view of the parking area from the building.
- At low-use times, close off unneeded parking areas or sections of large parking areas to concentrate people and cars for supervision.
- Require students and staff to sign up by name and have a sticker, even for nighttime or free areas.
- Eliminate nooks and corners in parking structures and fence parking areas.
- Get visitors to sign in and give them time limits.
- Build parking structures as slopes so that people on foot will have clear sight lines.
- Make visibility into parking structure stairwells easy.
- Orient buildings to face parking areas.
- Trim hedges and the lower limbs of trees around parking areas; avoid thick foliage.
- Post signs and organize the flow of traffic so that neither cars nor pedestrians will get lost.

Ronald Clarke has created a list of situational crime prevention techniques based on successful crime prevention programs; some of these techniques, along with examples, are illustrated in TABLE 3-3. Techniques such as those outlined by Clarke have been evaluated in many different contexts.

One of the earliest evaluations of planned crime prevention was a CPTED demonstration program directed by the Westinghouse National Issues Center. This was a 4-year (1974–1978) effort sponsored by the Law Enforcement Assistance Administration. One of the demonstration sites was Portland, Oregon, where the CPTED commercial demonstration program was designed to reduce crime in the Union Avenue Corridor (UAC). Due to socioeconomic changes, the UAC faced a rising crime rate and a rapidly deteriorating neighborhood. Businesspeople felt that crime was the single greatest obstacle to the successful operation of their businesses.

A number of tactics were implemented in the UAC to bring about changes in the physical and social environments, including the installation of high-intensity street lighting to create a safe street for the people. Survey results suggested that the CPTED changes contributed to a reduction in the consumers' fear of crime.[104] Furthermore, CPTED had a moderate degree of success in bringing about positive and lasting changes in the physical and social environments. It increased access control and surveillance (target hardening) in the area.[105] However, these commercial effects did not appear to carry over to residential neighborhood areas. A final study examined commercial burglary data from UAC to determine if CPTED applications were effective over time. The results indicated that commercial security surveys and street-lighting changes led to a significant reduction in commercial burglaries in the area. This effect had been maintained since the beginning of the project.[106]

For a number of reasons, situational crime prevention is more popular in other countries than in the United States. Indeed, since the 1980s, situational crime prevention has been the dominant strategy employed by the British government to reduce crime.[107] This focus led to a plethora of demonstration projects and evaluation research. For example, a 1997 study examined a program that sought to improve street lighting in an English neighborhood. Old streetlights were replaced with 129 high-pressure sodium lights in one neighborhood, but they were left intact in a similar (control) neighborhood. Over the next year, household victimization decreased in the experimental, but not in the control, neighborhood.[108] Other advantageous effects included an increase in the number of people on the street (especially women) after dark and a reduction in the fear of crime.

A more extensive program designed to reduce burglary also yielded favorable results.[109] The Safe Cities Program, in effect from 1985 to 1995, set up over 500 individual programs designed to prevent domestic burglary in British

TABLE 3-3

Examples of Situational Crime Prevention Techniques

Technique	Examples
Increase the Effort for Crime	
Harden targets	Steering column locks, tamper-proof packaging
Control access to facilities	Electronic access to garages (entry phones)
Deflect offenders	Street closures, tavern locations
Control tools/weapons	Smart guns, plastic beer glasses in taverns
Increase the Risks of Crime	
Extend guardianship	Travel in groups at night, carry a phone
Assist natural surveillance	Street lighting, defensible space
Utilize place managers	Two clerks in convenience stores
Strengthen formal surveillance	Burglar alarms, security guards
Reduce the Rewards of Crime	
Remove targets	Removable car radios, women's refuges
Identify property	Property marking, cattle branding
Reduce temptation	Rapid repair of vandalism, off-street parking
Deny benefits	PIN for car radios, graffiti cleaning
Reduce Provocations	
Reduce emotional arousal	Controls on violent pornography
Avoid disputes	Fixed cab fares, reduce crowding in bars
Discourage imitation	V-chips in TV
Remove Excuses for Crime	
Set rules	Rental agreements, hotel registration
Alert conscience	Roadside speed display boards
Control drugs/alcohol	Breathalyzers in bars, alcohol-free events

Source: Cornish, D., & Clarke, R. (2003). Opportunities, Precipitators, and Criminal Decisions: A Reply to Wortley's Critique of Situational Crime Prevention. In M.Smith & D. Cornish (Eds.). Theory for practice in situational crime prevention. Monsey, NY: Criminal Justice Press.

neighborhoods. Many of these programs involved situational crime prevention, such as improving household locks on doors and windows, providing gates for alleyways, and fencing backyards. When compared with similar areas where no improvements were made, the "improved" areas had substantially lower levels of burglary.

Despite such evidence, situational crime prevention is not without critics. The primary concern about such programs is the potential for **crime displacement**; that is, improving the environment in one area may simply shift crime to a different location. Far too often, the displacement effect of a crime control strategy is ignored. After all, most people are satisfied when crime is moved out of their area or neighborhood, no matter where it goes. Such a limited view ignores the fact that crime has social costs for everyone, regardless of where it exists. This criticism has been answered in recent years by research indicating "real" prevention.

In the Safe Cities Program, there was some evidence of displacement. There was also evidence of "crime switching," in which offenders switched from burglary to other forms of theft. In the areas where the most intense changes were made, however, there was actually a **diffusion effect**. The crime reductions occurred not only in the program areas, but also in surrounding areas.[110]

David Weisburd and colleagues designed a creative experiment to explicitly monitor crime displacement and diffusion. A combination of police crackdowns and situational crime prevention was implemented to curb prostitution at one site and drug sales at another. The researchers then waited in "catchment areas" to see if crime shifted to these adjacent spots. There was little evidence of crime displacement. In their words, crime did not simply "move around the corner."[111] A 2009 review of over 100 crime prevention studies supports this position. On average, studies found just as much crime diffusion as crime displacement. Even where displacement was evident, it did not typically outweigh the overall crime reduction.[112]

To be sure, situational crime prevention is not a panacea. Some crimes can be controlled through environmental design (e.g., vandalism, burglary), but they may have little or no effect on underlying problems. Further, many violent crimes (such as rape and murder) may be less amenable to situational crime prevention than property crimes. Nevertheless, based on the positive results thus far, it appears that momentum is building to expand this type of environmental design prevention program in the future.[113]

Conclusion

Theories from the classical school display the cyclical nature of criminological theory. To a great degree, Beccaria and Bentham were protest writers, attacking the arbitrary nature of punishment at the hands of the state. Their call for uniform sentencing was a direct assault on the unjust forms of punishment that existed then. They were critical of the exercise and abuse of power by the state. Conservative criminologists such as James Q. Wilson and Earnest van den Haag helped usher in the get-tough movement that brought the classical school back to the forefront. Their call for a return to determinate sentencing, incapacitation, and the death penalty was an attempt to strengthen crime prevention policies. Thus, ideas that were once liberal are now conservative. It should be noted, however, that not all parts of the get-tough movement are consistent with the classical school. Indeed, Beccaria's 1764 essay, "On Crimes and Punishments," argues for the abolishment of the death penalty.

Politically, many neoclassical policies blossomed in the 1980s because they gave the impression of being tough on crime. However, the research on the incapacitation and deterrent effect of long prison sentences calls into question the effectiveness of such policies. In addition, their proposed benefits are not achieved without great human and financial costs. The research suggests that crime control policies should focus on increasing the certainty of arrest, conviction, and sentencing rather than on lengthening prison sentences—yet, the first response to a perceived new threat is typically the reverse. Most likely, this is due to the fact that altering the severity of punishment is much easier (i.e., simply pass a new law) than increasing the certainty of punishment.

The most promising evidence in favor of deterrence theory involves increasing the certainty of punishment and the SCF model. Focused deterrence strategies represent a departure from the tendency to simply increase prison sentences. Indeed, a goal of many of these programs is to reduce the use of jails and prisons. This is achieved by convincing offenders, often through explicit notification, that their odds of getting caught and punished are very high. Arrests and incarcerations are used in a more selective way to drive this point home. In a recent review of the deterrence literature, targeted policing and other "certainty" evidence prompted Nagin and Durlauf to raise the possibility that effective deterrence could reduce *both* crime and imprisonment at the same time.[114] Advances in situational crime prevention are also a promising step in this direction. Here, opportunities to offender are reduced by "hardening" potential targets of crime and by increasing guardianship.

Of course, one has to be careful to not overstate the effectiveness of deterrence and situational crime prevention. The preventive potential of the classical approach remains limited by its initial assumption about criminal behavior: that all criminals are rational. Where the criminal is irrational (e.g., psychotic, high on drugs, or intoxicated), unimpressed by the threat of punishment, or lured by the promise of immense financial gain (e.g., drug sales, white-collar crime), deterrence will be ineffective. The potential for crime prevention under this approach is also limited by its reliance on formal legal controls. Informal social control theory emphasizes the prevention of crime through such ideas as self-control and social bonds. Despite these limitations, the classical school continues to have a significant impact on criminological theory and the operations of the criminal justice system.

TABLE 3-4 summarizes the key theories of the neoclassical school.

TABLE 3-4

Summaries of Neoclassical School Theories

Theory	Major Authors	Summary	Policy Implications
Deterrence	Cesare Beccaria Jeremy Bentham	Formal punishment that is swift, certain, and severe reduces crime.	Use the criminal justice system to increase the certainty, severity, and swiftness of punishment. For those who cannot be deterred, incapacitation (removing the opportunity to offend) is the only other option.
Rational choice	Derek Cornish Ronald Clarke	Offenders rationally choose whether and how to engage in crime.	Situational crime prevention
Routine activities	Lawrence Cohen Marcus Felson	Crime occurs because of the convergence of motivated offender, suitable target, and lack of capable guardian.	
Lifestyle approach	Michael Hindelang Michael Gottfredson James Garafolo	Certain groups of people have higher rates of victimization because of their lifestyle.	

WRAP-UP

CHAPTER SPOTLIGHT

- In the 1970s, rehabilitation was attacked as a goal of corrections. This amounted to an attack on the sociological and psychological theories that provide targets for rehabilitation programs. Conservative scholars argued for a return to classical school principles.
- Deterrence theorists assume that humans are rational and hedonistic. Therefore, formal punishments such as arrest and imprisonment should reduce crime by sending a message to both those being punished (specific deterrence) and the rest of society (general deterrence). The empirical evidence in favor of deterrence theory indicates that the certainty of punishment is more important than severity or swiftness.
- Rational choice theory is similar to deterrence theory, but it takes into account a wider array of "costs" for violating the law. Rational choice theorists distinguish between criminal involvement (i.e., crime versus other activity) and criminal event decisions (i.e., when and how to commit crimes).
- Routine activities theory highlights the ingredients necessary for a criminal event (motivated offender, lack of capable guardianship, suitable target) to occur. Similarly, the lifestyle approach highlights factors that influence victimization. The policy implication of these theories is situational crime prevention—the manipulation of the physical environment to reduce the opportunity for offending.
- Although not a theory of crime, incapacitation is a corrections policy advocated by some neoclassical theorists. Incapacitation reduces the opportunity to offend by isolating offenders from the rest of society.

1. Can criminal behavior be deterred? For what types of crime is deterrence likely to work?
2. Which part of deterrence theory (certainty, swiftness, severity) receives the most empirical support? Why do you think that is the case?
3. How is "focused deterrence" different from typical police crackdowns or saturation patrols?
4. In rational choice theory, what is the difference between the criminal event and criminal involvement?
5. Does incapacitation work? Is it a feasible policy?
6. Using the data in this chapter, construct a debate concerning the death penalty as a deterrent to murder.
7. According to routine activities theory, what makes a target suitable? Give an example of how you might influence guardianship of your own property.

KEY TERMS

Police Tape: © SkillUp/Shutterstock

brutalization effect A term used to illustrate the research finding that executions actually increase some forms of homicide.

correctional boot camps Like their military counterparts, these programs emphasize physical training and military drills. Research suggests that most of these programs have little effect on criminal behavior.

crime displacement The idea that when crime is suppressed in one geographical area, it may simply shift to a new location.

crime prevention through environmental design (CPTED) A policy implication of routine activities theory. The way an environment is designed can promote or prevent crime.

criminal event In rational choice theory, decisions about how, when, and where of a particular crime.

criminal involvement In rational choice theory, decisions about whether to engage in crime in general, as opposed to satisfying needs and wants with non-criminal alternatives.

diffusion effect A process whereby the benefits of crime prevention efforts in one area may seep into adjoining areas. This is the reverse of the notion of crime displacement.

focused deterrence A strategy that narrowly tailors sanctions to specific individuals and/or specific criminal behaviors (e.g., handgun violence among gang members). This model also involves directly notifying offenders that they will be heavily sanctioned if they engage in the specified behavior.

general deterrence Punishing criminals so that the general public will get the message that crime doesn't pay.

incapacitation The use of prison and the death penalty to prevent crime by removing offenders from society.

intensive supervision probation (ISP) Offenders are supervised in the community under strict conditions, including frequent drug testing, curfews, and contacts with a probation officer. These programs were designed to increase the punishing aspect of probation. Research suggests that ISP programs do not reduce criminal behavior any more than traditional probation.

just deserts A justification for punishment (e.g., prison) that emphasizes the pain caused and thus earned by the criminal. Punishment serves as a collective expression of society's disapproval for criminal acts.

Kansas City Preventive Patrol Study An experimental study of police patrols. The main conclusion from this experiment was that increased police presence has little effect on crime. Later research suggests that more dramatic increases in police presence can suppress crime.

marginal deterrence The idea that incremental increases in the certainty or severity of punishment should produce decreases in criminal behavior.

pulling levers An approach to policing where police use all available legal mechanisms to sanction those offenders who fail to heed explicit warnings against continuing specific crimes.

This approach has been employed in focused deterrence strategies.

retribution Similar to just deserts, retribution is a justification for punishment that suggests that criminals deserve punishment because they have violated the legal code from which everyone benefits.

specific deterrence Punishing criminals so that they will be less likely to commit crimes in the future.

swift-certain-fair (SCF) model Programs that emphasize swift and certain sanctions. In the HOPE program, those who fail drug tests are immediately arrested and jailed for short periods.

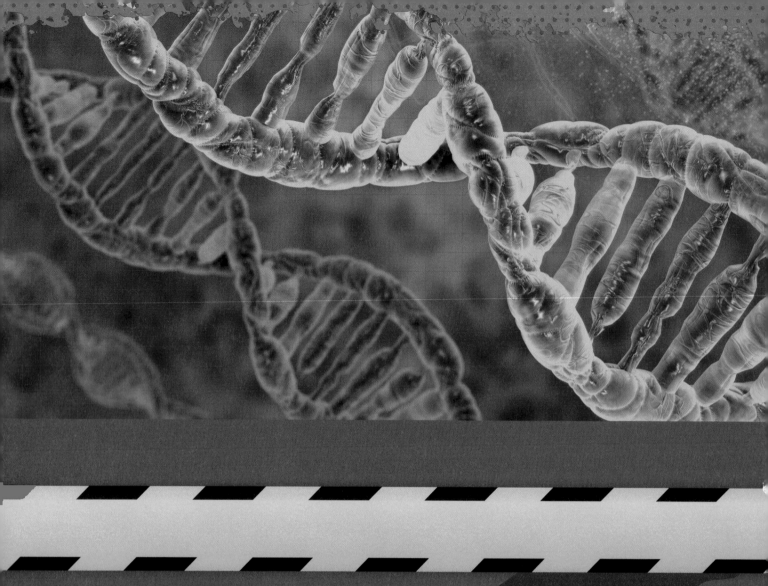

Never in the history of biocriminology has there been anything like this explosion of interest, this diversity of perspective and approach, or this intensity of research activity. Never before have governments funded biological research at current levels or scholars produced so many publications on biology and crime.

—Nicole Rafter, 2008[1]

Even the world's premier sociology journal, *American Sociological Review*, is beginning to publish molecular genetic research on crime and violence. Nobody would have dreamed that just fifteen years ago.

—Adrian Raine, 2013[2]

Biology and Crime

Objectives

- Learn the history of biological explanations of criminal behavior, including early biological theories and the policy implication of eugenics. Pgs. 68–72

- Understand the methodologies (such as twin studies, adoption studies, and molecular genetics) used by scientists in their attempt to establish a genetic basis for crime. Pgs. 72–79

- Grasp the known biological correlates of crime, which range from neurotransmitters to biological harms such as lead poisoning. Pgs. 79–85

- Understand biosocial theories of criminal behavior and how policy implications differ between modern biosocial explanations and early biological theories. Pgs. 85–89

- Understand the basis of evolutionary theories of criminal behavior and link this with a specific evolutionary theory. Pgs. 87–88

Introduction

Many criminologists regard biological studies of crime with a mixture of indifference and ridicule. As recently as 1990, only 20 percent of criminologists reported being receptive to the idea that genetic factors have an important influence on criminal behavior.[3] Certainly, this was not always the case. As noted in Chapter 1, many of the initial positivist school theories were biological. How and when did biological theories fall from grace? As the quotes from Adrian Raine and Nicole Rafter at the start of this chapter make clear, criminology is experiencing a resurgence of interest in biology. What is the reason for this resurgence? What are current biological (or "biosocial") theories of crime, and are they empirically supported? This chapter addresses these questions and explores the biology of crime. The opening section examines the early pioneers of a scientific approach to crime. The remainder of the chapter outlines the current contributions of biology to the study of criminal behavior.

Early Biological Theories

The biological approach can be traced back to the earliest history of criminology. Because many early criminologists were physicians, it was natural for them to use the body to explain crime.[4] As a result, these scientists believed that the presence of certain physical traits made it more likely that an individual would become a criminal. They scientifically studied, objectively quantified, and accurately noted a wide array of constitutional (physical) attributes, from body build to bumps on the head. Early biological research tended to point toward a single direct cause of criminality and to portray this cause as unchangeable. As will be noted, when a cause of crime is framed in this manner, the policy implications are rather narrow. Early biological theories are summarized in **TABLE 4-1**.

Phrenology

Phrenology was among the earliest schools of biological thought. Phrenologists believed that the brain was made up of roughly 30 separate "faculties," such as "combativeness" and "covetiveness." They theorized that activity within a faculty increased the size of that particular part of the brain. To estimate the size of a particular faculty, they examined the exterior of the skull. Thus, "bumps" on the head could indicate certain criminal tendencies. Theorists (e.g., Lavater, Gall, Spurzheim, and Caldwell) compiled cases for scientific inquiry and categorization. They systematized popular stereotypes about physical features and crime (e.g., the beady-eyed criminal). Yet, they were also among the reform-oriented,

TABLE 4-1

Summary of Early Biological Theories

Theorist	Theory	Core Elements
Cesare Lombroso	The "born criminal"	Lombroso used the concept of atavism—criminals as biological throwbacks on the evolutionary scale. Physical characteristics (stigmata) identified these atavistic criminals. With a cranial capacity smaller than the "normal" man, low foreheads, and broad noses, the criminal was born with a strong tendency toward law-breaking. He later modified this theory to recognize the influence of environmental forces. Subsequent research by Goring and Hooten did not support Lombroso's theory.
William H. Sheldon	Somatotype theory	This theory held that there was a strong link between body type and personality/behavior. Sheldon's study of delinquent boys found that they were likely to have the mesomorphic (muscular) body type. Subsequent research also documents this relationship. It remains unclear, though, why mesomorphy is related to delinquency.
Various, First Reported by Patricia Jacobs	XYY "supermale"	Because the Y chromosome dictates that the fetus will be biologically male, an extra Y chromosome was thought to make people "extra" male (more aggressive, violent). Initial studies on institutionalized men (and reports from the popular press) seemed to confirm this, but later studies did not. XYY males are no more likely to be violent than "normal" males, although they are moderately more likely to engage in criminal behavior. This may be due to other characteristics of the XYY anomaly, such as low intelligence.

arguing against brutal punishments that might negatively affect the mind.[5]

Lombroso's "Born Criminal"

Cesare Lombroso, a 19th-century Italian physician, led the movement away from the classical school toward scientific positivism. Lombroso's contributions extend beyond the biological school to highlight key features of the positivist approach, including:[6,7]

- A focus on the scientific study of the individual offender and conditions under which crime is committed.
- The application of scientific research methods and statistics, including the use of control groups.
- The use of typological methods to classify and study criminals (e.g., female criminals, persistent criminals) and to examine criminological phenomena (e.g., the relationship between epilepsy and violent crime).

Consequently, Lombroso is recognized as one of the "pillars of criminological thought" and as a person who transformed criminology "from an offshoot of phrenology to a full-fledged science."[8,9] Influenced by Charles Darwin's theory of natural selection, Lombroso applied the concept of **atavism** to criminological theory. He concluded that criminals were biological throwbacks (atavists) on the evolutionary scale. He believed that modern criminals shared physical characteristics, or "stigmata," with primitive humans. With low foreheads, broad noses, and cranial capacities smaller than that of "normal" men, criminals were born with a strong tendency toward law-breaking. While performing an autopsy of the brigand Villella, Lombroso experienced an epiphany:[10]

At the sight of that skull, I seemed to see all of a sudden, lighted up as a vast plain under a flaming sky, the problem of the nature of the criminal—an atavistic being who reproduces in his person the ferocious instincts of primitive humanity and the inferior animals. These were explained anatomically by the enormous jaws, huge cheekbones, prominent

superciliary arches, solitary lines in the palms, extreme size of the orbits, handle-shaped or sessile ears found in criminals, savages, and apes, insensibility to pain, extremely acute sight, tattooing, excessive idleness, love of orgies, and the irresistible craving for evil for its own sake, the desire not only to extinguish life in the victim, but to mutilate the corpse, tear its flesh, and drink its blood.

As his rather florid language attests, Lombroso believed the criminal to be an immoral person who had not evolved to the same social and biological level as other people. His classic book, *The Criminal Man*, was published through five editions. Eventually, Lombroso acknowledged that social factors can contribute to criminality. For example, he stated that aspects of the environment such as poverty, police corruption, high food prices, and immigration play an important role in crime causation. As he shifted his perspective from strict biological causation to a combination of nature and nurture, he came to identify types of criminals other than the atavist. The "insane" were driven to crime through changes or defects in the brain, while "criminaloids" were influenced by passion and other environmental factors.[11]

Further Study of Physical "Deficiencies"

Researchers who followed Lombroso rejected his notion of an "atavistic" criminal but continued to argue that criminals were biologically inferior to law-abiding citizens. Charles Goring's influential book, *The English Convict: A Statistical Study*, recounted his study of 3,000 English convicts, groups of college students, hospital patients, and soldiers.[12] Among other things, Goring found no significant differences in various "stigmata" between the criminal and the noncriminal. The only significant difference he discovered was that the criminal group was shorter and weighed less. Still, he concluded based on this finding that criminals were physically deficient. His most controversial finding, however, was that criminal behavior was related to "defective intelligence." The convicts did not appear to researchers to be as intelligent as members of the noncriminal sample. Goring presumed that this factor was true of the entire criminal population.

In another study, American anthropologist Earnest Hooten examined more than 20,000 persons to determine whether physical traits play a role in crime causation. He concluded that criminals were physiologically inferior, characterized by low foreheads, pinched noses, compressed faces, and narrow jaws. Based on this evidence, Hooten suggested that he could predict specific forms of criminality. Murderers and robbers, for instance, were tall and thin; forgers, tall and heavy; and rapists, small.[13]

The research conducted by Lombroso, Goring, Hooten, and others has been roundly criticized on a number of grounds. For example, the comparison groups for some of these studies consisted of soldiers, fire fighters, or other types of individuals who were selected for the jobs based

Cesare Lombroso, a 19th Century Itialian physician, was among the first scientists to explore criminality. Although his theory of "atavism" has been discredited, his contributions (particularly the use of scientific methods) are still widely recognized.

Courtesy of the National Library of Medicine

on physical stature. Should it be surprising that the average soldier or fire fighter is physically different from the average criminal? A more damaging criticism is that much of this research involved circular reasoning. Similarities between criminals and noncriminals, regardless of how extensive, were ignored. When even slight differences emerged, the researchers assumed that the differences meant that the comparison group was superior to the criminal group.

Sheldon's Somatotype Theory

William Sheldon was a physician who examined the relationship between body build and behavioral tendencies, temperament, life expectancy, and susceptibility to disease. Building on the earlier work of German psychiatrist Ernst Kretschmer, Sheldon identified three basic human body types:[14]

1. *Endomorphs:* fat, soft, and round; tend to be extroverts
2. *Ectomorphs:* thin and wiry; are easily worried, sensitive, and introverted
3. *Mesomorphs:* muscular; are gregarious, aggressive, assertive, and action oriented

Sheldon noted that these are ideal types, meaning that no pure body type or **somatotype** actually exists. In other words, every person has some qualities from each category. For that reason, each individual had to be ranked on a seven-point scale for each somatotype. This created 343 possible combinations of body type.

In a study of 200 delinquents, Sheldon found that the majority were mesomorphic. Like Lombroso, he concluded that physical factors, when triggered by the environment, were related to criminal activity.[15] Although Sheldon's

A mesomorphic physique.
© Istvan Csak/Shutterstock, Inc.

methodology, measurement of delinquency, and statistics have been exposed as flawed, later research using more sophisticated methodology has replicated the mesomorphy–delinquency relationship. Eleanor and Sheldon Glueck, a husband-and-wife team at Harvard University, examined a sample of 500 white male delinquents and nondelinquents matched by IQ, age, and ethnicity.[16,17] They also found that mesomorphs dominated the delinquent sample. While they concluded that body type is a factor in delinquent behavior, they were much more cautious in their interpretation of this relationship.

Sheldon advocated a strict form of biological determinism. He believed that the personality associated with a mesomorph body type led directly to criminal activity. The Gleucks and others, however, outline other explanations for the relationship between a mesomorphic body and criminal behavior. For example, the mesomorphic body type may have an advantage in the rough-and-tumble activities of street crime. Other persons may be more likely to "draft" a mesomorph for help in criminal activities. Also, the criminal justice system may view the mesomorphic criminal as a more serious threat to society. Perhaps the delinquent mesomorph is perceived as a threat and thus is more likely to be arrested and incarcerated. A recent reanalysis of the Gleucks' data supports this argument.[18] While mesomorphic body types predicted official delinquency, they did not predict self-reported delinquency.

The XYY "Supermale"

A final example of an early biological theory is actually quite recent when compared to the work of Lombroso and Goring. Although the initial publication linking **XYY** males to crime appeared in 1965, the "supermale" phenomenon is included here because, like other early theories, it supposedly identifies a single, direct, and immutable cause of crime. This theory involves a particular chromosomal abnormality. Each human has 23 pairs of chromosomes; one pair of chromosomes determines the biological sex of the person. For males, the normal chromosome pair is XY; the female structure is XX. Some individuals, however, have more unusual combinations. For example, some females have an XXX structure, and some males have an XXY structure (also known as Klinefelter's syndrome).

The British scientist Patricia Jacobs found that the incidence of the XYY disorder (males with an extra Y chromosome) was 20 times higher among inmates in a Scottish prison than in the general Scottish population. She also reported that the double Y chromosome caused males to be unusually tall, aggressive, and violent.[19] On the basis of this and other early research, these "supermales" were believed to be prone to extremely violent, heinous crimes.

In the 1960s, a number of violent cases involving XYY offenders came to the attention of the world. Murder cases in Australia, France, Scotland, West Germany, and the United States featured XYY offenders. For example, the case of Richard Speck was a major influence in the study of the XYY male and crime. In 1966, Speck brutally murdered eight student nurses in Chicago. He had a lengthy criminal record and the physical stigmata associated with the chromosomal pattern (i.e., lanky, pimpled). Immediately, the XYY theory gained prominence; only later was it discovered that Speck did not actually have the extra Y chromosome.

In all, there have been more than 150 studies regarding violence and the XYY chromosome structure. An extensive summary of this research highlights the following findings:[20]

- XYY men convicted of crimes are more likely to be guilty of property offenses and less likely than convicted XY men to have committed violent offenses. Thus, even if XYY males were "born criminals," they were not more likely to commit violent crime.
- The families of XYY inmates tend to have less history of crime or mental illness than do the families of XY inmates.
- The prevalence of XYY men is higher in mental and penal institutions than in the general population.

In sum, it appears as though XYY males may be more likely to engage in criminal behavior but not violent behavior. For example, an exhaustive Danish study of more than 4,000 males found little or no evidence of violence. However, the XYY males did commit more nonviolent crimes than a matched control group of XY males.[21] Even here, many question whether this is a direct link or whether crime among XYY males is caused by their lower intelligence. One thing is certain: Because the XYY chromosome structure is so rare (less than 0.1 percent of the male population has this pattern), it can only explain a tiny fraction of crime among males and none among females.

The Legacy and Policy Implications of Early Biological Research

As noted already, much of the early biological research on crime had serious problems with methodology and interpretation. Early biological theory tended to be simplistic, clumsy, and oftentimes explicitly racist and sexist. Early theories were similar in a number of ways: They focused on a *single factor* (e.g., body type, defective intelligence, XYY chromosome structure) that was *not amenable to change* and that *directly* caused crime. The policy implications of such theories are rather narrow. If the cause of crime cannot be changed, what can be done? One answer, of course, is to separate these individuals from society. For example, Earnest Hooten advocated large criminal reservations to separate "inferiors" from the rest of society:[22]

> *Of course, I think that the habitual criminals who are hopeless constitutional inferiors should be permanently incarcerated and, on no account, should be allowed to breed. Nevertheless, they should be treated humanely, and, if they are to be kept alive should be allowed some opportunity for freedom and profitable occupation within their own severely restricted area.*

This quote also illustrates a second option advocated by many early biological researchers; not allowing "defective" members of society to have children. Francis Galton coined the term **eugenics** (meaning well-born) to describe the process of improving the human race by not permitting persons of "bad stock" to reproduce.[23] Many leaders of the early biological approach were ardent supporters of eugenics. William Sheldon, for example, concludes his book on human physique "with a eugenic vision in which somatotyping will eventually enable us to breed better people and predict their choices in clothing style, home location, and life partner."[24] Among other things, the eugenics movement led to limitations on the immigration of southern and eastern Europeans into

In 1966, Richard Speck brutally murdered eight student nurses. Because he had the features associated with the XYY chromosome abnormality, this case generated a great deal of interest in the "supermale" theory of offending.

© CWH/AP Photos

the United States in the early 1920s and to the institutionalization or forced sterilization of the poor, deviant, and disabled.[25]

The eugenics movement lost all of its momentum by the end of World War II. Nazi atrocities, including the mass executions of Jews, Gypsies, homosexuals, and other groups, was justified in part as an attempt to create a biologically superior Aryan (e.g., blue-eyed, blond-haired) race. Still, policies based on the initial XYY supermale findings were evident as late as the 1970s. For example, at the Boston Hospital for Women, a group of doctors started screening newborn male infants for the extra Y chromosome. In 1972, the California Center for the Study and Reduction of Violence set up a program to screen junior high school males for the XYY chromosome.[26] Such efforts could have severely stigmatized XYY males or at least have had a negative influence on their civil rights.

These policy implications, combined with research that was often blatantly shoddy, led to a sharp decline in the popularity of a biological approach to crime. At the same time, sociologists who found biological explanations repugnant came to dominate the field of criminology. From the 1950s until relatively recently, the study of biological influences in crime was almost taboo. Indeed, a 1992 conference sponsored by the National Institutes of Health (NIH) entitled "Genetic Factors and Crime" was cancelled after NIH withdrew funding due to public pressure. Because African Americans are overrepresented in

> ### Despite a tarnished legacy, biological research on crime has made a comeback in recent years.

official crime statistics, opponents to the conference believed the proceedings were racist and intended to exclude sociological explanations.[27]

A Modern Biosocial Approach to Crime

Despite a tarnished legacy, biological research on crime has made a comeback in recent years. Indeed, the cancelled conference on genetics and crime was rescheduled and took place in 1995. Subsequently, the Human Genome Project and other advances in molecular biology have led to an explosion of interest in genetics across many social sciences. In this section, four modern areas of biological inquiry into crime are discussed: (1) behavioral genetics, (2) biological correlates of criminal behavior, (3) biosocial theories, and (4) evolutionary explanations of crime.

Behavioral Genetics

A major question posed by the biocriminologists is whether crime is "heritable." An affirmative answer would implicate some biological process in the creation of crime. This line of inquiry is typically referred to as **behavioral genetics**. Four approaches have been used to examine the relationship between genetic factors and crime: (1) family studies, (2) twin studies, (3) adoption studies, and (4) molecular genetics. These strategies are summarized in **TABLE 4-2**.

Family Studies

The earliest heredity studies focused on "degenerate" families and feeblemindedness. For example, Dugdale traced the descendants of a woman he called Ada Jukes and found that most family members were criminals, prostitutes, or welfare recipients.[28] In a similar study, Goddard traced nearly 1,000 descendants of Martin Kallikak from the time of the American Revolution and identified "feeblemindedness" as his illegitimate line's dominant trait.[29]

The glaring problem with these studies is that environmental influences (e.g., poverty, area of residence) could easily explain why crime or feeblemindedness seemed to run in these families. Dugdale's own description of the "habitat of the Jukes" suggests as much:[30]

> They lived in log or stone houses similar to slave-hovels, all ages, sexes, relations and strangers "bunking" indiscriminately . . . To this day, the "Jukes" occupy the self-same shanties built nearly a century ago. . . . Sometimes I found an overcrowding so close it

Sarah Jane Wiley in the former operating room at the old Virginia Colony for the Epileptic and Feebleminded in Lynchburg, Virginia. Wiley was one of thousands of people sterilized in this operating room during the eugenics movement.
© Steve Helber/AP Photos

TABLE 4-2

Methods Used to Separate Nature from Nurture

Method	Research Design	Findings	Criticisms or Limitations
Family studies	Early studies traced family history; modern studies look at how parents' crime relates to their children's crime.	Parental crime consistently predicts the criminal behavior of their children.	Environment (nurture) could easily explain this finding. For example, criminal parents may be less likely to make a strong investment in parenting or socializing their children.
Twin studies	Compare monozygotic (MZ) twins to dizygotic (DZ) twins. Because MZ twins are genetically identical and DZ twins are not, a genetic effect is assumed if concordance rates are higher for MZ twins.	MZ twins generally have higher concordance rates than DZ twins. This finding is more consistent early in childhood and in adulthood (but not during adolescence).	Because MZ twins look exactly alike, people (parents, teachers, etc.) may treat them more similarly than they do DZ twins. Also, MZ twins are more likely to share the same friends—including delinquent peers.
Adoption studies	Compare the criminal record of adopted children with their biological parents (who only contributed genes) and adoptive parents (who provide the environment).	Children's criminal behavior appears to relate more to the biological parents' criminal records than to those of the adoptive parents.	Adoption agencies might match the environment of the adoptive parents to that of the biological parents. The adoptive parents' criminal records are not a strong measure of environment. Adoptees from criminal parents might experience trauma in the fetal or infant stages that relate to crime.
Molecular genetics	Isolate particular genes that may be related to a criminal disposition.	Some genes have been identified that are related to a criminal disposition.	Any particular gene will have a minimal effect on human behavior. Most will slightly prod behavior in a particular direction. The environment can interact with genes and may influence whether and how genes are activated.

suggested that these dwellings were the country equivalents to city tenement houses.

In fact, recently discovered documents from archives in the State University of New York at Albany and from records in a long-forgotten county poorhouse appear to offer some redemption to the Juke family ("Juke" was a name given to the family by Dugdale; their true identity was kept confidential). The poorhouse records, discovered in 2001, revealed that many of the Jukes were not misfits or criminals. Indeed, many of them were prominent members in the local culture.[31]

Still, modern studies continue to find that crime runs in families. Specifically, parental criminality is a relatively strong and consistent predictor of delinquency.[32] Although scholars continue to debate the meaning of this finding,

many criminologists favor an environmental explanation. For example, criminal parents may be less effective at socializing their children and may be role models for deviant behaviors. Criminologists Robert Sampson and John Laub found that poor parenting explained the relationship between parent and child criminal behavior. Criminal parents were less likely to supervise their children and more likely to use harsh and erratic punishment. According to Sampson and Laub, "A central characteristic of deviant and criminal lifestyles is the rejection of restrictions and duties—especially those that involve planning, patience, and investment in the future."[33]

Twin Studies

Twin studies offer an alternative to simply tracing family histories or examining measures of parental crime. These studies typically compare identical (monozygotic) twins to same-sex fraternal (dizygotic) twins. **Monozygotic (MZ) twins** are products of a single egg and sperm, and thus are exactly the same genetically. **Dizygotic (DZ) twins** are products of two eggs and two sperms, and thus are as genetically similar as any two siblings within a family. Researchers infer a genetic effect when MZ twins have more similar outcomes than DZ twins. These studies typically express findings in terms of a **concordance rate**. The outcome (crime) is concordant if both twins exhibit the behavior. When one is a criminal and the other is not, the pair is discordant. The effect of the environment is "controlled" because both types of twins share environments. In other words, one might expect that both types of twins would have some concordance because they share similar environments (same parents, same household, same school, etc.). A genetic effect is assumed when the concordance rate for MZ twins is higher than that of DZ twins.

The most cited example of twin research is the Danish twin study—a study of more than 3,500 pairs of twins born between 1881 and 1910 in Denmark.[34] Here, the concordance rate for conviction among identical twins was 52 percent, as opposed to 22 percent in the fraternal twin sample. In other words, if one twin is a criminal, the MZ twin is more than twice as likely to be involved in crime as the DZ twin. Similar but lower concordance rates were reported for female twins. In Ohio, a researcher had a sample of identical and fraternal twins respond to a self-report questionnaire concerning the delinquent behavior of each twin and the other twin's friends.[35] The author reported that the self-reported rates of delinquency were more similar among identical twins.

A review of 42 twin studies estimated (based on differences in concordance rates) that, on average, the genetic influence explained about 40 percent of the variation in antisocial behavior.[36] Still, there are several limitations of twin studies that might inflate concordance rates for MZ twins. In other words, the difference in concordance rates might be due to factors other than genetics. For example, because MZ twins look alike, they may be more likely to be treated the same by parents, teachers, and peers than DZ twins. Also, identical twins tend to spend more time with each other and tend to have the same friends.[37]

This is important for several reasons. First, because association with delinquent friends is a strong predictor of delinquency, it may be that some of the concordance among MZ twins is the result of their shared peer group. Second, if MZ twins spend more time together, one may simply imitate the other's antisocial behavior. These processes were illustrated in a Danish study of MZ and DZ twins. After controlling for imitation and peer relations, the genetic effect was substantially reduced.[38] Thus, even twin studies find it difficult to fully separate the influences of environment and heredity. The examination of MZ twins reared apart may be an important research strategy for future understanding of crime.[39]

Adoption Studies

One other method of addressing the nature versus nurture debate is to use adoption as a natural experiment. In the adoption study approach, the behaviors of adoptees are compared with the outcomes of both their adoptive and biological parents. Similarities in outcome between adopted children and their biological parents are assumed to reflect a genetic effect. Similarities between the children and their adoptive parents are assumed to reflect their shared environment. The most widely read adoption study involved over 4,000 Danish boys and their biological and adoptive parents.[40] The results of this analysis are illustrated in **FIGURE 4-1**. As expected, boys whose adoptive and biological parents engaged in crime had the highest crime rate (24.5%).

The estimate of a genetic effect is obtained by moving from left to right in this figure. The data indicate that regardless of whether the adoptive parents had a criminal record, the criminality of the boys was related to that of their biological parents. For example, the bottom half of the table contains only those boys

Monozygotic (MZ) twins are genetically identical. Observed concordance rates for criminal behavior are higher for MZ twins than for dizygotic (DZ) twins. Skeptics wonder whether this finding is caused by people treating identical twins more similarly than fraternal twins.

© sf2301420max/Shutterstock, Inc.

whose adoptive parents had no criminal record. Within this category of boys, those who had criminal biological parents had a higher rate of criminal convictions (20%) than those who did not have criminal biological parents (13.5%).

The extent of the criminal career of the biological parents was also influential. Boys whose biological parents had three or more convictions were three times more likely than their counterparts with noncriminal biological parents to commit crimes. Thus, biological factors appeared to be more important than environmental ones. As was the case with twin studies, adoption studies tend to reach a similar conclusion—most uncover a moderate genetic effect. This finding, however, emerges only for property (and not violent) offending.[41]

The adoption research design has been questioned on a number of grounds. For example, critics correctly point out that the measure of adoptive parents' criminality is not a comprehensive measure of environment. Second, adoption agencies sometimes seek to match the environmental characteristics of the biological parents' home to that of the adoptive parents' home. This process could create the illusion of a genetic effect.[42]

In sum, both adoption studies and twin research attempt to separate nurture from nature and establish a link between genetics and crime. There is a great deal of disagreement over where the weight of the evidence lies with this issue. A well-regarded review of both of these methods calculated that genetics can explain roughly half of the variation in antisocial behaviors and crime, with the remainder being due to environmental influences. Such

> *Similarities in outcome between adopted children and their biological parents are assumed to reflect a genetic effect.*

evidence suggested to leaders in the field of developmental psychology that "twin and adoption studies are likely to prove very useful for a long time."[43] In stark contrast, a 2014 article in the prominent journal Criminology argued that twin and adoption studies were so flawed that attempts to estimate heredity should be abandoned. Pointing to research on how genes and environment intertwine, the authors refer to attempts to separate these ingredients as "biologically nonsensical."[44] Of course, the criminologists who use twin studies voiced their disagreement,[45] and so the debate continues.

Molecular Genetics: The Human Genome Project and Beyond

Twin and adoption studies attempt to demonstrate genetic effects without directly measuring genes. In contrast, molecular genetics research examines the heredity of crime by measuring specific genes and linking them to criminal behavior.[46] A full understanding of this research requires some rather detailed knowledge of biology (see **Theory in Action: The Language of Genetics**). Nevertheless, understanding the gist of this research requires only some basic terminology. Most people are familiar with deoxyribonucleic acid (DNA), which contains the chemical codes for all living organisms. DNA is made up of four chemicals, called bases, which bind together in different sequences. The specific order of bases within these sequences underlies all of the diversity in life. They dictate, for example, whether an organism is a human, a mosquito, or a grain of rice. A gene is a specific sequence of bases within a DNA molecule that works together to carry out a particular task. Current estimates based on the Human Genome Project indicate that humans have between 20,000 and 30,000 genes. Each gene, through the creation of different proteins, dictates the "instructions" for the development and function of a human being.[47,48]

Technology now permits scientists to sift through DNA structure in order to isolate and study specific genes. One strategy for this new technology is called gene-linkage analysis. Here, a single gene is followed through a particular family that evidences a particular disease or disorder. A high-profile study illustrates this analysis. Geneticist Hans Brunner and his associates studied a Dutch family line with a history of rather bizarre and violent behavior among males (but not females).[49] For example, one of the males raped his own sister, another forced his sisters to undress at knifepoint, another stabbed a prison warden with a pitchfork, and another attempted to run over his work supervisor. Two of the men had a propensity for starting fires.

	Do biological parents have a criminal record?		
Do adoptive parents have a criminal record?	**YES**	**NO**	
YES	24.5%	14.7%	"Environmental" Effect
NO	20.0%	13.5%	
	"Genetic" Effect		

FIGURE 4-1 Results of the Danish Adoption Study. The numbers in the table refer to the percentage of adoptees within each category who had a criminal record.

Data from Sarnoff A. Mednick, William F. Gabrielli, and Barry Hutchings, "Genetic Influences on Criminal Convictions," *Science* 224 (1984): 891–894.

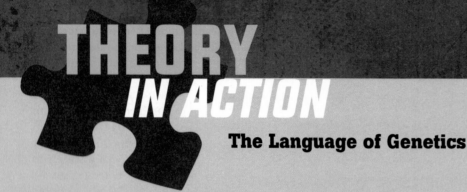

The Language of Genetics

One problem with a multidisciplinary approach to criminology is communication across disciplines. Students (and professors) interested in crime often lack any detailed understanding of genetics. This capsule is designed as a primer in the language of genetics. As noted in the text, the DNA of every organism contains four "nucleotide bases." These bases are adenine (A), thymine (T), cytosine (C), and guanine (G). DNA consists of two "polynucleotide" fibers that are bonded together in the shape of a double helix (see **FIGURE 4—2**). The bases can only join together in certain ways—A pairs with T, C pairs with G. For example, a hypothetical sequence of bases ACCTAAGTTA would have to be paired with the sequence TGGATTCAAT.

While all organisms have DNA made up of the same four bases, it is the sequence of the bases that distinguishes one organism from another. In human DNA, there are roughly three billion base pairs that are arranged in a particular order. The HGP identified this specific sequence of bases. A gene is simply a group of nucleotide base pairs that work together to carry out a particular task. More specifically, genes carry the instructions needed for the body to create proteins. Proteins are complex molecules that dictate physical characteristics (e.g., height, eye color) and produce the antibodies that fight off diseases. Scientists estimate that the human body contains over 20,000 genes. The genes are located on all of the 23 pairs of chromosomes inherited by humans. One of these chromosomes dictates sex, and the other 22 "autosomes" are numbered from smallest (1) to largest (22). Genes occupy a specific location on the chromosome. Thus, the HGP involved linking each gene with a particular spot on a particular chromosome. All genes are made up of two copies—one inherited from each parent. Most copies are identical, as genes are available in only one form. This produces the general human form (e.g., skin, eyes, nose, organs) and development. For a small percentage of genes, there are at least two alternative copies, or "alleles." It is these genes that produce variation in traits ranging from eye color to personality. There are different types of alleles. Some

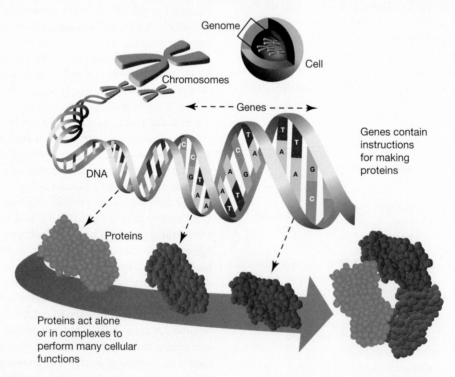

FIGURE 4—2 From Genes to Proteins.

Courtesy of U.S. Department of Energy Genome Programs http://genomics.energy.gov

are differentiated by a single difference in a base (TTAG-TAA vs. TTAGTAG). Others differ in their end-to-end length, which happens when sequences of bases are repeated more or less often. For example, a "3-repeat allele" has the same sequence repeated three times.

Research has identified alleles that appear to increase the risk of specific personality traits, crime, and mental disorders. For example, the "10-repeat allele" on the DAT1 gene located on chromosome number 5 has been linked to ADD, gambling, and criminal behavior. The search for a genetic basis for behavior continues to grow more complex. Researchers are now examining how specific genes interact with one another and the environment to produce behavior. Indeed, the cutting edge of genetic research involves *epigenetic* influences. Research in this area examines the complex

biochemical systems that mute or activate genes. Among the most interesting hypotheses under consideration is that changes in gene expression, caused by environment, can be transferred to the next generation. In other words, the social environment might become "biologically embedded."

Sources: Raine, A. (2013). *The anatomy of violence.* New York: Random House; Rowe, D. C. (2002). *Biology and crime.* Los Angeles: Roxbury; Beaver, K. M. (2009). Molecular genetics and crime. In A. Walsh & K. M. Beaver (Eds.), *Biosocial criminology.* New York: Routledge; U.S. Department of Energy, National Institutes of Health. (n.d.) Human Genome Project information. Retrieved May 20, 2010, from http://www.ornl.gov/sci/techresources/Human_Genome/project/about.shtml

After a decade of laboratory research, Brunner and his associates isolated and identified a particular mutated gene present in the males within this family. This gene was responsible for the production of **monoamine oxidase A (MAOA)**. MAOA breaks down two neurotransmitters (serotonin and norepinephrine) so that they can be removed from the body. The mutation in the gene rendered the body unable to perform this important function. Serotonin levels, in particular, have been linked to violent behavior.

It is important to note that, to date, this particular gene mutation has only been found in one Dutch family. Thus, this type of mutation is unlikely to provide a general explanation for crime. In all likelihood, traits consistent with a criminal disposition are based on a wide variety of genes: "the nudge from any particular gene is not strong, and it could easily be countered by a favorable balance from another gene."[50]

Because no single gene is likely to have a strong effect on criminal behavior, the search for genes related to criminal behavior is likely to take some time. Results from the **Human Genome Project (HGP)**, however, may aid in the search. Formally launched in 1990 and completed in 2006, the U.S. Human Genome Project was a coordinated effort by the U.S. Department of Energy and the National Institutes of Health to map the entire human genome.[51] **Genome** is a term used to describe the total DNA in an organism. The genome of humans (a copy of which is contained in almost all cells) consists of over 3 billion base pairs. Already, there is research from the HGP and from other genotyping that correlates the presence of specific genes to behavioral outcomes.

Much of the initial research focused on broad personality traits (e.g., novelty seeking) and childhood disorders such as attention deficit disorder (ADD) and conduct disorder (CD).

In turn, many of these traits and disorders are related to criminal behavior. For example, genes that help regulate the neurotransmitter dopamine have been linked to ADD, CD, impulsivity, novelty seeking, gambling, and alcoholism.[52,53] More recent research has directly connected some of the genes to criminal behavior. Using data from the National Longitudinal Study of Adolescent Health (Add Health), Guang Guo

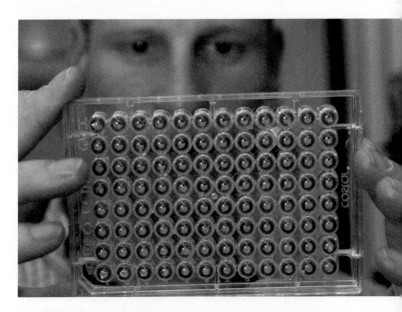

A lab technician examines a plate containing sample so purified DNA as it is prepared to be sequenced in the lab at MIT's Whitehead Institute in Cambridge, Massachusetts, as part of the Human Genome Project. Genetic research on criminal behavior has increased dramatically since the Human Genome Project was completed.

© Elise Amendola/AP Photos

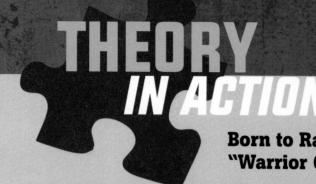

THEORY IN ACTION

Born to Rage? Media Coverage of the "Warrior Gene"

In 2010, National Geographic Channel aired a documentary titled, "Born to Rage?" The film is narrated by Henry Rollins, the former "bad boy" front man for the punk rock group Black Flag. Rollins opens the film with a provocative question and answer. "Are some people born to be violent? An extraordinary discovery suggests they are. A single gene has been directly associated with violent behavior." The gene at the center of this discussion regulates the enzyme monoamine oxidase A (MAOA). MAOA metabolizes neurotransmitters (e.g., serotonin, dopamine) that are related to impulse control and other cognitive functions. Importantly, there are different versions of this gene, and roughly 30 percent of people have one variation, the so-called "warrior gene," that creates low levels of MAOA.

In the documentary, Rollins is tested for the presence of this gene variation. His results are compared to others who are interviewed, including former gang members, outlaw bikers, mixed martial arts fighters, and Buddhist monks. Is this an example of media hype or an accurate portrayal of modern biocriminology? The documentary does review much of the science connecting MAOA to violence, including a 2002 study published in the well-respected journal *Science*. A careful look at this paper, however, also suggests reasons to be skeptical about the film. The researchers reported higher levels of antisocial behavior (including violence) among subjects who had *both* the low-MAOA version of the gene and a history of severe child abuse. In other words, the genetic variation alone did not predict violence. Subsequent research has confirmed the importance of this interaction between biology and environment.

While this caveat and the limits of research are discussed in the film, the whole premise of the documentary is

that the presence of the "warrior gene" alone might help to explain why some of the interview subjects have a history of violence. Additionally, many of those appearing in the show appear hopeful that they *will* have the genetic variation related to violence. They appear to equate a predisposition to impulsiveness and violence with masculinity and toughness. Embedded in both the science and the media coverage of the "warrior gene" is the issue of race. The base rate for the low-MAOA gene is different across racial populations, leading some to speculate about a genetic basis for racial differences in violence. In New Zealand, researchers pointed out that 56 percent of Maori males and 34 percent of Caucasian males have the low-MAOA gene. They suggested that this might help to explain both the warrior culture of the Maori as well as current racial differences in crime and other problem behaviors. Critics point out that racial differences in the base rate of the MAOA gene do not always correspond with differences in violence. They also raise important ethical concerns about the harm that such speculations might cause to particular populations.

Sources: Day, P. (2010). *Born to Rage?* Santa Monica, CA: Edge West; Raine, A. (2013). *The Anatomy of violence: The biological roots of crime.* New York: Pantheon; Caspi, A., McClay, J., Moffitt, T. E., Mill, J., Martin, J., Craig, I., et al. (2002). Role of genotype in the cycle of violence in maltreated children. *Science, 297,* 851–854; Kim-Cohen, J., Caspi, A., Taylor, A., Williams, B., Newcombe, R., et al. (2006). MAOA, maltreatment, and gene-environment interaction predicting children's mental health: New evidence and a meta-analysis. *Molecular Psychiatry, 11,* 903–913.

and his colleagues found that a specific form (10-repeat allele) of a dopamine transporter gene (DAT1) predicted violent delinquency in both adolescence and adulthood.[54]

Molecular genetics research is evolving quickly. Much of the current research examines the interaction between specific genes and environmental influences. For example, Avshalom Caspi and his coauthors documented an interaction between a gene that helps regulate MAOA and child abuse among a sample of males. Specifically, individuals in the sample who had both genetic (genes related to low MAOA activity) and environmental (experienced child abuse) risks were more likely to be convicted of violent crime in adulthood. Although these individuals made up only 12 percent

of the sample, they accounted for 44 percent of convictions for violent offenses.[55] This interaction has been confirmed in subsequent research.[56,57] Indeed, the specific gene variant measure in this research, dubbed the "warrior gene," has garnered a great deal of media attention (see **Theory in Action: Born to Rage? Media Coverage of the "Warrior Gene"**).

Moving beyond even gene–environment interactions, researchers have started to examine how combinations of genes affect criminality. Kevin Beaver and his colleagues found that a combination of two genes related to dopamine levels (DRD2 and DRD4) predicted both conduct disorder and an index of antisocial behavior.[58] It is important to note that many of the gene–crime links identified thus far are not particularly strong. Furthermore, researchers have not been able to replicate some of the links identified by initial research.[59]

Overall, there is support from a variety of sources for the idea that a person's propensity for crime is partially heritable. To be sure, this area of inquiry is extremely controversial, and many sociologically trained criminologists are still skeptical about the extent to which research supports a genetic basis for crime. While biology oriented criminologists believe that a gene–crime link has been clearly established, they point out that there is no "crime gene." Rather, they argue that some genes may *predispose* a person to antisocial behavior. What are the biological mechanisms (inherited or not) that relate to predisposition for criminal behavior? Some of the possible suspects are highlighted in the following discussion of biological correlates of crime.

Biological Correlates of Crime

Like the work of Lombroso and Sheldon, much of the current biological research focuses on physiological differences between criminals and noncriminals. Rather than skull features or body type, however, the modern approach focuses on a wide range of characteristics, including neurological (brain) functioning, the autonomic nervous system, hormones, and various "biological harms." Furthermore, unlike early positivistic theories, modern day scientists do not believe that biological differences can unequivocally identify criminals. Rather, the biology of criminals is likely to fall on a continuum with the biology of law-abiding citizens. TABLE 4-3 summarizes the biological correlates of crime.

TABLE 4-3
Summary of Biological Correlates of Crime

Biological Factor	Specific Measures and Conclusions
Neurological Factors	
Direct measures of the brain	Measures of brain structure (MRI scans) and brain activity (PET scans) suggest that there are differences in the frontal lobe of the brain between certain types of criminals and noncriminal control groups.
Neurochemical measures	Neurotransmitters allow cells to communicate with one another. Low levels of serotonin have been linked with impulsive and aggressive behavior.
Indirect measures	IQ and other "neuropsychological" tests predict delinquency. Some biocriminologists assume that this reflects underlying neurological deficits.
Autonomic Nervous System	
Heart rate	Some types of criminals have lower heart rates than noncriminal controls. Studies of skin conductance (sweat) yield mixed results.
Biological Harms	
Perinatal harms	Perinatal risks (maternal smoking and drinking during pregnancy) and delivery complications are associated with juvenile and adult crime. Some studies find that this effect is more pronounced in unstable families.
Exposure to lead	Lead is a highly toxic substance that produces biological damage, especially to children, who are still developing. Exposure to lead (through lead paint and other sources) has been linked to delinquent behavior. In one study, lead exposure was among the strongest predictors of delinquency.
Nutrition and diet	Some research suggests that diet (particularly sugar intake) relates to antisocial behavior. In particular, some raised the prospect that hypoglycemia might cause violent, impulsive behavior. Recent research fails to support these findings.
Hormones	
Testosterone levels	Higher levels of the male androgen testosterone have been linked to antisocial behavior. There is some evidence that premenstrual syndrome is related to female offending. This research, however, has been severely criticized.

Neurological Studies

Neurological factors may play a significant role in criminal behavior. In particular, researchers have focused on the **prefrontal cortex**, the part of the brain responsible for "executive functions." Executive functions include the ability to sustain attention, self-monitoring, abstract reasoning, and the inhibition of inappropriate or impulsive behavior. There are a number of avenues for studying the role of the brain in antisocial behavior. Technology now offers several direct measures of brain structure and activity, including positron emission tomography (PET) scans, and magnetic resonance imaging (MRI).

PET scans detect which regions of the brain are active (and the extent of this activity). To utilize this technology, subjects are first injected with a glucose solution that has a radioactive component. Next, they are asked to complete some cognitive task. Glucose provides "fuel" for the brain, so the most active regions of the brain will draw the radioactive-labeled glucose, which the PET scan then detects.[60] Adrian Raine and his colleagues used PET scans to compare the brain activity of murderers to matched (on age and sex) noncriminal control groups in two studies. In the initial study, murderers showed less brain activity in the prefrontal cortex than the control groups.[61] A second study of the same group of murderers examined the **limbic system**. The limbic system is located beneath the outer cortex and includes the hippocampus, amygdala, and thalamus. This more primitive area of the brain houses emotional life. Researchers classified the murderers as proactive (violence was planned, cold-blooded) or reactive (violence was the result of lashing out against some stimulus). While both murder groups had higher levels of limbic system activity, proactive killers had just as much prefrontal cortex activity as the control group. Raine explains that:

> . . . cold blooded killers have sufficient prefrontal regulatory resources to act out their aggression in a relatively careful and premeditated fashion. They feel as angry as anyone, but instead of getting mad, they get even. In contrast, while the hot-blooded killers also have a mass of angry feelings simmering away, they don't have sufficient prefrontal resources to express their anger in controlled and regulated fashion. Someone gets their goat, they see red, and they blow their lid.[62]

Other types of brain scans (primarily MRI) also reveal differences between criminals and noncriminals. One MRI study compared individuals diagnosed with antisocial personality disorder (APD) to three separate control groups—a "normal" group, a group with other psychiatric disorders, and a group with substance abuse problems. All of the subjects for the study were recruited from the general population. Through the use of powerful magnets, MRI scans provide a detailed three-dimensional picture of brain anatomy. In the study, the APD group had less "gray matter," in the prefrontal cortex than any of the three control groups.[63]

Another route to studying the effect of brain processes on criminal behavior is to look at the chemicals within the brain. Indeed, much of the molecular genetics research discussed in the preceding paragraphs focuses on genes related to neurotransmitters such as serotonin and dopamine. Leading biocriminologists offer this explanation for the link between neurochemical processes and human behavior:[64]

> Thoughts, behavior, and emotions are mediated by the transmissions of electrical impulses between neurons, the cells of the nervous system. Gaps that exist between neurons are called synapses, and communications between neurons requires the passage of electrical impulses across these synapses. Neurotransmitters such as dopamine, norepinephrine, and serotonin therefore form the basis for information processing and communication within the brain; and as a result they underlie all types of behavior, including sensation, perception, learning and memory, and—more controversially—antisocial behavior.

The neurotransmitter studied most extensively is **serotonin**. Serotonin essentially acts as lubricant for the biological braking system in the prefrontal cortex.[65] Recall that this area of the brain is responsible for regulating inappropriate or impulsive behavior. Thus, low levels of serotonin would interfere with the ability of the brain to stop impulsive or thoughtless acts. The serotonin system is the target of a class of antidepressant drugs that includes Prozac. Although this is a simplification of the process, Prozac relieves depression generally by increasing the availability of serotonin.[66] A number of research studies find that low levels of serotonin are related to impulsive, violent, or antisocial behavior. For example, one study found that low serotonin levels predicted both official and self-reported criminal behavior among a sample of young adults in New Zealand.[67] The relationship held only for males, but it appeared even after controlling for a host of physical and environmental variables. In a more novel study, a small sample of offenders (N = 10) was injected with a drug that increases the availability of serotonin. The researchers reported reductions in both aggression and impulsivity.[68]

Rather than studying neurotransmitters and brain structure, some researchers use psychological tests as an indirect measure of neurological differences. Tests that focus on executive functions (cognition, attention, impulsivity) are assumed to reflect differences in brain functioning. Thus, neuropsychological tests are simply psychological tests that are assumed to reflect neurological differences. There is a good deal of evidence that such test scores are related to delinquency and crime. For example, one longitudinal study examined the relationship between neuropsychological measures and criminal behavior. The data were drawn from the Dunedin (New Zealand) Multidisciplinary Health and Development Study—a birth cohort of several hundred males, ages 13 to 18. The study demonstrated that neuropsychological scores at age 13 predicted delinquency and criminal behavior in adulthood.[69] These researchers interpret IQ scores, as a measure of neurological health. Of course, there are other interpretations of what IQ measures. The relationship between IQ and crime is explored more fully in Chapter 5.

The Autonomic Nervous System

The autonomic nervous system controls heart rate and gland secretions, among other things. Generally speaking, it controls how the body reacts to stimuli. The heart rate, for example, increases in the presence of stimuli that are stressful or exciting, such as when walking into a room to take an exam. A substantial body of research suggests that criminals may have a lower resting heart rate than noncriminals. A review of 14 studies on this topic revealed that regardless of how the heart rate (simple pulse to sophisticated equipment) or crime (self-reports, official records, psychiatric diagnoses) was measured, heart rates consistently predicted antisocial behavior.[70] Measurements taken as early as age 3 predict later delinquency and crime. Furthermore, *elevated* heart rates lower the odds of crime and may help protect juvenile delinquents from becoming adult offenders.[71]

> *A substantial body of research suggests that criminals may have a lower resting heart rate than noncriminals.*

Skin conductance is another measure of how the body reacts to stimuli. In this type of research, electrodes attached to an individual's fingers measure how much a person sweats. The research in this area is much more mixed, with many studies finding no relationship between skin conductance and crime. Studies that document a significant relationship find that criminals have lower levels of skin conductance than noncriminals.[72]

Why would heart rate and skin conductance relate to criminal behavior? Both of these measures (as well as some brain scan evidence) suggest that criminals may have low levels of arousal; that is, they do not respond to stimuli as much as the average person. There are two main interpretations of this finding.[73] First, if a person is in a constant state of underarousal, they may seek out activities (including childhood aggression and crime) that are naturally arousing. Accordingly, this perspective is called sensation seeking theory. An alternative explanation is fearlessness theory. When faced with situations that typically induce fear, their heart rate remains relatively low, and they do not sweat profusely. During childhood, fearless children may be more difficult to socialize. Obviously, fearlessness would also be beneficial for those who carry out criminal behavior. A recent study of a sample of 335 adolescent boys from Pittsburgh tried to assess which theory was correct. In this study, the heart rate–aggression link was due to sensation-seeking rather than fearlessness.[74]

Of course, neither of these propositions explains why arousal produces criminal responses rather than noncriminal alternatives. For example, an underaroused individual might try racing motorbikes or mountain climbing. Similarly, a fearless person might defuse explosive devices for the military rather than engage in criminal behavior. A biological predisposition toward crime does not guarantee that a person will become a criminal, but it may increase the risk of criminal behavior.

Biological Harms

Biological differences that relate to criminal behavior might be caused by a host of factors. The infamous violent Dutch family reviewed previously suggests that in some cases, genetics can play a role. Another line of research involves examining the effects of various biological "harms," such as physical trauma, disease, or exposure to certain chemicals. Charles Whitman is perhaps the most celebrated case study relating a brain tumor to violence. In 1966, Whitman shot and killed 14 people from the Texas Tower at the University of Texas. Just prior to the shooting spree, he murdered both his wife and his mother. After the incident, investigators discovered that Whitman had sought psychiatric help because he was experiencing irrational and violent thoughts (including a fantasy about shooting people from the tower).[75] Whitman kept journals and left behind numerous letters (some suggest this hypergraphia was an additional psychiatric symptom). In one of his final notes, he typed the following:[76]

> *I don't quite understand what it is that compels me to type this letter. . . . I don't really understand myself these days. . . . Lately I have been a victim of many unusual and irrational thoughts. These thoughts constantly recur, and it requires a tremendous mental effort to concentrate. I consulted Dr. Cochrum at the University Health Center and asked him to recommend someone that I could consult with about some psychiatric disorders I felt I had. . . . I talked to a doctor once for about two hours and tried to convey to him my fears that I felt overcome by overwhelming violent impulses. . . . After my death I wish that an autopsy would be performed to see if there is any visible physical disorder. I have had tremendous headaches in the past and have consumed two large bottles of Excedrin in the past three months.*

An autopsy revealed a walnut-sized tumor, which was located in the hypothalamus region of the brain and was pressing against the amygdala.[77] As noted earlier, the amygdala is thought to be involved with emotion and memory formation. Of course, like the violent Dutch family, the case of Charles Whitman is a dramatic example of how biological trauma might lead to criminal behavior. More commonly, researchers in this area focus on other biological harms, including perinatal risks and birth complications, exposure to a variety of environmental toxins, and diet- and nutrition-related conditions.

Perinatal Risks and Birth Complications

A growing body of literature has examined the role that perinatal (at or around the time of birth) problems play in the development of criminal behavior. Generally, these studies focus on high-risk maternal behavior (e.g., smoking, drinking alcohol, using illicit drugs) during pregnancy, trauma suffered by the fetus during delivery, and low-birth-weight infants.

There is a great deal of evidence that maternal behaviors during pregnancy can adversely affect the health of the fetus. For example, maternal consumption of alcohol in high doses during pregnancy can result in fetal alcohol syndrome (FAS). FAS is a well-documented condition defined by a host of characteristics, including central nervous system dysfunction, growth retardation, and organ anomalies.[78] There is some evidence that even lower doses of alcohol may relate to childhood problems and criminal behavior.[79] Evidence also exists that maternal smoking during pregnancy is related to criminal outcomes for children. Research on a sample of Danish adult males revealed that maternal smoking predicted adult criminal outcomes.[80] Similar results have been found for maternal use of marijuana during pregnancy. By age 10, the children of these mothers showed increased levels of inattention, hyperactivity, and delinquency.[81]

Several studies have examined the impact of delivery complications on delinquency or criminal behavior. Researchers believe that complications (e.g., use of forceps to extract the fetus) cause injury to the fetus. One study, for example, examined the relationship between perinatal events and crime.[82] The researchers examined physical and criminal data from a birth cohort of Danish children. They reported that birth trauma-induced brain injury may have contributed to repeat violent offending. Specifically, they found that an index of delivery complications predicted adolescent and adult violent crime. A related line of inquiry considers the effect of low birth weight on childhood and adult outcomes.

Low birth weight can be caused by a host of factors, including maternal smoking or drinking during pregnancy. A substantial body of evidence indicates that low-birth-weight children are more likely than children of normal birth weight to have mild learning disabilities, attention disorders, hyperactivity, behavioral problems, low intelligence, poor academic achievement, and a difficult temperament.[83] Research suggests that low birth weight and environment (e.g., poverty, single-parent households, etc.) may work together to create crime. This combination of risk factors was related to the early onset of delinquency in a sample of inner city black males.[84]

A major criticism of the studies involving perinatal problems is that the results might be explained by environmental influences. For example, mothers who drink and smoke during pregnancy may not be effective parents during the baby's childhood. To get around this problem, one research study looked at the effect of wartime famine on crime.[85] During World War II, the German army blockaded food supplies to western portions of the Netherlands. Researchers examined children whose mothers were pregnant during this period of severe nutritional deficiency. In this case, the potential injury to the fetus was clearly not caused by the mother. They found that, compared to children born in eastern Netherlands (no blockade), those born in western Netherlands were more likely to have antisocial personality disorder as adults.

Exposure to Environmental Toxins: The Lead–Crime Link

Researchers have examined how a variety of environmental toxins (e.g., mercury, lead, cadmium) affect the human body. The toxin most commonly linked with criminal behavior is lead. Lead is a highly toxic substance. A large body of research links lead exposure or lead poisoning to a range of biological, neurological, and behavioral problems.[86] Lead exposure is especially damaging to children because their brains and central nervous systems are still being formed. For them, even extremely low levels of exposure can result in cognitive difficulties, ADD, behavioral problems, impaired hearing, and kidney damage. In severe cases, lead poisoning can even cause death. Although individuals can be exposed to lead from a number of sources, the two most likely suspects include gasoline and paint:[87]

> **The toxin most commonly linked with criminal behavior is lead.**

1. Many houses built prior to the 1980s contain lead paint. Although lead paint that is in intact condition is not necessarily dangerous, lead paint that is allowed to deteriorate creates a hazard by contaminating household dust as well as bare soil around the house, where children may play.
2. Between 1920 and 1996, the use of leaded gasoline contributed greatly to the number of cases of childhood lead poisoning in the United States. Though leaded gasoline was banned in 1996, the lead emitted by gasoline-powered vehicles continues to present a hazard today. This is because much of that lead remains in the soil where it was deposited over the years. This is especially true near well-traveled roads and highways.

Several recent studies, using a variety of methods, have linked lead exposure to criminal behavior. For example, one study linked estimates of air-based lead contamination with homicide levels across counties in the United States.[88] These results held, even after controlling for social correlates of crime (e.g., poverty, number of individuals in their crime-prone years).

A more comprehensive analysis found that the phase out of leaded gasoline, which began in the 1970s, contributed to the large decline in U.S. crime since the 1990s. Specifically, the pattern of state phase outs (states differed in the implementation of phase outs) predicted the pattern of crime declines.[89] These findings have since been replicated with data from a host of other countries, including Canada, France, Finland, Italy, and New Zealand.[90]

At the individual level, a study of 900 African American youths revealed that lead poisoning was one of the strongest predictors of male delinquency.[91] Recent results from the Cincinnati Lead Study (CLS) support this contention. The CLS is an ongoing research project designed to understand the effects of lead on the behavior of children. The sample for the study consisted of roughly 300 urban, inner city (where lead paint is more prevalent) youth. The examination of these individuals started even before they were born. Data from this project indicate that both prenatal and postnatal measures of lead levels predicted arrests for both crime generally and specifically for violent crime. Each 5 microgram increase in blood lead levels was associated with 40 percent increase in risk for arrest.[92]

The dangers of lead exposure have led to government intervention. Notably, the U.S. Environmental Protection Agency began phasing out leaded gasoline in the 1970s. The Lead-Based Paint Hazard Reduction Act of 1992, known as Title X, targets lead-based paint in older homes. According to this law, individuals selling a house built before 1978 must disclose any known lead hazards. Sellers and landlords must also provide a pamphlet on lead poisoning to the buyer or renter before the pre-1978 property is sold or rented. Some believe, however, that this law should be extended so that landlords are required to *fix* any known lead hazards, and some states have moved in this direction.[93]

Diet and Nutrition

The final biological harm to be considered is self-inflicted. If it is true that "you are what you eat," then perhaps there is a connection between nutrition and crime. Studies have examined the influence of a variety of dietary factors, including vitamin deficiencies and food allergies, on behavior. Much of the research in this area focuses on the effects of sugar and junk food. One commentator noted, "Sugar intake has been condemned as the cause of a large number of psychological

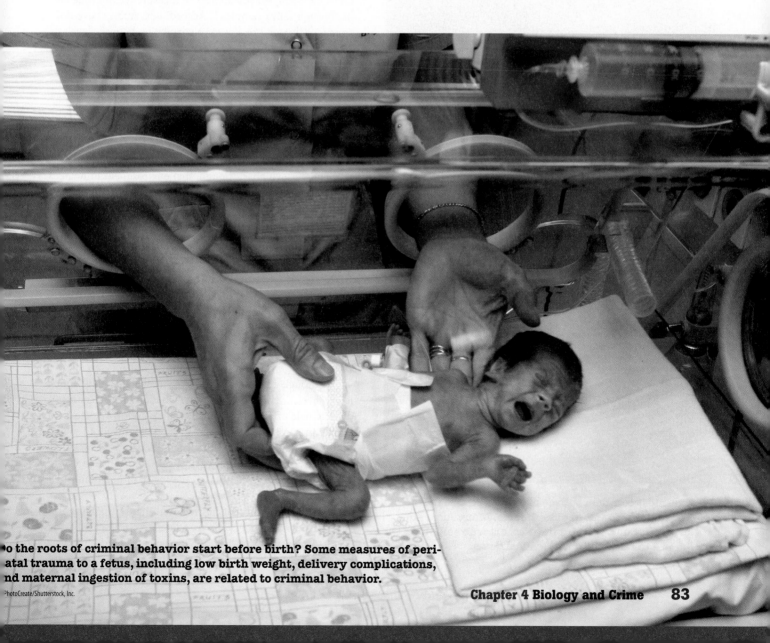

Do the roots of criminal behavior start before birth? Some measures of perinatal trauma to a fetus, including low birth weight, delivery complications, and maternal ingestion of toxins, are related to criminal behavior.

PhotoCreate/Shutterstock, Inc.

problems, including alterations in mood, irritability, aggression, and violent behavior."[94]

Of course, public perceptions about the evils of junk food do not necessarily mean there is a connection between sugar and crime. What does the empirical evidence suggest? One focus of research is hypoglycemia or low blood sugar. The brain has a chemical mechanism to control the level of blood sugar in the body. Some believe that excessive amounts of glucose (sugar) can cause hypoglycemia and, in some cases, trigger violent, antisocial behavior. Indeed, a number of research papers have documented a correlation between low blood sugar and violent behavior. Critics point out, however, that this relationship can be interpreted in a number of ways. For instance, people who engage in violence are more prone to alcoholism. Because chronic alcoholics often "drink" their meals, their inadequate nutrition might produce hypoglycemia.[95]

The most common source of lead exposure is lead-based paint found in older homes. Many local governments now require individuals who sell older homes to fix any known lead hazards.

© Tony Freeman/PhotoEdit

In contrast to sugar, the omega-3 fatty acids found in fish oils have been found to have numerous health benefits, including neurological health and the prevention of heart disease. A provocative study by a fish oil expert working for the National Institute on Alcohol Abuse and Alcoholism found that homicide rates had a strong negative correlation with country's level of fish consumption. In other words, countries such Japan, which have higher levels of fish consumption, experienced fewer homicides than countries with low fish consumption. Fish consumption has also been linked to aggression or crime within a single country. This research is relatively new and has yet to establish causal effects. Still, it raises the intriguing possibility that a healthier diet may reduce aggression and crime.[96]

Hormonal Influences

Most researchers studying hormonal influences on crime focus on the male sex androgen called testosterone. For the embryo carrying a Y sex chromosome, **testosterone** is the hormone responsible for development into a male fetus, and it influences secondary sex characteristics (e.g., body hair, muscle distribution). Technological advances since the 1960s have enabled researchers to measure testosterone levels through saliva samples.[97] Accordingly, studies have documented (though not always) a correlation between levels of testosterone and aggression or crime. For example, a study of adolescent boys ages 15 to 17 found that testosterone levels predicted both verbal and physical aggression as well as general "irritability."[98] A study of prison inmates found that those convicted of violent crimes had higher testosterone levels than those convicted of property or drug offenses. Furthermore, high-testosterone inmates were more likely to engage in confrontational misconduct while in prison.[99]

There is evidence, though, that environment influences the effects of testosterone. A study examining a sample of 4,462 American soldiers who served in Vietnam found that the association between testosterone levels and adult deviance was related to the level of the subject's social integration and prior delinquency involvement.[100] Men with lower levels of testosterone did not need a high level of social integration to keep them "in line." A more recent study of testosterone and delinquency considered the effects of peer associations. High-testosterone boys engaged in more antisocial behavior if they had delinquent peers. Testosterone actually had a positive effect (more likely to be chosen as team leaders), however, for boys who did not have delinquent peers.[101]

Although testosterone is present in females (at much lower levels), few studies examine whether testosterone predicts female criminal behavior. One exception is a study of female prison inmates. Similar to the relationship in males, the researchers discovered that higher levels of testosterone predicted aggressive behavior in prison.[102] Research on females, however, typically takes the study of hormones in a different direction.

The proposition that has received the most attention is that female menstrual cycles are related to criminal behavior. Prior to menstruation, hormonal changes (such as reduced estrogen) cause behavioral disturbances including anxiety, depression, irritability, aggressiveness, and mood swings for some women. Notably, during this period, there is also a drop in serotonin levels. The diagnosis of premenstrual syndrome (PMS) is made when such behavioral disturbances cause substantial disruption in a woman's life.[103] PMS can range in severity from mild to incapacitating in both a physical and a psychological sense.

The argument that PMS is related to criminal behavior has a long history. For example, a study published in 1945 found that 84 percent of women's crimes of violence were committed during the premenstrual and the early menstrual periods.[104] A few years later, a study of female inmates in New York reported that almost 80 percent of the women committed their crimes of violence during their menstrual cycles.[105] More recently, researchers reported that almost one-half of the 50 female prisoners they studied committed crimes of violence during their premenstrual period. They concluded that crimes are caused more by hormonal activity than by social or psychological factors.[106]

This body of research has been severely criticized. For example, one commentator noted that a PMS–crime link could be interpreted differently: The crime and the arrest could lead to changes in hormonal levels that triggered menstruation. Others argue that like the XYY supermale, the premenstrual syndrome thesis is "based upon stereotypical and unsupported views" of the sexes.[107] Diana Fishbein, a noted scholar in the area of biology and crime, however, contends that "there remains a general impression that a subgroup of women appear to be especially vulnerable to cyclical changes in hormone levels, causing them to be more prone to increased levels of anxiety and hostility during the premenstrual phase."[108]

Despite less-than-convincing scientific evidence, PMS has been successfully used as a criminal defense. Indeed, European courts recognized premenstrual defenses as early as the 1800s.[109] Two English cases in the early 1980s brought the PMS defense to the forefront. In both cases, female defendants in separate criminal actions successfully pleaded diminished responsibility or mitigating circumstances by establishing that they suffered from PMS. One of these defendants was found guilty of manslaughter rather than murder despite admitting that she had run over her lover with her car after an argument.

Legal experts continue to debate the use of PMS as a criminal defense. Some experts have argued that PMS should not be asserted as a complete defense of criminal conduct but should be used as a mitigating factor.[110] Even feminists are divided about the use of PMS as a defense or a mitigating factor during sentencing—such a defense may give some leniency to some women, yet it will also perpetuate stereotypes. Certainly, more research must be conducted on this subject before any definitive statements can be made.

> *Early biological explanations of crime tended to focus on a single, direct cause of criminal behavior*

Indeed, the medical profession continues to debate not only the symptoms of PMS, but also the validity of the syndrome itself.[111]

Biosocial Theory

Early biological explanations of crime tended to focus on a single, direct cause of criminal behavior (e.g., body type, feeblemindedness) that affected crime independent of the environment. In other words, biology was destiny. In recent theories, biological effects are often portrayed as indirect. Furthermore, they are shown to operate in conjunction with environmental influences. The biological findings discussed in the preceding sections identified a number of interactions between biology and environment that led to crime. For example, the interactions between testosterone and delinquent peer associations, and between a specific gene and child abuse both predicted antisocial behavior.

A review of research in this area documented 39 studies where significant biosocial interactions were discovered.[112] Modern theorists, then, do not advance a pure biological theory of crime. Instead, biosocial theorists argue that combinations of environmental and biological risk cause criminal behavior. A summary of biosocial and evolutionary theories covered in the text (see the following section) is provided in **TABLE 4-4**.

Eysenck's Biosocial Theory

Hans Eysenck was among the first to propose a biosocial explanation of crime. The core of Eysenck's theory is that personality differences, which are biologically rooted, explain criminal behavior.[113] For example, he argues that extroverted people (personality) have central nervous systems (biology) that are less responsive to the environment. The research on heart rate discussed previously supports this position. Eysenck suggests that underarousal may explain crime in at least two different ways. First (as already discussed), it might lead people to seek out extra stimulation, including criminal behavior. Second, underaroused individuals may not feel the sting of punishment.

In this regard, Eysenck suggests that parents may have a harder time conditioning their children out of unwanted behaviors through punishment. This proposition leads to a rather novel prediction. In prosocial environments (e.g., noncriminal parents), he expects that children who are difficult to condition would be more likely to engage in crime. In poor environments (e.g., criminal parents), he believes that biological deficits (low conditionability) would actually protect children from negative influences. Normal children, who are more easily conditioned, risk becoming socialized to their parents' criminal habits.

TABLE 4-4

Biosocial and Evolutionary Theories of Crime

Theorist	Theory	Core Elements
Biosocial Theory		
Hans Eysenck	Personality-based theory	Personality traits, which are driven by underlying biology, cause crime. In particular, children with low arousal will be difficult to "condition" and socialize. In criminal families, however, low arousal might prevent children from learning patterns of criminal behavior.
Terrie Moffitt	Life-course-persistent offending	Life-course-persistent offending (chronic offending that starts early in life) is caused by an interaction between neurological deficits and ineffective parenting.
Evolutionary Theory		
Various	Evolutionary theory of rape	Evolutionary processes allow males who are pushy and aggressive in the pursuit of sex to pass on their genes successfully.
Various	Cads and dads theory	Discusses two alternative strategies for reproductive success, the "cad" and "dad" strategies. Cads are essentially cheaters who pretend to want to make an investment in parenting but really want to reproduce with as many females as possible.

Some components of Eysenck's biosocial theory have been empirically tested. In fact, much of this research has already been discussed. For example, research on heart rate and skin conductance offers some indirect support. Those with lower heart rates and lower skin conductance are more likely to engage in crime. Personality research also supports some of Eysencks' propositions. Unfortunately, few have directly tested his conditionability argument.

Moffitt's Theory of Life-Course-Persistent Offending

The most widely recognized biosocial theory of crime is Terrie Moffitt's developmental theory of offending. Moffitt contends that there are two types of criminal offenders. **Life-course-persistent (LCP) offenders** start their criminal careers early in childhood and show remarkable stability in antisocial behavior throughout their lives. In contrast, adolescent-limited (AL) offenders tend to confine their criminal behavior to adolescence.

To explain LCP offending, Moffitt focuses on the neurological health of infants. She believes that biological processes within the nervous system influence psychological characteristics such as temperament, behavioral development, and cognitive abilities. As noted, countless factors may influence the neurological health of an infant. Examples include perinatal maternal drug or alcohol abuse, exposure to toxins such as lead, brain injury suffered due to pregnancy complications, or inherited individual differences in the nervous system.

According to Moffitt, even subtle deficits can produce an infant with a difficult temperament. These infants may be "clumsy and awkward, overactive, inattentive, irritable, impulsive, hard to keep on schedule, delayed in reaching developmental milestones, poor at verbal comprehension, deficient at expressing themselves, or slow at learning new things."[114] Such infants may be hard to socialize, even for the most competent parents. For a number of reasons, however, children with a difficult temperament are more likely to be raised in poor parenting environments.

For example, mothers who engage in behaviors that put unborn children at risk may be less apt at socializing their children after they are born. Also, low birth weight or exposure to toxins may be the result of adverse social conditions. In sum, this theory holds that a combination of neurological deficits and family adversity leads to a series of failed parent–child encounters. This results in an unsocialized (and therefore antisocial) child. As the child ages, he or she retains neurological deficits. Also, the child continues to provoke negative reactions (e.g., peer rejection, school failure) from the environment.

AL offending, on the other hand, is explained largely by environmental processes. Specifically, as children enter adolescence, they experience a "maturity gap." Biologically, they are ready for adulthood, but socially, many adult activities are restricted or prohibited. As adolescents struggle for independence, it becomes normative to engage in some forms of crime. Specifically, adolescents start to "mimic" the deviance (e.g., underage drinking, vandalism, drug use) of their LCP peers. Unlike their LCP peers, however, AL offenders quickly age out of this behavior. As people enter young adulthood, the maturity gap closes, college or careers begin, and it is no longer rewarding to rebel against parents. Desistance is made easier because AL offenders have neither the neurological problems nor the environmental baggage (e.g., school failure, drug addiction) of their LCP counterparts.[115]

Tests of the biosocial pathway in Moffitt's theory have received considerable support. The study of low birth weight discussed earlier is one example. The researchers found that those with both low birth weight and social disadvantage were most likely to engage in crime early in life. Results from Moffitt's New Zealand study indicated that boys with low neuropsychological test scores and adverse home environments had mean aggression scores that were four times higher than boys with just one of those characteristics.[116] A 2005 study using a sample of children from Pittsburgh found that neurocognitive impairments predicted antisocial behavior for LCP offenders.[117] Despite this positive evidence, Moffitt's theory is relatively new. Although some parts of the theory have been tested extensively (with mixed results), other aspects are still open to question. For example, there is growing evidence that there are more than two developmental pathways. Some antisocial children ("childhood recoveries") do not become LCP offenders, and some AL offenders continue to offend well into adulthood.[118]

Low Self-Control as a Biosocial Concept

In 1990, criminologists Michael Gottfredson and Travis Hirschi outlined a theory of crime with low self-control as the central concept (see Chapter 7). They characterized low self-control persons as impulsive, insensitive, physical (as opposed to mental), risk-taking, shortsighted, and nonverbal. They suggested that the primary cause of low self-control is ineffective parenting. While they conceded that individuals might differ biologically in ways that predispose them to low self-control, they argued that all children could be socialized to have self-control. It should also be noted that their concept of low self-control is similar to constructs (e.g., impulsivity, low constraint) from psychological theories.

As biological research has become more prevalent in criminology, some researchers have started to examine the relationship between biology and the development of self-control. For example, criminologists John Wright and Kevin Beaver used a sample of twin children in an attempt to separate the effect of parenting and genetics on low self-control.[119] They found that parenting had weak and inconsistent effects on self-control and concluded that genetics should be considered within this theory. Later research tied the development of self-control to the development of language skills (which were influenced by both environmental and genetic factors).[120,121] These researchers and their colleagues suggest that low self-control should be considered from a biosocial perspective, that is, originating as an executive function of the brain.[122]

> **They suggested that the primary cause of low self-control is ineffective parenting.**

A Biosocial Explanation of Female Delinquency

Although not a formal theory of crime, a group of researchers documented an interesting biosocial relationship that predicted female offending. The starting point for this study was previous studies indicating that early onset of puberty (a biological process) among females was related to criminal behavior. The researchers extended this line of inquiry by examining school settings among a sample of females.[123] In particular, early onset of puberty was related to offending for girls in mixed-gender school settings but not for those who attended all-female schools. The authors suggest that the females who started puberty early attracted the attention of older, crime-prone males. Female delinquency likely resulted from these associations.

Evolutionary Explanations

Evolutionary explanations of crime are based on the Darwinian principles of natural selection and survival of the fittest. Although entire textbooks are devoted to this topic, the gist of evolution is rather simple. In essence, those individuals who are best adapted to their environment will survive to reproduce and, therefore, will pass on their genes to their offspring (thus, the most genetically "fit" survive).

E. O. Wilson first proposed the idea of "socio-biology" to apply the principles of evolution to explain modern human behaviors (e.g., parenting, aggression, altruism). Richard Dawkins' *The Selfish Gene* also gave a push to what is now called evolutionary psychology.[124,125] Evolutionary theories assume that if a particular trait or characteristic is present in a population, it is likely to have contributed somehow to the reproductive success of ancestors. Theorists typically take a particular trait and work backward to craft an explanation of how this trait may have increased reproductive success. Importantly, these primeval genetic forces are hypothesized to be the deep-seated, unconscious roots of modern behavior. Thus, a trait may increase reproductive success without the person thinking about such matters.

There is no single evolutionary theory of criminal behavior; rather, a number of different theories exist. These theories tend to be rather narrow in scope, explaining, for example, only property crime or rape. Some evolutionary theories, however, do attempt to explain a wider range of criminal behavior.

An Evolutionary Perspective on Rape and Sexual Assault

Since evolutionary theory emerged, several explanations have focused on the crime of rape and sexual assault. The basic proposition here is that sexual aggression has been "selected" within males because they can invest very little in conceived offspring. Because they are relatively free of parenting responsibility (i.e., the female provides both the gestation and initial feeding), males benefit most from having multiple sex partners. Criminologists Lee Ellis and Anthony Walsh summarize this basic argument:[126]

> *According to the evolutionary theory of rape, male reproductive advantage derived from having multiple sex partners has resulted in natural selection favoring genes promoting brain patterns for "pushiness" in pursuit of sexual intercourse. In some males, genes may carry pushiness to the point of actual force, especially after less violent tactics fail to yield results . . . over generations, pushy males will probably be more successful at passing on their genes, including any genes coding for readily learning pushy behavior.*

One obvious prediction from this perspective is that males should predominate in the commission of rape (this is evident in crime statistics). A documented pattern of sexual promiscuity among some male criminal offenders also fits this theory. Of course, mainstream theories could also account for such findings. For example, they point to how males and females are socialized or to the difference in physical strength between the sexes. A more novel prediction from this perspective is that if natural selection plays a role in rape among humans, the same phenomenon should also appear in nonhuman species. Ellis and Walsh point out that forced copulation is perpetrated by the males of many animal species. Theories that tie rape to socialization (a uniquely human process) would not predict this type of behavior in lower animal species.

Cads and Dads

A number of evolutionary theories highlight the competition of alternative behavioral strategies for passing on genes. Typically, one behavioral strategy is rare and the other prevalent. Similar to an ecosystem with predators and prey, the prevalence of these strategies will fluctuate with each other over time. "Cads" and "dads" describe two evolution-based strategies for reproduction. The "dad" strategy involves investing the time and energy to help nurture and raise offspring. Females are attracted to dads because by virtue of their biological role in reproduction, females must make a similar investment. Unfortunately for females, other males give the illusion of a being a dad, but in reality they make only a minimal investment in parenting. Depending on the particular animal group, researchers call such male animals "cheaters," "satellites," "sneakers," or "cads."[127]

The main assumption behind this theory is that genetic predispositions underlie both of these strategies. In other words, a subpopulation of men has genetically evolved toward a strategy of minimal parental investment across as many females as possible. Some argue, however, that this behavior can also be learned. Because females are unlikely to find the "cad" strategy attractive, "cads" must be extremely deceptive (i.e., lie, cheat, etc.) and mask their true intentions.

This theory makes a number of predictions that are consistent with empirical evidence:[128]

- Criminality and psychopathy should be more prevalent among men than women.
- Criminals and psychopaths should be unusually promiscuous.
- Criminals and psychopaths should be more inclined to commit sexual assaults than males in general.
- The "cad" strategy should be more pronounced among males in the prime of their reproductive careers than in later life.

A Critique of Evolutionary Theory

Evolutionary theories have been criticized on a number of grounds. For example, many of these theories are difficult, if not impossible, to test. In essence, they are a "story" that is told about an already observed empirical finding. Thus, the hypotheses derived from these theories (e.g., men are more likely to rape than women) are often known empirical facts. It is relatively easy to conjure up a story about the evolutionary roots of a particular behavior. The late biocriminologist David Rowe, for example, suggested facetiously that the high prevalence of swimming pools in Phoenix, Arizona, is "adaptive" because the water cools men's sperm, making them more fertile.[129] Because of these difficulties and because these theories are relatively new, there are very few empirical tests.

 ## Conclusion

Overall, the findings from research on biology and crime suggest that a host of biological factors may be involved in criminal behavior. Some of these factors are thought to be inherited, while others result from biological harms. Current theorists argue that biological factors contribute to criminality under certain environmental circumstances. As unpalatable as it is for many to consider, humans may be partially driven toward crime by natural forces beyond their control. Keep in mind, though, that many environmental factors (e.g., poverty, neighborhood of residence) thought to cause crime are often outside the control of children and adolescents.

> *Current theorists argue that biological factors contribute to criminality under certain environmental circumstances.*

There is no question that, after many years of neglect, biological criminology is enjoying a revival. Perhaps signaling this revival, James Q. Wilson and Richard Herrnstein incorporated biological factors into their general explanation of crime. In their widely read (and controversial) 1985 book, *Crime and Human Nature*, the authors concluded that:[130]

> *Criminals are more likely than noncriminals to have mesomorphic body types . . . to have fathers who were criminals even in the case of adopted sons who could not have known their fathers . . . to be of somewhat lower intelligence . . . to be impulsive or extroverted . . . and to have autonomic nervous systems that respond more slowly and less vigorously to stimuli.*

In the 30 years following publication of their book, some biologically oriented theories of crime have become mainstream. Tests of biosocial theories also appear more frequently in leading criminology journals. An empirical review of criminology textbooks concluded that biological theories are currently given greater, and more favorable, coverage.[131] Indeed, there are now general criminology texts with a biosocial emphasis and several recent books on biocriminology.[132–134] One should be careful, though, not to overstate the popularity of the biological approach to crime. A quick scan of the citations in the notes for this chapter will show that most biological studies of crime still appear in journals devoted to the study of biology, psychology, or psychiatry. Indeed, many criminologists remain extremely skeptical of biological theories.

In light of this skepticism, criminologist Francis Cullen identifies three challenges for biocriminologists as they advance the biosocial paradigm. They will have to be able to educate fellow criminologists to make their ideas accessible and understandable, to relinquish their antagonism toward sociology, and to show how their new paradigm rejects its repressive heritage.[135] Indeed, it is the legacy of the eugenics movement, which aimed to sterilize and or incapacitate "biologically inferior" individuals, that gives pause to mainstream criminologists. However, current biological research points to a predisposition toward criminal behavior that may emerge *depending on the environment*. Thus, biology is not necessarily destiny. Furthermore, many of the biological harms (lead poisoning, perinatal injury, maternal pregnancy behaviors) are very much amenable to change.

In that sense, some commentators suggest that biological explanations of crime are becoming part of a general movement to define criminality as a "public health problem."[136] For example, the provision of intensive perinatal health care to at-risk pregnant women might help prevent some forms of trauma (e.g., alcohol, cigarettes, illicit drugs) to the fetus.[137] The most well known version of such a program was created by David Olds. Specifically, this program provided nine home visits to vulnerable pregnant women by nurse practitioners, with more than 20 follow-up visits during the first 2 years of the child's life. The nurses gave advice regarding prenatal care (e.g., reducing smoking and alcohol use) and served as a resource to help mothers meet the needs of their infants. A randomized study, where the control group received standard levels of care revealed impressive results when the children were 12 years of age. The home visiting program produced reductions of more than 50 percent in arrests and conviction and reduced alcohol consumption, truancy, and other harmful behaviors.[138]

Another common argument is that biological risk markers might identify children at risk for crime so that environmental counterbalances (e.g., parenting, social bonds) could be strengthened. Even here, there are serious ethical concerns. How exactly will people be screened for biological risk markers? Who will be screened? Will lower-class individuals automatically be the targets of policies? Certainly, stigmatizing those who have a characteristic that may be conducive to criminality would be unethical. These issues are magnified when considering molecular genetics. Gene-based criminology, it is feared, could justify the use of intrusive policies. For example, gene therapy might be offered as a condition for probation in lieu of prison. Even biocriminologists note that such concerns are valid:[139]

> *Perhaps a day will come when the strength of genetic dispositions can be predicted at birth, but it will not come soon. When, and if, it does come, let us hope that people have the wisdom to deal with that deeper knowledge of genetics and behavior.*

Finally, the biological approach often ignores white-collar, organized, and political crime. Rather, it tends to focus on aggression or antisocial behavior in children and so-called "street crime" in adults. Because minorities are overrepresented in street crime, there is the danger of misusing biology to provide unsound justifications for the control of minority populations. In fact, one reason biological criminology originally fell into disrepute was that it was a "kind of people" approach, comparing white "normals" to criminals of color.

In sum, many mainstream criminologists still regard the mixture of biology and criminology with skepticism and concern. Despite this fact, biosocial explanations are increasing in prevalence and popularity. Given advances in molecular genetics and other areas of biological study, it appears that this trend will continue.

Texture: © Malchev/Shutterstock; Police Tape: © SkillUp/Shutterstock

- Early biological explanations of crime pointed toward a single, direct, immutable cause of crime. For example, Lombroso believed that some criminals were atavists, or evolutionary throwbacks. One policy implication derived from these theories was eugenics—the attempt to create a better stock of humans by controlling who is allowed to have children.
- Early biological research was often shoddy. Researchers frequently used institutional populations to draw conclusions about all criminals. Furthermore, while researchers ignored physical similarities between criminals and noncriminals, differences (no matter how small) were assumed to reflect the superiority of noncriminals.
- The modern biological approach consists of a wide range of inquiry, including behavioral genetics (twin studies, molecular genetics), neurological functioning, and biological harms (perinatal risk, exposure to lead).

- Biosocial theories of crime emphasize the interplay between biology and the environment. For example, the LCP path within Moffitt's developmental theory of offending focuses on the interaction between neurological deficits and inadequate parenting skills. In contrast to early biological theories, modern theorists argue that biology often has a subtle, indirect effect on criminal behavior. Furthermore, some biological causes of crime (e.g., lead exposure, perinatal harms) are amenable to change.
- Evolutionary theory uses Darwin's concept of natural selection to explain criminal behavior. The underlying assumption is that the genetic predispositions for behaviors in the population (including crimes such as rape) were "selected" because they increase the chance of passing on one's genes.

PUTTING IT ALL TOGETHER

Police Tape: © SkillUp/Shutterstock

1. What are the common characteristics of early biological theories? Are they different from the modern biological perspective?

2. How is body type related to criminal behavior? What are the different explanations for this relationship?

3. How have scientists attempted to separate nature from nurture? Which factor do you feel is more responsible for crime: nature or nurture?

4. Identify and explain at least two biological correlates of criminal behavior.

5. What is a biosocial theory? Use a specific theory as an example in your answer.

6. What is eugenics? Do you feel that the biological approach to crime still leads to dangerous policy implications?

KEY TERMS

Police Tape: © SkillUp/Shutterstock

atavism Term used by Lombroso to describe people whom he believed were "evolutionary throwbacks" to a more primitive line of human beings.

behavioral genetics The scientific study of how genes and heredity affect particular behaviors.

concordance rate Focus of twin studies. The outcome (e.g., criminal behavior) is concordant if both twins exhibit the same behavior.

deoxyribonucleic acid (DNA) Found on each chromosome, it contains the molecular code for all living organisms. DNA is made up of four chemicals, called bases, that bind together in different sequences on a sugar phosphate backbone.

dizygotic (DZ) twins Fraternal twins who share the same amount of genetic similarity as non-twin siblings.

eugenics The goal of improving the human race through selective breeding. In the 20th century, eugenics led to limitations on the immigration of southern and eastern Europeans to the United States and the institutionalization or forced sterilization of the poor, deviant, and disabled.

fearlessness theory An explanation of the relationship between low levels of arousal and antisocial behavior. This theory suggests that persons with low arousal are more likely to commit crime because punishment does not stimulate anxiety and fear.

fetal alcohol syndrome (FAS) A well-documented condition caused when pregnant women ingest high levels of alcohol. FAS is defined by a host of characteristics, including central nervous system dysfunction, growth retardation, and organ anomalies.

gene A specific sequence of bases within a DNA molecule that works together to carry out a particular task.

genome The term used to describe an organism's complete set of DNA.

Human Genome Project (HGP) Begun formally in 1990 and completed in 2006, the HGP was a coordinated effort by the U.S. Department of Energy and the National Institutes of Health to map the entire human genome.

life-course-persistent (LCP) offenders A developmental pathway within Moffitt's theory of offending. LCP offenders exhibit deviance throughout their lives. This pathway is hypothesized by a biosocial interaction between biology (neurological deficits) and environment (social class, parenting, etc.).

limbic system A region of the brain located beneath the outer cortex that includes the hippocampus, amygdala, and thalamus. This more primitive area of the brain houses emotional life.

molecular genetics The study of the expression of genes accomplished by identifying the DNA sequences of chromosomes.

monoamine oxidase A (MAOA) An enzyme that breaks down neurotransmitters so that they can be removed from the body. The genes for MAOA and direct measures of this enzyme have been linked to crime.

monozygotic (MZ) twins Identical twins who are products of a single egg and sperm, and thus are exactly the same genetically.

prefrontal cortex The part of the brain responsible for "executive functions" (i.e., abstract reasoning, the ability to sustain attention, self-monitoring, and the inhibition of impulsive behavior). Biological studies suggest that deficiencies in this region of the brain may lead to a criminal disposition.

sensation seeking theory An explanation of the relationship between low levels of arousal and antisocial behavior. This theory suggests that low arousal is an unpleasant state, and therefore causes people to seek out stimulating behaviors.

serotonin A neurotransmitter that helps conduct the electrical impulses in the brain; low levels of serotonin hinder communication between cells. Research links low levels of serotonin with criminal behavior.

skin conductance A method for measuring how an individual's fingers sweat. Although research is mixed, some studies find that criminals have lower skin conductance than noncriminals.

somatotype The classification of human body types into three categories. Sheldon argued that body type relates to a person's personality or disposition. Endomorphs are fat, soft, and round, and they tend to be extroverts. Ectomorphs are thin and wiry, and they are easily worried, sensitive, and introverted. Mesomorphs are muscular, gregarious, aggressive, assertive, and action oriented. Some research suggests that the mesomorph is the dominant body type among delinquents.

testosterone For the embryo carrying a Y sex chromosome, the hormone responsible for development into a male fetus. Testosterone influences secondary sex characteristics (e.g., body hair, muscle mass). Research consistently demonstrates a relationship between levels of testosterone and aggression.

XYY A rare chromosome abnormality in which a male (typically XY) has an extra Y chromosome. Early research suggested that these individuals were unusually aggressive ("supermales"). Later research indicated that they are no more violent than others, but they are perhaps slightly more crime prone.

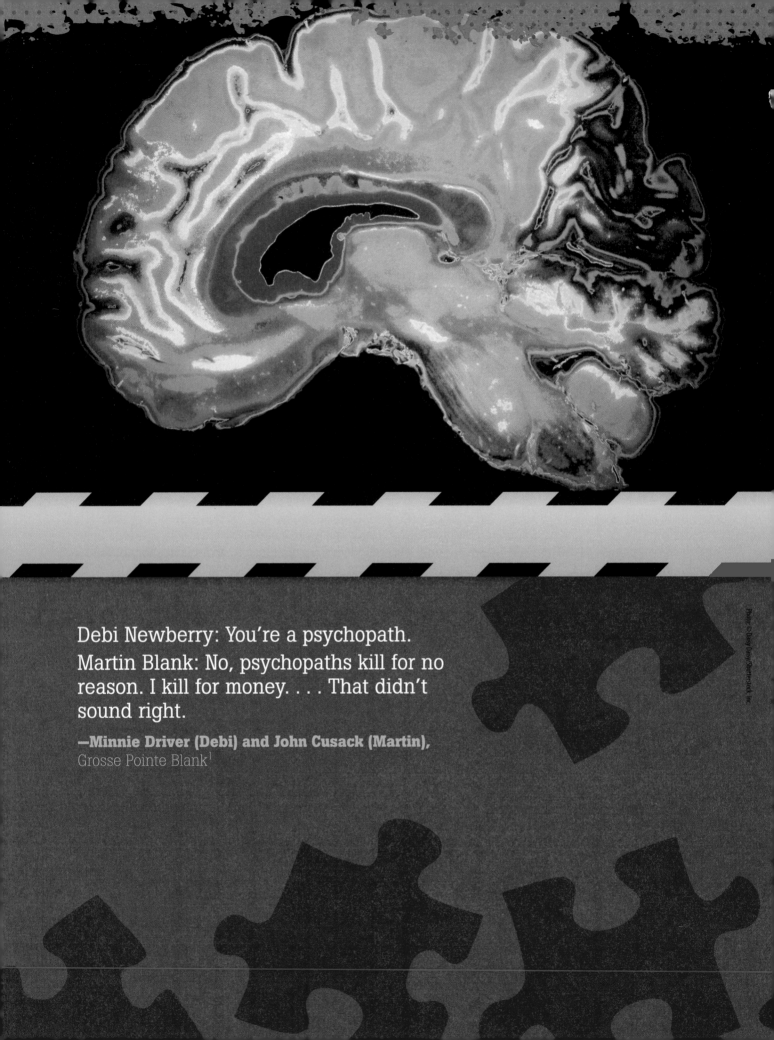

Debi Newberry: You're a psychopath.
Martin Blank: No, psychopaths kill for no reason. I kill for money. . . . That didn't sound right.

—Minnie Driver (Debi) and John Cusack (Martin),
Grosse Pointe Blank[1]

CHAPTER 5

Psychology and Crime

Texture: © Maiche/Shutterstock; Shooter: © Maiche/Shutterstock; Puzzle Piece: © Photodisc; Police tape: © SkillUp/Shutterstock

Objectives

- Understand the different types of contributions psychology makes to the study of crime. Pg. 94

- Know the fundamentals of psychoanalytic theory, including Freudian elements of personality and defense mechanisms. Pgs. 94–98

- Comprehend the three learning mechanisms—operant conditioning, classical conditioning, and observational learning—and how they relate to theories of crime. Pgs. 98–103

- Understand cognitive structure and cognitive content and how they have been applied to criminal behavior. Pgs. 103–104

- Distinguish between general personality research and research on a "criminal personality." Furthermore, be able to provide examples of general traits related to crime and the specific attributes of a psychopath. Pgs. 104–109

- Grasp the debate on the relationship between IQ and criminal behavior. Pgs. 109–111

- Know the policy implications derived from theories of learning, personality, and cognition. Pgs. 94–113

Introduction

Blockbuster movies and best-selling novels often star psychopathic killers. The killer is methodically tracked down by a psychologist who has a keen understanding of the criminal mind. This plot has been successful for Hollywood, but is there really such a thing as a psychopath or a criminal mind? How exactly does psychology contribute to the study of criminal behavior? This chapter introduces some of the basic psychological concepts developed to analyze and explain criminal behavior. Specifically, after a brief introduction to psychodynamic theory, we examine the contribution of four areas in psychology—behaviorism, cognition, personality, and IQ—to criminological theory and the effort to rehabilitate criminals.

Like the biological approach, psychological theories focus on how characteristics of the individual lead to criminal behavior. Indeed, researchers and theorists who are trained in psychology are typically open to the role of biology in explaining human behavior (see Chapter 4). Criminologists often contrast this individual approach with sociological theory. Sociological approaches tend to focus on how social structure causes crime. An important point to understand is that there is room for both types of explanations. For example, a sociologist might explain how conditions like poverty and residential mobility create high crime rates in a certain neighborhood. A psychologist might question why some individuals succumb to the criminal pressures of the neighborhood while others become successful, law-abiding citizens. Resilient people, for example, might have certain personality traits or problem solving skills that allow them to avoid the temptations of crime.

Psychology is also considered a "helping" discipline. That is, psychological research informs clinical work, with the long-term goal of improving people's lives. Psychologists, for example, have designed and evaluated many of the most effective rehabilitation programs in existence. Psychology intersects with the study of crime and the criminal justice system in a number of other ways. For example, forensic psychology is defined as research and application of psychological knowledge to the legal system. Forensic psychologists provide expert testimony at trials and consult with police departments (e.g., hiring decisions, counseling for officers).[2] Clinical psychologists and psychiatrists tend to operate from a medical model and treat individuals with mental disorders. Psychiatrists are medical doctors that can prescribe medication, whereas psychologists are not.

While most people do not consider crime to be a "disorder," there are disorders where crime is a central feature. **TABLE 5-1** provides details regarding conduct disorder (CD) and antisocial personality disorder (ASPD). Furthermore, the criminal justice

> *Like the biological approach, psychological theories focus on how characteristics of the individual lead to criminal behavior.*

TABLE 5-1
Mental Disorders That Include Criminal Behavior as a Central Feature

Conduct Disorder (CD): A serious behavioral and emotional disorder that is diagnosed in children and teens. Features include:
- Aggression toward people and animals (fighting, animal cruelty)
- Destruction of property (firesetting)
- Deceitfulness/theft (burglary, "conning" others)
- Serious violation of rules (truancy, running away)

Antisocial Personality Disorder (ASPD): A personality disorder diagnosed in adults, in which the central feature is a pervasive pattern of disregard for the rights of others. Specific features include:
- Failure to conform to social norms (acts that are grounds for arrest)
- Deceitfulness (lying, using aliases)
- Impulsivity (failure to plan)
- Irritability/aggressiveness (physical assaults)
- Reckless disregard for the safety of self or others
- Irresponsibility (inability to sustain employment)
- Lack of remorse (being indifferent to victims)

Data from American Psychiatric Association. (2013). *Diagnostic and statistical manual of mental disorders* (5th ed.). Washington, DC: American Psychiatric Association.

system encounters a large number of individuals with serious mental illnesses, such as schizophrenia, that are not directly related to crime (see **Theory in Action: Mental Illness, Crime, and the Criminal Justice System**).

Many psychologists are engaged in academic research on the causes of CD, ASPD, or more generally on criminal behavior. Psychologists study both environmental and personality influences on criminal behavior, along with the mental processes that mediate behavior. This chapter covers the psychological concepts of personality, learning, cognition, and intelligence/IQ. Prior to delving into current psychological approaches, we consider psychoanalytic theory as an important precursor.

Psychoanalytic Theory

Early theorists interested in the psychological aspects of crime focused on a variety of areas. For example, Henry Maudsley (1835–1918) studied the relationship between crime and insanity, especially "epileptic madness."[3] He believed that criminals suffered from "moral degeneracy"—a deficiency of moral sense. In writing of the criminal "who

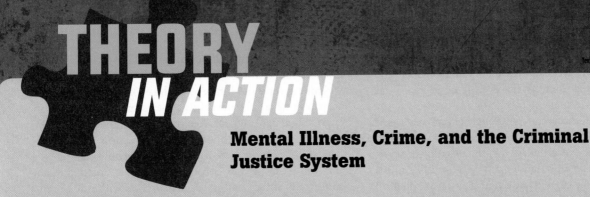

THEORY IN ACTION

Mental Illness, Crime, and the Criminal Justice System

Some of the most horrible mass homicides in recent years were committed by individuals who were alleged to have a serious mental illness. In Aurora, Colorado, James E. Holmes opened fire on an audience at the midnight screening of *The Dark Knight Rises*. Dressed in body armor and wearing a gas mask, he killed 12 people and wounded over 70 others. Holmes' defense attorney claims that the shooting was due to "psychotic episode" that resulted from schizophrenia. Holmes' pleaded "not guilty by reason of insanity" in his criminal trial that started in April 2015. At Virginia Tech in 2007, Seung-Hui Cho shot and killed 32 people and wounded 17 others in two separate attacks. Cho had been diagnosed with a severe anxiety disorder in childhood. At Virginia Tech, he was accused of stalking two female students. Just prior to the shooting, he was ordered into outpatient treatment by a special judge. These high profile cases lead the media, politicians, and the public to ask questions about mental illness, crime, and policy. How often does mental illness lead to crime? How should society and the criminal justice system handle the mentally ill? Should those with mental disorders be prevented from obtaining weapons?

As with most issues in criminology, the research evidence reveals that mental illness, crime, and the criminal justice system interact in complex ways. An understanding of the current situation requires some historical context. Prior to the 1960s, most states maintained large networks of mental health institutions. Between 1960 and 1980, a number of factors led states to deinstitutionalize people with serious mental illnesses (schizophrenia, bipolar disorder, major depression). In particular, improvements in psychotropic medicines allowed for the care of patients outside of institutions. Also, as public opinion towards mental illness became less prejudiced, laws emerged to prohibit the involuntary civil commitment of people unless they were deemed an imminent threat to themselves or others. As a result, treatment admissions to public psychiatric hospitals declined from 475,000 in 1971 to 47,000 in 2003. In theory, a "community treatment" model was supposed to allow for the care the mentally ill in the community. In practice, community treatment did not materialize.

Subsequently, many people with serious mental illness (PSMI) were swept up in the correctional building boom that occurred from 1980 to 2010. Indeed, because some of the largest providers of psychiatric care are large, urban jails, many believe that the criminal justice system has become the default mental health system. Mentally ill persons can end up in the criminal justice system for a variety of reasons:

- "Criminalization" occurs when PSMI are arrested for public order offenses such as disorderly conduct, minor property damage, or trespassing. These offenses are related to public expression of the symptoms (e.g., auditory hallucinations, delusions) of serious mental illness.

- PSMI are more likely to be homeless. This leads to more confrontation with police as well as crimes of "survival" (e.g., prostitution, shoplifting).

- A high proportion of PSMI have substance abuse problems. The strict enforcement of drug laws since the 1980s has increased the population PSMI in the criminal justice system. Substance abuse is also an independent risk factor for crime.

- PSMI are arrested for serious crimes that may or may not be related to their mental illness.

The last point raises the issue of whether PSMI are more likely to engage in crime than others in society. The research in this area is complicated and evolving. It does *not* appear, however, that having a serious mental disorder alone causes crime. In fact, the symptoms of some disorders such as schizophrenia and depression actually lower the odds of criminal behavior. Instead, many of the same factors (e.g., criminal thinking patterns, substance abuse) explain offending among both PSMI and non-PSMI populations. Thus, while it may be true that symptoms of mental illness may help explain some criminal events, simply having a serious mental disorder does not increase the risk for crime. Because of this, experts warn against sweeping policy changes that target PSMI. Indeed, to the extent that such policies stigmatize mental illness, they may lead fewer people to seek needed treatment.

Sources: Lurigio, A. J. (2013). Criminalization of the mentally ill: Exploring the causes and current evidence in the United States. *The Criminologist, 38*, 1–8; Peterson, J. K., Skeem, J., Kennealy, P., Bray, B., & Zvonkovic, A. (2014). How often and how consistently do symptoms directly precede criminal behavior among offenders with mental illness? *Law and Human Behavior, 38*, 439–449; Johnson, W. W. (2011). Rethinking the interface between mental illness, criminal justice, and academia. *Justice Quarterly, 28*, 15–22; Slate, R. N., Buffington-Vollum, J. K., & Johnson, W. W. (2013). *The criminalization of mental illness: Crisis and opportunity for the justice system* (2nd ed.). Durham, NC: Carolina Academic Press; Healy, J. (2015, April 27). Colorado shooting trial pits a calculated killer against an erratic mind. *The New York Times*, A14.

has such a strong interest in deceiving himself" and who is not thoroughly conscious of his crime, Maudsley anticipated the Freudian concept of the unconscious.[4]

As the father of psychoanalytic theory and psychoanalysis (a therapy derived from this theory), Sigmund Freud was perhaps the most influential psychological theorist at the beginning of the 20th century. Although psychoanalysis is still practiced, most acknowledge its limited application to criminal offenders. Nevertheless, psychoanalytic theory is discussed in some detail because many key concepts in this theory are utilized by current sociological and psychological theories of criminal offending.

Freud believed that one could understand human behavior best by examining early childhood experiences. These experiences, traumatic or not, can profoundly affect behavior without the individual being consciously aware of their impact. Freud developed psychoanalytic theory from the late 1800s through the early 1900s to explain both normal and abnormal behavior. The full theory is extraordinarily complex and often vague. Indeed, Freud himself changed his mind over time on a number of issues.[5] The key concepts, however, are fairly straightforward.

Sigmund Freud, the Austrian-born neurologist, is the father of psychoanalytic school of psychiatry and therapeutic technique of psychoanalysis. Many concepts from his theories and therapy techniques are apparent in modern theories.

Courtesy of Library of Congress, Prints & Photographs Division, [reproduction number LC-USZ62-1234]

Freudian Elements of Personality

Freud's greatest contributions to psychology include his distinction between the conscious and the unconscious mind, and his concepts of id, superego, and ego. If you've ever seen a cartoon where the devil (id) appears on one shoulder, an angel (superego) appears on the other shoulder, and the character (ego) must choose a course of action, you can understand the gist of these basic elements of personality.

Van Voorhis and Salisbury note that Freud did not conceive of these concepts as actual parts within the brain. Rather, they are best conceived as wishes or desires.[6] The **id** is the unconscious, instinctual aspect of the personality. Id wishes often include the immediate gratification of basic drives (e.g., sex, aggression). The primary rule for the id is: "If it feels good, do it!" The **superego** is akin to a conscience—the keeper of prohibitions ("Stealing is wrong") and wishes about what a person wants to be ("I am going to be just like my father when I grow up"). Parents, schools, and other social institutions serve as models for the content of the superego. Even though it lies in the realm of the unconscious, the superego manifests itself in the restraints imposed by moral, ethical, and societal values. The **ego**, a conscious part of the personality, is a "psychological thermostat" that regulates the savage wishes and demands of the id and the social restrictions of the superego. The ego delays certain behaviors until the time is suitable for their gratification and can entirely deny certain behaviors.

Freud was particularly concerned with anxiety. In psychoanalytic theory, anxiety stems from one of two sources. First, people feel anxious when a desire (whether conscious or not) is unmet. Second, people become anxious when an unconscious desire starts to become conscious.[7] Freud outlined a number of **defense mechanisms** that individuals employ (often unconsciously) to reduce or eliminate this anxiety. These mechanisms represent another major contribution of psychoanalytic theory to psychology and the study of criminal behavior (**TABLE 5-2**).

Based on the importance Freud placed on the unconscious mind, anxiety, and defense mechanisms, the treatment technique of psychoanalysis is designed to bring to awareness inner conflicts and emotional problems. Basically, the therapist attempts to get the patient to replay those feelings and events from the past that are influencing present behaviors and to make unconscious desires conscious. This is sometimes facilitated through **free association**, where the patient verbalizes—uncensored—anything that comes to mind.

Freudian Explanations of Delinquency

The basic assumption behind Freudian theory is that human nature is inherently antisocial. Due to the influence of the id, infants start life with antisocial drives. As infants grow and develop, however, they confront social rules to which they are expected to abide. Thus, they must give up the primitive drives of instant gratification, unbridled sexuality, and unrestrained

TABLE 5-2

Selected Freudian Defense Mechanisms

Defense Mechanism	Description or Definition
Denial	The truth of some experience is denied. For example, a child's father abandons the family, but the family acts as though he just went on a vacation and will return soon.
Rationalization	Finding a satisfactory reason for doing something inappropriate. For example, one indulges in fermented brews instead of studying and flunks a test the following day. The person reacts by saying, "That professor is a schmuck. . . . This class sucks. . . . I think I'll switch majors."
Repression	Desires or thoughts are forced back into the unconscious mind, and their existence is denied. For example, memories of childhood abuse are forgotten.
Reaction formation	An individual hides one instinct from awareness through the use of the opposite impulse. For example, love becomes a mask to hide hatred.
Projection	Attributing one's desires or wishes to someone else. For example, a person is angry at someone, but accuses that person of being the one who is angry.

aggression. Children develop a superego from experience and from role models such as parents and siblings who guide them along the path of appropriate behavior. Ego development helps children negotiate id demands for instant gratification with superego demands against such behavior. Any problem or trauma that upsets the development of the ego or superego can increase the risk of delinquency and crime.

The Freudian perspective on the psychological roots of delinquency and criminality has been developed by theorists such as Redl and Wineman, and Healy and Aichorn. Redl and Wineman applied psychoanalytic theory to a group of delinquent children as part of a treatment program.[8] They dismissed the possibility that abnormally strong id wishes resulted in delinquent behavior. Instead, they focused on the ego and superego. For example, they describe a **delinquent ego** that effectively blocks any potential restraint from the conscience (superego) and permits the delinquent to rationalize criminal behavior. Inappropriate role models might create a **delinquent superego**, which is guided by a delinquent code of behavior rather than appropriate values.

Yet another possibility is the **overdeveloped superego**. As noted earlier, the superego expresses displeasure (e.g., when its wishes are violated) in the form of anxiety. The result of this displeasure upon the personality is guilt. The more guilt the person accumulates, the more the person feels the need to be punished. It is only through punishment that the personality can truly be absolved of any guilt feelings. In this sense, some people may commit crimes because they want to be caught and punished.

As the concept of the overdeveloped superego indicates, Freudians often stress criminal acts as an indication of an underlying personality conflict. Aichorn, consistent with this Freudian principle, developed the concepts of "manifest" and "latent" delinquency. Aichorn wrote that manifest delinquency was the overt, expressed criminal behavior of stealing, robbing, and the like. Latent delinquency was the root cause

of this behavior—the instinctual wishes lurking in the background, waiting for an opportunity to break through for satisfaction. According to Aichorn, the challenge of psychoanalysis is to "seek the provocation which made the latent delinquency manifest and also determine what caused the latent delinquency."[9] For example, Freudian theorists believe that much delinquency has roots in repressed memories of traumatic experiences. A latent cause of criminal behavior, then, might be displaced hostility toward those who caused trauma.[10]

Policy Implications of Freudian Theory

The most obvious drawback of Freudian theory is that it is difficult, if not impossible, to study empirically. Concepts such as the id, ego, and superego cannot be directly observed or measured.[11] Moreover, motivations for delinquency are often hidden (unconscious), even to the offender. Psychoanalytic explanations of delinquency and crime therefore tend to be "after the fact" and untestable. As a rehabilitation technique, psychoanalysis is also wanting. Finckenauer notes that the effectiveness of psychoanalysis is limited to generally intelligent, articulate, adult neurotics. Conversely, the typical delinquent is less intelligent, inarticulate, and not neurotic.[12]

Not surprisingly then, studies of the rehabilitation literature confirm that insight-oriented therapies like psychoanalysis do not reduce criminal offending.[13] Finally, even if it were effective, psychoanalytic treatment lasts a long period of time (even a lifetime) and is expensive—traits unlikely to play well when the public foots the bill. Indeed, Redl and Wineman's treatment ended not because delinquents were deemed "cured," but because the funding ended. A complete treatment might have lasted several years.[14]

Despite these considerable drawbacks, psychoanalytic theory maintains an important place in the psychology of criminal behavior for a number of reasons. First, while most offenders are not neurotic adults, some crimes are tied to deep-seated (and perhaps unconscious) anxiety or hostility. Psychologist Ted Palmer suggests that such unresolved issues may create a barrier to any rehabilitation effort.[15] The results of a recent study of prison inmates appears to support this position.[16] Here, researchers found that a generally effective cognitive–behavioral rehabilitation program did not reduce crime for neurotic offenders.

Second, counselors who deal with offenders should be aware of the Freudian concepts of transference and countertransference.[17] Transference occurs when the client uses the counselor as a stand-in for someone in the client's past, such as a father or sibling. Countertransference occurs when the client "pushes the buttons" of the counselor so that the resulting anger and hostility interferes with treatment. Finally, many Freudian concepts appear, albeit sometimes altered and often with different terminology, in other theories of crime. Thus, concepts within Freud's theory have been modified so that they can be scientifically tested. Freudian defense mechanisms, for example, occupy a central role in current cognitive and social learning theories of crime. Current theories also point to the importance of "self-control" (ego strength) and of "morals" (i.e., superego) that are learned from role models.

Behavioral Psychology

The behavioral psychologist operates from a completely different perspective than a person trained in psychoanalysis. The focus of a behaviorist is on a specific behavior, and the orientation is very much on the here and now. A behaviorally oriented rehabilitation program would not spend time on the childhood emotions of an adult offender.[18] The basic principle underlying behaviorism is that all behavior is learned. The father of behaviorism, John B. Watson, believed that the purpose of psychology is to understand, predict, and control human behavior.[19] B. F. Skinner, another dominant figure in behaviorism, argued that criminals are not emotionally or morally "abnormal." Rather, they are simply responding to rewards and punishments within their environments.[20]

> *The focus of a behaviorist is on a specific behavior, and the orientation is very much on the here and now.*

Principles of Learning

Psychologists have identified three types of learning: classical conditioning, operant conditioning, and observational learning. Ivan Pavlov, a Russian physician, first identified classical conditioning. Pavlov's work focused on the relationship between stimulus and response (FIGURE 5-1). By pairing an unconditioned stimulus (meat) with a conditioned stimulus (a bell), he eventually reproduced a conditioned response (salivation) in dogs using only the bell.[21]

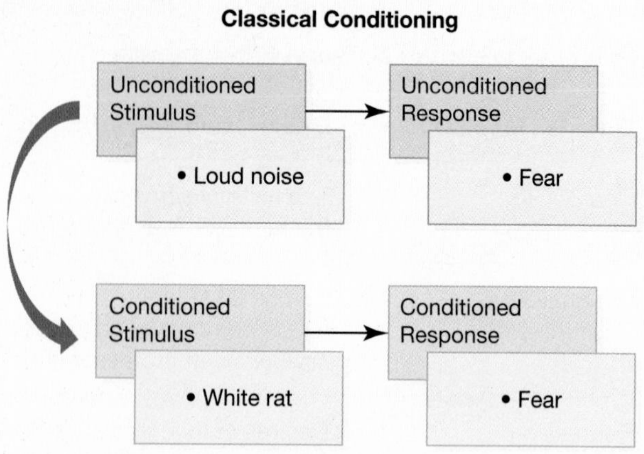

Classical Conditioning

FIGURE 5-1 Over time, the conditioned stimulus alone will produce a conditioned response. Although most crime is not learned via classical conditioning, aversion therapy uses this process as a form of correctional treatment.

John Watson later demonstrated this principle with a human subject, "little Albert." Initially, Watson used a loud noise, which produces the unconditioned response of fear in a child. Then, by pairing the loud noise with a white rat (the rat initially produced no fear), he was able to condition Albert to be afraid of the lab rat. Although this technology is still sometimes used to treat criminals (see the following section on aversion therapy), few would argue that classical conditioning explains why people originally engage in crime. Typically, psychologists point to either operant or vicarious learning to explain the acquisition of criminal behavior.

In operant conditioning, some behavior (often called a target behavior) must first be displayed. The target behavior can then be reinforced, which increases the likelihood of this behavior in the future. An undesirable target behavior (e.g., lying, stealing) can be punished, which decreases the likelihood of this behavior in the future (TABLE 5-3). Positive reinforcement increases the target behavior by rewarding the individual. This reward can be tangible (money, a treat) or social (praise, an approving look). Importantly, what is rewarding to each individual may be different. Many people confuse negative reinforcement with punishment. Negative reinforcement, however, increases the target behavior, while punishment has the opposite effect.

Negative reinforcement increases a target behavior by removing some unpleasant stimulus. For example, consider how small children often use behavior to manipulate others. Children are masters at using negative reinforcement to "train" parents. Suppose a child in a grocery store picks up a treat,

TABLE 5-3

The Operant Conditioning Process

Operant conditioning

Behavior → Reinforcement/punishment → Future behavior

Positive reinforcement: Awarding something (e.g., money, food, praise) when a desired action is taken in order to increase that behavior in the future.

Negative reinforcement: When target behavior is demonstrated, noxious stimuli (e.g., screaming, bad smell) is removed in order to increase the target behavior in the future.

Punishment: Introduction of noxious stimuli (e.g., scolding, spanking) to reduce or suppress a target behavior.

but is told "no" by the parent. The child then proceeds to fall on the floor screaming, crying, and attracting the attention of other shoppers. In behavioral terms, the child has introduced a noxious stimuli. When the frustrated and embarrassed parent relents, the child terminates the tantrum. The child has just used negative reinforcement—the removal of the tantrum and parental embarrassment. This increases the odds that the next time, the parent will relent more quickly and easily. The child may even throw in some positive reinforcement ("You're the best daddy ever!") to further the cause.

Unlike reinforcement, **punishment** (a scolding, spanking) reduces the odds of the target behavior being repeated. Through experimentation with both animals and humans, behaviorists have developed a knowledge base about the most effective way to condition behavior. One golden rule is that the consistency of reinforcement and punishment matters more than the severity. Indeed, parental use of harsh but inconsistent punishment is a good predictor of delinquent behavior.[22] Additionally, reinforcement shapes behavior more efficiently than punishment: psychologists recommend that reinforcers outnumber punishers by a ratio of four to one.[23] Finally, both punishment and reinforcement should follow quickly after the target behavior.

There is an interesting connection between operant conditioning and deterrence theory (see Chapter 3). In essence, philosophers such as Beccaria and Bentham, writing during the 1800s, correctly predicted that swift and certain punishment would be most effective in controlling human behavior. Indeed, at least one commentator has suggested that deterrence could be absorbed into a broader theory of learning.[24] Punishment through the criminal justice system would represent one form, among many, of operant conditioning that shapes human behavior.

Theorists across the disciplines of psychology and sociology tie delinquency to the failure of parents to effectively condition their children away from aggression, stealing, lying, and other antisocial behavior. Sociologists often refer to this as direct parental control (see Chapter 7). Research on children and adolescents has long supported the link between parental use of operant conditioning and delinquency.[25] Sheldon and Eleanor Glueck's study of 500 delinquent and 500 nondelinquent boys found that "harsh and erratic" punishment had a strong influence on

Who is in charge here? Children are masters at training their parents. One common technique that kids use to obtain what they want is to throw a temper tantrum. Stopping the tantrum negatively reinforces parents who cave into the child's desires.

© SW Productions/ Brand X Pictures/ Getty Images

delinquency.[26] Reviews of the literature find that other measures of parenting, including supervision and discipline, are among the stronger predictors of delinquency.[27,28]

Gerald Patterson and his associates at the Oregon Social Learning Center work extensively with delinquent children and their parents. Patterson's social interactional theory, derived from this work, has parental efficacy (effectiveness) as its central concept.[29] Parents who monitor their children closely, recognize deviant behavior, and use consistent punishment and reinforcement are more likely to rear nondelinquent children. Conversely, Patterson notes that parents of children who steal "do not track, they do not interpret stealing . . . as 'deviant,' they do not punish, and they do not care."[30] Patterson recognizes, however, that parenting efficacy is dependent (to some extent) on family environment (**FIGURE 5-2**). For example, single parents living on a marginal income might need to work two jobs and sacrifice some supervision over their children.

Patterson's theory and others that are similar are not without their critics. Judith Rich Harris' book, *The Nurture Assumption: Why Children Turn Out the Way They Do—Parents Matter Less Than You Think and Peers Matter More,* summarized a primary criticim.[31] This was a book designed for a popular audience, and her research was acclaimed in the media as "truly revolutionary" and "a paradigm shifter."[32] Harris' main thesis is that parental behaviors have few effects on the long-term development of their children. What does Harris make of the substantial amount of research linking parenting behavior to delinquency? She explains this relationship by arguing that the children are influencing parenting behavior.[33] In other words, difficult children *provoke* the very parenting characteristics—lax supervision and harsh/inconsistent punishment—highlighted in research.

One way to untangle the relationship between parenting skills and a child's behavior is to examine what happens when parenting practices change. If a change in parenting practices has no effect on the child, then Harris may be correct. If, however, changing parental behaviors reduces delinquency, Patterson's theory would be supported. Patterson and his associates have devised several methods for training parents. Those are discussed in greater detail later, but it is worth noting here that parent-training programs have reduced delinquency both as standalone programs[34] and as a common part of more comprehensive interventions.[35]

Although Harris dismisses the importance of parenting, she does believe that criminal behaviors are (in part) learned. Specifically, she argues that childhood playgroups and adolescent peer groups are an important source of childhood behaviors, including delinquency.

Modeling Theory

Research on peer effects usually focuses on **observational learning**—role modeling the behavior of others. Albert Bandura recognized that much of what is learned is not based on trial and error (operant conditioning). Rather, humans acquire behaviors simply by observing others. Bandura argues that although everyone has the capacity for aggression, they acquire the specific behavioral repertoire largely through observation.[36] Bandura and his associates demonstrated this principle in the now-famous "Bobo doll" experiments.[37] The researchers randomly divided a sample of children into two groups, both of whom watched a videotape of a playroom. In the first group, the video included people punching and kicking an inflated doll that was weighted on the bottom (the Bobo doll). The second group saw a similar video, but there was no violent behavior toward the doll. As one might expect, when the children were released into the playroom, only the group of kids who saw the Bobo doll kicked and punched in the video replicated this behavior.

Although this experiment is rather simple, the implications for explaining crime are immense. For example, children who observe their parents abusing each other or adolescents who observe their friends engaging in delinquency would be at risk for engaging in similar acts themselves. Of course, people do not randomly choose behaviors to model. Rather, people tend to imitate the behavior of those who are attractive and competent, especially if the role models are rewarded for the behavior.[38] Another important point is that people do not automatically use the behaviors that are acquired through observation.[39] Some are discarded without being used, while others are used extensively.

The impact of observational learning on criminal behaviors is difficult to study. Imagine how many observations one person could make in just one day! How would researchers

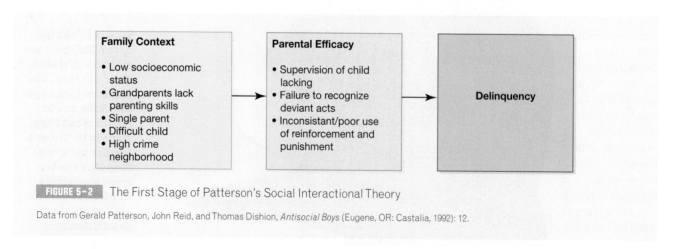

FIGURE 5-2 The First Stage of Patterson's Social Interactional Theory

Data from Gerald Patterson, John Reid, and Thomas Dishion, *Antisocial Boys* (Eugene, OR: Castalia, 1992): 12.

track the observation or know which observations were added to a person's behavioral repertoire? Given these limits, researchers typically use indirect measures of learning. The most common measure is whether or not a person has delinquent peers. The assumption here is that people imitate and role model the behavior of their peer groups. Indeed, the relationship between delinquent peer associations and delinquency is among the strongest in criminology.[40] Parents also have played a central role in the study of observational learning. A common explanation for the finding that crime runs in families is that children are modeling the behavior of parents. For example, a study of parolees from Buffalo, New York, found that children who observed their parents' violent confrontations were more likely to batter their partners during adulthood.[41]

Media and Crime

In addition to friends and family, psychologists have focused on the media as a role model for aggression, violence, and some forms of criminal behavior. A host of studies have shown that television, movies, and video games are laden with violent content, and that Americans spend a great deal of time engaged with this media.[42] The 2014 Nielson Company statistics, for example, revealed that the average American watches over 5 hours of television per day, with an additional 2.5 hours spend on the Internet.[43] U.S. children over 13 years of age report playing video games, on average, for almost 1 hour per day.[44]

Violence in the media is often portrayed in a way that is conducive to role modeling. For example, perpetrators of violence are not punished, the target of violence shows little pain, and there are few long-term negative consequences for the violence.[45] There is no shortage or reports where behaviors appear to be direct imitations of characters or events from video games, movies, television, or YouTube videos. Examples of such anecdotal evidence abound:[46]

- The video game *Grand Theft Auto* (GTA) has inspired numerous crimes, including homicide. In one case, an Alabama teen who was found sleeping in a stolen car by a police officer. While being questioned by the officer, he grabbed the officer's gun, shot him several times, and used the police squad as a getaway car. Upon capture, he stated that "Life is like a

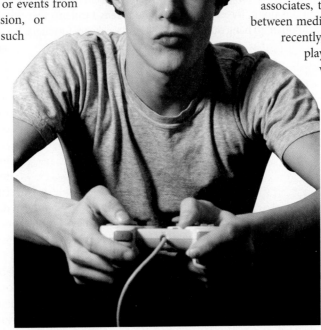

Do violent video games promote crime?
© charles knox/Shutterstock, Inc.

video game. Everybody's got to die sometime." At trial, his defense attorney revealed that he had been playing GTA III for several hours per day over the course of months. The "GTA-defense," however, was unsuccessful, and the teen was sentenced to death.
- The 2012 movie *Project X* has inspired several copycats. Teens who hosted "anything goes" flash mob parties have explicitly referenced this movie. Two *Project X*-style parties in Houston, Texas, caused over $100,000 in damage and led to the death of one teen.
- John Hinckley, Jr., who attempted to assassinate President Reagan, was imitating the main character in the movie *Taxi Driver*.
- The television series *Breaking Bad* has purportedly inspired multiple crimes, including the distribution of blue-tinted methamphetamine (courtesy of food coloring) and an attempt by a murderer to dissolve his victim's body in a plastic tub filled with acid.

Not surprisingly, roughly one-half of Americans believe that movies, television, and video games substantially contribute to violence.[47] Capturing this sentiment, presidential candidate Mitt Romney stated that "Pornography and violence poison our music and movies and TV and video games. The Virginia Tech shooter, like the Columbine shooters before him, had drunk from this cesspool."[48]

Is this anecdotal evidence and public opinion supported by scientific research? Researchers have studied this issue using a variety of methods, including survey research and laboratory and field experiments. Laboratory experiments, like the "Bobo doll" research by Bandura and his associates, typically demonstrate clear links between media violence and aggression. More recently, researchers had college students play either a violent or nonviolent video game for 20 minutes. They then asked half of each group to "ruminate" (think about the game and what they might have done better) about the game. One day later, males that had ruminated about a violent game were more likely to "noise blast" (the measure of aggression) a competitor.[49] Of course, "noise blasts" are a far cry from criminal violence. This is a crucial limit of lab-based experiments. When researchers have studied *criminal* violence through surveys, the findings are less consistent. One recent study that did find a media–crime effect examined children from 707 families over 17 years.[50] The researchers found that the amount of time spent watching television during adolescence predicted assault and robbery during adulthood. This relationship was evident, even after controlling for a host of environmental influences (e.g., family income, childhood neglect, neighborhood violence).

Reviews of this body of research find that regardless of the methodology, there is a moderate relationship between exposure to media violence and measures of aggression.[51] Much of the newer research has focused on the effect of violent video games. A recent summary of this emerging literature finds a moderate correlation between exposure to violent video games and both aggression and lack of empathy.[52] A review of only studies of *criminal* aggression, however, did not find that video gaming had a significant impact.[53] Skeptics of the link between media exposure and "real world" violence also point out that both cross-national research and American crime trends cast doubt on the existence of a large effect. For example, the Japanese are known both for their love of violent video games and their near-zero homicide rate. Furthermore, violent crime in the U.S. has declined for nearly 30 years in the midst of an explosion of new (and often violent) media.

Modeling Theory: A Summary of the Evidence

Generally speaking, because studies of observational learning often use indirect measures, their conclusions are open to question. For example, one common interpretation of the peer–delinquency relationship is that like-minded individuals hang out together. In other words, "birds of a feather flock together."[54] Similarly, critics of the media–violence link suggest that violence-prone individuals will seek out violent programming. If this logic is correct, then delinquent peers or television have no causal effect on a person's behavior. Common sense suggests there is some truth to this point; for example, one would not expect a hard-core delinquent to hang out with members of the chess club. These issues will be discussed in greater detail in the context of sociological learning theories (Chapter 7).

Again, one way to test whether a relationship is causal is to put it into practice. With regard to the peer–delinquency example, one might study what happens if a delinquent is denied access to his or her normal (delinquent) peer group. Regarding media effects, there is some evidence that reducing exposure to media violence reduces aggression among children. For example, Thomas Robinson and colleagues reported that one program designed to reduce television viewing significantly reduced aggression in a sample of third and fourth graders.[55]

Observational learning is a component in many theories of crime. Theorists in this area typically incorporate both operant and vicarious learning as well as cognitive aspects into a single "social learning theory." Because sociologists and psychologists have both advanced similar social learning theories, they will be addressed in greater detail in Chapter 7.

Policy Implications of Behaviorism

Perhaps the most appealing aspect of behavioral theory is that it translates easily into treatments and interventions for delinquents and criminals. Furthermore, unlike psychoanalysis, it does not require the presence of trained therapeutic personnel or years of therapy sessions. As a general principle, behaviorists argue that the same mechanisms involved in learning crime can be used to reduce crime.[56] In addition, criminals can learn prosocial behaviors to replace criminal actions. One practical application of classical conditioning, for example, is **aversion therapy**. Aversion therapy is used to eliminate links between stimuli and troublesome behaviors. For example, alcoholics can be conditioned to experience alcohol as noxious rather than pleasant, or sex offenders can be conditioned so that deviant images are repulsive rather than stimulating.

Aversion therapy works by pairing a stimulus that elicits pleasure with a noxious stimulus. For example, a therapist might show a pedophile a sexual image of a child while exposing him or her to a very noxious odor (rotting meat seems to be a favorite) at the same time.[57] After repeating this procedure over time, the deviant sexual image produces revulsion and nausea rather than sexual stimulation. For ethical reasons (how does one procure a sexually deviant image?) and because the general public finds this process itself somewhat repulsive, aversion therapy is used sparingly.

The principles of both operant and vicarious learning, however, are present in virtually every successful rehabilitation program. One simple application of operant conditioning is a **token economy**. Here, participants earn tokens if they behave in the appropriate manner and lose tokens for inappropriate behavior. Later, the participants can exchange the tokens for items that they desire, such as television privileges, weekend furloughs, or purchases from a store. In the same way that money motivates people in the outside world, tokens provide a way for institutions to establish a work-payment incentive system.[58] Token economies, when administered correctly, are efficient at reducing inmate misconduct and increasing desirable behaviors ranging from personal hygiene to academic achievement.[59,60] For this reason, they have become a mainstay of juvenile correctional institutions. Of course, the main drawback to a token economy is its artificial nature. A juvenile released from a correctional institution quickly discovers that studying for school or keeping a neat room no longer elicits "tokens."

To avoid the artificial nature of token economies, many psychologists advocate working with parents and children within their home. Gerald Patterson, for example, trains parents to monitor the behavior of children and use reinforcements in the home.[61] To encourage adequate supervision and

> *Observational learning is a component in many theories of crime.*

the consistent and correct use of reinforcement and punishment, he has parents chart out the frequency of problem behaviors (e.g., stealing, lying, staying out past curfew). Often, this is followed by a **contingency contract**, a formal contract signed by the parent and child that specifies behaviors that the child is to complete (chores) and avoid (stealing). In addition to the behaviors, the contract specifies how the child will be reinforced or punished based on his or her behaviors. Parent training programs have been moderately successful in reducing the delinquency of children.[62,63]

Note, however, that behavioral treatments are not a silver bullet for curing crime. In fact, behavioral programs that narrowly focus only on operant and/or classical conditioning (e.g., token economy, aversion therapy) have only a limited impact on offender behavior.[64] Aversion therapy is portrayed in movies as almost magical (as in the movie *A Clockwork Orange*), but the reality is that conditioning is relatively easy to overcome. An alcoholic conditioned to experience alcohol as nauseating, for example, needs only to "drink through the nausea" a few times before the conditioning wears off. Among the most effective treatments are those that combine behavioral principles with cognitive theory.[65]

Cognitive Psychology

Behavioral psychology is criticized by some for its portrayal of learning as a rather mechanical process. Cognitive psychologists believe that the human ability to engage in complex thought processes makes people different from other animals. Imagine, for example, checking your phone while walking down a crowded sidewalk on a busy city street. Someone walking in the opposite direction bumps a shoulder and almost knocks you down. What thoughts go through your mind? Perhaps, "That #@!! is disrespecting me!" or instead, "Whoa! I should watch where I'm going." Cognitive theorists believe that those thoughts, more than the actual shoulder bump, will impact how a person responds.

There is a great deal of overlap between cognitive psychology and behaviorism. For example, cognitions, like behaviors, can be learned. Once learned, a person's thoughts serve to prompt, reinforce, or punish behavior.[66] In other words, a person can use their thoughts as a form of operant conditioning to punish or reinforce their own behavior. With respect to crime, cognitive psychologists focus on two broad areas: the content of a person's thoughts (*what* is thought) and general thought structures (*how* a person thinks).[67]

Cognitive Structure

Cognitive structures refer to stable ways of thinking about one's self and the environment. Lawrence Kohlberg's theory of moral development fits well within this definition. Kohlberg argued that humans advance through predictable stages of moral reasoning, defined as how a person thinks about fairness, justice, and a right course of action. Kohlberg had subjects reason through various moral dilemmas and decide on a course of action. He was less interested in what

people decided than how they came to that decision. From this research, he developed six stages of moral reasoning (TABLE 5-4). Subsequent research on Kohlberg's stages revealed that many delinquents get stuck in Stage 2 type reasoning.[68] Moral education is now a component in many rehabilitation programs. Here, offenders work through moral dilemmas and with the aid of a trained leader, learn to think about such issues in a more complex manner.[69]

Of course, moral reasoning is just one aspect of a person's cognitive structure. Criminologists often discuss cognitive structure as a series of skills acquired through prior learning and applied consistently to different situations. Examples of cognitive skills other than moral reasoning include self-control, the ability to empathize (take the perspective of others), the ability to formulate short-term and long-term plans, the ability to anticipate the consequences of behavior, and the ability to recognize and control anger.[70,71] In the shoulder-bumping incident, someone who has high self-control, is empathetic, and

TABLE 5-4

Lawrence Kohlberg's Stages of Moral Development

Stage	Definition
Stage 1	The right course of action is determined by blindly obeying those with power and authority. Emphasis is on avoiding punishment. The interests of others are not considered.
Stage 2	The right course of action is to further one's own interests. The interests of others are important only as a way to satisfy self-interests.
Stage 3	Moral reasoning is motivated by loyalties to others and a desire to live up to other people's standards and to follow the Golden Rule.
Stage 4	Right is following the rules of society and maintaining important social institutions (e.g., family, community).
Stage 5	Moral decisions are made by weighing an individual's rights against legal principles and the common good.
Stage 6	Moral decisions are based on universal principles such as the concern for human dignity, a respect for life, and a desire for justice. These principles are considered across different contexts and are independent of the law.

Data from Lawrence Kohlberg, *Stages in the Development of Moral Thought and Action* (New York: Holt, Rinehart and Winston, 1969).

anticipates consequences well would probably be unlikely to respond in a violent manner. As you might have noticed, cognitive skills tend to focus on what a person is *not thinking* about, including the long-term consequences of his or her actions, how the victim might feel, and legal alternatives to the criminal act.[72] In contrast, the area of cognitive content addresses what offenders *are thinking* before, during, or after their crime.

Cognitive Content

The content of cognitions refers to *what* people think. Criminologists focus on rationalizations or denials (recall Freud's defense mechanisms) that support criminal behavior. Different theorists refer to such thoughts as criminal thinking errors, cognitive distortions, techniques of neutralization, or "stinking thinking."[73] All of these terms refer to illogical or irrational thoughts that can prompt or support behavior. For example, a criminal might rationalize a burglary by thinking, "They've got insurance; I'm not really hurting anyone." Almost without exception, research in this area finds that criminals or delinquents are more likely to express such thoughts than law-abiding citizens.

The primary criticism of this research deals with time ordering and causation. Do these thoughts actually cause criminal behavior, or are they simply after-the-fact excuses used to justify actions and deflect blame? To cognitive scholars, this is a relatively unimportant issue. Regardless of whether the thoughts happen before (a prompt) or after (reinforcement) the criminal act, they serve to reduce the guilt of the offender. Recalling the discussion of negative reinforcement, the thought allows the burglar to terminate a noxious stimulus (guilt/anxiety), which increases the likelihood he or she will burgle again. Such rationalizations are especially common for sex offenders, where guilt associated with the act is strong. Pedophiles, for example, will report that children enjoy sexual contact with adults; they feel that sex is "good" for children and that children often initiate sex and know what they want.[74,75]

Policy Implications of Cognitive Psychology: Cognitive–Behavioral Programs

Like behaviorism, cognitive theory translates easily into practice. In fact, most cognitive-oriented rehabilitation programs incorporate principles of learning. The cognitive component of such cognitive–behavioral interventions includes the content of thought, the structure of thought, or both. Cognitive skills programs focus on cognitive structure and attempt to teach offenders skills such as moral reasoning, self-control, or anger management. The therapist teaches these skills using the principles of learning. Typically, a behavior is modeled by the therapist, and offenders are given several opportunities to practice the skill. Offenders are then reinforced when they employ these skills in role-playing sessions and (more importantly) outside of a specific session.[76]

Cognitive restructuring refers to attempts to change the content of an individual's thoughts. In essence, criminal-thinking errors (e.g., rationalizations, distortions) are identified and forcefully rejected by the therapist. Often times, this is done in a group setting where offenders are taught to identify and correct others' thinking errors. A widely used intervention that attempts to teach cognitive skills and correct criminal-thinking is "Thinking for a Change." Offenders in this program learn and practice skills such as apologizing, active listening, and responding to anger. They also create "thought reports" to help themselves identify and correct cognitive distortions.[77]

Cognitive–behavioral treatments have accumulated a track record of success for reducing the criminal behavior of children, adolescents, and adults.[78,79] For example, a recent review of evaluations from cognitive–behavioral programs concluded "cognitive–behavioral programs can reduce recidivism rates by significant amounts. This was found to be true for the overall collection of cognitive–behavioral studies and also for the subcategories of social skills development training and cognitive skills training."[80]

The same study found that strictly behavioral programs (e.g., token economy, contingency contracting) were not as effective. In that sense, treatments that have multiple targets for change and those that operate in the "real world" have proven more successful. Multisystemic therapy (MST) is a good example of this type of treatment. Devised by psychologist Scott Henggeler and his associates, MST is a cognitive–behavioral treatment that emphasizes "providing home-based and family-focused services that are intensive, time limited, pragmatic, and goal oriented."[81] MST has proven successful at reducing offending for a variety of populations, including inner-city juvenile offenders, adolescent sex offenders, and abusive parents (see **Theory in Action: Multisystemic Therapy** for a detailed description of this program through a case study).

Personality and Crime

Personality theory provides further possible insights into the psychological aspects of crime. The primary assumption behind this perspective is that crime and delinquency are related to the presence of some personality trait. A personality trait is a characteristic of an individual that is stable over time and across different social circumstances. For example, an impulsive person is not likely to suddenly become a cautious person. Furthermore, one would expect the person to be impulsive in a variety of domains—from driving a car to shopping for groceries. A personality is therefore the sum of personality traits that defines a person. Psychologists

> *Personality theory provides further possible insights into the psychological aspects of crime.*

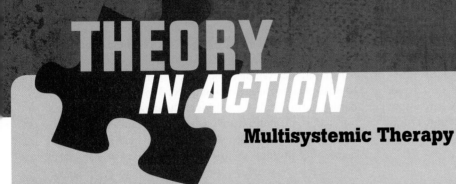

THEORY IN ACTION

Multisystemic Therapy

Many scholars have hailed multisystemic therapy (MST) as one of the best rehabilitation programs currently available. This praise stems from research findings that show MST reduces criminal behavior, even among very difficult populations. What makes MST unique is its comprehensive approach. While some cognitive–behavioral programs teach a set of skills or work with parents, MST targets many areas for change and uses many different techniques. Consider the case of "Homer," provided by MST creator Scott Henggeler and his associates:

> Homer is a 15-year-old Caucasian male with an extensive history of delinquent behavior, including assault and battery with intent to kill, simple assault and battery, malicious destruction of real property, trespassing, petty larceny, contempt of court, and resisting arrest. Homer had a reputation for fighting and bullying his peers and had been expelled in the seventh grade for assaulting a classmate and cursing at his teachers. Homer was in a gang of juvenile delinquents who affectionately called themselves "Death Row." Aside from his criminal record and association with deviant peers, Homer had an extensive history of abusing inhalants, marijuana, and alcohol. At the time of referral, Homer had recently been released from a 45-day juvenile justice evaluation facility. He resides alone with his mother, who is employed full-time and has a history of alcohol abuse. Homer also has a 17-year-old sister with a history of crack cocaine dependence. She was recently released from a state-supported treatment facility and at the time of referral was living with her boyfriend and his family. A maternal uncle also lived in the community, though he refused to have contact with Homer due to Homer's antisocial behavior.

The MST therapist (a graduate student) identified a number of targets for change, including:

- Homer's deviant peer group (he hung around with older, "streetwise" youth).
- Homer's refusal to go to school (he spent most days at home, getting high with friends).
- Homer's thinking biases (anyone who failed to comply with his requests was "dissing" him, and he felt justified in responding aggressively).
- Homer's mother failed to monitor or punish his behavior (Homer was allowed to stay out as long as he wanted and did pretty much as he pleased).

The therapist also identified a number of strengths:

- Homer's mother was still emotionally attached to her son and willing to learn new parenting skills.
- Homer was intelligent, could be quite personable, and excelled at sports.
- Both Homer and his mother wanted him to attend high school rather than continue in the seventh grade (Homer wanted to play high school football).

The therapist modified Homer's behavior by utilizing a number of behavioral techniques. For example, Homer's mother was trained to monitor Homer's whereabouts and punish his misbehavior (parent training). She produced a list of chores and responsibilities for Homer and consistently rewarded or punished him, depending on whether he completed his chores (contingency contract). The therapist also worked with Homer and his mother to get him admitted into high school. Once admitted, his time was more structured; he had less access to delinquent peers and more access to prosocial peers. Furthermore, playing football became a natural reward that helped shape Homer's behavior. Finally, as Homer's behavior improved, his uncle began to spend more time with him, serving as a good adult role model (observational learning).

While evaluations of MST are very promising, exporting the program to different jurisdictions has proven difficult. As originally conceived, MST is delivered in conjunction with a graduate program in psychology. PhD candidates act as the therapists, and the program developers supervise the therapists. While results of meta-analyses confirm the successes of the original MST programs, they also find that attempts to replicate the program using alternative structures (e.g., therapists who are not PhD-level students) have not been nearly as effective.

Sources: Henggeler, S. W., Cunningham, P. B., Pickrel, S. G., Schoenwald, S. K., & Brondino, M. J. (1996). Multisystemic therapy: An effective violence prevention approach for serious juvenile offenders. *Journal of Adolescence, 19,* 55–56, with permission from Elsevier; Cullen, F. T., & Gendreau, P. (2001). Assessing correctional rehabilitation: Policy, practice, and prospects. In *Criminal Justice 2000.* Washington, DC: National Institute of Justice; Petrosino, A., & Soydan, H. (2005). The impact of program developers on criminal recidivism: Results from meta-analyses of experimental and quasi-experimental research. *Journal of Experimental Criminology, 1,* 435–450.

Texture: © Nik Merkulov/Shutterstock, Inc.

typically link personality to criminal behavior in one of two ways. First, an offender may have specific traits within their personality that are conducive to crime. Second, some psychologists believe that certain criminal offenders, called psychopaths, sociopaths, or antisocial personality disordered, have a criminal personality. In other words, they have a specific cluster of personality traits that drives them toward crime.

Personality Traits and Crime

In general, personality theorists attempt to define and outline basic traits that form the building blocks of human personality.[82] Typically, a number of related traits are combined to form "super factors" or broad dimensions of personality. A common dimension of personality with which many are familiar is extroversion (i.e., outgoing, sociable) and introversion (i.e., reserved, private, cautious). A substantial number of general personality theories exist, each with its own traits and dimensions. Among the most popular is the **five-factor model**, which identifies five dimensions of personality (hence the name).[83] The dimensions include the following:

1. Neuroticism (emotional stability versus instability)
2. Extraversion (sociability)
3. Openness to experience (curiosity, interest in trying new things)
4. Agreeableness (antagonistic versus agreeable interpersonal strategy)
5. Conscientiousness (impulse control, ability to follow moral code, organizational ability)

Another example is Auke Tellegen's personality model.[84] Tellegen identifies three dimensions of personality: (1) positive emotionality, (2) negative emotionality, and (3) constraint. As outlined in **TABLE 5-5**, each of these dimensions is composed of several traits. An individual exhibiting high constraint, for example, would score high on traditionalism (desires conservative environment, endorses high moral standards), harm avoidance (avoids excitement or danger, prefers safe activities), and control (reflective, cautious, careful).

Personality researchers have constructed a number of personality inventories to measure the presence or extent of specific personality dimensions. Generally, these are paper-and-pencil questionnaires asking a broad array of questions that tap into a variety of personality traits.

Early research linking personality and crime was plagued by methodology problems. For example, the Psychopathic Deviate (Pd) scale in the Minnesota Multiphasic Personality Inventory (MMPI) correlates well with criminal behavior. However, the scale was designed to identify dangerous individuals within psychiatric populations. Criminologists correctly criticized the use of these scales to predict criminal behavior because the scales were constructed with questions that asked about failing on probation or engaging in crime.[85] It shouldn't surprise anyone that someone who reports failing on probation has engaged in crime.

Recent personality instruments do a better job of avoiding this pitfall. A 2015 meta-analysis found that several elements of the five-factor model predicted "bullying" acts.[86] In particular, children with lower levels of agreeableness and conscientiousness and higher levels of neuroticism and extraversion were more likely to bully their peers. Perhaps the most extensive study on personality and crime used the Multidimensional Personality Questionnaire (MPQ), which measures Tellegen's model, to predict criminal behavior. In an impressive

---

TABLE 5-5

Personality Dimensions in the Multidimensional Personality Questionnaire

Constraint

- **Traditionalism:** desires a conservative social environment; endorses high moral standards
- **Harm avoidance:** avoids excitement and danger; prefers safe activities even if they are tedious
- **Control:** is reflective, cautious, careful, rational

Negative Emotionality

- **Aggression:** hurts others for advantage; will frighten and cause discomfort for others
- **Alienation:** feels mistreated, victimized, betrayed, and the target of false rumors
- **Stress reaction:** is nervous, vulnerable, sensitive, prone to worry

Positive Emotionality

- **Achievement:** works hard; enjoys demanding projects and working long hours
- **Social potency:** is forceful and decisive; fond of leadership roles
- **Well-being:** has a happy, cheerful disposition; feels good about self and sees a bright future
- **Social closeness:** is sociable; likes people and turns to others for comfort

Source: Caspi, A., Moffitt, T. E., Silva, P. A., Stoughamer-Loeber, M., Krueger, R. F., & Schmutte, P. S. (1994). Are some people crime-prone? Replications of the personality-crime relationship across countries, genders, races, and methods. *Criminology, 32*, 163–195.

multinational study, researchers gave the MPQ to samples of youth in Pittsburgh, Pennsylvania, and Dunedin, New Zealand, to see what personality traits predicted self-reported, official (arrests), and parent/teacher-reported delinquency. Across samples and regardless of how delinquency was measured, individuals with low constraint and high negative emotionality were more apt to engage in delinquency.[87]

A review of personality–crime research considered evidence across four different models of personality (including both the Tellegen model and the five-factor model). The reviewers discovered that each model successfully identified traits that predicted antisocial behavior with moderate strength. Noting similarities across the personality models, the authors suggest a general personality profile of criminals:[88]

> *Individuals who commit crimes tend to be hostile, self-centered, spiteful, jealous, and indifferent to others. They tend to lack ambition, motivation, and perseverance, have difficulty controlling their impulses, and hold nontraditional and unconventional values and beliefs.*

Criminal Personality: The Psychopath

In contrast to personality theorists who focus on general traits common to everyone, some argue that there is a class of individuals who have a distinct criminal personality. The term *psychopath* is widely used (and misused) by both professionals and the general public to describe this personality. Variations on the concept of psychopathy have existed within the professional field since the early 1800s. Indeed, in an article that addressed the history of criminology, Rafter concluded that "moral insanity" was among the first explanations of criminal behavior.[89] Isaac Ray, a 19th-century psychiatrist, defined moral mania as a "cerebral disease" that could cause a person to commit horrible crimes without any motive or remorse.[90]

The term psychopathy was actually coined in 1845, and its meaning has changed over time. The current conception of a psychopath is usually traced to psychiatrist Hervey Cleckly's book, *The Mask of Sanity*, originally published in 1941.[91] Cleckly spent years working with psychiatric patients, and used case studies to outline key traits of a psychopathic personality. His laundry list of traits includes the following:

> *Superficial charm, manipulative, above-average intelligence, absence of psychotic symptoms, absence of anxiety, lack of remorse, failure to learn from experience, egocentric, lack of emotional depth, trivial sex life, unreliable, failure to follow a life plan, untruthful, suicide attempts rarely genuine, impulsive, antisocial behavior. . .*

As the title of the book suggests, psychopaths are unlikely to come across as "crazy." They do not suffer from paranoid delusions, hallucinations, or breaks with reality. So, how does one identify a psychopath?

Despite use of the term by researchers and clinicians, psychopathy has never been listed as a disorder within *Diagnostic and Statistical Manual* (*DSM*), the main tool used to diagnose mental disorders. Indeed, despite some vigorous debate during the revision process, the most recent version (*DSM-V*) continues to use antisocial personality disorder (ASPD), a similar but much broader concept (see Table 5-1). In part because psychopathy was not an official diagnosis, little research was done on psychopathy until the 1980s. That changed dramatically when Robert Hare, a Canadian psychologist, devised the Psychopathy Checklist (PCL). Hare refined Cleckley's description of psychopathy to create a list of 20 traits that comprise two "factors." Factor 1 traits involve underlying

Convicted serial murderer Dennis Rader walks into the El Dorado Correctional Facility in August, 2005. Rader, convicted of killing 10 people over the course of 30 years, showed some characteristics of psychopathy. In a court hearing, he described without any visible emotion described his murder victims as "targets" and his murders as "projects."
© Jeff Tuttle/EPA/Landov

emotions (e.g., glibness, lack of remorse) while factor 2 traits measure antisocial lifestyle (promiscuity, delinquency).[92] The PCL is administered by a trained interviewer who asks a number of questions in an effort to gauge whether a person exhibits each trait (TABLE 5-6). Each trait is scored as not applicable (0), possibly applicable (1), or definitely applicable (2). At some score (usually between 25 and 30), individuals are considered to be psychopaths.

The advent of the PCL led to an explosion of research on psychopathy. Much of this research attempts to distinguish psychopathic prison inmates from nonpsychopathic inmates. Hare estimates that 15 percent to 25 percent of prisoners and perhaps 1 percent of the general population are psychopaths.[93] Researchers comparing nonpsychopathic prison inmates to psychopaths find some interesting differences in emotions, learning, speech patterns, and biological measures. For example, psychopaths have difficulty recognizing emotions such as fear or disgust in others' speech.[94] They also tend to make more logically inconsistent statements and other speaking errors than nonpsychopathic criminals.[95] It is noteworthy that much of the biological research (see Chapter 4) focuses on either psychopathy or APD. Thus, with lower heart rates, lower levels of skin conductance, and lower "startle responses," psychopaths tend toward under-arousal and low levels of fear. The combination of low experienced fear and the inability to recognize the fear/disgust of others is believed to underlie the central feature of psychopathy: a lack of a conscience.[96]

Recently, Hare's PCL conception of psychopathy has attracted both criticism and competition. For example, while Hare has argued that the terms *sociopath* and *psychopath* describe the same individuals, others believe that there are important differences between these two constructs. Their basic argument is that sociopathy is caused by severe childhood trauma, such as parental abuse and neglect. In contrast, psychopathy has few known environmental causes.[97] Critics also point out that while crime is a central feature in Hare's "PCL-psychopathy," Cleckly's classic definition of psychopathy did not include criminal behavior.[98] Christopher Patrick and his colleagues have recently proposed a three-factor (triarchic) model of psychopathy (Table 5-6 illustrates the PCL and triarchic models of psychopathy). Notable in this model is the addition of "boldness," which contains many traits (calmness under pressure) that are adaptive and may relate to social success. Rather than viewing psychopathy as a unitary construct, this model suggests there may be several variants. For example, a boldness-disinhibition type psychopath may be less likely to end up in the criminal justice system.[99]

This is an important consideration because it raises the question of whether a substantial population of "successful" psychopaths exists who manage to avoid criminal behavior or detection. Indeed, some of the more exciting research in recent years examines psychopathic tendencies outside of prison populations. In an attempt to attract these "free range" psychopaths, criminologist Adriane Raine created a "temp

TABLE 5-6

Two Models of Psychopathy

Triarchic Model of Psychopathy	PCL Psychopathy
Disinhibition Impulsivity Negative emotionality Impaired affect regulation Poor planning Lack of behavioral restraint.	**Factor 1: Emotional/Interpersonal Traits** Glibness/superficial charm Grandiose sense of self-worth Need for stimulation/prone to boredom Conning/manipulative Lack of remorse or guilt Shallow affect Callous/lack of empathy Lack of realistic, long-term goals Failure to accept responsibility for own actions Pathological lying
Boldness Calmness under pressure Rapid recovery from stress Confident and socially poised Venturesome and brave Thrill-seeking	**Factor 2: Antisocial Lifestyle** Many short-term marital relationships Juvenile delinquency Criminal versatility Promiscuous sexual relations Poor behavioral controls Parasitic lifestyle Early behavior problems Impulsivity Irresponsibility Revocation of conditional release
Meanness Low empathy Avoidance of and contempt for close attachments to others Exploitative Empowerment through cruelty Rebellious	

Sources: Patrick, C. J., Fowles, D. C., & Krueger, R. F. (2009). Triarchic conceptualization of psychopathy: Developmental origins of disinhibition, boldness, and meanness. *Development and Psychopathology, 21*, 913–938; Hare, R. D. (1999). *Without conscience: The disturbing world of psychopaths among us.* New York: Guilford.

agency" and hired people to work in his lab. As he notes, "temp agencies are wonderful safe havens for psychopaths" because they suit the nomadic and parasitic lifestyles of these individuals. From his hires, Raine and his colleague created a sample of successful (no criminal convictions) and unsuccessful psychopaths, along with a control group (nonpsychopaths). Among their more interesting findings was that successful psychopaths outperformed both unsuccessful psychopaths and the control group on measures of executive functioning.[100] Robert Hare and his associates have recently turned their attention to psychopathy in the corporate world. Written with industrial psychologist Paul Bibiak, the book, *Snakes in Suits: When Psychopaths Go to Work,* is designed to help corporate leaders screen potential employees for psychopathy.[101]

The study of psychopathy remains in a great deal of flux, and scholars disagree about many aspects of this disorder. Indeed, one point of contention is whether psychopathy *is* a discrete disorder. Hare and others argue that the specific cluster of traits identify a unique, discrete disorder. Others suggest that these differences are in quantity only. That is, everyone has some traits consistent with psychopathy. Those we call psychopaths simply have more than others. Indeed, the PCL is scored on a continuum, and there is no universal "cut off" score that distinguishes psychopaths from others. Another contentious debate is whether or not psychopaths benefit from correctional treatment. By the end of his career, Cleckly came to believe that little could be done to change psychopaths. Indeed, some studies utilizing the PCL have even found that treatment programs can actually *increase* their criminal behavior.[102] Some newer research, however, suggests that the same types of interventions that work for ordinary offenders can also work among psychopaths.[103] It seems likely that research in the near future will help settle this debate.

Policy Implications of Personality Theory

In recent years, personality explanations of delinquency and crime have become more accepted in criminology. Much of this acceptance stems from the fact that personality traits consistently predict delinquency and crime. Despite this popularity, such theories are plagued by basic questions. How are personality traits formed? Where do they come from? Can traits be changed through rehabilitation programs? By definition, personality tends to be stable over the life course. Oftentimes, personality traits are portrayed as almost impossible to change. A cognitive theorist, though, might argue that "traits" such as impulsivity or lack of empathy are simply cognitive skill deficits that can be remedied through training. In the research with the MPQ described earlier, the authors suggest that low constraint may stem from ineffective parenting, whereas negative emotionality may be a biological function—inherited and difficult to alter.

Hans Eysenck, one of the first theorists to outline a personality-based theory of crime, believes that basic dimensions of personality stem from differences in biology. For example, he argues that arousal levels are related to the concept of extroversion, and "psychoticism" is related to testosterone

levels.[104] Similarly, psychopathy is believed by many to be a function of biology. Hare notes that "the elements needed for the development of psychopathy—including a profound inability to experience empathy and the complete range of emotions, including fear—are provided in part by nature and possibly by some unknown biological influences of the developing fetus."[105]

There is a danger of viewing personality traits as something inborn and unchangeable. In particular, the concept of psychopathy can be used by psychologists eager to make money from the criminal justice system. Prosecutors can hire these eager psychologists to testify at trial. The psychologists, often after spending only a short time with the offender, testify that a defendant is indeed a psychopath. This testimony can lead (perhaps unfairly) to very harsh prison sentences.[106] Another danger is that those labeled as psychopaths may be restricted from rehabilitation programs because of the belief that psychopaths do not benefit from rehabilitation. There is some evidence, however, that some programs may in fact be effective.[107] Apart from the criminal justice system, the belief that crime stems from sources outside of one's control may lead people to ignore environmental conditions that foster crime.

Intelligence and Crime

Early positivists believed that feeblemindedness was a primary cause of crime. The emergence of psychological testing, including IQ tests, further heightened interest in this relationship. Currently, many people view IQ scores as a measure of general, native intelligence. Others view IQ as something other than intelligence and believe that the environment affects scores. What exactly is IQ, and how does it relate to criminal behavior?

A Brief History of Intelligence Testing

IQ tests allegedly measure mental differences from one person to another. Experimental psychologists were the first to design psychological tests to measure intelligence. For example, Hermann Ebbinghaus (1850–1909) believed that a large part of intelligence could be quantified by measuring one's ability to memorize. Alfred Binet (1857–1911) began his research on intelligence by measuring skull size, but he quickly realized that this was insufficient.

Thus, in 1905, Binet and Theodore Simon developed a scale that would identify students who were performing poorly in school and in need of academic help. The scale was created by having children perform a hodgepodge of different tasks (e.g., counting coins, identifying which face was "prettier"). The tasks were labeled according to the age at which a child of normal intelligence should be able to complete them successfully. Children proceeded through increasingly difficult tasks until they were unable to complete a task. The age assigned to the last successfully completed task was considered their mental age. The concept of IQ, which stands for intelligence quotient, was born when a statistician later divided mental age by biological age and multiplied the result by 100.[108] Note that average intelligence, where a person's biological and mental age are equal, is therefore always scored as 100.

Binet was aware of how such a scale might be used by others because he once believed that intelligence was fixed at birth himself. He therefore included several caveats with the publication of his scale that can be summarized as follows:[109]

1. The scores are a practical device that does not support any theory of intellect. One cannot call what they measure intelligence.
2. The scale is a rough guide for identifying mildly mentally challenged children. It is not a scale for ranking "normal" children.
3. Regardless of the causes of difficulty identified, emphasis should be placed on improvement through training. Low scores should not be used to mark children as incapable.

Unfortunately for Binet, his work was translated into English and made accessible to the United States at a time when the eugenics movement was in full swing. Eugenicists believed that intelligence was inherited and immutable. Therefore, great importance was placed on the ability to identify different types of feebleminded individuals so that they could be isolated and/or sterilized. Indeed, several slang terms come from the categories created by scientists. H. H. Goddard coined the term "moron" to describe the most important type of person—one who is mentally inferior yet still able to function in society and therefore pass on genes.

In this light, Binet's testing procedures were modified and applied to various populations (e.g., World War I army soldiers, prisoners, immigrants) in an effort to identify mentally inferior people. Many of these early tests were obviously culturally biased, and testing was often carried out in a shoddy manner. Stephen Jay Gould illustrates cultural bias with three questions from an early IQ test:[110]

1. Crisco is: patent medicine, disinfectant, toothpaste, food product
2. The number of Kaffir's legs is: 2, 4, 6, 8
3. Christy Mathewson is famous as a: writer, artist, baseball player, comedian

Most can probably get the Crisco question, but what about the Christy Mathewson question? Imagine a recent immigrant grappling with such a test. World War I army recruits who took this exam averaged a mental age of 13 years (just above "moron" status). Rather than question the exam or their testing procedure (both were flawed), the researchers took the results as valid. When the testers found that immigrants who had been in the country for at least 5 years performed better, they might have become suspicious that their tests were biased. However, their conclusion was that recent immigrants came from "poor breeding stock" and were therefore less intelligent.[111]

Lewis Terman, a Stanford University professor, devised the first standardized tests based on Binet's earlier scales. The resulting Stanford-Binet test was mass marketed to schools and became the gold standard for future IQ tests. The original Stanford-Binet test (and current IQ tests) no longer identified a mental age. Rather, the test was statistically manipulated so that the average score would be 100, regardless of the person's biological age. Most modern IQ tests are simply distant relatives of the Stanford-Binet test that follow the same format—they tap into a variety of mental processes.[112]

How does one interpret modern IQ scores? Psychologists themselves disagree over the meaning of an IQ score. Although some interpret IQ as a measure of general intelligence that is mostly inherited and resistant to change, others argue that there are multiple forms of intelligence (learned, reflective, neural), some of which are very amenable to improvement.[113]

IQ and Crime

One of the earliest applications of mental testing was on criminals. Goddard, for instance, tested prisoners at various correctional institutions early in the 20th century and found that 70 percent were "feeble-minded."[114] This led him to conclude that criminality and feeblemindedness were interchangeable, and because one was tied in with the other, all such "affected" persons should be incarcerated and sterilized. However, by the 1920s, many people were critical of the IQ tests, noting their biases and flaws. Indeed, both Terman and Goddard recanted many of their own claims. Edwin Sutherland, a prominent sociologist, argued that as testing procedures improved and as IQ tests became less culturally biased, the gap in IQ between criminals and noncriminals would disappear.[115] For many years after that, criminologists ignored research on IQ.

As it turns out, Sutherland was only half correct. Although the IQ–crime relationship did indeed shrink over time, recent research suggests that an 8- to 10-point gap between criminals and noncriminals still exists. The first thing to recognize is that this is not a very large difference. Many offenders have above average IQ scores, while many law-abiding people have lower IQ scores. Still, what can one make of this difference? Several possibilities exist. It could be that smarter offenders commit less visible crimes and are less likely to be apprehended. The fact that IQ differences emerge even for self-reported delinquency (where detection of the crime is not an issue) casts this idea in doubt. It could also be that IQ tests are still biased so that blacks, Hispanics, or those in poverty might perform worse. If this were the case, then IQ might simply be a proxy for race or class—factors that are related to offending. Yet, the IQ–crime link appears, even after statistically controlling for race and social class.

Criminologists Travis Hirschi and Michael Hindelang revived interest in the IQ–crime link by suggesting that a child's IQ was at least as significant an indicator of delinquency as social class or race (important factors in many sociological theories of crime).[116] However, they also argued that intelligence had only an indirect effect on delinquency. IQ relates to poor school performance and possibly school failure, which in turn can lead to delinquency. More recently, Herrnstein and Murray renewed the argument that IQ measures a native, general intelligence. In their book, *The Bell Curve*, they claim that the effect of IQ on delinquency is direct: People who are mentally "dull" have difficulty understanding the rules of a complex society.[117] In other words, some people are not bright enough to learn right from wrong or legal actions from illegal behavior. They conclude that:[118]

People of limited intelligence can lead moral lives in a society that is run on the basis of "Thou shalt not steal." They find it much harder to lead moral lives in a society that is run on the basis of "Thou shalt not steal unless there is a really good reason to." The policy prescription is that the criminal justice system should be made simpler.

Leaving aside the controversy about whether IQ measures general intelligence, one might question whether an 8- to 10-point difference in IQ warrants their sweeping conclusions. In a response to *The Bell Curve*, Francis Cullen and his associates point out that IQ is not a very strong predictor of criminal behavior. When ranked on a scale with other known predictors of crime (e.g., attitudes, personality, delinquent peer associations), IQ ends up on the bottom of the list.[119]

Nevertheless, because the crime–IQ link is consistently documented, criminologists continue to study this relationship.[120,121] The bulk of research on this issue supports the indirect model outlined by Hirschi and Hindelang. For example, a 2004 study on a sample of 1,727 American youths found that youths with lower IQ scores were more likely to encounter deviant peer pressure and to have lower school performance and lower levels of self-control. In turn, these factors (e.g., school performance, peer pressure) predicted delinquency. In other words, IQ was related to crime because it influenced these other factors. Of course, there are other interpretations of the IQ–crime relationship. In Chapter 4, it was noted that biologically oriented criminologists view IQ as a measure of neurological health.

Policy Implications of the IQ–Crime Relationship

The policy implication of the IQ–crime relationship depends on one's view of IQ. Is IQ a measure of native intelligence or something else? It also depends on the interpretation of the IQ–crime relationship. Is IQ a direct cause of crime, or does it influence other factors, such as school failure or peer associations, that cause criminal behavior? The policy implication in the direct-cause model has already been discussed. Early positivists believed that feeblemindedness was a direct and unchangeable cause of crime. These early criminologists advocated a policy of eugenics. Many believe that the policy implications outlined in *The Bell Curve* take a similar stance. Although the authors did not recommend sterilizing offenders, they portray crime as an almost unavoidable consequence of being "dull," and their policy implication is to make the world simpler.

The vast majority of criminologists believe that IQ plays a minor and indirect role in criminal offending. If the IQ–crime link is indirect, the policy implications would focus on those things related to both IQ and crime. For example, a program might focus on keeping learning-disabled youth in school. Another policy implication deals with newer (cognitive–behavioral) rehabilitation programs. Many of these programs require extensive reading and journaling. Some suggest using IQ tests to identify offenders who may have difficulty with a reading/writing-intensive program.[122]

Summary of IQ and Crime

The meaning of IQ and its relationship to criminal behavior was neglected for many years in the field of criminology. Obviously, that situation has changed over the past 25 years. Modern studies consistently find that IQ is related to criminal behavior. Critics point out, however, that this relationship probably does not hold for many types of white-collar crime (e.g., insider trading). Also, they highlight the fact that IQ is a relatively weak predictor of criminal behavior. Most criminologists conclude that IQ matters because of its effect on other factors related to crime.

Conclusion

Psychology has made a number of important contributions to the study of crime. Each of the schools of thought has its own key concepts and theories concerning criminal behavior (see **TABLE 5-7** for a summary). Some of these theories (behavioral approaches, personality) are well supported by empirical evidence, while others (psychoanalytic theory) are not. The primary link between all of them, however, is their emphasis on the individual. Because of this emphasis, many psychological theories translate smoothly into treatment programs for offenders.

Psychologists Don Andrews and James Bonta are among the most strident supporters of a psychological approach to criminology. The authors contrast the "psychology of criminal conduct" with mainstream criminology. According to Andrews and Bonta, the psychology of criminal conduct "seeks a rational and empirical understanding of variation in the occurrence of criminal acts, in particular, a rational empirical understanding of individual differences in criminal activity."[123] Throughout their text, they argue that psychological constructs from cognitive, behavioral, and personality theory have much stronger associations with crime than traditional sociological factors, and they lament the "weak psychology" found in sociological theories. The authors argue that much of the support for mainstream theories of crime (sociology) is based on faith and ideology rather than scientific evidence.

As Canadian psychologists, Andrews and Bonta did not fall under the spell of the "nothing works" ideology that

The policy implication of the IQ–crime relationship depends on one's view of IQ.

TABLE 5-7

Summary of Psychological Theories

Theory	Key Theorists	Overview	Key Concepts
Psychodynamic theory	Sigmund Freud	Criminal behavior can be understood by examining early childhood experiences when personality is formed. Often, behavior is caused by unconscious memories, wishes, and desires.	Id, ego, superego Defense mechanisms Psychoanalysis
Behaviorism	Ivan Pavlov Albert Bandura Gerald Patterson	Criminal behavior is learned through classical, operant, or vicarious (observational) learning. Crime can therefore be "unlearned."	Reinforcement Punishment Token economy Aversion therapy Cognitive–behavioral treatment
Personality	Auke Tellegen Hervy Cleckly Robert Hare	Personality traits or a criminal personality (psychopathy) are stable characteristics of individuals who cause crime.	Multidimensional Personality Questionnaire (MPQ) Psychopath Antisocial Personality Disorder (APD)
Intelligence	Alfred Binet H. H. Goddard Stephen Jay Gould	IQ scores predict criminal behavior, but this effect is most likely indirect.	Intelligence Quotient (IQ)

pervaded American criminology from 1970 until the 1990s. Indeed they were part of small group of researchers that helped to "save" rehabilitation.[124] In their zeal for the psychological approach, however, they minimize the importance of sociological theories that are well supported in the literature. Many sociological theories do not focus on individual differences that predict offending; rather, they highlight macro-level factors thought to influence crime rates across time or different geographical locations. Psychological theories largely ignore

the "big picture," or macro-level influences. A behavioral theorist, for example, would have a difficult time explaining why violent crime rates in the United States are higher than in other countries. Are American parents that ineffective? If they are, then why does this ineffectiveness produce more violent crime but not more property crime? And why does crime rise and fall within the United States from year to year? Certainly, a personality theorist would have a difficult time explaining why the violent crime rate suddenly dropped in the 1990s.

Texture: © Malchev/Shutterstock; Police Tape: © SkillUp/Shutterstock

- Sigmund Freud is responsible for psychodynamic theory and psychoanalysis (a treatment derived from his theory). Freud deserves credit for devising a number of important concepts (e.g., ego, defense mechanisms) and distinguishing between the conscious and the unconscious. Although psychoanalysis is not appropriate for criminal offenders, many of Freud's ideas have found their way into modern criminology.
- Psychologists have identified three types of human learning: operant conditioning, classical conditioning, and observational learning. Operant conditioning (e.g., parents socializing kids) and observational learning (e.g., television violence) are both implicated in theories of crime.
- Cognitive psychologists have highlighted the importance of cognitive content and cognitive structure in the genesis of crime. Cognitive content refers to antisocial attitudes that prompt or reinforce criminal behavior. Cognitive structure focuses attention on how people think and specific cognitive skills such as empathy or self-control.

- Classical conditioning (aversion therapy), operant conditioning (parent training), and observational learning (modeling) have been used in attempts to rehabilitate offenders. Cognitive–behavioral programs have a track record of success in rehabilitating criminals.
- There is substantial evidence that certain personality traits are related to criminal behavior. A key issue in this research is how personality is formed.
- Psychopathy is among the oldest concepts in criminology. Here, the issue is whether or not a distinct, criminal personality (e.g., superficial, above average intelligence, pathological lying, egocentric) exists. In other words, are psychopaths qualitatively different from others, or do we all have a bit of psychopathy in our personalities?
- There is a consistently documented link between IQ and criminal behavior. This relationship, however, is not very strong, and there is substantial debate about how to interpret the IQ–crime link.

PUTTING IT ALL TOGETHER

Police Tape: © SkillUp/Shutterstock

1. Briefly describe the two general ways that psychologists have linked personality to criminal behavior.

2. How strong is the relationship between IQ and criminal behavior? Why are individuals with lower IQ scores more likely to engage in crime?

3. Discuss Freud's personality elements (id, ego, and superego). How might each of these elements produce criminal behavior?

4. What is a psychopath? How is psychopathy different from antisocial personality disorder? Is there a danger in using the term "psychopath"?

5. Describe the three types of learning outlined in this chapter. Give an example of each.

6. Discuss any two rehabilitation programs used by behaviorists. What type of learning (operant, classical, observational) do they use?

7. Make up a story using Gerald Patterson's social learning theory (see Figure 5-2). Explain how the person in your story becomes a criminal. Try to use as many elements in the theory as possible.

aversion therapy The use of classical conditioning to reverse an unwanted relationship between a stimulus (e.g., alcohol) and a response (pleasure).

classical conditioning By pairing an unconditioned stimulus (e.g., meat) with a conditioned stimulus (e.g., a bell), a conditioned response (e.g., salivation) is reproduced over time using only the conditioned stimulus.

cognitive restructuring A rehabilitation technique in which criminal-thinking errors (cognitive distortions) are identified and contested.

cognitive skills programs Rehabilitation programs that attempt to build thinking skills, such as moral reasoning, empathy, and anger management.

contingency contract A tool to promote parental use of operant conditioning. Parents and children sign a contract that lays out expected behaviors, reinforcements, and consequences.

countertransference A term from psychoanalysis; when the client "pushes the buttons" of the counselor so that the resulting anger and hostility interferes with treatment.

defense mechanisms Psychological ploys that individuals use (often unconsciously) to reduce or eliminate anxieties.

delinquent ego Application of Freudian principles to describe an ego that effectively blocks any potential restraint from the conscience (superego) and permits the delinquent to rationalize criminal behavior.

delinquent superego Application of Freudian principles to describe a superego that is guided by a delinquent code of behavior rather than appropriate values.

ego The conscious part of the Freudian personality; the "psychological thermostat" that regulates the savage wishes and demands of the id and the social restrictions of the superego.

five-factor model A personality structure that includes five main personality dimensions: neuroticism, extraversion, openness to experience, agreeableness, and conscientiousness.

free association A technique used in psychoanalysis in which the patient verbalizes—uncensored—anything that comes to mind.

id The unconscious, instinctual aspect of the Freudian personality. Id wishes often include the immediate gratification of basic drives (e.g., sex, aggression).

negative reinforcement The removal of a noxious stimulus (e.g., bad smell) to increase a target behavior.

observational learning Learning behavior by observing and modeling the behavior of others.

operant conditioning The use of reinforcement and punishment to shape behavior.

overdeveloped superego Application of Freudian principles to describe a superego that causes a person to seek out punishment.

people with serious mental illness (PSMI) Individuals who have a mental illness, such as schizophrenia, bipolar disorder, or major depression, that is defined by the law as serious.

personality The sum of personality traits that defines a person.

personality trait A characteristic of an individual that is stable over time and across different social circumstances.

positive reinforcement The use of rewards (e.g., praise, money, tokens) to increase a target behavior.

punishment The presentation of a noxious stimulus (e.g., spanking, scolding) to decrease a target behavior.

superego The conscience of the Freudian personality—the keeper of prohibitions ("Stealing is wrong") and wishes about what one wants to be ("I am going to be just like my father when I grow up").

token economy Application of operant conditioning to corrections. Individuals are reinforced and punished using "tokens" that can be exchanged for privileges.

transference A term from psychoanalysis to describe when the client uses the counselor as a "stand in" from the past.

Now Main Street's whitewashed windows and vacant stores. Seems like there ain't nobody wants to come down here no more. They're closing down the textile mill across the railroad tracks. Foreman says these jobs are going boys and they ain't coming back to your hometown.

—Bruce Springsteen[1]

Social Structure and Crime

Objectives

Introduction

Across the United States, many urban areas are undergoing drastic changes. Public housing projects, crime ridden and physically deteriorated, are being torn down in favor of townhouses and other forms of development. Nowhere is this more evident than in the city of Chicago. The "windy city" has long been known for crime-ridden public housing developments such as Cabrini-Green and the Robert Taylor Homes. The Chicago Housing Authority, following the lead of other cities, has started to demolish and remake these neighborhoods. Why are such communities continually overrun by crime? Will urban renewal projects change the characteristics of neighborhoods and reduce crime?

This chapter considers what role society may play in promoting or impeding criminal behavior, what social factors lead individuals to commit crime, and also what features of society relate to the crime rates of particular neighborhoods, cities, or countries.

> **In the early history of criminology, theories from psychology and biology dominated scientific inquiry into crime.**

High-rise public housing projects were havens for criminal activity. Will urban renewal projects reduce crime?

© Fred Jewell/AP Photos

In the early history of criminology, theories from psychology and biology dominated scientific inquiry into crime. Although these theories differed in terms of the exact cause of crime (e.g., atavism, feeblemindedness, moral insanity), they shared an important similarity: The cause of crime came from within individuals. Earlier chapters in this book considered the ways in which biological and psychological approaches to crime are still part of modern criminology. The dominance of these theories, however, was challenged in the early 1900s by a radically different perspective. During this time, the emerging discipline of sociology captured the imagination of many scientists interested in criminal behavior.

The major premise that drives the sociological approach is that criminality is rooted in and impelled by the very structure of society itself. In a way, the shift from individual to social responsibility for criminal behavior might have been expected.[2] Certainly, it makes sense given the social context of the early 1900s. During this period, the United States experienced rapid social change, based largely on the shift from an agrarian society to an industrial society. Major urban areas developed quickly. For example, Chicago's population increased from 4,100 residents in 1833 to 1 million in 1890 to more than 2 million in 1910. Lilly and associates note that this rapid population growth created sanitation, housing, and other critical social problems:[3]

> Like other citizens, criminologists in the 1920s and 1930s witnessed—indeed lived through and experienced—these changes that created bulging populations and teaming slum areas. It was only a short leap for them to believe that growing up in the city, particularly in the slums, made a difference in peoples' lives. In this context, crime could not be seen simply as an individual pathology; it made more sense when viewed as a social problem.

Interest in how the structure of society is related to crime eventually evolved into two distinct social structural traditions. The Chicago School tradition focuses on the structure of cities (and neighborhoods); the anomie tradition focuses more broadly on the structure of America. Behind both types of theories, however, is the work of Emile Durkheim.

Emile Durkheim and Crime

Considered a pioneer in the field of sociology and the father of French sociology, Emile Durkheim (1858–1917) became world renowned for his emphasis on the relationship between social structure and social problems. He defined crime as behavior that shocks the sentiments and "healthy

**Emile Durkheim, the "father of French sociology."
Durkheim's writings heavily influenced both the
social disorganization and anomie traditions in
American criminology.**

© British Centre for Durkheim Studies, Oxford.

conscience" of any civilized society.[4] Nevertheless, as noted in Chapter 1, Durkheim regarded crime as a natural and inevitable part of any human society. To Durkheim, the criminal is and will continue to be a functioning member of every society.

Durkheim viewed crime as serving several functions in a society. First, criminals can act as an agent for change. Some individuals anticipate a change in social norms and pioneer the future morality. Socrates, for example, was considered a criminal under Athenian law, primarily because of the independence of his thinking. Second, crime calls attention to social ills, identifies those persons who violate social norms, and labels them as such. This labeling process actually serves as social cement that binds the "good people" in a society to one another and against the "bad people."

Durkheim also distinguished two types of criminals: altruistic and common. The **altruistic criminal** is somehow offended by the rules of society and wishes to change those rules for the better. This criminal is motivated by a sense of duty to improve society. Students who burned their draft cards in protest of the Vietnam War would fit this profile. The **common criminal** rejects all laws and discipline and purposely violates the law without concern for the rightness of the acts. With no social conscience, this person takes whatever action is necessary to serve his or her interests.

Durkheim's theories, hypotheses, and assumptions about human nature serve as the foundation for most current sociological theories of crime. Major themes within his research and writing include:[5]

- The view that humans by nature are selfish and greedy. He believed that humans have unlimited desires that must somehow be capped or controlled.
- A focus on the social integration of members of society. Durkheim emphasized that social ties to families, friends, and neighbors helped restrain human ambitions and strengthen the communication of norms and values.
- Durkheim referred to norms and values as a society's "collective conscience." He argued that strong norms and values were essential to a stable society.
- Durkheim coined the term **anomie** to describe a state of affairs for which the norms and values of society weaken and are no longer able to control behaviors.

Durkheim was leery of rapid social change, particularly the movement away from rural societies characterized by **mechanical solidarity** and toward industrial societies based on **organic solidarity**. Initially, all societies start in a "mechanical" form in which homogeneity reigns. There are few or no specialized functions within society; social groups are self-sufficient, and there is little division of labor or specialization of talents. In societies with mechanical solidarity, laws seek to enforce uniformity by repressing deviation from group norms. Because such a society is close knit, there are high levels of social integration, and group norms are strong.

As societies grow more complex, however, organic solidarity necessarily results. Members of modern industrial societies perform diverse functions and fill social demands for various talents.[6] Durkheim recognized that this division of labor might foster some interdependence (i.e., members must interact to trade goods and services). He believed, however, that industrial societies were more prone to low social integration and a weakening of norms. He was particularly suspicious of industrial prosperity:[7]

Overweening ambition always exceeds the results obtained, great as they may be, because there is no warning to pause here. Nothing gives satisfaction and all this agitation is uninterruptedly maintained without appeasement.

In other words, when monetary wealth replaces the goal of self-sufficiency, human tendencies toward greed are enhanced. As social integration decreases, norms lose their ability to guide behavior (anomie increases) and cap human desires. Durkheim applied this line of reasoning to explain suicide rates. In particular, he noted that suicide rates increased during periods of rapid social change, because the caps on human desires became less clear and forceful.

Various American criminologists pursued different aspects of Durkheim's writings. By borrowing selectively from Durkheim, these scholars created distinct theoretical traditions. The sociologists who created the Chicago School and social disorganization theory followed the idea that low social integration weakens social control. The anomie tradition is largely based on the idea that norms might weaken in a society that places an emphasis on industrial prosperity.

Social Disorganization and Social Ecology

Social ecology is the study of how human relationships are affected by a particular environment. Crime is one aspect of social ecology. A central premise of this tradition is that causes of crime can be found in the social and physical structure of an environment; that is, the setting may promote crime. This approach was pioneered in several countries. In the United States, the city of Chicago became a hotbed for ecological studies of crime. The influx of immigrants and southern blacks into this city and the growth of organized crime during Prohibition made Chicago a case study in how neighborhoods develop and change. Notably, the first sociology program in the country was established at the University of Chicago in 1892. The theories and studies by sociologists in this program are now viewed as elements of the Chicago School of crime. The central question to the Chicago School was why certain areas had higher crime rates than others. In studying ecological forces, these criminologists attempted to understand the role of environment in criminal activity.

Early Social Ecology: Concentric Zone Theory

Robert E. Park, a former Chicago news reporter, believed that the city could be used as a laboratory to study crime. Influenced by prominent sociologists W. I. Thomas, George H. Mead, Erving Goffman, and Georg Simmel, Park saw a connection between how animals live in natural settings and how humans live in urban settings.[8,9] Park considered the city as a social organism within which neighborhoods survive, thrive, or fall apart. Using similar logic, Ernest W. Burgess (a colleague of Park) argued that cities, driven by economic forces, grew in a systematic way. Like ripples from a rock thrown in a lake, cities expanded outward from the central business district in concentric rings.[10]

Burgess organized 1920s Chicago into a series of concentric zones according to residential, occupational, and class characteristics **[FIGURE 6-1]**. The center zone, which contained industries and commercial activity, had access to transportation sources (e.g., waterways, trains). The nicer residential areas were farthest away from this central zone—away from the pollution, crowding, and poverty of the business district.[11] Burgess and his associates sought to understand how these urban zones changed over time and what effect this process had on rates of crime.

They identified the **zone in transition** as the major source of concern. As businesses expand into this area from the central zone and as zoning laws change to accommodate them, those residents who can afford to do so leave. With the stable wage earners gone, housing deteriorates and the zone becomes an undesirable place to live. Those who are left generally have little economic or political power. In the context of Chicago during the early 1900s, the zone in transition hosted waves of new immigrants who were too poor to live elsewhere. Burgess and other Chicago School sociologists argued that these patterns of city growth produced social disorganization—a weakening of the social ties that bind a community together (recall Durkheim's concept of social integration). They argued that social disorganization was the root cause of a host of social problems such as disease, infant death, and delinquency.

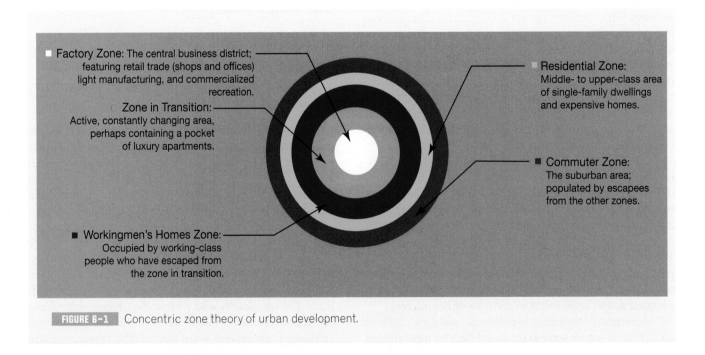

Factory Zone: The central business district; featuring retail trade (shops and offices) light manufacturing, and commercialized recreation.

Zone in Transition: Active, constantly changing area, perhaps containing a pocket of luxury apartments.

Workingmen's Homes Zone: Occupied by working-class people who have escaped from the zone in transition.

Residential Zone: Middle- to upper-class area of single-family dwellings and expensive homes.

Commuter Zone: The suburban area; populated by escapees from the other zones.

FIGURE 6-1 Concentric zone theory of urban development.

Social Disorganization Theory

Clifford Shaw and Henry McKay were not members of the sociology department; they worked at the Institute for Social Research in Chicago. They were well versed, however, in the theories flowing out of the University of Chicago. In particular, these researchers examined whether rates of delinquency would correspond with Burgess' concentric zones. Using court records, they methodically plotted the addresses of delinquents on a street map of Chicago. Shaw and McKay repeated this methodology in several studies on delinquency in Chicago over a 30-year period. Their studies confirmed Burgess' belief that delinquency is highest in the zone in transition—the farther one moved from this zone, the lower the rate of delinquency.[12]

Perhaps more importantly, their findings suggest that the characteristics of the people living in that zone mattered less than the particular geographical area. During the period they studied (1900–1930), the zone in transition was home to many different waves of immigrants (e.g., German, Irish, Polish, African American). Regardless of what ethnic group occupied the zone in transition, their children had high rates of delinquency. This finding ran counter to the popular belief that the poor moral fiber of certain racial or ethnic groups made them criminals. Also, by locating high crime rates within the zone in transition, Shaw and McKay disproved another common belief: the notion that the city was itself criminogenic. Instead, they found that only certain parts of the city fostered delinquency and crime.

In this sense, Shaw and McKay's research efforts advanced an understanding of the ecological nature of crime. Nevertheless, the key question has yet to be addressed: How exactly does the zone in transition generate delinquency? Shaw and McKay outlined a number of ecological characteristics of the zone in transition that might answer this question:

- Physical decay (e.g., crumbling or abandoned buildings)

In neighborhoods that lack cohesion, residents struggle to control street-corner youth.

© BananaStock/age fotostock

- Population heterogeneity (a mix of people from different ethnic groups)
- High population mobility (constant movement of residents in and out of the neighborhood)
- High poverty rates

The researchers argued that these ecological characteristics disrupted community organization (i.e., produced social disorganization).[13] In other words, they interfered with a community's ability to organize and reach common goals—including socializing and supervising children. For example, where population mobility is high, neighbors are less likely to know and trust each other. Therefore, they are less likely to intervene on behalf of one another. Social institutions, such as schools and community organizations that help to shape youth, are difficult to establish and maintain when community members hope to leave at the first available opportunity. Shaw and McKay also believed that once delinquency became entrenched, another process helped to keep crime rates stable. They argued that delinquent subcultures (gangs) developed and passed their norms and values across generations—a process they described as cultural transmission.

Social disorganization theory was a prominent explanation of crime from the 1950s through the 1960s. Interest in this theory declined in the 1970s, and it was relegated to the criminology "dustbin" for many years thereafter.[14] One reason for this decline was a general shift in emphasis from community-level studies to individual-level explanations. Additionally, social disorganization was criticized on a number of grounds:[15]

- Social disorganization is a pejorative term implying inadequacy and inferiority. If something is disorganized, it must necessarily be dysfunctional. Because the Chicago School theorists were generally middle-class white males, critics argued that perhaps the communities were not disorganized, but simply organized around different principles.
- Shaw and McKay relied on official (arrest) statistics. Thus, their findings may have reflected police practices more than actual levels of delinquency.
- Shaw and McKay sometimes spoke of delinquency as an indicator of social disorganization. If delinquency is part of social disorganization, it would be circular (tautological) to also say social disorganization causes delinquency.
- Shaw and McKay never directly measured social disorganization. They assumed that ecological factors (poverty, mobility) caused a breakdown in social controls, but they could not measure this process.

The theory of social disorganization has enjoyed a revival during the past 25 years. This resurgence started when scholars refined the propositions in the theory and clearly defined social disorganization as "the inability of a community structure to realize the common values of its residents and to maintain effective social controls."[16] In essence, they left behind the cultural transmission part of Shaw and McKay's work and focused on informal social control. Informal social control means that neighbors assume responsibility for each other through actions such as questioning strangers, watching each other's property, and intervening in local disturbances.[17] The other crucial factor was that researchers developed ways to directly measure this process. In other words, they were able to connect ecological factors such as poverty and residential mobility with community measures of social control.

In this regard, Sampson and Grove's 1989 analysis of the British Crime Survey (BCS) was a turning point. Using BCS data, these researchers demonstrated that ecological characteristics of British neighborhoods (family disruption, poverty, residential mobility) influenced both informal social control (supervision of street-corner youth) and neighborhood cohesion (friendship networks, membership in community organizations). In turn, measures of social control and cohesion predicted crime victimization. Since that time, Sampson and his associates have replicated these findings in Chicago.[18-20] In the **Project on Human Development in Chicago Neighborhoods (PHDCN)**, the researchers interviewed almost 9,000 residents within 343 Chicago neighborhoods. **FIGURE 6-2** outlines their research findings and is also a good summary of modern social disorganization theory.

This research once again found a relationship between ecological factors (residential mobility, concentrated disadvantage) and a neighborhood's level of cohesion and informal control. Because cohesion and control were strongly related, they combined these concepts under the title of **collective efficacy**. Sampson and his associates found that the level of collective efficacy predicted neighborhood violence, even after controlling for the characteristics of individuals living in the neighborhood.[21] In other words, it is not simply a collection of "bad apples" that makes a neighborhood prone to crime. Since this early work, others continue to document similar effects in other urban centers and even in more rural settings.[22] There is a strong consensus among reviewers of

the literature that certain neighborhoods are crime ridden because there is a lack of social cohesion and informal social control.[23]

The PHDCN continues to generate interesting findings. A 2010 study, for example, examined the relationship between collective efficacy and unstructured socialization with peers (e.g., hanging out with friends, going to parties). Typically there is a strong link between unstructured peer socialization and violence. The authors found that the negative impact of unsupervised peer socialization was reduced in neighborhoods with high collective efficacy.[24] Importantly, data from other areas and even other countries also confirm the importance of collective efficacy. One recent study, for example, found the basic collective efficacy model predicted delinquency in Iceland.[25]

Race, Place, and Crime

Some of criminology's most difficult and divisive questions have to do with the intersection of race, ethnicity, and crime. Statistics regarding race and ethnic disparities are startling. The incarceration rate, the number of jail or prison inmates per 100,000 citizens, varies dramatically by race. The incarceration rate for black citizens (roughly 4,700) is almost three times higher than the rate for Hispanics (1,800) and seven times higher (700) than that for whites.[26] At least part of these differences may stem from racial bias in the criminal justice system (see Chapter 8). However, there are also "real" differences in serious crime. For example, African Americans make up roughly 13 percent of the U.S. population, yet account for about 50 percent of homicide victims and 38 percent of known homicide offenders. The social disorganization perspective has emerged as a strong explanation for racial and ethnic differences in criminal offending.[27]

As noted in the discussion of Chicago during the early 1900s, waves of immigrants started out in the zone in transition. As they accumulated money, they were able to move to residential zones and were replaced by newly arriving immigrants. One of Shaw and McKay's central findings was that each group that lived in these distressed areas experienced high crime rates. Evidence collected over the last 40 years

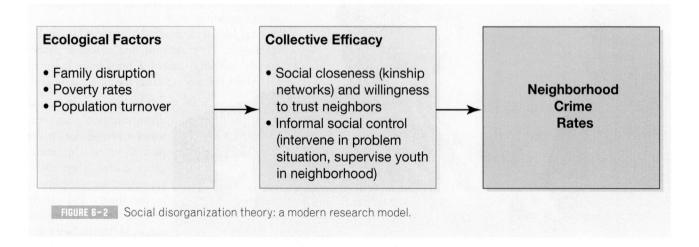

FIGURE 6-2 Social disorganization theory: a modern research model.

indicates that inner city residents, especially those of color, are less able to accumulate wealth and move to more desirable areas. They have become trapped within criminogenic neighborhoods.

William Julius Wilson has studied the development of the black "underclass" in the inner cities of America. His landmark 1987 book, *The Truly Disadvantaged*, makes the argument that racial differences in crime are due to differences in place.[28] Wilson contends that a concentration of disadvantage, in the form of poverty and joblessness, started in the 1970s and has continued to the present. During this time, several social forces collided in toxic fashion to foster its development: a legacy of racism, residential segregation, loss of manufacturing jobs in the inner city, and the failure of civil rights policies.[29] For many decades, manufacturing jobs allowed many European immigrants to earn a decent wage and escape the inner city. Over the past 35 years, this industry has largely left the inner city, and in many cases has left the United States altogether. The economy in the United States has become polarized. On one end are low-paying service jobs (e.g., working the counter at fast-food chain restaurants) that do not yield enough income to move up the social ladder. On the other end are high-wage jobs that demand a level of education and technical training that is largely beyond the reach of the underclass.[30]

Racial discrimination in housing also may have played a role in concentrating minorities in inner city neighborhoods. When minority residents earned enough to escape their environment, housing discrimination limited their options. Furthermore, high-rise public housing "projects" served to condense and isolate minority populations.[31] Other researchers point to the role of the criminal justice system. The strategy of incapacitation (see Chapter 3) has had particularly strong effects on the underclass. The incarceration rate for young black males who reside in the inner city is almost 10 percent on any given day and 33 percent in their lifetime.[32] These rates climb even higher within specific neighborhoods. Thus, incapacitation may interfere with the social organization of these communities by fostering joblessness, reducing the marriageability of men, and reducing the supervision of youth.[33] Wilson and others suggest that this geographically and culturally isolated underclass is now permanently outside the mainstream of American society. As with statistics on race and crime, the data on race and neighborhood disadvantage are clear. In Chicago, one-third of black children live in the densest areas of concentrated disadvantage. For whites, the percentage is zero.[34] Similar neighborhood segregation exists for Hispanics and in other urban areas in the United States[35]

What are the implications of this **concentrated disadvantage**? First, as noted earlier, because these locations inhibit informal social control, the underclass occupies criminogenic neighborhoods. Second, isolation from mainstream society and existence in concentrated high crime areas might have influenced the "cognitive landscape" of youth. Children in these areas are more likely to witness violence, be exposed to poor role models, and have easy access to weapons—especially handguns.[36] Violence, crime, and the values that support them become normalized.

Physical decay, such as abandoned buildings and unkept yards, are a hallmark of crime-prone neighborhoods.

© Charles Rex Arbogast/AP Photos

The strong relationship between race and neighborhood, and between neighborhood and crime, led Sampson and others to propose a **racial invariance hypothesis**.[37] They propose that race alone plays no role in generating crime. Rather, the race–crime relationship is due to the fact that both are related to place. This view of race, poverty, crime, and the underclass offers a strong rebuttal the tendency to see crime as the result of "bad choices" made by individuals. For example, James Q. Wilson argues that moral poverty (as opposed to financial poverty) is the primary cause of crime.[38] Wilson suggests there is no real root cause of criminal behavior; rather, some criminals are simply bad people and others simply make bad choices. What Robert Sampson, William Julius Wilson, and others make clear is that social structure and public policy shape the context of moral values. In other words, racial minorities and the poor are not inherently bad; instead, structural forces shape available choices.

Stark's "Deviant Places" Theory

In his theory of deviant places, Rodney Stark combines social disorganization with routine activities approach (see Chapter 3).[39] Stark poses the question: How can neighborhoods remain the site of high crime rates despite a complete turnover in their population? His conclusion: There must be something unique about certain places that sustains crime. Stark examines five variables known to affect the crime rate in a community: (1) density, (2) poverty, (3) mixed use, (4) transience, and (5) dilapidation. These variables interact with four others: (1) moral cynicism among residents, (2) increased opportunities for crime and deviance, (3) increased motivation to deviate, and (4) diminished mechanisms of social control. **TABLE 6-1** outlines Stark's theory in greater detail.

According to Stark, the nature of the neighborhood's ecology determines the crime rate. Even in low-income areas, the crime rate should be lower if the neighborhood is less densely populated, is more fully residential with less

TABLE 6-1

Propositions on "Deviant Places"

The greater the density of a neighborhood, the more contact there is between those most and those least predisposed to deviance.

The greater the density of a neighborhood, the higher the level of moral cynicism. People in dense neighborhoods will serve as inferior role models for one another—the same people would appear to be more respectable in less-dense neighborhoods.

When neighborhoods are dense and poor, homes will be crowded.

Where homes are more crowded, people will tend to congregate outside the home, where there are greater temptations and opportunities to deviate.

Where homes are more crowded, there will be lower levels of supervision over children.

Poor, dense neighborhoods tend to be mixed-use neighborhoods, where homes, apartments, retail shops, and even light industry are jumbled together (the Chicago School's zone of transition).

Poor, dense, mixed-use neighborhoods have high transience rates.

Dense, poor, mixed-use, transient neighborhoods tend to be dilapidated. Dilapidation is a social stigma for residents.

The larger the relative number of demoralized residents, the greater the number of available "victims."

Stigmatized neighborhoods will suffer from more lenient law enforcement. More lenient law enforcement increases moral cynicism and increases the incidence of crime.

Data from Rodney Stark, "Deviant Places: A Theory of the Ecology of Crime," *Criminology 25* (1987): 893–909.

crowded and dilapidated housing, has a low concentration of demoralized residents, and has a low police tolerance of vice. Although Stark's full theory has not been tested, many of his ideas have been incorporated into tests of social disorganization and routine activities theories. In that regard, those tests support the central concepts of a theory of deviant places.

Hot Spots of Criminal Behavior

Another application of social ecology is the study of "hot spots" of criminal behavior. Recall that commentators prior to the Chicago School believed that the city was criminogenic. As research on social disorganization makes clear, some neighborhoods clearly are more prone to crime than others. In other words, a focus on the city is much too broad. In the 1980s, policing researchers started to narrow the geographical area further, pointing to small, high crime areas within particular neighborhoods.

Lawrence Sherman and his associates in Minneapolis conducted the most well known study.[40] This study examined data on over 300,000 calls to Minneapolis police citywide over a 1-year period and found that only 3.5 percent of street addresses produced over 50 percent of all calls to the police. These hot spots, some as small as street intersections, were especially high in predatory crimes such as robbery, rape, and auto theft. As these findings suggest, certain

locales are more susceptible to crime. Although these geographical places are much smaller than neighborhoods, the social disorganization approach still appears be applicable. Spelman analyzed data on calls for police service for specific locations such as high schools, housing projects, subway stations, and parks in Boston. He found that the worst 10 percent of locations produced 50 percent of crime calls.[41] As with Shaw and McKay's research on neighborhoods, the locations with the most calls for service remained stable over time. In a related study, Spelman examined calls for service data from Austin, Texas, to determine if crime rates were higher on blocks with abandoned residential buildings (e.g., physical decay).[42] He found that blocks with unsecured buildings had over three times as many drug calls, almost two times as many theft calls, and more than twice the number of violent crime calls.

Criminology research on neighborhoods and "microgeographic units," such as street segments or intersections, use these locations as units of analysis. One interesting conclusion from this body of research is that "place" research can often mirror research on individual offenders. Lawrence Sherman maintains that the concentration of crime in hot spots is more intense than it is among individual repeat offenders.[43] Such places have characteristics that are like those considered in the development of offending among persons: onset, continuance, specialization, and desistance. A recent study of street segments (both sides of a street block between two intersections) found that the concentration of crime in these units was remarkably similar to the concentration of offending within cohorts of individuals. Across a number of large cities, roughly the same small percent (3–6%) of segments were responsible for more that 50 percent of crime incidents. This mirrors research finding that the "chronic 6%" of offenders cause over 50 percent of the crime in their cohort.[44]

The analysis of places extends beyond academics. The development of geocoding and geographical information systems (GIS) has made the identification of hot spots routine among police departments. Like individuals with a long "rap sheet," high crime locations have become targets of policing initiatives. Problem-oriented policing, for example, often depends on the identification of hot spots as a starting point. Aside from its application in policing, hot spots research reminds us not to make sweeping conclusions about whole neighborhoods and the people who live there. As criminologist David Weisburd points out, "there are crime hot spots in neighborhoods that are generally termed *good neighborhoods*, and most streets in even so-called *bad neighborhoods* have little or no crime."[45]

> **Like individuals with a long "rap sheet," high crime locations have become targets of policing initiatives.**

Policy Implications: Social Ecology and Social Disorganization

The policy implications of social disorganization theory and hot spots of crime depend on where one jumps into the chain of events that leads to crime. The general argument is that broad ecological factors, such as poverty, residential mobility, and physical decay, affect community cohesion and informal social control. Cohesion and control (or collective efficacy) impact crime. From a policy perspective, one might target the ecological factors; the cohesion and social process of a neighborhood; or both.

Shaw and McKay applied social disorganization theory by developing a large-scale delinquency prevention program called the **Chicago Area Project (CAP)**. The first projects started in 1932, and they were carried out into the early 1960s. The projects targeted high crime neighborhoods and attempted, among other things, to:[46]

- Mobilize local informal social organization and social control among law-abiding citizens by creating "community committees" consisting of existing community groups, such as churches and labor unions, as well as residents who were city leaders
- Overcome the influence of delinquent peers and criminal adults by assigning "detached" local adults to neighborhood gangs (e.g., work with

youth in nonorganized, informal setting) and through recreational programs designed to provide youth with associations with conventional peers and adults
- Improve sanitation, traffic control, and physical decay

Although there was no rigorous evaluation of the CAP, long-term assessments suggest that the CAP met with mixed results. For example, there is some evidence that delinquency rates declined in neighborhoods with strong community committees. In other CAP neighborhoods, crime remained stable or increased. A 50-year follow-up study suggested that CAP had a marginal (but positive) influence on delinquency. Unfortunately, this research was unable to tie differences in delinquency directly to the activities of CAP.[47]

When asked to comment on the policy implications of social disorganization theory, most people will mention neighborhood watch programs. In this type of program, residents conduct neighborhood patrols and generally engage in the type of informal control implicated in social disorganization theory. Unfortunately, neighborhood watch programs tend to be successfully implemented in neighborhoods that are cohesive. In other words, they tend to take hold in the communities that need them the least.

The Moving to Opportunity (MTO) program is a unique program with implications for ecological theory. In five cities, randomly selected families were given the opportunity to move out of high-poverty neighborhoods into more stable, low-poverty neighborhoods. Although the overall research record is mixed, there is evidence that arrests for violent crime declined among the youth of families who moved.[48] In a recent analysis of a Chicago MTO program, violence decreased for families that moved into suburban neighborhoods outside of the city limits. Unfortunately, families that moved to low-poverty neighborhoods *within* the city actually experienced *increased* violence. The data suggest that suburban neighborhoods offered youth higher quality schools and more control over their environment.[49] Although MTO programs provide important evidence for social disorganization theory, moving everyone out of poverty-stricken neighborhoods is probably not a realistic policy.

In contrast, "urban renewal" projects, like the renovation of Chicago's public housing projects (see **Theory in Action: The Demolition of Cabrini-Green**), are occurring in many communities. Here, programs attract higher income residents into poverty-stricken neighborhoods. On the surface, it may appear that such a move could increase social cohesion and political clout and reduce crime rates. As more affluent people move in, however, property values and taxes increase. Neighborhood services do improve, but poor

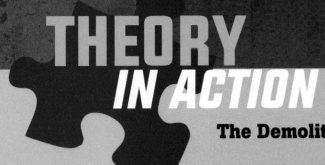

THEORY IN ACTION

The Demolition of Cabrini-Green

The Cabrini-Green housing development, cited by many as a national symbol for public housing gone bad, is being demolished. The development started with the construction of the Frances Cabrini Rowhouses in 1942. Originally known as "Little Sicily," the development primarily housed Chicago's Italian American community. By 1962, when the William-Green Homes were added to this composite public housing property, Cabrini-Green was one of the largest sites in the Chicago Housing Authority, with a mostly African American residential population. In its heyday, the Cabrini-Green development was home to about 15,000 residents and 3,500 public housing units. Over the years, physical deterioration, gang violence, and the proliferation of illicit drugs plagued Cabrini-Green.

The demolition of the high-rise public housing projects is part of a larger movement to revitalize inner city areas. The Urban Revitalization Demonstration Program was initiated in 1993 by the U.S. Department of Housing and Urban Development to "fundamentally reinvent" public housing by demolishing the most severely decayed housing projects and redeveloping them as mixed-use, mixed-income projects. A primary goal is to lessen the concentration of poverty within small geographical areas. In Chicago, the high-rise apartments are being replaced by a mix of affordable (20%), market-rate (50%), and public (30%) housing. While many applaud this plan, others are more critical. They fear that private owners are engaging in a land grab and that the promised "affordable" housing will fail to materialize.

On the surface, the physical makeover of Cabrini-Green appears to follow the policy prescription of social disorganization theory. In particular, mixed housing might produce more residential stability and give owners a stake in the well-being of the neighborhood. Richard M. Daley, the Mayor of Chicago during the formation of the plan, expressed hope that mixed-income housing would reconnect shunned sections of the city to services and investment. He believed the development would allow poor African Americans who had lived in concentrated disadvantage to reap the rewards of a middle-class lifestyle.

There is some cause for concern, however, because making some housing "market rate" will mean less available housing for the poor. What will become of those residents who are left out of the new project? There is also the potential for conflict between those who pay market rate and others who live in subsidized housing. Indeed, former Cabrini-Green residents who were given vouchers to find housing in private developments have found themselves subjected to high levels of scrutiny. Restrictions include criminal background checks, drug testing, regular "inspections" of the apartment, and strict guidelines about who could visit the rental units.

Commercial development in the Cabrini-Green area has already commenced. A Target store now occupies the site of one of the housing towers. In April 2015, the Chicago Housing Authority unveiled its detailed redevelopment plan for housing. Construction is expected to be completed by 2019. Nobody knows for certain how this urban renewal project will shape social life in this location. Whatever the outcome, social scientists will be watching this manipulation of neighborhood ecology with a great deal of interest.

Sources: Biasco, P. (2015, April 23). Cabrini-Green development includes over 2,300 homes. *DNAinfo.* Retrieved June 1, 2015, from http://www.dnainfo.com/chicago/20150423/old-town/cabrini-green-redevelopment-plans-include-over-2300-homes; Austen, B. (2012, May). The last tower: The decline and fall of public housing. *Harpers Magazine.* Retrieved October 21, 2014, from http://harpers.org/archive/2012/05/the-last-tower/3/; Ihejirika, M. (2010, July 1). Cabrini-Green tenants return to court. *Chicago Sun-Times*; Grossman, K. N. (2005, January 10). 14 Cabrini high-rises to close; CHA whittling complex to 3 buildings as residents fight to stay. *Chicago Sun-Times.*

residents are pushed out into adjacent areas—creating a new community with even less social organization.[50]

There are also two policy considerations that relate to the criminal justice system. The first is community policing, which involves the police taking an active role in working with neighborhood residents to identify and solve community problems. This approach is very much in keeping with the spirit of social disorganization theory. As with CAP, community policing efforts have revolved around organizing community members and building community relationships. To date, the evidence regarding community policing is mixed. Such efforts may reduce the fear of crime in some locations, but there is little evidence at this time that they substantially reduce criminal behavior.[51] The second consideration for the criminal justice system is that incarceration may have unintended consequences. As noted earlier, some research suggests that high levels of incarceration within a neighborhood might actually contribute to social disorganization and increase crime over the long run.

Neighborhood watch programs seek to foster community organization, kinship, and informal social control. Unfortunately, such programs are most likely to succeed in neighborhoods that already have high levels of informal control.

© Josh Reynolds/AP Photos

Criminologist Michael Tonry has written extensively about race, incarceration, and the war on drugs.[52] He notes that the war on drugs has resulted in black offenders being sentenced in numbers disproportionate to their presence in the community or among drug users. Tonry argues that long prison sentences for drug offenders led to the destruction of minority communities. He believes this was a foreseeable tragedy. Tonry makes a case for new drug laws that encourage the least restrictive sanction, provide judicial mitigation for special circumstances, and promote treatment over punishment. As attitudes toward illicit drug use have softened over the past several years, judicial and legislative reforms have indeed moved in that direction. There appears to be a growing consensus among liberal and conservative policymakers that drug-only offenders should not be incarcerated.

There appears to be a growing consensus among liberal and conservative policymakers that drug-only offenders should not be incarcerated.

The Strain/Anomie Theoretical Tradition

In 1938, in a 10-page article titled "Social Structure and Anomie," Robert K. Merton extended the work of Durkheim to create a rich theoretical tradition within criminology.[53] While Chicago School theorists used Durkheim's notion of social integration to explore neighborhood-level crime, Merton applied Durkheim's concepts of industrial prosperity and anomie to the context of the United States. In doing so, Merton borrowed more heavily and more explicitly from Durkheim. The most prominent idea that Merton borrowed was that institutionalized norms could be weakened in societies that place an intense value on economic success.

Merton believed the United States was unique in its emphasis on the cultural goal of monetary success. The "American dream" exhorted all to pursue material and financial wealth. Merton also believed that this cultural goal was almost universal—after all, part of the American dream is the idea that everyone has a fair and equal chance of becoming successful (anyone can go from "rags to riches" in America). What could be wrong with setting such a lofty cultural goal? Merton argued, much like Durkheim, that too much emphasis on the pursuit of money can weaken norms that dictate the proper way to achieve this goal. Thus, people will pursue financial success even if it means violating norms or laws. Similarly, members of society will pay less attention to how wealth is achieved, in comparison to *whether* wealth is achieved. In this scenario, "The technically most feasible procedure, whether legitimate or not, is preferred to the institutionally prescribed conduct."[54] This is the very definition of anomie.

This problem is compounded by the fact that, in reality, America is a stratified, or class-based, society. In this sense, different classes have different access to the means for success. An upper-class youth has access to high-quality education, business contacts, and other means for success. The lower-class youth, in particular, has little access to the legitimate, institutionalized means (education, contacts, good job) of achieving those goals.[55] For example, a common goal for middle-class Americans is to own a home. To achieve this goal, they will save their money for a down payment and then budget their income in order to make the mortgage payments each month. The means to realizing this cultural goal are finding legitimate employment and saving money. But what if there are no good jobs available and it is not possible to save enough money for a down payment? To quote the rock group The Violent Femmes, for some folks, "The American dream is only a dream."[56]

The intense pressure to succeed combined with a lack of conventional means to do so puts strain or pressure on many individuals. For this reason, Merton's theory is often called a strain theory. In sum, crime results when individuals are unable to achieve their goals through legitimate channels. Merton offers four possible adaptations to strain produced by the gap between the cultural goal of economic success and the reality of limited access to the proper means: innovation, ritualism, retreatism, and rebellion. Where there is no gap between the cultural goal of success and the means to achieve success, conformity is expected.

1. **Innovation.** The innovator buys into the culturally approved goals of society but pursues them through

unacceptable means. This type of adaptation is most likely to lead to criminal behavior. For example, in the television series *Breaking Bad*, a high school chemistry teacher with a terminal illness "innovates" by manufacturing methamphetamine. This adaptation strategy is more prevalent in the lower class where there are more obstacles in the way of achieving cultural goals legitimately. According to Merton, these obstacles account for the higher crime rate in the lower class.

2. **Ritualism.** This describes a person who, over time, abandons the goal of financial success. Despite this, they continue to embrace the accepted means. A ritualist seeks to play it safe. For example, Archie Bunker, from the 1970s TV show *All in the Family*, was a ritualist. Each night he came home from his job at the loading dock, hung up his coat and hat, sat down in his chair in front of the TV, and ordered his wife, Edith, to bring him a beer. He then would get up to eat his evening meal, watch some more TV, and go to bed. Every day, he performed the same weary ritual. Archie knew that the symbols of success in American culture (a nice car, a house in the suburbs, fancy clothes, and so on) were beyond his reach. His only "goal" was to make it through one more day and move on to the next. In modern times, a stereotypical ritualist might hold a dead-end service job, work for minimum wage, and barely make ends meet.

3. **Retreatism.** The retreatist is a social dropout. In Merton's words,

Robert K. Merton, with a short journal article, launched the theoretical tradition of anomie, or "strain" theories.

Courtesy of University Archives, Columbia University in the City of New York.

retreatists include "psychotics, psychoneurotics, chronic autists, pariahs, outcasts, vagrants, vagabonds, tramps, chronic drunkards, and drug addicts."[57] Like the ritualist, this type of person will not resort to illegitimate means to achieve widely shared goals. Retreatists may be morally opposed to violating the norms of society or simply be powerless to violate such norms. Unlike the ritualist who keeps plodding along, these individuals simply withdraw from society.

4. **Rebellion.** The person who opposes both the culturally dominant goals and the means to achieve these goals is a rebel. The rebel seeks to establish a new social order and embraces a different cultural goal. For example, "hippies" might pursue the cultural goal of "peace" through their own prescribed means (free love, living in a commune). In criminological terms, the terrorist (see Chapter 13) and perhaps some street gangs (see the following subcultural theories) best exemplify this mode of adaptation.

Critique of Anomie Theory

Merton's theory is primarily utilitarian in nature: People engage in crime because they lack the legitimate means to achieve success. In that sense, his theory is geared to explain monetary crimes (robbery, burglary) as opposed to expressive crimes like murder and rape. Furthermore, because strain stems from a lack of legitimate means, Merton's theory explains crime largely among the lower class. Because middle- and upper-class people generally have access to legitimate means, they are expected to conform. These limitations mean that strain theory has a rather narrow scope. In defense of Merton, strain theory was developed as a middle-range theory that would account for some, but not all, forms of deviant behavior.

The most damaging criticism of Merton's theory is that he fails to explain why people react to strain differently. In other words, why do people in almost identical social situations differ in their reaction to the feelings of helplessness? For example, why does one member of society (the ritualist) continue to pick up his or her lunch pail and trot off to work every day, while another (the innovator) deals drugs, and yet another (the rebel) joins a street gang?

In addition to these criticisms, Merton's strain theory has never received much empirical support. One of the first tests of this theory compared adolescents' educational aspirations (How far in school would you like to get?) with their educational expectations (How far in school do you think you'll get?).[57] Strain theory would predict that youth with high aspirations but low expectations would be most likely to engage in crime. Instead, this study (and others that followed) found that delinquents tended to have low aspirations. Other measures of strain theory, including perceptions of blocked opportunities for success, and satisfaction with current monetary status, have suggested some support for the theory.[59-61] Even here, these relationships tend to be weak when compared to other predictors of crime.

Indeed, during the 1970s, many scholars started to question whether poverty and social class were even related to

Because they seek to establish cultural goals using unconventional means (violence) terrorists such as Osama Bin Laden fit Merton's category of "rebellion."
© AP Photos

criminal behavior. For example, poverty and unemployment rates do not appear to fluctuate over time with crime rates in any meaningful, consistent manner. During some time periods, crime actually increases as poverty rates decline.[61] Furthermore, self-report studies of criminal offending suggest that income levels are only weakly associated with delinquency.[63] One should note, however, that self-report surveys tend to measure less serious forms of delinquency and crime. Thus, the relationship between class and crime remains an unsettled issue in criminology.

The combination of weak empirical support and narrow scope led some scholars to call for an abandonment of strain theory as a valid explanation of crime.[64] Others, however, attempted to modify Merton's propositions in order to address criticisms and put forth an empirically supported model.

General Strain Theory

In 1992, Robert Agnew proposed a substantial overhaul of Merton's strain theory. Titled general strain theory (GST), this explanation of crime takes a much broader view of the sources of strain. Agnew suggests three sources of strain:[65,66]

1. The failure to achieve positively valued goals (e.g., economic success, good grades)

2. The removal of positively valued stimuli (e.g., death of parent, break up with boyfriend/girlfriend)
3. The presence of inescapable negative stimuli (e.g., violent household, school troubles)

Strain in the context of GST is clearly available to all people, rich or poor. In that sense, Agnew addressed a major criticism of Merton's theory. Agnew also clearly explained how strain leads to crime. Specifically, he argues that strain produces negative emotional states, such as anger (violence) or depression (illicit drug use) that are conducive to many different types of delinquency and crime. Finally, Agnew addresses why some individuals react to strain in a nondelinquent manner, while others react with criminal behavior. Individuals who lack the coping skills (intelligence, creativity, problem-solving ability) necessary to deal with strain in a constructive manner are more likely to have a delinquent response. Furthermore, he outlines several factors (e.g., personality traits conducive to crime, delinquent peers) that may limit a person's response to strain.

Agnew's theory is much more complex and broader than Merton's modes of adaptation. FIGURE 6-3 outlines the major concepts in his theory. The crucial issue is whether this reformulation has increased the support of strain theory. Although this is a relatively new theory, the core aspects of GST have received consistent empirical support. For example, Paternoster and Mazerolle studied a sample of over 1,500 adolescents. The authors found that various measures of strain (negative life events, school/peer hassles, negative relations with adults) predicted delinquency. This relationship held even after controlling for measures from competing theories.[67] Numerous other studies have confirmed this strain–crime link.[68–71]

More recently, scholars have turned to the more complex aspects of this theory. Here, the research is more mixed. For example, some studies examining the role of negative emotions like anger or depression yield findings that are inconsistent with GST. In some studies, strain appears to "directly impact criminal behavior, bypassing negative emotions altogether."[72] In other research, negative emotions simply do not predict crime.[73] In addition to this negative evidence, one might question whether GST is in keeping with the spirit of Merton's strain theory. Merton focused on social structure and broad cultural goals, while GST focuses more on the role of psychological stress.

Institutional Anomie Theory

Messner and Rosenfeld provide a different twist on Merton's theory of anomie. Their theory of institutional anomie, proposed in 1993, took root from the recognition that Merton's writings were about more than just modes of adaptation. In particular, Messner argued that Merton actually offered a cultural explanation for why the United States was more crime prone than other countries.[74] In keeping with Merton's (and indeed Durkheim's) notion of anomie, Messner and Rosenfeld suggest that the high level and distinctive pattern of crime in the United States are due to the cultural values

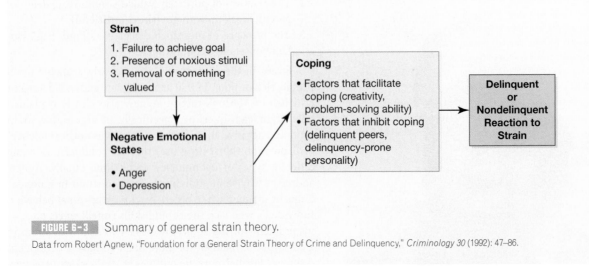

FIGURE 6-3 Summary of general strain theory.

Data from Robert Agnew, "Foundation for a General Strain Theory of Crime and Delinquency," *Criminology 30* (1992): 47–86.

in American society. They identify a cluster of values that constitute the American dream:[75]

- **Achievement.** The American culture exhorts people to make something of themselves, to "be all they can be." Personal worth is evaluated on the outcome of these efforts. The failure to achieve is akin to the failure to make any meaningful contribution to society.
- **Individualism.** Americans are encouraged to make it on their own. Fellow members of society are thus competitors in the rat race.
- **Universalism.** Everyone is encouraged to social ascent and everyone is susceptible to evaluation based on the basis of individual achievement.
- **"Fetishism" of money.** American culture values the accumulation of monetary rewards; money is literally the measure of success.

These core values of American culture place great pressure on Americans to achieve at any cost. The values are "highly conducive to the mentality that 'it's not how you play the game; it's whether you win or lose.'"[76] As with Merton's theory, Messner and Rosenfeld suggest that people are encouraged to use illegal ways to attain culturally approved goals (that is, U.S. culture promotes crime). Institutional anomie is different here in one important respect. Because there is no stopping point with regard to monetary success (How much is "enough" money?), the pressure to succeed is not dependent on social class. In other words, the theory can account for why some wealthy people might engage in crime.

Institutional anomie theory really departs from Merton regarding social structure. Merton discusses social structure almost solely in terms of economic status. To Messner and Rosenfeld, social structure revolves around social institutions such as the economy, education, family, and polity (government). These institutions perform different roles in a society. For example, the government allows members of society to achieve collective goals (build a highway system) and the economy provides basic necessities (food, clothing,

shelter). The family and the education system, among other things, allow members of society to socialize children.

The key concept in institutionalized anomie theory is the institutional balance of power. Institutions often compete with each other for scarce resources. What is good for the economy might not necessarily be good for the family or education. Therefore, any society can be measured on what institutions are valued over others. Messner and Rosenfeld suggest that in the United States, the economy towers over other institutions. The power of the economy weakens those institutions (family, education) that prevent crime. The authors provide a number of examples of how the economy dominates other institutions:[77]

- Noneconomic roles and values are devalued. For example, the homeowner is valued more than the homemaker. The excellent teacher does not receive the financial compensation relative to his or her business peers. The average childcare worker makes much less than the average bartender.
- Other institutions accommodate economic demands. For example, workers worry about finding time for their families, but never worry about finding time for their jobs. Few employers offer any form of paid parental leave, and few provide any childcare.
- Economic norms penetrate other institutions. For example, schools rely on grading systems similar to wages, and husbands and wives are now termed *partners* who manage the household *division of labor*.

In comparison to the United States, many European countries have strong safety nets (paid parental leave, long vacations, welfare payments) that balance the economy more equally against the family and the education system.

In sum, institutionalized anomie theory suggests that two forces shape crime in the United States: the cultural pressure to succeed financially and a social structure that weakens those institutions that socialize children **[FIGURE 6-4]**. This is a country- or society-level theory; institutionalized anomie predicts that countries that place exaggerated value on economic success and allow the economy to

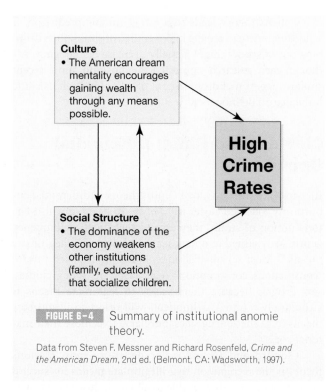

FIGURE 6-4 Summary of institutional anomie theory.

Data from Steven F. Messner and Richard Rosenfeld, *Crime and the American Dream*, 2nd ed. (Belmont, CA: Wadsworth, 1997).

Culture
- The American dream mentality encourages gaining wealth through any means possible.

Social Structure
- The dominance of the economy weakens other institutions (family, education) that socialize children.

High Crime Rates

dominate other institutions will have high crime rates. Direct tests of this theory would require rather detailed data from a large sample of countries. For this reason, most tests of institutional anomie theory have been partial and indirect.

One strategy has been to test the theory within the United States by comparing states or counties. A recent study examined instrumental crime rates—burglary, larceny, robbery, and auto theft—across 77 different geographical areas within the United States.[78,79] Areas with a high commitment to economic success (especially in the context of low commitment to legitimate means) had higher levels of instrumental crime. The strength of noneconomic institutions, such as family, appeared to help mitigate these negative effects. Although consistent with institutional anomie theory, it was not a cross-national comparison. The only available cross-national tests examine homicide rates. Several studies find that countries with stronger safety nets (e.g., the provision of pension, unemployment compensation) to buffer the effects of the economy have lower rates of homicide.[80,81]

Policy Implications of Anomie and Strain Theories

The policy implications of anomie or strain theory depend on the specific theory in question. The implication of Merton's modes of adaptation is that reducing poverty and increasing opportunity for lower-class people would reduce strain and therefore crime. Notably, during this theory's peak in popularity, it had a great deal of influence on public and political debate over crime. The Delinquency Prevention and Control Act of 1961 and President Lyndon B. Johnson's "War on Poverty" sought to increase educational and economic opportunities for the lower classes. Specific delinquency prevention programs that focused on poverty, because of their association with subcultural explanations of crime, are highlighted later.

General strain theory and institutional anomie theory lead to rather different policy implications. General strain theory highlights the importance of psychological strain and its relation to negative emotional states, such as anger. Those who cope with their emotions constructively are less prone to engage in delinquency. In that sense, cognitive–behavioral rehabilitation programs (see Chapter 5) that focus on skills such as anger management and conflict resolution are consistent with general strain theory. Of course, there are many other factors within this theory that one could target. Indeed, a major limitation of theories that lack parsimony is that it becomes difficult to figure out the exact policy implications.

Within institutional anomie theory, there are essentially two targets for change. First, Messner and Rosenfeld suggest a number of policy implications designed to strengthen the institution of family:[82]

> *Initiatives such as the provision of family leave, job sharing for husbands and wives, flexible work schedules, employer-provided child care, and a host of other "pro-family" economic policies should help alter the balance between the economic demands faced by parents and their obligations and opportunities to devote more time and energy to exclusive family concerns..*

Second, institutional anomie suggests that altering the American dream culture would also reduce crime. While a total transformation of American culture is "fanciful," it might be possible to push the culture in a less criminogenic direction. For example, goals other than the accumulation of wealth will need to be strengthened: "This implies greater recognition of and appreciation for . . . social roles such as parenting, 'partnering,' teaching, learning, and serving the community. . . ."[83]

Subcultural Explanations of Crime

Between the 1950s and early 1960s, several authors developed subcultural theories of delinquency. These theories branched off of the dominant explanations of crime during that period: the anomie and social disorganization perspectives. Subcultural theories share two common themes. First, they focus squarely on the lower class. Second, the theories attempt to explain the formation and activity of delinquent subcultures. A subculture is defined as a group, such as a street gang, that holds norms and values that are different from mainstream society.

Cohen: Status Frustration and Reaction Formation

In *Delinquent Boys*, Albert K. Cohen sought to explain why delinquent subcultures (gangs) developed and why they engaged in a particular kind of delinquency.[84] Cohen argued that most gang-related juvenile delinquency was nonutilitarian, malicious, and negativistic (e.g., vandalism, assaults). Even theft seemed to be based on factors other than the value of stolen goods (e.g., thrill, something to do). In this case, Merton's idea that "strain" produced innovation geared toward financial success made little sense. Still, Cohen argued that strain produced delinquency; he simply devised a different source of strain. In Cohen's theory, strain is caused by the failure of lower-class boys to achieve middle-class status. According to Cohen, most lower-class boys desire middle-class status and initially accept the goals and values (e.g., responsibility, delayed gratification, ambition, manners/courtesy, control over aggression, respect for property) of the middle class.

The turning point occurs when boys reach school age. Cohen noted that the school systems of the 1950s were "entrenched in middle-class values and social networks."[85] Lower-class boys, singled out by their dress, manners, and attitudes, failed to live up to this "middle-class measuring rod." Cohen suggested of the lower-class boy:[86]

> To the degree to which he values middle-class status, either because he values the good opinion of middle-class persons, or because he has to some degree internalized middle-class standards himself, he faces a problem of adjustment and is in the market for a "solution."

Like Merton, Cohen believed that different youth would react to this status frustration differently. A "college boy" will "buck up" and achieve middle-class status by working hard and achieving in school. Others will drop out and become "street-corner boys" (like Merton's retreatist). The delinquent solution involved the creation of a subculture that valued things in direct opposition to middle-class standards. Cohen borrowed the Freudian defense mechanism reaction formation to describe this process.

In essence, because the boys cannot achieve middle-class status, they create a culture that rewards the opposite values. Thus, for example, physical aggression, toughness, and hedonism are stressed. Members of these delinquent groups do not consider the future consequences of their behavior, but instead focus on immediate gratification of their desires. Gang members are openly hostile to the agents of conformity. Moreover, they oppose other delinquent groups and use force to ensure loyalty and conformity to their own group. In short, it is a culture all their own and of their own making.

Cohen's theory leads to a rather unique prediction. If school experiences are the major source of strain, then dropping out of school might actually decrease delinquency. Although early research supported this position, more recent studies suggest that dropping out of school in itself has little influence on delinquency.[87]

Cloward and Ohlin: Differential Opportunity

Richard Cloward and Lloyd Ohlin's theory of differential opportunity followed closer to Merton. In keeping with Merton's notion of strain, they argued that much delinquency is primarily aimed at obtaining wealth through illegitimate means.[88] Most serious delinquents are predisposed toward "conspicuous consumption" (e.g., fast cars, fancy clothes, sex, drugs). Because their access to legitimate means is structurally blocked, delinquents will resort to illegitimate means (e.g., theft, drug sales, burglary) to achieve their material goals.[89]

Cloward and Ohlin's major departure from Merton's theory is the recognition that illegitimate means for success are not automatically available to all youth. Just as legitimate means (e.g., education, a good job) are unequally distributed in society, so too are illegitimate means. In some neighborhoods, illegitimate opportunities for success are readily available. For example, there may be a well-entrenched organization that distributes illicit drugs. Such an organization provides an illegitimate avenue to pursue financial success. In other areas, neighborhood conditions deteriorate to the point that even illegitimate organizations are unable to survive. In this sense, Cloward and Ohlin draw together Merton's work with the Chicago School theorists (neighborhood organization, cultural transmission of criminal values and skills).

Thus, differential opportunity speaks both to the availability of legitimate opportunities (blocked opportunity creates delinquency) and to the availability of illegitimate opportunities for success. Cloward and Ohlin argue that the presence or absence of illegitimate opportunity dictates the form taken by the delinquent subculture. If illegitimate opportunities are available, criminal gangs will engage in more utilitarian activities (organized crime, drug distribution) in pursuit of money and status. Even here, some retreatist gangs develop. Retreatist gangs consist of "double failures"—those individuals who could not achieve success through either legitimate or illegitimate means. To the extent that illegitimate means are unavailable, conflict gangs will organize around violence—and engage in activities that "protect turf." The three different delinquent subcultures identified by Cloward and Ohlin are summarized in **TABLE 6-2**.

Some qualitative data (ethnographic research) drawn from gang members appear to support differential

> **Gang members are openly hostile to the agents of conformity.**

TABLE 6-2

Forms of Delinquent Subcultures

Criminal subculture: Follows the basic organized crime model. Areas where organized crime is firmly established provide a goal for delinquents. They rationally seek economic gain and view crime as a career.

Conflict subculture: Places high premium on violence. This subculture often occurs in neighborhoods populated with new immigrants, where the delinquent pursues opportunities lacking elsewhere.

Retreatist subculture: Emphasizes drug abuse or other forms of escape. This delinquent is a "double failure" who cannot achieve success in either the criminal or conflict subcultures.

Source: Reprinted with permission of Free Press, a Division of Simon & Schuster, Inc., from *Delinquency and Opportunity: A Theory of Delinquent Gangs* by Richard A. Cloward and Lloyd E. Ohlin. Copyright © 1960 by The Free Press. Copyright renewed © 1988 by Lloyd E. Ohlin. All rights reserved.

opportunity theory. John Hagedorn's study of gang involvement in the illicit drug market is a good example. Hagedorn demonstrates how gang drug dealing is a response to the absence of legitimate employment opportunities.[90,91] His studies are based on interviews and observations conducted in Milwaukee, Wisconsin, in 1987 and 1992. Drug organizations responded rationally to the demands of the market. When sales were made to low-income neighbors, they were done informally. New and more sophisticated structures were developed to handle sales to affluent whites and outsiders. There were differences in drug organizations across ethnic lines. Latinos maintained their gang membership but used kinship groups to expand operations. African American adult gang members were more likely to freelance or use small businesses as covers. Most white adult gang members held down full-time jobs and sold cocaine on the side.

Over time, Hagedorn found that four types of adult gang members developed:

1. Those few who had gone "legit" or had matured out of the gang
2. "Homeboys"—a majority of both African American and Latino adult gang members who alternately worked conventional jobs and took various roles in drug sales
3. "Dope fiends"—those addicted to cocaine and who were in business to maintain access to the drug
4. "New jacks"—those who saw the drug game as their career

Hagedorn argues that most gang members would accept legitimate employment. He believes that the key to their future lies in building social capital that comes from steady employment and a supportive relationship, without the constant threat of incarceration.[92] Employment, even a minimum-level of involvement in the legitimate economy, could be an effective deterrent to gang involvement. In that light, jobs programs should focus on ways to encourage private and public investment in poor neighborhoods and advocate for more community control of social institutions.[93]

On the negative side, few people have directly tested whether the availability of illegitimate means directly influences the activities of gangs. Furthermore, gang research often does not reveal typologies consistent with Cloward and Ohlin's framework. Rather, gangs tend to be diverse (e.g., drug use, drug sales, violence, property offenses) in their delinquency, rather than specialized in a particular vice.[94] Where evidence of specialization does exist, it does not match up with Cloward and Ohlin's typology.[95]

Miller: Focal Concerns of the Lower Class

Walter B. Miller outlines several focal concerns or values of the lower class that encourage deviance.[96] In essence, Miller's theory views the entire lower class as a unique subculture. He argues that members of the lower class, for example, place a high value on street smarts and toughness. In contrast, the middle-class values delayed gratification and restraint of aggression. The focal concerns of the lower class are summarized in TABLE 6-3. Unlike Cohen, who viewed the values of gangs as a reaction to the middle class, Miller suggests that gang values are actually absorbed from the culture of the lower class.

TABLE 6-3

Six Focal Concerns of Lower-Class Delinquents

1. **Trouble:** A preoccupation with getting into, or staying out of, trouble—trouble can refer to violent situations or interactions with the police

2. **Toughness:** The need to demonstrate that one can stand up to adversity and "take" whatever the street brings (e.g., run-ins with other gangs and the police)

3. **Smartness:** The high value placed on "street smarts"; one must know how to handle oneself on the street

4. **Excitement:** The view that "life" is all about the thrill of engaging in conflict and ripping people off

5. **Fate:** The belief that what happens in life is beyond one's control—whatever happens is meant to be

6. **Autonomy:** The intolerance of challenges to one's personal sphere—the need to stand up to anything or anyone

Source: Miller, W. B. (1958). Lower class culture as a generating milieu of gang delinquency. *Journal of Social Issues, 15*(3), 5–19. Reprinted by permission of John Wiley & Sons Inc.

Miller singles out the female-based household as another factor in producing gangs. He argues that in the lower classes, men do not fully participate in the rearing of children. Miller contends that young, lower-class males often go out on the streets to learn appropriate adult male behavior. In this context, the gang becomes the arena for demonstrating and exaggerating the core values (focal concerns) of the culture in an attempt to demonstrate manhood.

Qualitative data suggests that the focal concerns are an important influence in the development of gangs. For example, a former street gang leader interviewed by Weisfeld and Feldman stated that most members continued in crime because of adherence to the lower-class values of toughness, autonomy, and easy money.[97] The leader had become moderately successful as an independent businessman. He noted that crime is a bad bargain in the long run. Many of his friends had died on the streets. However, the advantages of legitimate work and the costs of crime are not apparent to most urban youths. He suggests, though, a policy implication more consistent with the work of Merton or Cloward and Ohlin—improving employment opportunities for young people.

Miller's work has been heavily criticized on a number of grounds. The strongest critiques center on his failure to put the focal concerns of the lower class in any kind of context. In other words, he essentially blames the lower class for having particular values without recognizing the effects that concentrated poverty and pervasive joblessness may play in generating values such as fate and autonomy.[98] Also, research suggests that many middle-class youth hold values and attitudes similar to those identified by Miller.

The work of Elijah Anderson appears to address some of these criticisms. Anderson argues that the "code of the streets" guides many lower-class youth.[99] This code is a set of informal rules that governs interpersonal public behavior. At the heart of this code is respect and fear of being disrespected, or "dissed." Under this code, actions that seem petty to middle-class people (e.g., maintaining eye contact for too long) may elicit violence. While similar to Miller's focal concerns, Anderson locates the cause of the code in the pervasiveness of racism, joblessness, alienation, and despair prevalent in the affected communities. Thus, the code is not simply attitudes held by particular individuals. Rather, it is a property of neighborhoods where poverty and despair are evident. He also points out that even in crime-prone areas, there are many "decent" families who have conventional, middle-class values.

A recent study found support for Anderson's central argument.[100] Using a sample of over 700 African Americans across 71 neighborhoods, the authors discovered that neighborhood street culture (e.g., responding to disrespect with violence, showing others that you cannot be intimidated) predicted violent delinquency. Neighborhood street culture mattered independent of an individual's own adoption of the code. In other words, living in an area where these values are promoted makes violence much more likely.

The experience of living in concentrated poverty also breeds cynicism toward social institutions. In particular, it can foster legal cynicism in which, "law and the agents of its enforcement are viewed as *illegitimate, unresponsive,* and *ill equipped* to ensure public safety."[101] Of course, this cultural belief is related to how people interact with police. When people experience the police as unresponsive, corrupt, or uncaring, they are less likely to report crime, or provide information about criminal activity to the police. The challenges of policing in such environments are explored in **Theory in Action: Place, Race, and Policing**.

A General Critique of Subcultural Explanations

In general, subcultural theories attempt to explain gang activity among lower-class boys. In other words, they have a very narrow scope. They cannot account for middle-class, upper-class (i.e., white-collar crime), or female offending. On the other hand, this perspective does provide a framework to study and examine gangs. The main theme is that gangs offer an opportunity to "be somebody" and achieve the status that has been denied by society.

Another general criticism is whether gangs are truly subcultures. The term *subculture* suggests that gangs are strong, cohesive units that have a distinct core of values that are subscribed to by all members. In contrast, some researchers portray many gangs as "near groups": less cohesive and structured than subcultural theories suggest.[102] Also, a substantial amount of research indicates that delinquents have rather conventional values but excuse or rationalize their criminal behavior. A related criticism of these theories is that they do not allow for individual deviance—individuals are always adequately socialized.[103] In subcultural theories, they are simply socialized toward the wrong set of values.

Policy Implications of Subcultural Theories

As touched on previously, subcultural theories have had an influence on social policy during the past three decades. The notion that blocked opportunities spawned crime was embraced by the Kennedy and Johnson administrations in the 1960s. In a sense, President Johnson's "War on Crime" and "War on Poverty" were fought on the same battleground, against the same enemies. Lack of economic and educational opportunities were viewed as the catalyst, breeding anomie or social hopelessness, which in turn led some individuals to crime.

Differential opportunity theory (along with strain theory) was particularly influential in the formation of delinquency policies and programs during this period. The Delinquency Prevention and Control Act of 1961 and President Lyndon B. Johnson's War on Poverty sought to increase educational and economic opportunities for the lower classes. The most notable example was the Mobilization for Youth Program (MFY) that Cloward and Ohlin actively supported. MFY attempted to attack the root causes of crime in New York City's Lower East Side by securing social services and establishing political structures in lower-class

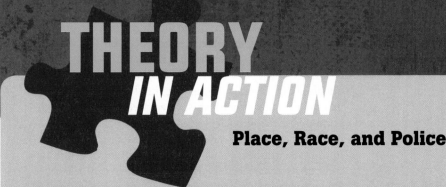

THEORY IN ACTION

Place, Race, and Police

Many of the theories in this chapter emphasize how crime becomes embedded in particular locations. Serious crime flourishes in areas with concentrated poverty, physical decay, weak social institutions, and limited opportunity for legitimate employment. This social context also creates a culture cynical toward social institutions, including law enforcement. Within American cities, these areas are disproportionately occupied by African American and Hispanic residents. This situation raises very difficult policy questions, especially for law enforcement. How should neighborhoods that are rife with both economic inequality and violent crime be policed?

As discussed in Chapter 3, law enforcement departments rely on different models of policing. Community oriented policing (COP) emphasizes police–citizen dialogue. Law enforcement officers are called upon to help strengthen neighborhoods and build a sense of community. Officers might walk a foot patrol, operate out of small neighborhood "substations," or organize informal neighborhood watch–type programs. In the language of social disorganization theory, police try to build collective efficacy. Research finds that many COP initiatives reduce fear of crime and improve police–citizen relations. Unfortunately, there is less evidence that the initiatives reduce crime.

In contrast, broken windows, or zero tolerance policing models advise aggressive police response to any form of disorder. The belief is that when disorder is allowed in public spaces, criminals become emboldened. Also, law abiding citizens start to avoid these areas. Here, police may saturate high crime neighborhoods, "stop and frisk" residents, and arrest many people for public order crimes such as loitering, public intoxication, drug use, and prostitution. Such tactics can suppress serious crime, especially in the short term. Over time though, heavy handed policing can create an "us versus them" mentality for both police and residents. Residents of the neighborhood become cynical about the criminal justice system, especially police. Racial divisions and allegations of police brutality further fuel mistrust.

The protests and riots that erupted in Baltimore in April of 2015 illustrate many of these issues. The flashpoint for the riots was the death of Freddie Gray, a black man who died while in the custody of police. According to police reports, Gray was arrested at the end of a long foot chase after he "fled unprovoked" from an area known for drug dealing. Although details are still emerging, Gray suffered a fatal spinal injury after being driven in a police van. An investigation from the *Baltimore Sun* revealed that this was not an isolated incident. In fact, the city had paid out almost six million dollars in the preceding 4 years for court judgments or settlements for police brutality cases. One reporter and lifelong resident of the city, citing the mix of pervasive poverty,

crime, hopelessness, and alleged policing brutality, stated that "it was just a matter of time before Baltimore exploded."

Certainly, police cannot be expected to fix the structural problems of these troubled communities. Still, many police departments are seeking a middle ground between zero tolerance and COP. The focused deterrence programs (see Chapter 3) of David Kennedy and his colleagues are one example. Within these programs, police work with researchers and community members to crack down on specific crimes (juvenile gang homicides, or a particular drug market) without targeting the whole community. The federal weed-and-seed strategy that operated from 1991–2010 is another example. The "weeding" occurred when chronic violent offenders were incapacitated. The "seeding" consisted of programs designed to bring human services to the area and promote economic and physical revitalization in neighborhoods. In this model, law enforcement works with the community to gain information regarding who needs "weeding" and to aid residents in obtaining information about community revitalization and seeding resources.

Sources: Puente, M. (2014, September 28). Undo force. *Baltimore Sun*. Retrieved June 10, 2015, from http://data.baltimoresun.com/news/police-settlements; Fletcher, M. A. (2015, April 28). What you really need to know about Baltimore, from a reporter who's lived there for over 30 years. *The Washington Post*. Retrieved June 10, 2015, from http://www.washingtonpost.com/blogs/wonkblog/wp/2015/04/28/; Seabrook, J. (2009, June 22). Don't shoot. *The New Yorker*, 32–42; Dunworth, T., & Mills, G. (1999). National evaluation of Weed and Seed. *Research in Brief*. Washington, DC: National Institute of Justice.

The death of Freddie Gray in April 2015, while in police custody, sparked protests and riots in Baltimore.
© Matt Rourke/AP Photo

neighborhoods. A focus on political structure differentiated this program from other community projects:[104]

> ... the problem with employment was not simply that minorities lacked skills but that they were excluded from union apprenticeships; the problem of poor educational opportunities was a matter not simply of youths lacking books in the home but also of policies that assigned the newest and least talented teachers to schools in slum neighborhoods.

As it turns out, the focus on politics was MYF's undoing. The program became embroiled in political struggles with city officials, was investigated by the FBI (but exonerated of any wrongdoing), and ultimately disappeared. On the one hand, there is little available evidence that MYF reduced delinquency. On the other hand, it suggests the enormous difficulty of trying to achieve broad social change.[105]

 Conclusion

This chapter outlines two broad theoretical traditions, the social disorganization and anomie/strain perspectives, and discusses how each contains themes and ideas from the work of Durkheim. **FIGURE 6-5** demonstrates the relationships among these theories. The key assumption shared by these perspectives is that aspects of the social structure can promote crime. Because of this, the theories focus on "big picture" issues that tend to otherwise get neglected.[106] In criminology, the vast majority of crime theories focus on individual offenders. In contrast, social structural theories often use macro-level units of analysis such as street segments, neighborhoods, and even societies. Since a street segment or neighborhood cannot simply be interviewed like a person, research in this area can be difficult. Yet, advances in data collection, computer software, and theorizing over the past 20 years have led to renewed interest in this type of research. **TABLE 6-4** outlines each of the theories covered in this chapter and describes their key concepts and policy implications.

Social disorganization theory, which evolved from the work of Chicago School theorists, highlights how ecological features of a neighborhood such as poverty and residential mobility can interfere with community cohesion and informal control. In turn, a lack of collective efficacy in a neighborhood allows crime to flourish. More recently, theorists note that over the past 30 years, such neighborhoods have become concentrated and isolated from mainstream society. An effective policy implication based on these insights remains elusive. Nevertheless, this theory of place speaks directly to some of criminology's most difficult questions regarding race, crime, and the criminal justice system. In particular, Shaw and McKay found high delinquency rates

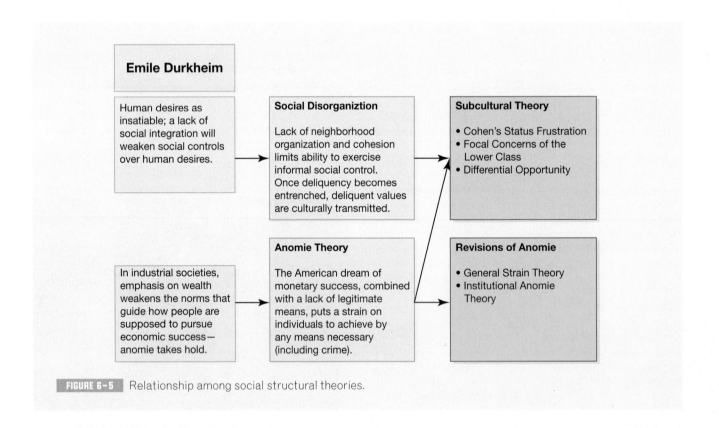

FIGURE 6-5 Relationship among social structural theories.

TABLE 6-4

Summary of Social Structural Theories

Theory and Major Authors	Core Elements	Policy Implications
Anomie/Strain Tradition		
Robert Merton Anomie/strain theory	Most people recognize culturally approved goals and means to achieve them. Anomie develops when access to the approved means is blocked. Adaptation to anomie takes forms: ritualism, retreatism, innovation, rebellion, and conformity. Crime is primarily the result of innovation; the criminal uses illegal means to achieve the culturally approved goal of success.	Reduce poverty; provide legitimate opportunities for success to members of the lower class.
Robert Agnew General strain theory	Strain comes from three broad sources: (1) failure to achieve a goal, (2) presence of a noxious stimulus, and (3) the removal of positively valued stimuli. Strain produces negative emotional states (anger, depression) that, without adequate coping skills, are conducive to delinquency.	Because most people will encounter strain, focus on the ability to cope with strain (e.g., anger management, cognitive skills).
Steven Messner and Richard Rosenfeld Institutional anomie theory	Macro-level (country/society) theory that predicts high crime rates based on culture and social structure. In cultures that place intense value on economic success, the norms guiding how a person attains wealth become weak. When the economy dominates and weakens those institutions responsible for socializing children (school, family), high crime rates result.	Push the culture of society away from a focus on money and toward the recognition that other roles are important. Increase the strength of socializing institutions—for example, employer-sponsored childcare.
Chicago School		
Clifford Shaw and Henry McKay Social disorganization theory	A macro-level (neighborhood) theory. Crime rates are stable and high in areas with certain ecological features (high poverty, population mobility, physical decay). These features impede social organization and cohesion and prevent informal control of delinquency. Once crime is prevalent, delinquent norms and values are culturally transmitted to others and compete with normative values.	Target for change those ecological factors that relate to cohesion and control (or collective efficacy). Promote neighborhood cohesion and informal social control.
Subcultural Theories		
Albert Cohen Status frustration	Delinquency is largely a lower-class phenomenon. The delinquent experiences status frustration and a loss of self-esteem. To combat this loss, the delinquent ridicules what is valued in society and develops a subculture that recognizes and rewards delinquent values.	Unclear; perhaps prepare lower-class youth for school (Head Start programs).

(Continued)

TABLE 6-4 (CONTINUED)

Summary of Social Structural Theories

Theory and Major Authors	Core Elements	Policy Implications
Richard Cloward and Lloyd Ohlin Differential opportunity theory	As with Merton's theory, strain is primarily caused by a lack of legitimate opportunities for success (good job, education) among the lower class. Blocked economic aspirations lead to a poor self-image and this frustration leads to delinquency. The form that delinquency takes, however, depends upon whether access to illegitimate means for success (drug dealing, pimping) are also denied. Where illegitimate opportunities are present, criminal gangs will occur. In neighborhoods without a criminal structure, conflict gangs are more likely.	Provide legitimate opportunities for success to members of the lower class.
Walter Miller Focal concerns of the lower class	Six focal concerns of the lower class foster delinquency: trouble, toughness, smartness, excitement, fate, and autonomy. The lower-class youth responds to these values and develops a subculture of delinquency. The predominance of female-based households contributes to this problem. Lower-class adolescents often go out on the streets to learn appropriate adult male behavior.	Unclear; theory suggests crime could be reduced by changing the values of the lower class or reducing the incidence of female-based, single-parent households.

in the zone in transition, regardless of what racial or ethnic group occupied this area. This is a powerful argument against those who view all crime as simply a personal and moral failure.

The anomie tradition also points to the importance of the social structure. Many of these theories suggest that economic stratification generates crime. In particular, they imply that blocked economic opportunity causes some to search for illegitimate ways to achieve status or monetary success. Thus, unless these economic forces are dealt with directly, a certain level of crime will be built into a society.

Some scholars note that there is a relationship between these two perspectives. For example, factors that promote strain, such as poverty and lack of opportunity, are most prevalent in socially disorganized communities.[107]

The subcultural theories of Cohen and Cloward and Ohlin also linked these two perspectives together. In these theories, strain causes the formation of delinquent subcultures, which are then maintained through a process of cultural transmission of values.

Of course, a focus on the lower class has drawn some criticism. With few exceptions (general strain theory, institutional anomie), these theories cannot explain white-collar crime or in many cases middle-class street crimes. Also, these theories tend to overpredict crime among the lower class.[108] In fact, the majority of people who reside in high crime areas are actually law-abiding citizens. Despite such limitations, social structural theories remain the most viable explanations of group differences (neighborhood, country) in crime rates.

- The major premise of social structural theories is that criminality is rooted in the very structure of society.
- Emile Durkheim's work serves as a foundation for the American theoretical traditions of social disorganization and anomie. Durkheim wrote about the importance of community ties and the need to control the insatiable desires of humans. He also believed that the pursuit of monetary wealth ("industrial prosperity") was criminogenic.
- The Chicago School of crime focused attention on ecological characteristics of the city. Early research by Shaw and McKay demonstrated that crime rates were consistently high in the "zone in transition." Eventually, social disorganization theory emerged as an explanation of why some neighborhoods are more crime prone than others. Modern social disorganization theorists argue that ecological factors (e.g., residential mobility, concentrated poverty) inhibit a neighborhood's collective efficacy, which in turn increases crime.
- The policy implication of social disorganization theory is to increase collective efficacy among neighborhoods or to change the ecological factors in a way (e.g., increase home ownership, repair or demolish dilapidated buildings) that would increase collective efficacy.
- Robert K. Merton argued that the disjuncture between culturally valued goals (the American dream) and the availability of the institutionalized means for success (e.g., job, education) produced a strain. Individual

reactions to strain might include rebellion, retreatism, ritualism, or innovation.
- Robert Agnew's general strain theory (GST) is a revision of Merton's theory that operates at the individual level. In GST, there are many causes of strain. Agnew argues that strain produces "negative emotional states," such as anger, that are conducive to crime. People react differently to strain based on their coping abilities.
- Institutional anomie theory updates Merton at the macro level. Messner and Rosenfeld argue that the American dream culture causes Americans to pursue success through any (including criminal) means. Furthermore, they believe that the economy dominates the institutions (e.g., family, education system) that are responsible for socializing children.
- The policy implications of the strain/anomie tradition depend upon the particular theory in question. Merton's theory suggests that increasing economic opportunity would reduce crime. GST points to factors such as anger management and constructive coping.
- Subcultural theories attempt to explain the formation and activities of street gangs. Cohen explains the content of street gang activity (e.g., malicious, negativistic) as a reaction to middle-class values. Cloward and Ohlin argue that the availability of both legitimate and illegitimate opportunities shape the formation of street gangs. Miller suggests that the lower class has a core set of values that differ from middle-class values—these "focal concerns" of the lower class are criminogenic.

1. Use Merton's anomie theory to explain the rise of a gangster such as Al Capone. In your own words, describe the societal pressures that might have been operating at that time and what means of adaptation that gangsters might have used.

2. Some theorists claim that juvenile gangs are subcultures. What evidence would you cite to support such a claim? What is the evidence against such a claim?

3. What is "concentrated disadvantage"? How does disadvantage become concentrated and isolated?

4. Merton's theory of anomie assumes that "money is the root of all evil." Does society's emphasis on material success cause crime?

5. Prior to the Chicago School, many argued that the city and immigrants of poor stock caused crime. How did the work of Shaw and McKay refute these arguments?

6. What is the policy implication of social disorganization theory?

7. Describe one revision of Merton's anomie theory. How is the revised theory similar and different from Merton's original theory?

KEY TERMS

altruistic criminal Defined by Durkheim as a person somehow offended by the rules of society who wishes to change those rules for the better. This "criminal" is motivated by a sense of duty to improve society.

anomie Term coined by Durkheim to describe a state of affairs in which the norms and values of society weaken and are no longer able to control behaviors.

Chicago Area Project (CAP) A large-scale delinquency prevention program developed by Shaw and McKay. The projects targeted high crime neighborhoods and created "community committees" to promote community organization; assigned "detached" local adults to neighborhood gangs; and made efforts to improve sanitation, traffic control, and physical decay.

code of the streets A set of informal rules that governs public behavior in some inner city neighborhoods. Caused in part by pervasive racism, joblessness, and alienation, the code emphasizes the importance of not being disrespected, or "dissed."

collective efficacy The combination of social cohesion and informal social control within a neighborhood.

common criminal Defined by Durkheim as a person who rejects all laws and discipline and purposely violates the law without concern for the rightness of the acts.

concentrated disadvantage The idea that poverty and unemployment have become concentrated within certain neighborhoods, leaving isolated pockets of "truly disadvantaged" citizens.

legal cynicism A set of cultural values that arise in communities with concentrated disadvantage and coercive policing. The law and the police come to be viewed as ineffective and illegitimate.

mechanical solidarity Term used by Durkheim to describe rural societies that are homogeneous, cohesive, and self-sufficient.

middle-class measuring rod Term used by Cohen to describe a school system that favored middle-class dress, mannerisms, and etiquette. Cohen argued that lower-class boys were often unable to meet these standards, and therefore experienced strain, or "status frustration."

Mobilization for Youth Program (MFY) A program that Cloward and Ohlin actively supported.

MFY attempted to attack the root causes of crime in New York City's Lower East Side by securing social services and establishing political structures in lower-class neighborhoods. The program became embroiled in political struggles with city officials, was investigated by the FBI (but exonerated of any wrongdoing), and ultimately disappeared.

organic solidarity Term used by Durkheim to describe industrial societies, which are more complex and based on exchanges of goods and services.

Project on Human Development in Chicago Neighborhoods (PHDCN) A program where researchers interviewed almost 9,000 residents within 343 Chicago neighborhoods. Research results have largely supported the theory of collective efficacy.

racial invariance hypothesis The idea that race differences in crime are due to differences in where people live. Because nonwhites are more apt to live in areas of concentrated disadvantage, they experience higher rates of crime.

social ecology The study of how human relationships are affected by a particular environment (the Chicago School is based on social ecology).

weed-and-seed strategy A federal initiative designed to reduce violent crime, drug abuse, and gang activity in targeted high crime neighborhoods across the country. The "weeding out" involves targeting chronic violent offenders for incapacitation. The "seeding" consists of programs designed to bring human services to the area and promote economic and physical revitalization to neighborhoods.

zone in transition In Burgess' concentric zone theory, this is the geographical area just outside the business district. Research by Shaw and McKay confirmed that the zone in transition had consistently high crime rates from 1900–1930.

The infectiousness of crime is like that of the plague.

—**Attributed to Napoleon Bonaparte**[1]

The question, "Why do we do it [crime]?" is simply not the question the theory is designed to answer.

The question is, "Why don't we do it?" There is much evidence that we would if we dared.

—**Travis Hirschi**[2]

Social Process and Crime

Objectives

Introduction

This chapter covers theories of crime that focus on the interplay between the individual and society. As with social-structural theories, process theories have developed within broad theoretical traditions. The theories in this chapter are organized into three such traditions: differential association/social learning, informal social control, and labeling.

The aim of social process theory is to discover how social influences like family life, employment, and friendships shape individuals over time. Social process theories assume that there is a vital interplay between the environment, the individual, and criminal behavior. Many of these theories emphasize the process of socialization. Socialization is the gradual process whereby a person learns the "proper" way to live, including the norms and values that guide human behavior. Because each of us belongs to society, the socialization process affects us all.

Two theoretical traditions within this chapter focus explicitly on socialization. Informal social control theories suggest that inadequate or incomplete socialization leads to criminal behavior. Often, these are referred to simply as control theories. The full name, however, distinguishes this tradition from the formal social control of deterrence theory (see Chapter 3). Social learning theories focus on adequate socialization toward the incorrect norms and values. In other words, children are indeed socialized, but they are socialized to accept criminal norms and values.

Within the social learning and social control perspectives, socialization occurs through interaction with social institutions. These institutions provide information regarding proper behavior and social expectations. Although some theories touch on education or religion, the primary socializing institutions are most often the family and the peer group.

Both the informal social control and social learning perspectives flow directly from the work of the Chicago School theorists and early versions of social disorganization theory. In social disorganization theory, characteristics of neighborhoods (e.g., poverty, residential mobility) increase crime rates because they limit informal social control within the community. Also, once crime rates increase, delinquent cultural values (recall the "code of the streets") emerge and spread through a process of "cultural transmission."

Different authors pursued these two aspects of social disorganization (a macro-level theory) and applied them at the individual level. Thus, authors who focused on cultural transmission pursued theories of differential association and social learning. Those who focused on informal control attempted to explain in detail how institutions socialized individuals. FIGURE 7-1 illustrates the relationship between the Chicago School and these theoretical traditions.

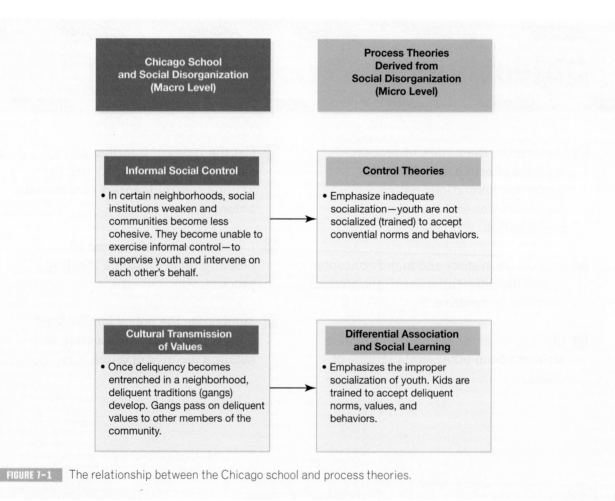

FIGURE 7-1 The relationship between the Chicago school and process theories.

The third type of process theory covered in this chapter is **labeling** theory. The labeling perspective focuses on how a person's self-concept may cause them to engage in crime. This tradition places emphasis on interactions between individuals and institutions of formal control (e.g., police, courts, prisons). In particular, labeling theorists suggest that contact with police and the courts may have a negative impact on a youth's self-image. Thus, formal interventions with children and adolescents may actually increase their criminal behavior.

A great deal of overlap exists between some sociological process theories and the psychology tradition of behaviorism. Sociologists have borrowed heavily from psychologists to explain how socialization unfolds over time. For example, sociological learning theories use operant conditioning and role modeling to explain criminal behavior. Control theories emphasize parental use of operant conditioning to directly control the behavior of their children. Learning, social control, and labeling perspectives are also evident in developmental theories of crime (see Chapter 9).

Differential Association and Social Learning Theory

Social learning theorists argue that people become criminals much as they become anything else—through learning. In other words, the same techniques are involved in learning to change a tire, rob a bank, or hide criminal activity. Convicted serial killer Ted Bundy, for example, once explained how he diminished his vulnerability to detection when disposing of bodies. He would park on a curve so that he could see cars approaching from either direction. He learned this technique from a movie about a killer who had done the same thing. Asked how old he was when he saw this movie, Bundy replied he must have been 12 or 13 years old. That movie did not turn Ted Bundy into a serial murderer; a whole variety of life experiences made him what he was. However, Bundy did learn this particular method of concealment.

Social learning theorists emphasize the influence of primary groups and significant others (admired individuals) on individual behavior. These are the key factors in the socialization process that help guide the individual into either criminal or law-abiding behavior.

Tarde's Law of Imitation

Nineteenth-century French criminologist Gabriel Tarde was unique in his rejection of the biological and physical theories

> *Social learning theorists emphasize the influence of primary groups and significant others (admired individuals) on individual behavior.*

of crime causation. Tarde launched an offensive against the idea of the "born criminal" (see Chapter 4). He argued that regional differences in crime rates were caused more by local variations in levels of poverty and alcoholism than biological factors.[3]

Tarde also believed that criminality was a "profession," learned through interaction with and imitation of others.[4] His **laws of imitation** attempt to explain criminality as a function of association with "criminal types."[5] In this sense, a criminal goes through a period of "apprenticeship," similar to that of a doctor, lawyer, or skilled worker. Tarde developed three laws of imitation to account for criminal behavior and imitation. The first law states that people are more likely to imitate one another if they are in close contact. Thus, in active, densely packed towns or cities, imitation is most frequent.[6] The second law states that inferiors imitate superiors; crime originates in higher ranks and descends to the lowest ranks. The third law states that when two fashions come together, one can be substituted for the other. When this process of insertion occurs, there is a decline in the older method and an increase in the newer method.[7]

Another aspect of imitation was that certain forms of crime tended to originate in capital cities. For example, cutting corpses into pieces became a trend in Paris in 1876.[8] In recent times, large metropolitan cities like Los Angeles or New York have often been the sites of new crime fashions, such as drive-by shootings and carjacking. These crimes have then cropped up in other parts of the country. Internationally, terrorist tactics such as hijacking planes or Internet-posted beheadings seem to follow a similar pattern.[9,10]

Sutherland's Theory of Differential Association

Edwin Sutherland moved Tarde's laws of imitation toward the general framework of the Chicago School of crime. Sutherland received his doctorate in sociology from the University of Chicago in 1913 and held a professorship there from 1930 to 1935.[11] In his 1939 *Principles of Criminology*, Sutherland outlined his **theory of differential association**. This theory speaks to the central Chicago School question: Why does crime remain stable in certain areas despite high population turnover? In keeping with the Chicago School, his theory elaborates on one Chicago School answer: the cultural transmission of delinquent values. It is important to note, however, that Sutherland did not buy into the full Chicago School explanation for crime. He argued, for example, that the lower class was not "disorganized." Instead, he preferred "differential social organization" to make clear that the lower class are not by nature either inadequate or dysfunctional.[12]

Sutherland expressed his theory of differential association as a series of nine fundamental principles:[13]

1. Criminal behavior is learned. Negatively, this means that criminal behavior is not inherited, as such; also, the person who is not already trained in crime does not invent criminal behavior, just as a person does not make mechanical inventions unless he or she has had training in mechanics.

2. Criminal behavior is learned in interaction with other persons in a process of communication. This communication is verbal in many respects, but also includes the communication of gestures.

3. The principal part of the learning of criminal behavior occurs within intimate personal groups. Negatively, this means that the impersonal agencies of communication, such as movies and newspapers, play a relatively unimportant part in the genesis of criminal behavior.

4. Learning criminal behavior includes learning the techniques of committing the crime, which are sometimes very complicated, and learning the specific direction of motives, drives, rationalizations, and attitudes.

5. The specific direction of motives and drives is learned from definitions of the legal codes as favorable or unfavorable. In some societies, an individual is surrounded by persons who invariably define the legal codes as rules to be observed, while in others he or she is surrounded by persons whose definitions are favorable to the violation of the legal codes. In American society, these definitions are almost always mixed, with the consequence that there is cultural conflict in relation to legal codes.

6. A person becomes delinquent because of an excess of definitions favorable to violations of the law over definitions favorable of the law. This is the principle of differential association. It refers to both criminal and anticriminal associations and has to do with counteracting forces. When persons become criminal, they do so because of contacts with criminal patterns and also because of isolation from anticriminal patterns.

7. Differential association may vary in frequency, duration, priority, and intensity. This means that associations with criminal behavior and also associations with anticriminal behavior vary in those respects. "Frequency" and "duration" as modalities of associations are obvious and need no explanation. "Priority" is assumed to be important in the sense that lawful behavior developed in early childhood may persist throughout life, and also that delinquent behavior developed in early childhood may persist throughout life. "Intensity" is not precisely defined but it has to do with such things as the prestige of the source of a criminal or anticriminal pattern and with emotional reactions related to the associations.

8. The process of learning criminal behavior by association with criminal and anticriminal patterns involves all of the mechanisms that are involved in any other learning. Negatively, this means that the learning of a criminal behavior is not restricted to the process of imitation. A person who is seduced, for instance, learns criminal behavior by association, but this process would not ordinarily be described as imitation.

9. Although criminal behavior is an expression of general needs and values, it is not explained by those general needs and values, because noncriminal behavior is an expression of the same needs and values. Thieves generally steal in order to secure money, but likewise honest laborers work in order to secure money. The attempts by many scholars to explain criminal behavior through general drives and values, such as the happiness principle, striving for social status, the money motive, or frustration, have been and will continue to be futile because they explain lawful behavior as completely as they explain criminal behavior. They are like breathing, which is a prerequisite for any behavior, but which does not differentiate criminal from noncriminal behavior.

In short, Sutherland believed that people learn how to commit crimes mostly through primary group interactions; that is, through contact with others in intimate personal groups. Intimate personal groups might include one's family or set of friends. Sutherland was obviously skeptical of the idea that crime was learned through impersonal sources such as movies or television. This skepticism remains in updated versions of Sutherland's theory. In general, sociologists have been more doubtful than psychologists that television and movies impact behavior. Lessons learned within the socialization process include not only the techniques of committing crime, but also the motives, attitudes, and rationalizations that support it. These are described as "definitions," or how one defines a situation or behavior. Definitions can either be consistent with or in opposition to the legal code. In particular, he noted that this process involved more than mere imitation—a reference, perhaps, to Tarde.

Sutherland's theory has been roundly criticized. The primary reason for this is the theory's vague concepts and phrasings, which make it difficult to test empirically. For example, what exactly is a definition and how might a person measure this concept? Also, to say that learning criminal behavior involves all of the mechanisms that are involved in any other learning does not really explain how behavior is learned. What exactly are the "mechanisms"?[14]

Still, there is little question that Sutherland's contribution advanced the scientific development of criminology beyond biological determinism. Differential association gave a new direction and intellectual respectability to American criminology.[15] Despite its limitations, this theory became a dominant paradigm in criminology.[16] More importantly, this dominance led to efforts to restate differential association in a clearer and more testable manner.

From Differential Association to Social Learning

The modification of differential association theory primarily involved borrowing principles of psychological behaviorism to explain the mechanics of learning. In the first revision, Ronald Akers and Robert Burgess created

Sutherland stated that the "impersonal agencies of communication" such as movies were relatively unimportant in causing crime. Would he still feel this way about modern mass media?

© Photos.com/Getty

differential reinforcement theory by adding the concept of operant conditioning (see Chapter 5).[17] Later, Akers added the concept of imitation and changed the title of the theory from differential reinforcement to social learning theory.[18] In addition to specifying the mechanisms of learning, these theorists also attempted to clarify the exact meaning of definitions. Akers' current social learning theory has four central concepts:[19]

1. **Differential associations:** In keeping with Sutherland, this is the notion that people are exposed throughout life to different sorts of people (role models) and different attitudes and values. Some of these people will model criminal behavior and communicate values or attitudes that are consistent with such behavior.

2. **Definitions:** Akers describes definitions as "one's own attitudes or meaning that one attaches to given behavior . . . that define the commission of an act as right or wrong, good or bad, desirable or undesirable, justified or unjustified."[20]

3. **Differential reinforcement:** The balance of anticipated or actual rewards or punishments that are consequences of behavior. These rewards can be social (praise, status)

or more tangible (money, property). Reinforcement can also be internal (reinforcing or punishing oneself).

4. **Imitation:** This concept is the same as vicarious learning within psychology. Others serve as role models for behaviors. Individual characteristics of the models, and whether the models' behavior is rewarded, determine whether the model is imitated.

The concepts of differential association and definitions stem directly from Sutherland, and differential reinforcement and imitation are drawn from psychology. Like differential association theory, Akers emphasizes that not all sources of definitions or role models are equal. Some people, such as parents and close friends, will be more important than others.

FIGURE 7-2 provides a basic sequence that organizes these concepts. Akers suggests that differential associations— exposure to different people and values—over time will produce an initial set of behaviors. To the extent that one is exposed to deviant role models and/or deviant values, delinquent behavior becomes more likely. Whether delinquency is repeated over time depends primarily upon reinforcement.[21] Recall that, according to behaviorism, behavior

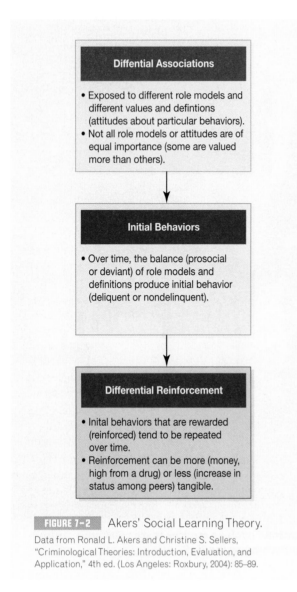

FIGURE 7-2 Akers' Social Learning Theory.

Data from Ronald L. Akers and Christine S. Sellers, "Criminological Theories: Introduction, Evaluation, and Application," 4th ed. (Los Angeles: Roxbury, 2004): 85–89.

Diffential Associations

- Exposed to different role models and different values and defintions (attitudes about particular behaviors).
- Not all role models or attitudes are of equal importance (some are valued more than others).

Initial Behaviors

- Over time, the balance (prosocial or deviant) of role models and definitions produce initial behavior (deliquent or nondelinquent).

Differential Reinforcement

- Inital behaviors that are rewarded (reinforced) tend to be repeated over time.
- Reinforcement can be more (money, high from a drug) or less (increase in status among peers) tangible.

is strengthened when positive rewards are gained (positive reinforcement) and weakened when punished.

Consider a hypothetical child named Johnny whose parents are true "children of the 1960s" and still regularly smoke marijuana. As Johnny grows up, he is likely to be exposed to attitudes that support marijuana use. His parents might say that marijuana is "no worse than alcohol" or that "the real crime is that marijuana is illegal." If the parents smoke in Johnny's presence, they are role modeling the specific techniques (smoking instruments, etc.) involved. In this context, it would be more likely that at some point, Johnny would try marijuana. To the extent that this experience is rewarding (Johnny likes the "buzz"; his status among peers increases), he is likely to repeat this behavior in the future. If he experiences punishment (he gets paranoid and "freaks out"; his peers disapprove), he is less likely to repeat the behavior.

Of course, social learning theory is more complex than either the outline or Johnny story indicate. The full explanation for Johnny's behavior would have to include all of the role models and attitudes he was exposed to over time, including those that did not favor the use of marijuana. Furthermore,

future role models and attitudes would continue to have an impact. As noted in the discussion of psychological theories of learning, tests of social learning tend to be (necessarily) limited and indirect.

Differential association and social learning theory have been the subject of a great deal of empirical research. Criminologist Travis Pratt and his colleagues reviewed the research conducted on social learning theory over the last 35 years. Their meta-analysis revealed strong support for measures of definitions (e.g., attitudes or beliefs that support crime) and differential associations (delinquent behaviors or attitudes among peers, siblings, or parents). Imitation (admired models witnessed) and differential reinforcement (peer/parent reactions to crime) had weaker relationships to crime.[22]

Akers and his associates studied a sample of more than 3,000 male and female children in Grades 7 through 12.[23] They found that measures of attitudes, associations, and reinforcement predicted both alcohol and drug use. Recent research continues to reveal strong relationships between measures of social learning and a wide range of outcomes, including smoking, computer crimes, gang-related delinquency, and other forms of criminal or delinquent activity.[24,25] For example, researchers surveyed 9th grade students in an attempt to explain gang involvement and gang-related delinquency. The researchers found that social learning measures predicted whether or not a person was involved in a gang, and their involvement in both gang and nongang forms of delinquency.[26]

Many studies on social learning focus exclusively on either antisocial attitudes or delinquent peer associations. In Chapter 5, antisocial attitudes were described as "criminal-thinking errors" in the context of cognitive psychology. In sociology, the most widely known terminology to describe this same concept is Sykes and Matza's **techniques of neutralization**. In one of the first tests of differential association theory, Sykes and Matza documented common rationalizations for delinquency among a sample of delinquents.[27] The techniques of neutralization are outlined in **TABLE 7-1**.

For example, delinquents denied injury, claiming they didn't really hurt anyone (The guy had insurance, didn't he?). Modern research continues to document relationships between neutralizations or other antisocial attitudes and different forms of crime. One study determined that older employees who stole and sabotaged production in their workplace engaged in both denial of injury and denial of the victim.[28] A case study of two hit men found that professional killers manage stigma through the neutralization process of "reframing." Basically, they redefined the victim as a "target" rather than a person. This allowed them to deny the victim, the injury, and responsibility.[29]

A common criticism of such findings is that such attitudes do not actually cause criminal behavior. Critics suggest that rationalization or justifications are utilized after the offense is committed and only when such behavior is called into question.[30] As noted in Chapter 5, even where this is

Social learning theorists argue that youths learn delinquent behavior from their peers. Critics believe peers and crime are related because, "birds of a feather flock together."

© Doug Menuez/Photodisc/Getty Images

true, it does not mean that rationalizations are unimportant. To the extent that these rationalizations neutralize guilt, they reinforce criminal behavior. There is evidence from the rehabilitation literature that changing these attitudes reduces crime.

Association with delinquent peers is by far the most common measure of the social learning theory. Indeed, many people consider delinquent peers and social learning synonymous. Social learning emphasizes associations with those who engage in crime because they serve as role models and communicate deviant values and attitudes. Therefore, individuals who are surrounded by others who engage in crime should be more prone to engage in crime themselves. In a review of this research, Mark Warr argues: "Few, if any, empirical regularities in criminology have been documented as often or over as long a period as the association between delinquency and delinquent friends."[31] He suggests that no characteristic of an individual is a better prediction of crime and delinquency than delinquent peer associations.

In virtually every study where a measure of delinquent peers is included, the measure strongly predicts delinquency or crime. Furthermore, this is not simply a matter of whether a person has one delinquent friend. Research has documented a

---

TABLE 7-1

Sykes and Matza's Techniques of Neutralization

1. **Denial of responsibility:** The offender argues that the act was caused by factors (e.g., a broken home, poverty, or peers) outside of his or her control. The youth thus claims to be a good person who was led astray.

2. **Denial of injury:** The offender insists no one was really hurt by the criminal act; that is, the injured party (e.g., wealthy person) can easily overcome the impact of the transgression (e.g., stolen property).

3. **Denial of victim:** The offender sees no real victim here. A social distance is placed between the offender and the victim. Beating up a rival gang member, "bashing the queers," and rolling street people are all examples of the victimization of devalued persons. The victims' status deprives them of their humanity.

4. **Condemnation of the condemners:** The offender rationalizes that "everybody is crooked" (e.g., public officials are "on the take" or "the cops beat innocent people"). By shifting the responsibility for their own delinquency to others, youths consider themselves undeserving of punishment.

5. **Appeal to higher loyalties:** The gang member often commits crimes "for the sake of the group." Loyalty becomes a license to commit crime and places gang members above the law.

Data from Gresham Sykes and David Matza, "Techniques of Neutralization: A Theory of Delinquency," *American Sociological Review* 22 (1958): 664–670.

connection between the proportion of a person's friends who were delinquent and their own delinquency.[32] Increases in this proportion corresponded with increases in delinquency. For example, youths who had all delinquent friends were twice as likely to engage in delinquency as youths with a mix of delinquent and nondelinquent friends.

There is even evidence that criminal behavior is learned through an explicit tutelage process. A recent study of Canadian inmates found that one-third of them were introduced into a criminal environment by a specific mentor. Typically, the mentors were much older and had a longstanding, strong relationship with the inmate.[33] Of course, researchers have also examined the effect of having criminal parents or siblings. As noted in earlier chapters, it is true that crime runs in families. Having a parent or sibling with a criminal history substantially increases the odds of a person engaging in crime.[34]

Although few criminologists question the strength of these relationships, many have questioned their meaning. For example, biology-oriented criminologists are likely to see crime within families as the result of genetics. A common non-social learning interpretation of the peer–crime correlation is that "birds of a feather will flock together."[35] In other words, kids are not learning criminal behavior from their friends. Rather, delinquent youths attract one another as friends. Untangling the peer–crime relationship is difficult, but more sophisticated research has provided some insight into the issue. One key has been the use of longitudinal research. For example, a study using data from five consecutive waves of the National Youth Survey found some evidence that like-minded delinquents attract each other. Those who engage in delinquency at an early point in time were more likely to have delinquent friends at a later time. Even so, peer relations (exposure to delinquent peers, time spent with peers, loyalty to peers) still had an impact on future delinquency.[36]

Jean McGloin took a slightly different approach to studying peers and crime. She examined the criminality of individuals and their closest friends. The largest changes in behavior over time were found among friends who had the largest differences in initial criminal behavior. A prosocial person with a crime-prone friend was more likely to engage in crime at a later time. Conversely, a crime-prone individual with a conventional person as a close friend became less likely to offend.[37] More recently, improvements in data collection and analysis techniques have allowed researchers to track entire "social networks" over time. Here, youth are provided with a list of other students in their school and are asked to indicate their friends. Information is then collected from all of the youth so that researchers can map both friendship and crime patterns over time. A recent study of social networks and crime in a sample of Dutch students found evidence that supports social learning theory. Youth with a higher average delinquency among their peers increased their own delinquency over time. Furthermore, leaving or joining an informal peer group was related to changes in delinquency.[38]

In short, some studies find that birds of a feather do sometimes flock together. Despite this, peers *also* appear to have a causal influence on future behavior. These findings led Akers to counter the bird metaphor with his own animal metaphor—people who "lay down with dogs, wake up with fleas."[39] The relationship between delinquent peers and delinquency continues to generate debate and controversy within criminology.

Aside from attitudes (definitions) and peer associations, researchers have examined the role of reinforcement. For example, an analysis of survey data from 1,600 high school students revealed that they engaged in substance abuse for the thrill of the experience. Illicit drug use was rewarding because it created a psychological high and provided excitement.[40] As noted in Chapter 3, successful robbers are reinforced by the money or property obtained and by less tangible rewards such as excitement or a boost in their reputation. As this connection suggests, there is a relationship between rational choice or deterrence theory and social learning. Each of these theories predict that when rewards outweigh punishments, certain types of behavior will result. As noted elsewhere, Akers believes that deterrence (formal punishment) could be easily absorbed into social learning theory.

In sum, Akers' social learning theory, which was built on the framework of differential association theory, has accumulated a great deal of empirical support. To be sure, the theory is not without criticism. Scholars still question the exact role that delinquent peers and delinquent attitudes play in generating delinquency and crime. Nevertheless, the weight of empirical evidence appears to support the theory's central propositions.

> Scholars still question the exact role that delinquent peers and delinquent attitudes play in generating delinquency and crime.

Policy Implications: Social Learning Theory

As should be clear, there is a great deal of similarity between the differential association/social learning perspective in sociology and social learning theories within psychology. In that sense, the policy implications are also similar. To reduce crime, it would be necessary to (1) reduce access to delinquent peers, (2) confront and change antisocial attitudes, and (3) change the balance of reinforcement so that it supports prosocial behavior. Many of the cognitive–behavioral programs described in Chapter 5 are therefore consistent with social learning theory. For example, cognitive restructuring programs attempt to change "criminal-thinking errors" common to offenders. Because thinking errors are similar to Sutherland and Akers' "definitions," the effectiveness of cognitive restructuring is viewed as evidence in favor of social learning theory.

In fact, some of the earliest experiments in this type of rehabilitation were explicitly designed to test principles of differential association. Psychologist D. A. Andrews used community volunteers (college students) to conduct group sessions with probationers and parolees.[41] In the typical group, several volunteers discussed various topics (e.g., the importance of rules, the limits of common rationalizations for offending) with several offenders. Andrews demonstrated that the community volunteers were able to reduce the antisocial attitudes (definitions) of the offenders. More importantly, improvement in attitude led to reductions in offending.

Cognitive–behavioral programs also focus on a variety of social learning concepts as targets for change. Reviews of the rehabilitation literature consistently indicate that such programs are among the most promising means for reducing crime.[42,43] On the other hand, such programs typically include targets (personality, cognitive skills) that are not relevant to differential association.

Informal Social Control Theory

Social control theorists assume that crime is naturally appealing because it is often a quick, easy way to fulfill desires. Standing other criminological theories on their heads, they ask, "Why aren't we all criminals?" Their answer is that most people are socialized against crime. Socialization creates control over individuals and prevents them from pursuing criminal acts that might otherwise be appealing.

Three Types of Informal Social Control

Many varieties of control theories exist. Every control theory, however, focuses on one or more of three general types of informal control:[44]

- Indirect control occurs when individuals have something valuable (a relationship, a good job) that ties them to conformity. In other words, a person has something positive that they do not wish to sacrifice by engaging in crime.
- Direct controls are exercised by those who have direct authority over others. For example, parents control their children by using punishments and rewards. In school, teachers exercise direct controls over their pupils.
- Internal control reflects the idea that individuals are able to exercise control over their delinquent

impulses. Different researchers have used different terms (e.g., self-control, self-concept, conscience) to describe this concept.

Early Control Theory: Walter Reckless and "Containment"

A number of informal social control theories were put forth in the 1950s. Most of these theories have since been absorbed into modern control theories. One of the more comprehensive theories during this time was outlined by Walter Reckless. Reckless felt that criminological theory had not explained why many individuals who were exposed to criminal influences did not turn to crime. Noticing that some youngsters who lived in high crime areas did not turn to delinquency, he concluded that they were somehow insulated.[45] Thus, his containment theory focuses on factors that insulate youth from crime. Reckless identified different types of inner containment and outer containment. A primary source of inner containment was self-concept. A favorable self-concept (a form of internal control) could protect an individual faced with a crime-promoting environment from a life of crime. Outer containment included direct controls, such as parental and school supervision. Containment theory also included various "pushes and pulls" (poverty, delinquent subcultures, anger/frustration) toward delinquency.[46] These are the factors that containment had to counter. **TABLE 7-2** lists Reckless' ingredients of inner and outer containment.

Reckless believed that internal containments were stronger, more important, and more effective crime control elements than outer containments. Individuals lacking a high degree of inner containment, Reckless suggested, would be unlikely to be saved by external containment. For example, if unemployment or lack of educational opportunity pushes juveniles toward crime, the last line of defense is the self-concept. If it is strong, the juvenile can resist the lures of delinquency.

Most research on containment theory therefore examined the role of self-concept. Reckless' research on self-concept indicated that "bad" boys had lower self-esteem than "good" boys.[47,48] Research conducted by Reckless' colleagues showed that the boys with a good self-concept avoided delinquency.[49] Follow-up research, however, failed to establish a firm link between self-concept and delinquency.[50] Part of the problem was that self-concept proved difficult to measure without referencing delinquency or misbehavior. More recent research provides little validity for Reckless' belief that high self-esteem insulates youth from delinquency. Not surprisingly then, an intervention project in Columbus, Ohio, junior high schools designed to improve the self-concept of predelinquent boys had no significant impact.[51]

Even though research on self-concept was not particularly fruitful, containment theory proved to be influential. Many aspects of inner and outer containment found their way into later control theories. Indeed, Reckless is cited as "one of the fathers of control theory laying the groundwork for the most sophisticated later versions of scholars like Travis Hirschi."[52]

TABLE 7-2

Ingredients of Containment

Inner containment	In addition to self-concept, Reckless outlined other forms of inner containment including: Self-control Ego strength Well-developed super ego (conscience) High frustration tolerance High resistance to diversions Ability to find substitute satisfactions Tension-reducing rationalizations Inner forces to resist the lure of criminal behavior
Outer containment	These elements represent the structural buffer in the person's immediate social world that is able to restrain the individual. They include: Presentation of a consistent moral front Institutional reinforcement of norms, goals, and expectations Existence of a reasonable set of social expectations Alternatives and safety valves Opportunity for acceptance

Data from Walter Reckless, *The Crime Problem* (New York: Appleton Century Crofts, 1967).

Hirschi's Social Bond Theory

Travis Hirschi is perhaps the most well-known and influential social control theorist. Hirschi's 1969 book, *Causes of Delinquency,* represented a shift in how criminologists presented theories and how the field of criminology classified theories in general. In the book, Hirschi laid out his own theory of delinquency, provided measures of each concept, and presented data from a sample of high school students that supported his theory.[53] Hirschi also defined a "pure" informal control theory and compared it with other theories of crime. According to Hirschi, assumptions about human nature clearly differentiate control theories from other theories of crime. Most theories of crime seek to explain why individuals engage in crime. In doing so, they identify factors (e.g., strain, association with delinquent peers) that propel or push people toward deviance. Since a person must be "forced" into crime, Hirschi argued that these theories assume that humans are naturally "good."[54]

In contrast, control theories ask, "Why don't all people engage in crime?" The underlying assumption is that humans are hedonistic and self-interested. Because crime is often a quick and easy way to meet self-interests, human nature tilts toward deviance. It is this assumption about human nature that connects control and deterrence theories. The difference between these theories is the type of control considered most important. Deterrence theories emphasize the formal controls of the criminal justice system, while control theories emphasize informal controls. Hirschi believed that human nature provided enough push toward crime that other pushes or (as in containment theory) were unnecessary. Instead, they need only explain why some people refrain from crime. His explanation was that humans refrained from crime because adequate socialization produced a "social bond" between an individual and society.

Hirschi's theory identifies four elements of the social bond that tie an individual to society: attachment, commitment, involvement, and belief. FIGURE 7-3 summarizes the four elements of the social bond. *Commitment* reflects a persons' investment in society. Conventional actions, such as taking a job or working hard in school build prosocial ties and discourage criminal involvement. Seeking success, the conformist will not risk their investments by committing crimes. Conversely, it is often said that the most dangerous person is one who has nothing to lose. *Attachment* refers to the emotional bonds that people form with others in society. Those who forge close relationships with parents, teachers, or friends, will care about the opinions of these people, and therefore refrain from crime. *Involvement* in conventional activity is a time-consuming process. The more heavily one is involved in conventional activities, the less time there is available to engage in deviant behavior. Finally, *belief* in the way society operates engenders sensitivity to the rights of others and respect for the laws.

Although Hirschi included some forms of direct control, his theory focuses mostly on indirect control. Attachment and commitment especially represent something that might be lost if a person engages in delinquency. For example, a youth considering delinquency might wonder, "What would my parents think of me if they found out I did this?" Similarly, a high school student might refrain

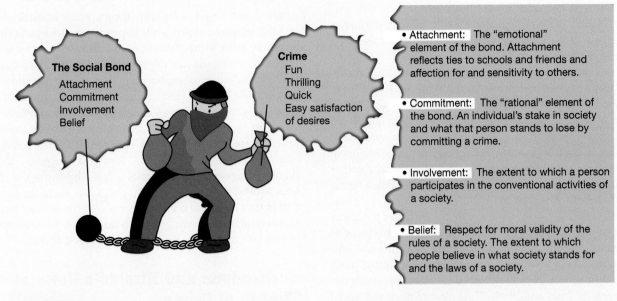

The Social Bond

Attachment
Commitment
Involvement
Belief

Crime
Fun
Thrilling
Quick
Easy satisfaction
of desires

- **Attachment:** The "emotional" element of the bond. Attachment reflects ties to schools and friends and affection for and sensitivity to others.

- **Commitment:** The "rational" element of the bond. An individual's stake in society and what that person stands to lose by committing a crime.

- **Involvement:** The extent to which a person participates in the conventional activities of a society.

- **Belief:** Respect for moral validity of the rules of a society. The extent to which people believe in what society stands for and the laws of a society.

FIGURE 7-3 Hirschi's social bond theory

Data from Ronald L. Akers and Christine S. Sellers, "Criminological Theories: Introduction, Evaluation, and Application," 4th ed. (Los Angeles: Roxbury, 2004): 85–89.

from drinking or using illicit drugs because they do not want to risk getting kicked off of a sports team. Hirschi argued that direct controls were less important because most delinquency occurs when kids are outside of the supervision of authority figures. He also rejected internal control. He felt that concepts such as low self-control, conscience, and self-concept were too subjective and too difficult to measure.

Hirschi's own empirical test generally supported his theory. Among a sample of high school students, he found that measures of attachment (respect and desire to emulate parents) and commitment (average grades, aspirations to continue school) and belief (respect for law) predicted delinquency.[55] Subsequent investigations support the relationship between certain elements of the social bond and delinquency. Massey and Krohn found that commitment was the most important element of the bond.[56] They also discovered that the elements of the bond predicted less-serious delinquency much better than more serious forms of delinquency. Finally, they noted that control theory is more applicable in predicting female rather than male delinquency. More recent research continues to reveal a similar pattern.[57,58] For example, researchers examined the impact of social control variables on the behavior of a sample of 5th graders in St. Louis.

All of the elements of Hirschi's theory were tested, but only attachment and commitment were related to conformity.[59] Overall, it appears as though some elements of the bond are weakly or moderately related to delinquency.

Research also indicates that a person's social bond might depend on personality characteristics. One such study examined survey data from 399 male and 300 female undergraduates enrolled in criminology and criminal justice courses at the University of Maryland.[60] Researchers tested the hypothesis that individuals who are more present oriented and self-centered invest less in social bonds, and therefore are less deterred from committing crime by

Informal social control theorists believe that parents are the key to proper socialization of children. Parents serve as sources of direct, indirect, and even internal forms of control.

© Photos.com/Getty

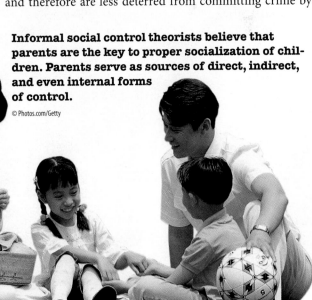

the possibility of damage to such bonds. They found that self-centered individuals were less likely to invest in personal capital: conventional attachments and commitments. There was some evidence that these individuals were less likely to be deterred from crime.

As this study illustrates, the relationships between the social bond and delinquency may be more complex than Hirschi believed. As with other theories of crime, social bond theory has a number of shortcomings. First, people have questioned the causal order put forth in the theory. Instead of weak bonds causing crime, it is plausible that delinquency or a delinquent disposition may weaken a young person's social bond. Another criticism speaks to the relative importance of indirect versus direct controls. Research consistently demonstrates that direct parental controls (supervising, discipline) are better predictors of delinquency than indirect controls such as attachment to parents.[61,62] Finally, Hirschi predicted that attachments to others, regardless of whether they were criminal, insulated youth from delinquency. Hirschi described relationships among delinquents as "cold and brittle."[63] As already discussed, social learning theory makes the opposite prediction—that association with delinquent peers should increase crime. Research on this issue consistently favors the social learning perspective. Studies of relationship quality suggest that relationships among delinquents are no different than relationships among nondelinquent youth.[64, 65] Furthermore, to the extent one attaches (forms strong relationships) to delinquent peers, they are more prone to delinquency themselves.[66,67]

Is a person's faith something that is risked to engage in crime? There is some evidence that religiousness deters criminal behaivor.

© Lisa F. Young/Dreamstime.com

Religion as a Source of Indirect Control

Although not a part of Hirschi's theory, many scholars suggest that religion can play a role in restraining delinquent impulses. In other words, faith or one's relationship with a god or gods is something that might be risked in order to engage in crime. Indeed, most studies do find an inverse relationship between religion and crime. A review of 60 studies of the crime–religion connection found that measures of religious behaviors (e.g., church attendance) and attitudes (e.g., belief in God, importance of religion) had a moderate effect on delinquent or criminal behavior.[68,69] Some have suggested that these findings may be noncausal—that religiousness is related to other factors (e.g., secular controls or social support) that in turn influence crime. A recent study, however, found that even after controlling for such influences, participation in religion consistently reduced the likelihood of crime.[70]

Gottfredson and Hirschi's General Theory of Crime

Travis Hirschi eventually came nearly full circle on his thinking about the causes of delinquency. As discussed, Hirschi's social bond theory focuses almost entirely on indirect social control. In their 1990 book, *A General Theory of Crime*, Gottfredson and Hirschi suggested (as Reckless had many years earlier) that internal control is the vital component. The authors boldly claim that **low self-control** is the *sole cause* of all criminal behavior, as well as behaviors that are analogous to crime.[71] In keeping with control theory perspective, Gottfredson and Hirschi assume that humans are born without self-control. The key question, then, is how does a person gain self-control? Their answer is proper parenting—a form of direct control. Borrowing heavily from Gerald Patterson (see Chapter 5), they argue that parents who supervise their children, recognize deviance, and punish deviant acts will build self-control in their children.[72]

Hirschi argued earlier, in his 1969 book, that internal control was too subjective and too difficult to measure. How do these authors avoid this problem? Gottfredson and Hirschi take a rather novel approach to outlining what they call the nature of low self-control. The authors begin by describing the nature of crime; that is, they identify what different forms of crime have in common. They argue, for example, that crimes are generally easy to commit and usually require a victim to suffer some pain. A summary of their characterization of crime is provided in FIGURE 7-4. They also point out that many acts (e.g., gambling, unprotected sex, adultery) that are not illegal share the same

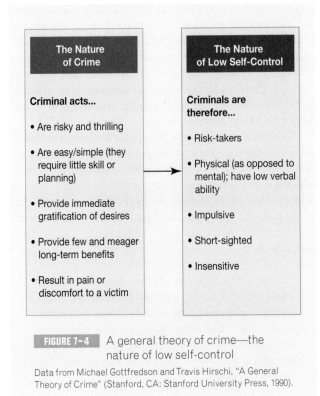

The Nature of Crime	The Nature of Low Self-Control
Criminal acts...	Criminals are therefore...
• Are risky and thrilling	• Risk-takers
• Are easy/simple (they require little skill or planning)	• Physical (as opposed to mental); have low verbal ability
• Provide immediate gratification of desires	• Impulsive
• Provide few and meager long-term benefits	• Short-sighted
• Result in pain or discomfort to a victim	• Insensitive

FIGURE 7-4 A general theory of crime—the nature of low self-control

Data from Michael Gottfredson and Travis Hirschi, "A General Theory of Crime" (Stanford, CA: Stanford University Press, 1990).

general "nature" as crime. They refer to such acts as behaviors analogous to crime. Gottfredson and Hirschi use the nature of crime to deduce the nature of low self-control. For example, if crime requires some pain and suffering to a victim, those with self-control should be insensitive to others. Through this process, they arrive at a definition of low self-control:[73]

> *In sum, people who lack self-control will tend to be impulsive, insensitive, physical (as opposed to mental), risk-taking, short-sighted, and nonverbal, and they tend therefore to engage in crime and analogous acts.*

Gottfredson and Hirschi argue that self-control is formed in early childhood. A person's level of self-control crystallizes around age 10 and remains stable thereafter. Given this argument and the description of low self-control, this theory is very similar to personality theories within psychology. Recall that the trait "low constraint," as outlined by a personality inventory, predicted delinquency and crime. Similarly, empirical studies consistently reveal that low self-control has a moderate to strong effect on both crime and analogous behaviors.

In a review of self-control research conducted in the first decade after publication of the theory, criminologists Travis Pratt and Francis Cullen note that measures of low self-control:[74]

- Predict both "analogous behaviors" (fast driving, cigarette smoking) and crime
- Are among the strongest (compared to predictors from other theories) predictors of crime

- Predict delinquency, crime, and analogous behavior regardless of sample composition (male or female, adult or juvenile, offenders or general population)

In a fairly short period of time, the concept of low self-control has garnered a great deal of empirical support.[75] However, the empirical support of Gottfredson and Hirschi's theory does have limits. Foremost, it appears that low self-control, although important, is not the sole cause of criminal behavior. Studies continue to reveal that regardless of one's level of self-control, other things such as delinquent peers, antisocial attitudes, and neighborhood problems continue to matter.[76]

Another issue deals with the genesis of self-control. Gottfredson and Hirschi claim that self-control comes completely from parenting. Recent research suggests that there are multiple sources of low self-control. For example, there is some evidence that attention deficit hyperactivity disorder is related to low self-control, regardless of parenting.[77] Furthermore, poor parenting practices appear to influence crime for a variety of reasons, not simply because of their contribution to low self-control. One recent study documented four different characteristics of children with conduct disorder that are affected by parenting: low self-control, a hostile view of relationships, anger/frustration, and the acceptance of deviant norms.[78]

Finally, some of Gottfredson and Hirschi's claims about the stable and rigid nature of low self-control appear overstated. The authors contend that around the age of 10, children lock into a certain level of self-control. They are very skeptical about whether planned interventions or changes in environment can alter a person's level of self-control. This position is meant to explain a common criminology finding: that criminal behavior tends to be stable over time. In other words, childhood misbehavior predicts juvenile delinquency; juvenile delinquency predicts adult crime; and so forth. Gottfredson and Hirschi can explain stability in crime because low self-control is also stable over time. Emerging evidence, however, suggests that self-control is both fluid over time and changeable through interventions.[79] A study of a Johns Hopkins University intervention program illustrates these points. In this study, 1st grade students from nine different Baltimore elementary schools were randomly assigned to either a control group or an intervention group. The intervention was designed to improve academic achievement and reduce conduct problems. One part of the intervention was an explicit attempt to improve parenting and therefore increase self-control within the children. Although the intervention occurred in 1st grade, subjects were followed through high school. This allowed researchers to examine levels of self-control over time, and to study the effects of the intervention. Findings indicate that "self-control is malleable, is responsive to intentional attempts to increase it, and continues to develop in response to the changing level of social control/bond at least up until grade 12 (17 years of age)."[80]

Despite these criticisms and limitations, it appears as though Gottfredson and Hirschi have identified and described an important concept (low self-control) that will continue to receive attention. The final control theory discussed in this chapter, however, reverts to Hirschi's "old" social bond theory as a starting point.

An Age-Graded Theory of Informal Social Control

The most recent development in control theory comes from two former students of Travis Hirschi—Robert Sampson and John Laub—who propose an extension of Hirschi's social bond theory. Hirschi's theory focuses on factors, such as school achievement and attachment to parents, that are most relevant to youth. These factors, however, become less important as adolescents become young adults. Sampson and Laub's "age-graded" theory emphasizes both direct (parenting) and indirect (social bond) controls during childhood and adolescence.[81] Later in the life course, they emphasize **adult social bonds**. They argue that a quality marriage and/or a quality job help to explain why most crime-prone youth eventually desist from criminal behavior during adulthood. The full theory, which was one of the first development altheories in criminology, is considered in Chapter 9. Here, we focus on adult social bonds.

As social bonds, marriage and jobs are important, to the extent that they produce informal control. They represent something that a person could lose by engaging in criminal behavior. This is why the quality of a job or relationship is important. A person considering crime would probably not be too upset about losing a low-paying job at a fast-food restaurant. That same person might think more carefully about disappointing a boss whose opinion they respect or losing a job that pays decent wages. Sampson and Laub found that marital attachment and job stability predicted desistence from crime among adults—even for those who had a history of juvenile delinquency.[82,83] Subsequent research has replicated these findings. For example, a recent study found that marriage reduced offending for both males and females. Importantly, crime reduction was greatest among males who were initially least likely to marry (based on other factors).[84]

Even in the short term, it appears as though relationships and employment insulate people from crime. In a recent study, researchers interviewed newly convicted male offenders and examined their month-to-month activity prior to their incarceration. As expected, they found that crime patterns were correlated with social variables, such as education, marriage, and employment. The authors conclude that:

> Persons with a high rate of crime may be unlikely to graduate from school, unlikely to maintain meaningful employment, and unlikely to stay in a stable, meaningful relationship. Even so, they may sometimes go to school, sometimes work, and sometimes live with a wife, and at those times they are less likely to commit crimes.[85]

What's Love Got to Do with It? Social Support and Altruism

Criminologist Francis Cullen offers a provocative critique of social control theory.[86] He does not dismiss control theories—indeed he notes that they have accumulated a great deal of empirical support. Instead, Cullen suggests that the control theory view of human nature as selfish and

Robert Sampson and John Laub contend that marriage is an adult bond that explains why some people desist from crime as they age. A quality marriage is something that a potential criminal would risk by engaging in crime. Also, marriage often changes routine activities and friendship patterns.

hedonistic is too simplistic. In addition to instant gratification, humans also seek out and engage in altruistic and unselfish behavior. He points out that elements of social supports, such as parental love, nurturing, and caring, are "preconditions" for effective social control. In other words, parents who love and support their children are more likely to do the hard work of socialization.[87] Furthermore, "lack of love and nurturance is related to a host of emotional and cognitive deficiencies—deficiencies that are precursors for later conduct disorders."[88]

Cullen's thesis is that whether social support is delivered through government social programs, communities, social networks, families, interpersonal relations, or agents of the criminal justice system, it reduces criminal involvement. In that sense, evidence that "religiousness" or "quality marriages" reduces crime might not only rest on social control. Rather, they may provide nurturance and support and therefore reduce crime.

A study using data from a national sample of adolescents demonstrates that both social support and social control have effects on delinquency. Parents who attended important events in the lives of their children; consistently used praise, affection, or compliments; and encouraged hobbies, were less likely to have delinquent children. The measures of social support were related to social control (parental discipline) but predicted delinquency independent of parents' level of control.[89] There is also evidence from studies conducted at the macro level.[90,91] One study found that higher levels of social altruism within cities reduces crime. Using a sample of more than 300 cities, researchers found that property and violent crime rates are higher in cities with lower United Way contributions.[92] As with many theories, however, some tests of social support theory are not supportive.[93,94]

Over the past 30 years, social control and social learning perspectives have battled for supremacy in criminology. Cullen's theory of social support is a newcomer to this battle. Although there is some supportive evidence, it remains to be seen how much interest social support theory generates compared with the dominant theories of crime.

Policy Implications for Theories of Informal Social Control

The policy implications for theories of informal social control depend somewhat on the particular theory or form (e.g., internal, direct, indirect) of control in question. There are, however, some common themes. All of the control theories discussed in this chapter point to the importance of families. Parents can strongly contribute

> *In addition to instant gratification, humans also seek out and engage in altruistic and unselfish behavior.*

to conformity by providing supervision for, by building a quality relationship with, and by communicating with their children. Depending on the particular theory, effective parenting increases a child's attachment, generates self-control, or simply acts as a form of direct control. Hirschi remains skeptical that child-rearing programs could generate broad reductions in delinquency rates.[95] As noted previously, however, parent training programs have indeed had some success at increasing self-control and reducing delinquency. The popularity of reality television programs, such as *Supernanny* and *Nanny 911*, suggest that many parents are indeed open to helpful parenting techniques.

The **Seattle Social Developmental Project (SSDP)** developed by J. David Hawkins and his associates is perhaps the best example of an intervention based on control theory. The SSDP targets both direct and indirect control in family and school environments to prevent childhood aggression and delinquency.[96] Within the program, teachers were trained in proactive classroom management—the proper use of rewards and punishment to promote a good learning environment. Teachers were also trained in a number of techniques (interactive teaching, cooperative learning) designed to strengthen children's bonds with the school. Parents were offered parent-skills training that focused on direct control (recognize deviance, punish consistently). Parents were also encouraged to increase social support (spend time together, involve kids in family activities, develop children's school abilities).

This program started with children entering 1st grade, when students were randomly assigned to the SSDP group or a control group. Study participants were monitored over roughly the next 20 years. Results throughout the project have been positive. By 5th grade, the SSDP kids were more committed and attached to school and slightly less likely to drink alcohol or engage in other misconduct.[97] At age 18, the SSDP youth maintained higher attachment and had higher academic achievement. Although the groups did not differ on many measures of delinquency, the SSDP youth were less likely to engage in violent forms of delinquency or heavy drinking. At age 21, the SSDP participants were more successful in school and work, and less likely to have a court conviction.[98] As they approached age 30, the SSDP were more involved and successful within their community, and had fewer mental health problems. Differences in criminal behavior and substance abuse, however, were no longer evident.[99]

Sampson and Laub's adult bonds would require a much different approach. To be sure, few criminologists would recommend marriage as a policy to reduce criminal behavior.

Employment—finding a quality job (i.e., stable, good pay, good relationship with employer) for those with prior criminal involvement—is more plausible. Still, many employers are reluctant to hire people with a criminal past (see **Theory in Action: Employment and Criminal History—Check the Box or Ban the Box?**).

Can't We All Just Get Along? Social Control, Social Learning, and Behaviorism

It is very easy to get confused about the difference between control theories and social learning theories. Moreover, it can be difficult to understand the difference between these perspectives and materials covered under the heading of behaviorism within psychology. Within sociology, informal control and social learning theory both discuss aspects of learning. In control theories, the focus is on parental use of rewards and punishment to control the behavior of children. In social learning theory, the emphasis is on role models and attitudes that promote delinquency. In the discipline of psychology, there is no such distinction. Rather, psychologists speak only to different learning mechanisms (classical and operant conditioning, observational learning).

The distinction within sociology comes largely from a debate about the nature of humans. Control theories view humans as self-interested and hedonistic and therefore in need of control; these theories emphasize how antisocial impulses are corrected through operant conditioning. Sociological learning theories view humans as more of a "blank slate" and are more likely to emphasize how deviant behavior is learned through observation and the communication of values and attitudes.

Not all criminologists agree that this distinction is crucial. Terrance Thornberry has put forth a theory that integrates social control and social learning measures into a single theory of crime. His interactional theory of delinquency suggests that a lack of informal control allows youth to come into contact with delinquent peers.[100] Although his theory has attracted some attention, most criminologists prefer to keep control and learning as distinct theories.

Labeling Theory

Unlike social learning and social control theory, the labeling perspective does not feature a handful of well-known theories. Rather, a number of different scholars

> **The gist of labeling theory is that government intervention in the lives of delinquents will make matters worse.**

have contributed concepts and ideas within the same general framework. Although many of these contributions occurred from 1930 to 1950, the general perspective did not receive much attention in the United States until the 1960s. A number of scholars have noted that labeling theory perspective was a good fit to that social context.[101] The 1960s was a period of great social conflict where many questioned the motives and intentions of the government. Reaction to protests over civil rights and the war in Vietnam, the Watergate scandal, prison riots, and other events suggested to many that the government could not be trusted. The labeling perspective echoes this view. The gist of labeling theory is that government intervention in the lives of delinquents will make matters worse.

The Roots of the Labeling Perspective

The labeling perspective is built around three themes: (1) a view of crime and deviance as "relative," (2) a focus on how power and conflict shape society, and (3) the importance of self-concept.

The first theme is a general position that no act is inherently evil, bad, or criminal. Whether an act is considered deviant or criminal depends on a number of factors, including: (1) when and where the act is committed, (2) who commits the act and who is the victim, and (3) the consequences of the act.[102] Consider, for example, the use of mind-altering drugs. In some societies, such substances are legal, although in others they are considered illicit drugs. Within the same society, the status of an act can change. For example, Colorado and Washington recently decriminalized marijuana. Alcohol, traditionally a legal drug was made illegal during Prohibition. Even violent behaviors, such as killing another person, are not always classified as homicide. During wartime, such behaviors are rewarded. Death from cancer caused by pollution is generally viewed as an environmental risk that is necessary for the economy.[103]

In short, the gist of this view is that no act is inherently evil or bad. Whether these acts are considered deviant depends on the society in which they happen, the particular historical context, and the circumstances of the behavior. In labeling theory, the crucial dimension is the societal reaction to the act, not the act itself. As Becker notes, ". . . deviance is not a quality of the act the person commits, but rather a consequence of the application by others of rules and sanctions to an 'offender.' The deviant is one to whom the label has successfully been applied; deviant behavior is behavior that people so label."[104]

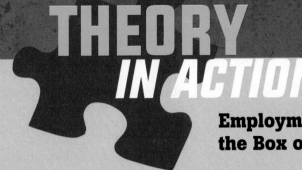

THEORY IN ACTION

Employment and Criminal History—Check the Box or Ban the Box?

Samson and Laub's theory of informal social control emphasizes the importance of adult social bonds—particular quality employment. In their theory, the authors point out that criminal convictions and incarceration reduce opportunities to obtain a good job later in life. A good job can act as a "turning point" that allows crime-prone individuals to become law-abiding citizens. Conversely, the inability to land a decent job may help foster crime through adulthood. Since roughly 30 percent of U.S. youth, and almost 50 percent of black males are arrested prior to age 25, this is an important policy issue.

Two features of modern society make it difficult for those with a prior record to obtain employment. First, most employers require applicants to check a box indicating whether they have ever been either arrested or convicted for criminal activity. Second, advances in technology and the availability of public data have made background checks standard practice for employers.

Research experiments on employment consistently reveal that employers are reluctant to call back (for an interview) anyone who discloses a felony offense. The findings are particularly discouraging for non-white job applicants. In fact the "call back" rate for *noncriminal* black applicants is actually lower than for *criminal* white applicants. African American men with a prison record are virtually disqualified from consideration for most employment. Findings such as this led a national civil rights organization to create a "Ban the Box" campaign. The campaign asks employers to "choose their best candidates based on job skills and qualifications, *not* past convictions." Of course, many employers feel that criminal history is a valid predictor of future employee behavior, and are reluctant to change hiring practices.

Over the past decade, legislators have tried to strike a balance between the employment rights of the accused and/or convicted, and the rights of employers. At least 10 states have now passed some form of Ban the Box legislation. These laws govern the type of criminal history data that can be used (arrest vs. conviction) and when during the job hiring process employers can conduct criminal background checks. Timing is important because research shows that personal contact with the applicant can mitigate the negative effect of a criminal history. An example of recent legislation can be found in the state of Minnesota. As of 2014, Minnesota employers are no longer permitted to ask about criminal histories until a job applicant has been selected for an interview or offered a job.

Sources: Pager, D. (2007). *Marked: Race, crime, and finding work in an era of mass incarceration.* Chicago: University of Chicago Press; Uggen, C., Vuolo, M., Lageson, S., Ruhland, E., & Whitham, H. K. (2014). The edge of stigma: An experimental audit of the effect of flow-level criminal records on employment. *Criminology, 52,* 627–654; All of us or none. (2015). *Ban the Box Campaign.* Retrieved June 5, 2015, from http://bantheboxcampaign.org/

The labeling perspective emphasizes the influence of powerful groups in society to both define and react to deviant behavior. Similar to conflict theory (see Chapter 8), labeling theorists argue that those in power (the middle and upper classes) will define and enforce laws in a manner that benefits themselves to the detriment of those who are less powerful. Becker described those who define and enforce rules as **moral entrepreneurs**. *Rule creators* are interested in the criminalization of certain forms of behavior that they view as profoundly evil. They typically espouse a doctrine that sounds increasingly dogmatic or regressive. They also tend to leave the application of their desired policies to others.

Rule enforcers are professionals who enforce the law unflinchingly, whatever its content. They must justify their position and win the respect of those above them. They face the double dilemma of showing that the problem still exists but proving that it is being dealt with efficiently. Becker believes that rule enforcers, in response to the pressures of the job, will enforce the law selectively. Importantly, labeling theorists do not equate selectiveness with randomness. Rather, selective enforcement will be directed at those who lack power and status. Arrest and incarceration are more likely for those who are male, young, unemployed, lower-class, nonwhite, and for those living in urban, high crime areas.[105]

A final piece in the labeling theory puzzle is derived from the general theory of **symbolic interactionism**. The thrust of this perspective is that people communicate through gestures, signs, words, and images that stand for, or represent, other things (symbols). In that sense, a single word (label) may contain a whole set of meanings. Labels such as "cool," "crack head," "psychotic," or "over-achiever" conjure up a particular image. These exchanges of symbols, among other things, help people understand and define themselves. In other words, people interpret symbolic gestures from others and incorporate them into their self-image.

Charles Horton Cooley described this process as the "looking-glass self." Here, one's own self-concept—how a person describes or thinks about themself—is the product of other people's conceptions or symbolic labels.[106] In turn, the self-concept can dictate behavior. Individuals attempt (consciously or not) to live up to their image. Put another way, the labels that others use to describe a person can become a self-fulfilling prophecy.[107] Symbolic interactionists argued that this was not a one-way process. The people being labeled could respond back—they could "negotiate" their self-concept.

Putting the Pieces Together—The Labeling Process

By combining the three central themes, labeling theorists describe a general process whereby official intervention (e.g.,

> ... people interpret symbolic gestures from others and incorporate them into their self-image.

arrest, trial) creates an unintended side effect. FIGURE 7-5 illustrates this general process. The starting point in the labeling process is the portrayal of childhood deviance as relative. Many children engage in various forms of deviance (there is no inherently evil act), including crimes such as shoplifting or vandalism. Such acts are typically portrayed in the labeling literature as unorganized and sporadic.[108]

Edwin Lemert termed these behaviors primary deviance. He suggested that if these acts go unnoticed, they have little impact. Most kids grow out of such behavior. Labeling theorists are therefore not concerned with the motivation behind the initial deviant acts.[109] Some acts, however, will be noticed. Frank Tannenbaum coined the phrase "dramatization of evil" to characterize the process whereby the primary deviance of certain people is singled out.[110] In other words, some individuals are tagged as delinquents or troublemakers. Once identified in this manner, others may see them in an entirely new light. They may retrospectively interpret past actions in light of the new label (e.g., "I always knew he was bad news").

Who is most likely to have their primary deviance singled out and how exactly are people labeled? The answer

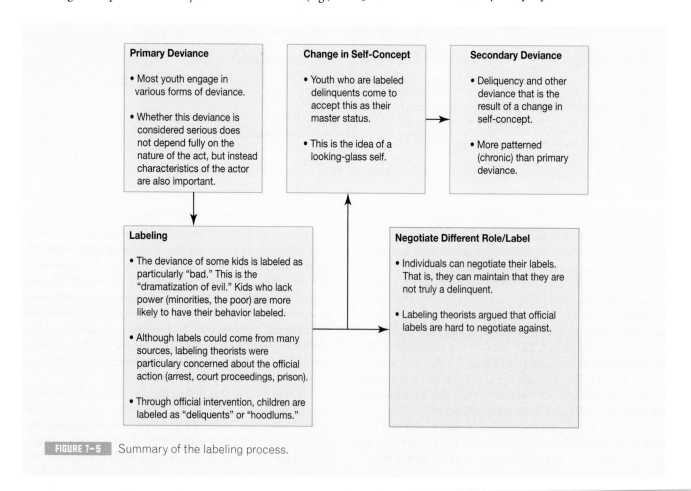

FIGURE 7-5 Summary of the labeling process.

for most labeling theorists is that police or other agents of the criminal justice system start the process. In turn, society responds to delinquent activity by negatively defining and rejecting the offender. This response and rejection serve to identify to society the "evil in its midst."[111] Furthermore, it is more important who the kid is (white or minority, wealthy or poor) than what he or she has done. In other words, people are tagged, not because of the particular act, but because of their status in society.

Drawing on the symbolic interactionism, labeling theorists point out negative consequences of this process. After the person is labeled, a change in self-identification may occur, so that an individual acts out the role of criminal. Thus, the label of "delinquent" becomes a self-fulfilling prophecy. Individuals organize their self-concept around deviance. They may even join with other "outsiders" in a delinquent subculture.[112] Lemert described delinquent behavior that results from this change in self-concept as **secondary deviance**. Others described it as deviance amplification. The criminal justice system, in effect, creates crime by trying to prevent it.

Recall that in symbolic interactionism, people could negotiate labels and their self-concept. Becker, for example, went to great pains to point out that not all labeled individuals will form a delinquent self-concept. For some, sanctioning might have the intended (deterrent) effect. Labeling theorists did argue, however, that the labels enforced by the agents of government would be difficult to negotiate. Once labeled as a delinquent, it is difficult to live down that definition.[113]

A Critique of Labeling Theory

Labeling theory has been severely criticized over the past 30 years. The most damaging criticism is that the central elements of the theory appear to have very little empirical support. Research appears to refute the following tenets of labeling theory:

- The characterization of primary deviance as relative, sporadic, and unimportant
- The idea that the nature of the person predicts official reaction more than the nature of the act
- The effect of official sanctions on future behavior (deviance amplification)

Labeling theorists cannot explain why some people engage in primary deviance, while others do not. Instead, they portray anything that happens before an official response as sporadic, unpatterned, and relatively unimportant. Studies of childhood and adolescent deviance indicate that this is not an accurate picture. Even young children demonstrate consistent, patterned, and chronic misbehavior.[114] Furthermore, they are unlikely to simply "grow out" of such behavior. The trend is that misbehavior, delinquency, or deviance continues over time, regardless of whether a child is officially labeled. Many critics also take issue with the complete relativity granted to deviant acts. This portrayal of deviance generates an underdog ideology that denies the heinous nature of certain crimes (some acts are bad) as well as the independence and responsibility of the actor.[115]

Another premise of labeling theory is that the social status of the offender rather than the particular offense dictates whether the person will be arrested and punished. To be sure, there is evidence of some racial bias in the criminal justice system. For example, despite procedural efforts to prevent it, death sentencing in the United States is plagued by racial bias. Studies of the capital sentencing process reveal that blacks who kill whites have the greatest probability of receiving the death penalty.[116] Some studies also find that race influences decisions to arrest or the severity of punishment (although others find that race doesn't matter). Even where racial bias is detected, though, it is a much weaker predictor of police or court decision making when compared with offense seriousness and prior record. In other words, the quality of the act is a more important determinant of whether or not the police make an arrest or whether a person is sentenced to prison.[117,118]

> The central argument in labeling theory is that the stigmatizing effect of criminal justice sanctions will increase (amplify) future criminal behavior.

The central argument in labeling theory is that the stigmatizing effect of criminal justice sanctions will increase (amplify) future criminal behavior. As noted with respect to deterrence theory (see Chapter 3), arrest or other sanctions alone do not have a consistent effect on future behaviors. In some cases, sanctions may reduce crime. There is also some evidence, including newer research, suggesting that sanctioning also may increase future crime.[119,120] In particular, there is evidence that imprisonment increases the odds of future criminal behavior.[121,122] This is worrisome, given that the United States now incarcerates over 2 million offenders. Still, while incarceration may increase future offending, it is unclear whether this is due to the classic labeling perspective. It is possible, for example, that incarceration decreases job prospects, which in turn is related to crime.

The bulk of research indicates that the same factors (e.g., delinquent peers, poor bonds, personality traits, parenting behavior) that produce early (primary) deviance also predict later delinquency and crime regardless of whether a person has been officially labeled. The lack of empirical support for labeling theory does not mean that labels or official

THEORY IN ACTION

Restorative Justice

Consider the following scenario. A criminal smashes a window in a garage and steals $800 worth of possessions. The police apprehend the offender—he is charged with burglary and sentenced to 6 months in jail. A restorative justice advocate would ask, "What has been accomplished?" The victim has not been repaid the $800, and the offender will be released from jail, having never directly faced his victim. In addition, he probably never will have received treatment, counseling, or rehabilitation.

Restorative justice is a broad, ambitious philosophy regarding the best way to view and react to criminal offenses. Perhaps the easiest way to understand this philosophy is to compare it with the present criminal justice system. In the criminal justice system, crimes are considered offenses against the state, and the victim is only minimally involved in the sanctioning process. The offender is held accountable for their actions through some form of punishment (e.g., probation, prison, jail). In the restorative justice model, the victim is central to the process, and the focus of all proceedings is to repair the harm caused by the crime to the victim and community. Thus, accountability revolves around repairing harm and directly addressing the victim.

This philosophy stems from theory and research on the labeling and deterrence perspectives. In some ways, it is a compromise between the two theories. In restorative justice, perpetrators of crime are held accountable, but within a format that keeps them connected to the community. Offenders are also "shamed," in a personal and meaningful way, by community members and victims, as opposed to by an impersonal criminal justice system. This follows empirical studies that suggest informal control is a more effective deterrent than formal control. Restorative justice programs include:

- **Victim–offender mediation:** The offender meets with the victim to discuss the offense and ways in which the harm can be repaired. The victim has the opportunity to ask questions of the offender and to describe how they have been affected by the incident. The mediation can also include family members of the offender.
- **Restitution:** Offenders literally pay back victims for the damage they caused.

- **Sentencing circles:** Members of the community, in concert with the victim, come up with a plan to restore the harm caused by an offense.

With regard to the opening scenario, restorative programming might include a face-to-face meeting between the owner of the garage and the offender, repayment of monetary damages, and a sentence agreed upon by the victim and members of the community.

Evaluations of restorative justice programs thus far are mixed. Programs such as victim–offender mediation generally increase both victim and offender satisfaction with the process. There is also some evidence that restorative justice programming can reduce criminal behavior. Despite this positive evidence, the restorative justice approach is not without criticism. Skeptics point out that restorative programming is limited, because it depends on voluntary participation from victims, offenders, and the community. In particular, for many offenses (e.g., rape), the victim may have no interest in restorative conferencing. Others worry that restorative programming might funnel money away from rehabilitation programs that have a better track record of success in reducing recidivism.

Despite this criticism, the popularity of the restorative justice approach has increased over the past 2 decades. As restorative programs spread, they will continue to generate empirical research. Ultimately, this research has the potential to inform criminological theory. To the extent that mediation, shaming, and other restorative programs "work," they support the underlying theoretical concepts such as Braithwaite's reintegrative shaming.

Sources: Menkel-Medow, C. (2007). Restorative justice: What is it and does it work? *Annual Review of Law and Social Science, 3,* 161–187; Latimer, J., Dowden, C., & Muise, D. (2005). The effectiveness of restorative justice practices: A meta-analysis. *The Prison Journal, 85,* 127–144; Bazemore, G., & Umbreit, M. (1995). Rethinking the sanctioning function of the juvenile court: Retributive or restorative responses to juvenile crime. *Crime and Delinquency, 41,* 296–316; McGarrell, E. F. (2001). Restorative justice conferencing as an early response to young offenders. *Juvenile Justice Bulletin.* Washington, DC: Office of Juvenile Justice and Delinquency Prevention.

action never produce negative consequences (including more crime). It is clear, though, that the label itself is much less important than other factors. As Cullen and Agnew note, "Labeling theory wishes to pretend that being raised in criminogenic conditions for 10, 15, or 20 years . . . pale in comparison to the effects, albeit over a more limited time, of being arrested and perhaps jailed."[123]

The most visible supporters of labeling theory (e.g., Becker, Schur, Lemert) later argued that labeling was never meant to be a "theory" of criminal behavior. Rather, they portrayed the perspective as a way to "sensitize" criminologists to issues regarding the effects of criminal justice actions.[124] In that respect, labeling theorists did call attention to issues that had been neglected in the study of crime.

Policy Implications of Labeling Theory

Labeling theory tells a story with an ironic twist. In trying to prevent crime, the criminal justice system actually produces or promotes more crime. As seen, however, this contention has not been empirically supported. Another irony is that despite a lack of empirical support, labeling was very popular for a brief period and influenced many policymakers. The policy implication of labeling theory is relatively easy to identify: Do not intervene in most matters of juvenile delinquency whenever possible. As Edwin Schur phrased it, engage in "radical non-intervention."[125]

Labeling theorists, for example, condemned the sanctioning by juvenile courts of status offenses—acts committed by juveniles that would not be considered crimes if committed by adults (e.g., running away, truancy). Schur maintained that these are moral judgments that make a bad situation worse. A runaway (primary deviation), placed in a juvenile institution, can become a burglar (secondary deviation) because of the labeling process.[126] In 1974, Congress enacted the Juvenile Justice and Delinquency Prevention Act, which appeared to follow the policy prescription of labeling theory. The act called for the deinstitutionalization of status offenders and encouraged states to remove status offenses from the general category of delinquency. During this time, **diversion programs** became very popular. These are programs designed to divert offenders away from the formal juvenile justice processing to programs run by other entities (social services).[127] Although interest in these programs lapsed in the 1980s, many are still around.

Extensions of Labeling Theory

Although interest in the labeling perspective declined substantially after the 1970s, there has been renewed interest in recent years. Some scholars continue to test variations of labeling theory. Recent tests tend to portray labeling as having a more minor role and to focus on the effect of *informal* labels used by parents and peers. One study found that some parents are quicker to negatively label their children than others, regardless of their children's actual behavior.

Furthermore, these labels do predict (although weakly) the child's future delinquency.[128]

Other theorists have attempted to find middle ground between deterrence theory and labeling theory. Labeling theory suggests that official sanctions will magnify delinquency, while deterrence theory suggests the opposite. In his book, *Crime, Shame, and Reintegration*, Australian criminologist John Braithwaite suggests that both perspectives may be partially correct. Braithwaite argues that effective punishment shames an offender, but does so in a reintegrative manner (e.g., hate the sin but love the sinner).[129] He points to cultures such as Japan, where ceremonies both shame offenders and recertify them as members of society after the shaming is complete. In contrast, punishment that stigmatizes creates societal outcasts, who are more prone to future criminal behavior.

Lawrence Sherman arrived at a similar conclusion from his observations of policing. Like Braithwaite, Sherman argues that sanctioning might produce different effects. He suggests that police sanctions can produce defiance (escalation in offending), deterrence (decrease in offending), or be irrelevant.[130] Both police behavior and social bonds determine an individual's response. Rude and/or discriminatory police action, for example, produces defiance rather than deterrence. As noted in the discussion of deterrence theory, sanction is more likely to deter offenders if they are socially bonded to society.

These new twists on labeling theory and Braithwaite's work in particular, have supported the emerging concept of **restorative justice**. Many envision restorative justice as an alternative way to handle delinquent and criminal behavior.[131] The central focus of this philosophy is that the goal of the criminal justice system should be to repair the harm created by the offense. The approach emphasizes victim–offender mediation, where crime victims have an opportunity to meet with offenders. The concept of restorative justice is featured in **Theory in Action: Restorative Justice**.

 ## Conclusion

In this chapter, three general perspectives on delinquency and crime are examined. All three share the assumption that the deviant behavior is the result of individuals interacting with social institutions over time. These institutions, including the family, education, peer groups, and the criminal justice system act as agents of socialization. The three types of theories discussed in this chapter are summarized in **TABLE 7-3**. Social control theories focus on inadequate socialization; that is, crime occurs because direct, indirect, or internal controls have not been properly established. Social learning theory suggests that delinquency results when individuals are socialized toward the wrong set of norms, attitudes, and behaviors. Each of these perspectives has generated a good deal of empirical support. Because they both focus on the role of learning, these perspectives have a great deal in common.

TABLE 7-3

Summary of Social Process Theories

Theory and Author(s)	Central Ideas	Policy Implications
Laws of imitation Gabriel Tarde	Criminals learn their behavior from other persons and imitate them. The law of imitation explains criminality as a function of association with criminal types. In imitation, the individual selects a role model and fashions behavior after that model. The three laws of imitation are fashion, custom, and insertion.	Use the principles of learning to • Reduce access to delinquent peers. • Confront and change antisocial attitudes. • Change the balance of reinforcement so that it supports prosocial behavior.
Differential association Edwin Sutherland	Criminal behavior is learned through communication within intimate personal groups. A person becomes delinquent when exposure to law-breaking attitudes is greater than exposure to law-abiding attitudes. Learning criminal behavior includes both techniques of committing crime and rationalizations and attitudes.	
Social learning theory Ronald Akers	Incorporates psychological learning principles (reinforcement and observational learning) into differential association theory. Delinquency is the result of exposure to delinquent role models or delinquent values/attitudes. Reinforcement determines whether delinquency is maintained.	
Containment theory Walter Reckless	Certain individuals who are exposed to criminal influences do not turn to crime or delinquency because they are insulated. The primary insulator is favorable self-concept.	Improve self-concept.
Social bond theory Travis Hirschi	Emphasizes indirect control. Individuals bonded to society are less likely to engage in delinquency. Elements of the social bond include attachment, commitment, involvement, and belief.	Increase attachment to school and parents. The Seattle Social Developmental Project is one example.
Low self-control theory Travis Hirschi and Michael Gottfredson	Emphasizes internal (self) control. Effective parenting (use of operant conditioning) produces self-control in children. Levels of self-control crystallize during early childhood and remain stable thereafter.	Train parents to effectively socialize their kids (consistent discipline).
Age-graded theory of informal social control Robert Sampson and John Laub	At different stages in life, different forms of control are more or less important. Direct parental controls, attachment to parents, and commitment to schools are important during adolescence. During adulthood, attachment to a spouse and holding a quality job help form an adult social bond.	Similar to Hirschi's social bond theory for adolescence. In adulthood, job opportunities are important.
Labeling theory Frank Tannenbaum, Edwin Lemert, and Howard Becker	Suggests that formal intervention with delinquents actually leads to an escalation in delinquency. This happens because youth come to define themselves as "delinquents."	Radical nonintervention. Diversion programs.
Reintegrative shaming John Braithewaite	The effect of formal punishment (e.g., arrest, court) on a person depends on how he or she is punished. Punishment that is both "shaming" and reintegrative will reduce future crime. Punishment that is stigmatizing will increase future crime.	Restorative justice.

In some respects, labeling theory also focuses on socialization. Through interactions with the criminal justice system, individuals are socialized to accept their delinquent identity. The classic labeling explanation is not strongly supported by research. Revisions of this perspective (e.g., informal labeling, reintegrative shaming) may prove more promising. As noted, labeling theory had a clear policy impact on the juvenile justice system during the 1970s.

WRAP-UP

CHAPTER SPOTLIGHT

Texture: © Malchev/Shutterstock; Police Tape: © SkillUp/Shutterstock

- Process theories focus on the interplay between the individual and society. They focus on how society (e.g., family, peers, religion) shapes individuals over time.
- The differential association/social learning tradition focuses on improper socialization. People learn values, attitudes, and behaviors that are consistent with violating the law. Edwin Sutherland believed that crime was learned through a process of communication within intimate personal groups. Ronald Akers extended this theory by specifying the learning mechanics (e.g., imitation, differential reinforcement) involved in this process.
- Research consistently reveals that delinquent peer associations and antisocial attitudes are among the strongest correlates of crime. Critics question whether these relationships are causal. For example, they point out that like-minded delinquents will attract each other as companions.
- Theories of informal social control suggest that crime results from inadequate socialization. Control theorists ask the question, "Why don't we all engage in criminal behavior?" Their answer, of course, is that we are controlled through our relationships with others in society.
- There are three basic forms of informal social control: direct control, indirect control, and internal control.

- Travis Hirschi's social bond theory and Sampson and Laub's age-graded theory both emphasize indirect control. To the extent that individuals have formed a societal bond, they will refrain from crime because they are unwilling to risk breaking this bond.
- Gottfredson and Hirschi's general theory of crime implicates both direct and internal control. In this theory, effective parenting (direct control) produces self-control (internal control) over time.
- Informal control theories have garnered significant empirical support. In particular, measures of direct parental control (e.g., supervision, discipline) consistently predict delinquency. There is also some evidence that adult bonds reduce criminality, even among those with a history of offending.
- Labeling theorists argue that formal punishment might actually amplify future offending. Youths who are arrested and brought to court are stigmatized as "deviant." To the extent that they believe this, they may modify their behavior to fit the label.
- Many criminologists are critical of labeling theory. There is little empirical evidence to support the proposition that arrest increases future crime. Furthermore, by the time many youths are first arrested, they have already established a pattern of chronic antisocial behavior.

PUTTING IT ALL TOGETHER

Police Tape: © SkillUp/Shutterstock

1. Compare any two social control theories of crime. What type of control (direct, indirect, internal) do they emphasize? Are the policy implications similar or different?

2. Why do social learning theorists believe that delinquent peer associations predict crime? How has this been criticized?

Chapter 7 Social Process and Crime

3. Discuss the role of social control in your own life. How might have direct, indirect, and internal controls contributed to you becoming a college student rather than a death row inmate?

4. What are the major criticisms of the labeling perspective?

5. Discuss the following statement: "It's not the quality of the act that accounts for the deviancy but rather the application of sanctions by those in power."

6. Discuss the assumption about human nature made by control theories and social learning theories. Which assumption do you think is more accurate?

KEY TERMS

adult social bonds An extension of Hirschi's social control theory from adolescence to adulthood. Adult social bonds include quality marriage and quality employment. They are a form of indirect control (something risked in order to engage in crime).

diversion programs Programs designed to divert juveniles away from official juvenile justice processing. A policy derived largely from labeling theory.

dramatization of evil Phrase coined by Frank Tannenbaum to characterize the process whereby the primary deviance of certain people is singled out and labeled as "bad."

informal social control The perspective that inadequate or incomplete socialization leads to criminal behavior.

inner containment A form of internal control (good self-concept) from Walter Reckless' containment theory.

labeling The perspective that a change in a person's self-concept, caused by criminal justice actions, may increase criminal behavior.

laws of imitation An early form of social learning theory. Gabriel Tarde identified three laws to explain how criminals learned to engage in crime.

looking-glass self The idea that self-concept is formed based on how other people respond to and react toward a person.

low self-control The key form of internal control in Gottfredson and Hirschi's general theory of crime. The authors believe that effective parenting produces self-control in children.

moral entrepreneurs Describes individuals (in the context of labeling theory) who seek to pass laws that prohibit particular behaviors.

outer containment A form of indirect control (supervision) from Walter Reckless' containment theory.

primary deviance Deviant behavior that occurs prior to any official reaction. Labeling theorists portray primary deviance as sporadic and relatively unimportant.

restorative justice A general philosophy that the proper role of the criminal justice system is to repair the harm caused by an offense. Victim–offender mediation is a central program in this perspective.

Seattle Social Developmental Project (SSDP) A project that implements many of the policy implications from the social control theory in an attempt to prevent childhood aggression and delinquency. The project attempts to increase direct control over youth, as well as to build attachment to parents and teachers and a commitment to education.

secondary deviance Deviance that is caused by the adoption of a delinquent self-concept. Without an official reaction to crime, secondary deviance would not be possible.

social bond From Hirschi's control theory. The social bond ties individuals to society so that they are not free to engage in crime. Elements of the bond include attachment, commitment, involvement, and belief.

socialization The gradual process whereby a person learns the "proper" way to live, including the norms and values that guide human behavior.

social learning The perspective that socialization toward the wrong norms and values produces criminal behavior.

symbolic interactionism A general perspective within sociology that emphasizes communication through symbolic labels and gestures.

techniques of neutralization Common excuses for delinquency identified by Sykes and Matza. These excuses neutralize the guilt associated with criminal behavior. This represents one of the first attempts to measure Sutherland's concept of "definitions favorable to law violation."

theory of differential association Edwin Sutherland's influential learning theory. He proposed that crime is learned in intimate groups through communication.

Is a person who kills another in a bar brawl a greater threat to society than a business executive who refuses to cut into his profits to make his plant a safe place to work? By any measure of death and suffering the latter is by far a greater danger than the former.

—Jeffrey Reiman[1]

CHAPTER 8

Critical Approaches to Law and Crime

Texture: © Malchev/Shutterstock; Shooter: © Malchev/Shutterstock; Puzzle Piece: © Photodisc; Police Tape: © Skillup/Shutterstock

Objectives

- Understand the difference between a consensus and conflict view of society, and the core themes of critical theories. Pg. 170

- Recognize how conflict among different interest groups shapes the content of the law and the operation of the criminal justice system. Pgs. 171–173

- Understand the evidence regarding the relationship between race, class, and criminal justice outcomes. Pgs. 173–177

- Know how radical criminologists explain the law, criminal justice system, and criminal behavior. Pgs. 179–185

- Recognize extensions of radical theory, including peacemaking criminology and critical realism. Pgs. 185–186

- Appreciate how gender may shape both criminal justice processing and theories of crime. Pgs. 187–190

- Link specific critical theories with their policy implications. Pgs. 170–191

Introduction

Are the crimes of wealthy individuals and corporate leaders treated with kid gloves compared with typical street crimes? If so, why does this situation exist? How did marijuana come to be legalized in some states but not others? The theories in this chapter raise just such questions. Critical approaches to criminology discuss why certain acts are illegal while others are not. Furthermore, they note that the criminal justice system only targets certain laws and certain individuals for full enforcement. In seeking to understand the content of the law and the operation of the criminal justice system, critical approaches are quite different from the mainstream theories covered in previous chapters.

Critical theories gained popularity in the United States in part because of the social context of the 1960s and 1970s. Prior to that time, American criminology was dominated by anomie or strain theories of delinquency and crime. Criminologists such as Cloward and Ohlin argued that broad social reforms, including the reduction of poverty, were necessary to reduce crime. Support for their Mobilization for Youth program and the general "war on poverty" indicated that many agreed with their position. By the 1970s, however, the social context had changed dramatically. The political vision of a "great society" wilted under the reality of the Vietnam War, the Watergate scandal, prison riots, the shootings at Kent State University, and civil rights demonstrations. Criminologists saw that crimes of the powerful (e.g., Watergate, FBI violations of civil rights, crimes against blacks) were ignored, while violations of victimless crimes (e.g., marijuana use, vagrancy) were pursued vigorously. Arguments for increasing support for the poor gave way to the belief that an economic and political system that created these class differences was corrupt beyond saving.[2]

Labeling theory emerged from this context as a popular explanation of crime. Labeling theorists stated that crime was a social construction and that government intervention only made delinquency worse. Theories that emerged during the 1970s, however, were "much more explicit about the connection between the criminal justice system and the underlying economic order, sometimes condemning the state itself."[3] Different commentators have referred to these theories as *critical criminology* or the *new criminology*. As will soon be noted, these general titles capture a very diverse body of theories, including conflict theory, Marxist/radical theory, and feminist criminology.

Despite this diversity, it is possible to identify a number of broad themes that tie these theories together:[4]

1. Inequality and power as central concepts: Power can be based on social class, race, gender, or other factors. The powerful will use their power to control the law and the operation of the criminal justice system.

2. Crime as a political concept: The law is not an objective, agreed-upon list of behaviors that cause the most social damage. Many acts by the powerful that cause damage are not considered criminal.

3. The criminal justice system as serving the interests of those in power: The criminal justice system targets those who lack power and ignores the crimes of those who have power.

4. The solution to crime as the creation of a more equitable society: Criminologists should work to foster social justice by supporting humane policies aimed at preventing harm.

In sum, the focus of critical criminology is much different than mainstream criminology. Until now, the theories discussed sought to explain why people engage in crime or why some neighborhoods are more prone to crime than others. The theories in this chapter focus more on the content of the law (What is illegal?) and the actions of the criminal justice system (What laws are enforced?).

> *Norms against certain behaviors begin as folkways and mores and are eventually codified into law.*

At the heart of critical theory is the belief that the law reflects the outcome of a struggle over power. Prior to this time, the popular view was that the law and its enforcement reflected societal consensus. In the **consensus model**, the law reflects common agreement over the fundamental values held by society; that is, it reflects the interests of the vast majority and the "shared popular viewpoint" in society.[5] Certain acts are prohibited because society generally agrees that this is necessary. Norms against certain behaviors begin as folkways and mores and are eventually codified into law. Law is a mechanism to resolve conflicting interests and maintain order. Here, the state is a value-neutral entity. Lawmakers resolve conflicts peacefully, the police enforce the law, and the courts arbitrate. Any biases that arise are temporary and unintended.[6]

In the **conflict model**, the law is the result of a battle between people or groups that have different levels of power. Control over the state—including the law and the criminal justice system—is the principal prize in the perpetual conflict of society.[7] In that regard, conflict theorists see bias in the criminal justice system as conscious and intentional. Those in power use the legal system to maintain power and privilege; the law and the criminal justice system reflect the interests of those who won the power struggle. Furthermore, crime can directly result from the conflict between competing groups in society.

A host of theories assume that conflict is a natural part of social life. Early conflict theories tended to be pluralistic; that is, they portrayed conflict as a result of clashes among many groups. The pluralistic perspective is discussed in this chapter under **conflict theory**. In the 1970s, theories focused on one central conflict: the battle between the very wealthy and the rest of the population. This perspective can be considered Marxist or **radical theory**.

 **Conflict Theory**

George Vold produced the first criminology textbook that prominently featured the conflict perspective. Vold argued that the content and enforcement of the law was the result of the values and interests of those in power: "Those who produce legislative majorities win control over the police power and dominate the policies that decide who is likely to be involved in violation of the law."[8] In the 1960s, a number of theorists, including William Chambliss, Richard Quinney, and Austin Turk heightened interest in how conflict shapes law.

Conflict Theory and the Law

As with labeling theorists, conflict theorists argue that mainstream criminology focuses too much attention on why people break the law, while ignoring the reasons that certain acts are illegal. As William Chambliss put it, "Instead of asking, 'Why do some people commit crimes and others do not?' we ask 'Why are some acts defined as criminal while others are not?'"[9] Their answer is that those with power and influence define the laws in a way that promotes their interests.

Within conflict theory, power is derived from a variety of sources. Power can come from membership in a more powerful group based on gender, social class, or race. In the United States, those who are white, male, and wealthy have more power than those who are poor, from a minority group, or female. Power is also equated with "resources," which might include money, organization, or access to the media. There are multiple sources of power and many different groups.[10] The competition among these groups creates a society defined by a continual state of struggle and conflict.[11] Still, many conflict theorists acknowledge that there is a high degree of consensus for some crimes—particularly violent acts such as murder, rape, and robbery. Even here, it is crucial to recognize that there is disagreement over how particular physical acts are defined. If a corporation causes someone's death by selling them an unsafe product or by polluting the air, is this "murder"?[12]

A substantial body of empirical evidence supports the conflict view of law. To be sure, research on public support for laws indicates a great deal of agreement among different segments of society for many crimes. There is also consensus on which crimes are more or less serious (violent crime vs. property crime, drug offenses).[13] Despite this agreement, a substantial amount of conflict also exists. Disagreements are apparent in laws regarding things like public order offenses (e.g., public drunkenness) and the regulation of consensual sex (e.g., prostitution).[14] Laws in these areas continue to evolve. Even where there is agreement on the law, there is conflict regarding how individuals who violate the law should be punished.

Few people would dispute the fact that political interest groups shape the criminal law in the United States. The power of interest groups is apparent in a diverse range of issues, including abortion, gun control, drug laws, pollution laws, and the death penalty. Groups such as the National Rifle Association, the American Association of Retired People, the Marijuana Policy Project, and the National Right to Life pay individuals to lobby members of Congress to push for laws consistent with their values and interests. Indeed, there are over 12,000 *registered* lobbyists in Washington, DC, and perhaps as many as 100,000 people working on behalf of interest groups.[15] On a larger scale, conflicts arising from social movements (e.g., the civil rights movement), broad segments of society (e.g., the "religious right"), and political parties (e.g., Republicans versus Democrats) also influence the development of law.[16] **Theory in Action: From Killer Weed to Medical Drug—Conflict over Marijuana Law** examines how individuals, interest groups and social movements have changed marijuana laws over time.

Conflict Theory and the Criminal Justice System

Those with power not only define the law to serve their interests, but also have an impact on the operation of the criminal justice system; that is, they have power over which laws are (or are not) enforced. Within the conflict framework, Austin Turk sought to understand crime through society's authority relationships. He suggested that criminologists should focus primarily on the process of criminalization, or the assignment of criminal status to an individual.[17] In other words, whose behavior is targeted for enforcement? Like labeling theorists, he believes that criminalization may depend less on the particular behavior of people and more on their relationship with authority figures.

Turk devised a number of concepts intended to explain criminalization. **TABLE 8-1** outlines some of his more important ideas. For instance, consider Turk's concepts of

Demonstrators gather on the Colorado State Capitol grounds to protest against the National Rifle Association's annual meeting, which took place after shootings at nearby Columbine High School. The debate over gun rights and gun control is an example conflict over the content of the law.

© Eric Gay/AP Photos

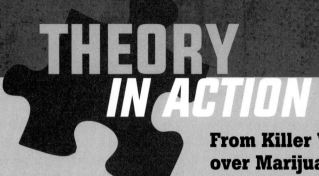

Texture: © Nik Merkulov/Shutterstock, Inc.

From Killer Weed to Medical Drug—Conflict over Marijuana Law

The consensus perspective suggests widespread agreement regarding the content of criminal laws. By and large, criminalization and penalties depend on degree of the harm caused by the act. Acts that are harmful to society become prohibited by law, and the most harmful acts have the most severe penalties. Much of the core of the legal code seems to conform to this logic. Homicide, for example, is treated more seriously than theft. Theories from the consensus perspective ask, "Why do some people violate the law?" In contrast, critical theories do not focus much on what causes crime. Instead they ask, "Why are some acts legal and others not?" In conflict theory, laws emerge from the battles among "moral entrepreneurs," interest groups, political interests, and broad segments of society. The conflict over marijuana use features all of these parties.

Most societies divide mood-altering drugs into "good/acceptable" and "bad/deviant" categories. Often, these categories have more do with history, culture, and conflict than the any measure of objective "harm" caused by the drug. It is not uncommon for drugs to become more or less accepted over time. In the United States, drugs such as caffeine, nicotine, and alcohol have a history of cultural acceptance. In contrast, during the past century, marijuana has largely been treated as a criminal substance. By most objective measures, alcohol and tobacco use cause much more direct harm (e.g., disease, death) to society than marijuana. How did marijuana come to be criminalized in the early 1900s, and why are some states now decriminalizing use of the drug?

Prior to 1900, most drugs were legal in the United States. Many over-the-counter cough syrups and "elixirs" contained cocaine, opium, or morphine. During this time, so-called "Indian hemp" from marijuana plants was used in many materials, and cannabis and hashish could be obtained legally at drug stores. The criminalization of most drugs (including alcohol) occurred throughout the early 1900s in the context of a general "temperance" movement. Influenced by religious doctrine and ideology, interest groups such as the Woman's Christian Temperance Union and the Anti-Saloon League pushed for bans on alcohol and other mood-altering substances. Although individual states began criminalizing marijuana in the 1920s, most sources credit Harry Anslinger with creating a national anti-marijuana campaign. Anslinger, the first commissioner of the Federal Bureau of Narcotics, used a mass media campaign to exploit existing racial tensions and moral sentiments to create a panic over marijuana. In his "gore files," he detailed (usually without any substantiation) gruesome crimes:

An entire family was murdered by a youthful addict in Florida. When officers arrived at the home, they found the youth staggering about in a human slaughterhouse. With an axe he had killed his father, mother, two brothers, and a sister. He seemed to be in a daze. . . . He had no recollection of having committed the multiple crimes. The officers knew him ordinarily as a sane, rather quiet young man; now he was pitifully crazed. They sought the reason. The boy said that he had been in the habit of smoking something which youthful friends called 'muggles,' a childish name for marijuana.

Consistent with previous drug scares, Anslinger capitalized existing social tensions by singling out and scapegoating African Americans, Mexicans, musicians, and other "dangerous classes":

There are 100,000 total marijuana smokers in the US, and most are Negroes, Hispanics, Filipinos and entertainers. Their Satanic music, jazz and swing, result from marijuana usage. This marijuana causes white women to seek sexual relations with Negroes, entertainers and any others."

The social construction of marijuana as a "killer weed" is captured in the 1930s propaganda film *Reefer Madness.* Financed by a church group, the movie depicts marijuana as worse than opium or heroin—a drug that causes rape, homicide, and insanity. After testimony from Anslinger and others (but with little debate) Congress passed the Marijuana Tax Stamp Act of 1937, which effectively outlawed marijuana. Since the 1970s, the federal government has classified marijuana as a "schedule I" drug—a class of drugs with a "high potential for abuse" and "no medical benefit."

Over time, attitudes toward and enforcement of marijuana laws have shifted substantially. From 1960 to the 1970s, "pot" became more popular among the affluent and middle classes. The more sinister exaggerations of marijuana effects were debunked, and many jurisdictions relaxed the punishments for possession of marijuana. *Reefer Madness* became a "cult" movie, used by legalization proponents to poke fun at government propaganda. In the 1980s, marijuana was lumped into the "war on drugs," and the pendulum swung back towards strict enforcement. Efforts to decriminalize marijuana increased in the 1990s, with the "medical marijuana" movement. A diverse set of interest groups (e.g., patient advocacy groups, drug policy groups) succeeded in redefining marijuana as medicine. By the 2000s, it was clear that attitudes toward marijuana had softened in the public. The change is reflected in the HBO series *Weeds*, where the drug is portrayed as a staple of upper-class suburban life. In 2012, Colorado and Washington became the first states to legalize the possession and sale of marijuana for recreational use since the Tax Act. Oregon, Alaska, and the District of Columbia followed suit in 2015. In each initiative, interest groups focused on the economic and social costs of incarceration, and the potential benefits of increase tax revenue. Laws were changed by direct-vote ballot measures rather than by legislative votes.

There is still a great deal of conflict regarding attitudes toward marijuana. Because the federal government and many states still view marijuana use as a serious crime, there is confusion regarding enforcement. As one example, banks and credit card companies, fearing federal trafficking laws, have been reluctant to deal with marijuana dispensaries in Colorado and Washington. Marijuana merchants, stuck carrying large amounts of cash, have fallen prey to armed robbery. Furthermore, because marijuana remains a schedule I drug, medical research about the benefits or hazards of medical marijuana is difficult. Perhaps the only certainty now is that conflict over this drug will continue in the near future.

Sources: Hari, J. (2015). *Chasing the scream: The first and last days of the drug war*. New York: Bloomsbury; Johnson, K. (2014, November 5). New marijuana initiatives loom as 3 win approval. *New York Times*, Retrieved July 6, 2015, from http://www.nytimes.com/2014/11/06/us/politics/new-marijuana-initiatives-loom-as-3-win-approval.html; Barcott, B. B., & Scherer, M. (2015, May). The highly divisive, curiously underfunded and strangely promising world of pot science. *Time*, 38-45; Lee, M. A. (2012). *Smoke signals: A social history of marijuana—medical, recreational and scientific*. New York: Simon and Schuster.

organization and sophistication. Criminalization is more likely for an organized but unsophisticated norm resister (e.g., delinquent gang member) than for an organized and sophisticated person (e.g., Mafia member). Turk's theory has recently found some support in research that analyzes police–citizen encounters.[18] A study of data from police observations found that organization and sophistication of the police and suspects significantly predicted overt conflict (use of force).[19]

William Chambliss and Robert Seidman authored another influential conflict-oriented text. The starting point for their analysis was the assumption that as society becomes more complex, dispute resolution will move away from "reconciliation" and toward "rule enforcement."[20] A complex society will therefore depend heavily on sanctioning (police action) to keep order among parties in conflict. In the United States, Chambliss pointed to the dominance of middle-class values. Thus, the middle class could impose its own standards and view of proper behavior upon others in society. Furthermore, the bureaucratic nature of the legal system meant that enforcement of the law would be biased against lower-class people. Bureaucratic agencies tend to maximize the rewards for and minimize the strains against the organization. As a result, police are expected to avoid enforcing crimes committed by the powerful (which might cause trouble) and focus on crimes of the poor. Those who lack power are less able to successfully resist enforcement.[21]

> *Bureaucratic agencies tend to maximize the rewards for and minimize the strains against the organization.*

Research on Race and Criminal Justice Processing

Conflict theory suggests that enforcement of laws will be biased against those who lack power. One way to test this proposition is to see whether the less powerful groups in society (e.g., racial minorities, the poor) receive harsher treatment from the criminal justice system. In other words, are black offenders more likely to be arrested, prosecuted, and imprisoned than white offenders? A simple inspection of arrest and prison statistics appears to support the conflict perspective. Minorities (especially African Americans) are overrepresented at every stage of the criminal justice system—from arrest to imprisonment. In 2012, white Americans were imprisoned at a rate of 463 per 100,000. African Americans had an imprisonment rate of 2,841 per 100,000; and Hispanics 1,158 per 100,000.[22] On the other hand, males are incarcerated at a dramatically higher rate than females—a finding that contradicts conflict theory because men have more power.

The fact that a particular group is overrepresented in the criminal justice system does not, however, definitively support or refute conflict theory. Many consensus theories predict that minorities or members of the lower class are more likely to be involved in serious forms of criminal behavior. Social disorganization theory (see Chapter 6), for example, predicts that because minorities often live in poverty-stricken, disorganized neighborhoods,

TABLE 8-1

Factors Influencing Conflict Between Authority Figures and Law Violators

Factor	Relationship to the Likelihood of Conflict
Organization	Conflict is more likely when those engaging in crime are organized. (Gangs and syndicate criminals will likely be more resistant to authority.)
Sophistication	The probability of conflict increases when the law violator is less sophisticated (a street thug as opposed to a white-collar criminal).
Relative power of enforcers and resisters	Criminalization is more likely when enforcers (police, prosecutors) have substantially more power than resisters. However, some resisters who have little power may be passed over and seen as being "not worth the trouble."
The correspondence of cultural and social norms	Cultural norms are "what is expected" (the letter of the law), whereas social norms refer to "what is actually being done" (how laws are actually enforced). When there is congruence between these sets of norms, criminalization is more likely.

Source: Turk, A. T. (1969). *Criminality and legal order.* Chicago: Rand McNally.

they are more likely to engage in crime. Conflict theory, on the other hand, would suggest that differences in arrest and imprisonment are not simply due to differences in criminal behavior. The key issue is whether **extra-legal factors** (e.g., race, class, and gender) have a substantial impact on criminal justice system decision making, regardless of **legal factors** such as offense seriousness and prior record.

At the least, it appears as though legal factors, particularly offense seriousness and prior record, are the strongest predictors of decisions made by the police, prosecutors, and judges.[23] This finding should not come as a shock to anyone. Common sense dictates that someone with prior felony convictions who is caught in the act of armed robbery has a greater risk of arrest and imprisonment than someone with no prior record who gets caught shoplifting. Still, an important issue is whether race, class, or other factors also matter. The vast majority of research in this area focuses on race. This research asks (sticking with the example), "Are a black and white shoplifter, each with similar criminal records, treated equally?"

Answering this type of question requires a multivariate analysis, which statistically controls for legal factors in order to examine factors such as race or class. That is the only way to find out whether the size of the black prison population is due to legitimate factors (e.g., more serious offenses, more severe prior record) or to discrimination.

The research examining race and the criminal justice system is extremely complex and often contradictory. Typically, a study examines official decision making within a jurisdiction, at a particular stage (e.g., arrest decisions, court decisions) of the criminal justice system. The most difficult decision makers to evaluate are the police. Police decisions typically occur on the streets, and there are no records of individuals who are let go without formal action. To overcome this problem, a number of researchers have directly observed the behaviors of police.

Reiss's 1966 observational study found that race in itself did not influence police decisions to arrest. Black suspects were more likely to be arrested because they were suspected of more serious crimes, were more hostile toward police, and were more likely to have complainants who demanded official action.[24] Later studies reached very similar conclusions. It is important to remember that hostility toward police does not arise in a vacuum; minority communities are subject to a stronger and often more aggressive police presence than other areas. Also, a few observational studies have found evidence of racial bias.[25] An important limitation of this type of research is that police might act differently—in a less biased manner—simply because they are being observed.

Over the past 30 years, **racial profiling** has become an extremely controversial issue. Many minorities believe that they are pulled over for traffic stops simply because of the color of their skin (i.e., "driving while black"). A great deal of evidence exists that indicates that African Americans are more likely to be stopped, to have their cars searched, and to be ticketed than would be expected given their numbers in the population.[26] Still, it is difficult to determine the cause of this difference. For example, it could reflect the fact that minorities are more likely to live in high crime areas that are heavily patrolled by police, to drive in areas where more traffic accidents occur, or to speed.[27] Recent research, using data from police stops and from surveys of the public on their interactions with police, finds evidence that race disparities cannot be entirely due to these factors.[28] Where does the weight of the evidence on the relationship between arrest and race lay? A meta-analysis of research conducted over the last 30 years found that "the most credible conclusion based on the evidence examined is that race does affect the likelihood of arrest."[29]

After a person is arrested, tracking decision making becomes much easier because a paper trail exists. Scholars have examined whether race impacts bail decisions, prosecution decisions (whether to charge or release a suspect), and sentencing decisions (both sentence length and whether or not a person gets prison time). Once again, there are no simple answers. Instead, different studies yield different results. As a starting point, consider Alfred Blumstein's research comparing arrest rates to incarceration rates at a national level. If there were no bias in the criminal justice system, the percentage of blacks arrested should be roughly equal to the percentage of blacks incarcerated. In two separate studies, Blumstein found that a large portion (76–80%) of the racial disparity in incarceration rates was due to disparities in arrest rates.[30,31] Still, incarceration rates were higher for blacks than would be expected given their arrest rates. Furthermore, as the seriousness of the offense decreased, arrest disparities were less important for explaining disparities in black incarceration.

This finding suggests that as discretion in the criminal justice system increases, blacks find themselves at a disadvantage. In a replication of this study in a single jurisdiction (Pennsylvania), researchers concluded that race differences in arrests accounted for even less (70%) of the race differences in imprisonment. In other words, 30 percent of the racial differences in incarceration were not due to racial differences in offending. For drug crimes, where criminal justice system discretion is higher, racial differences in offending accounted for only 20 percent of racial differences in incarceration.[32]

Another approach is to track offenders within a jurisdiction. Joan Petersilia conducted a detailed study of the California criminal justice system based on Offender-Based Transaction Statistics (OBTS). She found that minority suspects were more likely than whites to be released after arrest. Yet, following a felony conviction, minority offenders were more likely than whites to receive a long prison sentence. These differences held even after controlling for prior record, offense seriousness, previous violence, and probation or parole status. Additional information from the Rand prisoner survey in California, Texas, and Michigan revealed that minorities are not overrepresented in the arrest population compared with the number of crimes that they actually commit, nor are they more likely to be arrested.[33]

An analysis of more than 11,000 California offenders convicted of assault, robbery, burglary, theft, forgery, or drug crimes revealed a similar pattern. Although black and

African Americans have much higher arrest and incarceration rates than white Americans. Conflict theories suggest that this is due, in part, to the lack of power that this group has in American society.

© Mark Richards/PhotoEdit

Latino offenders were more likely to go to prison than white offenders, after legal factors (e.g., prior adult or juvenile history, use of a weapon) were controlled, race differences disappeared. In other words, knowledge of race, independent of legal factors, did not help predict who goes to prison versus who gets probation.[34]

Studies such as these led William Wilbanks to conclude that it was a myth that the criminal justice system is discriminatory. Wilbanks argues that although some persons in the system may make decisions on the basis of race, there is no systematic racial bias in the criminal justice system.[35] After other factors (e.g., prior record, offense seriousness) are held constant, the effect of race is minimal. Wilbanks's position, however, is by no means the final word on this subject. This body of research does not capture, for example, differences in police patrolling. In other words, police presence helps to determine who accumulates a prior record. In that sense, statistically controlling for prior record might mask racial bias in policing.[36] Furthermore, some studies do indeed find that racial bias exists and affects criminal justice decisions independent of legal factors.[37]

A final body of empirical research examines the relationship between the presence of a "threatening" social group and measures of punitiveness within a certain geographical area. The racial threat hypothesis suggests that increases in minority populations relative to the white population will provoke racial fear and prejudice and increase punitive criminal sanctions. This hypothesis has received some support in the literature.[38] Scholars have documented correlations between the percentage of black citizens and a diverse number of outcome measures, including lynching, the size of police forces, arrest rates, and sentencing practices.[39,40] For example, McGarrell tested a conflict model of incarceration rates in the United States for 1971, 1980, and 1988. He compared the effects of both social and structural variables and the crime rate. He determined that two variables (percentage of black population and the violent crime rate) were strong and consistent predictors of the incarceration rate.[41]

Critics note that "percentage of black citizens" is at best an indirect measure of threat—and one that does not capture ethnicity. This is important because Hispanics now constitute the largest racial/ethnic minority in the United States. A recent study attempted to address both of these limitations. They discovered that the growth rate of the Hispanic population (the measure of "threat") predicted public support for the use of ethnicity in criminal sentencing. Where the growth rate was high, people were more likely to agree that "Judges should be allowed to use an offender's ethnicity when determining how severe his or her punishment sentence should be."[42]

As should be clear from the preceding, the research on race and the criminal justice system is complex and oftentimes contradictory. On the broad question of whether the system is biased, there is no easy answer. Looking within certain categories of crime or punishment, however, sometimes yields a clear and disturbing picture.

Race and the War on Drugs

Conflict theory appears to be particularly relevant to a discussion about the law, race, and the criminal justice system in the context of illicit drugs. The history of legislation against drug use in the United States is in many ways a story of linking particular drugs with a "dangerous" (and powerless) class of citizens. In an effort to portray these drugs as particularly bad, opium was linked to Chinese immigrants and marijuana to Mexicans.[43] In essence, the "drug of choice" of the less powerful group is criminalized; laws against the particular drug are then enthusiastically enforced.

David Cole summarizes the conflict argument regarding the most recognizable target in the war on drugs—crack cocaine.[44]

> *Politicians impose the most serious criminal sanctions on conduct in which they and their constituents are least likely to engage. Thus, a predominantly white Congress has mandated prison sentences for the possession and distribution of crack cocaine 100 times more severe than the penalties for powder cocaine.*

When crack cocaine spread rapidly through urban areas in the 1980s, legislators responded with harsh penalties for possessing or selling this drug. Critics suggest that the major causality of the War on Drugs has been racial minorities.

© Janine Wiedel Photolibrary/Alamy Images

> *African-Americans comprise more than 90% of those found guilty of crack cocaine crimes. By contrast, when white youth began smoking marijuana in large numbers in the 1960s and 1970s, state legislatures responded by reducing penalties. . . .*

There is little doubt that police targeted the sale and distribution of crack cocaine throughout the 1980s and 1990s. Not surprisingly, a shift in focus from powder cocaine and other drugs toward crack increased racial disparities in drug arrests. In the 1970s, African Americans accounted for roughly 20 percent of drug arrests. By the early 1990s, they made up 40 percent of all drug arrests.[45] It is important to recognize that competition over crack cocaine markets created spikes in violence in many minority communities. In part, increased arrests and prosecutions were a response to this violence. Criminologist Michael Tonry has argued, though, that the overall effect of the war on drugs on the black community was a foreseeable tragedy:[46]

> *What was clear both then and now is that a program built around education, drug abuse treatment, and social programs designed to address the structural, social, and economic conditions that lead to crime and drug abuse would have a much less destructive impact on disadvantaged young blacks than would a program whose primary tactics were the arrest, prosecution, and lengthy incarceration of street-level sellers who are disproportionately black and Hispanic.*

There are clear signals that the drug war is winding down. Attitudes toward illicit drug use have shifted in American society. More than half of Americans now support the legalization of marijuana. Since 1990s, many states have legalized marijuana for medical use, and four states (Alaska, Oregon, Colorado, and Washington) and the District of Columbia have legalized recreational use. In this new landscape, the appetite for incarcerating drug offenders has waned among policymakers. At the federal level, these shifts are reflected in the Fair Sentencing Act of 2010, which reduced the so-called "crack multiplier" from 100:1 to18:1, and eliminated a 5-year mandatory sentence for simple possession of crack cocaine.[47] To be sure, this change has been slow and uneven, and enforcement disparities persist. An ACLU report released in 2013 found that marijuana arrests continue to account for half of all drug arrests in the country. Despite equal usage of the drug, blacks are almost four times more likely to be arrested for marijuana use than whites.[48]

Capital Sentencing and Race

Historically, race has also played a role in the imposition of the death penalty in the United States. In *Furman v. Georgia*, a number of the Supreme Court justices raised serious questions about discrimination and arbitrariness in the application of the death penalty. For example, Justice Douglas noted:[49]

> *It would seem incontestable that the death penalty inflicted on one defendant is "unusual" if it discriminates against him by reason of his race, religion,*

wealth, social position, or class, or if it is imposed under a procedure that gives room for the play of such prejudices.

At that time, a massive body of research indicated that racial bias clouded the capital sentencing process. In particular, it clearly demonstrated that blacks were far more likely to receive a death sentence than were whites.[50,51] Also, it was determined that whites were more likely to have their death sentences commuted to a lesser sentence.[52] Other studies found that capital sentencing was not only based on the race of the killer, but also was determined by the race of the victim. For example, one study found that Philadelphia blacks charged with murdering whites were more likely to receive a death sentence than any other offender–victim race combination.[53] This pattern was also present in rape cases; blacks convicted of raping whites were 18 times more likely to receive a death sentence.[54]

The *Furman* case led to a ban on the death penalty for the crime of rape, but did not go so far as to rule the death penalty unconstitutional. Rather, it questioned the unbridled discretion at work in the capital sentencing process. In 1976, the Supreme Court (*Gregg v. Georgia*) approved a new Georgia system. The Supreme Court ruled that Georgia's "guided discretion" statute provided adequate protection against the arbitrary and capricious application of the death penalty. In other words, the Supreme Court concluded that the Georgia process provided adequate protection against racial bias and other arbitrary, extra-legal influences.

The Georgia law had several significant features. First, it required a bifurcated trial. In the first phase of the trial, the jury addressed the issue of guilt or innocence. In the second or sentencing phase, the penalty was decided. Second, the law delimited specific aggravating (and later, mitigating) circumstances that juries would consider during the sentencing phase of the trial. The court eventually gave broad latitude to the defense regarding what could be introduced in mitigation. Third, the Georgia law required an automatic appeal of all death sentences to the state supreme court. The Court believed that these processes provided sufficient protection of the rights of the accused.

Unfortunately, research on capital sentencing conducted following *Gregg* indicates that race is still an important factor in the decision to execute. For example, studies of the capital sentencing process in Florida revealed that blacks who kill whites have the greatest probability of receiving the death penalty.[55] Other studies found evidence of this specific pattern of discrimination in different states, including Texas, Maryland, and Kentucky.[56–58] This pattern of racial discrimination was not a function of other factors. For example, cases in which blacks killed whites were not more aggravated or particularly heinous homicides.[59]

This research evidence was the focus of an evaluation synthesis conducted by the U.S. General Accounting Office (GAO).[60] This analysis was required under The Anti-Drug Abuse Act of 1988. Specifically, this legislation called for a study of capital sentencing procedures to determine if the race of either the victim or the defendant influenced the capital sentencing process. The GAO uncovered 53 studies of capital sentencing. They excluded those that did not contain empirical data or were duplicative. As a result, 28 studies were judged methodologically sound. Based on their review, the GAO concluded that:[61]

Thomas Miller-El gained a stay of execution from the U.S. Supreme Court in 2002. He was granted a new trial because of alleged racial discrimination in his first trial. Research consistently reveals that individuals who kill white women are the most likely to receive the death penalty.

© Brett Coomer/AP Photos

- In 82 percent of the studies, the race of the victim was found to influence the likelihood of being charged with capital murder or receiving the death penalty (especially those who murdered whites).
- The influence of the victim's race was found at all stages of the criminal justice system process. This evidence was stronger at the earlier stages of this process (e.g., prosecutorial decision to seek the death penalty or to proceed to trial rather than plea bargain) than in the later stages.
- Legally relevant variables (e.g., aggravating circumstances, prior record, culpability level, heinousness of the crime, and number of victims) were influential but did not fully explain the reasons for racial disparity in capital sentencing.

The GAO concluded that this evidence represented a strong race-of-victim influence over capital sentencing. Studies since the 1990s continue to find that the capital sentencing process is significantly influenced by race. Offenders who killed whites are more likely to be charged with a capital offense and to receive a death sentence, especially if they are black.[62]

The United States remains distinct from its Western European peers in its use of the death penalty. As with the drug war, however, American attitudes toward the death penalty have softened somewhat in the past decade. A 2015 Pew Center Research poll found that 58 percent of Americans support the death penalty. This was a 40-year low and a sizable decline from peak support (78%) in 1996. There remain profound racial divides regarding support for executions. In the United States, blacks and Hispanics typically express support levels that are 25–30 percentage points lower than whites.[63] The overall decline and the race and ethnic divides in support quite possibly stem from concern over the possibility that an innocent person could be executed. Indeed, since the advent of DNA technology in the 1980s, 20 death row inmates have been exonerated.[64]

Conflict Theory as an Explanation of Criminal Behavior

As noted earlier, the conflict explanation of the law and criminal justice system suggests that those who have power will make and enforce laws that are in their interests. Several sociologists, however, have extended conflict theory to explain criminal behavior. Criminal conduct may originate when a less powerful group adheres to its group norms while simultaneously violating those of another group. Basically, behavior that is valued in one group is denounced (and criminalized) by another. All the while, individuals believe they are acting appropriately.

Thorsten Sellin is most well known for developing this principle. Sellin was primarily concerned with the culture conflict faced by immigrants. He proposed that culture conflict was the result of the difference in norms between ethnic groups.[65] In complex societies like the United States, people from diverse ethnic, cultural, religious, and social backgrounds are living in close proximity to one another, yet they may not accept the values or divergent lifestyles of their neighbors. Moreover, in most social situations, each group has right and wrong ways of behaving. People are socially conditioned by these "conduct norms,"[66] but different groups have different norms. Culture conflict results when these groups meet.

Sellin defined **primary conflict** as that which may arise between an established culture and recent immigrants. Because immigrants bring divergent religious beliefs, norms, and values from their homeland, culture conflict is inevitable. What was considered appropriate conduct in the old country may be a crime in the new culture. To illustrate, Sellin cites the Sicilian father in New Jersey who murdered the youth responsible for seducing his daughter. The father expressed surprise at his arrest because he was merely defending his family's honor in the traditional Sicilian fashion. Here, customary behavior in Sicilian society clashed with American definitions of legal behavior.

A more recent example of primary conflict is the use of "khat" among East African (e.g., Somalian, Ethiopian, Yemeni) immigrants. Khat is a stimulant that is legal and culturally accepted in East Africa and the Arabian Peninsula, but is illegal in the United States. Khat has created conflict between East African immigrant communities and law enforcement.[67] Yet another example is the practice of circumcising females. Circumcision, which can include the removal of the clitoris, is still common in some cultures but has been denounced under American law.[68] In such situations, the norms of the dominant culture become the deciding factor in characterizing an action as crime.

Secondary conflict occurs within a single culture that has different subcultures, each with its own conduct norms. Here, Sellin anticipates the development of subcultural theories in criminology (see Chapter 6). Norm conflict can develop within a single culture when the norms of one subculture come into conflict with those of another. This theme is apparent in the study of 1,313 gangs conducted by Frederic Thrasher.[69] He reported the existence of a gang culture whose norms clashed with those of society. One dominant activity was orgiastic behavior: drinking, gambling, smoking, and sex. The values of the gang created an esprit de corps that carried over to all its activities. Similarly, Sutherland's culture conflict theory stated that the different values present in segments of society could lead an individual to criminal behavior.[70]

Sellin considered conduct norms to be universal and common to all forms of society. His theory was criticized, however, for being too narrow in its focus on norms, not people. As history shows, migrant groups are seldom accepted, and this rejection often leads to anomie and resentment. However, as succeeding generations of immigrants are socialized by the dominant culture, family ties as well as old-world cultural norms weaken. In short, Sellin overlooked the fact that heterogeneity must develop in modern, complex societies.

George Vold turned the attention of conflict theory toward a class of crimes that were more directly related to political conflict:[71]

- Crimes resulting from political protest movements (e.g., disorderly conduct arrests from clashing with police)
- Crimes that arise from strife between management and labor unions (e.g., the use of illegal tactics to "break" unions, employee sabotage of factory equipment)
- Crimes that result from attempts to change or upset the caste system that enforces racial segregation (e.g., lynching)

In such situations, Vold argues, "criminality is the normal, natural response of normal, natural human beings struggling in understandably normal and natural situations for the maintenance of the way of life to which they stand committed."[72] In this case, conflict directly produces criminal behavior. Furthermore, criminality depends on which side ultimately wins the conflict. Take, for example, the "Jim Crow" laws enforced by whites. These laws were passed by 19th-century legislatures of the southern states to segregate blacks and maintain a racial caste system. Blacks who violated these laws were seen as criminal; their churches were bombed and their leaders lynched. Ultimately, after the spread of civil rights, the white supremacists who enforced these laws were seen as criminals. In a similar vein, individuals who are a direct threat to a government regime are often branded as dissidents or terrorists and jailed. As power shifts, such criminals may become leaders of a new government.

A Critique of Conflict Theory

Within a certain realm of behavior, conflict theory appears to have some support, both as a theory of criminal behavior and as a theory of law. There is little disagreement that conflict is a central feature of democratic societies, nor is there argument against the idea that political groups attempt to shape the law in their favor. Conflict can (as in the case of labor strife or abortion protests) directly lead to criminal behavior. Early conflict theorists such as George Vold recognized that conflict theory should not be stretched to account for behaviors or laws that are outside of its scope. Chambliss, for example, points out that in many circumstances, there is no conflict whatsoever. There is wide public consensus that laws should prohibit crimes such as murder, assault, and rape.[73]

In that sense, conflict theory does not explain the core of the legal code, much of which seems to be agreed on and to benefit society as a whole. Furthermore, the vast amount of delinquent and criminal behavior is not political in nature, nor does it tend to pit one group against another. Rather, victimization studies clearly demonstrate that most crime occurs within the same groups. Minorities generally victimize other minorities; poor people generally victimize other poor people, and so forth. In this regard, conflict theory has been criticized for explaining too little. On the other hand, some have criticized conflict theory for not going far enough. In the 1970s, many conflict theorists shifted their attention toward one main source of conflict: the distribution of wealth.

 ## Radical Criminology

Over time, many conflict theorists came to believe that conflict results not from a struggle among many groups, but from a larger struggle between the very wealthy and the rest of society. Radical, or "Marxist" criminologists use Karl Marx's theories of social structure to explain both (1) the nature and extent of crime in society and (2) the content and enforcement of the criminal law. Although Marx did not address the issue of crime in-depth, his ideas do spotlight the linkage between capitalism and criminality.

Karl Marx and Crime

Marxist criminology focuses on the conflict among three socioeconomic classes:[74]

1. The **capitalists**, who own the means of production and exploit the surplus labor of others
2. The **bourgeoisie**, who hold salaried and management (i.e., middle-class) positions
3. The **proletariat**, who comprise the working class

Marxists view the enactment and enforcement of laws as an outgrowth of the conflicts created by the unequal distribution

Karl Marx wrote extensively about the evils of capitalism. Although he wrote little about crime, his ideas are an integral part of modern radical theory.
© Photos.com/Thinkstock/Getty

of wealth, power, and control within a capitalist society. In short, the law enforces the ideology of the capitalist ruling class.

Marx's critique of capitalism is relevant to the study of crime in several ways. Marx saw crime as largely a function of class conflict. The capitalist class owned the means of production: the use and distribution of tools, technical knowledge, and human labor. In addition, it profited from the creation of surplus value, or the value of commodities workers produce above what they are paid in wages.[75]

According to Marx, the capitalist economic system is supported by the **superstructure** of social institutions (e.g., law, education, and politics) that "lend legitimacy to both the class structure and the dominant set of economic relationships underpinning" the structure.[76] They were the foundation of the legal and political structures of the state. In this context, crime became an expression of the individual's struggle against unjust social conditions. Criminals were part of the **lumpenproletariat**—the dispossessed, unorganized workers' underclass. They did not contribute to the production of goods and services; instead, they made their livelihood from others who did work.[77] Criminal life was a natural reaction by those who were cut off from the fruits of capitalism and brutalized by under- or unemployment. Marx asserted that crime was a product of poverty and the conditions of inequality bred by capitalism. Because crime was the result of an unjust economic system, the only way to prevent crime was to change that system.

Engels and the Social Revolution

Friedrich Engels, Marx's friend, sponsor, and collaborator, directly addressed the issue of crime. To Engels, crime was a form of revolt—too primitive and unorganized to succeed—waged against the dreadful oppression of the capitalist industrial system. Society was the original offender. It created crime by depriving unfortunates of a place at the "feast of life." Engels believed that communism was the ultimate solution to crime:[78]

> To protect itself against crime, against direct acts of violence, society requires an extensive, complicated system of administrative and judicial bodies, which require an immense labor force. In communist society, we eliminate the contradiction between the individual man and all others, we counterpoise social peace to social war, and we put the ax to the root of crime. Crimes against property cease to their own accord where everyone receives what he needs to satisfy his natural and spiritual urges, where social gradations and distinctions cease to exist.

Bonger and Egoistic Capitalism

One of the first Marxist criminologists was Wilhelm Adrian Bonger. He expanded the definition of criminal behavior by viewing crime as an "immoral" act against a prevailing social structure. Bonger stated that unless the act injures the ruling class as well as the subject class, it was unlikely to be punished.[79]

Bonger believed that **altruism** was a defining characteristic of primitive societies: Production was for mutual consumption, not exchange; social solidarity was high. The problem with a capitalist society was that it transformed the basic nature of humankind. Capitalistic societies are characterized by **egoism**: Capitalists produce for themselves and attempt to build a surplus to create a profit. They are not interested in the needs of others. In this manner, capitalism builds social irresponsibility and creates a climate of motivation for crime.

Bonger also considered what he called rich men's crimes: Fraudulent bankruptcies, adulteration of food, stock market manipulations, land speculation, and the like. These types of crimes forced the masses to pay more than required for the necessities of life: "What an ordinary criminal does in a small way, they do on a gigantic scale; while the former injures a single person, or only a few, the latter brings misfortune to great numbers."[80]

According to Bonger, the solution was to create a socialist society. Socialism, he claimed, would cure many ills and allow the spirit of altruism to come forward and flourish.

He noted, however, that crimes would still be committed by persons with medical or psychiatric problems. Bonger's writings—especially his focus on the crimes of the wealthy, and his suggestion that capitalism corrodes empathy for fellow citizens—are still reflected in modern radical theories. Bonger's central ideas were also put to a recent empirical test. Using a sample of nations, researchers found that more "capitalistic" countries had higher homicide rates. This relationship, however, did not appear to stem from the spread of egoism, as predicted by Bonger.[81]

Rusche and Kirchheimer and Penal Systems

George Rusche and Otto Kirchheimer offered another early Marxist analysis of crime. They examined how criminal sanctions developed in a capitalist state. Until the rise of capitalism, they noted, punishments for criminal behavior were largely determined by one's ability or inability to pay a fine. Thus, they argued, it was only natural that punishments would become more severe as economic conditions worsened. For example, over 72,000 thieves were hanged in England during the reign of Henry VIII. However, when the potential of inmate labor power became apparent, convicts were transported to distant lands to provide more markets for the British Empire instead of being executed. Rusche and Kirchheimer regarded economic conditions as the central issue in penal policy:[82]

> The penal system of any given society is not an isolated phenomenon subject only to its own special laws. It is an integral part of the whole social system, and shares its aspirations and its defects. The crime rate can be influenced only if society can offer its members a certain measure of security and to guarantee a reasonable standard of living.

Rusche and Kirchheimer argued that imprisonment served as a solution to economic problems after Western society moved from feudalism to capitalism. They concluded that the complex legal systems found in capitalist societies provide only an illusion of security. They do not deal with the root problems of social inequality.

Rusche and Kirchheimer theorized that imprisonment served an important role in capitalist societies: the regulation of the labor force.[83] In essence, their argument implies that imprisonment should increase when surplus labor is high and decrease when there is a labor shortage. The research findings on this hypothesis are inconsistent. A multivariate analysis of time-series data on imprisonment in the United States from 1948 to 1981 found evidence of an effect of unemployment on prison admissions.[84] However, a historical analysis of the New York state prison system offered little support

> **The problem with a capitalist society was that it transformed the basic nature of humankind.**

to Rusche and Kirchheimer's claim that imprisonment is a consequence of the desire to exploit and train captive manufacturing labor.[85] A longitudinal study investigated the effect of unemployment rates on rates of pretrial jail incarceration in Florida and found no relationship between these variables at either the felony or misdemeanor levels.[86] This finding suggests that Rusche and Kirchheimer overstated this relationship. Pretrial incarceration was not used to control labor surpluses.

The Marxist influence has extended to modern criminology. Radical criminologists argue that the power of the capitalist state depends entirely on its ability to use the criminal justice system to maintain social order. The economic elite define and enforce the law to favor specific interests. The law reflects the unequal distribution of wealth in society and enforces the will of the ruling class. Moreover, they point out, the state is very selective about whom it punishes.

> **The economic elite define and enforce the law to favor specific interests.**

Richard Quinney: Class, Crime, and the State

Richard Quinney remains one of the most influential radical criminologists in the United States. Quinney's ideas have evolved substantially over time—from conflict theory in the 1960s to radical theory throughout the 1970s and 1980s, and finally to his most recent statements on peacemaking criminology. In his 1977 book, *Class, State, and Crime*, Quinney portrays the criminal justice system as the last supporting prop for a slowly decaying capitalist social order.[87] It controls a population that can no longer be restrained by employment or social services. Of particular interest is Quinney's definition of criminal behavior (see TABLE 8-2).

Quinney ties together the work of Marx, Engels, Bonger, and others to characterize most forms of criminal behavior as the result of capitalism. Quinney describes several types

TABLE 8-2

Richard Quinney's Typology of Crime

Type of Crime	Description
Crimes of Domination	
Crimes of control	Felonies and misdemeanors by law enforcement agents against persons accused of crimes (e.g., violations of the civil liberties of citizens).
Crimes of government	Actions by elected and appointed officials of the capitalist state to maintain political control over others (e.g., Watergate, Iran-Contra, warfare, political assassination).
Crimes of economic domination	Corporate crimes (e.g., price fixing, pollution, hazardous work conditions, marketing of unsafe products) that protect and further the accumulation of capital. Organized crime also seeks to perpetuate the capitalist system because it invests some of its profits from illegal goods and services in legitimate businesses.
Social injuries	Denial of basic human rights (e.g., sexism, racism, economic exploitation) that are not typically defined as crime.
Crimes of Accommodation	
Predatory crimes	Crimes such as burglary, robbery, and drug dealing that are produced out of a need to survive. These are reproductions of the capitalist system.
Personal crimes	Violent crimes (e.g., murder, rape, robbery) usually directed against members of the same class and pursued by those who have already been brutalized by the capitalist system.
Crimes of resistance	Crimes that are an expression of political consciousness (e.g., the sabotage of factory equipment) directed at the capitalist class.

Data from Richard Quinney, *Class, State, and Crime*, 2nd ed. (New York: Longman, 1980): 56–66.

of crime committed by capitalists in order to maintain their control over society. Consistent with radical theory, Quinney argues that law enforcement exists primarily to control members of the lower class. "Crimes of control" result when police violate the civil rights of others (e.g., police brutality). "Crimes of economic domination" include most forms of white-collar crime (e.g., price fixing, pollution). The capitalist elite also engage in socially injurious behavior, such as the denial of basic human rights (e.g., sexism, racism, economic exploitation), that are not defined as criminal. These denials are not defined as criminal because the capitalists control the definition of criminal behavior and are unlikely to pass laws against their interests.

Apart from crimes committed by capitalists, Quinney portrays crimes among the lower class as acts of survival. Because they are economically exploited, members of the lower class rob, steal, and burglarize in order to meet basic needs. Ironically, by exploiting other members of their class, these predatory offenders reproduce the capitalist system. He argues that acts of violence (murder, rape, assault) are a reaction to the brutality of the capitalist system. Ultimately, Quinney advocates the development of a socialist society to halt the abuses of the capitalist state.

Radical Explanations of the Law and the Criminal Justice System

Quinney's work clearly suggests that criminal law and the criminal justice system are used solely as tools to control the lower classes. Considered **instrumental Marxism**, this type of theory argues that the law and criminal justice system are always instruments to be used by the capitalist class.[88] The purpose of radical analyses within this perspective is to demonstrate the true purpose of the criminal law and the justice system. A major weakness of instrumental Marxist analysis is that there is a substantial body of law that appears to run against the interests of the capitalist class. Why, for example, would economic elites allow laws against pollution, price fixing, or false advertising?

Structural Marxism grants the government, at least in the short term, a degree of political autonomy. In other words, some laws may indeed run counter to the desires of the capitalist class. Furthermore, capitalists are not portrayed as a single homogenous group. Rather, some laws may serve the interests of particular factions of the capitalist elite, but not others.[89] In the long run, both perspectives argue that the content of the legal code and enforcement of the laws will benefit the economic elites. What is the evidence to support this position?

Jeffrey Reiman's *The Rich Get Richer and the Poor Get Prison* is a classic treatise on this issue. Reiman argues that dangerous actions perpetrated by the wealthy are often not even defined as criminal. For example, studies estimate that over 12,000 Americans die from unnecessary surgeries each year. Countless more die from pollution, hazardous work conditions, and unsafe products. Even where these actions are defined as criminal, they are framed as actions that require regulatory oversight rather than criminal prosecution. To the extent that white-collar criminals convicted of acts

such as insider trading, embezzlement, and fraud are even sanctioned, their penalties pale in comparison to the typical sanctions for street crimes.

Reiman argues that at virtually every stage of the criminal justice system, the wealthy and middle-class members of society are weeded out, leaving predominantly poor individuals to fill U.S. prisons. Reiman highlights research that indicates that (1) the police are more likely to take formal action when the suspect is poor; (2) the wealthy are less likely to be formally charged for an offense; and (3) even when charged, the wealthy are often able to avoid punitive sanctioning.[90]

Moreover, crimes that are likely to be committed by wealthy individuals (e.g., insider trading, embezzlement, violations of occupational safety standards, bribery, consumer fraud) are viewed as less serious and are less likely to be enforced. Reiman highlights the savings and loan scandal in the 1980s, and corporate crime sagas of the 1990s (e.g., Enron, Arthur Anderson, Tyco). Where prison sentences were handed out for these crimes, they were very light compared with the typical sentence for a comparable street crime. For example, the savings and loan scandal in the 1980s cost

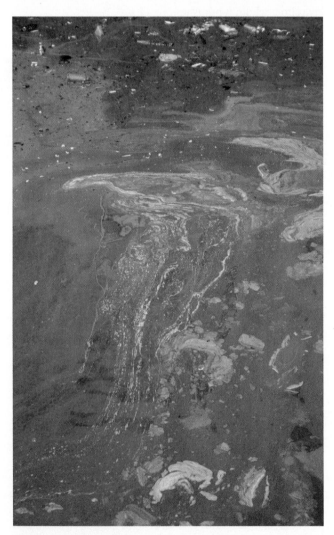

Would more vigorous enforcement of the law reduce corporate and white collar crimes such as pollution?

© george green/Shutterstock, Inc.

American taxpayers over $480 billion, but it led to only a handful of convictions of company executives. Of those convicted, most ended up serving between 1 and 4 years in prison.[91]

Recently, federal criminal prosecutions of white-collar offenders have actually *decreased*. Over the past decade, the Justice Department has been stung by legal setbacks in several high-profile cases. Furthermore, after the 9/11 terrorist attack, many white-collar investigation resources were diverted to fight terrorism. Between the mid 1990s and 2012, white-collar prosecutions, as a percent of total federal cases dropped from almost 18 percent to 9 percent.[92] Thus, despite dwarfing past corporate scandals in magnitude, the mortgage and credit crisis that led to the "Great Recession" of 2008 produced no prison sentences for Wall Street executives.

Instead of prison sentences, the Justice Department and federal regulatory agencies have focused on reaching settlements while demanding corporate reform. Banks and other financial firms, including JP Morgan Chase ($31B), Bank of America ($58B), and Citigroup ($13B) have paid out over $150 billion in fines, fees, and restitution for their role in the mortgage meltdown.[93]

The most recent trend in the prosecution of corporations is the use of deferred (DPA) or non-prosecution agreements (NPA). Here, corporations agree to certain conditions in exchange for avoiding criminal prosecution. This practice is explored in detail in **Theory in Action: Too Big to Jail? Conflict Theory and Corporate Crime**.

Critics point out that many of these settlements require no admission of wrongdoing, and that the fines are often a

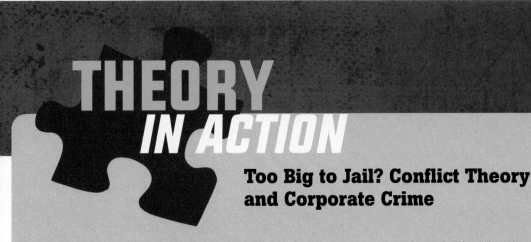

Texture: © Nik Merkulov/Shutterstock, Inc.

Too Big to Jail? Conflict Theory and Corporate Crime

Conflict and radical theories seek to understand how power shapes the content of the law and the operation of the criminal justice system. Radical theories in particular point out how the wealthy elite use their power to stay above the law. In the book *Too Big to Fail: How Prosecutors Compromise with Corporations*, Brandon Garrett explores how difficult it can be to deter the criminal activities of powerful multinational corporations. Under U.S. federal law, corporations can be prosecuted for criminal conduct. With "no soul to be damned, and no body to kick," however, a corporation can obviously not be jailed. Instead, criminal sanctions are limited to fines and/or disbarment from seeking government contracts. Over the past decade, there has been a spike in the amount of money collected through criminal fines. Most of the money was paid in a small number of blockbuster cases. Indeed, it seems as though the government has announced "record" fines almost yearly.

Many of these fines were the result of a new trend in the criminal pursuit of corporations—deferred (DPA) or non-prosecution agreements (NPA). In a typical arrangement, the prosecutor agrees to hold off (or end) prosecution if the corporation agrees to meet certain demands. The demands usually include payment of a criminal fine, cooperation with the investigation (including cases against individual

employees) ethics training for employees, and sometimes oversight from a third party. Deferred prosecution was developed, and is still used today, as method to reform criminal offenders. Individuals agree to stipulations, such as drug treatment, in order to avoid prosecution for their offense. In the 1990s, the U.S. corporate sentencing guidelines extended them in an effort to change corporate culture and encourage companies to admit their wrongdoing.

Why has there been a sharp increase in the use of DPA or NPA for corporate crime? There appear to be several reasons. Corporate crime can be difficult to prosecute, especially against huge multinational corporations that can mount an expensive and skilled defense, and drag the case out for years. In corporate prosecutions, notes Garrett, the federal government is David and the corporations are Goliath. Therefore, DPAs allow prosecutors to save scare resources by relying on the corporation to investigate its own wrongdoing and to monitor its own compliance under new procedures or rules. Prosecutors can also request the corporation make an admission of wrongful behavior. This stands in contrast to civil suits, where companies pay a fine but admit to no wrongdoing. Another reason to prefer a DPA is the desire to avoid "collateral consequences" of a full prosecution for non-involved employees, shareholders, and even the economy. In 2002, the successful prosecution of accounting firm Arthur Anderson led to unemployment for thousands of employees, most who had no involvement in crime. The case centered on the company's shredding of documents related to the auditing of Enron. Employees gathered outside the trial wearing shirts with the slogan, "I didn't shred, my kid needs to be fed."

Garrett notes, however, that DPAs and other corporate plea bargaining grant leniency to the most powerful individuals and corporations in the world and often ask little in return. In corporate crime, the "biggest fish" get the best deals. They plead to lesser crimes and get smaller fines. Compliance conditions that sound impressive turn out to be difficult to enforce. For example, while billion dollar fines may sound impressive, they amount to less than 1 percent of the corporation's market value, and are often a fraction of the profit made from the criminal offense. Garrett found that in two-thirds of DPAs, no individuals were punished. Individuals who *were* singled out for prosecution were lower level employees rather than corporate leaders.

Consider the pharmaceutical giant Pfizer. In 2009, as part of a DPA, the company paid a then record $2.3 billion in civil and criminal fines for flagrantly illegal marketing activities, including bribing doctors to promote "off-label" use of drugs. Whistle-blower John Kopehinski, a former Pfizer employee, described a corporate culture driven by sales, where "if you didn't sell drugs illegally, you were not seen as a team player." In the "historic" settlement, Pfizer also agreed to an "expansive corporate integrity agreement" to detect and report future illegal conduct.

While the press releases from the government made this settlement sound like a victory, there is much to criticize. First, industry analysts suggest that the fines were only a fraction of the profits gained from the illegal activity. Second, this was Pfizer's fourth DPA involving illegal marketing activities since 2002. Each of the previous DPAs had similar compliance stipulations that did not appear to have been effective. Finally, as with the previous DPAs, none of the senior executives who were alleged to have known about (and sometimes coordinated) the illegal activity were prosecuted as individuals. Indeed, the criminal prosecution of corporate executives is rare. Demonstrating the criminal intent of executives is difficult. Garrett notes that executives can invoke several variants of the "ostrich defense" (they were not aware of the criminal activity). Furthermore, with almost unlimited resources, they can outgun federal prosecutors at every stage of criminal justice proceedings.

There is little doubt that wealth and power influence the enforcement of law and criminal justice proceedings. The pursuit of corporate criminals often stands in stark contrast to the pursuit of street criminals. Do prosecutors worry about "collateral consequences" (e.g., will the offenders' children be cared for) when convicting a drug offender? Would a shoplifter commit more crimes if they were fined $10 for stealing $500 worth of goods from a store?

Sources: Garrett, B. L. (2014). *Too big to jail: How prosecutors compromise with corporations.* Cambridge, MA: Belknap Press; Rakoff, J. S. (2015, Feb 19). Justice deferred is justice denied. *The New York Review of Books.* Retrieved June 10, 2015, from http://www.nybooks.com/articles/archives/2015/feb/19/justice-deferred-justice-denied/; Harris, G. (2009, September 3). Pfizer to pay $2.3 billion to settle inquiry over marketing. *The New York Times.* Retrieved June 10, 2015, from http://www.nytimes.com/2009/09/03/business

fraction of the profit gained from illicit activities. Instead of being framed as moral wrongs worthy of shame, corporations view these penalties as simply a "cost of doing business." The disparity between the treatment of white-collar and street crime helps to create the public image of an offender as a young, black, inner-city resident. Ironically, from a deterrence theory perspective, white-collar offenders would seem to be more vulnerable to criminal sanctions than street offenders. This is because many white-collar crimes are rational and involve cost–benefit calculations, and many white-collar offenders are people for whom prison would be particularly painful.

Historical Support for Marxist Criminology

Many aspects of radical theory can be difficult to test. Historical analyses of the law and systems of formal control offer one method to examine Marxist theories. William Chambliss uses such a historical analysis to support his theory. For example, he argues that the English vagrancy law of 1349 was enacted solely to provide a pool of cheap labor and to combat the collapse of the feudal system:[94]

> *The law was clearly and consciously designed to serve the interests of the ruling class at the expense of the working class. The vagrancy laws were designed to alleviate a condition defined by the lawmakers as undesirable.*

The vagrancy law was later amended to protect the transportation of goods and to control recidivism by branding the letter "V" on the forehead of repeat offenders.[95] In this way, enforcement of the vagrancy law was adapted to meet changing social conditions. Although his study has been severely criticized, it remains a classic work in criminology.

Another example of how history has been used to support Marxist theory is Anthony Platt's study of the origins and development of the juvenile court system in the United States.[96] To Platt, this system was formed to control immigrant youths and instill discipline. It was dominated by wealthy upper-class matrons who promulgated the values of the white, Anglo-Saxon, capitalist class:[97]

The child saving movement was heavily influenced by middle-class women who extended their housewifely roles into public service and economic resources to advance the cause of child welfare. The child savers defended the importance of the home, of family life, and parental supervision. These institutions traditionally gave purpose to a woman's life.

Platt charges that, under the guise of the child-saving movement, delinquency was invented to control the behavior of lower-class youths. The combination of a capitalist society (which creates a surplus labor pool) and the child labor laws (which prevent children from working) created a dangerous class that necessitated control. Platt argues that the juvenile courts were created largely to serve this purpose.

A Radical Critique of "Traditional" Criminologists

Critical theorists have even subjected the discipline of criminology itself to scrutiny. They contend that mainstream criminology concentrates on the behavior of the offender, accepts the legal definitions of crime, and largely ignores the proposition that crime is created by political authority. Thus, criminologists serve as agents of the state who provide information that the government uses to manipulate and control those who threaten the system.[98]

Radical criminologists point out, for example, that most mainstream theories of crime are actually theories of street crime that largely ignore crimes of the affluent.[99] Consider, for example, Gottfredson and Hirschi's theory of low self-control. Most persons in a position of power have demonstrated enough self-control to accumulate the credentials (e.g., employment, education) to rise to their position. Robert Merton's modes of adaptation virtually require offenders to be poor (i.e., only the poor lack legitimate means for achieving success). Criminologists also lend legitimacy to the image of criminals as urban, poor, and non-white by relying on the FBI's Uniform Crime Report (UCR) data. The UCR does not track corporate or government crime.[100] Furthermore, despite recent attempts to remedy this situation, the UCR does not provide reliable information on other forms of white-collar crime.[101] Radical scholars urge mainstream criminologists to question this preoccupation with street crime and to scrutinize the political and social institutions that support the crimes of the powerful.

A Critique of Radical Criminology

Radical criminology has been criticized on several grounds. First, there is the question of whether radical criminologists offer much that is new.[102] For example, like Durkheim, radical criminologists assert that crime is normal and that diversity should be tolerated. Like labeling theorists, they emphasize rulemaking, not rulebreaking. In fact, some scholars argue that the only thing the radicals managed to do was to politicize traditional criminological theories.[103]

Second, some claim that radical criminologists have been unable to clearly define the ruling class.[104] Are the capitalists all powerful? Can they really decide exactly how the law is made and enforced? In some ways, radical criminologists portray crime policy as a conspiracy theory. Critics are also leery of radical theory's dependence on historical analysis, which is essentially someone's interpretation of historical events.[105]

Third, Criminologist Jackson Toby argues that the radicals provide an idealized view of the deviant as a rebel. This underdog mentality appears to excuse all lower-class criminality. He notes that crimes of the elite, however, do not legitimate other crimes. Toby also asserts that the radicals must acknowledge that imperfect justice is the product of an imperfect world: "What the radical criminologists refuse to recognize is that the political process in a reasonably open society is responsive (not perfectly) to public opinion."[106]

Finally, radical criminologists must now contend with the failure of communism in the Soviet Union and Eastern Europe. Certainly, these states were not model Marxist societies; they were more bureaucratic and party dominated than Marx would have liked. However, they did represent an attempt to put Marxian theory into practice, and their demise supports the view that Marx's utopian vision of society is difficult, if not impossible, to carry out. Even more damaging is the fact that some capitalist countries (e.g., England, Japan) have relatively low crime rates. If capitalism is the sole cause of criminal behavior, how is this possible?

Does the failure of communism and the low crime rates of some capitalist countries mean that the radicals were wrong? Perhaps, but their work has forced criminologists to broaden their perspective. Criminal law *can* be used as a weapon to oppress the public, and it can be overextended in damaging and self-defeating ways. Radical theorists also deserve credit for highlighting the difference in sanctioning between crimes of the powerful and crimes of the poor. As discussed briefly earlier (and will be seen more clearly in Chapter 15), crimes of the powerful are far more destructive than street crime. Radical theorists also act as a conscience for the discipline of criminology. They remind criminologists not to allow their discipline to be co-opted by the status quo.

Extensions of Radical Criminology

Interest in the more hard-line versions of Marxist and radical theories of crime peaked in the early 1980s and has declined thereafter. Since that time, there have been several attempts to reinvigorate radical theory. We explore three of these attempts—critical realism, market society capitalism, and peacemaking—in the next section.

Critical Realism

Radical criminologists have always been concerned with praxis, or "action that is guided by theory and that has social change as its goal,"[107] yet they also have been criticized for relying on a socialist revolution to solve social problems. Radical theories also tend to focus on criminal law, class conflict, and crimes of the powerful. Often, concern over street crime was virtually dismissed because it drew attention away from the "real" conflict. Where it was discussed, it was framed as a "proto-revolutionary" activity. From a policy perspective, this excluded radicals from the public conversation about how to reduce street crime. Instead, right-wing strategies that emphasized law and order and the use of surveillance and policing dominated the policy debate.

Critical realism (also called British realism, or left realism) emerged from British scholars as an attempt to maintain a critical stance while also treating street crime as an important issue. They argue that street crime is a serious problem for the working class and not a "proto-revolutionary activity" of the oppressed masses. Working-class people are victimized not only by the powerful classes in society, but also by the poor.[108] The British realists are critical of the policies developed by the government to deal with street crime. They question conservative crime policies that emphasize deterrence, military-style policing, and increasing use of prisons. As an alternative solution, left realists suggest the use of minimal policing and police accountably to local communities.[109] Specifically, minimal policing calls for maximum public initiation of police action, minimal coercion by the police, minimal police intervention, and maximum public access to the police.[110]

From a theory perspective, critical realists have proposed a "square of crime" that captures the main components involved in the construction of crime—the offender, the victim, the state, and the public. Robert Matthews describes this approach, in which "The role of theory is to reveal the underlying processes or determinants on which the complex realities of everyday life are built. Thus social theory is a primary concern of critical realism, but it has to be useful and useable. It is not an end in itself."[111]

Elliott Currie: The United States as a "Market Society"

The gist of radical theory is that capitalism causes crime. Elliott Currie suggests the following update: *Some forms* of capitalism encourage crime. Currie uses the concept of a market society to explain the difference.[112] A *market economy* is based on the principles of capitalism—and capitalism is an important aspect of the global economy. Many societies with capitalist economies nevertheless have relatively low crime rates (e.g., Japan, Great Britain). Currie refers to the economic and social arrangements in these countries as compassionate capitalism. In other words, the government curbs the free market by ensuring that economic inequality does not become too severe and provides strong safety nets for those who are not involved in the economy. In contrast, a **market society** involves the following:[113]

[T]he spread of civilization in which the pursuit of personal economic gain becomes increasingly the dominant organizing principle of social life; a social formation in which market principles, instead

of being confined to some parts of the economy, and appropriately buffered and restrained by other social institutions and norms, come to suffuse the whole social fabric—and to undercut and overwhelm other principles, that have historically sustained individuals, families, and communities.

In other words, a market society is a completely Darwinian society with a sink-or-swim mentality. There are few cushions against disabilities or misfortunes in the labor market. This central idea is very similar to Messner and Rosenfeld's institutional anomie theory. In both cases, that adherence to a hard-core form of capitalism produces America's high rates of violent crime. As a critical criminologist, however, Currie takes this central idea in a more radical direction.[114] He identifies seven mechanisms that link a market society to high rates of violence. The mechanisms are outlined in **TABLE 8-3**.

In particular, Currie points out that a market society tolerates high levels of inequality and poverty. The idea of having a strong safety net, with job training and relocation, child care, and universal health care, runs counter to the "everyone-for-themselves" mentality of a market society. Even the regulation of handguns is very limited, when compared with other advanced countries. These characteristics interfere with the childhood development (poverty), informal control (job relocations, lack of child care), and other buffers against high levels of crime. Thus, while Marxist radicals support a revolution to overthrow capitalism, Currie suggests that a softer, gentler capitalist society—allowing a little socialism to creep in might suffice.

Criminology as Peacemaking

Another new direction in radical thought involves using criminology to promote a peaceful society. This approach draws on many religious traditions (e.g., Buddhism, Quakerism, Judaism) that see crime as a form of suffering from both the criminal's and the victim's perspective:[115]

Crime is suffering passed on from one person to another; one kind of suffering becomes another; we have to suffer with the criminal to put an end to the suffering the criminal inflicts upon others. As long as we persist in trying to make the criminal suffer for us, the problem will get worse.

One concrete example of a course of action is mediation. Mediation transforms criminal disputes into civil matters by bringing victims and offenders to the bargaining table. It attempts to offer forms of reconciliation that are constructive for both parties.[116,117] This approach also calls for the development of a "nonviolent criminology of compassion and service."[118] This, Quinney suggests, runs counter to the interests of the criminal justice system, which he says is driven by violence:[119]

It is a system that assumes that violence can be overcome by violence, evil by evil. Criminal justice at home and warfare abroad are of the same principle of violence. This principle sadly dominates much of our

TABLE 8-3

How a Market Society Breeds Violent Crime

Premise	Explanation
1. A market society breeds violent crime by destroying livelihood.	In a market society, labor is always a cost to be reduced rather than a social institution valued in its own right. Benefits and wages are cut, and the number of working poor is high. A lack of stable or rewarding work breeds alienation and undercuts the idea of having a stake in society.
2. A market society has an inherent tendency toward extremes of inequality and material deprivation.	Income inequality in the United States is more dramatic than in other advanced countries. Poor children are more prevalent in the United States, and they are poorer than in other industrialized countries. Children living in poverty (especially extreme poverty) are more likely to be physically abused and neglected and less likely to develop intellectually.
3. A market society weakens public support.	A market society is opposed to the provision of public support that may inhibit violent crime. For example, while other countries provide nearly universal child care to working parents, the United States "allows" parents to take unpaid leave without getting fired for certain family emergencies.
4. A market society erodes informal social support.	Employers' desire for a flexible workforce means that workers continuously move locations, uprooting them from their communities and families. This interferes with social organization and removes a source of social support.
5. A market society promotes a culture that exalts brutal individual competition and consumption.	A culture of materialism (or "hypermaterialism") emphasizes money, rather than other values, such as a job well done. In such a culture, throwing people out of a job is not considered bad, but rather good business practice.
6. A market society deregulates the technology of violence.	The virtual absence of national-level gun control distinguishes the United States from virtually every other advanced nation.
7. A market society weakens alternative political values and institutions.	The prevailing ideology (or myth) is that inequality and deprivation are simply the nature of things. Labor unions or political parties that address the needs of the poor or disenfranchised are weak or nonexistent.

Source: Currie, E. *Theoretical criminology,* Vol. 1, Issue 2, 147–172, © 1997 by Sage Publications. Reprinted by Permission of SAGE.

criminology. Fortunately, more and more criminologists are realizing that this principle is fundamentally incompatible with a faith that seeks to express itself in compassion, forgiveness, and love.

The warlike image of the criminal justice system, so this argument goes, contributes to the crime problem. Criminologists must seek to make peace by confronting such issues as homelessness, sexual assault, and the use of prisons.[120] The primary criticism of this perspective is that most of its proponents (though there are exceptions) reject any effort to scientifically study crime or crime control. Rather, it is simply a call to love thy neighbor. In that sense, peacemaking criminology no longer portends to be a theory of criminal behavior.[121,122]

Feminist Criminology

Historically, females were largely ignored in criminology. Most empirical tests used data on males to explain male offending; theories of crime explained why boys or men engaged in crime.[123] Until the last 40 years, only a handful of scholars directly addressed female criminality. Even here, the portrayal of female offenders was often blatantly sexist. In essence, because female offenders deviated from their "natural temperament" (e.g., warm, passive, caring), they were viewed as biologically or psychologically defective.[124] Over the past few decades, this situation has changed substantially. A major turning point was the women's movement and the fight for gender equality. Among other things, this movement created a wave of female criminologists by paving the way for women to enter graduate school.[125]

As **TABLE 8-4** illustrates, the feminist perspective takes different forms.[126] Liberal feminists, who emphasize equal opportunity and the importance of sex-role socialization, had the most influence in the early days of the feminist movement. Critical (e.g., socialist and radical) feminists emphasize the structural inequality in power between men and women. This approach links male and female crime to patriarchy—a cultural arrangement where males exert dominance

TABLE 8-4

Three Feminist Perspectives on Crime

Perspective	Description
Liberal feminism	Highlights problems arising from gender discrimination and stereotypical views concerning the traditional roles of women in society. It emphasizes the use of affirmative action and equal opportunity as major weapons of change. This perspective has been criticized as limited because it ignores class and race differences among women. It has also been characterized as less threatening because it does not strongly question "white, male, and/or capitalist privilege" and typically uses the traditional scientific, quantitative (positivist) methodology to study crime.
Socialist feminism	Views gender discrimination as a function of capitalist society, which fosters both social class divisions and patriarchy. The criminality of males and females varies in frequency and type because of the social relations of production (class) and reproduction (family). Patriarchal capitalism creates two groups: the powerful (males and capitalists) and the powerless (females and the working class). The opportunity to commit crime is limited by position in the social structure.
Radical feminism	Views the origins of patriarchy and subordination of women in male aggression and the control of female sexuality. For example, radical feminists have redefined rape as a crime of violence and male power, control, and domination rather than as a sexual crime.

Source: Simpson, S. S. (1989). Feminist theory, crime, and justice. Criminology, 27, 605–632.

over females through financial and physical power. In a patriarchal society, male behaviors are defined as "normal," and male control of females is viewed as legitimate.[127]

In a now-classic article, Kathleen Daly and Meda Chesney-Lind outlined two central problems for a male-dominated criminology.[128] The **generalizability problem** suggests that (in part, because most criminology theorists are male) mainstream criminological theories may not be applicable to female offending. The **gender-ratio problem** speaks to the empirical observation that males account for the vast majority of delinquent and criminal offending. The key task before researchers is to identify factors that account for this gender difference.

The Gender Ratio

There is little doubt that males are more prone to crime than females. UCR data from 2012 shows that males account for the vast majority of arrests made for homicide (89%), rape (99%), robbery (87%), and aggravated assault (77%). The gender difference is smaller for property crime, where males constituted roughly 63 percent of all those arrested.[129] The National Crime Victimization Survey reveals a similar pattern: Males account for roughly 80–85 percent of violent offenders identified by victims.[130,131] Self-report studies that measure serious forms of delinquency tell a similar story. The central issue for theorists is explaining male overrepresentation in criminal behavior. It is hard to overstate the importance of this issue. If, as many believe, the gender gap is due to environmental influence such as different parenting practices, the policy implications are enormous. Sticking with the example of parenting—if parents "parented" their boys as they do girls, male offending would be expected to decline

dramatically. Ironically, though, the first investigations into the gender ratio did not seek to explain its existence. Rather, they argued that the gender ratio was shrinking.

In 1975, two controversial works appeared. Freda Adler's *Sisters in Crime* and Rita Simon's *Women and Crime* argued that the women's movement provided greater opportunities for females in both legitimate and illegitimate enterprises.[132] The assumption was that feminism would thus lead to a growth in the female crime rate. According to this "liberation hypothesis," female offenders were now capable of committing the same offenses as men, and female criminality would approach that of males in both nature and volume.

Both Adler's and Simon's studies were criticized by feminists because they:[133]

> [P]roposed ideas about women's criminality that were troubling to feminists because they were largely an outgrowth of the unexamined assumption that the emancipation of women resided solely in achieving legal and social equality with men in the public sphere. Although the books reached different conclusions, they touched a raw nerve by linking women's crime to the women's movement and to the goal of equality with men in the public sphere.

In fact, while there is some evidence that the gender ratio has declined over time, analysis of crime statistics reveals that such changes have not been radical. Furthermore, there does not appear to be a large shift toward female offending in "male-oriented" crimes such as robbery. Indeed, the largest increases in female offending involve property crimes such as theft.[134] Evidence also suggests that recent gender-ratio declines in violent offending are due to sharp decreases in male offending rather than in an increase in female offending.[135]

Overall, female involvement in crime remains far less than that of males. This pattern is not limited to street crime. Women convicted of white-collar crimes tend to be clerical workers, not managers or administrators, as with their male counterparts.[136] Female white-collar offenders are also more likely to act alone and to profit less from their offenses than males.

Over the past 20 years, several scholars have devised empirical tests to examine and explain the gender gap. Typically, these studies use variables from mainstream theories of crime (e.g., social learning and social control) to account for the difference in offending across genders. The assumption in this research is that male and female offending is caused by the same factors but that males are exposed to more risk factors than females. These investigations have yielded mixed results. Typically, researchers find that they can account for some, but not all, of the gender gap. Generally, social learning variables (e.g., delinquent peers, antisocial attitudes), social control variables (self-control, social bonds), and sex-role attitudes (e.g., traditional gender beliefs, masculinity) do the best job of explaining gender differences in offending.[137–139]

The Generalizability Issue

Virtually all theories of crime, until recently, were created by men to account for male offending. An important question is whether such "male" theories can also explain female offending. The general finding is that variables derived from mainstream theories of crime also explain female offending.[140] Hirschi's social bond theory (see Chapter 7) actually explains female offending better than male offending. More commonly, authors find little difference in how well theories predict offending across gender. Paul Mazerolle's analysis of general strain theory (see Chapter 6) is a good example. Mazerolle found that, for the most part, measures of strain (e.g., negative life events, peer hassles) explain both male and female offending.[141]

The fact that mainstream theories can explain female offending does not necessarily mean that they offer a *complete* explanation. Feminist scholars point out that the male perspective may overlook factors that are unique to females. Past victimization in general, and in particular sexual

Because females constitute less than 10% of all prisoners, most states have only one female prison.

© Ron Chapple/Thinkstock/Alamy Images

victimization, is implicated in much female offending.[142] Studies on incarcerated girls reveal that between 40 percent and 73 percent had been sexually abused.[143] Importantly, abuse can lead to girls (and boys) running away from home. Prostitution, theft, and other crimes result from the attempt to survive in this environment.

Criminologist Kathleen Daly used presentence investigation reports and other court records to examine what factors led females to engage in crime.[144] **TABLE 8-5** presents Daly's typology of female offending. Street women, for example, are those who have experienced high levels of abuse and are arrested primarily for prostitution, theft, and drug-related offenses. Battered women were typically arrested for harming (and in some cases, killing) their abusers. Results from a more recent study of women from the Baltimore City Detention Center confirmed several of Daly's typologies, especially the harmed and harming women, drug-connected women, and battered women pathways. This study also found some support for distinctive pathways based on age of onset. Child onset offenders were more apt to have been sexually abused as children than were later onset offenders and were more heavily involved in drug dealing, property crime, and violence in adulthood. On the other hand, adolescent onset offenders were no more likely to have been sexually or physically abused as children.[145]

Over the past decade, criminologists have sought to "gender" mainstream theories of crime. In other words, they have tried to explain how theories such as social control, social learning, strain, and rational choice might explain female crime and the gender gap.[146–147] Heimer and De Coster use the feminist perspective to "gender" differential association theory. The authors believe that definitions favorable to law violation have different sources for males and females. Among males, pro-violence attitudes are learned when parents fail to correct their violent acts (e.g., "boys will be boys"). Females, because of their greater concern for interpersonal relationships, are more likely to learn violent attitudes when there is a breakdown of relationships in the family.[148]

Feminist explanations of female offending, such as Daly's typology and Heimer and De Coster's revision of differential association, represent an exciting new area in criminology. After much neglect, it appears as though the female perspective and feminist theory are gaining a voice within criminology. This relatively new area of criminology will continue to generate important insight into the gender gap, the issue of generalizability, and female (as well as male) offending in general.

TABLE 8-5

A Typology of Female Offenders

Type of Offender	Description
Street women	Street women have experienced high levels of abuse, which is their primary reason for living on the street. This type of woman is likely to be arrested for prostitution, theft, or drug-related offenses.
Harmed-and-harming women	These offenders, abused and/or neglected as children, are labeled as "problem children." They are more likely to be addicted to alcohol or drugs, have psychological problems, and engage in violent behavior.
Battered women	Battered women are currently in a relationship with an abusive partner. Often, they are in court for harming the person who is battering them.
Drug-connected women	This type of offender distributes drugs in conjunction with her boyfriend, husband, or family.
"Other" women	"Other" women are those who do not fit in other categories. They are more likely to be in court for crimes of greed, such as embezzlement or fraud, which are not committed to meet basic needs.

Data from Kathleen Daly, *Gender, Crime, and Punishment* (New Haven, CT: Yale University Press, 1994).

Gender and the Criminal Justice System

What predictions would a feminist criminologist make on the relationship between gender and the law? A patriarchal society is by definition male dominated. Following the logic of other critical theories, those who lack power should have their behavior criminalized and should be singled out by the criminal justice system for punishment. Also, crimes against the less powerful should be given less priority. Disparities in the treatment of women in the criminal justice system have been studied by both conflict and radical theorists. Are persons treated equally under the law, or is gender a key indicator of how a case will be handled?

As with race and class, research on this area examines whether gender has an impact on criminal justice decision making independent of other factors. The general pattern found in this research is that if there is a gender effect, it benefits females.[149] In fact, Daly notes that gender decisions favoring women are found more often than race decisions favoring whites.[150] As with race, significant gender effects tend to be small and appear at different stages of processing.

The finding that females are treated more leniently within the criminal justice system was long ago tabbed the chivalry hypothesis. Because police, prosecutors, and judges are predominately male, they may have a chivalrous attitude toward women and be more inclined to treat them with leniency. Evidence suggesting the differential processing of women in the criminal justice system is mixed, however. Visher found that police make arrest decisions about women based on the image the woman projects, not the type of offense (violent versus property). The officers were more likely to be chivalrous toward older, white females and to arrest their young, hostile, black counterparts.[151] A study of plea bargaining in Washington, DC, showed that women were less able to bargain and were more willing to plead guilty than men. In other words, they were not rewarded for pleading guilty with a lesser sentence.[152]

Even where females receive more lenient treatment, feminists are more inclined to regard this as paternalism. A paternalistic response, unlike a chivalrous response, could lead to leniency but also to a punitive response if it serves to keep women in a submissive role.[153] Bishop and Frazier's examination of Florida delinquency processing suggests a degree of paternalism. For more serious offenses, boys were treated more harshly, and for most status offenses, there were no differences across gender. For contempt-of-court cases, which resulted largely from repeated attempts to run away from home, girls were more likely to be incarcerated than boys.[154]

Like conflict theorists, feminists have also highlighted certain crimes that were not enforced because women lacked power and status. Male violence against women, particularly nonstranger rape and battering of intimates, was traditionally not sanctioned or penalized by the state.[155] Only through sustained campaigning and activism have feminists managed to alter this situation. Terms such as date rape and marital rape, unheard of only a short time ago, are now part of the common vocabulary. Furthermore, intimate violence has been reframed as a crime of violence rather than a personal problem between intimates.

Conclusion

Critical theories highlight the manner in which laws are made and enforced. Conflict, Marxist, and feminist theories of criminology often challenge the basis and legitimacy of the criminal justice system and of law enforcement. Collectively, they have changed the manner in which crime is studied, considered, and analyzed. They remind society that crime is not an objective behavior, but rather a politically constructed label. In

> *They remind society that crime is not an objective behavior, but rather a politically constructed label.*

this sense, they have significantly broadened both the definition and the scope of criminology. Critical theories also challenge criminologists to explain crimes often neglected in the mainstream literature. Feminist theories call attention to female criminality and the male–female offending gap, and radical theories call attention to white-collar, government, and corporate crime. Critical analysis of the operation and nature of the criminal justice system must be continued if criminology is to have a beneficial impact on society.

WRAP-UP

CHAPTER SPOTLIGHT

- Although critical (e.g., conflict, radical, feminist) theories of crime include a diverse body of theories, they share some commonality. In particular, they view crime as a political concept, where those in power shape both the content of the law and the operation of the criminal justice system.
- Conflict theory is based on a pluralistic view of power. There are many interest groups that shape the law. Conflict is primarily used to explain the law and the actions of criminal justice agents, but conflict can also explain some forms of criminal behavior (e.g., an abortion clinic bombing).
- Radical theory stems from the work of Karl Marx. Radical theorists emphasize the conflict between the wealthy elite and the working class. They point out that many harmful acts perpetrated by the wealthy are not defined as criminal. To the extent that such acts are defined as criminal, they are not strongly enforced. Those prosecuted for white-collar crimes rarely receive long prison sentences.
- A central empirical issue in radical theories is whether criminal justice decisions (e.g., the

decisions to arrest and to prosecute) are related to race and class. This body of evidence is extensive, complex, and often contradictory. There is some evidence of racial disparity in criminal justice decision making. Racial disparity is most clear in the areas of illicit drug use and capital sentencing.
- Modern extensions of radical theory include Currie's concept of a "market society" as well as peacemaking criminology and left realism.
- Feminist scholars point out that most criminological theories were written by males and about male criminality. They question whether such theories apply to females. Furthermore, they point out that mainstream theory cannot adequately explain why males are more likely than females to engage in crime.
- As with race and class, researchers have studied whether gender has an effect on criminal justice processing. There is some evidence that females are treated more leniently by the system. For some acts (e.g., contempt of court cases arising from repeated runaways), however, the reverse holds true.

1. Is the criminal justice system racist? What factors would you have to take into consideration to research this question?
2. Does American society operate under a consensus or a conflict model?
3. Describe the gender-ratio and generalizability problems.
4. What does Currie mean by a market society? How does a market society breed violence?
5. Think of a current scandal involving wealthy individuals or corporations engaging in crime. How might radical theorists explain this?

KEY TERMS

Police Tape: © SkillUp/Shutterstock

altruism According to Bonger, altruism was a characteristic of primitive societies. In these societies, social solidarity was high, and individuals were more selfless and looked after one another's needs.

bourgeoisie Within Marxist theory, those who hold salaried and management positions.

capitalists Within Marxist theory, the owners of the means of production.

chivalry hypothesis The idea that females are treated leniently by the criminal justice system because police, prosecutors, and judges are predominately male and have a gracious attitude toward women.

conflict model The belief that the law is the result of a battle between people or groups that have different levels of power. Control over the state (including the law and the criminal justice system) is the principal prize in the perpetual conflict of society.

conflict theory Theory that emphasizes a pluralistic perspective: Multiple groups within a society wield different levels of power.

consensus model The belief that the law reflects common agreement over the fundamental values held by society.

egoism A lack of consideration for others. According to Bonger, capitalism encourages selfishness, greed, and insensitivity to others.

extra-legal factors Characteristics such as race, class, and gender that can affect criminal justice decision making.

gender-ratio problem A key issue for criminologists is to explain the empirical observation that males

account for the vast majority of delinquent and criminal offending.

generalizability problem Because most criminology theorists are male, mainstream criminological theories may not be applicable (i.e., may not generalize) to female offending.

instrumental Marxism This type of Marxist theory argues that the law and criminal justice system are always instruments to be used by the capitalist class.

legal factors Factors such as offense seriousness and prior record that play a role in criminal justice decision making.

lumpenproletariat Within Marxist theory, the dispossessed, unorganized workers.

market society A country (such as the United States) where the capitalist economy dominates all other spheres of life. This is a sink-or-swim society that does not provide a strong safety net for citizens.

primary conflict A concept from Thorsten Sellin's culture conflict theory. Primary conflict may arise between an established culture and a less powerful culture. For example, recent immigrants may conduct themselves based on codes from the old country that may be criminal in the dominant culture.

proletariat Within Marxist theory, the working class.

racial profiling Racially biased law enforcement; targeting individuals for law enforcement based primarily on their race.

racial threat hypothesis The idea that as minority populations increase relative to the white population, they will be viewed as a threat and punitive measures against them will increase.

radical theory Theoretical perspective that emphasizes conflict between the wealthy elite and the rest of society.

secondary conflict Concept from Thorsten Sellin's culture conflict theory. Secondary conflict occurs within a single culture that has different subcultures, each with its own conduct norms.

structural Marxism This type of Marxist analysis grants the government (at least in the short term) a degree of political autonomy. Some laws may run counter to the desires of the capitalists.

superstructure The system of social institutions (e.g., law, education, and politics) that lend legitimacy to capitalist arrangements.

Introduction

In 1940, Harvard researchers Sheldon and Eleanor Glueck started an ambitious research project. They compiled a sample of 500 delinquent boys who were sent to a reform school in the 1930s. They then added an additional sample of 500 "non-delinquent" boys that were matched to the first sample on factors such as age, race, IQ, and neighborhood of residence. From each sample, the Gluecks collected an impressive amount of data on a wide range of physical, psychological, and social factors that might predict crime. After following the boys for almost a decade, they published *Unraveling Juvenile Delinquency*, a book unprecedented in scope and depth. A central finding in the book was that many of the strongest predictors of delinquency, such as inconsistent parenting, emerged during the boys' early childhood. Indeed, they included statistical predictions of delinquency using measures from when the boys were as young as 6 years old.[3] How was this book received by mainstream criminology? Not well.

Edwin Sutherland, considered by many the father of criminology, had for years attacked the Gluecks' work. Sutherland compared their search for traits that distinguished delinquents from nondelinquents to early biological theories such as Lombroso's. He rejected their "multiple-factor approach" as atheoretical. Thus, the sociological-oriented criminology largely relegated *Unraveling Juvenile Delinquency* to the criminology dustbin—where it stayed for over 40 years. The Gluecks had insisted on large scale longitudinal research designed to predict criminality at different stages of life. Instead, over several decades, criminologists pursued theories that focused almost exclusively on adolescence and young adulthood.[4]

In the 1980s, several factors converged to refocus criminology on different stages in life. The first step in this direction was the emergence of the "career criminal" perspective. Sparked by interest in chronic, or "career," offenders, this area of research examined how offending patterns change over time. By the 1990s, criminologists had come full circle—back toward the study of early childhood and the framework outlined by the Gluecks some 40 years earlier. As we will see, one modern theory was literally developed from the Gluecks' *Unraveling Juvenile Delinquency* data. The life-course criminology perspective that emerged seeks to understand the development of crime and its precursor behavior from childhood through adulthood. Doing so raises very interesting questions. Do chronic adult offenders usually have a history of childhood misbehavior? How common is it for juvenile delinquents to

> *A central finding in the book was that many of the strongest predictors of delinquency, such as inconsistent parenting, emerged during the boys' early childhood.*

reform themselves in adulthood? Do the causes of crime change at different stages of life?

In a very short period of time, this perspective has generated an impressive amount of research, theory, and policy. Indeed, addressing the American Society of Criminology in 2010, the prominent criminologist Frank Cullen proclaimed that life-course criminology *is* criminology.[5] This chapter explores the study of crime over the life course. We begin by looking at the career criminal paradigm—a precursor to life-course criminology. This includes early case studies of career criminals, as well as research on criminal cohorts. Next, we examine the emergence of the life-course perspective and theories that stem from this point of view. Finally, we discuss policy implications drawn from this literature.

The Criminal Career Perspective

The idea of career criminality is based on the assumption that some criminals are committed to a life of crime. In other words, they have a worldview built around criminal activity. They define themselves as criminals and tend to associate with other criminals. Their careers accelerate or progress as they become more skilled and engage in different types of offenses. In addition, career criminals view crime as a profession, like law or medicine, in that it involves the acquisition of specialized knowledge and skill.[6]

The **criminal career perspective** was based on two different sorts of studies. First, since the early 1900s, criminologists have done in-depth interviews with offenders in an attempt to determine the characteristics and motives of career criminals. These case histories provide a rich portrait of particular types of criminals. Second, beginning in the 1970s, criminologists published findings based on whole cohorts of individuals born in a particular location. Some of these cohorts were tracked for several decades to examine offending patterns.

Case Studies of Criminal Careers

Early studies of career criminality were based on case studies—descriptive life histories of particular individuals that focus on offenders who engage in particular types of crime. The aim of these studies was to gain in-depth knowledge about the motives and methods of criminals engaged in certain crimes. Case studies can lead to the development of theories to explain criminal behavior and thus they have the ability to inform policies and programs that are aimed at crime prevention and rehabilitation.

Many of the assumptions about criminal careers originated in Edwin Sutherland's classic work, *The Professional Thief*.[7] This study followed the career of Broadway Jones and served as part of the basis for Sutherland's theory of differential association. Sutherland distinguished between the career criminal and the occasional offender and developed the idea that crime can be viewed as a profession. According to Sutherland, professional thieves use their wits and talking ability rather than force to commit crimes; they also develop techniques acquired through education from other professional thieves. Status in the profession is based on their technical skill, financial standing, connections (to other thieves and power brokers), power, dress, and manners. According to Sutherland, thief is an honorary title bestowed on persons who have proven their skill.

Moreover, Sutherland believed professional thieves have a set of norms that govern their behavior. They work together without serious disagreement because of their shared values, and strong group loyalties develop. They view the law as a common enemy. Thieves are not expected to cooperate with authorities; to them, "squealing" is a heinous offense. Crime becomes organized in the sense that unity and reciprocity are common among members. When the group recognizes the individual as a professional, status is secured. The group will select and tutor certain individuals, but only those who are successfully recognized as professional thieves.

Several criminological studies followed Sutherland's lead and used the case study approach to examine the career criminals who chose to specialize in a particular kind of crime. Carl Klockars examined the secret world of a professional fence, Vincent Swaggi (a pseudonym).[8] Klockars found that in order to attain the status of a professional fence, one must be a consistent and profitable dealer (both a buyer and a seller) in stolen property for a considerable period. The fence must also have a reputation as a successful dealer among both thieves and law enforcement officials. In short, Klockars discovered that fencing is an acquired status based on skills and knowledge that are not readily available to just anyone—a finding that echoes Sutherland's research. In particular, the fence must learn how and what to buy, how to sell it, and how to deal with the traditional business issues of capital, supply, demand, and distribution. Swaggi said that people are less likely to buy a good from him unless they believe that it is stolen and that they are getting a bargain. To become successful, then, the fence must have knowledge of the product, avoid getting caught, and have the convincing appearance of a law-abiding business.

Jerome E. Jackson did field research and conducted interviews with fraud masters—individuals who conducted fraud as their personal business.[9] These masters of fraud operated like professional businesspeople while taking advantage of their access to the illegal opportunities to commit crime. Credit card thieves often traveled to different cities and states for the sole purpose of engaging in their craft and tended to avoid their hometowns (where they were more likely to be recognized). They were career criminals—on average, specialists with more than a dozen years of experience. They siphoned the funds of victims either quickly or over a prolonged period of time, victimizing friends, acquaintances, or strangers.

Cohort Research: The Chronic Six Percent

Although case studies are useful, they cannot provide estimates of the number of chronic offenders in society. In contrast, large scale longitudinal studies can track a sample of individuals over time to provide these estimates. Cohort research is a specific type of longitudinal research. A **cohort** is a group of individuals who share the same experience in time. A birth cohort includes individuals who were born in the same year. Cohorts are often used to study individuals over an extended period of time. Through the cohort, life patterns can be examined and criminal careers reconstructed. Cohort

A woman enters her credit card information to make a purchase over the Internet. How might the Internet have changed how credit card thieves operate?

© SuperStock/Alamy Images

studies show that there is a group of offenders who make up a relatively small percent of the population, yet cause much of the social damage. Because of this, these chronic offenders have been a sort of "holy grail" in criminology.

Researchers at the University of Pennsylvania were the first to conduct cohort research in order to examine criminal behavior. Their first cohort consisted of over 10,000 boys born in Philadelphia in 1945.[10] The researchers obtained information from school and police reports to draw conclusions about offending patterns. The most pertinent and influential finding of the 1945 Philadelphia birth cohort study was that a small group of 627 chronic offenders—roughly six percent of the sample—was responsible for the majority of crimes committed. Studies of the second Philadelphia birth cohort (1958) confirmed the existence of these chronic offenders. Chronic offenders in the 1958 cohort were a larger group and committed a higher percentage of the total number of offenses. Although the percentage of chronic offenders in the entire cohort declined from the 1945 levels, they still accounted for the majority of serious violent crime committed by the group.[11,12] Specific offense rates for both cohorts are presented in TABLE 9-1. As this table indicates, the chronic offenders in the 1958 cohort committed a greater number of crimes than those in the 1945 cohort and their crimes were more serious.

Other longitudinal studies also find small groups of chronic offenders. In his study of offenders in the National Youth Survey (NYS), Elliott reported that the activity of serious violent offenders followed a progression. Like the chronic groups from the Philadelphia birth cohort studies, the serious violent offenders were less than 5 percent of the NYS sample, but they accounted for 83 percent of the index offenses and half of all offenses reported.[13] Similarly, Hamparian and her colleagues studied the criminal careers of 1,138 youths born in Columbus, Ohio, between 1956 and 1960.[14,15] They also found a group of chronic offenders. Although the chronic offenders accounted for only 2 percent of the Columbus cohort, 60 percent of them were arrested at least once as a young adult (before age 20) for a felony offense. These youths also tended to be arrested

> *Through the cohort, life patterns can be examined and criminal careers reconstructed.*

more often (at least five times), to have spent time in a juvenile correctional facility, and to have committed serious crimes earlier and more frequently. They accounted for two-thirds of the crimes committed by the entire cohort, and two out of every five arrests were made for violent index crimes.[16]

Females as Chronic Offenders

As noted in Chapter 8, criminologists neglected the study of female offenders until relatively recently. As such, the rich history of case studies evident for males does not extend to females. Nevertheless, females were part of the second (1958) Philadelphia birth cohort analyses. The delinquency pattern for females in this research was very different from that of the males. Only about 14 percent of the women studied had at least one police contact before age 18. The delinquency rate for males was about two and a half times higher than that for females. Females were primarily one-time delinquents (60 percent of their cohort). Thus, the female offenders were more likely to commit one crime and then desist (or one and a half times more likely to desist than the males).[17]

Female rates of offending were much lower for every type of crime (personal or property). Only half as many violent offenses committed by females caused grave harm to victims (e.g., death or hospitalization). For theft, victims of males had a higher median dollar loss per offense ($40) than the victims of females ($25). However, this offense pattern varied by race. Nonwhite females in the cohort committed more crimes than white females. Nonwhite females committed about three and a half times more serious felonies and about five and a half times more violent crimes than white females.[18]

The pattern of crime among female *chronic* offenders in the 1958 Philadelphia birth cohort was also unlike that of males. Only 1 percent of the females were chronic offenders and they were responsible for 27 percent of the total number of crimes. Female chronic offenders accounted for 26 percent of the serious felonies committed by females whereas male chronic offenders committed 68 percent of the total serious felonies.[19] Both males and females who began their criminal careers early persisted as criminals into adulthood and had

TABLE 9-1

Offense Rates of Chronic Offenders in the 1945 and 1958 Birth Cohorts (Percentage of Entire Cohort)

Year	Cases	Offense	Murder	Rape	Robbery	Assault
1945	6.3	52	71	73	82	69
1958	7.5	61	61	75	73	65

Data from Paul E. Tracy and Kimberly L. Kempf, *Continuity and Discontinuity in Criminal Careers* (New York: Plenum Press, 1996).

more diverse patterns of offending than those who began later in life. Thus, male and female career criminals, while they differ in the types of offenses they commit, are similar in their pattern and persistence of offending over time.[20]

In his assessment of 500 career criminals, Matt DeLisi found a group of chronic female offenders who were more likely than their male counterparts to engage in forgery, fraud, and prostitution. They were also younger, less mobile, and had shorter criminal careers than males, but their presence in the cohort indicated that females also could be habitual offenders.[21]

Stephen Lab and William Doerner compared female delinquency patterns to that of the males in the three Racine, Wisconsin, birth cohorts. These cohorts consisted of all males and females born in Racine in 1942, 1949, and 1955 that stayed in that city through their adolescence. They reported that over time, female delinquency rose for status, victimless, and minor property offenses. However, in terms of major property and personal offenses, the female rates did not match that of their male counterparts.[22]

From "Criminal Career" to Life-Course Criminology

The criminal career perspective started to fade in the 1980s. Gottfredson and Hirschi were among the most vocal critics of this area of research. They contended that the known facts about crime contradicted much of the career criminal view and that most offenders do not follow a "career" in the traditional sense. Instead, they have a short-term, hedonistic orientation and tend to pursue immediate pleasure without regard to future consequences. In addition, offenders often are socially disabled and have problems managing the ordinary tasks of life—getting an education, working, supporting a family—and staying "straight." Furthermore, Gottfredson and Hirschi believe that the decline in crime with age characterizes even the most active offenders.[23]

Gottfredson and Hirschi also make a case that most criminal activities yield little in the way of tangible rewards. The majority of crimes are attempted rather than completed, and the average "take" on completed property crimes is rather meager. They took particular exception to the portrayal of criminals as "specialists." Indeed, criminal careers research revealed little specialization, with "cafeteria style" offending as the common pattern. Chronic offending had more to do with the volume than the pattern of their criminal activity.[24,25] Burglars also engaged in drug use, violence, or other criminal activity and so forth. Overall, they conclude that the word "career" is a poor metaphor for what appears to be chronic criminal behavior.[26] By the end of the 1980s, debate over the criminal career had reached somewhat of a stalemate. Those interested in chronic criminals abandoned the metaphor of criminal careers. They remained interested in how crime progressed through life, but started to speak using a different perspective and language. This new perspective is called either developmental or life-course criminology.

Life-Course Criminology

At the center of life-course criminology is one of the most well established relationships in criminology—the age–crime curve. The curve, based on official arrest data, shows that criminal behavior emerges during the teenage years, peaks prior to age 21, and declines quickly thereafter (**FIGURE 9-1**). This age–crime curve is remarkably similar for males and females, across different societies, across time, and for different crimes.[27,28] In a nutshell, this suggests that crime is a young person's game—crime emerges during early adolescence and declines by adulthood. Most mainstream theories of crime are therefore really theories of adolescent delinquency. Hirschi's *Causes of Delinquency*, for example, focused on social control during adolescence. He identified factors such as commitment to school and identification with parents that are most germane to that developmental stage.[29] Similarly, Merton's strain theory focuses on the period from adolescence to young adulthood, when youth realized that they could not achieve the American dream legitimately.[30]

Life-course criminologists argued, however, that the picture of crime painted by the age–crime curve was distorted. They pointed out that the age–crime curve traced the roots of crime only to early adolescence because it was based on *arrests*.[31] What happens if instead of arrest or conviction, the focus becomes antisocial behavior or deviance? Childhood precursors to crime such as conduct disorder, severe temper tantrums, and other antisocial behaviors emerge much earlier than adolescence. Furthermore, studies indicate that such behaviors are among the best predictors of adolescent delinquency and adult criminality.[32–34]

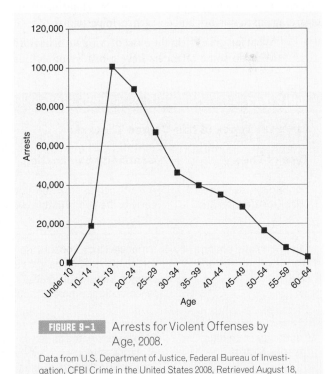

FIGURE 9-1 Arrests for Violent Offenses by Age, 2008.

Data from U.S. Department of Justice, Federal Bureau of Investigation, CFBI Crime in the United States 2008, Retrieved August 18, 2010, from http://www2.fbi.gov/ucr/cius2008/data/table_38.html

For example, Lee Robbins' longitudinal study of a cohort of black males indicated that an adult diagnosis of antisocial personality disorder virtually required antisocial childhood behavior.[35,36] Reviews of the literature on childhood antisocial behavior revealed that lying, aggression, and theft were strong predictors of later delinquency and criminal offending. Furthermore, those children with (a) the highest levels of problem behaviors, (b) problem behaviors in multiple settings, and (c) an early onset to delinquency tended to be antisocial in later life and were more likely to exhibit chronic offense patterns.[37,38] As the quote by psychologist Terrie Moffitt on the opening page of this chapter suggests, there is a great deal of stability, or continuity, in antisocial behavior. Because of this stability, the search for the chronic criminal was pushed back into early childhood. Since research by the Gluecks and others had decades ago established that parenting and other childhood factors predicted adolescent delinquency, this was more of a rediscovery.[39]

The final piece of life-course criminology involves the most obvious feature of the age–crime relationship. Simply put, most people eventually desist from crime. Despite all of the stability evident in offending, there is also a great deal of change. Recall that the age–crime curve of arrests drops steeply during adulthood. Studies that follow antisocial children find that many "recover" and do not become adolescent delinquents. Roughly half of delinquents never accumulate an adult criminal record.[40] Thus, finding adult chronic offenders and looking backward in time, stability is the rule. Following children with serious behavioral problems demonstrates a great deal of change. It is this puzzle of stability and change that is central to life-course criminology.

Central Life-Course Questions

Life-course criminology approaches crime by asking questions regarding onset, stability, and desistence. In particular:[41,42]

- What factors explain the *onset* of criminal behavior? Why do some offenders have a history of serious misbehavior dating back to early childhood? Why do some offenders appear to begin offending during adolescence?
- What are correlates of crime at different developmental stages from childhood through adulthood?
- What explains the stability of antisocial behavior? Why does childhood misconduct predict adolescent delinquency?
- Why do most offenders, regardless of their criminal history, age out of crime? Why do many children and adolescents appear to recover from early conduct problems prior to adulthood?

 # Life-Course Theories

Over the past 20 years, a number of theories have been developed to answer these questions. The theories differ in their explanation of stability, change, and the causes of crime across different stages of life. Francis Cullen and Robert Agnew offer a very useful **typology** to organize these theories.[43] **TABLE 9-2** illustrates this typology.

Continuity Theories

Continuity theories are designed to explain the emergence of deviance in childhood and the stability of such behavior through life. This type of theory locates the cause of both initial deviance and stability in the existence of some trait such as impulsivity or low self-control. For this reason, they are also called "trait" theories. Gottfredson and Hirschi's theory of low self-control, discussed in Chapter 7, is a good example of a continuity theory. In this theory, self-control is the result of parenting. Parents who supervise their children and punish them consistently build self-control within their children at an early age. In contrast, low self-control is described as a cluster of traits (impulsiveness, insensitivity, risk-taking

TABLE 9-2

Different Types of Life-Course Theories

Type of Theory	Continuity Explanation	Change Explanation
Continuity (trait) theories Gottfredson and Hirschi	A trait such as "low self-control" emerges early in life and is stable over time.	Trait theories have difficulty accounting for change.
Continuity and change theories Sampson and Laub	Initial deviance impacts a person's environment, including parents and peers. This creates a snowballing effect where desistence becomes more difficult over time.	Although the social environment often makes crime patterns more entrenched, it also opens up the possibility of change. Crime-prone youth may find a quality job or a prosocial spouse that leads them off a criminal pathway.
Continuity or change theories Moffitt	Stability is created largely by a small group of chronic offenders. Their deviance starts very early in life and is resistant to change.	Change is created by a large number of youth who engage in crime during adolescence but desist during young adulthood.

Data from Francis T. Cullen and Robert Agnew, *Criminological Theory*: Past to Present 4th Edition (New York: Oxford, 2011): 454-460.

orientation) that stabilizes in early childhood.[44] Thus, this theory can explain childhood precursors to delinquency by focusing on parenting practices. The stability of antisocial behavior is accounted for in the enduring trait of low self-control. The problem with such a theory is explaining why many people with low self-control desist from crime. In defense of their theory, Gottfredson and Hirschi argue that since almost everyone desists from crime (it is near universal), it is unnecessary to explain why it happens.[45] Of course, many criminologists disagree with this view.[46]

> The problem with such a theory is explaining why many people with low self-control desist from crime.

Continuity and Change Theories

A second type of life-course explanation for crime is the stability *and* change theory. Here, both processes are present within a single explanation of crime. Theories of this type often rely on the concept of **cumulative continuity**.[47] This is the notion that early deviance has an impact on a child's environment. Parents, teachers, and peers all react to antisocial children, often in a negative way. In turn, negative reaction from the environment (e.g., peer rejection, parental withdrawal, school failure) increases the odds of future deviance. In essence, early deviance "snowballs" into a trajectory that is difficult to escape.[48] Still, because this type of explanation includes environmental forces, change is possible. Even though deviant children are likely to face peer rejection and school

failure, it is possible for a deviant child to befriend a prosocial peer or encounter an exceptional teacher. Such circumstances may help explain why many children appear to recover from childhood deviance.

Sampson and Laub's age-graded theory of informal social control, discussed briefly in Chapter 7, is an example of a continuity *and* change theory. Their 1993 book, *Crime in the Making: Pathways and Turning Points Through the Life Course* is considered a classic for a number of reasons. First, it was one of the first books to outline the idea of life-course criminology. Second, they presented a life-course theory based on data from the Gluecks' *Unraveling Juvenile Delinquency* study. The data was restored and computerized after John Laub's remarkable discovery, in 1986, of boxes containing the Glueck study records in the basement of Harvard Law School. Finally, their data and theory allowed them to examine how and why even chronic offenders desist from crime. This had been a neglected area of research.[49]

FIGURE 9-2 illustrates the central concepts in Sampson and Laub's age-graded theory of social control. As the title of the book suggests, Sampson and Laub portray the development of crime in terms of pathways and turning points. Antisocial pathways represent continuity in behavior across the life course—including antisocial behavior. A host of factors help establish antisocial pathways. Some of these factors—difficult temperaments and conduct disorder—are consistent

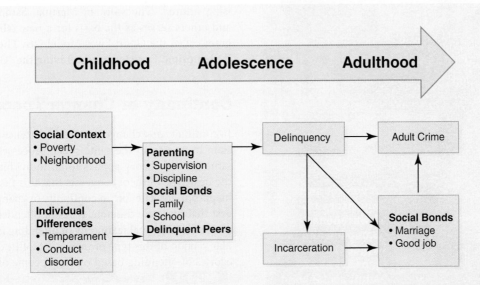

FIGURE 9-2 A summary of Sampson and Laub's age graded theory of social control.

Data from Robert J. Sampson and John H. Laub (1993). *Crime in the Making: Pathways and Turning Points through Life* (Cambridge, MA: Harvard University Press).

with trait theories. Other influences, such as an unstable family context and economic disadvantage, are social in nature. Cumulative continuity helps to explain why individuals stay on a delinquent pathway. Factors from early childhood (conduct disorder, social context) have an impact on later influences like parenting and commitment to school. Thus a pattern is established in which misconduct and delinquency decrease future social controls (parental supervision, bonds to family and school). While the pattern is stable, the types of social control change over time. For example, crime during adolescence and young adulthood weaken the adult social bonds of marriage and employment. In turn, the lack of adult social bonds keeps individuals on the antisocial pathway.[50]

Despite this likelihood of continued antisocial behavior, adult social bonds can also serve as turning points—processes that deflect people off of a criminal pathway. Indeed, Sampson and Laub found that individuals who obtained *quality* jobs or *good* marriages were most likely to desist from crime.[51] The nature of employment and marriage matters because they serve as a social bond—something to risk losing by engaging in crime. Thus, a low-wage fast food job would not be much to risk. To further study **desistence**, Sampson and Laub conducted follow-up interviews with men, now in their late 60s, from the Glueck sample. This follow-up confirmed their central idea that marriage, employment, and military service create opportunities for change. However, they came to view the desistence process as more complex than forming an "adult bond." Specifically, they note that structural life changes such as marriage and employment:[52,53]

A worker sorts inventory in a warehouse. Sampson and Laub argue that quality jobs act as an adult social bond that encourages desistence from crime.
© AbleStock/Getty

- Cut off the past from the present, providing an opportunity for identity transformation
- Provide increased supervision and monitoring, and also opportunities for social support and growth
- Change routine activities by providing more structure

Laub and Sampson note that desistence often happens by default rather than through any conscious decision to quit crime. A person gets married, becomes a parent, begins hanging around with a different crowd, and drifts away from crime. They also note, though, that there is a "human agency" involved. In other words, people are more than just empty vessels being filled by social factors. A person can find a quality job or good marriage and not take advantage of this new opportunity.[54]

Sampson and Laub's theory and studies have led to a surge in research on the desistence process. For example, one recent study capitalized on the aftermath of Hurricane Katrina in New Orleans to see whether a change of residence could act as a turning point for parolees. Moving to a new neighborhood might allow ex-inmates to knife off the past from the present and to assume new, noncriminal identities. After Hurricane Katrina, some offenders who were released from prisons in Louisiana were unable to return to their old neighborhoods because of extensive property damage. The study showed that parolees who moved to a new area were less likely to be reincarcerated in the following 3 years.[55]

Desistence is also a central theme in the work of Shadd Maruna. Maruna's classic Liverpool desistence study chronicled the life stories of a sample of chronic offenders to see why some desisted while others remained active offenders. He was particularly interested in "scripts," the stories people told themselves and others to explain their criminality. He found that desisters were able to form "redemptive scripts" that asserted their essential goodness. As with a change in address or new employment, the script allowed offenders to psychologically sever their criminal past from a more promising future.[56] The work of Maruna, Sampson and Laub, and others serves as the basis for a new rehabilitation program called the Good Lives Model (see **Theory in Action: Redemption, Desistence, and Living the "Good Life"**).

Continuity or Change Theories

In continuity *and* change theories, desistence and persistence stem in part from the same social processes. Similarly, the same general theory applies to all individuals. In contrast, the next type of theory suggests that this thought process is inappropriate. The "or" in continuity or change theories suggest that there are different types of offenders. Psychologist Terrie Moffitt's dual taxonomy of offending is the most popular version of this type of theory.[57] Moffitt created two categories of offending based on how people offend over time (**TABLE 9-3**). **Life-course–persistent (LCP) offenders** begin their offending early in life and show a great deal of stability in their antisocial behavior. The LCP group is similar to the "chronic six percent" identified by cohort research. They make up a small percentage of any cohort, but cause much of

TABLE 9-3

Moffitt's Two Types of Offenders

Type Offender	Onset of Antisocial Behavior	Explaining Stability	Explaining Desistence
Life-course–persistent (LCP)	Very early onset, caused by the interaction between neurological deficits and an adverse environment.	Neurological deficits remain. Additionally, initial deviance has a negative impact on the environment. LCP youth face peer rejection and school failure.	LCP youth are less likely to desist from crime. However, because stability is caused in part by the environmental influences, it is possible that these influences may also produce desistence.
Adolescent-limited (AL)	Onset of offending during adolescence. Caused by the "maturity gap." AL youth begin to mimic the behavior of their LCP peers.	Unlikely to remain criminal after young adulthood, though some may become "snared" in the consequences of their adolescent deviance.	The maturity gap closes and offending is no longer rewarding. AL youth have little negative baggage so they are able to desist.

Data from Terrie E. Moffitt, "Adolescent Limited and Life-Course-Persistent Antisocial Behavior: A Developmental Taxonomy," *Psychological Review* 100: 674-701.

the crime for that cohort. In contrast, **adolescent-limited (AL) offenders** do not begin offending until adolescence. The AL group makes up a large percentage of a cohort—50 percent or more. As the name suggests, criminal behavior in the AL group is largely limited to adolescence. Most AL offenders desist by young adulthood.

Within this theory then, change comes primarily from the AL group, while stability arises from the LCP group. The two groups of offenders generate different sorts of research questions. Why does the LCP group start their misbehavior so early in life and why do they continue into adulthood? Why do AL offenders start later, and why do they desist so readily?

As discussed in Chapter 4, Moffitt proposes that the LCP group begins life with subtle neurological deficits. The deficits may be caused by a host of factors such as prenatal harm to the fetus, low birth weight, exposure to toxins, or even genetic predisposition. According to Moffitt, even subtle neuropsychological deficits can produce an infant with a "difficult temperament." Specifically, these infants may be "clumsy and awkward, overactive, inattentive, irritable, impulsive, hard to keep on schedule, delayed in reaching developmental milestones, poor at verbal comprehension, deficient at expressing themselves, or slow at learning new things."[58] Such an ill-tempered infant may be hard to socialize and evokes challenges for even the most competent, loving parents. For a number of reasons, however, these children are more likely to be raised in less ideal parenting environments.

This is true because many of the possible causes of neurological problems mentioned earlier (e.g., low birth weight, maternal smoking during pregnancy, heredity) co-occur with poor parenting and adverse social conditions. For example, mothers who engage in behaviors that put an unborn child at risk may be less likely to have the characteristics associated with good parenting. Alternatively, exposure to toxins may be the result of adverse social conditions. Thus, the LCP pathway begins with poor prenatal care followed by difficult

children being raised by parents not equipped to handle them.[59] LCP children tend to stay antisocial for two reasons. First, their neurological deficits continue to cause problems. Second, LCP youth will tend to alienate themselves from prosocial peers and the school environment. Failure in these domains may limit these children's abilities to acquire and practice prosocial skills (e.g., empathy, self-control).

In contrast to the LCP path, the explanation for adolescent-limited offending must explain why offending starts later in life and why it stops quickly. Moffitt suggests that the root of AL offending is a gap between biological and social age. Biologically, adolescents are ready for adult roles and behavior. Socially, they are prohibited from many adult behaviors—alcohol use, sex, and so forth. This maturity gap causes youth to rebel, often times in a delinquent manner. During this time, delinquent acts such as underage drinking and illicit drug use become normative. AL offenders begin to mimic the behavior of their LCP counterparts.[60]

AL offending stops during young adulthood for two reasons. First, the maturity gap closes. Rebelling against parents is not as rewarding to a 25-year-old person as it is to an adolescent. Second, AL offenders do not have the same deficits as LCP offenders. They have no neurological deficits and have not built up as much negative baggage (e.g., school failure, peer rejection). Moffitt notes, however, that is it possible for AL offenders to get sucked into an antisocial lifestyle. For example, their illicit drug use may develop into a drug addiction. Still, the most likely scenario is that they enter adulthood and take on adult roles and responsibilities.

Moffitt's theory has generated a great deal of research.[61] A recent review of 61 studies published in the 20 years since she proposed her theory found "support for the hypothesis that life-course–persistent antisocial behavior is a neurodevelopmental disorder which emerges in the transactions between individual vulnerabilities and environmental adversity."[62] A general

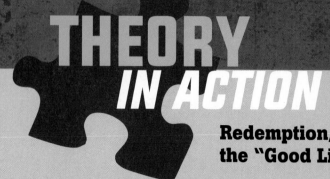

THEORY IN ACTION

Redemption, Desistence, and Living the "Good Life"

From its start, the discipline of criminology has focused on causes of crime. Criminologists have uncovered a host psychological, biological, and sociological factors that help to explain why people start and/or persist in criminal behavior. By the 1990s, however, life-course criminologists were asking a different question. They wanted to understand why people *stopped* engaging in crime. Sampson and Laub were among the first to propose a life-course theory of crime that included an explanation of desistence. They argued that "turning points," such as employment, marriage, and military service served to deflect people from criminal pathways. As their theory evolved, they came to believe that "human agency" played a central role in desistence. That is, the offender must have the *will* to keep a good job or to nurture a good marriage.

This new perspective received support from Maruna's now classic study of chronic offenders in Liverpool, England. Maruna collected the life histories of two carefully matched groups of offenders. Both groups grew up in tough neighborhoods and had many risk factors (e.g., drug/alcohol abuse, low employment, childhood abuse and neglect) for crime. Although both groups also had extensive histories of criminal behavior, one group had desisted from crime and other group remained active. What accounted for desistence? Maruna focused on the "scripts" or "self-stories" that offenders used to explain their lives to themselves and others. The narratives help offenders deal with the stigma and voids that a criminal history creates.

Active offenders told stories that followed a *condemnation script*. They lacked personal agency and instead saw themselves as pawns, driven to crime by criminal associates, drug addiction, or other forces. They viewed their future prospects for survival in the "need not apply" straight world as dim and felt they had nothing left to lose. This narrative provides psychological shelter, since it is easier to give up on purpose than to continually struggle and fail. Active offenders framed happiness in terms of material consumption and the "big score." For example, most bought lottery tickets and thought about what they could do with the winnings. In contrast, those who had desisted from crime had self-stories that followed a *redemption script*. They told optimistic "comeback stories" about beating the odds. They framed their criminal past as an "it" that happened (e.g., "it was the drugs") as opposed to viewing it as part of their identity. This script allowed them to claim a good "true self" (e.g., "I was always a good person") that could be salvaged from the criminal past. Desistence was framed as an act of rebellion against a system that fosters crime, and not an act of "giving in" to the demands of authority figures. The redemption script also incorporated the idea that something good can come from past struggles. Desisters expressed the desire to give something back—to help the next generation avoid similar mistakes.

Research on desistence from crime has obvious policy relevance. Policies that can foster desistence would reduce crime. The policy implication from Maruna's research is that redemptive scripts should be encouraged and fostered. For example, Maruna and his colleagues recommend employment of formerly incarnated persons as counselors or paraprofessionals to work with newly released inmates. This nurtures the desire of those who have desisted from crime to give back to the community and takes advantage of their skill set (ability to overcome stigma, coping ability, prosocial attitudes). This "wounded healers" concept is already evident in substance abuse counseling, where many counselors are recovering addicts. In a more broad sense, the work of Mauna and others has fostered a new approach to rehabilitation called the Good Life Model (GLM).

The GLM was created by New Zealand psychologist Tony Ward and his colleagues throughout the 2000s. This rehabilitation model starts with the assumption that all humans (offenders included) seek basic goals. These goals, termed "primary human goods" include knowledge, relatedness, autonomy, play, physical health, and mastery. Ward and his colleagues believe that a combination of internal and external factors led criminals to meet these human needs through deviant methods. The main treatment goal is to have offenders pursue these goals in a prosocial manner. The key insight that ties GLM with the work of Maruna is that for offenders to make this difficult change, they must feel like change is possible. Thus, therapists encourage "agency" by encouraging offenders to visualize a more positive future. This is especially important for people (e.g., sexual offenders) carrying a great deal of stigma, shame, and hopelessness. With the aid of a therapist, offenders develop a realistic but hopeful "good life plan." In the language of Maruna's research, the good life plan creates a redemptive script for the offender to follow. While there is some promising research on the GLM, this new model has yet to accumulate rigorous scientific support. Studies over the next decade should indicate whether the GLM effectively reduces crime.

Sources: Maruna, S. (2001). *Making good: How ex-convicts reform and rebuild their lives.* Washington, DC: American Psychological Association; LeBel, T. P., Richie, M., & Maruna, S. (2015). Helping others as a response to reconcile a criminal past: The role of the wounded healer in prisoner reentry programs. *Criminal Justice and Behavior, 42,* 108–120; Ward, T., Mann, R. E., & Gannon, T. A. (2007). The Good Lives Model of offender rehabilitation: Clinical implications. *Aggression and Violent Behavior, 12,* 87–107; Ward, T. (2015). Ethical practice in the treatment of sex offenders: Addressing the dual relationship problem. In D. Wilcox (Ed.), *Sex offender treatment: A case study approach to issues and interventions.* Oxford, UK: Wiley-Blackwell.

Texture: © Nik Merkulov/Shutterstock, Inc.

critique of typologies is that they are too simplistic—individuals in the real world often defy categories. Indeed, career criminal research emerging in the late 1980s documented several specific offending trajectories, such as early starters, later starters, persisters, desisters, occasionals, and chronics.[63] For example, there is evidence that her AL pathway may not describe all adolescent offending. Research indicates that severe antisocial behavior can emerge later in adolescence and persist into adulthood.[64] Nevertheless, it is clear that Moffiit's theory has made an important contribution to criminology, and that it will continue to generate research interest in the near future.

An Integrated Life-Course Theory

Although most life-course theories fall within one of the three categories discussed above, there have been attempts to integrate these perspectives. Most recently, Travis Pratt has proposed modifying self-control theory to bring it into line with research findings and to integrate it with other theories.[65] Stated in a series of propositions, the gist of the theory is that self-control is dynamic (rather than a purely static trait), and self-control is an important cause of the life events (such as "turning points") that are assumed to influence criminal behavior. **TABLE 9-4** outlines the core propositions in this theory.

The Policy Implications of the Criminal Career Perspective and Life-Course Criminology

The criminal career perspective and life-course criminology have spurred a great deal of theoretical debate and research. As with any area in criminology, theory and research yield policy implications. Thus, one goal of this research is to determine the most effective time to intervene in a criminal career, for either crime control or rehabilitative purposes. What does the debate and research generated by these areas tell us about bringing a criminal career to an end—for both the protection of the public and the salvation of the criminal?

Many of the policy implications are directed toward chronic offenders, as it is clear that they represent a significant threat to society. In one cohort of 500 adult criminals, offenders totaled over 29,000 arrests, including 58 homicides, 201 rapes, 55 kidnappings, 405 armed robberies, and 1,101 aggravated assaults. These activities led to 2,801 felony convictions and 1,739 prison sentences. Given this level of activity, the authors estimated that these habitual offenders generated over $415 million in victim costs,

> *. . . one goal of this research is to determine the most effective time to intervene in a criminal career, for either crime control or rehabilitative purposes.*

required over $137 million in criminal justice systems costs to process them, and over $14 million in lost earnings. In sum, the crimes of this group of career criminals cost society over $550 million in victimization costs.[66]

As with other policy decisions, scholars, researchers, and policymakers disagree about the best way to reduce the damage caused by chronic offenders. Traditionally, conservatives prefer a criminal justice oriented (e.g., punishment) response. Indeed, one common sense reaction to the existence of the "chronic six percent" is to "lock 'em up!" Like conservatives, liberals see chronic offenders as the key to crime reduction. Liberals, however, seek to use life-course theory to identify and change the variables (such as self-control, parenting, and employment) that cause serious crime. Because the roots of chronic offending go back to early childhood, early preventive programs may hold a great deal of promise. We consider both of these strategies in the following sections.

Criminal Justice Responses

As noted in Chapter 3, the implicit goal of corrections in the United States since the 1980s has been incapacitation. As rehabilitation came under attack in the 1970s, influential scholars, based in part on the cohort research discussed here, argued that locking up high-rate offenders for long periods of time would reduce crime rates dramatically. If six percent of a cohort committed over 50 percent of the crime, then incarcerating this group should have substantial impacts on crime.[67] Although crime has indeed declined over the past 25 years, it is unclear how much of this decline is due to incapacitation.[68,69] For example, states that largely resisted the incarceration binge that occurred through the 1980s and 1990s experienced crime drops similar to those in states with an aggressive incarceration policy (research on incapacitation is reviewed in Chapter 3).

One factor that greatly limits the impact of criminal justice programs is the difficulty in *prospectively* identifying which offenders will eventually become the chronic six percent. As John Laub notes, "the old adage goes—lives are lived forward but can only be understood backwards."[70] Thus, statisticians armed to the teeth with data cannot predict with much accuracy which young criminals will become chronic offenders. Criminal justice agencies, operating with even less information, often fare worse. One result of this emphasis has been a burgeoning incarceration rate. As noted previously, the United States has the highest incarceration rate of any industrialized country. The goal of incapacitation has been pursued by implementing a wide range of criminal

TABLE 9-4

Core Propositions for an Integrated Self-Control/Life-Course Theory of Crime

Proposition	Explanation
Self-control predicts problematic behavior at all relevant points of the life course.	As Gottfredson and Hirshi contend, low self-control fosters stability.
Self-control varies within individuals at all relevant points of the life course.	Self-control may not be as stable as predicted. A person's level of self-control may get "depleted" under stressful conditions.
Following the peak crime years, self-control increases within individuals over time.	Desistence may result from an increase in self-control as people age.
Self-control influences selection into negative life events and coping strategies following negative life events.	Suggests an overlap between self-control and Agnew's general strain theory.
Self-control is a key factor linking neuropsychological deficits to early onset offending.	Suggests an overlap between self-control and Moffitt's life-course–persistent pathway.
Self-control influences late adolescent/teen sensitivity to the maturity gap.	Suggests an overlap between self-control and Moffitt's adolescent-limited pathway.
Self-control influences individuals' sensitivity to informal and formal social control at all points in the life course.	Individuals with high self-control will respond more to criminal sanctions and informal control.
Self-control influences social ties and turning points over the life course.	Self-control impacts whether and how people experience marriage, employment, and other turning points.

Data from Pratt, T. C. (2015). A self-control/life-course theory of criminal behavior. *European Journal of Criminology*. Published online before print May 31, 2015, doi: 10.1177/1477370815587771

justice policies, most often using police initiatives and the correctional system. We will explore these two areas in greater detail.

Policing Initiatives

Over the years, several police programs have been developed to support the arrest of chronic offenders. One early form of this sort of initiative was the **repeat offender program (ROP)**, pronounced "rope." ROPs selectively focus police resources on chronic offenders.[71] These programs take a proactive approach by having the police target offenders or certain types of crime and try to catch the offenders red-handed rather than waiting for a citizen's call.[72] Typically, ROP squads focus their efforts on two sorts of offenders. Those already wanted on arrest warrants are arrested on sight. Those believed to be criminally active but not currently wanted are aggressively investigated. Working in close conjunction with prosecutors, these programs attempt to apprehend career criminals and effectively incapacitate them. Early ROP initiatives were developed in Washington, DC, and Phoenix, Arizona.

In Washington, DC, an 88-officer team used investigative and undercover tactics to apprehend high-rate offenders.

> *Over the years, several police programs have been developed to support the arrest of chronic offenders.*

Specifically, the ROP officers targeted those persons believed to be committing five or more UCR Part 1 offenses (e.g., rape, robbery, burglary) per week. An experiment designed to evaluate the performance indicated, that by many measures, it was productive. The researchers found that ROP increased the likelihood of arrest, the seriousness of the criminal histories, the probability of felony prosecution, and the sentence lengths of its arrestees.[73] They also noted, however, that ROP reduced the arrest productivity of police and was expensive to implement.

In an experimental evaluation of the ROP in Phoenix, Arizona, offenders were randomly assigned as to an experimental (ROP-enforced) group or a control group. The rate of conviction and incarceration for ROP cases was higher than the control group. Once convicted, ROP offenders were more likely to be sentenced to prison for longer periods. On average, convicted ROP offenders received an additional 9.4 months.[74] Of course, incarceration through ROP only works in the long term to the extent that incapacitation reduces overall crime (a point we return to later).

More recent policing models often stress preventive deterrence over arrest and incarceration. In Chapter 3, we explored the violence reduction programs (Boston's Operation Ceasefire, Cincinnati Initiative to Reduce Violence) that operate under the focused deterrence model pioneered by professor David Kennedy. Here, police use the explicit threat of arrest and sanction to prevent criminal activity. For example, police hold "call ins" for youth gang members to inform them that if any gang member engaged in gun violence, the whole gang would be targeted for arrest and prosecution. At another site, police notified drug dealers that they were building a case against them and would arrest if the drug dealing didn't stop.[75]

Modern policing, such as that advocated by Kennedy, often depends on gathering and analyzing information. Such approaches have benefited from the shift to "intelligence-led policing." Ratcliffe defines intelligence-led policing as a business model and managerial philosophy in which data analysis and crime intelligence are pivotal to an objective decision-making framework that facilitates crime and problem reduction, disruption, and prevention through both strategic management and effective enforcement strategies that target prolific and serious offenders.

Intelligence can help police deal with crimes that they can impact—especially street-level violence and order-maintenance crimes.[76] For example, focused deterrence against gang violence requires intelligence on gang membership and involvement in violence. In the Cincinnati initiative, analysts discovered that the tiny fraction (0.3%) of the population that was involved in violent gangs or groups caused 75 percent of the homicides in a year.[77]

Sentencing/Corrections Initiatives

As noted earlier, chronic offenders have always been the "holy grail" of policymakers. Selective incapacitation strategies seek to identify and incarcerate members of the "chronic six percent" for long periods of time. Unfortunately, even with detailed life histories, scholars cannot accurately identify these offenders until late in their criminal careers. Criminal justice policies operate with much less information. Typically, criminal history is used as a rough indicator to identify chronic offenders. Since the early history of prisons, "habitual offender" statutes called for longer sentences for repeat offenders. As incapacitation strategies came to dominate the American political landscape, many states also passed "mandatory minimum" sentences.

Among the most popular have been the so-called "three strikes" laws that emerged in the 1990s. Sixteen states (California, Colorado, Connecticut, Florida, Georgia, Indiana, Kansas, Louisiana, Maryland, New Jersey, New Mexico, North Carolina, Tennessee, Virginia, Washington, and Wisconsin) eventually adopted three-strikes legislation. These laws typically call for a term of life imprisonment without possibility of parole for persons convicted for a third time of certain specified felony crimes.[78] California, until recently, had one of the more sweeping laws. In this state, the three-strikes law was passed following the notorious case of Richard Allen Davis, an unrepentant repeat offender who abducted 12-year-old Polly Klaas from a slumber party and murdered her. Davis had been paroled after serving half of his 16-year sentence for kidnapping. The case became a hot political issue. As a result, the three-strikes law proposal was placed on the 1994 California ballot with strong support from petitions. It passed with over 71 percent of the votes cast.[79] The aim of the law was to reduce serious crime while incapacitating and also deterring others from becoming repeat offenders.[80] If an offender commited any of 500 listed felonies when they already had one "strike" (conviction), the new sentence was automatically doubled. If the offender had two strikes, a new felony conviction carried a prison sentence of 25 years to life.[81] The California law differed from other states in that this sentence enhancement could be invoked when the offender had only one prior conviction for a serious crime. In addition, the crime that triggered the enhancement did not need to be violent. This is important because the vast majority of felony offenses are property crimes, such as theft.

Because California's law was construed so broadly, the state ended up incarcerating thousands of offenders—four times as many inmates as all of the other three-strike states combined.[82] According to one estimate, nearly two-thirds of these California offenders have been imprisoned for nonviolent offenses.[83] Research on the impact of the California law reveals that it did not achieve its goals. It failed to lower the crime rate, even in those counties that used it the most.[84] While it is unclear the exact role that the three-strikes law played, California now faces severely crowded prisons. In 2011, the Supreme Court placed a population limit on the prison system because prison officials were unable to provide adequate health care to inmates. In 2012, California citizens passed Proposition 36, which limits use of three-strikes legislation to serious, violent felony offenses. The new law also authorized re-sentencing for offenders currently serving life sentences if their third-strike conviction was not serious or violent.[85]

Negative Consequences of Getting Tough

There is some evidence that punitive criminal justice responses may produce unintended negative consequences. For example, career criminals interviewed in an Bureau of Alcohol, Tobacco, and Firearms (ATF) study clearly stated their views on a mandatory-sentence gun law:[86]

If a guy makes a living with a gun, he is going to do what he has to do and believes he is not going to be caught. Criminals will shoot at officers to avoid facing the 15 years; it's a life sentence anyway.

Yes, if I got out today I'd have a gun today. If a government agent showed up at my doorstep, I'd kill her. I'm not going down again. This law is creating a monster—it's creating a lot of people who will kill agents because you've made them hardened criminals—what does he have to lose? A guy facing mandatory sentences will resort to violence.

Yes, if a cop pulls up on me after this, we will hold court right there. I won't do 15 years again for carrying or having a gun.

These blunt quotes taken from interviews indicate that cracking down on career criminals may have unintended and undesirable side effects. There is some evidence that career criminal laws may place law enforcement officers in danger. A study of the impact of California's three-strikes law revealed notable increases in arrest rates, resisting and assaulting officers, and a significant increase in the Los Angeles area of two- and three-strikes crimes with a police officer victim.[87]

Additionally, there is some research suggesting that the strategy of incapacitation may backfire and actually *increase* crime. Incarcerating a high percentage of adults from already disadvantaged neighborhoods can further destabilize these areas, leading to higher crime rates.[92] Also, there is evidence indicating a negative effect on individuals who are incarcerated. Most inmates are eventually released from prison. The longer the time served, the more difficult it is to reintegrate these ex-inmates back into society.[88]

In sum, the policy of incapacitation seems simple on the surface—incarcerate chronic offenders to reduce crime. However, it is difficult, if not impossible, to accurately identify who these individuals are and to take action before many of their crimes are already committed. A truly proactive approach is impossible because society cannot take action against citizens until they actually commit a crime. While there is some evidence that mass incarceration reduces some types of offenses, it is very expensive to build and maintain prisons. Also, such a strategy inevitably faces the "law of diminishing returns." The more individuals who are incarcerated, the fewer high-risk individuals there are for future incarceration.[89] Finally, many incapacitation strategies run afoul of a central finding in life-course criminology—almost everyone ages out of crime by late adulthood. Policies that lock up offenders "for life" may generate a prison population of elderly inmates that pose little threat to society.[90] For these reasons, many criminologists recommend a policy model based on prevention and rehabilitation.

Prevention and Rehabilitation

Punishment and incapacitation are not the only policies called for to interrupt, or effectively prevent, a destructive career in crime. Selective incapacitation was a seductive policy because locking up a relatively small percentage of offenders could generate large reductions in crime. For the same reason, policies that *prevent* individuals from starting down an antisocial pathway are also very appealing. Since a chronic offender generates a great deal of social damage over the life course, eliminating the factors that cause early deviance and crime could generate huge cost savings. Even programs geared toward older offenders can reduce crime by encouraging early

> Since a chronic offender generates a great deal of social damage over the life course, eliminating the factors that cause early deviance and crime could generate huge cost savings.

desistence from chronic offending. Thus, policymakers have capitalized on life-course theory and research that identifies and attempts to change the risk factors for crime at different developmental periods. There is now a large body of evidence demonstrating that some of these rehabilitation and prevention programs are effective.[91,92]

We have noted elsewhere that criminologists have "rediscovered" the importance of childhood in the development of crime. The general policy implication from this emphasis is that prevention and rehabilitation programs should be started as early as is feasible. Indeed, programs to improve the health of newborns have become much more popular in recent years. Some are yielding promising results.[93,94] In particular, home visiting programs, where nurses visit mothers before and after the birth of their child, have shown a great deal of promise. We discuss these initiatives in more detail in **Theory in Action: Home Visitation Programs**.

Life-course theories such as Moffitt's dual taxonomy and Sampson and Laub's age-graded theory of informal control focus on the role of parenting and parental skills. Family-based interventions, such as training programs to provide parental management skills, have accumulated a track record of modest success.[95–97] For example, the most recent "second-generation" family-based intervention from Gerald Patterson and his colleagues is called the Family Check-Up (FCU). This program aims to reduce childhood conduct problems by targeting disrupted or unskilled family management. This is important because conduct problems such as oppositional and aggressive behaviors place children at risk for future behavioral problems in school and the community.[98] Recall, for example, Moffitt's description of life-course–persistent (LCP) offenders. Their early conduct problems provoke peer rejection, school problems, and parental rejection, all of which help keep them on the LCP pathway.

The FCU is a brief, three-session intervention with an optional parent management training component. The three sessions are constructed as follows:[99]

- The first session is a 1-hour assessment where a staff member reviews and discusses concerns with the caregiver, focusing on family issues that are most critical to the child's well-being. Specifically, the interview covers the parent's goals and concerns within the family.
- In the second session, a therapist engages the family in a variety of in-home videotaped tasks of parent–child interactions, while caregivers complete questionnaires about their own, their child's, and their family's functioning. During this session, staff completes ratings of parental involvement and supervision.

Home Visitation Programs

Since the late 1980s, criminologists have "rediscovered" the importance of childhood. In particular, a host of studies using different methodologies revealed that early childhood behavioral problems predict delinquency and crime. Children diagnosed with conduct disorder, or those who are reported by parents and teachers to lie, steal, or bully, are more likely to become delinquent youth. The new emphasis on childhood raises the question of whether these initial behaviors can be prevented. Life-course theories suggest a host of factors that might reduce childhood deviance. Programs that train parents in effective child-rearing practices are one policy option. Some programs go even further back into childhood.

Criminologist Elliot Currie has long advocated a prevention approach to crime reduction. He points to promising research on a number of early intervention strategies. In particular, programs that support at-risk mothers of new babies have had a great deal of success. Typically, the programs involve a nurse or a paraprofessional visiting the new mother at her home. These professionals provide support, education, and pragmatic help (e.g., finding better living conditions, obtaining employment, finding child care), and are able to connect women with additional services. Research consistently indicates that home visiting programs have a variety of positive effects. In particular, they:

- Improve prenatal health of the baby
- Reduce childhood injuries
- Reduce the rates of subsequent pregnancies and births
- Increase maternal employment
- Reduce women's use of welfare
- Reduce children's mental health problems
- Increase children's school readiness and academic achievement

Because of these positive effects, cost–benefit analyses consistently reveal that home visiting programs reduce overall costs to government and society. Although research findings are less clear, many home visiting programs have been successful at reducing child abuse and neglect. Furthermore, there is also some evidence that as the children of these programs age, they are less likely to become chronic criminals.

Growing evidence for the effectiveness of some home visitation programs has prompted support at the federal level. In 2008, Congress approved $10 million to fund 17 evidence-based home visitation programs. Very quickly, this initial investment blossomed into a program called Maternal, Infant and Early Childhood Home Visiting (MIECHV). Between 2010 and 2014, MIECHV provided $1.5 billion in grants for states to invest in home visiting programs. In March 2014, Congress authorized an additional $400 million for fiscal year 2015. As children from these programs mature, researchers will learn more about the effects of home visiting.

Sources: Rodrigue, E., & Reeves, R. V. (2015, Feb. 15). Home visiting programs: An early test for the 114th Congress. *Brookings Institute*. Retrieved June 4, 2015, from http://www.brookings.edu/blogs/social-mobility-memos/posts/2015/02/05-home-visiting-funding-reeves; Stolzfus, E., & Lynch, K. E. (2009). *Home visitation for families with young children*. Washington, DC: Congressional Research Service; Currie, E. (1998). *Confronting crime: An American challenge*. New York: Pantheon Books.

- The third meeting is a feedback session where the parent consultant can summarize results of the assessment and work with the parent to assess his or her motivation and willingness to change problematic behavior. This final session also includes an overview of the behaviors and/or practices that need additional attention. At that time, parents are offered a maximum of six follow-up sessions to continue improving their parenting practices and family management skills.

Because FCU is new, it is not yet known whether the program reduces delinquency or crime. The National Institute of Justice considers it "promising" based on evidence that it does reduce childhood problem behavior and increase positive parenting practices.

Another approach to early intervention is intensive preschool. The most well known intervention of this type is the Perry Preschool Project. This program was conducted from 1962–1967 in Ypsilanti, Michigan. The program randomly assigned a sample of 123 African American youth aged 3–4 years who were considered at high risk for school failure into one of two groups. The program group received a high-quality preschool education based on an "active learning" model, while the comparison group received no preschool program. Follow-up studies consistently showed that the Perry youth outperformed the control group on measures of financial success, academic success, and reduced criminal behavior. In 2005, when participants were around 40 years of age, differences in outcomes were still stark. Preschool participants were more likely to have obtained a high school diploma and to be earning over $20,000 per year. Regarding crime, the Perry participants (36%) were less likely to be chronic offenders than the control group (55%). A cost–benefit analysis based on findings from the project found that over the lifetime of the participants, the initial $15,000 cost of the program yielded almost $200,000 in public benefit.[100]

During adolescence and young adulthood, life-course theories identify a host of risk factors related to individuals, school, family, and peers. As noted in Chapter 5, cognitive–behavioral interventions that target these risk factors have established a track record of success. Generally speaking, programs that target more risk factors across multiple domains are the most effective. Multisystemic therapy (MST), discussed in detail in Chapter 5, is one of the most comprehensive and effective programs for serious youth offenders. In this program, a team of therapists work to correct any systems (family, peer, school) that are contributing to crime (see Chapter 5 for details).[101]

Later in the life course, there are a number of programs that are designed to foster desistence. Consistent with Sampson and Laub's notion of adult social bonds, programs to improve education and employment can increase social ties to the community and social capital. For example, the Good Lives Model (GLM), discussed earlier in this chapter, is based in part on adult bonds and the desistence model described by Sampson and Laub. The GLM builds human "agency" by encouraging offenders to visualize a more positive future and devise a plan to achieve this future.[102] More broadly, there has been a renewed focus on the importance of prisoner reentry. The Second Chance Act of 2007 authorized federal grants to government agencies and nonprofit organizations in order help people to avoid reincarceration. A

host of demonstration programs are now underway to provide employment assistance, substance abuse treatment, housing, family programming, mentoring, victim support, and other services to people returning to the community from prison.[103]

In sum, there is a range of prevention and rehabilitation programs that target antisocial behavior across the life course. As David Farrington notes, it is "never too early, never too late" to intervene successfully to reduce offending. It is worthwhile to support early interventions that prevent childhood conduct problems and later programs that prevent delinquency and crime during adolescence or encourage desistance during adulthood.[104]

Conclusion

The study of crime across the life course is one of the most exciting new areas in criminology. Life-course criminology focuses on how crime develops over time, through different developmental stages. In particular, researchers have examined the onset of crime, continuity in antisocial behavior, and desistence from offending. Since the 1990s, several new theories have been designed and/or modified to explain stability and change. Taken together, these theories demonstrate recognition of the complexity of the causes of crime. Research and theory in this area has had an impact on policymakers. The recognition that a small fraction of offenders commit the majority of crimes in their cohort has generated calls for incapacitation and prevention.

WRAP-UP

CHAPTER SPOTLIGHT

- The idea of career criminality is based on the assumption that such criminals are committed to a life of crime; in other words, they have a worldview built around criminal activity. They define themselves as criminals and tend to associate with other criminals. Their careers accelerate or progress as they become more skilled and engage in different types of offenses. In addition, career criminals view crime as a profession, like law or medicine, in that it involves the acquisition of specialized knowledge and skills.

- Many of the assumptions about criminal careers originated in Edwin Sutherland's classic work, *The Professional Thief*. This study followed the career of one professional criminal and served as the basis for Sutherland's theory of differential association.

- Birth cohorts are often used in criminology research because they permit the study of individuals over an extended period of time. Through review of the cohort, life patterns can be examined and criminal careers reconstructed. Two of the most influential birth cohort studies in criminology were conducted in Philadelphia.

- Cohort and other longitudinal research demonstrate that a small fraction of offenders (roughly six percent) accounts for the majority of offending in their cohort.

- Life-course criminology is concerned with three major themes: the onset of antisocial behavior, continuity (or stability) in offending, and desistence from crime.

- A central finding in life-course research is that there is continuity in offending. The best predictor of juvenile delinquency is childhood

- misconduct (lying, bullying, severe temper tantrums, diagnosis of conduct disorder).
- Despite the evidence of stability/continuity, there is also much change. Most offenders eventually "age out" of crime. Furthermore, the majority of antisocial children do not become serious delinquents or adult offenders. It is this puzzle of continuity and change that interests life-course researchers.
- Life-course theories can be grouped into three broad categories: continuity theories, continuity *and* change theories, and continuity *or* change theories. Each type of theory accounts for stability and change differently.

- Criminal justice policies aimed at coping with chronic offenders include repeat offender projects, three-strikes laws, and intelligence-led policing. While there is some evidence that such programs can reduce crime, they may also generate unintended consequences.
- Prevention/rehabilitation programs include family-based interventions, investing in school programs to improve education and employment, and drug treatment programs. Some of these programs have accumulated a track record of success in crime reductions.

PUTTING IT ALL TOGETHER

1. Describe the career criminal perspective. Why did critics believe that "career" was a poor metaphor?
2. Describe the most important findings from the Philadelphia birth cohort research. How do males and females differ in their offending patterns?
3. Describe the central areas of life-course criminology, including stability and desistence.

4. Illustrate the three different types of life-course theories discussed in this chapter by using specific theories.
5. Identify and describe two policy implications drawn from life-course research and/or theory.

KEY TERMS

adolescent-limited (AL) offenders In Moffitt's taxonomy of offenders, this group starts their deviance in their mid-teens, and desists from crime quickly.

chronic offenders Persons who habitually engage in crime; in both Philadelphia birth cohorts (all persons born in 1945 and then 1958), the small group of offenders who were responsible for the bulk of serious crimes committed by the entire array.

cohort A group of individuals who share the same experience in time. Birth cohorts are often tracked to determine the groups that have the highest rates of offending.

criminal career perspective An area of criminology that characterized crime as a profession, like law or medicine, in that it involves the acquisition of specialized knowledge and skills. The focus on how crime develops over time now falls under the umbrella of life-course criminology.

cumulative continuity An explanation for stability whereby initial deviant acts affect a person's environment in a negative way (e.g., job loss, peer rejection). These social outcomes then make desistence from deviance less likely.

desistence The cessation of offending and/or other antisocial behavior by individuals.

life-course criminology An area of criminology that seeks to understand crime and its precursor behavior from childhood through adulthood. Central to this area is explaining the onset and persistence of criminal or antisocial behavior and desistence from offending. Some scholars refer to this as developmental criminology.

life-course–persistent (LCP) offenders In Moffitt's taxonomy of offenders, this group starts offending early in life and persists. They are akin to the "chronic offenders" described in cohort studies.

repeat offender program (ROP) Projects that selectively focus police resources on career criminals and take a proactive approach. Police target offenders and try to catch them in the act.

selective incapacitation Strategies that seek to identify and incarcerate chronic offenders for long periods of time in order to reduce crime.

typology A framework and theoretical construct that is used to describe and compare different forms of criminal behavior.

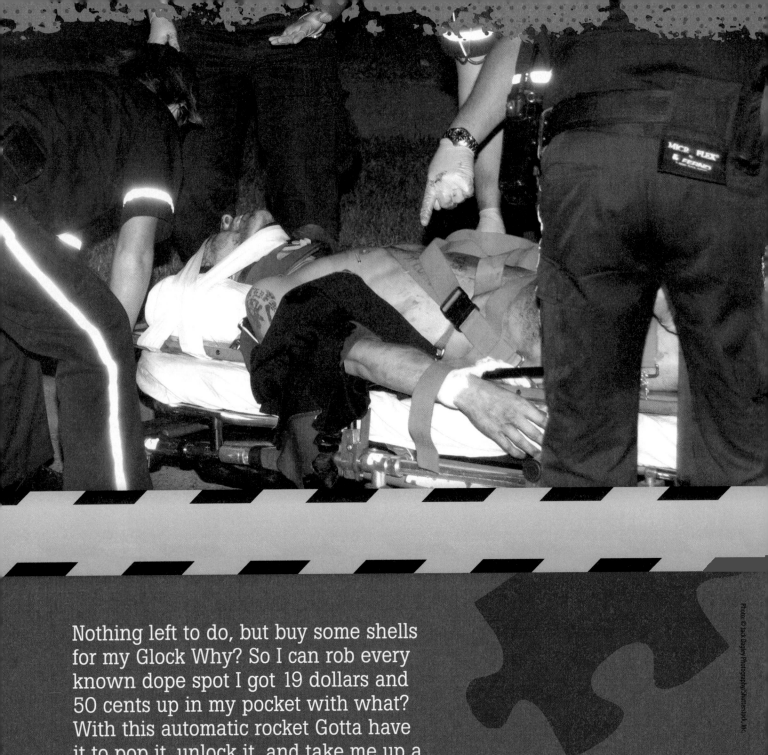

Nothing left to do, but buy some shells for my Glock Why? So I can rob every known dope spot I got 19 dollars and 50 cents up in my pocket with what? With this automatic rocket Gotta have it to pop it, unlock it, and take me up a hostage.

—Snoop Dogg[1]

CHAPTER 10

Crimes of Violence

Objectives

- Define violent crime, including the various forms of homicide, rape, robbery, and assault. Pg. 214

- Know the current rates and trends for violent crimes in the United States. Pg. 214

- Review and understand typologies of all forms of violent crime. Pgs. 221–231

- Be aware of homicide levels and trends in the United States; grasp the nature of homicide and understand explanations for differences in homicide rates between the United States and other industrialized countries. Pg. 215

- Know the prevalence rates for various forms of rape, the proposed motivations for rape, and explanations of rape and sexual assault. Pg. 224

- Understand the nature and prevalence of intimate partner violence and stalking. Pg. 227

- Grasp the level and trends of robbery rates in the United States, know what distinguishes robbery from other forms of violence, and understand explanations of robbery. Pg. 236

- Understand the nature and prevalence of assault in the United States. Pg. 239

- Understand how criminological theories are used to explain violence. Pg. 240

Texture: © Malchev/Shutterstock; Shooter: © Malchev/Shutterstock; Puzzle Piece: © Photodisc; Police Tape: © Skillup/Shutterstock

Introduction

More than any other type, violent crime has the greatest impact on the public's perception of crime in general: People fear violent crime. Although people are much more likely to be victims of burglary, larceny, and car theft, what affects people's behavior and attitudes toward crime is their fear of homicide, rape, robbery, and assault. Fear of violence leads people to stay in at night, refuse to open their doors to strangers or help strangers in need, travel in groups when walking the streets and refuse to visit certain areas of their cities and neighborhoods. There is little doubt that the public's fear of violent crime is related to the media. Newspapers, television (both the news and dramas), movies, and other media outlets portray violence (especially violence perpetrated by strangers) as a "typical" rather than rare form of crime.[2] This is not to say that Americans' fear of violence is irrational. Although rare, violent crimes can have a life-altering effect on victims and/or their families.

Although rare, violent crimes can have a life-altering effect on victims and/or their families.

Why do some people behave violently? Why are some societies or communities more violent than others? Criminologists, sociologists, psychologists, and many others have attempted to address such questions throughout history. Most agree that no single explanation exists for violent crime. This chapter explores the nature and extent of the most common types of violent crime—homicide, rape, robbery, and assault.

Violent Crime Trends in the United States

Although people may have valid reasons for their fears, violent crime—like crime in general—has been on the decline throughout the early part of the 21st century. Uniform Crime Report (UCR) data reveal that in 2012, an estimated 1,214,462 violent crimes occurred nationwide, an increase of 0.7 percent from the 2011 estimate, but a decrease of 12.9 percent from the total amount of violent crime reported to the police in 2008. The **violent crime index rate** was 386.9 per 100,000 citizens—similar to that recorded in 2011.[3]

The examination of violent crime rates and trends raises many questions. For example, why has violent crime declined across the nation? What explains this multiyear trend? Despite the recent decline in overall violent crime rates, Americans remain more likely to murder each other than citizens of other industrialized countries. Why then, in contrast to other countries, does the United States experience stubbornly high levels of homicide? This chapter explores these questions (and others related to the causes of violence) through the examination of homicide, rape, domestic violence, robbery, and assault.

Homicide

Homicide is the taking of life by another human. Not all homicides are illegal. Most societies allow some agents of the state—police officers and soldiers, for example—to kill in certain situations. Also, some homicides are considered justifiable. A justifiable homicide, such as a homicide committed in self-defense, occurs when the death of the other person is unavoidable or is in some fashion warranted. There is no malice or negligence involved, and the law acknowledges that any other prudent and socially aware person would have acted in the same manner under similar circumstances.

As  indicates, there are a number of ways to classify criminal homicide. **Murder** is a homicide that includes the element of malice aforethought. Malice aforethought is the manifestation of a deliberate intention to take the life of a fellow human. First-degree murder is committed

TABLE 10-1	
Examples of Different Forms of Homicide	
Types of Homicide	**Examples**
First-degree murder	Husband kills wife for the insurance money after months of planning
Second-degree murder	Husband impulsively kills wife during an argument over the monthly bills
Voluntary manslaughter	Husband kills wife after walking in on her with another man
Involuntary manslaughter	Husband is driving under the influence and crashes his car; his wife dies.

with premeditation and deliberation. Premeditation means that the act of fatal violence was consciously considered beforehand; deliberation means that the killing was planned and not a spontaneous or impulsive act. In second-degree murder, there is also malice aforethought, but not premeditation and deliberation. Murder can also include the killing of another person in the process of committing another felony.[4] Murder is typically considered the most serious offense in the United States. This is reflected in the fact that in most death-penalty states, murder is the only crime for which an offender can receive the death penalty. Furthermore, murder is one of the few criminal offenses for which there is no statute of limitations; killers may be brought to justice any time after their crime has been committed.

Manslaughter is the unlawful taking of a human life without malice. Voluntary manslaughter is the killing of another person in some circumstance where emotions cloud the offender's judgment. In involuntary manslaughter, the death is neither deliberate nor premeditated; rather, it is the result of some type of negligent behavior.

Murder Levels and Trends

In 2012, an estimated 14,827 persons were murdered in the United States. This was a 1.1 percent increase from the 2011 estimate, but a 9.9 percent decrease from the 2008 figure, and a 10.3 percent drop from the number in 2003. There were 4.7 murders per 100,000 people. The murder rate rose 0.4 percent in 2012 compared with the 2011 rate. The murder rate was down from the rates in 2008 (12.8 percent decline) and 2003 (16.9 percent drop).[5]

Despite this decline, the U.S. homicide rate is still substantially higher than that of most other industrialized nations. Across the world in 2012, almost half a million people (437,000) were the victims of homicide. A United Nations Drugs and Crime report[6] compared homicide rates among several countries. Again, the 2012 U.S. murder rate was 4.7 per 100,000 citizens.[6] Most other industrialized countries, such as the United Kingdom (1.0), France (1.0), Canada (1.6), and Germany (0.8), Austria (0.9) and Australia (1.1) had murder rates lower than that of the United States. Countries with homicide rates higher than the United States in 2012 included Venezuela (53.7), South Africa (31.0), Columbia (30.8), Mexico (21.5), Myanmar (15.2), the Russian Federation (9.2), and Pakistan (7.7).[7]

Within the United States, homicides are not equally distributed across the country. Historically, the Southern region has had higher homicide rates than other parts of the country.[8] In 2012, the Southern region had a higher homicide rate (5.4) than the Northeast (3.8), Midwest (5.0), or West (4.2).[9] Murders were more likely to occur in urban rather than rural areas, but there is also wide variation among large metropolitan areas. Consider the differences in 2012 murder rates per 100,000 in Philadelphia (9.1), Chicago (8.2), Houston (5.7), Los Angeles (5.0), Denver (3.9), New York City (3.8), and Boston (3.7).[10]

Homicide investigation is a specialized skill.
© Jack Dagley Photography/Shutterstock, Inc.

The average American over the age of 11 has a 1 in 14,706 chance of becoming a homicide victim. The homicide rate among blacks is more than six times that among whites, and the risk of homicide is about 60 percent higher among Hispanics than all others. When older persons are attacked, they are more likely to be killed.[11] Attacks involving firearms produce far more deaths per incident than those committed with a knife or club or no weapon. In 2012, UCR data indicated that 69.3 percent of homicides involve handguns, shotguns, rifles, and other firearms. Handguns alone accounted for about 72 percent of the homicides committed by firearms.[12]

Circumstances Leading to Homicide

How does the typical homicide unfold? Marvin Wolfgang's classic 1958 study classified one-quarter of homicides as "victim precipitated." Wolfgang defined a homicide as victim precipitated when the victim was the first to use physical force.[13] Later research using alternative definitions suggests that the rate of victim precipitation in homicides might be much higher.[14] For those homicides in which the circumstances are known to the police, the UCR also sheds some light on the context of homicides. In 2012, the most common pathway to homicide was by argument (25.3%). This lends some credence to the role of victim precipitation. Just over 14 percent of homicides are classified as felony murder. In other words, these homicides were committed while the offender engaged in a separate felony offense (e.g., rape, robbery, arson). Other circumstances include juvenile gang killings (5.6%) and gangland killings (1.2%).[15]

Offender and Victim Characteristics

Homicide research has determined that a relatively stable number of factors are consistently related to homicide rates. First, the greater the level of population size and density, the higher the homicide rate—a factor that is supported by routine activities theory (see Chapter 3). Namely, these population factors are likely to put attractive homicide victims (targets) in contact with motivated offenders in the absence of capable guardians. Second, consistent with strain and social control theories, persons living with high rates of poverty are more likely to be homicide victims. Similarly, divorced males and unemployed persons are more likely to be murdered.[16]

In 2012, about 65 percent of the offenders arrested for murder were male.[17] Male offenders were responsible for more than 88 percent of male homicide victims and over 91 percent of the female victims. Males also represented roughly 70 percent homicide victims.[18] About 95 percent of the homicide offenders in 2012 were over age 18.[20] The same can be said of homicide victims—more than 91 percent were under age 18.[19]

In 2012, the majority of homicides occurred within racial groups. Over 91 percent of black homicide victims were killed by black perpetrators. In cases of white victims, the perpetrators were also white in almost 84 percent of the cases.[20] Finally, over 77 percent of homicides where a suspect was named, involved offenders and victims who were known to each other.[21]

Intimate Partner Homicide

A type of homicide in which the offender and victim are current or former intimate partners is known as intimate partner homicide (IPH). Several attributes highlight IPH. First of all, females are much more likely to be killed by an intimate partner than males. Cohabitation is a significant factor in IPH. Females who cohabitate with their partner are 9 times more likely to be killed by their intimate partner than are married females, while male victims who cohabitate are more than 10 times more likely to be murdered by their intimate partner than men who are married. For females, the highest risk for homicide is when the victim leaves the relationship.[22] The majority of IPH perpetrators are under the influence of substances before the crime is committed. Alcohol abuse and firearm ownership are strong predictors of female intimate partner homicides.[23]

There is a correlation between IPH and intimate partner abuse: IPH is often preceded by physical, emotional, or sexual abuse. This link is important for both female victims and offenders. Studies have found that women tend to kill during domestic disputes. This is typically after a long history of physical and psychological abuse at the hands of their male intimate partner, after the male "victim" initiated the attack, and more often than men, women claim self-defense.[24–27] Men who kill often have a long history of abuse toward their female intimate partners. Men are also significantly more likely to kill their female partners or ex-partners and then commit suicide.[28,29]

Criminologists have developed or applied theories to explain the causes of IPH. In their pioneering work, Wilson and Daly offered two theoretical explanations—male sexual proprietariness theory and self-defense theory.[30–34] Since the previously mentioned factors indicate that males are most often the perpetrators of IPH, these theories attempt to explain the motivations of males in these encounters. Male sexual proprietariness theory holds that men kill their intimate women partners because of jealousy (the suspicion of female infidelity) or because the woman has threatened to leave or end the relationship. Women kill their intimate male partners to protect themselves. Male partners have often severely abused their female partners and often have records of violence in other cases.

Another theoretical attempt to explain IPH comes from strain theory (see Chapter 6) as applied by Erikkson and Mazerolle.[35] Strain theory is used to explain the motivations of both males and females in IPH situations. Under strain theory, male perpetrated IPH is a function of the strain caused by a loss of control over the relationship (including the threat of separation and child custody disputes) as well as arrests and protection orders against males. This strain generates anger, rage, and jealousy that, coupled with such factors as low constraint, condoning attitudes toward violence, proprietary/entitlement attitudes toward and low attachment to the female partner, leads to IPH. Sources of strain for female IPH perpetrators include the ideal maintenance of a close relationship, restricted freedom, loss of identity, exposure to violence, child abuse, and anticipated abuse. For females, strain leads to IPH by fueling negative emotions (fear, desperation, terror) coupled with low perceived social support against the male perpetrator, and limited access to resources. Taken together, these theoretical explanations offer a balanced view of IPH.

In response to research linking intimate partner abuse to IPH, some states have made attempts to develop risk assessment tools to enable criminal justice personnel to intervene in cases most likely to escalate into IPH. Studies have demonstrated that the availability of domestic violence programs have produced greater reductions among whites and married couples than among blacks and unmarried intimate partners. However, rising divorce rates have also contributed to the decline, as more women exited relationships with violent or abusive partners.[36]

Explaining America's Homicide Rate

Cross-national victimization surveys of crime reveal that American violent crime rates are on par with those of other industrialized nations.[37] As noted previously, homicide rates are the exception to this conclusion. Simply put, Americans are much more likely to kill each other than are members of most other industrialized countries. What accounts for this finding and for cross-national differences in homicide generally? Three common explanations include (1) the availability of firearms, (2) a violent national history, and (3) economic inequality.

Firearm Availability

Many criminologists and commentators believe that there is a rather simple reason for high homicide rates in the United States—the readily available supply of firearms in general and, specifically, handguns. The estimated total number of guns (both illicit and legal) owned by American civilians is between 270 and 310 million—a rate of over 101/100,000 people and about 34 percent of all American households in 2012.[38] Indeed, American handgun possession rates exceed those of any nation for which data are available.[39]

Typically, self-protection is the major reason given by Americans for gun ownership.[40] Yet, statistics indicate that a gun kept in the home is more likely to be used to commit or attempt a suicide than to be used in

self-defense. Most suicides (60%) are committed with firearms.[41] Therefore, gun ownership is a particularly dangerous proposition. Another indication of this danger is that, due to of the availability of firearms, violent incidents (an argument/brawl or robbery) are more likely to become lethal. If this hypothesis is correct, what is the policy implication? The typical response is a call for more stringent gun control.

The Gun Control Debate

Gun control is among the most hotly debated public policy issues in America. Gun control advocates argue that reducing the availability of firearms (especially handguns) and keeping them out of the hands of criminals will reduce homicides and other forms of violence. Others believe that gun control laws will either have no impact on violence or that gun control actually increases violence because criminals will feel freer to victimize unarmed citizens. Clearly, America's lax gun laws are unlike those of other developed countries that ban private handgun ownership.[42,43]

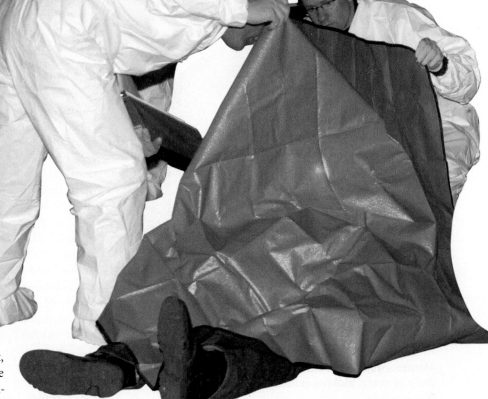

A homicide investigation team collects and preserves physical evidence.

© Jack Dagley Photography/Shutterstock, Inc.

Different forms of gun control legislation operate at the local, state, and federal level. One strategy is to regulate those who sell firearms. The Federal Gun Control Act requires firearms dealers to be licensed, to carefully document each sale or purchase, and to refrain from selling guns to those prohibited (e.g., minors, felons) from owning firearms. The "Brady Bill" (named after former White House Press Secretary James Brady, who was shot in the attempted assassination of President Ronald Reagan) was passed in 1993 and mandated a 5-day waiting period before a licensed dealer could sell a handgun to a non-licensed person. In 1998, this law was amended and now requires a background check (which can be instant) to see whether the buyer is prohibited from owning firearms. Research results on the effect of the Brady Law are mixed. One study determined that states that had implemented the Brady Law did not have lower homicides rates, while a later study by La Valle found that the Brady Law had an effect on both gun-related and total homicides.[44]

However, a study by the Community Preventive Services Task Force of the U.S. Centers for Disease Control studied the impact of various types of firearms laws on reduction of violence. Overall, they determined that the research evidence on the ability of the following types of gun control restrictions to reduce gun violence was inconclusive:[45]

> ### Gun control is among the most hotly debated public policy issues in America.

- Bans on specified firearms or ammunition
- Restrictions on firearm acquisition
  - Waiting periods for firearm acquisition
  - Firearm registration and licensing of firearms owners
  - "Shall issue" concealed weapons carry laws
  - Child access prevention laws
  - Zero tolerance of firearms in schools
  - Combinations of firearms laws

Criminologist James Jacobs suggests several reasons why laws aimed at restricting licensed arms retailers in America are ineffective:[46]

- Criminals tend not to buy guns directly through licensed dealers; they may use a third party (relative, friend) with a clean record to buy guns indirectly.
- The secondary market (e.g., gun shows, classified ads) is completely unregulated.
- Firearms can be purchased illegally "on the street."
- Those ineligible to buy a gun may steal guns during burglaries or borrow a gun from a friend or relative.

Criminologists have particularly assessed the impact of handgun bans. A study on the effect of the Washington, DC, ban on the possession and sale of handguns in 1975 found some evidence that it led to a reduction in suicides and homicides. Specifically, while gun-caused homicides and suicides decreased, non-gun suicides and homicides remained steady.[47] Critics correctly note, however, that similar patterns emerged during this same time frame in cities without a handgun ban. Handgun bans by two Illinois cities (Morton Grove and Evanston) in the early 1980s appear to have had no effect on gun-related crimes.[48] An assessment of the impact of gun control and ownership in 170 U.S. cities with a population of at least 100,000 determined that: (1) gun prevalence levels generally have no net positive effect on total violence rates; (2) homicide, gun assault, and rape rates increase gun prevalence; (3) gun control restrictions have no net effect on gun prevalence levels; and (4) most gun control restrictions generally have no net effect on violence rates.[49]

The debate over gun control shows no sign of being resolved. In fact, over the past 2 decades, many states have enacted conceal-and-carry or shall-issue legislation. Conceal-and-carry legislation directs local authorities to grant citizens who meet certain criteria (e.g., non-felon, no history of mental disorders) a permit to carry a concealed firearm. Economist John Lott lends support to such legislation with his provocative book that bluntly argues, "more guns" mean "less crime."[50] The conceal-and-carry debate and the argument that armed citizens deter crime are explored in the **Theory in Action: Do More Guns Mean Less Crime?**

Community involvement can help prevent violent crime.

© Lomaney/Shutterstock, Inc.

THEORY IN ACTION

Do More Guns Mean Less Crime?

With the title of his book, *More Guns, Less Crime: Understanding Crime and Gun Control Laws,* economist John Lott, Jr., gets his main (and controversial) point across. Conventional wisdom among criminologists (and many Americans) is that the U.S. homicide rate is due in part to the widespread availability of firearms. Lott and others turn this argument on its head by arguing that less gun control (and more guns) will actually decrease crime. The gist of their argument is that the criminal element will be more leery of a well-armed citizenry. From a rational choice perspective, arming citizens increases the expected cost of crime. Furthermore, when offenders do choose to victimize, armed citizens will be able to protect themselves and fend off criminal attacks.

Much of Lott's work focuses specifically on right-to-carry (RTC) laws, which are designed to make it easier for citizens to carry concealed weapons in public places. In the absence of such laws, states generally have may-issue regulations, where county-level authorities have the discretion to issue permits, based on broad criteria, such as the applicant having "good moral character." In contrast, shall-issue regulations direct local authorities to issue permits unless the applicant fails to meet some objective criteria (e.g., no history of mental disorder or alcohol/drug abuse, no felony conviction, successful completion of a gun-safety course). RTC laws have been adopted by 34 states and are currently under consideration in others.

While Lott clearly believes that such laws reduce crime, critics contend that RTC laws will have little effect on crime. For example, skeptics note that very few people (even in RTC states) apply for permits. Moreover, many who apply for permits already had been carrying weapons (illegally) for protection. What does the empirical evidence indicate? More than two dozen studies have been conducted on this topic; most compare states that adopted RTC laws with those that did not and assess the impact of this legislation on violent crime over time. Unfortunately, different researchers reached very different conclusions: Some find that RTC laws reduce violent crime, some find slight increases in violence for RTC states, and others find that the laws have no impact. The divergence in findings is partly a function of the complex statistical models used in this research: Altering statistical assumptions or changing the time period of the study substantially changes the findings. A 2003 study moved beyond simple measures of whether a state has an RTC law and focused instead on the usage of these laws. The authors found that the number of permits issued under the law had no effect on violent crime. A study of 25 RTC laws from 1977 to 1999 found that they neither increased nor decreased the number of mass shootings. Research by Donahue and Ayers also found that RTC laws had no effect on

crime rates. Finally, a review of the research on RTC laws by the National Research Council concluded that there is no credible evidence that they either decrease or increase violent crime.

Apart from whether a concealed weapon serves as a general deterrent is this question: Can a victim successfully fend off an attack by brandishing or using a weapon? That is, once a criminal event has started, does possession of a handgun help the victim? Throughout his book, Lott provides compelling case examples of defensive gun use (DGU) such as the following:

> As more than 30 diners sat in Sam's St. John's Seafood [in Jacksonville, Florida] about 7:20 p.m., a masked man entered the eatery and ordered everyone to the floor, said co-owner Sam Bajalia. The man grabbed waitress Amy Norton from where she and another waitress were huddled on the floor and tried to get her to open the cash register. At that point, [Oscar] Moore stood up and shot him. Another diner pulled out a .22-caliber derringer and fired at the man as he ran out of the restaurant. . . . "I'm glad they were here because if that girl couldn't open the register, and he didn't get [any] money, he might have started shooting," Bajalia said.

Empirical evidence from the Violence Policy Center reveals that there were approximately 338,700 incidents of DGU to prevent property and violent crimes from 2007 through 2011. Research reveals that DGU is effective at thwarting robbers, burglars, and assault situations, although there is some evidence that it also increases the victims' odds of suffering injury or death. Others caution that the benefit of DGU might be outweighed by the harm caused by the presence of handguns. For example, there is evidence that the "house gun" kept for one's own defense is more likely to kill someone in the household or to be used in a domestic quarrel than to defend against an attack. A study of gunshot victims in Philadelphia, Pennsylvania, found that among gun assaults where armed victims had some chance to resist, their odds of being shot in the assault were 5.45 times greater than unarmed victims. DGU remains a hotly debated topic in criminology and there is little doubt this topic will generate more research.

- What are the gun control laws in your state?
- Has RTC legislation been recently passed, or is it under consideration?
- How does the RTC debate relate to neoclassical theories of crime?

Sources: Lott, J. R., Jr. (2013). More guns, less crime: *Understanding crime and gun control laws*. Chicago: University of Chicago Press; Fagan, J. (2003). Guns, science, and social policy. *Criminology and Public Policy, 3*, 359–362; Kovandzic, T. V., & Marvell, T. B. (2003). Right-to-carry concealed handguns and violent crime: Crime control through gun decontrol? *Criminology and Public Policy, 3*, 363–396; Donohue III, J. (2003). The final bullet in the body of the more guns, less crime hypothesis. *Criminology and Public Policy, 3*, 397–410; Donohue, J., & Ayers, I. (2003). The latest misfires in support of the more guns, less crime hypothesis. John M. Olin Center for Studies in Law, Economics, and Public Policy Working Papers. Paper 278. Retrieved May 14, 2014, from http://digital commons.law.yale.edu/lepp_papers/278; National Research Council. (2004). *Firearms and Violence: A Critical Review*. Washington, DC: The National Academies Press; Wells, W. (2002). The nature and circumstances of defensive gun use: A content analysis of interpersonal conflict situations involving criminal offenders. *Justice Quarterly, 19*, 127–157; Kleck, G. (1997). *Targeting guns: Firearms and their control*. New York: Aldine de Gruyter; Cook, P. J., & Ludwig, J. (2009). Firearm violence. In M. Tonry (Ed.), *The Oxford handbook of crime and public policy*. New York: Oxford University Press, pp. 71–101; Duwe, G., Kovandzic, T., & Moody, C. E. (2002). The impact of right-to-carry concealed firearm laws on mass public shootings. *Homicide Studies, 6*, 4, 271–296; Violence Policy Center. (2013). *Firearm justifiable homicides and non-fatal self-defense gun use*. Washington, DC: Violence Policy Center; Branas, C. C., Richmond, T. S., Culhane, D. P., Ten Have, T. R., & Wiebe, D. J. (2009). Investigating the link between gun possession and gun assault. *American Journal of Public Health, 99*, 11, 2034–2040.

Economic Inequality

Apart from firearms possession, the United States is distinct from other industrialized countries in terms of social structure. Specifically, the country has a high level of economic inequality and a low level of social support (e.g., no national child care, limited national health care, low support for the unemployed). Both Messner and Rosenfeld's institutional anomie theory[51] and the work of Elliott Currie[52] suggest that the failure to provide a buffer (or safety net) for the less advantaged members of society ultimately breeds violence.

Two relatively recent cross-national studies appear to support the link between inequality and homicide. In Messner and Rosenfeld's own test of their institutional anomie theory, a "decommodification index" (a measure of the strength of the safety net in any society) predicted homicide rates. A 2002 study that examined 46 nations found that countries with both high levels of economic inequality and low levels of social support (such as the United States) experienced higher levels of homicide.[53,54] A similar study of 56 nations found that societal measures of economic inequality were a strong predictor of homicide rates.[55] An analysis based on UCR data in this country also found that economic inequality was a significant predictor of felony murders.[56] Similarly, Like determined that indicators of city-level white and black residential segregation and economic inequality were significant predictors of risks for violent victimization among blacks and whites, but both measures of racial inequality were associated with increased risks for blacks but decreased risks for whites.[57]

In sum, the relationship between economic equality and homicide is consistent with strain theory (see Chapter 6).

 **Multicide**

The term multicide refers to murders that feature multiple victims. Here, we review two types of multicide: mass and serial murder.

Mass Murder

Mass murder is defined as the intentional "antisocial and non–state-sponsored killing of multiple victims during a single episode at one or more closely related locations."[58] It has also been termed *autogenic (self-generated) massacre* because it involves individuals who kill in pursuit of personal goals—the killing is generated from the offender's problems, attitudes, and psychopathology.[59,60]

From 1976 to 2011, there were 672 mass murder incidents that involved at least four victims.[61] Some of the most infamous mass killings include the following crimes. In 1965, Charles Whitman fatally shot 15 people and wounded 14 others from the top of a tower on the campus of the University of Texas in Austin. James Oliver Huberty killed 21 customers and wounded 19 others at a McDonald's restaurant in San Ysidro, California, in July 1984. Ronald Gene Simmons killed 14 family members and two coworkers near Russellville, Arkansas, in December 1987. On August 20, 1986, former postal worker Patrick Sherill walked into his old post office in Edmond, Oklahoma, and shot 21 people, killing 14. In a movie theatre in Aurora, Colorado, James Holmes shot and killed 12 people and wounded 58 others on July 20, 2012.

Schools and universities have been notable sites of mass murder. On April 20, 1999, Eric Harris and Dylan Klebold, students at Columbine, Colorado high school, shot and killed 13 people and wounded more than 20 other victims before taking their own lives. Virginia Polytechnic Institute and University was the site of the deadliest shooting rampage in U.S. history on April 16, 2007. Seung-Hui Cho killed 32 people on the campus before committing suicide. On December 13, 2013, Adam Lanza shot and killed his mother and then went to Sandy Hook Elementary School in Newtown, Connecticut, where he then murdered six adults, including the school's principal, and 20 children before committing suicide.

In one of the latest incidents, Elliot Rodger killed six people in Isla Vista, California, on May 24, 2014. Rodger then committed suicide. This mass murder event will serve an example in the following sections.[62]

Characteristics of Mass Murderers

Fox and Levin[63] have characterized five primary examples of mass murder motives:

1. *Power*: a "pseudo-commando" style massacre perpetrated by some marginalized individual attempting to wage a personal war against society.
2. *Revenge*: A deeply disgruntled individual seeks payback for a host of failures in career, school, or personal life.
3. *Loyalty*: A devoted husband/father kills his entire family and then himself to spare them all from a miserable existence on earth and to reunite them in the hereafter.
4. *Profit*: A gunman executes the customers and employees at a retail store to eliminate all witnesses to a robbery.
5. *Terror*: A political dissident destroys government property, with several victims killed as "collateral damage," to send a strong message to those in power.

Applying these motives to the Isla Vista, California case, Rodger sought revenge. He expressed frustration from sexual rejections that he had experienced since adolescence.[64] Rodger killed three women in front of their Alpha Phi sorority home. Mass murderers were often rejected and alienated by their peers, resulting in feelings of inadequacy, fear, and hostility.[65] Rodger stabbed three people to death in his apartment, including his two roommates whom he described as "repulsive."[66]

Perpetrators of mass murder are not impulsive in their actions. On the contrary, these events typically involve assaults planned over long periods of time, including such factors as whom to kill (target selection), weapons (typically firearms), and location.[67] Rodger expressed his desire to carry out his plans in his manifesto:[68]

> *May 24, 2014 was the final date. There is no postponing it anymore, no backing out. If I don't do this, then I only have a future filled with more loneliness, rejection ahead of me, devoid of sex, love, and enjoyment.*

Rodger's planning was carried out meticulously over a 3-year period. He stockpiled semi-automatic weapons and ammunition in his apartment and practiced at a shooting range.[69]

Mass murderers share several common attributes. Research reveals that they are overwhelmingly male (95%), most often white (nearly two-thirds Caucasian), and over age 30 (more than half).[70] In terms of psychological and behavioral characteristics, mass killers tend to suffer from depression, resentment, social isolation, a tendency to externalize blame, and have a fascination with graphically violent entertainment and keen interest in weaponry.[71]

In terms of location, most of these massacres tend to occur in small town or rural settings. These offenses typically feature the use of firearms, particularly semi-automatic weapons that offer the possibility of harming a large number of victims, while not requiring expertise that is difficult to acquire.[72] Again, revenge is the typical motive and may account for the methodically planned nature of these massacres. Mass killers often view themselves as victims of injustice and seek payback for unfair treatment by targeting those that they hold responsible for their misfortune due to what they have done or what they represent. They externalize blame and never hold themselves responsible for their personal predicaments.[73]

There appear to be a number of contributing factors or "triggers" for mass killings. These include a sudden sense of loss (unwanted separation from a person or place), financial or educational difficulties (unemployment or flunking out of school), marital conflict (separation or divorce), and bullying. These factors seem to have a cumulative effect on males, threatening their masculinity and self-image. Therefore, they may account for the fact that most mass killers are male. Mass killers often exacerbate these factors by isolating themselves from intimate relationships that could offer them some form of emotional support and by living alone for extended periods of time.[74] In some rare instances, mass murderers have suffered from brain pathology (head traumas, tumors, epilepsy) that was accountable for the violent event that was not consistent with their personality.[75] Finally, perpetrators of mass murder have been found to have personality traits consistent with the offense such as: antisocial personality, narcissism, hostility, oversensitivity, obsessiveness, a sense of entitlement, and impulsivity.[76]

In terms of criminological theory, strain theory, coupled with control and routine activities theory, combine to offer an explanation for mass murder. Levin and Madfis developed a five-stage model of *cumulative strain* that they applied to school shooting massacres.[77] The stages are:

1. *Chronic strain*: The offender is confronted with frustration caused by their inability to achieve personal objectives. These failures include negative experiences and disappointing social relationships at home, school, work, or in the neighborhood. The lack of social ties to peers or family members fails to mediate homicidal behavior.
2. *Uncontrolled strain*: Lack of social bonds contributes to feelings of alienation and marginalization.
3. *Acute strain*: Short-term, but particularly troubling, events occur that seem catastrophic to an individual who is beleaguered, frustrated, isolated, and unable to cope with adversity.
4. *Planning stage*: Feeling no stake in conformity to conventional norms, lacking a supportive environment with

frustration mounting, the offender is inspired to "get even."

5. *Massacre at school*: The offender attempts or executes the plan to massacre people.

The school target is a product of routine activities theory. Suitable targets are readily available and guardianship is absent. All factors are favorable: multiple, despised victims congregated closely in classrooms or public places; an absence of armed officers in the immediate area; and a motivated offender(s) willing to kill their classmates.[78] Since it is difficult to change these factors and strengthen the target, Levin and Madfis recommend the use of long-term prevention techniques (such as anti-bullying programs) to ensure that students do not develop the desire to engage in a school massacre in the first place.[79]

Recent events support the conclusion that primary prevention, attention to the offender prior to an offense, is certainly in order. Fox and DeLateur note the difficulties in preventing mass murder. Many of the espoused solutions do not seem to be effective or possible. For example, they note that greater attention to telltale warning signs may not lead to prevention of the murderous act.[80] In the Isla Vista, California incident, police had visited Rodger's apartment in early April but did not have probable cause to search for weapons. At the eleventh hour, his parents discovered his 140-page manifesto that outlined his deadly plan, but police were unable to prevent the attack.[81] In addition, legal efforts to keep firearms out of the hands of mentally disturbed offenders were not effective in this case.[82] California law has provisions to bar individuals from obtaining firearms if they are considered a threat to themselves or others, or if they make a threat against a specific person to a therapist who reports it to law enforcement officials. Again, Rodger's manifesto was discovered long after he had obtained weapons.[83]

Serial Murder

The term **serial murder** refers to the killing of a number of people, usually three or more, over the course of more than a month.[84] This type of multicide has captured the attention of the American public since the early 1970s, following the convictions of notorious serial killers such as Ted Bundy, Randy Craft, John Wayne Gacy, David Berkowitz, Arthur Shawcross, and Gary Ridgeway.

Ted Bundy was executed in 1989 in Florida for three murders, and he is suspected of killing more than three dozen other victims in as many as 10 states. Randy Craft, the "Score Card Killer," was sentenced to death in 1989 for killing 16 victims in California between 1972 and 1983. He is also believed to have been involved in the death of more than 60 victims in California, Oregon, and Michigan.[85]

> *Since offenders take great pains to avoid apprehension, serial murder is a hidden crime.*

John Wayne Gacy, the "Killer Clown," was convicted of 33 murders of young men in Illinois. Although he consistently maintained his innocence, more than 20 bodies were dug up from the crawl space under his home. David "Son of Sam" Berkowitz was convicted in the killing of six young women in New York City. In 1991, Arthur Shawcross was convicted in the murder of 10 women. When asked what the police should do with him, Shawcross remarked that he should be put in jail for the rest of his life because if he ever got out he would kill again.[86]

During the 1980s and 1990s in the Portland and Seattle area, one serial killer continued to find victims while the case remained unsolved. It was not until 2002 that Gary L. Ridgeway, the "Green River Killer," was finally apprehended. In November 2003, Ridgeway admitted to killing 48 women (all of whom were prostitutes) in the greater Seattle area. Ridgeway admitted to these killings and offered some explanations for his crimes: He hated prostitutes because of the crime and disease they spread and was therefore helping police by murdering them. He also chose prostitutes because they were easy to pick up without being noticed. He believed that they would not be reported missing and that he could kill as many of them as he wanted without getting caught.[87]

Dennis Rader, the notorious "BTK Killer," terrorized the residents of Wichita, Kansas, during the 1970s and was finally apprehended in early 2005. He pled guilty to 10 murders spanning almost 30 years. Rader has said that he was possessed by a "demon" from an early age and could not contain himself.

Characteristics of Serial Murder and Murderers

Criminologists have struggled with determining the amount of serial murder. Since offenders take great pains to avoid apprehension, serial murder is a hidden crime. Although official crime data is often most valid for homicides, this is not the case for serial murder. Egger (1984) has noted that law enforcement agencies suffer from "linkage blindness" in serial murder cases. These offenses take place over time and space and cross jurisdictional boundaries. Uncovering them requires sharing of information and the ability to link data elements together to form a pattern—tasks that are not easily accomplished.[88] For these reasons, estimates of serial murder have varied. Quinet compiled serial murder databases and estimated that from 1970–2009, there were 502 solved serial murder cases in the United States that involved 3,228 victims.[89] During this time period, 52 percent of the offenders targeted female victims only, 15 percent male victims only, and 33 percent targeted both males and females.[90] Overall, 32 percent of these serial murder cases involving female victims featured prostitute victims.[91] Serial killers target strangers (making the ability to solve the homicide more difficult and striking fear in the hearts of communities) and vulnerable victims (prostitutes, drug users, hitchhikers, children, the elderly) who are more easily abducted.[92]

A study that compared samples of single and serial homicides confirmed the findings of studies on the attributes of serial murder alone. Serial murderers tend to be young, white males. Serial murder is a male dominated crime (95 percent of the offenders were male). As noted above, serial murderers target female victims. They use strangulation, kill for sexual reasons, and exhibit planning by moving the victim or body from one location to another, by using restraints, and by disposing of the body in a remote location.[93] Contrary to their "drifter" image, spatial analysis of serial murders has determined that serial murderers tend to offend relatively close to their home. The majority of serial murderers confine their activities to the same general location or area and only just over one-third travel wide distances to dispose of bodies.[94] Body disposal location also tends to be related to intelligence (serial murderers with high IQs traveled further from their homes to dispose of bodies) and the availability of transportation.[95]

Although most serial killers are male and white, criminologists have uncovered the existence of both female and African American (black) offenders. An infamous case of serial murder involved Aileen Wuornos. She was convicted of killing six of her clients while serving as a prostitute. She was executed in Florida on October 9, 2002. Her life and case were the subject of the film *Monster*.[96] Keeney and Heide found some important gender differences in their study of female serial killers.[97] Female serial killers were more likely to be passive than predatory in their method of killing (e.g., smothering or poisoning), were more likely to "lure" their victims to their death, were more likely to be diagnosed with a broad range of mental disorders, and were older than their male counterparts. Kelleher and Kelleher hypothesized that female serial killers have a variety of motives for their crimes, including: the Black Widow (who poisons multiple spouses, partners, or family members), the "Angel of Death" (the lethal caretaker who kills charges dependent upon their services), sexual predators, revenge, profit or crime, team killers (females often join male serial killers), question of sanity, unexplained, or unsolved.[98] A study of a sample of solo female killers determined that their victims were likely to be adults personally known to the offender (adult children and siblings, husbands, lovers, parents, their own young children and stepchildren, grandchildren, nieces, and nephews).[99] Poison was confirmed as the method of choice for female serial killers but they also used asphyxiation and guns. Most of these offenders confined their activities to a specific location or area (house, hospital, or a particular city or state) and did not travel long distances to commit crimes. They committed their crimes for a combination of motives, rather than one clear-cut reason—indicating that their motives are not easily explained.[100]

Branson documents the cases of 153 black serial murderers operating in the United States from 1915–2010.[101]

He states that their exclusion from the analyses of serial murder is a race-based political correctness that hinders law enforcement and endangers communities when their predation is undetected. The most pertinent example here is the "DC Sniper" investigation in October, 2002, where profilers repeatedly suggested that the perpetrators were white males when in fact they were two black males (John Allen Muhammad and Lee Boyd Malvo killed 10 and critically wounded 3 victims) who had evaded detection across time and space due to their organized methodology.[102] These studies demonstrate that serial murderers cross gender and racial boundaries and further complicates their detection and apprehension.

A Typology of Serial Murderers

Attempts have been made by practitioners and academics alike to profile serial murderers. As previously noted, their characteristics defy easy classification. The one characteristic they do often share is the ability to blend into society and appear to be normal citizens. They are so exceptionally skillful in their presentation of self that they are often beyond suspicion and difficult to apprehend.[103] This is precisely what makes them so dangerous. Typically, these profiles focus on the motivation and psychological attributes of the killers.

One of the earliest and most influential serial murder profiles was compiled by Holmes and DeBurger and contains four basic types:[104]

1. *The visionary*. This killer is propelled to kill because he or she hears a voice or sees a vision that commands the murderous acts. The apparition may take the form of God, a devil, a demon, or an angel. Serial killer Joseph Kallinger was commanded by a floating head named Charlie to kill everyone in the world.[105] The visionary serial killer is truly psychotic, suffering a severe break with reality. He or she is ordinarily geographically stable. The crime reflects the disoriented personality: The crime scene is chaotic with a great deal of physical evidence.

2. *The missionary*. This killer takes it upon himself or herself to rid the community or the world of an undesirable type of person. Although not psychotic or compelled by outside influences such as voices or visions, the missionary has a "job" to do. For example, one serialist killed those whom he had judged to be prostitutes (although none of the three female victims were indeed prostitutes) because it was his job to rid his community of "bad" women and sexually transmitted diseases.

3. *The hedonist*. This killer has made the vital connection between fatal violence and personal/sexual gratification. He or she may commit acts of necrophilia, mutilate bodies, and collect personal souvenirs. Jerry Brudos, the convicted killer of at least four young women in Oregon, kept an ankle of one victim, one breast of another, and both breasts of a third, and he sent electrical shocks through the dead body of his fourth victim.[106]

4. *The power/control seeker.* This killer achieves gratification from the complete possession of the victim. The power/control killer has eroticized possession of the victim as an object in the same fashion as the hedonistic killer has eroticized aggression.

The power/control motive is often a dominant one. Serial killers engage in expressive violence, enjoying the act of murder accompanied by the screaming and begging for mercy. They tie up their victims, then rape, sodomize, and mutilate them in order to degrade their victims and make them feel superior.[107]

Serial murderers tend to have detailed and elaborate fantasies ("scripts of violence") that follow themes of dominance. This script can change over time, fueling more violence as the killer updates the fantasy. They typically collect hard-core pornography with themes of bondage, dominance, and violence. They collect memorabilia and souvenirs of their crimes including photos, clothing, and body parts from victims.[108]

Despite the profiling of motives and methods, serial murderers have proven difficult to psychologically characterize. They do not tend to suffer from mental disorders (like schizophrenia) or delusions. Typically, they understand the nature of their crimes and the difference between right and wrong. Typically, they have been diagnosed as sociopaths (see Chapter 3); that is, persons who lack a conscience, feel no remorse, and care only for their own pleasure, using others as instruments of gratification. Another categorization applied to serial killers is the borderline personality disorder marked by instability in mood, relationships, and self-image. They are able to compartmentalize their feelings, dehumanize their victims, and are able to kill people without remorse or guilt.[109]

Comparing Multiple and Single Homicide Offenders

Profiles are typically based on the comparison and analysis of individual cases rather than statistical analysis of samples. Delisi and Scherer examined an exploratory sample of 160 multiple homicide offenders (MHOs—both mass and serial murderers) and a control group of 494 single homicide offenders to consider the personal attributes and the development of their criminal careers (see Chapter 9).[110] Compared to the single homicide offenders, MHOs were male, older (average age over 39), and unlike the previous profiles, came from an array of ethnic backgrounds (Caucasian, African American, Hispanic). MHOs who committed rape or burglary during the course of their homicide case were significantly more likely to kill multiple victims. Of the MHOs, 38 percent had no official criminal history prior to their homicide event, but the majority of them had persistent criminal records (an average of nearly four arrests, three felony convictions, and one prison sentence). Yet, the MHOs did not fit the typical pattern of Moffitt's life-course persistent offenders (see Chapter 9). These killers were not arrested until their adulthood.[111] This study demonstrates the potential that traditional analysis of criminal cases has to improve

profiling. Profiles have an investigatory purpose—to assist in the discovery of the crime and in identification and apprehension of MHOs.

 **Rape and Sexual Assault**

Rape has been recognized as a crime since the earliest written legal codes. Here, rape is defined as unlawful sexual intercourse by force or without legal or factual consent.[112] Rape can occur among strangers, dating partners, marital partners, heterosexuals, people of the same sex, young and old, and with either men or women as victims. Moreover, rape may involve anal, oral, vaginal–penile intercourse, or even assault using a foreign object.

Rape: Incidence, Prevalence, and Trends

Statistics on rape vary greatly. It is estimated that rape is among the most underreported crimes. Data from a national telephone household probability sample revealed that rape victims were unwilling to report the offense to the police several reasons including:[113]

- Not wanting others to know about the rape
- Not acknowledging the rape as a crime (not believing it was serious enough to report, fear of being seriously injured or killed during the assault, fear of reprisal from the perpetrator or others, and feeling personally responsible for the event due to drinking or voluntarily taking substances)
- Having concerns about how they would be treated by the criminal justice system due to myths and stigma attached to alcohol- and drug-related assaults, fear of being blamed for the rape, encountering negative reactions from law enforcement officials, and fear of potentially facing their assailant during the process

One of the major causes of non-reporting in rape incidents is the existence of rape myths that shift blame for the offense to the victim.

A meta-analysis of 37 studies on rape myth acceptance (RMA) found that men displayed significantly higher endorsement of RMA than women. It was also determined that RMA was more prevalent among persons who expressed feelings of racism, sexual aggression, and hostile attitudes and/or other aggressive behaviors toward women. RMA was also related to "playboy behavior," sociosexuality, and the use of degrading images. RMA was lessened by the number of sexual partners, frequency of sex, and number of sexual thoughts. However, male pathology and psychopathic traits were not related to RMA. It appears that hatred toward women plays a major role in RMA that helps to perpetuate underreporting of this crime.

These factors cloud the accuracy of crime figures regarding the prevalence and incidence of rape. According to UCR data, there were an estimated 84,376 forcible rapes reported to law enforcement in 2012. This estimate was 0.2 percent

Raising awareness is a key crime prevention tool.

Courtesy of UN Action, www.stoprapenow.org

higher than the 2011 estimate, but 7.0 percent and 10.1 percent lower than the 2008 and 2003 estimates, respectively. The rate of forcible rapes in 2012 was estimated at 52.9 per 100,000 female inhabitants.[115] Crime figures from the National Crime Victimization Survey (NCVS) combine rape and sexual assault figures. In 2012, the rate of rape and sexual assault per 1,000 persons age 12 and over was 11.5, down from 15.2 in 2003.[116] It was also estimated that the number of reported rapes in 2012 was 6,842,590—down about 11 percent from 2003.[117] However, the NCVS also reported that only 28 percent of rape and sexual assaults were reported to the police—a figure that has declined dramatically from 56 percent in 2003.[118]

However, survey results of lifetime prevalence rates suggest that rape is all too common. The National Violence Against Women Survey (NVAWS) interviewed a national, random sample of 8,000 women and 8,000 men. This survey indicated that about 18 percent of women and 3 percent of men (1 in every 6 women and 1 in every 33 men) experienced a completed or attempted rape in their lives (including during childhood).[119] A victimization study of college women revealed that about 1 in 36 college women experience a completed or attempted rape during an academic year. The study authors calculate that during the course of a college career, rape victimization (completed and attempted) among women at higher education institutions might be as high as 20 to 25 percent.[120]

Victims of Rape and Sexual Assaults

Most rape victims know their rapist. The NVAWS reported that only 16.7 percent of female and 22.8 percent of male victims were raped by a stranger.[121] In the survey of college women just described, about 90 percent of the offenders were known to the victim. Acquaintances included boyfriends (or ex-boyfriends), classmates, coworkers, and friends.[122]

Data on rape and sexual assault from the NCVS from 2005–2010 have revealed the following patterns:[123]

- Females who were age 34 or younger, who lived in lower income households, and who lived in rural areas experienced some of the highest rates of sexual violence.
- Of sexual violence incidents, 78 percent involved an offender who was a family member, intimate partner, friend, or acquaintance.
- The offender was armed with a gun, knife, or other weapon in 11 percent of rape or sexual assault victimizations.

For all racial and ethnic groups, the rate of sexual violence was lower in 2005–2010 than it was in 1994–1998. Within each time period, few differences existed in the rates of sexual violence across racial and ethnic groups. Non-Hispanic white females and black and Hispanic females had a similar rate of sexual violence over time. However, Hispanic females had lower rates of sexual violence than black females in 1999–2004 and in 2005–2010.[124]

Drugs and alcohol play an important role in rape victimization. About two-thirds of women and men who were raped as adults reported that their rapist was using drugs and/or alcohol at the time of the incident. In addition, 19.8 percent of female victims and 38.3 percent of male victims said they (the victims) were using drugs and/or alcohol at the time of the rape.

Effects of Rape and Sexual Assault Victimization

Those who are victims of rape and sexual assault experience a range of physical and psychological harm. The percentage of female victims of sexual violence who received medical treatment increased between 1994–1998 and 2005–2010. In 2005–2010, 58 percent of female victims of sexual violence suffered a physical injury during the victimization, such as cuts, bruises, internal injuries, broken bones, gunshot wounds, or rape injuries.[126] Data from the NVAWS documents the mental health and social costs of rape victimization. Of those raped since age 18, 33 percent of the female rape victims and 24.2 percent of the male victims said they received counseling from a mental health professional as a direct result of the incident. The survey found that 19.4 percent of the female victims and 9.7 percent of the male victims raped as adults said their victimization caused them to lose time from work.[127]

People close to the sexual assault victim (e.g., spouses, partners, peers, siblings) are often affected by it and are sometimes considered secondary victims. Husbands or partners of rape victims, for example, must help the victim cope and recover. While the spouse or partner may play a positive role in the recovery process, some may become withdrawn or partially blame the victim.[128]

The Criminal Justice Response to Rape

It is often said that rape victims are victimized twice—once by the actual rapists and again by the criminal justice system if they decide to report their rape. There is often a stark difference between what is "good" for the victim and the goals and organizational nature of the criminal justice system. The primary goal of police and prosecutors is to prove beyond a reasonable doubt that a crime occurred. The successful prosecution of a case hinges on physical evidence and corroborating witnesses. In most rape and sexual assault cases, the sole witness is the victim. The process begins with reporting the crime to the police. As previously noted, the percentage of rape or sexual assault victimizations reported to police increased to a high of 56 percent in 2003 before declining to 35 percent in 2010, a level last seen in 1995.[129]

The hospital is the key institution for rape investigation, because this is often the first place that victims go after a sexual assault. The hospital is responsible for a medical examination and the collection of physical evidence. Physicians and hospital staff have been called the "reluctant partners" in systems that work with rape victims.[130] Rape victims are often not viewed as "real" patients (especially if there is no physical injury), and doctors are reluctant to perform rape exams (they are long and intrusive) and to testify in court.[131] Even where physical evidence confirms sexual relations, it often cannot speak to whether the sex was consensual.

The primary role of police officers is to "build a good case."[132] Police officers, attempting to get a thorough and clear statement, often come across as "interrogating" the victim. Accordingly, victims often feel as though the police do not believe their story.[133] Prosecutors generally strive to secure a conviction that results in punishment appropriate to the level of harm caused by the crime. Prosecutors represent the state rather than the victim and generally prefer plea bargaining (a sure conviction) to trial. Research suggests that prosecutors are more likely to either dismiss or plea bargain rape cases than other types of criminal cases.[134] There is

also evidence that prosecutors try to find discrepancies in a victim's statements, determine if the victim had ulterior motives for alleging rape, and see if the victim fits the criteria for a "typical" victim when deciding whether to charge a rape case.[135] Prosecutors may also be more leery about accepting the victim's testimony as the truth and may require the victim to take a polygraph test. Prosecutors justify these actions by noting that coercion is difficult to prove, which makes it hard to secure convictions for rape and sexual assault cases.[136]

For the rare case that goes to trial, the victims must face defense attorneys who are bound by an ethical code to vigorously advocate (e.g., do whatever is necessary) for their clients. Prior to the 1980s, defense attorneys were allowed to bring up the victim's past sexual behavior, her chastity (or lack thereof), or any motive she might have to falsely claim that a consensual encounter was rape. Rape shield laws now prohibit defense attorneys from bringing up the promiscuity or character of the victims. However, the defense can generally skirt these laws by indirectly attacking the victim's character.[137]

Aside from rape shield laws, can the justice process be made more victim-friendly to victims of sexual assault? In a recent book that examines organizations, networks, and people who work with rape victims, Patricia Martin suggests that a rape crisis center (RCC) should serve as the primary interface between victims and other agencies (e.g., police, prosecutors, and hospitals). Within these other agencies, rape victims are only a small part of what workers confront. In contrast, RCCs, because their sole focus is victim support, may be the missing link that can bring all of these organizations into a network that is most favorable for the victim.[138]

In general, rape victim respondents in the NVAWS gave the criminal justice system mixed reviews. Of the female rape victims who reported their most recent rape to the police, 47.7 percent said they were satisfied with how the police handled their case. This figure increased to 65 percent when only those victims whose rapist was arrested or detained by the police were considered. Similarly, 48.6 percent of the female victims who came in contact with the courts—because their rapist was prosecuted, they obtained a restraining order against their rapist, or both, said they were satisfied with how the courts treated them.[139]

Explaining Rape and Sexual Assault

A central controversy surrounding the explanation of rape is the motivation of the offender. Historically, most social scientists viewed rape as a sexually motivated crime and used Freudian analysis to explain its occurrence.[140] More recently, many scholars have viewed rape from the perspective of its victims—that rape is actually an act of violence in which sex is used as a weapon. In this case, rape is analogous to acts such as assault or battering. Feminist scholars discuss rape within the political/historical context of men's oppression of women. For example, Brownmiller argued that rape is "nothing more or less than a conscious process of intimidation by which all men keep all women in a state of fear."[141] Men rape, Brownmiller contends, to keep women in their place and to validate their masculinity.[142] Other motives have also been put forward by scholars—sexual gratification, the desire to hurt and humiliate, proving masculinity, and "sexual aggression," that is, power, control and domination.[143] The aim of ascertaining motives for rape include the desire to solve the crime, to establish moral culpability, and to convict the offender.[144]

Psychological Typologies of Rapists

One way to approach the study of rape motivation is by constructing typologies. Researchers (typically psychologists) develop typologies for a number of reasons. Typologies are a useful starting point for research on the causes of rape; they may help police identify potential offenders (based on circumstances of crime) and can suggest useful forms of treatment for offenders.[145] They often blend motive and method. One traditional schema has focused on the motives of power, anger and sadistic rapists.[146]

1. *Power rapists*: exercise strength, authority, and control over their victims to compensate for feelings of inadequacy and to affirm their masculinity. They typically use a minimal amount of force (often using verbal threats), do not intend to injure victims using the level of violence necessary to commit the assault. Their attacks may be premeditated or opportunistic, repeated over a period of time, and often increase in aggression. They are often disappointed because the attacks do not meet their expectations or fulfill their needs. There are two basic subtypes of power rapists:
   a. *Power-reassurance rapists*: Often referred to as "gentlemen rapists" because they display false concern and care for their victims. They use minimal force, often compliment their victims, ask for evaluations of their performance, and even apologize after the assaults. They attempt to overcome self-dissatisfaction by exerting physical control and strength over their victims. Their sexual assaults serve as a way to reassure themselves of their masculinity and to compensate for a perceived lack of a positive self-image.
   a. *Power-assertive rapists*: attack to assert their masculinity. They use a moderate amount of force and may attack their victims repeatedly during the duration of the crime. They show little concern for their victims and exercise physical and verbal abuse.
2. *Anger rapists*: intend to harm, humiliate, and degrade their victims. Their attacks express rage, release anger, or obtain revenge. Since their offenses are often precipitated by a buildup of frustration or induced by life circumstances, they are typically spontaneous and unplanned. They use excessive amounts of violence and force and view the sex act with disgust as a way to punish their victims. They usually attack for a short period of time and then flee the scene of the crime. There are two subtypes of anger rapists.
   a. *Anger-retaliatory rapists*: are often triggered by events that evoke strong emotion, their assaults are forms of vengeance and retribution. Their victims are symbolic of whomever they are seeking to avenge. The use of unnecessary violence against victims frequently results in hospitalization following the attack. Due to the unorganized manner of their attacks and uncontrollable rage, their victims are often hospitalized or may be murdered even though the offender only intended to commit a sexual assault.
   a. *Anger-excitation rapists*: are sexually aroused by the physical and psychological suffering of their victims. Their assaults are committed to achieve pleasure by observing physical and emotional torture of the victim. They engage in extensive planning and preparation prior to the attack; however, their victims are not preselected. They are chosen at random. These assaults usually last for a number of hours or over the course of several days.
3. *Sadistic rapists*: are also sexually aroused by the physical and psychological suffering of their victims. They are motivated by sexual satisfaction obtained through victim suffering. These offenders use excessive force, such as bondage, torture, rape with objects, sexual mutilation, and even murder. They may also perform other acts of degradation, such as cutting hair, burning with cigarettes, and sexual intercourse with a corpse following murder. Their attacks are carefully planned and prevent discovery. They are likely to engage in elaborate violent fantasies.

To reiterate, these typologies can assists the criminal justice community, especially in its efforts to profile, track, and eventually apprehend specific types of sexual offenders and lead to development of effective and specialized treatment programs.[147]

Intimate Partner Violence

The manifest purpose of the family is to provide a physically and emotionally safe place for all of its members; unfortunately, not all families do so. Each year, thousands of children, spouses, and intimate partners are abused. Public awareness of **intimate partner violence (IPV)** has risen and this crime has increasingly become defined as a crime problem. Unfortunately, it is also one of the most difficult crimes to control because so much of it occurs outside of the public eye. It has been said that intimate partner abuse (IPA) and child abuse (along with sexual assault) may be among the least reported crimes.[148] Reasons for the low report rates include fear of reprisal, not wanting the abuser to get in trouble, not defining the behavior as abusive, and not wanting others to find out. This section discusses some of the issues surrounding domestic violence. Included are discussions of IPA, stalking (the majority of stalking cases involve persons who were or are intimately involved), and child abuse.

Intimate Partner Abuse

According to a 2013 United Nations data review, 35 percent of women worldwide have experienced IPV or non-partner sexual violence in their lifetime, and 70 percent of American women have been the target of IPV in their lifetime.[149]

We reviewed current statistics for this crime type in Chapter 2. Intimate partner violence is an inclusive term that encompasses both spousal abuse and violence that occurs between couples who are not living together. It includes rape or sexual assault, robbery, aggravated assault, and simple assault committed by the victim's current or former spouse, boyfriend, or girlfriend.[150] IPV includes current or former heterosexual or homosexual intimate partners. A considerable amount of recent research indicates, however, that the majority of the victims of IPA are women and their abusers are men.[151-153]

Types of abuse include psychological as well as physical methods. Psychological abuse includes limiting or controlling the victim's activities or behaviors, isolating the victim from contact with friends or family, limiting or denying the victim's access to basic or financial resources, destroying the victim's personal property, abusive behavior toward a victim's loved ones, verbal threats, humiliation, put-downs, and any other behaviors intended to cause emotional pain, embarrassment, diminishment, or powerlessness.[154]

Between 1993 and 2011, the following patterns emerged for IPV:[155]

- The rate of IPV declined 64 percent from 9.8 to 3.6 victimizations per 1,000 persons age 12 and older.
- IPV has declined more than 60 percent for both males and females during this time period.
- About four out of five victims of IPV were female.
- Females 18–24 and 25–34 had the highest rates of IPV.
- Females living in households comprised of one female adult with children experienced IPV at a rate more than 10 times higher than households with married adults with children and 6 times higher than households with one female only.
- IPV declined for females of all marital statuses.

Given the recent laws and programs devoted to the prevention of domestic violence and increased public awareness of this type of crime, the decline in intimate partner victimization is encouraging.

Many theories exist to explain IPA. The theory of intergenerational transmission of violence posits that individuals who either observed violence as children or experienced violence themselves are more likely to engage in IPA as adults or to be victims of IPA themselves as adults than those who did not.[156-158] Studies have found a correlation between observing and/or experiencing violence as a child and later offending or victimization as an adult.

Feminist theories focus on male domination as the key explanation for IPA perpetrated by men against their female partners and ex-partners. Feminists argue that men's use of violence against women arises from men's power over women in the family and in society.[159-161] In patriarchal societies, historically, men have been socialized to be aggressive and even encouraged to use violence to keep women in line.[162] Evidence does suggest that IPA is more prevalent in patriarchal societies. A central component of patriarchy is the predominance of violence by both men and male-dominated organizations. Physical violence by men, then, is a manifestation of patriarchy. IPA against women results naturally from patriarchy: Males act violently to maintain dominance and control over women.[163]

Typically, IPV follows a vicious cycle:[164]

> ## A central component of patriarchy is the predominance of violence by both men and male-dominated organizations.

1. *Tension-building stage*: The batterer vents extremely high stress on objects or by acting aggressively in other ways. Acting jealous of the partner or attempting to isolate them from family and friends is commonplace.

2. *Explosive stage*: The batterer releases stress, directing violence at the partner in the form of physical and/or sexual violence. The batterer believes that the victim has caused the stress and needs to be "put in their place" so that the batterer can regain control of the situation. Batterers may appear to be cool, calm, and collected while the victim is confused, hysterical, terrified, shocked, angry, afraid, and degraded. Batterers often lie about the situation and use the victim's responses to deny what has happened.

3. *Honeymoon stage*: The batterer attempts to convince the victim that they have changed in order to maintain their relationship. Promises are made and presents are given as expressions of love and commitment. Batterers may also promise to go through treatment and minimize the abuse that they have committed. Victims may believe these promises but also feel depressed, helpless, hopeless, and trapped. This stage often cycles back to the tension-building stage.

A study of a cohort of 317 batterers arrested in Massachusetts used trajectory methodology to track their domestic violence and non-domestic violence arrests over a 10-year period. Individuals who had a prior domestic violence and/or drug/alcohol offense were significantly more likely to be assigned to a high rate domestic violence arrest trajectory. They also significantly increased their probability of assignment to a low or high rate non-domestic violence trajectory. Older offenders were less likely to be assigned to either trajectory and marriage to the victim also decreased membership, but its effect was not statistically significant. These findings were consistent with life-course theories that indicate that offense specialization is rare (see Chapter 9), and that batterers may also need substance abuse counseling to avoid engaging in the offense.

The Criminal Justice Response

In the first three-quarters of the 20th century, the traditional criminal justice response to cases of IPA was dominated by the belief that it was a personal matter. For that reason, the formal system did not respond. The traditional police response to cases of IPA was dominated by the "overriding goal to extricate [themselves] from the dangerous and unpleasant duty with as little cost as possible and to re-involve [themselves] with 'real' police work."[166] The typical response of both police and court personnel was to do nothing or to respond with minimal action. In the 1960s and 1970s, in response to pressure from feminists and battered women's advocates, to lawsuits against criminal justice personnel alleging inadequate responses to IPA, and to new research concerning police response, many police chiefs, politicians, and criminologists began to review and debate the existing police and court practices regarding IPA.

A study of 102 female victims of IPA reported that 90 percent of them did not contact the police when they were victimized again. More than half of them did not report another victimization because of the way they were treated in the past. They felt that the police treated them poorly and did not agree with the outcome of their previous case. Revealing their ignorance of mandatory arrest policy in these cases (see Chapter 1), many victims did not support the arrest and/or conviction of their partner. The second most common reason was that they felt that the incident was not serious enough to report or that they would not be taken seriously. About one-quarter of the victims failed to report out of fear that life circumstances for themselves and their children would be negatively affected. Another 22 percent failed to report out of love or the desire to protect their partner, while the final main reason was out of fear that their partner would retaliate. In addition, there was evidence that friends of victims advised them not to report the case.[167]

IPV victim programs can help to mediate these feelings. An evaluation of a program designed to assist IPA victims after they report the crime to the police found that program participants were significantly more likely to fully engage with prosecutors and were more likely to go to court (especially ethnic women) than victims not served by the program. However, women who engaged in treatment were not more likely to have their cases end with no charges filed/refused, dismissed, or have no charges entered—an effect that was even more pronounced among women who continued to live with their abuser.[168]

Today, mandatory and presumptive arrest policies are the norm across the nation. If there is probable cause, the police are mandated to arrest a suspect in an IPA situation. Thirty-nine states and the District of Columbia allow victims of dating violence to apply for orders of protection against a perpetrator. Although many have cheered these policies, there continues to be room for improvement in the criminal justice response to IPA. Eleven states do not recognize dating violence in their statutes.[169]

Stalking

Stalking is defined as a pattern of harassing or threatening tactics used by a perpetrator that is both unwanted and causes fear or safety concerns in the victim. It includes such features as:[170]

- Unwanted phone calls, voice or text messages, or hang-ups.
- Unwanted emails, instant messages, or messages through social media.
- Unwanted cards, letters, flowers, or presents.
- Watching or following from a distance, spying with a listening device, camera, or global positioning system (GPS).
- Approaching or showing up in places such as the victim's home, workplace, or school when it was unwanted.
- Leaving strange or potentially threatening items for the victim to find.
- Sneaking into victims' home or car and doing things to scare the victim or let the victim know the perpetrator had been there.
- One in 6 women (16.2%) and 1 in 19 men (5.2%) in the United States have experienced stalking victimization at some point during their lifetime in which they felt very fearful or believed that they or someone close to them would be harmed or killed.
- Two-thirds (66.2%) of female victims of stalking were stalked by a current or former intimate partner; men were primarily stalked by an intimate partner or an acquaintance (41.4% and 40.0%, respectively).
- Repeatedly receiving unwanted telephone calls, voice, or text messages was the most commonly experienced stalking tactic for both female and male victims of stalking (78.8% for women and 75.9% for men).
- More than one-half of female victims and more than one-third of male victims of stalking indicated that they were stalked before the age of 25; about 1 in 5 female victims and 1 in 14 male victims experienced stalking between the ages of 11 and 17.

On this basis, stalking is a campaign of offenses that take place over a long period of time rather than a singular act. These acts are threatening and elicit fear from the victim. They typically involve the "unwanted pursuit of intimacy" through the violation of physical and/or symbolic privacy.[171]

Stalking includes a variety of different behaviors. Using factor analysis, Coleman identified two categories or types of stalking behaviors. She identified violent behavior stalkers as those who broke into or attempted to break into the victim's home or car; violated restraining orders; threatened, attempted, or physically harmed the victim; physically harmed or threatened to harm themselves; stole/read mail; and damaged property of a victim's new partner. Coleman's harassing behavior stalkers were typified by those who called the victim at home, work, or school; followed or watched the victim; made hang-up calls; came unwanted to the home, work, or school of the victim; sent unwanted gifts, letters, or photos; left unwanted voice messages; or made threats against or harmed the victim's new partner.[172] Similarly, Burgess and her colleagues identified the following forms of stalking behavior: written and verbal communications; unsolicited and unrecognized claims of romantic involvement on the part of the victims; and surveillance, harassment, loitering, and following that produces both intense fear and psychological distress to the victim.[173]

Stalking Motives

Motivations for stalking vary. One study cited control, obsession, jealousy, revenge, and anger as possible motives for stalking.[174] A meta-analysis of 175 studies of stalking determined that the victims knew their pursuer and were romantically involved with them in the majority of cases. Motives of stalkers compiled under these studies included:

- *Intimacy*: abandonment/loss issues, dependency, infatuation, jealousy/envy, love, obsession, reconciliation, a developing relationship, and sex
- *Aggression*: anger/revenge, attack, control/possession, and intimidation
- *Disability-based motives*: drugs, mental illness/disability, and task conflict or issues (e.g., gain access to children or property[175]

Two related psychological theories attempt to explain how a stalking incident can continue over time, attachment theory and relational goal pursuit theory. Attachment theory has two dimensions: the mental model of self and the mental model of others. A positively viewed self is worthy of love and support while a negatively viewed self is not. Positively viewed others are viewed as reliable and supportive partners and negatively viewed others are not. In this framework, stalking is an attachment pathology. Studies in this meta-analysis found that stalkers were most frequently those who had lost a primary caregiver in childhood; lost an important personal relationship in the last 6 months; manifested love styles based on obsessiveness, possessiveness, and desperation; and had greater difficulty dealing with a breakup.[176]

Relational goal pursuit theory states that people tend to seek and possess relationships with others that they view as both desirable and feasible. Under this theory, stalkers continue to pursue relationships that the other person does not desire. Obsessional relationship pursuers feel that their self-worth and happiness are tied to the achievement of the failed relationship and continue vigorously when faced with rejection. They tend to view rejecting behaviors as encouragement. Negative views of the desired relationship are downplayed and overlooked and their motives are rationalized as the result of love. Therefore, stalkers have particular difficulty in relinquishing a terminated romantic relationship.

Most stalking incidents are the result of a distorted vision of courtship and romantic relationship failure.[177]

A review of the research literature reveals some of the risk factors associated with stalking. First of all, victims who had a previous relationship with the perpetrator are at a substantially higher risk for violence. Stalkers who have vengeful motives are more likely to physically assault the victim. These perpetrators have previously threatened the victim and are likely to carry out their threats. Substance abuse aggravates the stalking situation, especially when the perpetrator evidences mental health problems. The best predictor of the duration of the stalking is the existence of a prior intimate relationship with the stalker. The risk of recurrence is heightened under circumstances where the victim must maintain some contact with the perpetrator (children, shared property). Victims may suffer from "psychological terrorism," the feeling of being under a constant state of siege, paranoia, depression, anger, and helplessness.[178]

Interviews with 42 victims of obsessive relational intrusion (ORI) and stalking revealed turning points by the pursuer over time that often mirrored ordinary attempts to escalate intimacy in a developing relationship. These turning points were not reciprocated by, increasingly annoyed, and eventually threatened the victim. They included harassment, threats, and assaults that the victim viewed as spiteful and aggressive. Even after long periods of time, victims suffered emotional stress due to uncertainty that the pursuit had ended. These findings underscore the recommendation that victims should reject unwanted pursuits in a direct, succinct, and unambiguous fashion and not attempt to assuage the feelings of their pursuer.[179]

A survey of 118 faculty and 485 college students at a Southeastern university provides information about stalking in this situation. The majority of faculty (almost 68%) reported some form of unwanted pursuit from students. Consistent with feelings reported by stalking victims in the research, female faculty reported more pursuit incidents than male faculty and were more likely to express fear. The most serious cases crossed sex categories—male faculty reporting pursuit by female students (often for romantic motives) and female faculty stalked by male students who were typically angered about a grade or evaluation of their academic performance.

Relational goal pursuit theory was offered as an explanation for this behavior. Some students view their performance in a course as related to their life plans for a career and professional success while others seek relationships with faculty that are rejected and not reciprocated. However, the faculty reported that anger was much more likely to be a stalking motive than was romantic interest.[180]

A sample of college students (N = 2,783) found that self-reported stalkers evidenced insecure anxious attachment and "hyperactivation"—increasing efforts to reconnect with the objects of their romantic pursuit, regardless of opposition or rejection. They pursued failed relationships despite the negative reactions of their former partner. Only one psychological variable, anger, was related to stalking. Understanding of insecure attachment could help identify individuals who pose a risk for future problems and identify a method of treatment for preventive purposes.[181]

Stalking Typologies

Research has identified several different categories of stalking. Miller summarizes stalking typologies into three categories: (1) stalking for the purpose of acquiring a new relationship; (2) stalking for the purpose of intimidation, harassment, coercion and/or punishment over a rejection from a prior relationship; and (3) stalking primarily motivated by power and control.[182]

Michael Zona and his colleagues found three types of stalkers: erotomanic, love obsessional, and simple obsessional. Erotomanic stalkers hold the delusional belief that they are passionately loved by their stalking victims. They most often stalk people whom they do not know except through the media, entertainment, and/or politics. Stalkers in the love obsessional group may also hold the delusion that their victims love them, but the erotomania is only one part of their delusion. They are also delusional about other issues in their lives. They stalk people whom they do not know. In contrast, simple obsessional stalkers have a prior relationship with their victims, and many start stalking when the relationship ends or when they perceive some sort of mistreatment on the part of the stalking victim.[183] Holmes distinguishes between six types of stalkers:[184]

> *Michael Zona and his colleagues found three types of stalkers: erotomanic, love obsessional, and simple obsessional.*

1. *The celebrity stalker*: similar to the erotomanic or delusional stalker
2. *The lust stalker*: a sexual stalker who stalks strangers who possess certain characteristics because of a depraved sense of sexual lust
3. *The hit stalker*: a stalker who is hired by someone to kill someone else
4. *The love-scorned stalker*: stalkers who want and think that they have a relationship with a known victim
5. *The domestic stalker*: stalkers who are currently or were previously intimately involved with the victim
6. *The political stalker*: stalkers who stalk political personalities for the sake of expressing their political ideology

The relationships between stalkers and their victims can be characterized in one of three ways: intimates or former intimates, acquaintances, or strangers. Victims are most often the current or former spouses or intimate partners of their stalkers.[185] Studies show a high correlation between stalking and verbal and physical abuse in intimate relationships.[186]

Another influential typology of stalking is the RECON (relationship and context-based) typology. The RECON typology of stalking derived from a large non-random database of 1,005 North American stalking cases.[187] The RECON typology classifies stalkers into four groups based on two domains. In Type I, the stalker had a previous relationship with the victim with two possible subcategories: (a) *intimate stalkers*: a married, cohabitating or dating/sexual partner and (b) *acquaintance stalkers*: relationships with friends, acquaintances, or coworkers. Type II stalkers have no prior relationship with the victim and only limited or incidental contact with the victim and two subcategories: (a) *public figure stalkers* and (b) *private stranger stalkers*.

Intimate stalkers were the largest group (N = 502, 50% of the cases) and also the "most malignant"—dangerous and violent predators. They tended to be men who used or threatened to use violence, exhibited suicidal behavior, and engaged in drug/alcohol abuse. They were recidivists who were undeterred by protection orders or incarceration. Acquaintance stalkers (N = 129, 12%) had a strong desire to begin a relationship and would engage in sporadic but relentless pursuit, often over a long period of time. One-third of them eventually assaulted their victims.

Public figure (celebrity) stalkers (N = 271, 25%) featured female perpetrators (27% of the subgroup) and male victims (30%). They were older, had less violent criminal records, and a history of major mental disorder. They were less likely to escalate their behavior, threaten, or assault the victim. Private stranger stalkers (N = 103, 10%) tended to be mentally ill men who evidenced suicidal behavior and were significantly less likely to engage in substance abuse or have violent histories in comparison to intimate stalkers. They were most likely to communicate with, rather than pursue their female victims. Overall, this study confirmed patterns revealed in other research on stalkers. The majority of them (with the exception of public figure stalkers) threaten their victims. Intimate stalkers are the most violent and dangerous group. The severity or disruption of a sexual pair bond and physical proximity to the victim were risk predictors of violence. It has been recommended that systems such as RECON continue to be developed and tested in the hope of establishing effective treatment strategies for managing stalking incidents.[188]

Criminological Theories and Stalking

Criminological theories are also utilized to explain how stalking takes place. Routine activities, strain, social learning, and self-control theories have been applied to stalking behavior. For example, a survey of 861 college students from nine universities found that stalking victimization was related to women who got drunk in public and drank at home more often, bought illegal drugs, did not live on a college/university campus, and go to shopping malls more often.[189] Thus, their routine activities were predictors of stalking victimization (see Chapter 3).

Analysis of data from the 2006 NCVS stalking supplement revealed that male and female victims differed in their perceptions of the incident. Males acknowledged stalking victimization if they had been physically attacked, experienced both cyber and traditional stalking, had their pursuer suddenly show up at commonly frequented places, and had their pursuer spy on them. In addition to these factors, females agreed that they were stalking victims when the pursuer entered their homes or cars illegally during the incident and if they lost time from work. Women who acknowledged the incident were more likely than males to feel anxiety, fear, and feel physically sick. Younger and non-white female victims were also more likely to report the incident as stalking.[190]

Further analysis of this NCVS subsample considered strain theory as a framework to explain stalking victimization.[191] Female victims evidenced lower levels of anger and higher levels of negative emotions than males and were more likely to engage in legitimate coping mechanisms (changing their daily activities, taking protective measures, asking others for help, moving, and contacting the police). Females who experienced concurrent negative emotions (anger times fear, anger times anxious, anger times helpless) were more likely to seek support from others and call police—concluding that anger requires an additional emotion to move victims to take action against stalking strain (see Chapter 6).

Social learning theory was applied to the activities of recidivist stalkers. A Dutch study of 709 recidivist stalkers followed the group for 5 years to examine their behavior on release. It uncovered the existence of a small group of highly obsessive stalkers. The majority of stalkers (53%) committed a new crime but most of these offenses had nothing to do with stalking. They did not specialize in a particular type of crime, however they did engage in stalking once again—24 percent of the new crimes were in one way or another related to stalking. The majority of the time (85%), their previous victim was targeted once again. These repeat stalkers used Sykes and Matza's "techniques of neutralization" to justify their actions (see Chapter 7). Most often, they invoked "denial of injury" (45% of the cases) stating that their behavior resulted from their love for the victim. They also called upon "denial of responsibility" and rejected the intention to harm the victim. Through the use of these neutralization techniques, the stalkers validated their recidivism. Even after a court conviction and personal actions taken by their victims (installing alarms, moving), they proved very difficult to deter.[192]

Application of control balance theory to explain stalking behavior was tested with a sample of 2,783 college students. Tittle's control balance theory posits that individuals with low self-control will be more likely to commit deviant acts that requires personal contact (see Chapter 7).[193] The results revealed that both males and females with a perceived control imbalance were more likely to engage in stalking.[194] Consistent with previous findings, women were more often the victims of stalking.

Further analysis of this sample also found support for social learning theory (see Chapter 7). Stalkers were more likely to report one or more friends who also engaged in stalking and noted that they were less likely to react negatively to friends who did so. They also thought that stalking was acceptable in some situations. Similarly, stalking victims were more likely to know others who had been victimized, that their friends would react to their victimization with less sympathy, and that they believed that stalking was sometimes justifiable.[195]

However, simultaneous consideration of these theories on stalking victimization revealed some different patterns. Men and women who exercised low self-control were more likely to be stalking victims. Men who lived off campus were more likely to report stalking victimization. Among female victims, social learning theory variables, peer definitions, and a balance of definitions favorable to victimization were significantly related to stalking. When considered in combination with other variables, those reflecting control balance or deficit were not related to stalking victimization for men or women. These results indicate that strengthening self-control may be effective in reducing risk for stalking victimization.[196]

Effects of Stalking on Victims

Research examining the link between IPA and stalking has found that stalking is highly correlated with both psychological and physical abuse.[198-199] Studies that have examined this link focused on the relationship between abuse and stalking—when stalking begins in an IPA relationship—and the effects and consequences of stalking on the victim. In a study examining IPA victims' experiences with stalking, stalking appears to be more correlated with psychological abuse than physical abuse—the emotional abuse variables in the study predicted stalking better than the physical abuse variables did. Regarding the relationship between the abuser and the victim, Mechanic and her colleagues found that stalking in the relationship escalated among women who left their partners. Stalking victims were also found to be plagued by depression, posttraumatic stress disorder (PTSD), and increased levels of fear, anger, and distress.

Perceptions of Stalking

As noted, the perpetrators of stalking typically are persons who have a previous relationship with the victim—a current or former intimate partner. A study of police officers and citizens in the UK determined that, when viewing stalking scenarios, both groups were more likely to attribute the case to stalking when a stranger, rather than an intimate partner, was the offender. This stereotype held even though most police officers who had experience with stalking cases were significantly less likely to blame the victim for the offense.[200] A survey of residents of the United States, the UK, and Australia supported the view that victims were viewed as least responsible for stalking and the perpetrator most responsible when the offender was a stranger.[201]

A survey of college students documented male ignorance about stalking facts. The survey found that women were more likely than men to believe that stalking occurred frequently and was harmful to the victim—regardless of whether they had been stalking victims. Men also felt that famous persons were most likely to be stalked and that it was primarily the province of strangers. While women correctly viewed stalking as a common occurrence and a product of a personal relationship that was harmful to the victim, men viewed stalking motivations differently and were more likely to blame the victim.[202] Stalking scenarios were given to 349 college students in order to determine their perceptions of this action following a romantic breakup. Consistent with previous studies, the majority was significantly more likely to express concern and recommend official action when the case featured a female victim and a male stalker. Men pursued by women were viewed as more capable of handling the incident.[203]

Coping Behaviors of Stalking Victims

A number of studies have examined how victims of stalking coped with the problems caused by the victimization. A survey of 1,050 college students (62% female) was used to examine the effectiveness of coping strategies on obsessive relational intrusion (ORI) and stalking. The findings indicated that ORI and stalking perpetrators utilized threats, harassment, and aggression strategies against their victims. Once again, female victims expressed greater levels of fear and label their experience as stalking than males. Coping strategies failed to reduce stressful symptoms including: moving inward (diminishing or denying the reality, seriousness, or imminence of the threat), moving away (cautiously distancing or detaching from the pursuer), moving with (talking things out with or confronting the pursuer), and moving against (frightening, threatening, or coercing the pursuer) the perpetrators. In fact, engaging in these coping strategies may make matters worse.[204] Social support strategies slightly reduced the trauma felt by stalking victims, although female victims felt that social support was less adequate when ORI and stalking increased.[205]

Another study surveyed college students who were targets (N = 158: 95 women, 62 men, 1 unreported) and pursuers (N = 138: 80 women, 58 men) in unwanted pursuit (UP) and stalking incidents—permitting an analysis from both sides of the situation. Pursuers thought that victims responded to their aggressive tactics with threats, physical aggression, and by using self-protection and taking legal action. Both groups reported that "acting nicely" was the most common coping response and this may be due to the former existence of a romantic relationship. Due to this factor, targets were hoping that the pursuer would become discouraged and just fade away. Both groups also considered that the most dramatic actions (taking legal action, moving to another area, making threats, and assertive verbal confrontation) were the most effective ones. They also both endorsed avoiding and not communicating with the pursuer as an effective tactic.[206]

Finally, Miller offers the following suggestions to stalking victims that are culled from experts on the subject.

1. *Send a clear message and cut off contact.* Make the rejection firm and crystal clear: Do not contact me again, at any time, for any reason.
2. *Keep a paper (and electronic) trail.* Keep a secure record of all correspondence with the stalker (without responding to it) to preserve evidence and establish documentation of the stalker's actions and activities.
3. *Reduce target salience.* In crime prevention terms—harden the target! Make it as difficult as possible for the stalker to contact you in any way.
4. *Protect yourself.* Make your home as secure as possible, plan and vary travel routes, get training in physical and weapon protection.
5. *Enlist aid.* Report all violations to the police and never directly respond to the perpetrator. Gain support from friends, family members, mental health professionals, and support groups.
6. *Use the criminal justice system.* If the offender is known and has exhibited dangerous behavior, take out a restraining or protection order.[207]

The Criminal Justice Response

In 1990, the California legislature responded to a series of homicides by stalkers by establishing the nation's first stalking law and criminalizing "the repeated harassment or following of another person in conjunction with a threat."[208] Today, all states and the District of Columbia have stalking statutes. Research shows that the criminal justice system response to this crime has varied.

An analysis of data from an NCVS 2006 supplement on stalking determined that victims were more likely to report the crime to the police when: they were threatened and frightened, the perpetrator had a known criminal record, and when they acknowledged the behavior as stalking.[209] Reyns and Engelbrecht also examined these data to see how fear was expressed during the stalking encounter. They found that expressing fear was more likely: when the crime was seriousness of the crime, when the victims acknowledged the stalking, as contact with the stalker increased, and among females. Married victims were less likely to express fear (increased guardianship under routine activities theory; see Chapter 3).[210]

A study of 210 women who had obtained protection orders against their pursuers revealed that stalking continued in 35 percent of the cases despite this legal tactic. Women stalked by violent partners experienced the greatest amount of harm. Further interviews with criminal justice professionals and victim counselors reported differences in their perceptions and responses. Criminal justice respondents took a far less serious view of the stalking incidents than victim service representatives. Both encouraged victims to report the offense to the criminal justice system, but 36 percent indicated that they would tell them to document the behavior—a common recommendation for victims.[211]

A study of a police anti-stalking unit provides some indication of how stalking cases can be effectively handled. Storey and Hart reviewed how these officers dealt with stalking cases and uncovered some of the extra-legal methods that they adopted. One method was the adoption of a united front between the police, the victim, and relevant others (e.g., family members) to help convince the offender that their behavior was not condoned by the victim and to insure that the victim not seek any contact with the offender. In particular, the police can utilize their experience to provide victims with a view of the stalker's thoughts and reinforce that

THEORY IN ACTION

Campus Sexual Violence

It is estimated that 1 in 5 women on college campuses has been sexually assaulted during their time there—1 in 5. These young women worked so hard just to get into college, often their parents are doing everything they can to help them pay for it. So when they finally make it there only to be assaulted, that is not just a nightmare for them and their families, it's an affront to everything they've worked so hard to achieve. It's totally unacceptable.

—President Barack Obama

President Obama made these comments in relation to a study on campus sexual violence. Findings from this report include:

- Many women (88%) have never consumed a drink left unattended or consumed a drink given to them by a stranger (76%).

- One-quarter of the sample (25%) reported consuming alcohol or drugs before sex at least once a month, and slightly fewer (23%) were drunk or high during sex at least once a month.

- Eighteen percent experienced an attempted (13%) and/or completed (13%) sexual assault since entering college.

- Among the total sample, 5 percent experienced a completed physically forced sexual assault, but a much higher percentage (11%) experienced a completed incapacitated sexual assault.

- Sexual assaults were most likely to occur in September, October, and November, on Friday or Saturday nights, and between the hours of midnight and 6:00 a.m.

- Most victims of physically forced or incapacitated sexual assault were assaulted by someone they knew (79% and 88%).

- Freshmen and sophomores are at greater risk for victimization than juniors and seniors.

One of the most common risk factors is alcohol abuse. Research on alcohol use and sexual aggression among men has determined that men who drink heavily in dating and sexual situations are at risk for committing sexual assault. This effect of alcohol consumption is exacerbated if other risk factors for sexual aggression are also present (hostile masculinity, impersonal sex, and peer approval). Survey results from 255 men experienced in consensual sex from a large northwestern public university found that fraternity members were pressured by their peers to engage in sex, increasing the likelihood of sexual assault. This membership also indirectly predicted sexual assault by promoting alcohol consumption and illegal drug use. Self-control was related to sexual assault due to its relationship to abusive attitudes (pornography consumption and gender role views) and risky behavior (alcohol use). These findings support the routine activities model since these men had frequent contact with college women due to their Greek affiliation and have increased opportunity to engage in sexual assault. Since sexual assaults tend to occur when both the victim and perpetrator have been drinking heavily, colleges must address their alcohol policies to limit and curtail heavy drinking.

In addition to the traumas caused by sexual assault, there is evidence that such incidents have a deleterious impact on college performance. A survey of college students found that sexual assault during the first semester was associated with lower GPA scores. The severity of the assault also had differing impacts. GPAs of less than 2.5 were more common among rape victims.

Research reveals that victims fail to report sexual assault on college campuses. Most often, victims felt that the incident was not serious enough to report. They were more likely to report the incident to a female friend (who often encouraged them to "move on"). Students were typically unaware of the availability of campus services for sexual assault victims and did not make use of them due to shame and embarrassment. College programs must strive to reach these victims, make their services known, and encourage victims to report. They should encourage bystanders to intervene, especially when the potential victim and perpetrator are intoxicated. Colleges should consider mandating orientation programs that provide information on factors that place students at increased risk for sexual assault, the policies in place to prevent such behavior, and enforce violations as well as promote the availability of campus services.

Sources: Abbey, A., Wegner, R., Woerner, J., Pegram, S. E., & Pierce, J. (2014). Review of survey and experimental research that examine the relationship between alcohol consumption and men's sexual aggression perpetration. *Trauma, Violence, & Abuse. 15*, 265–282. Retrieved June 29, 2014, from http://tva.sagepub.com/content/early/2014/04/20/1524838014521031; Franklin, C. A., Bouffard, L. A., & Pratt, T. C. (2012). Sexual assault on the college campus: Fraternity affiliation, male peer support, and low self-control. *Criminal Justice and Behavior, 39*, 11, 1457–1480; Jordan, C. E., Combs, J. L., & Smith, G. T. (2014). An exploration of sexual victimization and academic performance among college women. *Trauma, Violence, & Abuse*, *15*, 3, 191–200; Krebs, C. P., Lindquist, C. H., Warner, T. D., Fisher, B. S., & Martin, S. L. (2007). *The campus sexual assault (CSA) study*. Washington, DC: National Institute of Justice; McMahon, S., & Banyard, V. L. (2012). When can I help? A conceptual framework for the prevention of sexual violence through bystander intervention. *Trauma, Violence, & Abuse*, *13*, 1, 3–14; Palmer, R. S., McMahon, T. J., Rounsaville, B. J., & Ball, S. A. (2010). Coercive sexual experiences, protective behavioral strategies, alcohol expectancies, and consumption among male and female college students. *Journal of Interpersonal Violence*, *25*, 9, 1563–1578; Orchowski, L.

M., & Gidycz, C. A. (2012). To whom do college women confide following a sexual assault? A prospective study of predictors of sexual assault disclosure and social reactions. *Violence Against Women*, *18*, 3, 264–288; Sabina, C., & Yo, L. Y. (2014). Campus and college victim responses to sexual assault and dating violence: Disclosure, service utilization, and service provision. *Trauma, Violence, & Abuse*, *15*(3), 201–226; The White House, President Barack Obama. Remarks by the President and Vice President at an Event for the Council on Women and Girls. Retrieved June 29, 2014, from http://www.whitehouse.gov/the-press-office/2014/01/22/remarks-president-and-vice-president-event-council-women-and-girls

they not give the offender any attention that could encourage them—including actions intended to discourage and deter them that could be misinterpreted by the offender.

These detectives also took pains to establish an informant relationship with the stalker. This strategy gave the offender someone to talk to and provide direct information on the mood of the perpetrator, their progress, and whether further intervention was in order—especially a referral to community services for low risk offenders. They also made a singular effort to refer offenders to mental health professionals when they demonstrated signs of mental illness. The authors stress that victims should be counseled to avoid any actions that would put them in danger and that they (and their families) not seek out the perpetrator and attempt to manage the situation on their own.[212]

Child Abuse

The abuse of children has an enormous impact on society. Many theorists argue that child abuse plays a large role in the intergenerational transmission of violence—the idea that violence is learned and passed on from generation to generation. **Child abuse** includes the following:

1. Non-accidental physical injury
2. Sexual abuse or exploitation
3. Emotional or psychological injury
4. Neglect or maltreatment to a person under the age of 18 years (or the age specified by the law of the state)

Many children will experience a variety of these behaviors during one incident.

The extent of child abuse is difficult to estimate for several reasons:[213]

- Children are unlikely to report because they do not know any better.
- They still love their abusers and do not want them to be punished.

- They have been threatened not to report.
- They do not know where to report the abuse.
- They are not readily believed when they do report abuse.
- Child abuse can be disguised as a legitimate and believable injury and can be covered up by the abuser.

Statistics on child abuse in the United States for 2012 reveal the following patterns:[214]

- A report of child abuse is made every 10 seconds. An estimated 686,000 children were victims of abuse and neglect.
- More than four children die every day as a result of child abuse. Of the fatalities, 80 percent were caused by one or more of the parents of the victim.
- It is estimated that between 50–60 percent of child fatalities are due to maltreatment and are not recorded as such on death certificates.
- Approximately 70 percent of children that die from abuse are under the age of 4.
- More than 90 percent of juvenile sexual abuse victims know their perpetrator in some way.

Child abuse occurs at every socioeconomic level, across ethnic and cultural lines, within all religions, and at all levels of education.

- About 30 percent of abused and neglected children will later abuse their own children, continuing the horrible cycle of abuse.
- The estimated annual cost of child abuse and neglect in the United States for 2008 is $124 billion.

Child abuse is also related to criminal behavior.

- In the U.S. prison population, 14 percent of men and 36 percent of women were abused as children, about twice the frequency seen in the general population.

- Children who experience child abuse and neglect are about 9 times more likely to become involved in criminal activity.
- As many as two-thirds of the people in treatment for drug abuse reported being abused or neglected as children.
- More than a third of adolescents with a report of abuse or neglect will have a substance use disorder before their 18th birthday, three times as likely as those without a report of abuse or neglect.

The negative consequences of child abuse are considerable. Girls are at higher risk of sexual abuse than boys, but boys appear to be at higher risk for severe physical abuse and serious injury, particularly at younger ages. Physical abuse during childhood is associated with reduced life chances, including greater risk of delinquency and of becoming a child abuser later in life. Individuals who were abused in the first 5 years of life were less likely to graduate from high school, more likely to have been fired in the past year, more likely to have become a teen parent, and at a greater risk for being arrested as juveniles for violent, nonviolent, and status offenses.[215]

Research on fatal child abuse and neglect cases reveals patterns about the nature of these crimes. An analysis of the National Child Abuse and Neglect data set compared the attributes of fatal and nonfatal child maltreatment cases. Boys, younger children, and African American children were more likely to become fatalities. Perpetrators of fatal cases were more likely to be young. Families that experienced child fatalities were more likely to live in inadequate housing, experience financial difficulties, and less likely to use an array of services (family supports, foster care, court appointed representatives, case management, counseling, education and training, information and referral assistance, and mental health services).[216]

Two Oklahoma-based studies provide some information on child fatality cases. A study of 685 Oklahoma fatal child maltreatment (FCM) cases over a 21-year period determined that African American and Latino children were overrepresented in these fatalities. Most child FCM victims died from neglect and were not involved with child welfare services prior to their death. Fatal neglect was also linked to a greater number of children living in the home—causing resources diminished by poverty to be stretched even further and aggravating the ability of a parent to provide supervision. Males (fathers, stepfathers, and mother's boyfriends) were more likely to commit physical abuse and females were more likely to perpetrate neglect. These males should be targeted for evidence-based programs to prevent child abuse. Children living in families with a history of child welfare involvement for any child in the home were at greater risk for death from child neglect than from physical abuse.[217] A second 22-year Oklahoma-based study of fatal child neglect cases (N = 372) uncovered an overwhelming presence of supervisor neglect in these cases. Children who lacked adequate supervision were significantly more likely to die due to neglect. Children under age 2, the youngest child in a family,

and African American and Native American children had increased risk for fatalities.[218]

Finally, a meta-analysis of 155 studies that examined 39 different risk factors for child maltreatment found that the two strongest risk factors for child neglect were the parent/child relationship and the parent perception that the child was a problem. For child physical abuse, the strongest risk factors were parent anger/hyperactivity and family factors (high family conflict and low family cohesion). These results indicated that prevention of these problems requires attention to the mental health needs of abusive and neglectful parents.[219]

The Criminal Justice Response

Until fairly early in the 20th century, children were regarded as the property of their parents both by law and by the parents. This meant that parents could legally mete out many forms of punishment as they saw fit, short of death or gross physical injury.

By the late 19th century, increased attention was paid to the lives and treatment of children. Child labor laws were enacted, and in 1899, the first juvenile court was founded in Cook County, Illinois.[220] One premise of the juvenile court system is that the courts operate in *parens patriae* (in place of the parent). Recognizing their responsibility to protect children, juvenile courts have acted in cases related not only to delinquency, but also to physical and later, sexual abuse.

In 1974, Congress passed the Child Abuse Prevention and Treatment Act. This act provides federal funding at the state level for prevention and response to child abuse. With this act, many states strengthened their responses to child abuse and established child abuse statutes in which parents may be prosecuted for abusing their children. Many parents have been prosecuted and children taken out of the home; however, the typical response is to try to do everything possible to avoid taking the child away (i.e., enter the family into treatment and monitor the family). Regardless of the legal response to child abuse, it is possible that much child abuse never comes to the attention of the criminal justice system and is, unfortunately, never dealt with.

Robbery

The UCR defines **robbery** as taking or attempting to take anything of value from the care, custody, or control of a person or persons by force, threat of force or violence, and/or by putting the victim in fear. The two key elements in the legal definition of robbery are (1) the taking of another person's property, and (2) the possibility of force. Because violence is either threatened or used to take a person's possessions, robbery is typically classified as a violent (rather than property) crime.

Characteristics of Robbery and Robbers

The UCR tracks robberies for both commercial (e.g., gas station, bank) and personal victimization, while the NCVS covers only personal robberies. Both sources indicate that

Surveillance cameras can help solve crimes.

© Little Rock Police Department/AP Photos

robbery rates have been decreasing since the early 1990s. The UCR recorded the following facts about robbery in 2012 nationwide:[212]

- There were an estimated 354,520 robberies. The 2012 estimated number of robberies decreased 0.1 percent from the 2011 estimate and 20.1 percent from the 2008 estimate.
- The estimated robbery rate of 112.9 per 100,000 inhabitants in 2012 showed a decrease of 0.8 percent when compared to the 2011 rate.
- In 2012, robberies accounted for an estimated $414 million in losses. The average dollar value of property stolen per reported robbery was $1,167. Banks experienced the highest average dollar loss at $3,810 per offense.
- Among the robberies for which the UCR program received weapon information in 2012, strong-arm tactics were used in 42.5 percent, firearms in 41.0 percent, and knives or cutting instruments in 7.8 percent. Other dangerous weapons were used in 8.8 percent of robberies in 2012.

The NCVS estimates that roughly 741,760 robberies occurred in 2012. This robbery rate (2.8 per 1,000 citizens) represented a slight increase over that of 2011.[223]

Several characteristics of robbery distinguish this offense from other forms of violent crime. In 2012, NCVS data revealed that:[224]

- Males (3.9 per 1,000) and blacks (5.2 per 1,000) had the highest rate of robbery victimization.
- Persons ages 21 to 24 had the highest rate of robbery victimization (5.9 per 1,000).
- Robbery was most likely to be committed by a stranger (61 percent of the total number of robberies).

Statistics on robbery from 2000 to 2005 reveal other attributes of this crime:[225]

- Most robbers are male (more than 90%), young (74% under 30), and black (54%).
- Most robberies do not yield high profits for robbers (only 29 percent led to cash), but nearly one-half of victims are physically attacked.
- Robberies with guns are less likely to result in victim injuries than are other robberies, but are much more likely to result in death.

Explaining Robbery

The primary motivation for robbery (i.e., the value of money and/or property) is obvious. Still, there are differences

TABLE 10-2

A Typology of Robbers

Type of Robber	Defining Characteristics
Professional robber	For this type of robber, crime is considered a profession or a source of livelihood (they are unlikely to hold any steady, legitimate job). Professional robbers are more likely to work in groups, to carefully plan their crimes, and to go after a few "big scores" (e.g., bank, store) each year.
Opportunistic robber	Opportunistic robbers tend to steal relatively small amounts of money from vulnerable targets (e.g., cabbies, drunks, people walking alone at night). They tend to be young and belong to a racial minority. Their crimes reflect little planning, organization, or sophistication.
Addict robber	This type of offender robs to get money in order to support a drug habit. Addict robbers are less likely to plan their crimes than the professional robber, but are more cautious than the opportunistic robber.
Alcoholic robber	Alcoholic robbers often commit robberies while they are drunk and disoriented. Their primary motive is to secure more alcohol. Their robberies are almost never planned, and they are unlikely to use a weapon.

Data from Conklin, J. (1972). *Robbery and the criminal justice system.* New York: Lippincott.

among robbers. John Conklin's classic typology of robbers (see TABLE 10-2) highlights such differences. For example, professional robbers carefully plan for the "big score" and treat robbery as their main livelihood. Addict and alcoholic robbers rob in order to sustain their substance use. Here, money from robbery is a means to purchase illicit drugs or alcohol. Recent research suggests that while money is a factor, there may be other motives for robbery.

For example, criminologist Jack Katz argues that the "take" from a typical robbery is too small to be the sole motivation for the crime. He points out that other forms of crime (e.g., drug sales) are much more lucrative. Instead of (or in conjunction with) monetary motivation, Katz suggests that robbery helps individuals maintain a "bad ass" street reputation. Robbery proves the participants' willingness to use violence even in the face of legal and physical threat.[226] A study of 86 active armed robbers lends some support to both Conklin's typology and the Katz critique against money as the primary motivation for robbery. Akin to Conklin's portrayal of some robbers as alcoholics, opportunists, or addicts, the robbers suggested that robbery netted "fast cash" that fueled participation in "street culture," which includes gambling, hard-drug use, and heavy drinking. One robber made the following comments:

> I [have] a gambling problem and I . . . lose so much so I [have] to do something to [get the cash to] win my money back. So I go out and rob somebody. That be the main reason I rob someone. I like to mix and I like to get high. You can't get high broke. You really can't get high just standing there, you got to move. And in order to move, you got to have some money.[227]

Interviews with other active robbers revealed different motivations for robbery. Some robbers reported enjoying a psychological thrill; others reported using robbery as a way to intimidate or get revenge against others.[228] This motive may explain why a substantial number of robberies are among acquaintances. There is evidence that among acquaintance robberies, the primary motive may be revenge rather than monetary reward.[229]

Robbery and Rationality

A good deal of evidence shows that robbers (even those who are opportunistic) are rational in their approach to robbery. For example, robbers will point to the advantages of robbery as opposed to other forms of crime. Robberies take less time than alternatives such as burglary or drug sales, and successful robberies typically yield cash rather than property. For this reason, robbers avoid many of the middlemen (pawn shops, fences, drug dealers) associated with other offenses.[230] Robbers display rational behavior by preying on "vulnerable" victims. Among the most vulnerable targets are those who are also involved in crime. For example, drug dealers or men who seek prostitutes are both likely to carry cash and are unlikely to report the robbery to the police.

A study of spatial patterns of tourism robbery in New Orleans applied routine activities theory to analyze this crime. Tourist robbers targeted weary and often inebriated tourist victims wandering through dark and unfamiliar streets. In about 20 percent of these incidents, victims contributed to the offense by placing themselves at a triple disadvantage—being an isolated stranger in an unfamiliar area in search of some illicit action. As a special victim type, tourists can increase their vulnerability by reducing guardianship and making themselves attractive to motivated perpetrators.[231]

If robbers are at least somewhat rational in their actions, then robbery should be a crime that is amenable to situational crime prevention. Discussed in Chapter 3, situational crime prevention is the idea that the environment can be altered in a way that would make crime less likely. There is evidence that target-hardening techniques (adding surveillance cameras, having two clerks on duty) can make convenience stores and gas stations less susceptible to robbery. For individuals, the policy implication is clear: Avoid being viewed as a vulnerable target. Examples include traveling in a group (rather than alone), avoiding the display of cash in public places, and refraining from criminal activity (such as the solicitation of prostitutes). These tips are also consistent with routine activities theory and rational choice theory—increasing guardianship can prevent robbery.[232]

Spatial patterns were also considered in a Philadelphia-based study that examined the impact of public housing proximity on street robberies. The results indicated that public housing facilities should not be automatically considered as crime generators. To prevent the incidence of robbery in such circumstances, locating public housing communities more than two blocks apart, excluding non-residential facilities (such as halfway houses, high schools, homeless shelters, pawn brokers and subway stations) a similar distance, and reducing the number of residents were recommended.[233]

🧩 Assault

The UCR (and most jurisdictions) divide assault into two categories. **Aggravated assault** involves the "unlawful attack by one person upon another for the purpose of inflicting severe or aggravated bodily injury."[234] Aggravated assaults usually involve a weapon or other means likely to produce death or serious bodily harm. Simple assaults do not involve a weapon and do not result in serious injury to the victim.

The UCR includes only aggravated assault among its Part I offenses, while the NCVS measures both aggravated and simple assaults. The following pattern of aggravated assault was reported in the UCR for 2012:[235]

- There were an estimated 760,739 aggravated assaults in the United States in 2012. The estimated number of aggravated assaults in 2012 increased 1.1 percent when compared with the 2011 estimate.
- In 2012, the estimated rate of aggravated assaults was 242.3 per 100,000 inhabitants. A 10-year comparison of data from 2003 and 2012 showed that the rate of aggravated assaults in 2012 dropped 18.0 percent.
- Of the aggravated assault offenses in 2012 for which law enforcement provided expanded data, 26.8 percent were committed with personal weapons, such as hands, fists, or feet. Firearms were used in 21.8 percent of aggravated assaults, and knives or cutting instruments were used in 18.8 percent. Other weapons were used in 32.6 percent of aggravated assaults.

> *According to the NCVS in 2012, female victims knew their assailants in over 50 percent of the assault incidents.*

According to the NCVS in 2012, female victims knew their assailants in over 50 percent of the assault incidents. In over 94 percent of the female victim assault incidents, a weapon was used. Black males experienced the highest rates for aggravated assault (6.0 per 1,000).[236]

Studies of aggravated assault indicate two particular variables associated to place: the availability of alcohol and the incidence of this crime in public housing properties. A Miami, Florida–based study considered the effect of the availability of alcohol on aggravated assaults and robberies among the Latino and black communities. Higher alcohol outlet rates were associated with higher numbers of assault and robbery victims for Latino but not black communities. Alcohol availability also promoted neighborhood instability in Latino neighborhoods. Consistent with social disorganization theory (see Chapter 6), this factor could lead to more victims by undermining collective efficacy and the ability to exert social control. Qualitative analyses determined that alcohol availability was unrelated to these crimes in black communities because they exhibited much higher levels of concentrated disadvantage (homelessness, poverty, unemployment, abandoned buildings) than the Latino communities in Miami.[237] A similar study in Cincinnati, Ohio, determined that the density of off-premise alcohol outlets was significantly related to a higher rate of assaults for block groups. Consistent with routine activities theory (see Chapter 3), off-premise alcohol outlets (gas stations, convenience stores) lack formal social control and fail to provide guardianship that could prevent an alcohol-fueled assault from taking place. They may be perceived as a deviant place where the use of violence to solve disputes is tolerated and promoted (see Chapter 6). Zoning laws and liquor license regulations can provide controls for this crime when it is evidenced.[238] Analysis of these data also revealed that elements of social organization (presence of community organizations, residential stability) may entirely negate the effect of alcohol outlet density on aggravated assault.[239]

THEORY IN ACTION

Explaining the Drop in Violent Crime

Criminologists, journalists, and other commentators have no shortage of explanations for increases in violent crime—but can they explain a crime drop? Most forms of crime have been on the decline in the United States for more than a decade. The most dramatic reductions, however, have been among violent crime. The drop in violent crime over the past decade calls into question the accuracy (or completeness) of many common explanations for crime increases.

Many legislators have been quick to point to criminal justice policies as the reason for the crime drop. Explanations include:

- Rise in imprisonment rates
- Increase in police presence
- Diminishing drug markets
- Improving economy of the 1990s
- Gun control policies

In New York City, people point to innovative and aggressive police tactics. An exhaustive analysis of the effectiveness of the Compstat program by Zimring reveals that New York City experienced a decline in seven major crime categories (homicide, rape, robbery, assault, burglary, larceny, and auto theft) that was greater than the nine other largest U.S. cities during the period 1990–2009). Others point more generally to the increases in prison populations and argue that the country is finally seeing the fruits of the get-tough movement.

In the book, *The Crime Drop in America,* some of the most widely recognized criminologists in the country contributed research that sought to explain the change in crime rates. Readers of this book will find research regarding many of the "usual suspects," including economic conditions, changes in demographics (fewer crime-prone youth, more elderly Americans), increases in prison population, and police tactics (community-oriented and zero tolerance policing). Conklin's research predominantly attributes the crime decline to the impact of incapacitation attributable to high incarceration rates.

Bruce Johnson and his associates provide research on the relationship between illicit drugs and inner-city violence in New York City. Although the city of New York is used as a case study, they also tie the relationship between drugs and violence to the broader context of the United States. The authors conclude that the use of three drugs (marijuana, cocaine, and heroin) has been cyclical. They refer to the 1960s as the "heroin injection era," the 1980s as the "cocaine/crack era," and the 1990s as the "marijuana/blunt era" (blunt refers to marijuana rolled into cigar leaves). They suggest that

increases in violent crime corresponded with the popularity of heroin in the late 1960s and with cocaine (crack) in the mid- to late-1980s. The preferred drug for those born in the 1970s has been marijuana—a drug not generally associated with violent crime.

Taking a different approach, Blumstein points out that much of the increase in violence during the 1980s was confined to a small segment of America—black youth residing in inner-city areas. He suggests that two primary factors, the increased availability of handguns and the crack cocaine epidemic, explain this surge in violence. In essence, a good deal of the violence created in the 1980s was caused by clashes over control of a new drug market. As the crack epidemic subsided (and control over the illicit distribution of crack stabilized), so too did the violence.

Finally, the Committee on Causes and Consequences of High Rates of Incarceration of the National Research Council studied the reviewed research literature on incarceration and crime rates and made the following recommendation:

> *The incremental deterrent effect of increases in lengthy prison sentences is modest at best. Because recidivism rates decline markedly with age, lengthy prison sentences, unless they specifically target very high-rate or extremely dangerous offenders, are an inefficient approach to preventing crime by incapacitation.*

Sources: Reckdenwald, A., & Parker, K. F. (2009). Homicide. In J. M. Miller (Ed.), *21st century criminology: A reference handbook* (Vol. 1). Thousand Oaks, CA: Sage, pp. 500–501; Zimring, F. E. (2012). *The city that became safe: New York's lessons for urban crime and its control.* New York: Oxford University Press; Blumstein, A., & Wallman, J. (Eds.). (2000). *The crime drop in America.* New York: Oxford University Press; Conklin, J. E. (2003). *Why crime rates fell.* Boston: Allyn & Bacon; Johnson, B., Golub, A., & Dunlap, E. (2000). The rise and decline of hard drugs, drug markets, and violence in inner-city New York. In A. Blumstein & J. Wallman (Eds.), *The crime drop in America.* New York: Cambridge University Press; Blumstein, A. (2000). Disaggregating the violence trends. In A. Blumstein & J. Wallman (Eds.), *The crime drop in America.* New York: Cambridge University Press; National Research Council. (2014). *The growth of incarceration in the United States: Exploring causes and consequences.* Committee on the Causes and Consequences of High Rates of Incarceration; Travis, J., Western, B., & Redburn, S. (Eds.). Washington, DC: The National Academies Press.

Assault is the most common form of criminal violence.
© Design Pics/age fotostock

 **Conclusion**

In public housing communities, one study compared aggravated assault rates for residents from two cities. In both cities, female residents of public housing who were assault victims knew their assailants—and at a much higher rate than those typically recorded by the NCVS. These were clearly cases of IPV that were committed in a private place, inside the public housing residences in City X, but more likely to be in public places in City Y. The differences in these assault patterns were attributed to elements of situational crime prevention. City Y's much smaller housing development created natural surveillance of the movements of both residents and visitors that could be seen and/or heard by neighbors. Therefore, it may be possible to increase guardianship in public housing communities to prevent the incidence of crime.[240] The conclusion was reaffirmed by the experience of Louisville, Kentucky, where public housing properties were demolished but assaults were displaced to areas where residents were relocated.[241] With careful attention, public housing communities can be prevented from becoming crime magnets.

This chapter explored the prevalence, trends, and nature of several types of violent crime. Many commonalities exist across these different forms of violence. Foremost, data from both the UCR and the NCVS reveal substantial declines for all types of violent crime over the past 10 to 15 years. Another theme that emerges is that for most violent crime (robbery is the exception), the majority of perpetrators are known to the offender. This runs counter to the common image of the offender as a stranger lurking in the shadows. Despite recent declines, violent crime is still an all-too-common feature of life in the United States. Victims of such violence may experience immediate physical harm and/or long-term emotional trauma. For this reason, Americans fear violent crime more than any other type of criminal behavior.

Ultimately, criminological research on violent crime seeks to uncover the causes of violence and develop effective public policy. The chapter reviewed many theories of violent crime, and each theory holds some promise for policy. For example, research on robbery reveals a rational component, which suggests that situational crime prevention may be an effective policy. There are also implications for the operation of the criminal justice system. Rape shield laws and the use of rape crisis centers have helped to make the criminal justice system more victim-friendly for rape survivors. Despite advances in knowledge, much is still to be learned about the roots of violent crime. Only by gaining a greater knowledge about the dynamics of violent behavior can law officials help to develop and implement policies, not only for the detection, apprehension, and treatment of offenders but also for the protection of citizens.

WRAP-UP

CHAPTER SPOTLIGHT

- The rate of serious violent crime (robbery, rape, homicide, aggravated assault) has declined since 1991. U.S. rates of violent crime are generally now similar to those of other industrialized nations, with the exception of homicide. American homicide rates are much higher than those of most other industrialized countries.
- Three explanations for the high homicide rates in the United States were reviewed: firearm availability, economic inequality/low social support, and the country's history of violence.
- Homicide perpetrators and victims are disproportionately young, male, and African American. Homicide is largely an intraracial crime.
- Multicide includes both mass murder and serial murder. Because it is so difficult to typify this kind of killer, law enforcement faces serious hurdles in preventing these crimes.
- In general, rapes are committed by sole offenders who had a previous relationship with the victim. Two forms of acquaintance rape include date rape and intimate partner rape.
- IPA can take on a number of forms that have serious consequences for victims.

- Stalking consists of the willful, repeated, and malicious following, harassing, or threatening of another person. The majority of stalking incidents involve individuals who are or were intimates or acquainted, with a high correlation existing between stalking and IPA.
- Child abuse includes non-accidental physical injury, sexual abuse or exploitation, emotional or psychological injury, and neglect or maltreatment to a person under the age of 18 years. The full extent of child abuse in this country is unknown, and it has proven difficult to arrive at a reliable figure.
- Robbery includes two legal elements: taking another's property and the use of force. Unlike other violent crimes, robbery tends to be perpetrated by strangers and is often an interracial crime. Explanations for robbery typically focus on money and property as motivation; there is evidence that robbers act rationally. Some scholars suggest that there are additional motives for robbery such as maintaining a street reputation and exacting revenge.

PUTTING IT ALL TOGETHER

1. How different is the U.S. homicide rate from that of other industrialized countries? What might account for this difference?
2. What have different scholars proposed as the primary motivation for rape? Describe a rape scenario that appears to fit each of these motivations.

3. Describe one macro-level and one individual-level theory that may explain violent crime.
4. What has been the violent crime trend in the United States over the past decade? What might account for this trend?
5. Debate the potential effects of gun control legislation on violent crime. Why do some believe

that RTC legislation will reduce violent crime? Is there evidence for this position?

6. Discuss the major differences between mass murder and serial murder.

7. Explain the relationship between IPA, stalking, and child abuse.

8. Select a nationally known serial killer. According to the typology of serial killers presented in this chapter, what type—visionary, missionary, hedonist, or power/control seeker—is he or she? Why?

9. Go on the World Wide Web and update the UCR and NCVS crime statistics presented in this

chapter. Have crime patterns stayed the same, or have they changed?

10. Is the drop in the national crime rate still in effect?

11. Review the crime typologies presented in this chapter. For each type of crime, what are the attributes than indicate high risk?

12. What policies and programs are in place on your campus to prevent and treat sexual assault? Review and discuss these policies and programs with your classmates and how you can contribute to the prevention of this crime.

KEY TERMS

Police Tape: © SkillUp/Shutterstock

aggravated assault The "unlawful attack by one person upon another for the purpose of inflicting severe or aggravated bodily injury.

child abuse Includes non-accidental physical injury; sexual abuse or exploitation; emotional or psychological injury; and neglect or maltreatment to a person under the age of 18 years (or the age specified by the law of the state).

felony murder Homicides committed while the offender is engaged in a separate felony offense (e.g., rape, robbery, arson).

homicide The unlawful taking of life by another human.

intimate partner homicide (IPH) A type of homicide in which the offender and victim are current or former intimate partners.

intimate partner violence (IPV) Encompasses both spousal abuse and violence that occurs between couples who are not living together. It includes rape or sexual assault, robbery, aggravated assault, and simple assault committed by the victim's current or former spouse, boyfriend, or girlfriend.

mass murder The intentional antisocial and non–state-sponsored killing of multiple victims during a

single episode at one or more closely related locations. It has also been termed *autogenic (self-generated) massacre* because it involves individuals who kill in pursuit of personal goals—the killing is generated from the offender's problems, attitudes, and psychopathology.

rape Unlawful sexual intercourse by force or without legal or factual consent.

relational goal pursuit theory People tend to seek and possess relationships with others that they view as both desirable and feasible. Under this theory, stalkers continue to pursue relationships that the other person does not desire.

robbery The taking or attempting to take anything of value from the care, custody, or control of a person or persons by force, threat of force or violence, and/or by putting the victim in fear.

serial murder The killing of a number of people, usually three or more, over the course of more than a month.

stalking A pattern of harassing or threatening tactics used by a perpetrator that is both unwanted and causes fear or safety concerns in the victim.

Offenders typically decided to commit a residential burglary in response to a perceived need. In most cases, this need was financial, calling for the immediate acquisition of money. However, it sometimes involved what was interpreted as an attack on the status, identity, or self-esteem of the offenders. Whatever its character, the need almost invariably was regarded by the offenders as pressing, that is, something that had to be dealt with immediately.

—Richard T. Wright and Scott Decker[1]

Property Crimes

Objectives

 **Introduction**

The major property crimes examined in this chapter include larceny-theft, burglary, arson, and motor vehicle theft. People are most likely to be victims of this set of crimes. There were almost 9 million property crimes reported to the police in 2012.[2]

As with other offenses, the data available to criminologists on property crime come from three main sources: (1) official data from the FBI in the Uniform Crime Report (UCR), (2) data gathered from victims of crime in the National Crime Victimization Survey (NCVS), and (3) offender-based research.

Property Crime Trends

According to the UCR, property crime (e.g., burglary, larceny-theft, motor vehicle theft) rates decreased 14.1 percent between 1993 and 2012 (TABLE 11-1). The NCVS household victimization rates revealed a much larger decrease for this time period of about 56 percent (TABLE 11-2). It is important to note that the UCR and NCVS measure property crime rates differently. The UCR rates are listed per 100,000 of the population while the NCVS uses a rate per 1,000 households. In addition, the NCVS shows that only 34 percent of all property crime victimizations were reported to the police in 2012.[3] However, they both register a decline in property crime rates for this time period.

In terms of cost, the FBI reported that property crimes accounted for an estimated loss of $15.5 billion in 2012.[4] Property crimes were more prevalent in the South (3,226.8/100,000 population) than in any other region.[5] Overall, there were over 1.6 million property crime arrests in 2012.[6]

NCVS property crime data for 2012 reveals that lower income households had higher rates of overall property crime (155.8/1,000), household burglary (67.9/1,000), motor vehicle theft (7/1,000), and property theft (198.1/1,000).[7] Households in the lowest income group (less than $7,500 per year) experienced property crime rates that were about 42 percent higher than the rates for households earning $75,000 or more per year. Burglary rates were more than 72 percent higher in the lowest income household group.[8] Property crime rates were also directly related to household size in 2008. For every type of property crime, households with six persons or more experienced higher victimization rates than smaller households—property crime total (316.1/1,000); household burglary (42.3/1,000); motor vehicle theft (8.2/1,000); and property theft (265.7/1,000).[9] A study of NCVS data from 1993–2010 determined that burglary and household larceny rates were highest during the summer months.[10]

Burglary

Several movies over the past decade (e.g., *The Italian Job, Ocean's Eleven*) have highlighted complex burglary schemes involving people who use their various skills to pull off the

TABLE 11-1

Estimated Rate of Property Crimes Known to Police (per 100,000 Inhabitants), 1993–2012

Year	Property Crime	Burglary	Larceny-Theft	Motor Vehicle Theft
1993	4,740.0	1,099.7	3,033.9	606.3
1994	4,660.2	1,042.1	3,026.9	591.3
1995	4,590.5	987.0	3,043.2	560.3
1996	4,451.0	945.0	2,980.3	525.7
1997	4,316.3	918.8	2,891.8	505.7
1998	4,052.5	863.2	2,729.5	459.9
1999	3,743.6	770.4	2,550.7	422.5
2000	3,618.3	728.8	2,477.3	412.2
2001	3,658.1	741.8	2,485.7	430.5
2002	3,630.6	747.0	2,450.7	432.9
2003	3,591.2	741.0	2,416.5	433.7
2004	3,514.1	730.3	2,362.3	421.5
2005	3,431.5	726.9	2,287.8	416.8
2006	3,346.6	733.1	2,213.2	400.2
2007	3,276.4	726.1	2,185.4	364.9
2008	3,214.6	733.0	2,166.1	315.4
2009	3,041.3	717.7	2,064.5	259.2
2010	2,945.9	701.0	2,005.8	239.1
2011	2,905.4	701.3	1,974.1	230.0
2012	2,859.2	670.2	1,959.3	229.7

Data from Federal Bureau of Investigation. *Crime in the United States, 2012: Property crime.* Retrieved June 16, 2014, from http://www.fbi.gov/about-us/cjis/ucr/crime-in-the-u.s/2012/crime-in-the-u.s.-2012/tables/1tabledatadecoverviewpdf/table_1_crime_in_the_united_states_by_volume_and_rate_per_100000_inhabitants_1993-2012.xls

"perfect" crime. Although films glamorize the offense and present the burglaries as being meticulously planned, a great deal of empirical evidence suggests that burglaries are more about easy or "soft" targets and opportunity than elaborate schemes.

TABLE 11-2

Property Crime Victimization (per 1,000 Households), 1996–2008

Year	Property Crime	Burglary	Larceny-Theft	Motor Vehicle Theft
1993	351.8	63.9	268.6	19.3
1994	341.2	62.9	259.1	19.1
1995	315.5	54.4	243.9	17.1
1996	289.3	52.8	222.6	13.8
1997	267.1	48.4	204.6	14
1998	237.1	42.9	182.7	11.6
1999	210.6	38.4	162.3	10
2000	190.4	34.3	147.4	8.8
2001	177.7	31.1	137.2	9.4
2002	168.2	29.5	129.5	9.2
2003	173.4	32	132.4	9
2004	167.5	31.1	127.2	9.2
2005	159.5	30.6	120.3	8.6
2006	169	32.9	127.4	8.7
2007	154.9	29.9	116.8	8.3
2008	142.6	28.6	107.4	6.6
2009	132.6	27.9	98.7	6
2010	125.4	25.8	94.6	4.9
2011	138.7	29.4	104.2	5.1
2012	155.8	29.9	120.9	5

Data from Bureau of Justice Statistics, *NCVS Victimization Tool (NVAT)*. Retrieved June 16, 2014, from http://www.bjs.gov/index.cfm?ty=nvat

Burglary is defined under the UCR as the unlawful entry (whether or not force was used) of a structure (apartment, barn, house, house trailer, houseboat, office, railroad car, vessel) to commit a felony or theft.[11] Burglary differs from robbery in that no interaction between the victim and offender may occur during burglary, and thus there may be no violence against the victim during the crime.

Official data sources distinguish between residential burglaries and nonresidential (business) burglaries. Data from the NCVS reflect only residential burglaries, because it takes its sample from households only. According to the NCVS, 55 percent of the burglaries that took place in 2012 were reported to the police.[12] People may fail to report the burglary to the police because the objects were recovered, the offender was unsuccessful, or the victim believed there was a lack of proof; some victims indicated that they felt as though the police would not want to be bothered. Since the UCR accounts for both residential and nonresidential burglaries reported to the police, it may be a better overall indicator of the extent of this crime.

Burglary Trends

In 2012, there were an estimated 2.1 million burglary offenses committed in the United States—a decline of 3.7 percent from 2011. Residences were the site of most of these burglaries (more than 70%). From the data in Table 11-2, we can calculate that UCR burglary rates have declined by about 39 percent since 1993. Calculations also reveal that the NCVS burglary victimization rates register an even greater drop of more than 53 percent during this time period.

The Nature of Burglary

Data show that residential properties (26 percent of the reported burglaries in 2012) are more likely to be the targets of burglaries than nonresidential properties. A majority of these properties are targeted during the daytime hours from 6 a.m. to 6 p.m. Burglars use various tools to gain entry to target homes, including crowbars, hammers, bolt cutters, and other tools. In 2012, over 59 percent of reported burglaries involved forcible entry.

Burglary victims are not only harmed by the monetary loss (2012 national total was $4.7 billion in property loss; an average of $2,230/burglary), but also often face psychological damage.[13] Many people who have experienced a burglary in their homes struggle with feelings of violation.

Dawnette Knight reacts to her 3-year prison sentence for stalking the movie actress Catherine Zeta-Jones.

© Nick Ut/AP Photos

The results of a random telephone survey of 727 Houston, Texas, residents reported that fear of burglary varied along three demographic lines. Homeowners and victims of previous crimes expressed a heightened fear of burglary. Being African American and feeling satisfaction with local police work lowered residents' fear of burglary. These results show that African Americans have a lower fear of crime, because they are more likely to experience the concentrated disadvantages in their lives that make crime a routine occurrence. Homeowners may fear losing valuable possessions via burglary. The police can impact fear of burglary through the use of effective crime prevention techniques such as community, problem solving, and hot spot policing.[14]

Rented households are more likely to be victimized by burglary than households that are owned. Burglars can easily identify soft targets within rental properties and can carry out their activities in a more secretive fashion because they are better able to blend into the crowd. The mobility of residents within rental property areas also creates more suitable targets. Victimization reports show that dwellings occupied for less than 6 months are victimized more often than homes occupied for 5 years or more.[15] Residences are most likely to be burglarized if they are close to major thoroughfares or located at the corner of a street block; are detached or semi-detached; border playgrounds, woods, or other nonresidential areas; and if parts of the house are not visible to the street.[16] A study of incident-level crime data from Albuquerque and Bernalillo County, New Mexico, examined the relationship between crime and the social and demographic features of neighborhoods. Regarding burglary, block groups with elementary schools had over 13 percent fewer incidents. This finding shows that elementary schools may provide an element of guardianship that helps lessen burglary victimization.[17] A study of crime patterns from a Merseyside, UK, police district determined that burglary risk was lower on cul-de-sacs and that it was higher on major roads and the street segments connected to them. This result shows that cul-de-sacs may be a beneficial urban design feature to sponsor burglary prevention.[18]

Burglars do their work in disadvantaged urban neighborhoods with poor social control. They prefer unoccupied dwellings that are easily accessible and visible from the street. They seek items that are **CRAVED (concealable, removable, available, valuable, enjoyable, and disposable)**, especially cash. Victims rarely know the offenders. Burglaries most often occur when residences are unoccupied.[19]

Research on burglary supports a neighborhood effect—offenders are more likely to see soft targets within their own neighborhoods and communities.[20] Habitual offenders in lower income neighborhoods seek homes in that location even when they are friendly toward the occupants. There is a greater chance of an offender being identified as a suspicious stranger in a neighborhood they are not likely to have visited in the past. Additionally, lower victimization rates are apparent in higher income neighborhoods because they are more likely to have security measures in place to combat the possibility of burglary. Home ownership is another factor in

burglary victimization. Homeowners may take more precautions to ensure that their property is safe and may also live in areas where neighbors are likely to look out for one another. People who rent their homes or apartments may move more frequently, diminishing their ability to establish strong bonds with neighbors.

Research also highlights that neighbors could in fact be a key to preventing certain types of property crime.[21] Apartment complexes have many people coming and going from them and create a greater potential guardianship to combat burglary. Yet, individuals in apartments may have fewer security measures in place to protect their property. Many apartment complexes have open parking areas, which make stealing items from cars (or stealing the cars) much easier. Conversely, houses are more likely to have a driveway and/or garage, making it difficult for thieves.

Several other factors affect burglary attempts. A Newark, New Jersey, study of residential and commercial burglaries reported to the police examined the how the features and characteristics of businesses, their products, and customers affected the risk of burglary. For residential burglary, increased risk of victimization was associated with the number of occupied housing units, food stores (24% increase), and burglarized residences (60% increase). Reductions in residential burglary risk were noted for the presence of educational services (22% decrease) and bus stops (3% decrease). The risk of commercial burglary victimization increased with the presence of automotive retail sales (75%), automotive repair and/or rental facilities (25%), food stores (58%), eating and drinking establishments (33%), educational services (25%), and bus stops (4%). Proximity to burglarized commercial establishments increased victimization risk by 36 percent and to burglarized residential units by 8 percent. Unexpectedly, the presence of business services decreased commercial burglary victimization risk by 31 percent. Consistent with routine activities theory, these unit-based variables increase guardianship (educational and business facilities) or increase the traffic of motivated offenders due to the attraction that their services provide.[22]

Once burglars identify suitable targets that convey a low risk of apprehension and punishment and gain familiarity with the areas they are in, these targets become more attractive and burglary risk increases accordingly. Studies of repeat burglaries have consistently found that homes have an increased risk of victimization once neighbors have been burgled.[23] A study of the relationship between unemployment and weekday residential burglary in 10 states revealed support for routine activities theory. The increased guardianship provided by the unemployed appeared to decrease the rate of weekday residential burglaries in these states. However, no effect was found for weekend residential burglaries.[24]

Interviews with active residential burglary offenders have portrayed them as rational criminals who, though they could maximize the rewards from the crime and minimize the risk of apprehension, were still vulnerable to detection.[25] A British-based study of residential burglaries examined the targeting strategies of offenders. Daylight burglars minimized their risk of apprehension by selecting upscale targets with better front covers. At night, they were more likely to choose townhouses with less cover. Age was also a factor in burglary decision making. Older offenders typically worked alone and at night while younger burglars worked in daylight, in pairs and on foot. Therefore, older burglars were seeking to minimize their risk of apprehension while younger offenders were more willing to accept it.[26]

Similarly, interviews with 50 experienced burglars in Britain found that money was the primary motivation for the crime, followed by the excitement of performing it. Thus, the profitability of the location was a major factor in target selection, although secondary to means of escape and the attraction of unoccupied residences. They stole profitable and easily disposed of items (cash, jewelry, and portable electrical merchandise). Their search methods were speedy yet methodical, and they were alert to cues that indicated the presence of guardians. They gained entry to residences through open or forcing vulnerable windows and doors. Both the motivations and methods of these burglars were habit driven.[27]

Finally, a study of the factors influencing the occupancy decision making of burglars found that they rationally considered such cues as: Are the curtains open? Is a vehicle parked outside?[28]

Typologies of Burglars

In previous chapters, we have reviewed criminal profiles for various types of crime. Burglary is no exception to this analysis. In one of the first analyses of burglars, Shover reported that *amateur burglars* were unskilled and haphazard in their approach and sought out targets close to where they live in order not to appear as a stranger in the neighborhood. Amateurs are more likely to seek a quick turnaround to acquire goods and selling to get cash. They will offend when the need arises, which can be often depending upon the lifestyle they are leading.

Professional burglars were fairly competent and skilled in their abilities to assess a potential target and successfully carry out the act. They gained a certain amount of profit from their activities and were better at eluding law enforcement than amateurs. Within the criminal subculture, professional burglars have a certain reputation that allows them to get information quickly on potential targets. It must be stated that burglars are not necessarily loners in their illegal activities. Residential burglars in particular work in groups, gaining information, assessing the attractiveness of a target, and carrying out the offense. A "good"

burglar is an individual who can get along well with others within a group's context; this is crucial given how many of these offenses are carried out.[29]

Bernasco found that burglars have three general property selection criteria:[30]

1. *Exposure*: distance from the street, absence of trees or hedges that block sightlines, and absence of lighting
2. *Occupancy*: people at home, presence of noise or light in the house, car in the driveway, toys in the garden, absence of unopened mail
3. *Accessibility*: easy entry to the property

These factors show that victims can prevent burglary by changing or altering the conditions or behaviors that promote it.

Women are also involved in burglary. Research reveals that women involved in burglaries fell into two categories: accomplices and partners. Female accomplices play subservient roles in the burglary event and are more likely to be the lookout or driver. Female partners in the burglary event take part as "equals" and the tasks are usually divided equally among male and female offenders. In the research conducted by Decker and his associates, older friends, family members, or street associates often introduced future offenders to the burglary scene.[31,32]

> **Research reveals that women involved in burglaries fell into two categories: accomplices and partners.**

Both male and female burglars are motivated to commit burglaries for financial gain and to help finance a party-type lifestyle filled with drugs and other activities. Females, however, noted that some of their financial gain went to support their children, while males used the financial gain to pursue sexual conquests. There was variation in how males and females selected targets. Males were more likely to have a job (e.g., cable television installer, construction worker, or gardener) that provided information on potential targets. Females could not access information on such a scale and relied on information from their male counterparts in the social network of burglars.[33]

Recent typologies of burglars focus on both their experience and motivation for the crime. Fox and Farrington used latent class analysis (LCA) to develop burglar profiles from a sample of solved Florida cases. LCA is used to identify latent classes in a group of individuals based on two or more measures. Their analysis created four types of burglars based on their criminal histories.[34]

1. *Starters*: (40% of the sample) lack criminal experience and a high rate of offending. This burglary was their first criminal offense. They had an accomplice (co-offenders). Although their age at onset was during adolescence, 38 percent of this subsample had criminal onset in adulthood. The dominant subgroup were *older white males* (38% of this subsample), over age 25, with brown or blond hair, brown or blue eyes, an average to large size build (28% overweight), and tall.

2. *Low rate offenders*: (27% of the sample) had committed one or two known offenses over a 5-year period and were most likely to have previous arrests for burglary and drug crimes. Age at criminal onset was during adolescence or later. They engaged in co-offending and were unlikely to know their victim. This subgroup had a high proportion of white offenders under age 25 (*younger whites*), female offenders (38%), short stature (65%), thin (84%) with brown eyes and hair.

3. *High rate offenders*: (14% of the sample) also had short criminal careers but had committed at least three known offenses during the time period with arrests for burglaries, thefts, and drug crimes. Age at criminal onset was during adolescence but almost one-quarter offended in childhood. They also engaged in co-offending and were unlikely to know their victim. They were mostly male, older (59% over 25), and either black (78%; *older black males*) or Hispanic (18%). They had black or brown hair, brown eyes, an average build, weight, and height.

4. *Chronic offenders*: (19% of the sample) had an arrest record with 94 percent offending for over 5 years. They were arrested for three or more prior crimes: burglary (36%), theft (38%), drug crimes (39%), and violent crimes (32%). Their criminal onset occurred prior to adolescence but about one-quarter committed crimes at that stage. They majority did not co-offend and were slightly more likely to know their victim. This subgroup had the highest number of adolescents (*younger minorities*; 15% of the entire sample). They had a high proportion of females (22%), blacks (70%), and Hispanics (nearly 30%). They tended to be short and thin.

This research also identified four classes of burglaries in terms of their offense characteristics.[35]

1. *Opportunistic offense*: (48% of all offenses) burglaries with no forced entry where offenders entered the premises through an open door, window, or garage. The offenders brought no tools to the site and took advantage of an opportunity that presented itself while the residents were away. However, nearly 40 percent of these crimes were unsuccessful because the burglars were interrupted, scared off, or apprehended at the scene. Overall, this burglary type tended to be committed by *younger minorities* (58%).

2. *Highly professional*: (27%) burglaries that indicated some level of planning and foresight with most offenders bringing a tool and taking it with them when the crime was completed. High value items were stolen in the majority of these cases. These burglaries also featured scenes left in a tidy state with no forensic evidence while occurring at unoccupied residential dwellings during daylight. These burglaries were successful 75 percent of the time.

3. *Disorganized offense*: (14%) burglaries characterized by a lack of preparation with crime scenes left in disarray and a high likelihood of tools and evidence left behind. These burglaries also featured forced entry of an unoccupied target, committed during the daylight hours, and often at a commercial site. In most cases, nothing was actually stolen.

4. *Highly interpersonal*: (12%) These burglaries featured a confrontation between the perpetrator and the victim and were motivated by anger or a dispute between them. They occurred at night when the premises were occupied and in most cases, nothing was stolen. No burglary tools were brought or used, the scene was tidy, and the offenders escaped. *Older black* (39%) and *white* (almost 33%) *males* committed most of this burglary type.

Therefore, these burglars committed offenses that were both organized and disorganized—not one particular pattern type. As with other offender profiles, the ultimate purpose is to be able to identify suspects on the basis of the attributes of the crime and lead to apprehension of the offender.

Latent profile analysis was used on a sample of 456 career criminals to develop a burglary profile. The profile yielded four subgroups of burglars:[36]

1. *Young versatile*: these burglars were distinguished by their youth and the variety of offense types they committed but showed a lack of a unique characteristic career pattern.

2. *Vagrants*: burglars who committed numerous offenses related to their transient status; they were likely to commit burglary for material gain to survive the winter months, and they may present mental illness issues and lack employable skills.

3. *Drug-oriented*: had numerous drug possession and trafficking charges plus high levels of theft and weapon offenses. They committed burglary to get funds to purchase drugs to sell and for their own use.

4. *Sexual predators*: the most violent group, with prior records that feature rape and other sexual offenses. They had the longest criminal careers (over 30 years) and the earliest age at offense onset. Their burglaries were the result of sexual compulsion to enter a dwelling and confront a victim they have stalked—a very dangerous and persistent criminal type.

This burglary typology tied to criminal career history revealed the motivations of the offenders from a broad perspective.

> **As with other offender profiles, the ultimate purpose is to be able to identify suspects on the basis of the attributes of the crime and lead to apprehension of the offender.**

Response to Burglary

Burglaries have considerably low clearance rates. According to the FBI, law enforcement agencies in 2012 cleared 12.7 percent of reported burglaries in the United States.[37] Law enforcement officials face significant hurdles when attempting to investigate burglaries, including the lack of physical evidence, the victim's inability to identify what was taken, and the time needed to investigate the crime. Especially problematic to police is the fact that other burglaries may have been carried out by the same offender who leads a criminal career lifestyle, and it takes time to investigate a series of burglaries, connect the leads, balance the caseloads before them, and relate evidence.

Because the police cannot patrol every street, community education (i.e., teaching people how to make their homes and businesses less attractive targets for would-be burglars) is necessary for burglary prevention. Neighborhood Watch programs also have been created to reduce the incidence of property crimes. These groups of neighbors and business owners actively patrol their neighborhoods and report suspicious activity to the local law enforcement agency.

Arson

Arson is traditionally defined as "any willful or malicious burning or attempting to burn, with or without intent to defraud, a dwelling house, public building, motor vehicle or aircraft, personal property, etc."[38] The UCR categorizes the types of structures that are damaged by arson as structural, mobile, and other. Each year, arson accounts for hundreds of millions of dollars in property damage. The crime of arson is a more intense form of property crime because it can cause so much damage.

The UCR compiled the following information on arsons committed in 2012:[39]

- In 2012, law enforcement agencies reported 52,766 arsons.
- Nearly 47 percent (46.8%) of all arson offenses involved structures (e.g., residential, storage, public, etc.).
- Mobile property was involved in 23.1 percent of arsons, and other types of property (such as crops, timber, fences, etc.) accounted for 30.1 percent of reported arsons.
- The average dollar loss per arson was $12,796.
- Arsons of industrial/manufacturing structures resulted in the highest average dollar losses (an average of $42,133).
- Arson offenses increased less than one-tenth of 1 percent in 2012 when compared with arson data reported in 2011.

Nationwide, there were 18.7 arson offenses for every 100,000 inhabitants in 2012.

A review of data on intentionally set fires (2008–2010) by the U.S. Fire Administration determined that:[40]

In July 2005 in Sparta, Tennessee, seven arson fires inflicted heavy damage on two churches and burned five vacant houses.

Courtesy of District Chief Chris E. Mickal/New Orleans Fire Department, Photo Unit

- An estimated 16,800 intentionally set fires in residential buildings occur annually in the United States.
- These fires result in an estimated 280 deaths, 775 injuries, and $593 million in property loss each year.
- Of all residential building fires, 5 percent were intentionally set.
- Lighters (22%), heat from other open flame or smoking materials (19%), and matches (15%) were the leading heat sources of intentionally set fires in residential buildings.
- The majority (76%) of intentionally set fires in residential buildings occurred in one- or two-family dwellings. An additional 19 percent of fires occurred in multifamily dwellings.
- Of the intentionally set residential fires, 41 percent occurred in vacant buildings.
- Rubbish, trash, and waste (8%); magazines, newspapers, and writing paper (7%); and uncontained flammable liquids or gas (6%) were the items most often first ignited in intentionally set fires in residential buildings.

Research on Arson and Arsonists

A review of the literature on arsonists revealed the following common characteristics:[41]

- Most arsonists are male, but the proportion of female offenders is increasing.
- The high-risk age group for arson is late adolescence through early adulthood.
- Arsonists are often unmarried, poorly educated, live alone, and are unemployed (unskilled laborers).
- They are also likely to be socially isolated and introverted, less physically attractive, and less assertive than other mentally disordered offenders.
- Female arsonists have been sexually abused.

- Most arsonists have criminal histories but not for arson or firesetting.
- Between 19 and 56 percent have a history of suicide attempts.
- Most have been referred for psychiatric evaluation and have a history of substance abuse disorders (especially alcohol).
- They are 20 percent more likely to be diagnosed as schizophrenic.
- They are likely to be mentally retarded, have low intellectual functioning, and antisocial and borderline personality disorders.

Some argue that the presence of these mental disorders among arsonists speaks to the need for the development of cognitive behavior treatment programs for them.[42]

A study of a random sample of arson cases from Finland revealed a pattern of crime scene actions and offender characteristics. Arson has elements of violent crime. These offenders identified jealousy, hatred, or revenge directed against another person as a frequent motive for their crime. They had mental health problems and/or a criminal background. The arsons were person- or object-oriented and expressively or instrumentally motivated.[43]

Although arson is a crime that is predominantly perpetrated by males, females also engage in this offense. A study of a sample of male and female arsonists from a large southern state between 2000 and 2005 reported significant differences between the two groups. Females were more likely to report a crisis during the past year and higher rates of childhood maltreatment and suicidal ideations. Female arsonists came from unstable homes and had little or no contact with one parent. Female arson offenses were committed at school, often as the result of an impulsive or accidental act. Males were more likely to evidence a delinquent lifestyle with prior delinquency involvement (including gangs) and a prior history of arson arrests. They were also more likely than girls to have a mental health diagnosis (both multiple mental health and ADHD diagnoses).[44] **TABLE 11-3** lists additional common motives for arson.

Arson Typologies: Mentally Disordered and Serial Arsonists

Mental disorders are another factor related to arson. Interviews with 23 mentally disordered arsonists resulted in a firesetting offense chain model with four stages predicated on risk factors for this crime.[45]

- *Phase 1—Background factors*: The majority of these offenders experienced negative relationships with caregivers, particularly with their mothers. There was a notable family history of mental health issues and/or substance abuse. As a result, this group was separated from their families and often exposed to abuse (especially in childhood). At this stage, risk factors included: early firesetting, strong affect toward fire and fire interest, antisocial activity (early criminal behavior), mental health problems (depression, schizophrenia, obsessive compulsive disorder),

TABLE 11-3

Common Motivations for Arson

Financial reward
To cover up another crime (e.g., about 1% of murders are carried out using fire as a method)
Political purposes
Mixed motives (e.g., depression, as a cry for help, under the influence of alcohol)
Mental disorder
Revenge
To get attention
Sexual satisfaction or excitement

Source: H. Prins, G. Tennet, and K. Trick, "Motives for Arson (Fire Raising)," *Medicine, Science and the Law 25*: 275–278.

and maladaptive coping (substance abuse, social isolation, interpersonal aggression, self-harm).
- *Phase 2—Early adulthood*: Early risk factors and problematic behaviors lead to the inability to develop and maintain healthy intimate relationships with others.
- *Phase 3—Pre-offense period*: In the 1-year period prior to the offense, these subjects experienced mental health deterioration and were admitted to a psychiatric facility or sought mental health services in the community. They also exhibited poor problem solving skills before their offense, not knowing how to deal with the previously-cited issues they faced. Motives for the firesetting included revenge, a cry for help/suicide, fire interest, boredom, and protection (use of fires as a tool to protect them from harm).
- *Phase 4—Offense and post-offense factors*: This period refers to how the mentally disordered offender started the fire. Some had experience with firesetting while others did not and whether they watched the fire or not.

Overall, this study revealed that their early experiences with fire influenced how these mentally disordered offenders committed arson. The presence of mental health problems exacerbated the other predictive risk factors. The findings highlight the need to explore early experiences with fire and how mentally disordered offenders react to them. How to manage these risk factors then becomes the major question for treatment of these offenders.

Research on serial arsonists has revealed varied motives for the crime. An analysis of 148 Australian arson cases from 1980–1998 (with at least three incidents per case) resulted in a typology of serial arson crimes. All of these offenders had been convicted and incarcerated. Statistical analysis provided five patterns of serial arson attacks. In the first pattern, the dominant factor was planning and the observation that there was some relationship between the offender and the victim. These arsonists entered structures prior to burning to steal items and start small fires, even when security and fire retardant devices were present—showing a brazen aspect of serial arson.

The second pattern, the thrill pattern, was a sporadic one with multiple targets often attacked and the use of various resources to start a fire. The thrill target was some form of bush, forest, or vegetation. In terms of physical appearance, the thrill offenders had poor dental work and some form of outstanding physical feature (like scarring). These crimes featured multiple offenders who were employed, lived with others, and used drugs and/or alcohol before the crime. They were older, socially competent individuals who appeared to derive some satisfaction from destroying property. Offenses were usually committed on spring or summer weekends. The fires were set in a highly visible location where they might be identified and caught. Upon apprehension, they were likely to confess to other crimes.

Anger was the motive for the third pattern of serial arson. The offender burned residential properties or motor vehicles to inflict personalized harm. They entered the residence and destroyed personal items before lighting the fire. Perpetrators were financially stable, foreign nationals who used vehicles to commit the crime. They promptly left the scene after the fire was lit.

The fourth or wanton pattern of serial arson featured attacks on educational facilities (schools and universities) and/or commercial business properties. Offenders lit some items within the target that had some personal meaning to them prior to the main fire. These offenders had a prior criminal history and were likely to commit their offenses on weekends.

The fifth and final pattern of serial arson was sexual in nature. These offenders associated the ignition of fires with sexual excitement and gratification. There was evidence of sexual activity at the crime scene. The target was a state-owned public site (trash receptacles, post boxes, public toilets) that was easily accessible. These attacks were minor in size and did not result in great destruction. These offenders did not travel far to commit the offense and lit fires on weekends during the winter months. They had a tendency to stay at the crime scene to observe the fire and even its extinguishment.[46]

As with other crime typologies, arsonist profiles can be used to prevent crime. They can form the basis of hypotheses of offender characteristics at an unsolved crime scene and as a guide to offender treatment following apprehension. In terms of a law enforcement response, a review of arson prevention strategies employed in Great Britain from 1999–2006 determined that the establishment of arson task forces and the clearing of abandoned vehicles were effective in reducing arson.[47]

Larceny-Theft

The crime of larceny-theft entails several different actions taken by an offender. The definition includes the unlawful taking, carrying, and leading or riding away of property from the possession of another; attempts to commit these acts are also included. The Uniform Crime Report includes shoplifting; pocket-picking; purse-snatching; thefts from motor vehicles; theft of motor vehicle parts and accessories; and bicycle thefts where there is no force, violence, or fraud involved. Larceny-theft can take two forms: grand larceny and petit (or petty) larceny. Grand larceny involves the theft of property worth more than a certain amount of money, usually $300. Petit larceny involves the theft of property worth less than $300. The former is usually considered a felony and the latter a misdemeanor.

Larceny-Theft Trends

In 2012, the UCR noted that larceny-theft accounted for more than 68 percent of all property crimes known to the police.[48] Data from Table 11-1 reveals that the UCR rate of larceny-theft declined by more than 35 percent between 1993 and 2012. Analysis of data from Table 11-2 reveals that the NCVS larceny-theft victimization rate plummeted by more than 55 percent during this time period. However, it must be noted that the NCVS accounts for those individuals who were victimized by theft, but accounts for it differently than the UCR. For instance, the NCVS does not account for businesses that may have been victimized by shoplifters, making the extent of the offense even more difficult to assess.

Nature and Extent of Larceny-Theft

Larceny-theft is a heavily underreported crime. According to the 2012 NCVS, only about 32 percent of thefts were reported to the police.[49] According to UCR figures, just over 28 percent of the 2012 larceny-theft arrestees were males under age 18. The average value of property taken during larceny-thefts was $987

Shoplifting is one of the most prevalent crimes and it costs retailers millions of dollars each year.
© Mauritius/age fotostock

per offense—the loss to victims nationally was nearly $6 billion. Thefts of motor vehicle parts, accessories, and contents made up the largest portion of reported larcenies (24%).[50]

Research on Larceny-Theft: A Focus on Shoplifting

Obvious among the motives of larceny-theft is financial gain. Juveniles may engage in theft to acquire things they do not have or in a group setting to prove something to their peers. Adults have stolen to support drug habits, for financial gain, and because they enjoy the thrill of it. Self-report studies on shoplifting, police arrest records of shoplifters, and observation of shoplifters by researchers and security personnel are inconclusive when it comes to identifying a specific profile of a shoplifter based on race, gender, or even age.[51-53]

Types of shoplifters include impulse, occasional, episodic, amateur, and semiprofessional.[54] Impulse shoplifters include kleptomaniacs who shoplift because of an uncontrollable urge to do so; they usually give little thought to what may happen if they are caught. Occasional shoplifters may be heavily influenced by peers and engage in the behavior out of boredom. Episodic shoplifters do so to satisfy specific needs, and they may also use a ritualistic process.

Amateur shoplifters commit the crime when they are unwilling to pay for an item and see an opportunity arise. Semiprofessional shoplifters are those who steal to resell the goods for money.[55] Understanding the motivations of these offenders can lead to the development of prevention strategies for store personnel and law enforcement.

Cromwell and associates, in their study of 320 shoplifters, identified the following motivations for shoplifting:[56]

- The individual wanted the item but did not want to pay for it.
- Peers pressured the individual.
- Individuals, in some instances, steal for a living.
- The individual wanted the item but could not afford it.
- "I don't know why. It was an impulse thing."
- "I was under the influence of drugs or alcohol."
- "I enjoy the thrill/rush/danger involved."
- "I was under a lot of stress."
- "I can't help myself. It's compulsive."

These motives were also noted in other studies of shoplifters. Caputo and King interviewed female drug abusers who supported their habit via shoplifting.[57] These offenders viewed shoplifting as another form of work. The shoplifters engaged in planning what they would do, when, and how. Time was viewed as a resource that could be spent wisely

> *Juveniles may engage in theft to acquire things they do not have or in a group setting to prove something to their peers.*

to increase profit. Stores were targeted by the value of their merchandise. Care was taken with their style of dress to allow them to blend in with other customers and belong in the environment. All preparation also included a willingness to accept risk. The ability to keep one's head under pressure was a requisite skill. Their goal was to make themselves invisible by confronting the risk of apprehension and dealing with it.

These shoplifters said that they had to decide how long to stay to "make the slip" (conceal and take control of the merchandise), "get over" (attract no suspicion), and "get out" of the store successfully. Here again, time was a crucial element because leaving too late or too early would arouse suspicion and increase the probability of apprehension, depending on the merchandise or store targeted. They showed flexibility in their methods of stealing, adapting them to the situation (the store and type of merchandise targeted). They determined risk through their experience and sense of the danger in the situation ("hunch, vibe, or instinct"). They acted on such perceptions and adapted their methods accordingly—clear evidence of a rational aspect to their decision making. In sum, they viewed shoplifting as an occupation that generated a source of income. They used techniques and methods that were both feminine and masculine in their expression and execution. They exercised an entrepreneurial spirit, including the willingness to assume risk and engage in strategic planning of their operations. They adopted businesslike methods of seeking targets, merchandise, and distribution and sale of their stolen goods.

Workplace theft is a specialized form of shoplifting where workers, rather than potential customers, are the offenders. Analysis of interview data from 44 restaurant employees illustrates how "techniques of neutralization" (see Chapter 7) were used to condone and justify their theft of items from the workplace. Workers who committed theft used these methods to avoid blame and maintain a positive self-image. They legitimized their thefts by stating that they only stole "a little, a lot" and that no one really cared about their crimes. They stole from the workplace but in limited amounts and without exceeding the bounds of custom. These justifications allowed them to deny their responsibility both individually and collectively.[58]

Criminal Justice System Response to Shoplifting

Many people feel that the law enforcement response to shoplifting should be more aggressive; shoplifters are rarely caught and, if they are, they are not necessarily likely to be prosecuted or given an appropriate sanction. Kraut found that the shoplifters felt they were less likely to be caught and less likely to experience severe consequences if caught than other types of offenders.[59]

One reason for the lack of sanctioning may be that the crime often goes unobserved. In a study designed to simulate a shoplifting incident, only slightly over one in four clerks observed the staged pilfering. Research shows that store personnel observe about 10 percent of actual shoplifting cases. To compound the problem, store customers are unwilling to report cases.[60,61]

To reduce shoplifting, the retail industry has launched training programs, conducted awareness seminars, and pursued other strategies. For example, retail personnel are instructed in the basic characteristics of shoplifters and their typical methods of stealing. Some retailers have arranged sale items in a conspicuous place where surveillance is possible. Some stores attach tags to merchandise that trip a sound alarm when the item is removed from a designated area. In addition, many sales clerks are instructed to require everyone to present a sales receipt before exchanging goods for cash.

Combining the rational choice and routine activity theories with situational crime prevention (see Chapter 3) can lead to testing a method to prevent shoplifting. A randomized, controlled experiment in 57 U.S. stores over an 8-week period used the packaging and placement of Gillette Mach 3 premium razor blade replacement packs to determine if these techniques could lower product loss and beneficially effect product sales. The stores were randomly assigned to one of three conditions: (1) special protective product handling procedures; (2) special protective product display fixtures; and (3) no treatment (control). The study found that both situational crime prevention measures reduced losses compared to control locations. Although protected product sales did not increase in the treated stores compared to the control, they did not decrease either. Hardening the target proved effective in this trial.[62]

From a mental health perspective, there is some movement toward recognizing that many shoplifters can benefit from counseling and treatment. Caputo examined a sample of adults who were arrested for shoplifting and found that most were poor and uneducated and that they stole to improve their style of life.[63] The offenders benefited from their exposure to the program and, although the rate of recidivism was not reported, the author reported that the plan had been adopted by other mental health agencies.

Motor Vehicle Theft

Motor vehicle theft (MVT) is defined as the theft or attempted theft of a motor vehicle (e.g., automobiles, trucks, buses, motorcycles, snowmobiles). What is excluded from this definition by the FBI is the taking of a motor vehicle for temporary use by persons having lawful access. Data from Table 11-1 shows that the UCR MVT rate dropped by about 62 percent between 1993 and 2012. Data from Table 11-2 reveal that the NCVS MVT victimization rate fell by about 57 percent during that time period. Traditionally, MVT is the crime most likely to be reported to the police. In 2012, about 79 percent of all MVTs were reported to the police.[64]

According to the UCR, more than $4.3 billion was lost to MVTs in 2012. The average dollar loss per stolen vehicle was $6,019. More than 73 percent of all motor vehicles reported stolen in 2012 were automobiles.[65]

Patterns of Motor Vehicle Theft

Traditionally, motor vehicles have the highest recovery rate of all stolen property. Most auto thefts take place near the victim's home during the nighttime hours. Among motor vehicles, automobiles are most likely to be stolen, and the probability of this victimization is related to how secure the vehicle is, how attractive it is to thieves, its age, and crime patterns in the area. Victims of auto theft are likely to be from households with incomes between $15,000 and $25,000 that are located in urban areas.[66,67] Motives for auto theft include: joyriding, short- and long-term transportation needs, profit, stealing a vehicle for use in another crime, to obtain parts, and for insurance fraud.[68] Although many vehicles now have antitheft devices, research on auto thieves shows that, mostly, they are fairly competent at disarming security measures in cars.[69] An analysis of MVT data from the NIBRS system (see Chapter 2) found that recovery of stolen vehicles was less likely for autos valued at less than $1,000. Proximity to a major port or the U.S.–Mexico border also decreased the likelihood of vehicle recovery. The odds of recovery increased when the police used stolen vehicle tracking systems.[70]

Patterns of MVT vary. A study of MVT rates in 310 U.S. cities examined the differences between temporary and permanent auto theft. Temporary MVT offenders tend to steal vehicles that are readily available to them regardless of type. Permanent MVT offenders are motivated by financial gain and focus on expensive vehicles. The analysis determined that temporary MVT was related to the size of the juvenile population that would engage in joyriding, and that they have less experience committing the crime. Temporary MVT was also related to the lack of access to a household vehicle. Permanent MVT was associated with the size of the adult male property offender pool, the unemployment rate, and a close distance to the U.S.–Mexico border.[71]

An examination of MVT locations in Louisville, Kentucky, determined that this pattern was clustered in certain parts of the city. Neighborhoods

People who steal cars may not be overly concerned about getting caught.

© Corbis

with a greater number of church parking lots had higher rates of MVT. Such a location would make attractive vehicles available to thieves. The crime was also related to neighborhoods with high levels of social disorganization (poverty, unemployment, vacant houses) that would offer less guardianship to prevent MVT.[72]

Methods and Motives of Car Thieves

All car thieves wish to avoid apprehension. One method they use to deal with risk is restrictive deterrence. Restrictive deterrence has four dimensions: (1) offense frequency, (2) seriousness, (3) detectability, and (4) displacement. Research from interviews with active auto thieves determined that they go through a three-step process in target selection. The first, discretionary target selection, involves strategies on what types of vehicles to steal and the locations in which to steal them. Three elements make up discretionary target selection: choosing regular, low-key cars, the use of geographically remote locations, and low risk times and approaches. Once the vehicle was in their possession, auto thieves engaged in normalcy illusions—managing their appearance to avoid apprehension. Here, five methods were in operation: changing license plates, short vehicle retention times, impression management (appearing normal to observers and police), manipulating driving routes, and the use of proxy drivers. They engaged in defiance or flight when the two previous methods failed. In this aspect, five decision making methods were used by the auto thieves: conditional assessment of police attention when pulled over, flight, crossing jurisdictions, and bailing. These thieves believed that these measures would help thwart the authorities.

Restrictive deterrence involves the impact of potential sanctions on how offenders then think and behave. The arrest avoidance strategies used by auto thieves increases the probability that their crime will be successful. In addition, they make risk more palatable to offenders by sponsoring composure and managing the anxiety of committing the crime.[73,74]

Interviews with 35 male and female car thieves in St. Louis, Missouri, examined gender differences in the commission of this crime. Female car thieves were mentored by males in methods of how to select targets, break into, and start vehicles. Using a flathead screwdriver to expose the ignition and inserting it into the exposed switch was the method used by both men and women. The major difference between male and female auto thieves was their differential access to methods for disposing of stolen vehicles. Female car thieves noted their lack of knowledge about and access to chop shops and stolen car networks that were male dominated. Therefore, they stole vehicles for joyriding and personal transportation.[75]

Interviews with 42 car thieves revealed the extent and nature of their fears when committing the crime. Their apprehensions were both formal and informal. Their level of experience was a key mitigating factor. Inexperienced auto thieves expressed little fear of the risk of arrest and felt it would be inconsequential. Experienced auto thieves were more concerned about this probability due to their more extensive criminal record. Both groups noted that their greatest fear was detection by victims and the potential for a violent altercation. In terms of informal threats, inexperienced auto thieves expressed a heightened fear of familial consequences and auto accidents because of the crime. The inexperienced and younger offenders had greater ties to their family while older, experienced car thieves were concerned about the possibility that family members may turn them in for the offense. The experienced car thieves noted that fear delayed but did not prevent them from committing the offense. Fear had little impact on their criminal careers as auto thieves.[76]

One method to harden the target and prevent car theft is the use of electronic keys to gain entry to and start the vehicle. However, interviews with car thieves revealed how these offenders have adapted to this change in opportunity. Auto thieves can use the presence of a key to present an image of normalcy—that they did not break into and damage the stolen car. These offenders took advantage of immediate opportunities for car theft that were presented when car owners failed to lock their car and take their keys. Other methods of getting keys included carjacking, burglarizing homes and businesses, and fraudulently obtaining keys from car repair or dealership businesses. It was recommended that vehicle owners take particular care to lock their cars, take their keys, and keep spare keys at home in a secure location.[77]

However, Cherbonneau and Wright argue that auto theft is unlikely to be deterred: "Simply put, the criminal justice system is incapable of deterring many would-be auto thieves, and persistent thieves are keenly aware of this. Offenders are unlikely to be detected, a small fraction of the 12 percent who are arrested each year will be prosecuted, most of these

> **The arrest avoidance strategies used by auto thieves increases the probability that their crime will be successful.**

THEORY IN ACTION

Which Cars Are the Most Popular Targets for Car Thieves?

A report from the National Insurance Crime Bureau (NICB) lists the model and type of cars most likely to be stolen between 2009 and 2012. During this time period, 31,586 large and mid-sized vehicles were reported stolen in the United States. Of the stolen vehicles, 70 percent were in the mid-sized class. Here is a list of the top 10 makes and models:

Large and Mid-Sized Car Thefts by Make and Model, 2009–2012

Make	Model	Thefts	Class
Toyota	Camry	4,619	Mid-sized
Chevrolet	Impala	3,608	Large
Nissan	Altima	3,103	Mid-sized
Chevrolet	Malibu	3,035	Mid-sized
Ford	Fusion	2,819	Mid-sized
Dodge	Charger	2,808	Large
Hyundai	Sonata	1,847	Mid-sized

Make	Model	Thefts	Class
Honda	Accord	1,712	Mid-sized
Dodge	Avenger	1,321	Mid-sized
Chrysler	300	1,045	Large

The top 10 models accounted for 82 percent of the overall thefts. The Toyota Camry accounted for 15 percent of all theft. California was the state that led these car thefts (5,094), followed by Florida (3,306), Michigan (2,604), Texas (2,247) and New York (1,769). In terms of metropolitan areas, the Detroit–Warren–Livonia area led with 2,405 thefts followed by New York–Northern New Jersey–Long Island (2,165), Los Angeles–Long Beach–Santa Ana (1,818) and Miami–Fort Lauderdale–Pompano Beach (1,586).

Only 6 percent of the large and 7 percent of the mid-sized vehicles were recovered by 6/30/2013. Stolen Toyota Camrys were the least likely vehicle to be recovered.

Source: Rust, J. (2013). *Data analytics forecast report: Mid-sized/large vehicle thefts in the United States*. National Insurance Crime Bureau.

---

prosecutions will not result in a felony conviction, and fewer than half of felony convictions will involve a prison sentence. It is unlikely that this trend will be reversed anytime soon."[78]

 ## Conclusion

Property crimes have unique characteristics in terms of the way they are defined by law, how they are committed, who commits them, and the response by law enforcement and other agencies. A common theme among the property crimes in this chapter is the instrumental motive of gaining money or property through illegal means. Unfortunately, many property crimes are not high on the list of police priorities because they are less serious than drug-related offenses and violent crimes. Research in property crime is expanding and promises to help law enforcement track and stop offenders.

Texture: © Malchev/Shutterstock; Police Tape: © SkillUp/Shutterstock

- Major property crimes include burglary, arson, larceny-theft, and motor vehicle theft.
- Property crime rates have decreased since the 1980s; victimization rates have also declined. Mainly adult males commit property crimes.
- Home ownership and residential mobility play a role in the amount of victimization that takes place among households in the United States.
- Burglaries occur in both residential dwellings and businesses and most involve forceful entry. Research on burglary shows that burglars may consider certain factors before carrying out the act. Included in these factors are the accessibility of the dwelling and several environmental factors (e.g., lighting, shrubbery, security devices). Burglary poses a challenge to law enforcement investigators and, as a result, has low clearance rates.

- Research on arson suggests that there are many motives for this crime. Arsonists are treated more harshly by the criminal justice system than other property crime offenders.
- Larceny-theft is one of the most prevalent forms of property crime and accounts for millions of dollars in money and property that is unlawfully taken each year. It includes acts of shoplifting, pocket-picking, and purse-snatching.
- The major focus of research on larceny and theft is in shoplifting. No evidence exists to suggest that there is one identifiable shoplifter based on age, race, or gender.
- Research on motor vehicle theft shows that offenders steal cars for financial reward, but they may also do so for the thrill of the experience.

PUTTING IT ALL TOGETHER

Police Tape: © SkillUp/Shutterstock

1. What may make a home or dwelling a less suitable target for burglars? How might this help law enforcement?

2. What do the burglary typologies in this chapter tell us about the motives and methods for this crime? How can this information be used to prevent burglary?

3. What do the arson typologies in this chapter tell us about the motives and methods for this

crime? How can this information be used to prevent arson?

4. How can shoplifting be prevented?

5. How can motor vehicle theft be prevented?

6. This chapter presented information on gender differences for offenders who engage in property crime. What was the nature of these differences? How do they compare? How do they differ?

Police Tape: © SkillUp/Shutterstock

arson Any willful or malicious burning or attempting to burn, with or without intent to defraud, a dwelling house, public building, motor vehicle, aircraft, or personal property. The UCR categorizes the types of structures that are damaged by arson as structural, mobile, and other.

burglary Defined under the UCR as the unlawful entry (whether or not force was used) of a structure (apartment, barn, house, house trailer, houseboat, office, railroad car, vessel) to commit a felony or theft. Burglary differs from robbery in that no interaction between the victim and offender may occur during the burglary, and thus there may be no violence against the victim during the crime.

CRAVED (concealable, removable, available, valuable, enjoyable, and disposable) The desirable attributes of stolen property.

grand larceny Theft of property worth more than a certain amount of money, usually $300; considered a felony.

larceny-theft The unlawful taking or attempted taking of property from another person.

motor vehicle theft Theft or attempted theft of a motor vehicle.

petit larceny Theft of property worth less than $300; considered a misdemeanor.

shoplifting Unlawful attempted or accomplished concealing, taking, and carrying away of goods from a commercial establishment.

For the criminal law at least, man has an inalienable right to go to hell in his own fashion, provided he does not directly injure the person or property of another on the way. The criminal law is an inefficient instrument for imposing the good life on others.

—**Norval Morris and Gordon Hawkins**[1]

CHAPTER 12

Public Order Crimes

Objectives

- Understand the concept of "victimless" crime. **Pg. 262**

- Examine how moral entrepreneurship relates to public order offenses. **Pg. 263**

- Discuss the broken windows theory as a method to explain public order offenses. **Pg. 267**

- Examine how the moralistic perspective is used to examine both prostitution and gambling. **Pg. 273**

- Examine how the law and order perspective is used to examine both prostitution and gambling. **Pg. 276**

Introduction

Crimes of public order are offenses that violate the customs, norms, and values of a society and thus vary from country to country. They have a moralistic tone and are harmful to citizens. It is difficult to precisely define public order crimes because the term is used to refer to a diverse collection of offenses. There is no standard list of public order crimes. Although these offenses are considered to be less serious than the major index crimes, they can have important effects on public health and safety, the economy, and public perception about the quality of life in a neighborhood or community.

In TABLE 12-1, examples of public order offenses are grouped by two basic perspectives: (1) morality and (2) law and order. Both aim to protect the public, but their concerns are different. The morality perspective seeks to use the criminal law to impose minimum standards of morality on citizens. Here, the laws defining offenses against public morality set standards for acceptable behavior. Examples include crimes of vice such as prostitution, illegal gambling, and drug use. The law and order perspective views enforcement of these laws as a way to maintain peace in the community. It sends a clear message that these dangerous behaviors will not be tolerated. These crimes make the public feel uneasy and unsafe and may even promote the occurrence of more serious offenses. However, these classifications are arbitrary. For example, driving while intoxicated (DWI) is a moral and a safety issue. Prostitution and illegal drug use constitute criminal offenses and also impact public health.

Another criminological perspective views public order offenses in a different way. Because the participants in these activities do not complain to the police, they are often referred to as **victimless crimes**—crimes that affect the person committing them. Because of the absence of a complaining victim, some people question whether it is appropriate to label activities such as gambling and prostitution as crimes. However, the "victimless" label is controversial. Often, there are third parties harmed by these behaviors (e.g., the families of drug addicts). These acts affect a significant number of people and disrupt members of society. For example, the father who is a compulsive gambler hurts both himself and his family when he gambles away his weekly paycheck. Many people also feel that acts such as prostitution are a threat to the moral fabric of American society and thus are harmful to all.

> *Many people also feel that acts such as prostitution are a threat to the moral fabric of American society and thus are harmful to all.*

In addition, questions exist about whether the participation of some, such as prostitutes, is consensual and whether prostitution is itself victimization. Many of these activities result in social ills, such as the spread of disease, addiction, and lost work productivity.[2,3] Historically, however, the laws prohibiting these offenses originated with concerns about upholding moral standards.

Some criminologists feel that enforcement of public order offenses causes rather than prevents problems for society. For example, Norval Morris and Gordon Hawkins believe that the "**overreach of the criminal law**" to govern such behaviors causes several secondary problems that aggravate the crime problem:[4]

1. Where the supply of goods or services is concerned (e.g., drugs, gambling, and prostitution), the criminal law acts as a "crime tariff," which makes the supply of such goods and services profitable for the criminal by driving up prices and discouraging competition by those who might enter the market were it legal.
2. It creates large-scale organized criminal groups and provides them with the funds to expand other criminal enterprises in which they engage.
3. Criminal prohibition and law enforcement help to drive up the cost of drugs and thus cause persons to engage in crime to support their habit.
4. The criminal laws lead to the growth of a criminal subculture that is subversive and does not support social order.
5. Overreach of criminal law depletes the time, energy, and manpower available for dealing with the crime problem.

TABLE 12-1

Public Order Crimes

Morality Perspective	Law and Order Perspective
Prostitution	Public intoxication
Gambling	Driving while intoxicated
Sodomy	Reckless driving
Obscenity (pornography)	Selling alcohol to minors
Drug use and trafficking	Weapons possession
Incest	Public urination/ defecation
Bigamy and polygamy	Disturbing the peace
	Unlawful assembly
	Disorderly conduct
	Panhandling
	Loitering
	Vagrancy
	Vandalism

6. Enforcing such laws contributes to two major problems for the police. First, it promotes corruption because the police are bribed to ignore crimes such as drug use and prostitution. Second, enforcing these laws often leads the police to use illegal means of law enforcement to capture offenders.

Therefore, Morris and Hawkins feel that the unwarranted extension of the criminal law into public order offenses is "expensive, unwarranted, and criminogenic," and the law should not "intervene or attempt to regulate the private moral conduct of the citizen."[5]

In sum, public order offenses strain the relationship between law and morality more than other kinds of crimes. The aim of enforcement is societal protection and crime prevention, but it is often difficult to establish and maintain a clear focus on these goals. With major crimes such as robbery or assault, a victim is harmed and violated by the offender. This relationship is less apparent in crimes such as prostitution, pornography, gambling, and drug use.

Besides reviewing some of the various public order offenses, this chapter considers three issues relevant to criminal justice policy: (1) the relationship between law and morality, (2) the relationship between public order and more serious crime, and (3) whether enforcement of these laws amounts to discrimination against the poor. Consideration of the theoretical bases for the morality and law and order perspectives helps clarify the differences between them concerning the purpose of enforcing laws against public order offenses.

🧩 The Morality Perspective

Moral Entrepreneurs

It has often been repeated that "you can't legislate morality," yet people assume that the law is grounded in and properly reflects moral standards for society. The major or index crimes reflect a high level of agreement regarding what is morally right and wrong. People agree that murder and robbery are illegal because they are morally wrong. Some research has even shown considerable consistency across such culturally different societies as the United States, India, Indonesia, and Iran.[6] Such widespread agreement is referred to as **consensus**. Compared with the index or major crimes, there is weaker consensus about the morality of public order crimes. Although some people question particular details of the law or disagree about whether a particular killing was justifiable, no one seriously advocates that murder should be legal.

In comparison, 52 percent of the American public believes that marijuana use should be legal.[7] There is little chance that a movement to decriminalize armed robbery will arise, but there are organizations that advocate for the decriminalization or legalization of marijuana (for example, NORML, the National Organization for the Reform of Marijuana Laws, advocates the decriminalization of marijuana laws and the medical use of marijuana). More than 30 percent of the U.S. population lives under some form of marijuana legalization as of 2014. Twenty two states have legalized medical marijuana for patients with such illnesses as epilepsy, cancer, Crohn's disease, and Parkinson's.[8] The fact that some public order crimes are not universally condemned as immoral raises questions about the relationship between law and morality.

Religion, particularly the Judeo-Christian tradition in the West, has been the source of much of the morality expressed in legal codes. For example, the criminal law against theft reflects the biblical injunction: "Thou shalt not steal." To some extent, the **legitimacy of the law**—the belief in the rightness of the law and public support for the law—was grounded in the presumed connection to religious ideas. However, most laws that originated from religious beliefs have purposes that can be identified and supported in secular terms.[9] Christians, Jews, Muslims, and atheists can all agree that murder is immoral and should be illegal—however, the direct connection between

Rally to promote awareness of domestic violence.
© Patrick Schneider, The Charlotte Observer/AP Photos

religion and law eroded as society became more secular and diverse.

Sometimes individuals or groups mobilize to create or enforce rules based on their particular values. Persons who take such a stance are known as moral entrepreneurs. They concern themselves with the moral well-being of society, appointing themselves as watchdogs who seek to maintain "honorable" standards for all. They presume that they serve the community by protecting its virtue.[10] These beliefs cause considerable law enforcement problems. Moral entrepreneurs can help make the laws and determine their enforcement. However, enforcing morality poses tremendous, and perhaps insurmountable, problems for the police. Enforcing morality laws requires the police to use undercover operations that can lead to legal issues such as entrapment. Enforcing laws against prostitution, for instance, requires police officers to pose either as clients or prostitutes and thus leads to the same legal and even ethical problems of enforcement. Unlike other crimes where there is a complaining victim, these crimes require the police to catch someone in the act and do more than respond to a call for service.

Moral entrepreneurs also raise public awareness about certain behaviors and demand that something be done about them. Mothers Against Drunk Driving (MADD) have publicized facts about alcohol-related automobile fatalities and pressured politicians to enact more stringent laws against driving while intoxicated. Laws requiring the use of seat belts

and prohibiting gambling largely resulted from the efforts of moral entrepreneurs and special interests rather than public demand. Such efforts have a long history in both North America and England. For more on moral entrepreneurs, read **Theory in Action: Candy Lightner—A Moral Entrepreneur**.

The Puritans who settled the Massachusetts Bay Colony acted as moral entrepreneurs, writing their religious doctrine into law. They believed that the purpose of the law was to deter and punish sin and uphold the patriarchal family. Thus, Puritan law strictly regulated sexual behavior and criminalized nonproductive pleasurable pursuits such as gambling and sports. Many of these ideas were written into the statutes of the various states after the American Revolution. Perhaps most exemplary of the Puritan influence are the laws regulating sexual behaviors, such as fornication and sodomy, and the "blue laws" that prohibited or restricted certain activities and the sale of goods on Sunday. These persisted until recently; in fact, remnants exist in some states, notably the prohibition against selling alcohol on Sunday. Sometimes the law reflects the efforts of interest groups and moral entrepreneurs. For example, organized labor supported the laws prohibiting businesses from opening on Sunday. Their support was not so much for religious reasons as it was to shorten the work week.[11]

The evolution of vagrancy laws offers another example of how public order crimes are shaped by moral entrepreneurs. Chambliss described how the laws against vagrancy were used in England following the enclosure movement. Enclosure meant that peasants were forced from the land as feudal landlords converted farmland to pasture to

A Mothers Against Drunk Driving rally.
© Roger L. Wollenberg/UPI/Landov

In 1980, 13-year-old Cari Lightner was struck down and killed by a drunk driver who had a previous history of four driving while intoxicated (DWI) convictions. The offender was sentenced to 2 years in prison but served time in a work camp and halfway house instead.

Outraged, Candy Lightner vowed to do something constructive about her daughter's death. She changed public attitudes toward DWI so it would be recognized as a serious offense. Mothers Against Drunk Driving (MADD), the organization that Lightner founded, has promoted the passage of tough legislation against DWIs. For example, MADD helped introduce legislation to prosecute drunk drivers for a blood alcohol content of 0.08, down from the previous higher legal level of 0.12. Lightner was recognized for her efforts and received the U.S. President's Volunteer Action Award.

Do you think that Candy Lightner is a moral entrepreneur or a law and order crime fighter?

Source: Mothers Against Drunk Driving (MADD). Cari Lightner and Laura Lamb Story. Retrieved June 25, 2014, from http://www.madd.org/about-us/history/

produce wool for the fast-growing textile industry. Arresting those without work or "any visible means of support" was a way of maintaining social order and encouraging those displaced persons to become part of the emerging industrial working class. Thus, in the early stages of the industrial revolution, vagrancy law was adapted to meet the need of landlords to control displaced peasants and the need of industrial capitalists for laborers. As the need for laborers was met, vagrancy law was used to control surplus labor. During the Great Depression, California used the tactic of arresting people for vagrancy to discourage migration. Gradually, the focus of vagrancy law shifted from controlling labor to the control of "the undesirable, the criminal, and the nuisance."[12]

The United States has become a morally diverse society, with a culture that defines many moral issues as a matter of personal preference. The puritanical tradition is one theme in U.S. culture. Although this tradition continues to shape the values of many, particularly conservative Christians, countervailing trends of individualism and hedonism have eroded its dominance. This erosion is manifest in the declining enforcement of laws regulating sexual behaviors such as fornication, sodomy, and adultery.

Fornication is sexual intercourse between unmarried persons. Adultery is sexual intercourse between individuals when one of the participants is married to another person. Sodomy varies in definition. It refers to sexual acts that were once defined as "unnatural" or "crimes against nature," including oral and anal sex and bestiality (sex with animals). Most states have eliminated the laws that make fornication a crime. As of 2009, 13 states (Florida, Idaho, Illinois, Massachusetts, Michigan, Minnesota, Mississippi, North Dakota, Pennsylvania, South Carolina, Utah, West Virginia, and Wisconsin) had valid fornication statutes. Twenty one states never had fornication laws, 10 states repealed such statutes, and these laws have been declared unconstitutional in 4 states.[13]

As of 2010, about two dozen states had adultery laws on the books. Consensual sex between adults is largely considered to be a private matter rather than a violation of public morals, and these laws are rarely enforced.[14] Even in earlier times, these laws were enforced normally only when the actions were "open and notorious;" they were intended to maintain public morality.[15]

As of 2014, 12 states (Alabama, Florida, Louisiana, Idaho, Kansas, Michigan, Mississippi, North Carolina, Oklahoma, South Carolina, Texas, and Utah) have sodomy laws—legal penalties for consensual sexual behavior between a person's sexual organs and the mouth or anus of another.[16] In one famous case (*Bowers v. Hardwick*, 1986), the law against sodomy was enforced. Michael Hardwick was arrested when an Atlanta police officer who was attempting to serve a search warrant observed Hardwick and another man engaged in oral sex. The case went all the way to the Supreme Court, which ruled in a five-to-four decision that Georgia's sodomy law was constitutional.[17] The court ruled that Georgia could outlaw consensual homosexual intercourse. The religious basis of this belief was evident in Chief Justice Burger's concurring opinion, in which he stated, "Condemnation of those practices is firmly rooted in Judeo-Christian moral and ethical standards." The court overturned this decision in 2003 in *Lawrence v. Texas* when the court cited a constitutional right to privacy.[18] The ruling specifically stated that because a governing majority traditionally believed a practice was immoral was not sufficient grounds for overriding the right to privacy, and anti-sodomy laws were struck down.

Ideally, most people expect law to reflect morals. As society diversifies, however, there is declining consensus on certain moral and ethical issues. If there is a range of morals, which group's values should the law represent? The example of sodomy laws illustrates this problem. Public order crimes often reflect the tension between values of individual liberty and community order. When some laws are believed to represent the values or interests of a particular group rather than an agreed-upon principle, the legitimacy of the rule of law may be eroded.

Drugs, Alcohol, Moral Entrepreneurs, and Interest Groups

Imagine that alcohol was illegal and marijuana was legal. This was the case in parts of the United States in the 1920s. Marijuana was easily available and not outlawed in many parts of the country. The criminalization of marijuana resulted from efforts of moral entrepreneurs and interest groups. Their efforts culminated in the passage of the Marijuana Tax Act in 1937, which effectively criminalized the possession, sale, or distribution of the drug.

Ethnic conflict and prejudice were the background for the push to make marijuana illegal. In the western states, marijuana use was associated with migrant Mexican laborers, while in the South it was associated with African Americans, especially jazz musicians. Newspapers and magazines of the time ran stories attributing outrageously exaggerated effects to the drug, such as claiming that "the man under the influence of hashish . . . runs through the streets hacking and killing everyone he meets," and stating that "you can grow enough marijuana in a window-box to drive the whole population of the United States stark, staring, raving mad."[19] During the 1930s, the nation was in the worst economic crisis in its history. Fearful of their poorly paid laborers turning violent under the influence of "Mexican opium," the land-owning classes in the western states lobbied for marijuana to be made illegal. They had allies in the alcohol industry, which feared competition from marijuana as they returned to business following the repeal of Prohibition in 1933. A small group of legislators, newspaper editors, and concerned citizens pressured Congress to enact anti-marijuana legislation.

Harry Anslinger, commissioner of the Bureau of Narcotics (1930–1962), took up their cause, even though he had previously testified before Congress that marijuana was a drug of little or no concern. Anslinger apparently changed his mind about marijuana, coming to believe it was the "assassin of youth" depicted in the popular press. Anslinger led the moral crusade, contributing his own hyperbole to the media accounts, mistakenly referring to marijuana as a narcotic, popularizing unsupported stories of murderous rampages committed by users and playing on racial prejudice regarding such events as "colored students" using marijuana to seduce white female students.[20] Anslinger has been described as a shrewd bureaucrat who used the fear of marijuana to strengthen his agency's power and increase its budget.

Alcohol was banned in the United States from 1920 to 1933, the era known as Prohibition. The 18th Amendment to the U.S. Constitution took effect in 1920. It outlawed the manufacture, sale, or transportation of intoxicating liquors for "beverage purpose." It is noteworthy that mere possession of alcoholic beverages was not mentioned and the phrasing of the law was widely interpreted as permitting alcohol for medicinal purposes. The passage of the Volstead Act (which defined intoxicating beverages as those containing more than 0.05 percent alcohol and laid out rules for enforcing the law) was the result of political pressure by a coalition of crusading groups collectively referred to as the Temperance Movement. The Temperance Movement originated in the Puritan/Protestant values of the New England elite middle class. Their values equated sobriety and abstinence with respectability, personal virtue, and social acceptance. The social dominance of the old middle class was threatened by the influx of immigrant groups whose values were different. The Temperance ideology merged with Protestant revivalism, and thus reflected ethnic and religious conflict.[21]

Probably the best-known organization of the Temperance Movement was the Women's Christian Temperance Union (WCTU) formed in 1873. The WCTU protested—sometimes violently—against saloons and bars, which the WCTU claimed were responsible for drunkenness and alcoholism and, therefore, wife beating, child abuse, and the destruction of families.[22] Working with other temperance groups to elect congressional candidates who favored prohibition and pressuring other legislators, the Temperance Movement had enough votes by 1917 to enact Prohibition. The First World War was an important factor, as many feared that "liquor sapped the nation's strength and will power."[23]

The "noble experiment" of Prohibition is widely regarded as a failure of social policy. Although in its early years there were some positive effects, such as declining rates of alcohol-related deaths, eventually those death rates rose again.[24] People continued to drink, often in illegal nightclubs known as speakeasies. Criminal gangs controlled the illegal liquor industry in the major cities. The violence and corruption associated with organized crime created an intolerable situation.[25] Franklin D. Roosevelt included a promise to repeal Prohibition in his presidential campaign platform. Shortly after becoming president, he signed the legislation that became the 21st Amendment, which was quickly ratified. Social policy toward alcohol shifted from prohibition to regulation, with criminal justice sanctions aimed at underage drinking, driving while intoxicated, and public drunkenness.

With the repeal of Prohibition and the enactment of the Marijuana Tax Act, alcohol became legal and marijuana illegal. The criminalization of each reflected the efforts of moral crusaders, interest groups, and class and ethnic conflicts. These factors also played a role in the criminalization of hard drugs, such as opiates and cocaine. These drugs were legal and widely used prior to the Harrison Narcotics Act enacted in 1914. When it was first marketed, Coca-Cola contained cocaine. It was intended to be a "temperance drink," a safe alternative to alcohol.[26]

Heroin was a brand name trademarked by the Bayer Company, the company better known today for its aspirin. Prior to 1914, opiates were legal and virtually unregulated. In fact, fortunes were made by British and American merchants who imported opium into China, where recreational use had become popular. Great Britain fought two wars with China in the first half of the 19th century to force the Chinese government to keep opium legal and remove trade restrictions on opium imports. When thousands of Chinese immigrated into the western United States, many brought the practice of smoking opium with them. When racial tensions flared, Chinese opium dens were frequently the target of vigilante and mob action by white Americans. Just as marijuana was associated with Mexicans, opium smoking was associated with the Chinese. Moral panics surrounding the corrupting influences of these drugs emerged when they were feared to be spreading to white youths.

In the United States in the late 1800s, the typical narcotic addict was not smoking in Chinese opium dens but living in the average household. The drug could be acquired from family doctors and, often unbeknownst to the user, in so-called patent medicines. Opiates and alcohol were the active ingredients in numerous elixirs and syrups sold as miracle cures for many common ailments, including morphine addiction. Manufacturers were not required to display the ingredients in their products.

Muckraking journalists exposed the fraudulent claims of the patent medicines around the turn of the century. It was actually public outrage over the dangerous and unsanitary practices of the meat-packing industry, famously revealed in *The Jungle* by Upton Sinclair that spelled the end of the patent medicines. In 1906, Congress passed the Pure Food and Drug Act, requiring the listing of ingredients. The press had waged an effective campaign against narcotics and the market for patent medicines declined.[27] The Harrison Narcotics Act of 1914 outlawed opiates. Originally, the Harrison Act was intended, like the Pure Food and Drug Act, to regulate drugs rather than criminalize the estimated 200,000 narcotics addicts. The Treasury Department, however, interpreted the law as making it criminal for doctors to prescribe narcotics to treat addiction.[28] Moral entrepreneurs like Charles B. Towns, who claimed to have a cure for addiction, and Mrs. William K. Vanderbilt, a member of the wealthy class, lobbied for legislation that further criminalized narcotic use. The typical addict as medical patient was replaced by the feared addict as criminal.[29] As with alcohol, the prohibition of narcotic drugs was followed by the creation of illegal black markets and the involvement of organized crime. Whether a return to legal status would break the drugs–crime connection remains a point of contentious debate.

In sum, the morality perspective calls for the enforcement of public order offenses to protect the public and to underscore the moral order that moral entrepreneurs seek to promote.

The Law and Order Perspective

From the law and order perspective, public order means the normal, peaceful conduct of social interaction conducted within social boundaries of decency and civility. Offenses against the peace are actions that interfere with the ability of the public to go about their daily business, use public space, or enjoy their private property. For example, aggressive panhandling (begging) can make sidewalks and subways uncomfortable and even threatening. Citizens want the police to deal with these behaviors to provide order and feelings of safety.

Wilson and Kelling: Broken Windows Theory

In 1982, two influential analysts of policing, James Q. Wilson and George L. Kelling, published their view of methods in policing and offered their interpretation of them.[30] This article had a great impact on policing. It called for reform and change in policing operations in the United States.

Wilson and Kelling commented on studies on the return to foot patrolling as a method of policing. Although the research results revealed that foot patrol had no effect on crime rates, these studies also showed that community residents felt safer when police officers patrolled their neighborhoods on foot. From their point of view, foot patrol had restored law and order to their community by controlling the street.

To support their views, they cited another study showing that once one window was broken in an abandoned building, eventually all the remaining windows would be destroyed. Tolerating one broken window led to the conclusion that no

> **Manufacturers were not required to display the ingredients in their products.**

one cared. Wilson and Kelling carried this argument over to neighborhoods:

A piece of property is abandoned, weeds grow up, and a window is smashed. Adults stop scolding rowdy children; the children, emboldened, become more rowdy. Families move out, unmarried adults move in. Teenagers gather in front of the corner store. The merchant asks them to move, they refuse. Fights occur. Litter accumulates. People start drinking in front of the grocery, in time, an inebriate slumps to the sidewalk and is allowed to sleep it off. Pedestrians are approached by panhandlers.[31]

Thus, failing to provide order leads to the deterioration of a neighborhood. Community controls break down and the police cannot prevent crime.

Wilson and Kelling called for a return to the order-maintenance function of policing. This function was abandoned when policing emphasized professional crime fighting and moved away from direct contact with the community. Wilson and Kelling stressed that when the police maintain order, they reinforce the control mechanisms in the community. The police must return to their duty of protecting communities and preventing "broken windows."

. . . the police must get out of their cars and spend more time in public spaces such as parks and plazas, confronting and assisting citizens with their private troubles. This is mundane, prosaic work, but it probably beats driving around in cars waiting for a radio call. Citizens would surely feel safer and, perhaps, might even be safer.[32]

In sum, Wilson and Kelling state that:

- Disorder breeds fear among neighborhood residents.
- If misbehavior is ignored, it signals that no one cares about the community and leads to more serious crime.
- If the police are to deal with disorder to reduce both crime and fear, they must rely on citizens for help.

Their argument caught on. It is now one of the rationales for developing police reforms such as Compstat, the form of crime analysis and suppression established in the NYPD under Commissioner William Bratton. For example, criminologist Gary Sykes argues that police provide a functional role by dispensing "street justice." Responding to community demands, the officer often plays the role of judge, jury, and punisher. As a result, the officer is caught in a bind between the demands of the public and those of the due process-oriented, professional model of policing. He declares that order maintenance is an important and vital role for police departments.[33]

George Kelling and Catherine Coles created a preventive model based on the tenets of the broken windows theory and community policing. This model features a partnership between the police and the community that recognizes that "citizens themselves must once again accept mutual responsibility for their own prudent, effective, and legally permissible involvement in crime prevention and order maintenance."[34] Kelling and Coles also cite research findings from New York City as evidence of the effectiveness of this approach (when the transit police and the entire department were under the direction of William Bratton):[35]

. . . robbery has been dramatically reduced in the subway, and murder is declining in the city. While we do not yet understand the precise nature of this linkage, and current police efforts extend beyond order maintenance activities alone, many police posit a direct correlation between restoring order and reducing violent crime in New York City. . . . the number of persons engaging in selling, buying, and using drugs decreased by 85%, and the number of people involved in "positive" activities increased by 79%. Furthermore, the presence of some officers, either stationed in one spot or on directed patrol, appeared more critical to affecting conditions than the absolute number of officers.

Central to these results was the establishment of the New York Police Department's Compstat program. Basically, Compstat formalized a crime control strategy for the NYPD that established clear and measurable goals for the department. Compstat stressed that:

- The core function of the police is crime control, aimed at disorder, fear, and index crime.
- The police have the capability to prevent crime.
- Officers must be both aggressive and respectful in their activities—"being aggressive in crime control does not require being combative, nor does being respectful of citizens embody weakness."[36,37]

One reason that the broken windows theory became so popular was that it "gave police officers something to look out for and intervene about when they were on foot."[38] Because public order offenses are considered to be less serious than the index crimes, some question whether it is a waste of valuable resources to punish loiterers, johns, and panhandlers when communities face high rates of murder, rape, robbery, and burglary. Again, the broken windows theory asserts that disorder and crime are causally linked. Put into practice, it implies that the police can reduce crime by cracking down on minor disorder.[39]

Kelling and Coles attribute the dramatic decrease in crime in New York City in the early 1990s to implementing these policies.[40] One example is the police crackdown on New York's infamous "squeegee men" (and women). Squeegeeing is the "unsolicited washing of car windows," expecting to receive tips. Many squeegee men conducted this activity in an aggressive, menacing style intended to intimidate drivers. Some sprayed soapy water or spit on car windows. Sometimes groups of three or four would surround a car, washing the windows whether the driver wanted them to or not, and then refusing to get out of the way until they received their "tips." A 60-day study, during which squeegee men were observed, videotaped, and arrested revealed that, far from being homeless men down on their luck, most had residences, and half had prior convictions for felonies. Squeegeeing was a minor infraction that was punishable by a fine and community service. Therefore the action taken against squeegee men by police officers was to write them a desk appearance ticket (DAT). DATs were routinely ignored by the recipients. Although squeegeeing was not punishable by jail, failure to appear was. The police had warrants for nonappearance routed directly to the officer who issued the DAT. Thus the officer could make an arrest and the offender would serve jail time. Soon squeegeeing was a thing of the past and residents and commuters felt safer.[41]

Research from the District of Columbia found that broken windows policing impacted violent crime. The results showed that police disorder arrests reduced violent crime (especially assault with a deadly weapon) in areas where resident based controls were low. The implication is that broken windows policing may be most effective in neighborhoods were community involvement is minimal and residential instability is high.[42]

However, other studies of broken windows policing have generated mixed results. A study of the effect of police crackdowns on crime hot spots determined that order maintenance methods promulgated under the broken windows theory may have unanticipated effects. Hinkle and Weisburd found that in Jersey City, New Jersey, fear of crime expressed by citizens increased even though crackdowns had lowered the crime rate. This finding underscores the necessity that the police communicate with citizens and explain their methods in order to be effective.[43] An analysis of Texas crime data from 1990–2004 on the 35 largest municipal police agencies found that broken windows policing raised clearance rates for burglaries and auto thefts (less significant) but actually decreased clearance rates for larceny-theft.[44] Examining county crime data from California, Worrall found a significant relationship between broken windows policing and burglary rates. However, there was no evident impact upon larceny-theft crimes in these areas.[45]

One reason for these mixed results might be that physical and social disorders are different factors that lead to differing results. Studies show that people have different perceptions of these two forms of disorder whereas broken windows theory assumes they are related. A telephone interview survey with respondents from two southeastern U.S. cities found that physical disorder, rather than social disorder, affected their opinions about the quality of life in their neighborhoods.[46] These findings suggest that police efforts to reduce social disorder may not affect the quality of life in areas. Data from Jersey City, New Jersey, from a telephone survey of residents and an observational study of blocks, determined that evidence of physical disorder affected their notions of social disorder in neighborhoods. Therefore, the police may wish to include methods to reduce physical disorder (like graffiti removal) when conducting broken windows policing.[47] An analysis of survey data from Washington State also determined that people have difficulty discerning their perceptions of physical disorder and crime. People who felt that their neighborhood was disorderly were more likely to make distinctions between disorder and crime.[48]

Some questions have also been raised about the social benefits of broken windows policing. Kramer notes that the efficacy and benefits of broken windows policing have been widely and fully accepted by political elites in New York City. Regulating crime and disorder (squeegee men and graffiti) may represent an attempt to "package" the city to make it available to certain customers of urban space in a way in which not all social groups will benefit. The monetary gains of a "safe" city do not mean that private interests who benefit from such policies will ensure fair distribution of monetary gains.[49]

🧩 Gambling

Gambling is defined as the operating or playing of a game for money hoping to gain more than the amount played or as a wager between two or more persons.[50] In American society, gambling has been historically tolerated and has become increasingly normalized. In various forms, gambling has been legalized across the country and its economic benefits have been promulgated. The availability of slot machines has been expanded to horse racing tracks. These "racinos" have a tax rate of 40 percent, far higher than the typical state tax rates on casino operations. They provide states with revenue that can be used for valued public benefits like education without increase taxes. Native Americans have also entered the casino business. More than 200 tribes now operate legal gambling operations.[51]

> **In American society, gambling has been historically tolerated and has become increasingly normalized.**

As various state and local governments faced fiscal crises in the 1980s, many turned to gambling as a quick-fix solution. For example, Wellford determined that:[52]

It is now legal in all but three states, and 37 states have lotteries. More than 8 in 10 adults say they have played casino games, bet on races on and off the track, bought lottery tickets, or in some other way engaged in recreational gambling. In a single recent year, Americans collectively wagered more than half a trillion dollars.

A report from the University of Nevada, Las Vegas Center for Gaming Research estimated that casino gambling in 28 states generated a total revenue of about $39 million—an increase of over 16 percent since 2004.[53] In addition, internet gambling has rapidly expanded with an estimated revenue of more than $12 million per month.[54]

Gambling has become increasingly normalized in American society.
© Andor Bujdoso/Shutterstock

Dombrink offers several reasons why the legalization of gambling does not create the same type of backlash as drugs and prostitution:[55]

1. Gambling does not challenge existing paradigms. Gambling has been an accepted practice, even when it was against the law.
2. Gambling lacks successful opposition. Gambling opponents cannot strictly provide moral arguments against it.
3. Gambling lacks a successful anti-gambling frame. Opposition to organized crime did not mobilize public opinion. The public has accepted government-sanctioned lotteries. Casinos have mobilized and implemented measures to deal with the problem of addictive gambling and its level of abuse is lower than that for drugs and alcohol.
4. Gambling plays an important role for states by providing tax revenues and funding economic development.

However, the fact that legalized forms of gambling have become so widespread has not eliminated the harm caused by gambling.

The Morality Perspective: Compulsive Gambling

Compulsive or pathological gambling—the inability to resist the impulse to gamble that may grow progressively worse—is seen as a symptom of a psychiatric disorder. It has several harmful consequences to both the gambler and his or her family.[56] These harms include:[57]

- Increasing indebtedness and bankruptcy
- Poor relationships with family and friends
- Suicide
- Committing crimes such as theft, embezzlement, domestic violence, and child abuse and neglect
- Drug abuse
- Alcoholism

The extensiveness of these problems underscores the moralistic view that gambling is wrong because it is injurious to the individual and others. Gambling involvement is often a gateway to future difficulties. Survey results from samples of Australian college students and residents who were screened for gambling problems found that gambling involvement and self-reported problems were highly related in both groups. Problem gamblers were more likely to visit multiple gambling venues and engage in a wider range of gambling activities both on- and offline. Problem gambling was also linked to online poker games, playing cards, and sports wagering.[58]

Gamblers Anonymous is one organization designed to help pathological gamblers; this organization is "a fellowship of men and women who share their experience, strength and hope with each other that they may solve their common problem and help others to recover from a gambling problem."[59] One of the leading anti-gambling organizations is the National Coalition Against Legalized Gambling (NCALG). Their mission is to "provide resources to assist citizens in making an informed decision that all forms of legalized gambling are detrimental to economic, political, social, and physical well-being of individuals, the community, and the nation."[60] NCALG contends that the revenues generated by legalized gambling are not worth the costs to the fabric of society.

There is some evidence that education programs can be established to prevent problem gambling. An evaluation of a school-based gambling prevention program in Alberta, Canada ("Stacked Deck"), reported that students exposed to the program evidenced more negative attitudes toward gambling, improved knowledge about gambling risks and problems, improved resistance to gambling fallacies, improved decision making and problem solving, decreased gambling frequency and decreased rates of problem gambling.[61]

The Law and Order Perspective: Casinos and Crime

States that have or are considering having legalized gambling are confronted with other negative consequences. For example, do casinos increase the amount of crime in a community? Routine activities theory suggests that casinos are likely hot spots for crime for both residents and tourists who frequent the casinos by flooding the area with motivated offenders.

However, research findings on the relationship between casinos and crime are inconsistent. Some studies have noted the introduction of casinos can led to an increase in crime. A review of persons seeking admission to Niagara Falls, Ontario, following the opening of Casino Niagara found that the number of criminally inadmissible individuals increased during this period. Thus, the study offered some support because casinos attract the criminal element.[62] A study of Wisconsin counties determined a link between the presence of a casino and increased crime—an impact that spilled over to adjacent counties.[63] A U.S. county-level examination of the association between UCR index crimes and casinos (before and after casino introduction, 1977–1996) found a positive relationship between the two (except for murder). The presence of a casino in a county increased property crimes by 8.6 percent and violent crime by 12.6 percent. Overall, the casino effect was low shortly after opening but grew over time.[64]

Other studies determined that the increased presence of tourists due to casino presence may account for the crime increase. A study based on offenses known to the police in Reno, Nevada (2007), found that the presence of tourists in casino areas was largely responsible for an increase in crime. Of the reported crime, 75 percent occurred within 600 feet of the casinos and decreased markedly in the areas outside of the casino zones. The tourist effect contributed to the increase in crime but neighboring areas were not affected significantly.[65] Research in Spanish provinces from 2000–2008 supports this conclusion. It determined that tourist arrivals had a significant and positive impact upon personal and property crimes. Specifically, a one percent increase in the number of tourists led to a 0.1 percent increase in minor and a 0.35 percent increase in serious property crime. In terms of personal crime, a one percent increase in the number of tourists led to a 0.1 percent increase in crimes against the person. Increased private security and police presence were recommended methods to deal with the crime threat to tourists and citizens.[66]

Additional research on casinos and crime finds no relationship between the two. An analysis of the effects of casino gambling on crime and the quality of life in seven communities (Alton and Peoria/East Peoria, Illinois; Sioux City, Iowa; St. Joseph, St. Louis, and St. Louis County, Missouri; and Biloxi, Mississippi) that had introduced riverboat gambling over a 10-year period compared to a set of control communities yielded mixed results. Three casino communities experienced an increase in crime while three others had a crime decrease and one had few significant differences in either direction.[67,68] Wilson found that the establishment of a riverboat casino failed to significantly affect the crime rate (e.g., driving while intoxicated, disorderly conduct, prostitution) in two nearby Indiana communities.[69] An analysis of the effect of Detroit casinos on the UCR crime rate (from 1996–2002) concluded that "there was no alarming indication" that the volume of crime increased in the 3 years following casino development in the city.[70] The relationship between casinos, hotels, and UCR crime in Indiana counties (1994–2004) found that the introduction of more hotel rooms seemed to reduce levels of larceny and motor vehicle theft. However, the presence of a casino did not seem to increase crime rates. In fact, rates of larceny, motor vehicle theft, aggravated assault and robbery decreased after casinos opened.[71] An examination of the impact of the presence of Michigan casinos (in 83 counties from 1994–2010) on burglary, robbery, larceny, and motor vehicle theft found no evidence of an impact upon these crimes. In fact, motor vehicle theft rates fell 16 percent in the presence of a casino and as a casino ages, robbery rates decline.[72] Research on the relationship between crime reported to the police (1997–2007) and the presence of casinos in Alberta, Canada, reported no association between the two for the crimes of breaking and entering, credit card fraud, drug possession, illegal gambling, and prostitution.[73]

This research evidence is further supported by another finding on crime reports from areas of the city that contain casinos and areas that did not have such establishments. Research in Reno, Nevada, examined police calls for service and crime incidents to examine temporal variations in crimes in casino and non-casino zones. No substantial temporal differences were found for violent, property, and disorder crimes between the two zones and any that did exist were a product of the 24-hour per day, 'round the clock' culture associated with casino life.[74] Research on other supposed risks posed by introducing casino gambling found no evidence of a detrimental effect. A study of the impact of casino gambling upon Michigan, Indiana, Ohio, and West Virginia found no significant impact on changes in unemployment, bankruptcy, or crime rates after casinos opened.[75] Analysis of the association between casino presence and fatal alcohol-related traffic deaths in 131 U.S. counties (between 1990–2000) found that the magnitude and effect of the relationship depended upon the population size of the area where the casino opened. Rural and moderately sized counties with casinos registered an increase in fatal alcohol-related traffic accidents, but their urban (or greater than average population) counterparts exhibited a decrease in these deadly events. Here, the number of miles driven by an intoxicated casino patron returning home may be related to the quantity of the effects generated.[76]

Despite the mixed findings on casinos and crime, police chiefs in casino communities have said that law enforcement agencies must know of the possible effect of a new casino on crime in the area. They believe that police agencies should establish good working relationships with casino security and keep accurate track of crime rates in the area.[77]

> *The onset of prostitution occurs most commonly in adulthood, except for juvenile runaways, child trafficking, and homeless people.*

Prostitution

Prostitution is the practice of engaging in sexual activities for hire.[78] It has a long history that dates back to ancient civilizations. In the Near East, it often represented service to a goddess as a religious duty. Ancient Hebrews prohibited prostitution among their own women and limited it to foreign women. In ancient Athens, Solon established houses of prostitution and the Temple of Aphrodite accommodated client sailors. Rome required prostitutes to adopt distinctive dress and dye their hair as distinguishing features. Religion played a major role in denouncing prostitution. The rise of Christianity during the Middle Ages attempted to prevent prostitution and Protestantism followed suit.[79]

In some cultures, prostitution is tolerated or even condoned. In 2010, 77 countries had legalized prostitution. It was still considered a crime in 109 countries. In the U.S., Nevada is the only state that has legalized prostitution.[80] A study by The Urban Institute focused on the illegal sex trade in eight U.S. cities (Atlanta, Dallas, Denver, Kansas City, Miami, Seattle, San Diego, and Washington, DC) in 2007. Across these cities, the estimated worth of the underground sex economy (massage parlors, brothels, escort services, and street and internet-based prostitution) was between $39.9 and $290 million. Pimps and traffickers interviewed for the study took home between $5,000 and $32,833 per week.[81]

The FBI Uniform Crime Report (UCR) data include arrests for prostitution and commercialized vice. This category combines selling sex with related offenses such as soliciting, pimping, or transporting prostitutes. In 2012, the FBI estimated that there were more than 43,000 arrests for prostitution and commercialized vice (both men and women; **TABLE 12–2**). This figure has declined about 34 percent since 1995. However, it is important to remember that these are arrest data and reflect police activity as much, if not more, than the actual prevalence of illegal activity.

Women arrested for prostitution are disproportionately minority—African American, Asian, and Hispanic—and are street workers. The onset of prostitution occurs most commonly in adulthood, except for juvenile runaways, child trafficking, and homeless people. There is a strong connection between drug use and prostitution, either to support a drug habit or to deal with the stress of this occupation. In addition, prostitutes have high rates of physical and sexual abuse.[82]

Types of Prostitutes

Prostitutes are often classified into different types, related to the setting in which business is transacted. Most researchers who study prostitutes place the types into a status hierarchy within the profession. The amount of freedom in choice of clients, working conditions, hours, safety, and freedom to leave the business vary with status.

Streetwalkers occupy the lowest status. As the label suggests, they ply their trade on the streets, approaching potential customers who cruise by in automobiles or walk by on the sidewalks. They may also work in hotel lobbies, bars, and nightclubs. Streetwalkers are the type of prostitutes arrested for obvious reasons: They are more visible and therefore

TABLE 12–2

Arrests for Prostitution and Commercialized Vice, 1995–2012

	1995	2012	Percent Change
Males	25,098 (38.2%)	14,024 (32.3%)	−44.1%
Females	40,680 (61.8%)	29,371 (67.7%)	−27.8%
Total	65,778	43,395	−34.0%

Sources: Federal Bureau of Investigation, *Crime in the U.S. 2008–Prostitution and commercialized vice*. Retrieved May 7, 2010, from http://www.fbi.gov/ucr/cius2008/data/table_42.html; Federal Bureau of Investigation, *Crime in the U.S. 2012 Prostitution & Commercialized Vice*. Retrieved June 28, 2014, from http://www.fbi.gov/about-us/cjis/ucr/crime-in-the-u.s/2012/crime-in-the-u.s.-2012/tables/42tabledatadecoverviewpdf

Streetwalkers approach potential customers who cruise by in automobiles or walk by on the sidewalks.
© Photographee.eu/Shutterstock, Inc.

more likely to be reported as a nuisance by the public, plus they are more vulnerable to police sting tactics. They are likely to be members of minority groups. They are also the most likely to be studied. Some argue that the research literature is disproportionately based on streetwalkers and thus misrepresents the facts about prostitution.[83]

Higher status is afforded those who work indoors in massage parlors, brothels, escort services, or as "call girls."[84] Call girls are the elite of the profession, charging much more than streetwalkers. One of the women who worked for Heidi Fleiss, the Hollywood Madam, charged $10,000 for a single "date."[85] Call girls are more selective with their clients and more discreet in the conduct of their business.

An exception to the status hierarchy appeared with the epidemic of crack cocaine in the 1980s. Prostitutes who worked in crack houses exchanged sex for drugs rather than money and were disparaged even by the streetwalkers.[86] Where prostitution is legal or condoned, it occurs indoors, in a brothel or club. In the Wild West frontier period, brothels (or "cat houses") were often multipurpose community institutions.

Farley and Kelly downplay the status hierarchy, arguing that: (1) many women engage in several types of prostitution, and (2) there are more similarities in the lives of the different types of prostitutes, such as the risk of violence, than are acknowledged.[87] Women who engage in prostitution at any level experience stigmatization and take the chance that others will see them as legitimate targets, responsible for their own victimization.

Entry into the Profession

Why do some women (and men) become prostitutes? Reasons for becoming a prostitute can be sorted into attracting,

predisposing, and precipitating factors. Narag and Maxwell summarize the three common views of prostitution:[88]

1. *Fall from grace*: View prostitution as a crime and a sin; those holding this perspective also consider prostitutes as weak, with low self-esteem and impulse control—women who should have sought legitimate employment. Terms like *whore* and *hooker* evoke stigma. It can lead to a "double standard"—harsh treatment of prostitutes but leniency toward the customer. Rates of violent crime, including murder and rape, are elevated among prostitutes.
2. *Voluntary*: Female sex workers freely choose to engage in prostitution. Prostitution is a legitimate and normal way to explore sexual pleasures. It is inevitable in a society that represses sexuality. Prostitution can provide income for the state and can sustain traditional institutions like marriage. Those who freely engage in prostitution have higher self-esteem.
3. *Involuntary and coerced*: Prostitutes are victims of their personal and environmental circumstances who need to be helped. Besides the prevalence of HIV and other STDs, they suffer from high rates of post-traumatic stress disorder, anxiety, depression, and other forms of trauma.

These views are considered in the following section.

The Morality Perspective: The Dangers of Prostitution

Research studies have identified drug use, violence, sexual abuse, and homelessness as important precursors of prostitution. Studies based on interviews with women currently or formerly in prostitution often reveal unusually high rates of physical and sexual abuse in childhood. For example, in a study of 123 women attempting to exit prostitution, 85 percent reported a history of incest, and 90 percent reported a history of physical abuse.[89] In one study, current and former prostitutes were compared to a sample of women clients of a community clinic for sexually transmitted diseases. These researchers found that, compared with non-prostitutes, the prostitutes were much more likely to have had sexual intercourse before age 11 and much more likely to have used injection drugs at a young age.

> **Research studies have identified drug use, violence, sexual abuse, and homelessness as important precursors of prostitution.**

Drug use, violence, and homelessness are linked to prostitution in different combinations. A typical pathway to prostitution goes something like this: A young girl is sexually abused by a family member or associate, such as her mother's boyfriend. As she matures, she becomes sexually promiscuous, either in search of intimacy or out of rebellion. She may experiment with drugs. Unable to get along with the family, she runs away from home or is kicked out. Lacking the skills to support herself in legitimate work, she drifts into turning tricks.[90]

These factors apply to juvenile prostitutes. Differential association and life course theories provide a framework for the analysis of interview data from 40 female prostitutes from five U.S. cities. Adolescent entry into street prostitution (age at onset) was not only related to running away from home to escape assaults but was also viewed as an acceptable, even glamorous avenue due to the example provided by family and friends who engaged in sex work. Prostitution was a way to support their drug habit and provide money to combat economic instability. The identification and treatment of these factors during adolescence was a method used to combat juvenile entry into street prostitution.[91]

Entry to juvenile prostitution was also the subject of a New York and Atlantic City interview-based study of more than 600 individuals engaged in sex work as either prostitutes or pimps in 2008. Contrary to traditional beliefs that juvenile prostitutes are coerced and recruited, about 2 percent of the prostitutes in both locations had a violent pimp. These juvenile prostitutes acted on their own and, if involved with a pimp, left him when they became more experienced. About 2 percent of the prostitutes noted that they would seek help from a social service agency if they were in trouble. Overall, life crises, rather than a trafficker, were responsible for their involvement in prostitution.[92]

Other research cites violence as both a precursor to prostitution and a fact of everyday life. Prostitutes risk violence from pimps and customers. Almost all of the women in one study had been sexually assaulted, and 75 had reported being raped by one or more customers.[93] Besides the sexual assaults, prostitutes are physically assaulted and robbed.[94]

Face-to-face interviews with 59 street prostitutes in an East Coast city determined that most of them had been raped, robbed, and/or hospitalized while working.[95] Yet, one study of 2,300 arrested customers concluded that most customers were nonviolent and that a relatively small proportion are responsible for most of the violence.[96] Although they may take steps to protect themselves, prostitutes almost never report the victimization to the police.[97]

The risk of violence is not restricted to streetwalkers. Some researchers reject the claim that life is different and safer for the high-class call girl, asserting that women in all forms of sex work report high rates of sexual violence.[98] Perhaps, it is the illegal status of prostitution that links it to violence and victimization. Policies to regulate prostitution in Nevada protected profitability by providing safety that extends to prostitutes. Preventing the spread of STDs protects both prostitutes and johns. Interviews with prostitutes determined that legalization provided a safer haven to conduct business by eliminating systematic violence and danger. However, such policies still leave open the question of whether prostitution is oppression.[99]

Other dangers faced by prostitutes are endemic to the job. Arrest and conviction is a possibility when anyone engages in an illegal business. Socially, prostitutes face the risk of social stigma once their status is public. Perhaps the most severe risk faced by prostitutes is the increased exposure to sexually transmitted diseases, including HIV/AIDS.[100,101] This risk is enhanced by unprotected sex for drugs (especially crack cocaine), transactions in which street prostitutes often engage.[102]

Exploitation or Sex Work?

Two schools of thought exist regarding prostitution: (1) prostitution as exploitation and (2) prostitution as sex work. Those who view prostitution as exploitation emphasize the coercive aspects of the business: They see prostitution as part of a continuum of abuse, the ultimate form of gender discrimination.[103] Adherents of this view rarely favor legalization, although they advocate for more lenient treatment of prostitutes, who they see as victims. Citing a "growing moral panic over prostitution and sex trafficking," Weitzer summarizes this victimization pattern:[104]

- Prostitution involves male domination and exploitation of women regardless of historical time period, societal context, or legal status.
- Violence is omnipresent in prostitution.
- Female prostitutes are victims because they do not actively make choices to enter or remain in prostitution.
- Legalization or decriminalization will make the situation worse because it would grant the blessing of the state to a despicable institution, increase the supply and demand for services, and thus amplify the victimization of female prostitutes.[105]

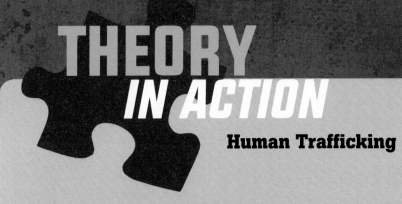

THEORY IN ACTION

Human Trafficking

Human trafficking is defined as the sale and enslavement of human beings who, after being bought and sold multiple times, are forced to labor against their will.

There are two basic types:

- *Sex trafficking* involves the recruitment, harboring, transportation, provision, or obtaining of a person for the purpose of a commercial sex act. Women from poor countries are coerced or enticed into prostitution, drawn in by the promise of lawful employment and a better life, only to find themselves in the hands of criminals who force them into the sex trade.

- *Labor trafficking* is the recruitment, harboring, transportation, provision, or obtaining of a person for labor service that is induced through force, fraud, or coercion.

Thus, human trafficking refers to forced prostitution and other forms of sexual exploitation, forced labor or services, and slavery. Both forms of human trafficking are spurred by global poverty and political instability that creates a vulnerable supply of victims seeking improved life opportunities.

The amount of human trafficking is difficult to estimate. Trafficking began when the fall of the former Soviet Union led to unprecedented mobility due to opening boarders and lessening of severe restrictions on movement. Milivojevic and Pickering have questioned these figures as fueling a moral panic and creating the perception of traffickers as dangerous people with transnational organized crime ties and victims as undesirables, thus justifying the restrictions established by anti-trafficking laws. Yet, here are some official statistics on human trafficking from the United States:

- In 2011, the U.S. Department of Justice (DOJ) charged 118 defendants in forced labor and adult sex trafficking cases, representing a 19 percent increase over the number of defendants charged in the previous year and the highest number ever charged in a single year. The same year DOJ prosecuted 125 total human trafficking cases (including sex trafficking of minors) and convicted 70.

- Approximately 8 in 10 of the suspected incidents of human trafficking investigated by federally funded task forces were classified as sex trafficking, and about 1 in 10 incidents were classified as labor trafficking.

- Between January 2008 and June 2010, 2,515 trafficking incidents were investigated by federally funded task forces. Of these incidents, 82 percent involved sex trafficking allegations, of which 48 percent involved allegations of adult prostitution and 40 percent prostitution or sexual exploitation of a child.

Much of the sex trafficking results from outright abduction or selling into prostitution. Recruitment often takes place through acquaintances, friends, or relatives. Vulnerable girls and women are forced into prostitution and manipulated through bullying and violence. Kleemans notes that women are not only victims. They also play a key part in sex trafficking in prominent roles as recruiters, transporters, or exploiters.

There is evidence that sex traffickers engage in rationalizations in defense of their crimes. Techniques of neutralization here include such tactics as denial of victim and denial of injury. The trafficker often believes that these women are better off than they were before he or she entered their lives. The women now have money, good food, homes, clothing, and jewelry. Therefore, they are profiting from sex slavery. Sex traffickers also deny responsibility by claiming that they just recruit women and have nothing to do with them after they enter the country. They also "condemn the condemners"—criticizing law enforcement officials for taking bribes and the public for taking advantage of the services of the prostitutes. They view the sex slave trade as a business transaction.

Recent studies on the U.S. document that the criminal justice system has difficulty uncovering and prosecuting these crimes. Police are often unaware of the problem and believe that it does not exist in their communities. They are also unwilling to devote the amount of resources necessary to deal with the problem. Research from North Carolina also found that the police have difficulty uncovering labor trafficking cases. Unlike the sex trafficking cases, police have little or no expertise investigating labor violations that may include labor trafficking.

In terms of prosecution, Farrell and her colleagues examined 140 human trafficking cases in 12 U.S. counties and found that suspects in these cases were not charged with the offense. About one-third were not prosecuted at all, while the remaining cases were charged with other types of sex offenses, including compelling or transport for the purposes of prostitution. Prosecutors noted that they were influenced by the credibility and willingness of victims to cooperate. They view victims as complicit in the crime.

Combating human trafficking requires an international response that is being made by several countries (including the United States) and the United Nations. The responses include technical help and training programs for law enforcement and prosecutors about these crimes, public awareness campaigns, and treatment and support programs for the victims themselves.

Sources:

Antonopoulos, G. A., & Winterdyk, J. A. (2005). Techniques of neutralizing the trafficking of women: A case study of an active trafficker in Greece. *European Journal of Crime, Criminal Law and Criminal Justice, 13*, 136–147.

Barrick, K., Lattimore, P. K., Pitts, W. J., & Zhang, S. X. (2014). When farmworkers and advocates see trafficking but law enforcement does not: Challenges in identifying labor trafficking in North Carolina, *Crime, Law & Social Change, 61*, 205–214.

Farrell, A. (2013). Environment and institutional influences on police agency responses to human trafficking. *Police Quarterly, 17*, 1, 3–29.

Farrell, A., Owens, C., & McDevitt, J. (2014). New laws but few cases: Understanding the challenges to the investigation and prosecution of human trafficking cases. *Crime, Law & Social Change, 61*, 139–168.

Gjermeni, E., Haxhiymeri, H., & Van Hook, M. (2006). Sexual trafficking of women: Tragic proportions and attempted solutions in Albania. *International Social Work, 49*, 29–40.

Human trafficking. Retrieved June 1, 2014, from http://www.victimsofcrime.org/logged-out/library/crime-information-and-statistics/human-trafficking

Kleemans, E. R. (2009). Human smuggling and human trafficking. In M. Tonry (Ed.), *The Oxford handbook of crime and public policy*. New York: Oxford University Press, pp. 409–427.

Milivojevic, S., & Pickering, S. (2013–2014). Trafficking in people, 20 years on: Sex, migration and crime in the global anti-trafficking discourse and the rise of the 'global trafficking complex.' *Current Issues in Criminal Justice, 25*, 2, 585–604.

San Miguel, C. (2009). Human trafficking. In J. M. Miller (Ed.), *21st century criminology: A reference handbook* (Vol. 1). Thousand Oaks, CA: Sage, pp. 599–611.

Shelley, L. (2003). Trade in and from the former Soviet Union. *Crime, Law and Social Change, 40*, 231–249.

Wilson, D. G., Walsh, W. F., & Kluber, S. (2006). Trafficking in human beings: Training and services among law enforcement agencies. *Police Practices & Research, 7*, 149–160.

Policing prostitution is thus viewed as gender discrimination, because prostitutes are arrested more than their customers or their managers and pimps. One leader in this fight against sexual exploitation is the international Coalition Against Trafficking in Women (CATW). Its main premise is that freedom from all forms of sexual exploitation is a fundamental human right and that women and girls have the right to sexual integrity and autonomy.[106]

The prostitution-as-sex-work perspective views prostitutes as exercising control over their lives.[107] As the label suggests, this viewpoint defines prostitution as work similar in important ways to legitimate jobs. One study concludes that, as sex workers, prostitutes shape their urban environment so it facilitates the selling of sex.[108] This position is more common among those who favor legalization. The negative aspects of prostitutes' lives are attributed to its illegal status. Each of these perspectives emphasizes different aspects of the research literature. The sex-work perspective emphasizes the differences among types of prostitution, whereas the exploitation perspective downplays those differences.

The Law and Order Perspective: Policing Street Prostitution

Enforcing laws against prostitution is promoted as both crime prevention and a public health benefit.[109] Consistent with the premises of the broken windows theory, street prostitution creates an environment where other crimes can occur. For example:[110]

- The site of street prostitution can also become a marketplace for the sale of illegal drugs.
- Street prostitution may generate profits that eventually attract members of organized crime.
- Prostitution attracts strangers and criminals to a neighborhood. Bringing these two groups into close contact opens up the possibility of more crime, such as assault and robbery.
- Prostitutes create parking and traffic problems where they congregate.

Police crackdowns on street prostitution are thus viewed as an example of problem solving.

Several methods have been proposed to deter both prostitutes and their clients. Law enforcement methods against street prostitution may thus include:[111]

- Enforcing laws prohibiting soliciting, patronizing, and loitering for prostitution. However, this is often a costly strategy because each prostitution arrest costs thousands of dollars to process. It also opens the police up to the possibility of corruption and civil rights abuse charges. This method may also be ineffective because it may simply cause the market to move to another area.
- Enhancing fines/penalties for prostitution-related offenses committed within a specified high-activity zone. Here again, the intention is to close down the marketplace however the problem remains and may be displaced somewhere else.
- Banning prostitutes or clients from geographic areas. This option is used as a condition of probation

for convicted prostitutes or their clients. They are ordered to stay out of certain areas where street prostitution is prevalent.

- Encouraging community members to publicly protest against prostitutes and/or clients. Here, the intention is to mobilize community residents against prostitution in their neighborhood, thus disrupting the marketplace. However, if the citizens are overzealous, they may violate the rights of the prostitute and their client or even be retaliated against.
- Identifying and targeting the worst offenders. This is an attempt at a high-impact strategy to remove the most active offenders and also discourage the lower level players operating in the area.

Thus, enforcing laws against prostitution is viewed as a method of containing a public nuisance tied to other serious social problems and preventing site creation for other types of crime.

Miller summarizes four legal paradigms developed to address prostitution:[112]

1. *Prohibition*: regards prostitution as a morals offense that disrupts public order and is related to other types of crime. It increases the stigma of the crime, heightens risks for victimization, and strips prostitutes of legal protection.
2. *Abolition*: views female prostitutes as victims in the commerce of sexual exchanges. Therefore, this market should be eliminated. It does not recognize the women's right to choose prostitution as a legitimate occupation.
3. *Decriminalization*: argues that prostitution should be recognized as sex work and a legitimate occupational choice. Women become involved in the sex trade due to economic and structural barriers that prevent them from earning sufficient salaries in the legitimate world.
4. *Legalization*: most often follows state tolerance via government regulation that gives officials direct control over the marketplace through licensing, registration, and health requirements.

The argument is that criminalization sends a strong deterrent message to prostitutes, pimps, and their customers. Legalization promotes idleness, promiscuity, and enhances the risk of spreading HIV and other STDs. Legalization recognizes that criminalization creates problems, including the corruption of political and law enforcement systems. Legalization proponents do not endorse child prostitution and human sex trafficking. Their position applies to sex workers that are endorsed and regulated by the government. Regulation will prevent the harms caused by prostitution by keeping track of registered workers, including conducting regular physical check-ups for both prostitutes and their clients. "Depenalization" is a combined approach advocated by those who view prostitution as violence and a human rights violation. They assume that prostitution is coerced. Therefore, prostitutes should be helped, and facilitators and customers should be punished.

Several studies have found mixed results from how the police deal with prostitution. Case files of 126 youths allegedly involved in prostitution from six U.S. cities were examined to determine how the police viewed their culpability. About 40 percent of the cases were considered to be serious by the police. They processed juvenile females as prostitutes rather than victims in need when they were acting on their own, failed to cooperate with them, had a prior record, and were not local residents. Training was recommended to help the police develop the skills necessary to deal with this population.[113]

Street surveys were used to determine the impact of a broken windows style of policing prostitution in Washington, DC. In 2005, the city council passed a law establishing "prostitution-free zones" in the city. Survey results showed that police abused and mistreated people they profiled as prostitutes in these areas. Less than half of the respondents were engaged in sex work when approached by the police but they were targeted because of their location. They noted that the police engaged in humiliation, verbal abuse, extortion (for sex), strip searches, assault, and confiscation of safe sex supplies. Younger persons (18 to 24), Latinos, and transgendered people were fearful of and abused by police practices. In addition, the police could not conceive of these people as potential crime victims who needed help. They were simply told to "move along!"[114]

A comprehensive review of the literature on law enforcement demand reduction efforts for prostitution and sex trafficking listed the extent of such programs. A plethora of approaches were reviewed including: reverse stings, shaming (publicizing johns by name and/or pictures; sending "Dear John" letters home), seizing autos, suspending drivers' licenses, establishing geographic exclusion zones, sentencing to community service, using surveillance cameras at prostitution sites, establishing john schools, neighborhood action targeting johns, and establishing public awareness/education programs. The report noted that the majority of these efforts were aimed at supply and distribution of prostitution rather than attempting to limit demand.[115]

Johns are often the target population for such programs because they are the source of demand for prostitution. A sample of posts from web forums for prostitute customers in 10 U.S. cities found that johns openly discussed methods to reduce the risk of apprehension and to promote safety. They carefully monitor areas and prostitutes to determine whether police are in the location and/or operating undercover. They obey traffic laws to decrease their visibility and take steps to protect themselves from victimization by the prostitute. By sharing their experiences on line, johns provide advice to other potential clients and make the task of law enforcement more difficult. The police could monitor such websites and turn the tables on johns.[116]

San Francisco's first offender prostitution program (FOPP) educated johns about the risk of soliciting prostitutes. An evaluation of FOPP found that the annual 1-year recidivism rate for arrested johns fell from 8.8 percent to 4.5 percent after the program operated. The reduction in recidivism was immediate and was sustained for the subsequent decade.[117]

Conclusion

Public order crimes present the criminologist with several interesting issues. Prostitution and gambling are mostly voluntary transactions between adults. The participants not only do not complain to the police, many times they also perceive their activities to be equivalent to legal pursuits. Some citizens ask: "Why is it a good thing to buy a state lottery ticket but a crime to place a bet in a numbers game?" or "Why can I drink alcohol and get drunk but get arrested for doing essentially the same thing with a marijuana joint?" Outlawing these activities does not eliminate the demand for them and organized crime is inevitably associated with the resulting illegal markets. Granted, there are serious social and personal harms associated with public order crimes—but how far should society go in using the criminal law to protect people from themselves?

The moral perspective brings attention to the social stigma that is often attached to public order offenses and the harm caused by them. Thus, the moral entrepreneurs pressure lawmakers and the law enforcement system to "do something" about public order offenses. They also stress that these crimes represent threats to the broader public—that prostitution spreads sexually transmitted diseases and gambling leads to compulsive behavior that can harm families. The law and order perspective stresses the ties between public order offenses and their tendency to be associated with other, often more serious, criminal activity. Perhaps the answer lies in the continued scientific and empirical study of the exact role and influence of public order offenses.

WRAP-UP

CHAPTER SPOTLIGHT

- The term *public order crimes* refers to a diverse collection of offenses. Considered to be less serious than major index crimes, they still can have important effects on public health and safety, the economy, and public perception about the quality of life in a neighborhood or community.
- Many consider public order crimes to be "victimless" because they affect only the perpetrator. The absence of a complaining victim causes some people to question whether it is appropriate to label activities such as gambling and prostitution as crimes.
- Public order offenses strain the relationship between law and morality more than other kinds of crimes. Here, the aim of enforcement is societal protection and crime prevention, but it is often difficult to establish and maintain a clear focus on these goals.
- Two basic perspectives can be used to classify public order crimes: the morality perspective and the law and order perspective. The morality perspective seeks to use criminal law to impose minimum standards of morality on citizens. The law and order perspective views the enforcement of these laws as a way to maintain peace and order in the community.
- A central question associated with crimes such as gambling and prostitution is how far society should go in using the criminal law to protect people from themselves.

PUTTING IT ALL TOGETHER

1. Why do public order crimes generate such a controversy? Do moral entrepreneurs reflect the attitudes of most Americans?
2. How can public order offenses be characterized as "victimless crimes"? Do you agree or disagree with this concept? Why or why not?
3. Morris and Hawkins decry the "overreach of the criminal law" regarding the enforcement of public order offenses. Do you agree or disagree with their position? Why or why not?
4. Construct a debate between a moral entrepreneur and a law and order advocate on the issue: "Do casinos contribute to crime?"
5. What are the public costs of prostitution?
6. Which perspective on prostitution do you find more persuasive: exploitation or sex work?

consensus Widespread agreement in society that laws against crimes such as murder should be strictly enforced.

legitimacy of the law The belief in the rightness of and public support for a law.

overreach of the criminal law Norval Morris and Gordon Hawkins contend that the attempt to govern public order offenses like prostitution causes a number of secondary problems that aggravate the crime problem.

victimless crimes Crimes that affect only the person committing them. Because of the absence of a complaining victim, some people question whether it is appropriate to label activities such as gambling and prostitution as crimes.

CHAPTER 13

Terrorism

George Richards
Edinboro University

Objectives

Introduction

This chapter summarizes terrorism and describes certain terrorist groups in the United States and abroad. Although concern about terrorist activities has influenced American public policy since the 1960s, the events of September 11, 2001 (9/11), caused both public servants and private citizens to take the concept of security in the United States more seriously. Things change, but sometimes becoming accustomed to the change and the consequences of that change are difficult.

For much of our history, the United States enjoyed the benefits of geographic security. Bounded to the east by the Atlantic Ocean, to the west by the Pacific, and to the north and south by friendly and non-threatening neighbors, having enemies in close proximity was something with which America did not overly concern itself. Yet technological advances in both travel and communication proved these natural defenses could be overcome. Our notions of protection were dashed by the Cold War arms race, in which both sides rushed to build intercontinental ballistic missiles that could reach across the globe to destroy the enemy.

Sometimes when our focus is centered on a difficult, if not overwhelming challenge, things that should get our attention or cause us concern go unnoticed. It would be grossly unfair to say that American policymakers and public servants realized that small and determined groups could pose a serious threat to national security, and that they did not take these threats seriously. They did. However, national security strategies from the late 1940s to the early 1970s focused primarily on the "Communist menace," not on terrorist cells.

It may be said that 9/11 served many purposes. If so, one of the most important, if not the most important, is that it woke the American people from the peaceful slumber they fell into during the wake of the Cold War's end and alerted them to the very real danger that we had another enemy. Unlike the Soviet Union, this enemy was not defined by boundaries and ideologies alone. The enemy was a form of warfare—terrorism. In the wake of 9/11, the United States declared a "War on Terror." In doing so, we are fighting a means of war. While some terrorist enemies, such as **Al Qaeda**, Hezbollah, and the Islamic State in Iraq and Syria (ISIS) remain static, others enter and leave the fray when their issues have been resolved or their resources diminish.

For people of my generation, there was a certain, unspoken fatality regarding the relationship between the United States and the Soviet Union. At some point in time, a mad man would press a button and nuclear holocaust would be unleashed upon the Earth. This fatalism was instilled early. While most of you who read this never had to do the "drop, duck, and cover" exercise under your elementary school desks, my classmates and I did. This was to protect us from the blinding flash associated with a nuclear explosion. Hiding under our desks would also protect us from falling rubble. Nothing was said about fallout and radiation sickness. We were young and knew nothing beyond what our parents and teachers told us—or the reality they hid from us.

A similar fatalism now exists among younger Americans regarding terrorism. It is also viewed as inevitable. Yet there is a subtle difference between the fatalism attached to terrorism and the fatalism derived from Cold War fears. The Cold War ended on a more peaceful note than many predicted, whereas there is no conceivable end for terrorism. For some, it is believed to be the only viable means of combating a political or social situation that has become intolerable. One aspect of the human condition that has always been with us is that regardless of the society in which you might find yourself, there will always be those who are, or believe they are, marginalized.

Terrorism Defined

A cursory examination of the literature pertaining to terrorists and terrorism will reveal many definitions of what terrorism is and what it entails. Much of the difference in opinion on what constitutes terrorism depends on the experience and orientation of the writer. Groups that perpetrate terrorist acts while not viewing their mission as one of terror further convolute a workable definition. Thus, terrorism is pejorative. A negative connotation is attached to its use and to those who use it. As Jenkins stated, "What is called terrorism thus seems to depend on one's point of view. Use of the term implies a moral judgment; and if one party can successfully attach the label terrorist to his opponent, then it has indirectly persuaded others to adopt its moral viewpoint."[1]

Hoffman maintained that how terrorism is viewed depends on how one views the victims or perpetrators of terrorist violence.[2] If they are sympathetic to the harm the victim has suffered, they view the act as terrorism. If they understand the rationale behind the act and see it as necessary, the act is not terrorism, but a form of political or social protest. An example of how the labeling of terrorism depends upon one's worldview is the kidnapping and murder of 11 Israeli athletes at the 1972 Munich Olympics. The group responsible for this was Black September, which had ties to Yasser Arafat's Fatah organization.

The Secretary-General of the United Nations (UN) Kurt Waldheim was quick to condemn this act. It was his opinion that the UN should not stand idly by, but take immediate, proactive measures to prevent this violence from occurring in the future. Although a majority of member states concurred with Waldheim, opportunities to discuss this were curbed by representatives from some Arab, African, and Asian countries. Their argument was that violence, even against unarmed noncombatants, was justified when people struggle to rid themselves of colonial control and influence.[3]

Also further confusing what constitutes terrorism is the labeling of acts heretofore seen as only criminal with the added sobriquet of terror. The Federal Bureau of Investigation (FBI) includes John Allen Muhammad and Lee Boyd Malvo, otherwise known as the Beltway Snipers, as terrorists.[4] During October 2002, Muhammad and Malvo shot and killed 10 people and wounded 3 in the greater Washington, DC, area over a 3-week period. While in prison, Malvo wrote of being on a *jihad* against the United States. If Malvo's statement accurately reflected his and Muhammad's motivation, it would change the cumulative nature of their perpetration of serial murder to that of terrorism.

An encompassing and proper definition of terrorism continues to elude both practitioners and researchers. According to Herschinger, for nearly 40 years, the United Nations has sought to define terrorism.[5] She credits governments that have varying national interests and cites their subsequent improbability of ever reaching any sense of unanimity regarding what makes up terrorism. The fluid nature of terrorism and the changing perspectives on what comprises it also resist the encapsulation of defining this phenomenon.

For the purposes of this chapter, this definition of terrorism will serve as the ideological vehicle for our discussion: **Terrorism** is the use or implied use of force, violence, and/or coercion to influence the political, social, and/or religious attitudes and behaviors of individuals or groups in a desired manner.

Why Terrorism?

William Shakespeare's' pastoral comedy *As You Like It* contains one of the playwright's best-known monologues:

> *All the world's a stage*
> *And all the men and women merely players;*
> *They have their exits and their entrances,*
> *And one man in his time plays many parts* (As You Like It, *Act II, Scene VII*).

Consistent with Shakespeare's notion we are all, to some extent, players on a stage is the contention that terrorism is a communicative device, and not merely a criminal act. Jenkins held terrorism was theater. Each act and part is staged to draw the most attention to the overall production. For any stage performance to be successful, there are two essential elements: the company and the audience. Terrorists need an audience. They need people to listen, watch, and comment on the acts they are witnessing. Similar to how a seasoned actor may move an audience's emotions through his or her performance, terrorists can influence the attitudes and behaviors of a populace through their message of violence.

To say that Americans are addicted to television and the

> **For any stage performance to be successful, there are two essential elements: the company and the audience. Terrorists need an audience.**

Internet would be to oversimplify the issue regarding factual depictions of terrorism. However, the dependence we have on media is significant. The notion that without an audience to view their actions, terrorist-like behavior would not be as significant is correct. On August 19, 2014, the Islamic State in Iraq and Syria (ISIS) beheaded American hostage James Foley. The journalist had been held captive in the Middle East since 2012. The video, titled "A Message to America," of his murder was uploaded to YouTube. It was quickly taken down, but continues to show up on various Internet sites. That Foley had been kidnapped was common knowledge, but it was not until his beheading was broadcast internationally that ISIS became a household name in the United States.

The motivations of terrorist groups will dictate their *modus operandi*. A terrorist organization or cell that has a political or secular agenda is more apt to perpetrate selective, surgical strikes with a high probability of media attention, but relatively low levels of civilian casualties. The rationale behind this is to avoid a backlash of opinion. This also shows that controlled, targeted violence is the work of a rational organization, and not a group purely motivated by raw emotion. Earth First!, an organization aimed at reducing the impact of humans on the environment, has hampered logging operations through tree sitting and further sabotaged lumber production through tree spiking. Their actions, though limited and generally nonviolent, have garnered them considerable media attention.

For religiously motivated terrorist groups, loss of life is of little consequence. Those labeled as nonbelievers deserve death, and all who do not share similar beliefs are the enemy. Causing their deaths is a moral duty. When sympathizers are harmed through a religiously inspired act of terror, the perpetrator's rationale is that their reward awaits them in Paradise.

The choice of target reflects the belief systems of terrorists. Institutions representing authority are preferred for those in secular terror groups: government offices, military installations, and corporate facilities. The individuals chosen for reprisals by these groups are those with particular importance to the political and economic structure they are seeking to disrupt. An example of this would be the 1946 bombing of the King David Hotel in Jerusalem. The attack was carried out by the Irgun, a pro-Zionist underground organization. Zionism can be roughly defined as advocating a Jewish state in Palestine. In this bombing, 91 people were killed and 46 were wounded.

On August 27, 1979, Louis Mountbatten, the 1st Earl Mountbatten of Burma, was killed off the coast of Ireland while on a fishing holiday. Lord Mountbatten, a former First Sea Lord and the last Viceroy of India, was selected as a target by the Provisional Irish Republican Army

The burning of the Two Elks Mountain Resort in Vail, Colorado. An environmental group took responsibility for this act, indicating that it was protesting the growth of the resort town. How should such an act of terrorism be classified?

© Mark Mobley/AP Photos

(IRA) because of his celebrity and his close relationship with the British royal family. The night before Mountbatten was scheduled to depart, an IRA operative slipped aboard the boat and planted a radio-controlled bomb. After the boat left the harbor, the bomb was remotely detonated by an IRA operative. Mountbatten, who was 79 years of age, was thrown in the water by the explosion where he quickly succumbed to his wounds and drowned.

Terror groups motivated by religion target similar types of institutions and individuals. However, there is a tendency among these groups to create greater physical devastation. The attacks of 9/11 by Al Qaeda operatives living in the United States are representative of this brand of targeting. On the morning of September 11, two airliners, American Airlines Flight 11 and United Airlines Flight 175, were hijacked and deliberately crashed into the north and south towers respectively of the World Trade Center. A short time after the World Trade Center was attacked, American Airlines Flight 77 was purposely flown into the Pentagon. A fourth plane, United Airlines Flight 93, was intended to target the U.S. Capitol building; however, heroic action on the part of the

passengers and crew prevented this attack. In the struggle to retake the plane, Flight 93 crashed in a rural field in southwestern Pennsylvania. The Pentagon and the U.S. Capitol building remain identifiable symbols of American political culture and military might. The World Trade Center was a symbol of American economic strength and was viewed by some as a testament to the capitalistic ethic.

This was not the first attack on the World Trade Center by a terrorist organization. On February 26, 1993, a Pakastani named Ramzi Yousef helped to mastermind a car bombing in the underground parking garage in Tower One. The goal was to collapse the tower and bring down the other one. Their plan failed, but still resulted in 6 deaths and 1,042 injured.

Holidays and significant dates also hold particular importance. The anniversary of a particular event or a religious holiday can serve to inspire a terror strike. **Timothy McVeigh**, a U.S. Army veteran and security officer, detonated a truck bomb in front of the Murrah Federal Building in Oklahoma City, Oklahoma, on April 19, 1995. Until the 9/11 attacks, this was the most devastating act of terrorism perpetrated on American soil. One hundred sixty-eight people died because of the ensuing blast. McVeigh's rationale for selecting the date of April 19 was inspired by the FBI's raid on the Branch Davidian compound near Waco, Texas, exactly 2 years prior to the Oklahoma City bombing. During the fire that broke out during the raid, 76 Branch Davidians were killed. McVeigh later claimed he was acting in retaliation for atrocities committed by the federal government at Ruby Ridge, Idaho, and at the Branch Davidian compound.[5]

Stuart Wright, a professor of sociology at Lamar University, has written that the attack on the Branch Davidian compound justified the existence and ideology of extremist, right wing groups. The response of federal agencies, particularly the ATF and FBI, was viewed as sign of government overreach. The preference of federal operatives for militaristic solutions to the standoff undermined possible negotiations and fostered sympathy for Koresh and his followers.

A common belief among terrorist groups is that change for what they perceive as better, whether it is political, social, or religious change, cannot occur unless accompanied by violence. Violence in this context is viewed as essential to bringing about a new order. This is referred to as *millenarianism*. In Christian eschatology, it is held that the second coming of Jesus Christ will serve as a prelude to the establishment of a Kingdom of God. This kingdom will last 1,000 years.[6] Many faith-based groups maintain that current forms of governments are corrupt or wrong. Regardless, they believe the illicit leaders of these governments will be brought down and subjected to judgment. It is common among these groups to believe that a conspiracy or conspiracies is controlling events and people at the helm of governments and large corporations. What is essential to remember is that belief systems that use views like millenarianism may justify both the expectation and use of violence. It is also important to remember that because of belief systems such as these, policymakers cannot afford to view these people as criminals whose motivations are materialistic and selfish. Their actions are not self-serving, but instead are motivated by what they believe to be a higher, nobler purpose.

> **Cells rarely have the resources to inflict sufficient damage to an enemy over long periods of time, whereas larger terror-oriented groups do have this capability.**

🧩 Organization and Support

Unlike a law enforcement officer or a soldier, terrorists often have considerable freedom to orchestrate and carry out a mission. There is a hierarchical chain of command in which a single leader or council dictates policy. However, due to the fluid nature of terrorism, it is common for terrorists to operate in small groups known as *cells*. Small bands are harder to penetrate by outsiders due to the intimate nature of the group and the people involved in them. The overall strategy and general goals of the organization are decided on by the leadership. The tactics of carrying out the organization's mission are left to those who perpetrate these acts. The cell structure was used effectively by the IRA in their struggle against the British occupation of northern Ireland. It was understood that cells operated in spontaneous and autonomous fashion by carrying out acts of violence and sabotage against government agents and/or military forces.

Patriot and militia organizations prevalent in the United States during the 1990s were organized around cell structures. Cooperation and coordination among patriot and militia cells for training and for sharing equipment and intelligence was common. Yet, it was understood each cell was autonomous and self-governing. The rationale for cell organization was articulated in Louis Beam's essay "**Leaderless Resistance**."[7] Beam held that a pyramidal structure would leave the chain of command open to identification and capture. Small cells operating independently of each other, but with similar goals, would stymie the efforts of an illegitimate power structure. However, cells would not be absolutely unknown to each other.

An examination of the historical record pertaining to terrorism will reveal cells have been the predominant form of terror organization. Yet the recent growth and influence of groups such as Al Qaeda, al Jihad, and Hamas has shown that although cells are necessary at the micro-level, decision making and coordination at the macro-level ensures the sustained influence of the organization. Cells rarely have the resources to inflict sufficient damage to an enemy over long periods of time, whereas larger terror-oriented groups do have this capability. A consistent, orchestrated terror campaign can influence government policies. This has been demonstrated by the machinations of ISIS in their current campaigns in Iraq and Syria. ISIS fighters are outnumbered in their own ranks by support personnel brought in for logistical support. ISIS, which is dependent on the revenue from selling oil on the black market, has publicly stated that they need qualified technical personnel to assist them in managing newly acquired assets.

Terror campaigns are not limited to being carried out by private individuals and small groups on the fringes of society. *State terrorism* is terrorism against perceived enemies of the state by government agents or quasi-government agents. The arenas in which state terrorism may be implemented are either internal, in which domestic enemies are selected for persecution, or external, against perceived foreign dangers to the state. Defining state terrorism is nearly as elusive as defining terrorism itself. However, one need only look to the historical record to see examples of where a state acts as perpetrator against its citizens. Shortly after the French Monarchy fell in 1793, a revolutionary dictatorship was established that sought to cement its power through the persecution and execution of anyone deemed an enemy to the new regime. Known as the *Reign of Terror*, its most common implement of death was the guillotine.

The persecution of German and European Jews during World War II began shortly after the Nazi party assumed power in Germany in 1933. The restriction of Jews from holding professional office, the implementation of racial purity laws, and the organized boycotting of Jewish businesses and services were precursors to significantly more violent government policies such as *Kristallnacht* (the night of the broken glass) and eventually the mass extermination of Jews living in Nazi-occupied Europe. Many German Jews had sought to migrate when it became obvious that anti-Semitism was no longer limited to the private sector, but was instead an actual government policy supported by policymakers and implemented by the bureaucracy. Jewish immigration to the United States was prohibited by policies of the U.S. Department of State, in particular the machinations of an assistant secretary of state, Breckinridge Long. Long warned consuls in European countries that Jews were trying to flee and advocated that they place every possible obstacle in their way for obtaining visas. Only 10 percent of visas applied for were granted by the United States. It is believed that if all visas requested by European Jews to the United States were granted that an additional 190,000 people could have been saved from Nazi atrocities.

Efforts by European Jews to migrate to British-occupied Palestine also were restricted by British policies prohibiting immigration. Jewish paramilitary groups operating in Palestine at the time, notably the *Irgun*, began a campaign of subversion and terror targeting British troops and installations. The headquarters of the British Army in Palestine was the King David Hotel in Jerusalem. On July 22, 1946, agents of the Irgun bombed the King David Hotel. The explosion resulted in 91 people killed and nearly 50 wounded. This led to a decrease in British military morale and a lack of public support among British citizens for the occupation of Palestine.[8]

Support for terrorist operations can come from a variety of sources. Nations may provide training sites for terror groups. Bulgaria, Cuba, Lebanon, Libya, North Korea, and Syria[9] are among those countries that have provided safe havens for terrorists to train. The means by which some nations sponsored terror operations changed dramatically after the breakup of the Soviet Union. Cuba still offers groups such as the *Euskadi Ta Askatasuna*, better known as the ETA, secure places to train. Through violence and intimidation, the ETA has sought a separate Basque homeland and has long been the recipient of Cuban hospitality. When Cuba enjoyed the sponsorship of the Soviet Union, it could offer financial support to terror groups in addition to providing a locale in which to sharpen their paramilitary skills.[10]

There are four countries identified by the U.S. State Department as sponsors of terrorism: Cuba, Iran, Sudan, and Syria. Besides the previously mentioned Cuba, Iran has been an active supporter of terrorist groups such as Hamas, Lebanese Hezbollah, and the Taliban fighting in Afghanistan. Iran's Islamic Revolutionary Guard Corps (IRGC) elite branch known as the *Qods Force* is the predominant means by which Iran identifies and supports terrorist activities. In addition to financial support and training, Iran also supplies groups such as the Taliban with small arms and other forms of weaponry. Among the munitions supplied by Iran are rocket-propelled grenades, mortar rounds, and plastic explosives.

Iran has long been on the U.S. Department of State's list of terrorist sponsors. Al Qaeda terrorists in Iran fostered the Riyadh compound bombing in 2003 with Iranian government complicity. A group with reputed ties to Iran, the Iranian Revolutionary Guards, was credited with bombing an Israeli embassy worker in New Delhi. No one was killed in this attack, but several were wounded. Kenyan officials have also been engaged in counterterrorism actions against Iranian-sponsored terrorists. In 2012, two Iranians were arrested on suspicion of planning to bomb U.S., British, Israeli, and Saudi targets in Kenya.

Sudan remains on the U.S. Department of State's list of terrorist sponsors. However, the U.S. government has recently credited the Sudanese government with increased cooperation with American efforts regarding counterterrorism. Even so, Hamas, Palestine Islamic Jihad (PIJ), and Al Qaeda continue to operate within certain Sudanese areas with impunity. Syria, noted as a state sponsor of terror since 1979, continues to provide support to terrorist organizations such as Hezbollah, Hamas, and the Popular Front for the Liberation of Palestine (PFLP). Of particular concern is Syria's largely cash-oriented economy and the opportunities this economic climate offers for money laundering, smuggling, and munitions purchases on the black market.[11] While it may seem unwieldy from a Western economic perspective to manage large amounts of cash, this arrangement works efficiently. Known as the *Hawala*, it is an informal banking network responsible for the transferring of funds on a global scale.

Terrorist organizations and interests that support them are innovative in funding their operations. Operating legitimate businesses, soliciting charitable donations, and creating charities are some avenues used to increase financial holdings. Charities are difficult to investigate. The true purpose of the organization may not be stated. Recipients of the charity's generosity may serve in a "straw man" capacity and funnel money on to a third-party terrorist group. In 1992, the Benevolence International Foundation (BIF) was established as a tax-exempt, not-for-profit charitable entity in the state of Illinois. The mission of the BIF was to conduct humanitarian relief operations globally. BIF operations were conducted in Bosnia, China, Pakistan, and Russia. It was later found that the chief executive officer of the BIF, Enaam Amaout, had close ties to Osama bin Laden and was operating the BIF as a racketeering operation to give aid and support to Al Qaeda.[12]

While some terrorist groups depend largely on the largesse of countries that share similar political, social, or religious ideologies and others operate legitimate businesses to support themselves, some terrorist operations have demonstrated a willingness to support themselves financially through a variety of illegitimate enterprises. Among the types of crimes that terrorists have used to support their activities are:

- Burglary
- Document fraud
- Embezzlement
- Extortion
- Identity theft
- Money laundering
- Political corruption
- Protection
- Robbery
- Smuggling
- Trade in illegal arms[13]

The opportunities for terrorist groups to generate income by smuggling are significant. Arms, drugs, diamonds, and cigarettes are among the most highly prized items to smuggle. These items are easily hidden during transport due to their size. Cigarette smuggling is particularly appealing to terrorist groups such as Hezbollah, Hamas, Al Qaeda, and the IRA. A Hezbollah cell operating in Charlotte, North Carolina transported cigarettes illegally to Michigan for resale. North Carolina has a low tobacco tax rate. Cigarettes could be purchased there and resold in Michigan, which has a higher tax rate on tobacco products. Traditionally, contraband items such as cigarettes were sold out of the trunks of cars and with the help of complicit retail outlets. This cell was able to fund the purchase of legitimate businesses in Michigan to serve as fronts to resell illicit cigarettes.[14]

The avenues that criminal enterprises offer terror organizations for funding their operations are significant. Of particular concern to transnational law enforcement efforts is the burgeoning field known as *narco-terrorism*. Peruvian President Belaunde Terry coined the term narco-terrorism in 1983 when he was asked to describe attacks on Peruvian police by drug traffickers. These attacks used terrorist strategies and tactics. Terry and Peruvian law enforcement officials believed the *Shining Path*, a Maoist-influenced rebel group, was cooperating with regional cocaine producers.

Davids stated that U.S. efforts to influence the Peruvian government to reduce cocaine trafficking was inadvertently responsible for fomenting the relationship between the Shining Path and cocaine producers. Efforts by Peruvian officials to eradicate coca-growing operations were viewed by the peasantry as intrusive. What little income they earned came from coca production. The Shining Path was able to offer protection to local farmers from counter-narcotics operations. They were also able to offer local coca growers protection from the drug cartels. Prior to the Shining Path being involved in drug operations, when local growers did not meet their quota, they were executed by the drug cartels as both a punishment and as a warning to others. These practices stopped abruptly when the Shining Path inserted itself as protector of the local peasantry. They were also eventually able to offer security to Columbian drug traffickers in protecting private airstrips from Peruvian counter-narcotics raids.

The heavy-handed tactics of the Columbian drug cartels reached their zenith on November 6, 1985. Guerillas involved with the 19th of April Movement, a revolutionary Columbian socialist group, stormed the Columbian Palace of Justice in Bogota. Upon seizing the palace, the guerillas took over 250 hostages. Of the hostages, 95 were killed, including 11 of the 24 justices of the Columbian high court. For several months prior to this, Columbian justices had been receiving death threats and bribes concerning extradition of drug traffickers to the United States.[15]

Narco-terrorism has evolved from the emulation of terrorist tactics by criminal groups to influence policy. It is now viewed as an economic staple of terrorist groups. Peters maintains that involvement in the drug trade in Afghanistan

Osama Bin Laden, flanked by his top aide Ayman al-Zawarhi, broadcasts his praise for the September 11 attacks on the United States, vowing that America "will never dream of security" until "the infidel's armies leave the land of Muhammad." How would Al-Qaeda be classified under the definitions of terrorism provided in this chapter?

© Al Jazeera/AP Photos

has altered the perception of the Taliban and Al Qaeda from being terror groups, whose ideologies are fueled by fundamentalist religious dogma, to that of being organized crime syndicates that have religious overtones. According to Peters, illicit drug money is now responsible for roughly $500 million in annual income for both terrorist organizations.[16] It is crucial to note that while the Taliban is assumed to get much of its financing by dealing in drugs, Al Qaeda is not. Al Qaeda is funded primarily through the contributions of wealthy sympathizers.

With thousands killed at the hands of few terrorists, new names and groups emerged to become a part of the American lexicon. Osama bin Laden became a household name. Likewise, the Taliban and Al Qaeda were groups unknown to most Americans before 9/11. Now all three are known to most Americans and linked to murder, suffering, and terrorism.

> **Terror groups operating within the United States are usually labeled as either left wing or right wing.**

Osama bin Laden had been known to the intelligence community in the United States since at least 1980. The 17th of 52 children born to wealthy construction magnate father, bin Laden graduated from King Abdul Aziz University with a degree in civil engineering in 1979. After his limited involvement in the Iranian Revolution and the Soviet invasion of Afghanistan, he became involved in raising money, rebuilding roads, and compensating the families of dead soldiers. Operating in a limited role until the invasion of Kuwait in 1990, he became more visibly involved in anti-Western ventures only to be rejected by the royal family of Saudi Arabia. They rejected his citizenship in 1994 and confiscated some of his monies. Bin Laden then moved to Afghanistan and became involved with the Taliban and Al Qaeda. In 1996, he issued a Declaration of Jihad in which he called for U.S. troops to be withdrawn from the Arabian peninsula, the liberation of Muslim holy sites, and pledged support to Islamic revolutionary groups across the globe.

Based on a presumed link voiced by President George W. Bush in response to the 9/11 attacks, he was hunted by armed forces of the United States and other allies as a terrorist and threat to the safety of millions of people. He linked himself to Al Qaeda by adopting the mission to expel all "nonbelievers" from the Middle East. The group encourages all Muslims to fight the battle of terrorism against all who fail to live according to their extremist interpretation of Islamic ideals. As bin Laden said on many occasions, there is no distinction made between those who wear the uniform of an "infidel" and those who do not. This coincides with the terrorist's belief that there are no innocents. Through *fatwas* (rulings on Islamic law), bin Laden stated that U.S. troops on the Arabian peninsula were to be attacked.

On May 2, 2011, approximately 25 U.S. Navy Seals breached a compound in Abbottabad, Pakistan, where bin Laden was in hiding. After a 40-minute firefight, bin Laden's death was confirmed by one of his wives. He was buried at sea in a service that adhered to Islamic law.

Domestic Terror Groups

While concern over the threats posed by international terror groups became all too real in the wake of 9/11, attention to domestic terrorist groups waned. However, there is a tradition of people banding together and arming themselves against what they view as societal inequities or unjust governmental interference. Terror groups operating within the United States are usually labeled as either left wing or right wing. Like the term *terrorism*, which was inspired by the Reign of Terror, the expressions of left and right on the political spectrum were also inspired by events that occurred during the French Revolution. After the revolution, the political orientation of members of the French Chamber of Deputies could be identified by where they sat in the legislative chamber. If one sat on the left side of the chamber, they favored change and supported the ideals of the revolution. If a member sat on the right side, they were more apt to be cautious regarding change and favored the status quo. Today, a left wing or leftist political agenda is looked upon as one that seeks political and/or social change with a view toward the creation of a more egalitarian society.

During the 1960s, America struggled with its political and social identification. Civil rights and the Vietnam War served as ideological vehicles through which people and organizations that wanted change and those who wanted to preserve the status quo argued the merits of their positions. Although the debates could become vituperative, violence was used by the extremists in the groups, not the core membership. Those who viewed violence as a legitimate response to the political subjugation of society by the "Establishment" were often influenced by Marxist ideals and ". . . championed contemporary revolutionaries and movements, such as the Cuban, Palestinian, and Vietnamese revolutionaries."[17] Two leftist groups that used violence to promote their messages were the Weathermen and the Symbionese Liberation Army.

The Weathermen was formed in 1969 when the Students for a Democratic Society (SDS) organization splintered. Sometimes referred to as the Crazies, the Weathermen's membership consisted of young, well-educated students from middle-class backgrounds. The nature of the group was violent from the beginning. In October 1969, shortly after the group was created, the Weathermen distributed leaflets in Chicago announcing their Days of Rage initiative. For 4 days, the Weathermen committed acts of vandalism and had continual run-ins with Chicago police. By 1975, the Weathermen (then known as the Weather Underground Organization [WUO]) had perpetrated over 40 bombings and members were assimilated back into society through a process they referred to as inversion.[18,19]

The Symbionese Liberation Army (SLA) was also the subject of notoriety during the 1970s. Founded in Berkeley, California, by escaped thief Donald DeFreeze and Mimzoon Soltysik, the SLA quickly gained a reputation for violence. In November 1973, the group murdered Marcus Foster, the superintendent of the Oakland school district, using cyanide-coated bullets. One of the SLA members, Emily Harris, worked in the registrar's office at the University of California Berkeley. Her position allowed her access to the personal information of members of the student body. Harris' attention and that of the SLA focused on an heiress to the Hearst newspaper fortune, student Patricia Hearst.[20]

On February 4, 1974, the SLA kidnapped Hearst from her apartment near campus. For the next several weeks, they made demands on the Hearst family for ransom and free food for the poor. By April of 1974, attitudes regarding the kidnapping of Hearst changed when security camera footage of a California bank that the SLA robbed was released that showed Patricia Hearst fully participating in the robbery. The film showed Hearst brandishing an automatic weapon at bank patrons. She adopted the name "Tania" to honor the paramour of Che Guevara. In May, DeFreeze and other members of the SLA were killed in a shootout with Los Angeles police. Hearst was arrested shortly after and was convicted of robbery and firearms charges. President Jimmy Carter commuted her sentence in 1979.[21]

The 1960s were a time of significant social and political upheaval in the United States. The discussion of political ideas and compromise between political opponents was hamstrung and stretched due to the unwillingness of participants to listen to other parties. Historian Richard Hofstadter wrote an article for *Harper's Magazine* in November 1964 in which he maintained that the arena of American political discussion was becoming home to "uncommonly angry minds." His article, "The Paranoid Style in American Politics," described what he referred to as the "political paranoid." While not all paranoid causes were harmful to a democratic state, Hofstadter held they were usually associated with "bad causes." The 11 points of the paranoid in American politics has been frequently used to describe both left and right wing extremists groups in the United States.

Similar to the efforts of left wing extremists to force political and societal change through aggression and bloodshed, right wing extremists use violence to maintain what they believe to be order and control. Some of these groups use Christian dogma to justify their actions. Christian Identity churches and affiliated groups have a Eurocentric view of Christianity with some individual churches maintaining that non-Caucasian peoples have no souls. There is no strict denomination of Christian Identity churches. Instead, these places of worship form loose alliances with other churches that believe as they do. Salvation, according to Christian Identity adherents depends upon redemption and race. Christian Identity is closely tied to British Israelism that dictates that many Caucasian Europeans are descendants of the 10 tribes of Israel that were taken into captivity by the armies of Assyria.

This dogma is central to the plot of *The Turner Diaries* by William Pierce (published under the pseudonym Andrew McDonald). In this book, a futuristic America is caught in a race war between Caucasians, African Americans, and Jews. Enjoying a marginal reading prior to the Murrah Federal Building bombing, *The Turner Diaries* enjoyed a resurgence in popularity once it was found that Timothy McVeigh was inspired by a similar incident in the book in which the FBI headquarters was destroyed in a similar manner.[22]

Other groups, which were identified as both right wing and possibly terroristic, were part of the **patriot and militia movement**. The patriot and militia movement enjoyed the height of its popularity during the 1990s. The membership of these groups was made up of disenfranchised Caucasians who were fearful of government intervention in areas of professional and personal life they considered their own domain. A cornerstone of their concern was gun control legislation spawned by the passage of the 1993 Brady Bill. Patriot and militia members use a literal interpretation of the Second Amendment to the U.S. Constitution. Other factors that contributed to the growth of these groups were the ongoing economic ramifications of the Farm Crisis and expansion of the Rust Belt. Of concern to the general public was the training in which these groups engaged. Dressed in camouflage and armed with a variety of weapons, these cells trained in a paramilitary fashion.

Taking advantage of highly publicized incidents such as the Ruby Ridge standoff and the deaths of the Branch Davidians at Mount Carmel, patriot and militia adherents used these events to paint the federal government as increasingly tyrannical. After McVeigh was found to have been involved with the Michigan Militia, the movement lost active followers. Some believed this would be the death knell for the movement. That was not the case. Although membership dropped and lead to the dissolution of some groups, those that remained under the specter of harsh public scrutiny provided a core group of true believers.

Two things led to the demise of the patriot and militia movement. The first was the lack of central leadership and focus. Several individuals were identified as leaders and spokespersons for the group. These were James "Bo" Gritz, John Trochmann, and James Johnson. Gritz, a former U.S. Army Green Beret Lieutenant Colonel, helped to get Randy Weaver to surrender to federal authorities and acted, unsuccessfully, as a mediator between the Montana Freemen and federal authorities. He was also a Populist Party candidate for President of the United States in 1992 campaigning on the slogan of "God, Guns, and Gritz." John Trochmann, a U.S. Navy veteran, formed the Militia of Montana with his brother David. The Militia of Montana was active in maintaining a website promoting patriot ideology. Trochmann also traveled extensively, speaking about his concerns about the growth of federal power and loss of individual freedoms. James Johnson, the head of the now-defunct Ohio Unorganized Militia,

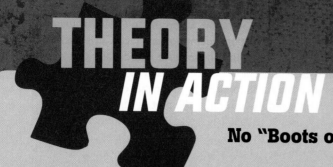

THEORY IN ACTION

No "Boots on the Ground"

On September 17, 2014, President Obama promised an audience at McDill Air Force Base in Tampa, Florida, that the United States would not be drawn into a ground war in Iraq against the forces of the Islamic State in Iraq and Syria (ISIS). Instead, the president has depended on using air strikes against ISIS targets in Iraq and Syria and building a coalition of nations willing to assist in the destruction of ISIS as a credible threat to western security.

Do you think air strikes alone will sway the determination of ISIS to seize power in this area of the world or do you believe the United States will have to send additional troops to the Middle East to combat ISIS?

Do you think it is feasible that ISIS might perpetrate an attack on American soil?

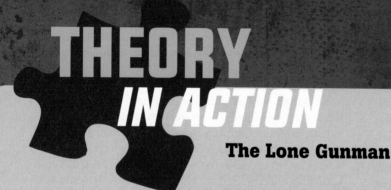

THEORY IN ACTION

The Lone Gunman

A group that has regular meetings, contact information, and a website is easy to follow, and therefore, easy to investigate. Cells and individuals operating in secrecy are not. Using Beam's model of "Leaderless Resistance" as your guide, discuss how you would create strategies to investigate these groups. How do you determine who is a threat when the threat wishes to remain anonymous and underground until they strike?

You may want to read more about how Timothy McVeigh and Terry Nichols planned the Oklahoma City bombing for more insight into how people operating as individuals strategize and execute their plans.

Sources: Beam, L. (1992, February). Leaderless resistance. Retrieved from http://www.louisbeam.com/leaderless.htm; Michel, L., & Herbeck, D. (2001). *American terrorist: Timothy McVeigh and the Oklahoma City bombing*. New York: ReganBooks.

was unique among the movement's leadership. Johnson is an African American. In 1995, he accompanied Trochmann to testify before the U.S. Senate Subcommittee on Terrorism, Technology, and Government Information. Other than Trochmann's and Johnson's cooperation before the Senate hearing, cooperation between militia and patriot leadership was rare. Criticism of other leaders of patriot and militia groups was commonplace at public events. One problem the movement faced was the lack of a cohesive, centralized leadership structure to guide the movement nationally.

The second factor was Y2K. Beginning in 1998, public concern grew out of the possibility that computers and global computer networks would cease to operate beginning on January 1, 2001, at 12:00 a.m. Many computers were only programmed with a 2-digit year and thus could not differentiate between 1980 and 2080. Thus, when the millennium arrived, the operating systems of computers could not read their programming. With the increased dependence on computers, this was seen by some as being a catastrophic event that would lead to a breakdown of both government and society.

Patriot and militia leadership called for supporters to be prepared for the coming crisis. "Preparedness expos" were held throughout the United States where attendees could be trained how to survive off the land. There were also vendors there who hawked items such as emergency generators, food dehydrators, and bulk quantities of food. When Y2K proved to be much ado about nothing, many who were stuck with unneeded generators and rotting food lost faith in the movement and its leadership.

 ## Responses to Terrorism

Responsible policymakers realize that terrorism will continue to be a part of the global political reality. Responses to terrorism from a law enforcement perspective may include SWAT teams, hostage negotiation squads, a perceived hardening of the judiciary system's attitude toward terrorism, and increased security at airports, train stations, and public facilities.

No intelligence organization and no one country, whatever its resources, can combat terrorism alone. The chief of the Security Specialties Division of the Federal Law Enforcement Training Center in Glynco, Georgia, has called for greater cooperation among global powers to fight terrorism around the world. Overall, the United States, despite being the target of more than 100 acts of terrorism, has been successful in this ongoing battle. There are several reasons for this success. Our intelligence apparatus has been upgraded since 9/11. There has been a growth in human intelligence (HUMINT) gathering and increased cooperation among federal and state agencies. This success can also be partially attributed to courses offered across the country for law enforcement personnel. With an increased awareness of the threat posed by terrorists, law enforcement in America is serious about the problem.[23]

One important strategy used by the United States is the Antiterrorism Assistance Program within the U.S. Department of State. Since 1983, more than 70 countries and 11,000 international government officials have taken part in this program. The Antiterrorism Assistance Program focuses on three objectives:

1. Enhancing the antiterrorism skills of participating countries
2. Strengthening the bilateral ties of the United States with friendly countries
3. Fostering an increased respect for human rights by sharing modern, humane, and effective antiterrorism techniques with international civil authorities

Perhaps through these and other similar efforts, inroads will be made against the real and present danger of domestic and international terrorism.[24]

Since 9/11, the U.S. government has taken an aggressive posture to fight terrorism. One controversial measure has been the USA Patriot Act, which enhances the U.S. government's powers in fighting terrorism. The act includes funding for counterterrorist activity and enhanced technical support, broadens the government's ability to collect electronic evidence, provides guidelines for detaining terrorists, and gives the FBI greater power to perform "warrantless" seizures when national security is in jeopardy. Proponents argue that it will strengthen our response to terrorism by giving the government the tools it needs. They maintain that the greater powers given to the government are necessary and worth the small infringement on American citizens' rights. Opponents argue that this act goes against our core civil and individual rights. They are most concerned with the government's power to monitor the lives of average American citizens, and debate and controversy still exist over the act. Time will tell whether its impact on the United States' fight against terrorism has been positive.

The Homeland Security Act of 2002 created the Department of Homeland Security (DHS) to protect the nation from terrorist attacks. The department is charged with coordinating the efforts of law enforcement agencies, especially at the federal level, to combat terrorism. Besides combating terrorism, DHS has also assumed the lead in managing natural disasters such as Hurricane Katrina.[25]

The necessity of communication and cooperation between federal, state, and local agencies cannot be overstated. With few exceptions, the first responder to a terrorist act will be a local law enforcement officer or other public safety official. It was an Oklahoma State Trooper who initially stopped Timothy McVeigh for driving without a license plate. McVeigh, along with Terry Nichols, perpetrated the 1995 bombing of the Murrah Federal Building in Oklahoma City. McVeigh admitted to the trooper that he was carrying a concealed weapon. McVeigh had a gun permit, but it was not legal in

> ### Responsible policymakers realize that terrorism will continue to be a part of the global political reality.

Oklahoma. He was arrested for driving without license plates and illegal firearms possession. Three days later, while in jail, he was identified as the bomber of the Murrah building.

While the local response to the attack on September 11, 2001, on the World Trade Center has been credited as largely a fire department response, over 2,000 New York City and Port Authority of New York and New Jersey police officers responded to the chaos in the wake of the collapse of the towers. The New York City Police Department (NYPD) lost 23 officers that day. The NYPD has made changes since then in order to address the phenomenon of terrorism in what is considered by some to be the world's most vibrant city.

Prior to 9/11, the NYPD had fewer than two dozen officers assigned to counterterrorism operations. Since 9/11, that number has grown to over a thousand. The NYPD now has offices in London, Tel Aviv, Singapore, and Abu Dhabi. They also oversee networks of informants who have connections to groups suspected of having terrorist ties and sympathies.

In the wake of the release of the 9/11 Commission Report, Congress mandated the creation of the Office for State and Local Law Enforcement (OSLLE) in 2007. The OSLLE seeks to coordinate activities between the Department of Homeland Security (DHS) and local, state, and tribal police departments. It also seeks to serve as the chief liaison between the DHS and nongovernmental organizations in counterterrorism.

Former DHS Secretary Janet Napolitano stated that "homeland security is hometown security." The necessity of committing to improved relations by federal agencies with local and state law enforcement was evident in this statement. Adequate homeland security begins at the community level. Prior to 9/11, information sharing was practically non-existent between agencies at any level of government. The tenets of federalism were not adhered to. Since 9/11 things have changed considerably regarding sharing information. Fusion centers have been established at the state and local levels to receive, analyze, and distribute information pertaining to terror threats.

More efforts are made at interagency cooperation in a meaningful manner. The FBI's Joint Terrorism Task Force (JTTF) has attempted to bring selected individuals from certain state and local agencies to their headquarters for counterterrorism training. Citizens have been encouraged to be more vigilant in their own communities regarding reporting suspicious behavior. Because of increased outreach efforts at all levels of law enforcement, relations with Muslim communities in the United States have improved. As state and local agencies struggle with budget demands, federal agencies have sought to provide equipment such as HazMat and biohazard suits in case of a weapon of mass destruction attack. In addition, the ability of agencies to communicate effectively during a disaster has improved through the sharing of radio channels. The Federal Emergency Management Agency (FEMA) has also created trainings regarding disaster preparedness for state and local departments.

WRAP-UP

CHAPTER SPOTLIGHT

Texture: © Malchev/Shutterstock; Police Tape: © SkillUp/Shutterstock

- Terrorism is the use or implied use of force, violence, and/or coercion to influence the political, social, and/or religious attitudes and behaviors of individuals or groups in a desired manner.
- There is no consistent reason why people resort to terrorism. It may be political, social, or religious. It may also be a combination of these factors.
- Terrorists use the media as a tool to disseminate information.
- Terrorist acts may be perpetrated to bring attention to their cause or causes.

- Terrorists may use a variety of means, some illegal, to raise money for their operations.
- Not all terrorism focused at American policy comes from foreign groups. There have been successful terrorist operations launched by "home-grown" terror cells.
- A successful strategy for combating terrorism must have cooperation between agencies at the federal, state, and local levels.

Police Tape: © SkillUp/Shutterstock

1. What are the challenges in creating a comprehensive definition of terrorism?
2. Is there a correlation between economic conditions and support for terror activities?
3. What is the difference between left wing and right wing groups?
4. Do you believe the Department of Homeland Security has been successful in curbing terrorist activity in the United States?
5. Why is the United States currently at war in Afghanistan? What do American policymakers hope this accomplishes?
6. Who are the players in a comprehensive terror reduction plan?
7. Will the Islamic State in Iraq and Syria (ISIS) continue to be a threat to the security of the United States?
8. How have some so-called religious groups helped to foster hate toward other groups and individuals?

KEY TERMS

Police Tape: © SkillUp/Shutterstock

Al Qaeda A terrorist group with Islamic leanings that supports terror operations globally. Osama bin Laden, held to be the titular leader of Al Qaeda, is believed to have been involved in the planning of the 9/11 attacks on the United States.

leaderless resistance Articulated by Louis Beam, this model of organizational structure is designed to avoid infiltration.

patriot and militia movement Active in the 1990s, this movement was characterized by paramilitary training and a deep-rooted fear of tyranny at the hands of the federal government. It lost considerable support after the sense of panic that Y2K caused waned.

terrorism The use or implied use of force, violence, and/or coercion to influence the political, social, and/or religious attitudes and behaviors of individuals or groups in a desired manner.

Timothy McVeigh A U.S. Army veteran, who, along with Terry Nichols, perpetrated the bombing of the Murrah Federal Building. McVeigh received the death penalty for his crimes.

Cyberdeviance is a fascinating mix of old crime and new opportunity. . . .

—Jeffrey Arbaugh

Introduction

...ter crime has been an issue in criminal justice and ...ology since the 1970s. In this venue, the types of com-...rimes have been categorized in two ways. First, a prev-...ctivity was criminals stealing computers. For example, ...final exams at your university, while studying, a stu-...aves his or her computer to use the restroom. When the ...: returns, they discover that someone has taken their ...er. Second, criminals use computers to commit crimes. ...pularity and development of the personal computer in ...0s allowed any individual to be able to own and use ...uter. Before this period, computers were large, bulky, ...pensive. In the early 1960s, a global communication ...was the dream of J.C.R. Licklider. His idea was to in-...nally connect a set of computers that would allow for ...ess to information. Licklider named his idea "galactic ...." At the present time, this galactic network is known ...ternet. As the Internet has grown in development, use, ...ularity, it has provided criminals with another place to ...their acts. Taken as a whole, the development of the ...computer and the Internet has provided the tools for ...ging area of criminal behavior called *cybercrime*.

...bercrime is a criminal act that is committed using a ...r and that occurs over the Internet. The Internet has ...the source for multiple types of crimes and different ...perform these crimes. The types of cybercrime may ...ly grouped into three categories. First, the Internet ...r the creation and maintenance of cybercrime mar-...ond, the Internet provides a venue for fraudulent ...(i.e., cyberfraud). Third, the Internet has become ...or the development of cybercriminal communities. ...pose of this chapter is to outline and provide exam-...hese different forms of communities; the chapter ...ts into describing policy steps to reduce some forms ...rime.

Cybercrime Markets

...rnet allows for illicit markets to be created and ...ed. The Internet provides its users with an opportu-...de their identities and to be in remote locations to ...d be part of illicit markets. For instance, cybercrim-...use various websites to trade (i.e., buy or sell) mer-...illegally, either through legitimate sites (e.g., eBay) ...h illegal sites (e.g., Silk Road). Some these websites ...e traced back to their original sources. While a ...icit markets exist (e.g., illegal adoptions, surrogate ...egg donors, banned substances, donor organs, for-...imals, endangered species, and illegal gambling), ...ets will be discussed here.

...important form of cybercrime is digital piracy.[1] ...iracy is defined as the illegal act of copying digi-...software, digital documents, digital audio (music ...ce), and digital video for any reason other than ...without explicit permission from and compensa-...copyright holder.[2] **TABLE 14-1** presents different

behaviors that may be deemed part of the larger concept of digital piracy.

The Internet has facilitated an increase in digital piracy in recent years. Four characteristics of the Internet that have enabled individuals to easily commit criminal activity: (1) it allows anonymous communication, (2) it is transnational, (3) it has created a shift in thinking from ownership of physical property to ownership of ideas, and (4) it is relatively easy.[3] Additionally, some contend that the Internet facilitates piracy because it allows the offense to occur in a manner that is completely detached from the copyright holder or owner. This provides the offender with the perception that the act is victimless.[4] The percentage of teenagers who perpetrate these acts is summarized in **TABLE 14-2**.

Several researchers have acknowledged sub-forms of digital piracy (i.e., audio and video piracy) as being increasingly pervasive.[5,6] Some have defined audio and video piracy as the "illegal act of uploading or downloading digital sound or video without explicit permission from and compensation to the copyright holder."[7] Higgins, Fell, and Wilson used data from college students to examine the roles of self-control and learning—mentioned in previous chapters—in understanding digital piracy. Their results indicate that people with low self-control are likely to learn the techniques necessary to perform digital piracy. Higgins et al. then showed that once the techniques are learned, the individual is likely to develop intentions to perform digital piracy. Beyond an individual's level of self-control and learning the techniques to perform digital piracy, technological advancements are partly

TABLE 14-1

Summary of Forms of Digital Piracy

Type of Digital Piracy	Example
Software piracy	Downloading or using software without properly securing the copyrights to the software.
Music (i.e., audio)	Downloading or sharing music without the express written consent of the copyright holder. In other words, the individual does not pay for the music that they have obtained.
Voice	Obtaining someone else's voice for use from the Internet.
Video	Downloading or sharing video without the express written consent of the copyright holder. In other words, the individual does not pay for the video that they have obtained.

Courtesy of George Higgins.

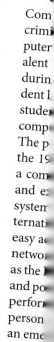

Cybercrime

George E. Higgins, PhD
University of Louisville

Com
crim
puter
alent
durin
dent l
stude
comp
The p
the 19
a com
and ex
system
ternati
easy ad
netwo
as the
and po
perfor
person
an eme

Cy
compu
become
ways to
be loos
allows
kets. Se
behavic
a place
The pu
ples of
then shi
of cyber

The Inte
maintai
nity to h
create ar
inals car
chandise
or throu
cannot
host of i
mothers,
bidden a
four mar
One
Digital
tal goods
and/or v
to back u
tion to th

Objectives

TABLE 14-2

Summary of Teenage Perpetration of Digital Piracy

Year	Percentage
2004	60
2006	43
2007	36

Sources: Business Software Alliance—Fact Sheet: Youth and Downloading Behavior. (2007); see also http://www.bsa.org/country/Research%20and%20 Statistics/~/media/5D4CE35FE06A4AE394059943D1B3B28E.ashx

responsible for the increased ease and accessibility of digital piracy. Some industry monitors have estimated that one in three music disks purchased around the world is an illegal copy.[8] The International Federation of the Phonographic Industry (IFPI) further estimates that 37 percent of all CDs purchased in 2006 were pirated, resulting in 1.2 billion illegal copies purchased worldwide. In fact, the IFPI concludes that pirate CD sales outnumbered legitimate CD sales in 30 markets across the world and resulted in a loss of $4.5 billion from the music industry.

Similar issues take place in the context of the movie industry. To be clear, industry figures indicate that the costs of unauthorized copying and redistribution of movies via physical media (i.e., video cassettes, DVDs, VCDs, etc.) exceed several billion dollars annually. In 2005, over 90 percent of the movies that were pirated were illegal recordings made with camcorders in movie theaters.[9] The Internet allows movie pirates to be able to illegally download these movies.[10] In 2005, the Motion Picture Association of America (MPAA) reported that $2.3 billion were lost due to Internet piracy.

Several researchers have argued that college students are likely to pirate almost all forms of digital media. In one instance, Hinduja used a sample of college students to show that piracy is a prevalent behavior. Hinduja established a profile of the individuals that are likely to perform this behavior.[11] Specifically, the likely pirate is:

- Male
- Asian
- Between the ages of 17 to 20
- At the freshman level

According the Business Software Alliance, the rate of piracy among college students has fallen slightly in 2007 compared with data from 2003 and 2005.[12] TABLE 14-3 summarizes these trends.

Importantly, two-thirds of students still believe that it is okay to swap or illegally download software without paying for it (TABLE 14-4). This is an example of the techniques of neutralization. Techniques of neutralization allow an individual to take a "moral holiday" to perform a deviant or criminal act.

Since the Copyright Act of 1976, digital piracy has been defined as a criminal act.[13] Mass copyright violations of movies and music were made a felony offense in 1982 by the Piracy and Counterfeiting Amendments Act of 1982; this was amended to include the distribution of copyrighted materials over the Internet via the No Electronic Theft Act in 1997.[14] That is, when an individual burns an extra copy of music CD, downloads music from the Internet without paying, or uses a peer-to-peer network to download music information, they are pirating music. This is especially true for digital music piracy that is committed through a multitude of modus operandi (e.g., CD burning, peer-to-peer networks, LAN file sharing, digital stream ripping, and mobile piracy [see IFPI. org for a discussion of these techniques]). The penalties from these acts and legislation may be civil (e.g., $10,000 per pirated copy) and criminal (e.g., possible jail sentences).[15]

Several criminologists have shown that criminological theories may be able to explain digital piracy. For instance, researchers demonstrated that Gottfredson and Hirschi's version of self-control theory has a link with digital piracy.[16] Individuals weigh the pleasure of digital piracy against the potential pain of digital piracy.[17] When the pleasure of digital piracy outweighs the pain, the individual is inclined to perform the act. The individual is more likely to be inclined

TABLE 14-3

Summary of College Student Piracy Rates

Year	Percentage
2003	68
2005	61
2007	55

Source: Business Software Alliance—Fact Sheet: Higher Education Unlicensed Software Experience—Student and Academics. (2007); see also http://www.bsa.org/country/Research%20and%20Statistics/~/media/F3F0E9C1C2AB4B308D5D6D0E3042A5A7.ashx

TABLE 14-4

Summary of College Student Beliefs: Okay to Swap

Year	Percentage
2003	23
2005	32
2007	33

Source: Business Software Alliance—Fact Sheet: Higher Education Unlicensed Software Experience—Student and Academics. (2007); see also http://www.bsa.org/country/Research%20and%20Statistics/~/media/F3F0E9C1C2AB4B308D5D6D0E3042A5A7.ashx

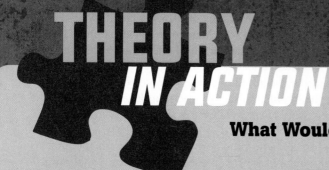

THEORY IN ACTION

What Would You Do to Get the CD?

Chris just heard that a popular CD has just been released to music stores nationwide. All of Chris's friends have heard the CD and said that it is great and that he has to get it! Unfortunately, every time that Chris tries to go to get the CD, he cannot because it is always sold out. However, a friend tells him about an online website that has posted an underground copy of the entire CD. The site will only allow members to download the CD. Chris really wants the CD, so he thinks about it for 2 days and then becomes a member and downloads the CD.

Use two criminological theories to explain Chris's decision to join the online website and download the CD. Contrast how different theories arrive at their explanations.

Source: Higgins, G. E., Fell, B. D., & Wilson, A. L. (2006). Digital piracy: Assessing the contributions of an integrated self-control theory and social learning theory. *Criminal Justice Studies, 19*, 3–22.

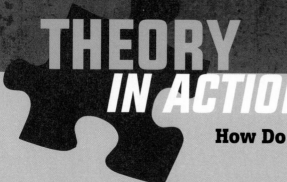

THEORY IN ACTION

How Do You Explain This Much Identity Theft?

In October 2002, an FBI team searched a house in New Rochelle, New York. The officers thought that they had completed their search, but one officer was not convinced and was not about to let months of investigation go for nothing. That officer returned to a bedroom that seemed to have oversized furniture. The officer pulled the draping back from oversized canopy over a bed and discovered hundreds of individuals' identities that had been used in an intricate scheme that had netted nearly $50 million.

At the time, this was described as the biggest case of identity theft ever uncovered in the United States. Two individuals were the perpetrators of this crime. One individual had contacts with a ring of Nigerian street criminals,

and the other individual was a help-desk clerk at a software company. They used several means of obtaining the identities that included Internet access. Their activities victimized at least 30,000 people nationwide. Some of their activities included taking out as much as $65,000 in loans. Do you think that this was identity theft or identity fraud? What theory might explain the activities of the perpetrators?

Sources: O'Brien, T. L. (October 24, 2004). Identity theft is epidemic. Can it be stopped? *The New York Times*. Retrieved March 18, 2009, from http://www.nytimes.com/2004/10/24/business/yourmoney/24theft.html

to perform the act if they have low self-control. Impulsive individuals are not likely to wait to own the copyrights of digital media (e.g., songs or movies).[18] That is, individuals that have low self-control are less likely to see the consequences of their digital piracy. Other researchers have found similar results using self-control theory.[19,20]

Other researcher have applied social learning theory to software piracy.[21] Their logic was that individuals who associated with others who performed digital piracy (i.e., differential association) were likely to acquire attitudes (i.e., definitions) that are favorable to performing digital piracy. In addition, the individual would find digital piracy rewarding, but they would have to learn the techniques for digital piracy from their friends through imitation of the behavior. Others have found support for this premise, including software piracy and an expanded definition of digital piracy.[22–24]

Researchers have also applied rational choice/deterrence theory to understand how to reduce instances of digital piracy. Other researchers showed that deterrence theory can be applied to software piracy.[25] For instance, Higgins, Wilson, and Fell used a sample of college students to examine the role of deterrence. They used a factorial design (i.e., a type of experimental design) to determine whether different factors for communicating certainty that piracy would be discovered and severity of punishment once piracy was discovered would deter the students from performing software piracy. In addition, Higgins et al. used some parts of contemporary deterrence theory (i.e., shame and family discovery). The results indicated that certainty of discovery, shame, and family discovery were the most relevant factors to deter individuals from performing software piracy. Specifically, they argued that rational individuals would be less likely to perform software piracy when the chances of being detected increase and the likelihood of punishment is certain and severe.

 Cyberpornography

Cybercrime includes the promotion and the distribution of pornography. This is known as **cyberpornography**. The promotion of pornography is defined as distributing unwanted emails or solicitations to view pornography. The distribution occurs when emails are provided that include pornography attached or within the message. While pornography may not be criminal for those age 18 or over, the Internet does not discriminate based on age. That is, teenagers' fantasies about nudity are replaced by hard-core pornographic images of every conceivable sexual activity.

In the academic literature, some researchers have shown that cyberpornography is an emerging behavior. For instance, researchers used data from children and young adults to examine exposure to cyberpornography.[26] They showed that individuals who sought out cyberpornography were likely to be male, 14 years of age and older, and more depressed. Individuals younger than 14 were more likely to be exposed to pornography through traditional exposures—movies and magazines.

Organizations and researchers have examined reasons why people view pornography. For instance, the Pew foundation found that 2 percent of adult Americans were likely to visit an adult website, and it has been shown that 70 percent of pornography is downloaded between the hours of 9 a.m. and 5 p.m.[27]

Stack, Wasserman, and Kern used the General Social Survey (GSS) to examine who viewed pornography using the Internet and the reasons why.[28] This study included several thousand responses from individuals in the United States. They demonstrated that individuals with weak religious ties, unhappy marriages, and past sexual deviance are more likely to view pornography via the Internet. Specific factors influence the access of cyberpornography. One study showed that when employment status increased, technology does play a role in the access to cyberpornography.[29]

The Internet also allows cybercriminals to participate in underage liaisons. One form of this particular type of cybercrime is online solicitation of children for sex. This is exploitation that involves an adult who engages in discussion with a child online and uses his or her manipulation skills to coerce the child to meet in person for sexual purposes.

Research shows that cyberpornography, especially child pornography, is an important issue. Cohen-Almagor reviews the literature in this area to show that this behavior not only occurs at alarming rates, but some forms of countermeasures are possible and needed to curb the activity.[30] Others have noticed that this is an important issue as well. Marcum, Higgins, Freiburger, and Ricketts used data from a random sample of police agencies to investigate the link between having a task force, training, performing an investigation, and making arrests for child pornography. Their results indicate that having a specialized task force for child pornography has a larger impact on performing investigations of child pornography and making arrests than does specialized training. Marcum et al. suggest that law enforcement agencies develop more of these task forces. The effect of these task forces would not only be an increase in the amount of investigations and arrests, it will also provide more information about the extent of the behavior taking place.[31]

The anonymity of the Internet allows cybercriminals the ability to disguise their postings, responses, and identities. This affords cybercriminals the opportunity to disappear at a moment's notice. In short, the Internet allows cybercrimes to be performed more easily and simply, while making their detection, apprehension, and prosecution more difficult. Therefore, the Internet makes cybercrimes through illicit markets more difficult to examine.

 Cyberfraud

Cyberfraud includes behaviors that occur with guile and deceit. One example is identity theft that may lead to identity fraud. Unfortunately, the definition of identity theft varies, requiring that one definition be determined for the purpose of clarity. For instance, one definition of **identity theft** is, "the unlawful use of another's personal identifying information."[32] Others have defined identity theft as, "involv[ing] financial or other personal information stolen with intent of establishing another person's identity as the thief's own . . ."[33] The FTC sees identity theft as, "occur[ring] when someone uses your personally identifying information, like your name, social security number, or credit card number without your permission, to commit fraud or other crimes."[34] This chapter adopts the FTC's definition of identity theft, although some may regard this definition as being identity fraud. In one sense, identity fraud involves using financial or other private information that is stolen or invented in order to make purchases or gain access to financial accounts.[35]

The FTC's definition clarifies some of the potential forms of personal information that may be used in identity theft. Other forms of personal information include address, date of birth, alien registration number, and government passport. While these forms of personal information and the definition of identity theft provide some context, identity theft can be summed up as constituting the unauthorized use of someone else's personal information for criminal activity.

The crime of identity theft has received substantial coverage from a wide variety of legal mechanisms. A substantial number of federal and state statutes relate to the criminality of identity theft and those who suffer from victimization. In the federal arena, the laws relating to identity theft are convoluted. They can, however, be divided into (1) statutes that relate to criminality, and (2) penalties and statutes that provide consumers with information or rights. The primary criminal statute in the federal system is the Identity Theft and Assumption Deterrence Act of 1998. Specifically, 18 U.S.C. § 1028 makes it a federal crime when anyone "knowingly transfers or uses, without lawful authority, a means of identification of another person with the intent to commit, or to aid or abet, any unlawful activity that constitutes a violation of Federal law, or that constitutes a felony under any applicable State or local law." In 2004, the Identity Theft Penalty Enhancement Act was enacted.[36] This act provides for enhanced punishments for identity thieves. For example, the act requires an additional 2 years of punishment for violators who use another's identity in the commission of a crime and 5-year sentences for the use of a false identity in the commission of a terror offense.[37] Sentencing discretion is also restricted, in that sentences may not run concurrently for offenses and probation is prohibited for those convicted under the statute.

Other federal statutes provide some aid for victims of identity theft.[38] The Fair Credit Reporting Act establishes procedures for people seeking to correct mistakes on their credit record and ensures that credit histories are only provided for legitimate business needs.[39] The Fair and Accurate Credit Transactions Act allows consumers to obtain free copies of their credit reports as well as restricts what information can be placed on a sales receipt. Similarly, The Fair Credit Billing Act establishes procedures for resolving billing errors on credit card accounts and establishes limits on a consumer's liability for fraudulent credit card charges.[40] Finally, the Electronic Fund Transfer Act focuses on transactions using debit cards or electronic means to debit or credit an account and limits the liability for unauthorized electronic fund transfers.[41]

Because the majority of all criminal prosecutions occur in state court systems, state legal schemes are critically important. All 50 states and the District of Columbia have criminal laws relating to identity theft.[42] Thirty-one states have created "freeze laws" for persons fearing identity theft. These laws generally lock access to credit reports, credit scores, and limits. While these laws vary greatly, there is generally no charge for the creation, temporary lifting, or complete termination of a freeze (a so-called "credit thaw") for the victim of identity theft. Others wishing to limit their risks may have to pay between $5 and $20. While freezes will not completely shield a consumer from victimization they will halt the creation of any new victimization where the issuer relies upon a credit report to provide credit. A few states have credit information blocking statutes that require the credit reporting agencies to block false information from consumer victims' credit reports within a certain time frame or upon the receipt of a police report.

California was the first state to pass a mandatory disclosure law for people whose information has been compromised. Currently, at least 35 states have some form of breach notification statute. These laws vary greatly by state.[43] The threshold for notification may be mandatory upon a security breach. For example, like California, Massachusetts recently passed a similar mandatory notification law. Other states use a risk-based analysis requiring notification only in cases of substantial risk of harm. These laws are based on three rationales. First, with timely notice consumers can take preventive measures to limit or reduce the potential for identity theft. Second, reporting provides an ability to accurately measure the true number of breaches and thus aids in research on identity theft. Last, the social and pecuniary costs associated with notification provide substantial motivation to protect consumer information.[44] Notification laws differ from fraud alert protections. An alert requirement forces notification if a person's credit file receives an inquiry. A breach notification law requires that a consumer be informed if his or her information has been compromised.

Identity theft or identity fraud is responsible for a large number of issues due to the theft of information. Identity thieves commit fraudulent acts to obtain identities of other individuals. For instance, identity thieves may "hack" (i.e., break into network databases) via the Internet to obtain personal information. Another form of fraudulent activity is the use of "phishing." Phishing is when an identity criminal goes online and poses as a corporation (e.g., Western Union, Amazon, eBay, or PayPal) or an individual in need (e.g., travel scams, stock frauds, financial transfers; nondelivery of merchandise, Internet auction fraud, credit card fraud) and requests personal information. An emerging form of identity theft is "pharming." Pharming is when a hacker redirects an individual from a legitimate site to a fraudulent site without the users' knowledge.

These forms of Internet identity theft are costly to the economy and to the victim. For instance, it has been shown that the U.S. economy was particularly susceptible to identity theft, and in the United States, identity theft has resulted in actual losses ranging from $442 million to $745 million over a span of 3 years.[45] Others have estimated identity theft costs to be between $53 and $73.8 billion per year.[46] While this gives some perspective, the true extent of identity theft is unknown. Identity theft can also have profound individual costs. For instance, a victim can expect to pay up to $3,000 and spend a substantial amount of time restoring his or her identity.[47]

TABLE 14-5 presents the different types of identity theft. The most common complaint is credit card fraud, followed by telephone and utility fraud. These forms of frauds are closely followed by employment and bank fraud. Not shown but some report that the most common form of identity theft bank fraud is electronic funds transfer (EFT)–related identity theft.[48] These forms of identity theft are followed by government documents/benefits fraud and loan fraud.

Hacking

Another important form of cybercrime is hacking. **Hacking** refers to an individual or organization that attempts to access a computer system, network, or data source that does not have expressed consent from the system owner or operator.[49,50] Hackers may be categorized in two ways. First, hackers may be individuals or organizations that are merely interested in the structure of a system. To clarify, the hacker trespasses in a system to learn how the system works or how the system is built. In this sense, the hacker does not have any malicious intent or perform any malicious acts, other than trespassing.

The second category is cracking. A hacker that is cracking—often referred to as a cracker—is an individual or organization that is trespassing with the intention to perform malicious acts. For instance, the individual or organization may spread malicious programs (i.e., viruses). The malicious programs that hackers produce and spread may have major effects. The programs may capture keystrokes, disrupt traffic, delete or corrupt files, and create an infected system that can be used in the future. Capturing keystrokes allows the individual or organization gain valuable information (e.g., passwords, documents, or other pieces of information). Hackers' malicious programs may have the capability of disrupting traffic flow. This means that the program has the ability to impede email transmission, Internet transactions, and Intranet transactions. Malicious programs can also delete or corrupt files that render the computer system useless. Unfortunately, malicious programs have the ability to lie dormant so that they may be used in the future by the hacker. The cracking may have harmful effects that may be felt immediately and into the future.

Two forms of research—qualitative and quantitative—provide some insight into hackers. Qualitative research indicates that a major issue with hacking is peer association. Holt shows that hackers need introduction to the behavior.[51] Peers, real and virtual, provide training and support for this type of behavior. The link between peers, in the context of hacking, tends to become close. Research indicates that hackers tend to stay connected to individuals either on- or off-line.[52] The subculture thrives on the connection among peers and the sharing of deep knowledge of technology. The closeness of the links creates a subculture. Within the subculture, hackers are consistently demonstrating their knowledge of the technology by either performing traditional hacking behaviors or cracking behaviors. For instance, subcultures harbor some individuals that seek to understand computer operating systems (i.e., hackers). Several companies, about 75 percent, reported that hacking is likely from employees, and 45 percent of businesses reported unauthorized access by insiders.[53] Other sources indicate that hackers are responsible for numerous attacks on businesses. Either of these behaviors generates a certain amount of credibility within the subculture. This credibility leads to reinforcement that perpetuates the subcultural value of credibility.

TABLE 14-5

Summary of Forms of Identity Fraud

Type of Identity Theft	Example
Credit card fraud	Using someone else's credit card identity without their knowledge.
Phone or utilities fraud	Establishing phone or utility services in someone else's identity without their knowledge.
Employment related fraud	Gaining employment-related benefits using someone else's identity.
Bank fraud	
Government benefits fraud	
Loan fraud	
Other identity theft	
Attempted identity theft	

Courtesy of George Higgins.

What to Do to Minimize Risk of Identity Theft/Fraud

Quantitative research in this area indicates that hacking may have multiple causes. Among college students, hacking is a behavior that comes from social learning (i.e., peer behavior), self-control deficits, and neutralizations. Holt and Kilger show that individuals who begin hacking started the behavior because of lower levels of self-control, but the hacking was minor and unsophisticated (i.e., usually password guessing).[54] For the individual to progress to more sophisticated forms of hacking, the individual needs to learn (i.e., educationally or socially) the techniques and skills that are necessary. Therefore, hacking may be explained as an interaction between these two theories. Marcum, Higgins, Ricketts, and Wolfe show that this behavior occurs among juveniles. They also show that low self-control and learning are important in a juvenile sample as well.[55]

Another theory that is important to hacking is neutralization. Hackers tend to neutralize their behavior. This allows them to take a moral holiday and absolve themselves from their responsibility in the behavior. Researchers consistently document that hackers believe that the individuals or organizations that they trespass against or the spread of malicious programs only harms those that "had it coming to them."

Overall, hacking is an important behavior. Hacking does not just occur among adult populations but also takes place among juveniles. Hackers form their own communities or subcultures where they learn the techniques or skills.

 Cybercrime Communities

The Internet provides a place for cybercriminal communities to exist and flourish. These communities may be seen as subcultures. Subcultures are cohesive cultural systems that vary in form and substance from the dominant culture. To be clear, a subculture maintains its own values, beliefs, and traditions that differ from the dominant culture. Thus, the individual performs behaviors that are consistent with those of their subculture, but that differ from the dominant culture. Some subcultures may be based on ethnic groups, delinquent gangs, and religious sects. Others may take place through the Internet or the cyber-environment.

Other deviants or criminals may also be part of an online subculture (i.e., pedophiles, depressives, anorectics, and bulimics). Cybercrime communities are important because they are seen as a venue where their criminal or deviant activity is reinforced and encouraged. Cybercrime communities provide an opportunity for transmittal of knowledge that makes their criminal behavior more effective and it legitimizes the behavior. In short, a person participating in these deviant subcultures learns new techniques for performing their behavior and how to handle potential issues (i.e., outsiders, legal or medical services). Cybercrime communities provide a place for the sharing of knowledge to take place on a level playing field. That is, in these communities, individuals are not alienated,

Some weeks, 20,000 people contact the Federal Trade Commission about recovering from identity theft (FBI).

© jokerpro/ShutterStock, Inc.

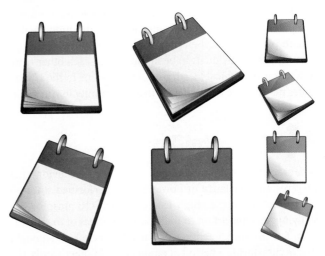

It took the Senate almost five years to ratify the Council of Europe Convention on Cybercrime, the major international treaty that allows governments to work together to combat cybercrime. Suspected cybercrime havens such as Lithuania and Romania ratified it years before the United States did (Council of Europe).

© juliengrondin/ShutterStock, Inc.

Cybersecurity research accounted for 1% of the Department of Homeland Security's science and technology research budget. The research funding for biological attack countermeasures was roughly 22 times as large (Department of Homeland Security, American Association for the Advancement of Science).

© get4net/ShutterStock, Inc.

There were 326 data breaches during 2006. Only five thieves were successfully prosecuted for data breaches throughout the year (Privacy Rights Clearinghouse).

© Andrew Buckin/ShutterStock, Inc.

rebuked, or ostracized based on age, race, sex, marital status, ethnicity, or socio-economic status. All this is required is a computer and an Internet connection and the individual is able to participate. Cybercrime communities provide an opportunity for individuals to be in touch with each other from different geographical locations. Thus someone in the United States may be able to participate in a community in Australia.

Cyberbullying

Cyberbullying is intentional, aggressive behavior that involves an imbalance of power that is performed through electronic means (i.e., high-tech devices).[56] To grasp cyberbullying, it is important to pull apart the pieces of the definition. For instance, intentional means that there is forethought that occurs during a period of rationality.[57] In other words, the individual that performs cyberbullying is someone who has thought about their actions before they performed the actions, and they deemed that cyberbullying would bring them pleasure.

In addition to being an intentional behavior, cyberbullying includes aggression. Aggression can occur verbally and physically. Given that cyberbullying takes place using high-tech devices, a direct physical event is not likely; however, an indirect physical event may occur. For example, someone may share or post an image or video of someone being physically harmed. Aggression may be also be verbal. Verbal aggression that takes place in cyberbullying may increase the instances of emotions.

Cyberbullying not only includes instances of intentionality and aggression, but it also includes instances of imbalance of power. The imbalance of power involves one individual having the ability to apply more aggression consistently. Power imbalances are relevant for the reinforcement of the behavior. The reinforcement of the behavior increases the likelihood that the victim will be harmed consistently.

The nature of cyberbullying does not just rest in the definition of the behavior; the persistence of the behavior is important. Hinduja and Patchin argued that instances of cyberbullying should take place more than once.[58] While a single instance of the behavior may cause emotional and potentially physical harm, multiple instances are necessary to confirm that cyberbullying is taking place. Further, they argue that many individuals are able to withstand one instance of cyberbullying, but that the continuation of cyberbullying will produce longstanding harm. Determining the repeat nature of cyberbullying is difficult to discern. For instance, an individual may post a cyberbullying message one time, but the message may get circulated through a community of individuals multiple times. Because the individual posted the message once, the repeat nature of the cyberbullying is in question. This has led Wolak, Mitchell, and Finkelhor to argue that one cyberbullying post is enough to constitute the behavior.[59]

Cyberbullying can and does take place using different forms of high-tech devices. This behavior may occur using a telephone, computer, or tablet. In other words, cyberbullying may occur using devices that allow for written and image (i.e., photographic or video) communications to take place.

While using high-tech devices, cyberbullying can take place using social networks (e.g., Facebook). In social networks, text messages, posting messages, chat rooms, and email provide the vehicles for cyberbullying to take place. The different parts of social media provide the opportunity to post messages or to send and receive written or image communications. Given the size of social networks, the impact or trauma that may arise from cyberbullying could be harsh.

Not only does cyberbullying occur in various ways, but the characteristics of the bully and the victim are disparate. In other words, individuals who bully and victims of bullying may be from any demographic. Despite these disparities, Hinduja and Patchin argue that cyberbullies are generally aggressive (i.e., proactive or reactive), short tempered (do not handle high pressure situations easily), lack empathy (do not care about anyone else), and are easily frustrated.[60]

Conclusion

The Internet environment is a new venue for criminal activity. While some argue that the behaviors that take place there currently occur on the streets, the Internet also provides a venue for new forms of criminal behavior. For instance, the Internet has created new marketplaces for criminal activity, venues to view and transmit pornography, methods for committing fraudulent behavior, and new communities that promulgate crime and deviance. Thus, as the Internet grows, so does the opportunity for criminal activity. This creates a necessity for understanding the activity and those who commit these crimes.

Forms of Cyberbullying

- *Harassment* in the cyber form entails repetitive messages that are generally offensive to the recipient. The offender may send emails or instant messages insulting or taunting the victim.

- *Outing* and *trickery* refers to the unintended sharing of personal information with others. A victim may have his or her social security number, telephone numbers, or sexual preference exposed without permission.

- *Flaming* occurs in a public setting, such as a chat room or discussion board, and is a brief exchange of insults between two or more parties. This could be considered a virtual argument.

- *Denigration* involves posting information about another that is disparaging and untrue. For example, an offender may post on a victim's Facebook page that she is a drug addict, a slut, or has no friends.

- *Exclusion/ostracism* is creating the perception of feeling left out or isolating the victim.

WRAP-UP

Texture: © Malchev/Shutterstock; Police Tape: © SkillUp/Shutterstock

- Cybercrime is an emerging criminal activity.
- Cybercrimes occur and have developed several markets that fall under the umbrella of digital piracy (i.e., stealing of music, movies, and software).
- Pornography is a form of cybercrime when teenagers are participants. Teenagers may be participants in the making of pornography or viewing the pornography. Each method of participation is a criminal act.

- Cyberfraud encompasses identity theft and identity fraud. Identity theft and identity fraud are fast growing criminal behaviors. These activities cost the American economy billions of dollars each year.
- Cybercrime communities are important because they provide havens for cybercrime and deviance that occur using the Internet. For instance, these communities may help hackers become more effective.

PUTTING IT ALL TOGETHER

Police Tape: © SkillUp/Shutterstock

1. Define cybercrime and provide examples of this behavior.
2. What are the main categories for thinking about cybercrime?
3. What is a subculture and how do they work with cybercrimes? Use two theories to help guide your response.
4. Discuss the importance of cyberfraud.
5. Define and describe cyberbullying.

KEY TERMS

Police Tape: © SkillUp/Shutterstock

cyberbullying Intentional, aggressive behavior that involves an imbalance of power that is performed through electronic means (i.e., high-tech devices).

cybecrime A criminal act that is committed using a computer that occurs over the Internet.

cyberpornography Promotion and the distribution of pornography using the computer or Internet.

digital piracy The illegal act of copying digital goods, software, digital documents, digital audio (including music and voice), and digital video for a reason other than to back up without explicit permission from and compensation to the copyright holder.

hacking The activity of an individual or organization that attempts to access a computer system, network, or data source that does not have expressed consent from the system owner or operator.

identity theft When someone uses your personally identifying information, such as your name, social security number, or credit card number, without permission, in order to commit fraud or other crimes.

"Drug warriors" and "legalizers" alike ground their policy recommendations on partial and one-sided analyses of the relationship between drugs and crime. By creating black markets, prohibition can cause crime. But intoxication and addiction can also cause crime, even when the underlying drug is legal. Thus, the answer to the question "Do drugs, or drug laws, cause crime?" is "Yes."

—David A. Boyum and Mark A. R. Kleiman[1]

CHAPTER 15

Drugs and Crime

Texture: © Malchev/Shutterstock; Shooter: © Malchev/Shutterstock; Puzzle Piece: © Photodisc; Police Tape: © Skillup/Shutterstock

Objectives

- Discuss the relationship between drugs and crime. Pg. 308

- Compare the research findings on drug use among the general public and people in jail and prison. Pg. 310

- Describe the Goldstein models of drug use and how they explain drugs and criminal behavior. Pgs. 312–313

- Discuss research findings on the effectiveness of treatment, especially the drug court model. Pg. 321

- Discuss the economic impact of both the illegal drug trade and drug abuse. Pg. 322

- Explain the arguments for and against the legalization of drugs such as marijuana. Pg. 323

Introduction

Drugs, although never completely absent from American life, have varied in the type and level of use throughout history. The U.S. Constitution has profoundly influenced the evolving interpretation of, and the legal response and consequences to, drugs. State and police powers now regulate the health professions and drug availability. Results of this regulation have been mixed, producing a free economy in drugs until the late 19th century, when state antidrug laws were enacted.

The opening quote captures the nature of the relationship between drugs and crime. Analyzing this relationship drives research on drugs and criminal behavior. This chapter summarizes the history of drug abuse in the United States, explores the research evidence concerning criminal behavior and substance abuse, examines trends in drug use by juveniles, discusses specific drugs and their classification, and analyzes the strengths and weaknesses of key policy issues, such as treatment and legalization.

Drug Use: A Historical Perspective

Narcotic drugs, introduced in the mid-19th century, offered promising applications for pain relief. However, by 1900, there were deep misgivings about the overuse of such drugs.

Opium, widely available to Americans in the 18th and 19th centuries, was used in a variety of medicines and concoctions.[2] Morphine, first isolated from opium in 1805, could be taken orally, applied topically, and injected.[3] Such extraction of purified active ingredients and their direct injection led to careless overprescription. Physicians incorrectly believed that, because the amount given by injection was so much smaller than the dosage given by mouth, there was little chance of addiction.

When cocaine was introduced in 1860, no restrictions were imposed on its sale or distribution. Alcohol extracts were marketed as tonics that provided energy and endurance. An early formulation of Coca-Cola (minus the alcohol) was modeled after such a tonic.[4] However, concerns about cocaine mounted. The Shanghai Opium Commission of 1909 and a 1911 conference in The Hague were international responses to the growing problem of opium and cocaine.[5] Marijuana, although regarded by many as benign, became the target of increasing scrutiny in the 1930s. In 1937, the Marijuana Tax Act became law.

In the United States, laws against narcotics at all levels reflected a growing antagonism toward their use.[6] Ironically, as the use of drugs decreased, the severity of punishment increased; by 1955, the federal penalty for providing heroin to anyone under the age of 18 years was death.[7]

In the 1960s, the recreational use of drugs increased. Marijuana; hallucinogenic drugs, such as LSD and peyote; depressants; barbiturates; and opiates (heroin), were widely used. The Comprehensive Drug Abuse Act of 1970 led to softer penalties for federal drug violations, offsetting the punitive laws of the Harrison Narcotic Act of 1914.

Tolerance for drug use continued to rise until the late 1970s. However, in the decades since, this tolerance has decreased as the fear of drug use has risen. Extensive antidrug campaigns were conducted in the 1980s and programs such as Drug Awareness Resistance Education (DARE) underscored the Reagan Administration's motto, "Just say no."

During the 1980s, the war on crime became primarily a war on drugs as public concern over the problem increased dramatically.[8] In 2001, 58 percent of a national sample identified drug abuse as the most important problem facing the country. By 2014, the percentage of Gallup poll respondents who considered drug abuse the most serious problem facing the country plummeted to 34 percent. In fact, by October 2013, a majority of respondents favored legalizing marijuana (58%).[9]

However, this decline in concern about drug abuse did not match the reported use of illicit drugs in the country. In 2012, an estimated 23.9 million Americans aged 12 or older (9.2% of the population) had used drugs illegal (marijuana/hashish, cocaine, heroin, hallucinogens, inhalants, pain relievers, tranquilizers, stimulants, and sedatives) in the month prior to the survey. This rate increased from 8.1 percent in 2008 to 9.2 percent in 2012. The rate in 2012 was similar to the rates in 2009 to 2011 (8.7–8.9%), but it was higher than the rates in the years from 2002 to 2008 (7.9–8.3%).[10]

One study followed the alcohol and marijuana use trajectories of 29 consecutive cohorts of high school seniors (graduating from 1976 to 2004) surveyed under the Monitoring the Future project. The results revealed that, while marijuana use remained stable, heavy drinking (consuming five or more drinks in a row) increased threefold for males and sixfold for females between the ages of 18 and 22. The findings show that antidrug and anti-alcohol efforts aimed at youth have been successful, but the unanticipated side effect is that young adult heavy drinking has dramatically increased.[11]

Similarly, a 2013 survey of 8th- to 12th-grade students in the United States, determined that their use of certain drugs (amphetamines, methamphetamine, crystal methamphetamine, cocaine, and crack cocaine) in the previous year had increased by between 1 and 2 percent for each grade group. However, marijuana drove this increase while the use of other illegal drugs held steady. The perceived risk associated with marijuana use had declined sharply among these student groups and may have contributed to amplified use.[12]

Parent's attitudes toward drug and alcohol use have some relationship to substance use among adolescents. Research on the effect of risk and protective factors (RPFs) for adolescent drug use and delinquency reported differences between adolescents in the United States and Netherlands. For both groups, the RPFs were similar, but the Dutch students perceived their parent's attitudes toward drinking to be more favorable than U.S. students and this led to more alcohol consumption (and smoking) for this group. However, when parents held favorable attitudes regarding alcohol consumption for the U.S. youths, higher rates of delinquency resulted.[13] Survey results from over 7,300 10th-grade students tested the effect of social control theory on adolescent substance abuse.

Weak parental controls (poor family management, favorable parental attitudes regarding drug use and delinquency) increased substance abuse among adolescents. However, three elements of expressive parental control (reinforcement of pro-social behaviors and attachment to mothers and/or fathers) were uniformly effective in reducing drug use.[14]

Substance abuse is linked to higher rates of mental illness and related problems. Structured psychiatric interviews with a representative sample of over 43,000 Americans found that abstainers (individuals with no lifetime use of drugs or alcohol) were substantially less likely than partakers to suffer lifetime from mood, anxiety, or personality disorders.[15] Data on over 34,000 cases from the National Epidemiologic Survey on Alcohol and Related Conditions (from 2004 and 2005) determined that individuals with histories of severe mental illness were more likely to be violent than persons with no evidence of mental or substance abuse problems. People with both severe mental illness and substance abuse problems had the highest rate of violence. In terms of their life history, persons who suffered from child abuse and neglect, household antisocial behavior, binge drinking, and stressful life circumstances were also at risk for violent behavior.[16]

Substance abuse has different impacts on women. Kandall notes that female addiction has been due to inappropriate, overmedication practices by physicians and pharmacists, media manipulation, or attempts by females to cope with and overcome social and occupational barriers that promoted inequality and blocked self-fulfillment. Addicted women were on the margins of society, their addiction levels were underestimated and treatment was largely unavailable until the 1970s.[17] Results from an analysis of the National Drug Use Survey on over 180,000 Americans (2006–2010) found that drug and criminal justice–involved males and females were more likely to have physical and mental health problems associated with short-term behavioral risk. Women had significant problems with lung cancer, cirrhosis, and possession of a dual diagnosis while males had evidence of suicide ideation and alcohol dependence.[18]

Such findings have contributed to the debate on what to do about drug abuse and have generated several different policy suggestions.[19] Since 1980, there have been four major antidrug bills:[20]

1. The Comprehensive Crime Control Act of 1984 broadened the criminal and civil asset-forfeiture laws and increased the federal criminal sanctions for drug offenses.
2. The Anti-Drug Abuse Act of 1986 provided money for treatment and prevention, but also restored mandatory prison sentences for large-scale distribution of marijuana and imposed new sanctions for money laundering.
3. The Anti-Drug Abuse Act of 1988 was an amendment to the 1986 act and it increased the sanctions for crimes related to drug trafficking and put new federal sanctions into place.
4. The Crime Control Act of 1990 doubled the appropriation for drug law enforcement grants to states and strengthened forfeiture and seizure statutes.

All of these bills had a specific focus on reducing the supply of drugs. Although other reduction strategies had been tried in the past, history went forward and lessons were not learned.

Historic attempts to reduce drug use include:

1. *Prohibition*: Focused on banning illegal drugs by meting out severe penalties for use, distribution, and sale. Here, illegal substance abuse is seen as a primary cause of crime. Therefore, the transport, possession, and sale of certain drugs are illegal. It also includes "hard-line" solutions such as interdiction and enhanced criminal sentences for offenders. The expectation is that these methods would force potential sellers to seek other economic pursuits. In addition, the violence generated by the drug marketplace and the crime committed by persons to support their habit would be eliminated.
2. *Legalization*: Calls for the elimination of drug laws and the institution of government regulation on the use of drugs that are presently illegal.
3. *Decriminalization*: The removal of criminal penalties for the possession of illegal drugs.
4. *Medicalization*: Giving physicians the responsibility for treating drug abusers, including the decision to maintain some users on the drug on which they have become dependent.
5. *Harm reduction*: Emphasizes the use of a public health model to reduce the risks and consequences of drug abuse.
6. *Prevalence reduction*: Reducing the number of users.
7. *Micro-harm reduction*: Reducing the average harm per dose, including harm to users and nonusers.[21]

> By attempting to keep marijuana from being imported, the United States has inadvertently encouraged domestic cultivation of new, more potent strains of marijuana.

These policies have attracted the attention of criminologists in the United States and elsewhere. When discussing marijuana use and its history in the United States, the legal sanctions and control ("The War on Drugs")—not treatment, prevention, and education—have dictated policy. This hard line has often backfired. By attempting to keep marijuana from being imported, the United States has inadvertently encouraged domestic cultivation of new, more potent strains of marijuana.

By 2014, marijuana has been decriminalized in 14 states.[22] While the overwhelming majority of marijuana users do not move to serious drugs, there appears to be a progression among serious drug users in which minor drug use leads to marijuana use and subsequently to more serious substances.[23] Drug use progresses through four stages: (1) alcohol or cigarettes, (2) marijuana, (3) other illicit drugs, and (4) medically prescribed drugs.[24]

Drugs and Criminal Behavior

The Incidence of Substance Abuse Among Offenders

"Does drug use cause crime or does crime cause drug use?"[25,26] This is a classic chicken-or-egg question that appears to go both ways. Drug use may increase criminal behavior by introducing the user to a high-risk subculture that promotes crime over legitimate, low-paying jobs to raise money. Thus, the marketplace for illegal drugs contributes to crime by diverting inner-city youths away from legitimate pursuits of school and employment.[27] Conversely, criminals may be more likely to use drugs because they already are part of this subculture.[28,29] Thus, it is difficult to separate these two behaviors and determine which causes the other. The drugs–crime relationship is summarized in TABLE 15-1 .

Research evidence reveals a strong link between substance abuse and criminal behavior. Gropper summarized research showing that offenders with a substance abuse problem commit a high percentage of the violent crimes (e.g., robbery: 75%). Drug addicts commit more crimes while they are under the influence—some four to six times more than when clean.[30] Research on heroin addicts in treatment uncovered a small group of "violent predators" responsible

for a disproportionate amount of crime even when they were not actively addicted.[31] In his analysis of the relationship between drugs and crime, Inciardi concluded that "narcotics use freezes its users into patterns of criminality that are more acute, dynamic, violent, unremitting and enduring than those of other drug-using offenders."[32]

Substance-abusing offenders are considered responsible for crime.[33] In 2006, 85 percent of the U.S. prison and jail population (2.3 million inmates) abused drugs and 1.5 million inmates met medical criteria for substance abuse or addiction. Another 458,000 inmates did not meet the abuse criteria but had histories of substance abuse and were under the influence of alcohol or other drugs at the time of their crime, committed their offense to get money to buy drugs, were incarcerated for an alcohol or drug law violation, or shared some combination of these characteristics. In 2006, alcohol and other drugs played a role in:

- 78 percent of violent crimes
- 83 percent of property crimes
- 77 percent of public order, immigration, or weapons offenses and probation/parole violations.

Alcohol was implicated in the incarceration of more than one-half of all inmates in America; illicit drugs were implicated in three-fourths of incarcerations.[34]

Wish and Johnson found that greater levels of illicit drug use are related to higher rates of drug distribution offenses and other serious offenses. More than half of those charged with murder, manslaughter, robbery, or burglary in Manhattan tested positive for one or more drugs upon arrest.[35] Similarly, Collins reports that offenders who are problem drinkers are disproportionately involved in violent crime.[36] Research also shows that offenders with active drug or alcohol abuse

TABLE 15-1		
Summary of the Drugs–Crime Relationship		
Drugs–Crime Relationship	**Definition**	**Examples**
Drug-defined offenses	Violation of laws prohibiting or regulating the possession, use, distribution, or manufacture of illegal drugs.	Drug possession or use; marijuana cultivation; methamphetamine production; cocaine, heroin, or marijuana sales.
Drug-related offenses	Offenses in which a drug's pharmacologic effects contribute; offenses motivated by the user's need for money to support continued use; offenses connected to drug distribution itself.	Violent behavior resulting from drug's effects; stealing to get money to buy drugs; violence against rival drug dealers.
Drug-using lifestyle	Drug use and crime common aspects of a deviant lifestyle; likelihood and frequency of involvement in illegal activity increased because drug users may not participate in the legitimate economy and are exposed to situations that encourage crime.	Life orientation with an emphasis on short-term goals supported by illegal activities; opportunities to offend resulting from conflicts with offenders and illegal markets; criminal skills learned from other offenders.

Data from Drug Policy Information Clearinghouse, Office of National Drug Control Policy. (2000). *Drugs & crime data—fact sheet: Drug-related crime*. Washington, DC: U.S. Department of Justice, p. 1.

problems are likely to continue their criminal behavior.[37] For example, cocaine use is often accompanied by alcohol use, and the combination may be more-than-addictively potent in unleashing aggression.[38]

This level of involvement is related to criminal behavior. A long-term study of addicts involved in treatment programs determined that dependence on cocaine and/or heroin led to a greater diversity in offending and a specialization in violent, predatory crimes.[39] The drug trade itself also promotes violence. Interviews with 18- to 25-year-old incarcerated men (135) and women (69) found that almost 50 percent of the men and 16 percent of the women had carried a gun prior to their imprisonment. These percentages were higher for individuals who sold crack cocaine or other drugs. Such offenders were also more likely to have been shot at.[40]

One of the consistent findings in criminological research is the existence of a chronic offender group that is predominantly responsible for crime (see Chapter 9). An analysis of data from the 2000–2001 from the National Epidemiologic Survey on Alcohol and Related Conditions (N > 43,000) uncovered a severe class of just over 5 percent of the respondents who were pathologically involved in varied and intensive forms of antisocial behavior. These individuals were prone to extensive psychiatric disturbance and confirmed previous findings on career criminal and life-course-persistent criminality on the existence of a small, persistent group of offenders.[41]

Much of the crime committed by heroin addicts is devoted to obtaining funds to purchase more drugs. Research shows that the crime rate among heroin addicts is higher during periods of active addiction.[42] This pattern apparently holds true for both blacks and whites.[43] Another study found that most heroin addicts began committing minor property crimes before becoming addicted. Then, as their drug use increased, their rate of property crime increased. They also engaged in drug dealing to support their habit.[44]

Ball and his colleagues interviewed a sample of 243 heroin addicts from a population of 4,069 males arrested by the Baltimore Police Department between 1952 and 1971. Over an 11-year period, these addicts committed over 473,000 crimes—averaging 178 crimes per offender per year. The dominant offense was larceny-theft, but over 60 percent of the sample were arrested more than once

for violent crimes. Arrest and incarceration had little deterrent effect on their criminal careers.[45]

Similarly, Ball compared crime rate findings on three groups of male heroin addicts enrolled in methadone-maintenance programs in New York City, Philadelphia, and Baltimore. Addicts from these three cities had comparable offense rates. During an average addiction year, these offenders committed 603 (New York City), 631 (Philadelphia), and 567 (Baltimore) offenses. In each city, the most frequent offense was trafficking in drugs, followed by thefts from stores and forgery (checks). There were no notable differences in either the volume or pattern of offenses committed by the three groups of heroin addicts.[46]

However, research shows that the patterns of crime committed by heroin users are severe. An analysis of studies of heroin, cocaine, and meth over the life course determined that heroin users were among the highest use group, had earlier onsets of drug use and criminal behavior, were among the least employed and had higher rates of incarceration.[47] Research results from a random sample (N = 200) of heroin addicted inmates in treatment determined that younger male addicts engaged in severe criminal activity. Although they were likely to deal drugs, they also showed a proclivity for violent crime.[48]

The profitability of crimes committed by heroin addicts varies.[49,50] A study of 105 New York City addicts, for example, showed that during a single day, they committed 46 robberies (average take: $79), 22 burglaries ($112), and 41 thefts ($51). On average, addicts held onto only 5 percent of their money 1 day later. Robbers were

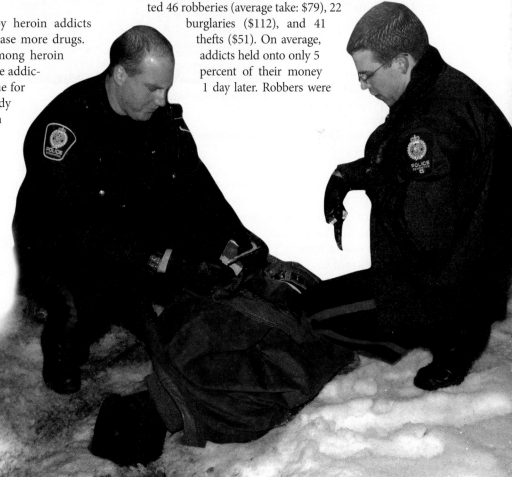

Police arrest a suspect in a drug bust.
© Jack Dagley Photography/ShutterStock, Inc.

the offenders most likely to spend their funds on cocaine and heroin.[51]

Another argument is that drug use fuels crime because heroin addicts need money to purchase additional drugs. However, Inciardi strongly questions this **enslavement theory of addiction**: that monopolistic control over the heroin black market forces addicts into lives of crime to support their habit.[52] The research on the crime rates among heroin and other drug addicts has "convincingly documented that while drug use tends to intensify and perpetuate criminal behavior, it usually does not initiate criminal careers."[53] Similarly, the Chaikens assert that among predatory (violent) offenders, drug use enhances the continuation and seriousness of a criminal career.[54]

Research shows that drug-using lifestyles are also major contributors to the U.S. crime problem. In 2012, the Office of National Drug Control Policy (ONDCP) sponsored the Arrestee Drug Abuse Monitoring II (ADAM II) data collection program in five U.S. counties. Data collected in 2012 revealed the following patterns concerning drug use and crime:[55]

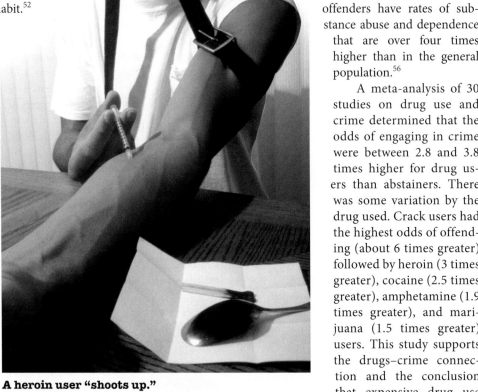

A heroin user "shoots up."
© Tony Freeman/PhotoEdit

- Over 80 percent of adult male booked arrestees in all ADAM II sites in 2012 reported a prior arrest history (arrested at least once prior to the current arrest). In other locations, arrests (two or more per year) ranged from 15 percent (Denver) to 24 percent (Atlanta).
- From 17 percent (Atlanta) to 27 percent (Chicago) of ADAM II arrestees in 2012 had a violent crime as one of the charges recorded for the current arrest. New York experienced a significant decline in the proportion of violent crime charges since 2007, while in Sacramento and Chicago there was a significant increase in violent crime charges since 2007 and 2008. In Atlanta and Denver, the proportion of ADAM II arrestees with a violent crime charge has remained the same since 2007.
- Of ADAM II arrestees in Denver, 19 percent had current drug charges pending, compared to 38 percent in Sacramento and 43 percent in Chicago.

- The percentage of adult male booked arrestees charged with a property crime in 2012 ranged from 15 percent in Denver and Sacramento to 33 percent in New York.

In addition, the National Institutes of Health estimates that offenders have rates of substance abuse and dependence that are over four times higher than in the general population.[56]

A meta-analysis of 30 studies on drug use and crime determined that the odds of engaging in crime were between 2.8 and 3.8 times higher for drug users than abstainers. There was some variation by the drug used. Crack users had the highest odds of offending (about 6 times greater) followed by heroin (3 times greater), cocaine (2.5 times greater), amphetamine (1.9 times greater), and marijuana (1.5 times greater) users. This study supports the drugs–crime connection and the conclusion that expensive drug use (heroin, crack, and cocaine) is linked to income-generating crime.[57] This evidence reveals that frequency of drug use is related to increased criminal activity and shows that a reduction in drug use could lead to declines in both violent and property crime.[58]

The Goldstein Models

Paul J. Goldstein explains how drug abuse sponsors violent behavior. His focus is on the effect of the drug as a promoter of violent crime—specifically, drug-related homicides. There are three different models:[59]

1. The **psychopharmacological model of drug crime**: Violent crime results from the effect of the drug on the offender and/or the victim. The drug sponsors irrational and violent behavior.[60]
2. The **economic-compulsive model of drug crime**: The offender commits a violent crime (e.g., murder or assault) during the course of a robbery. The addict commits crime to get money to support a drug habit.[61]
3. The **systemic model of drug crime**: Some violent crimes are committed because of the pattern of drug

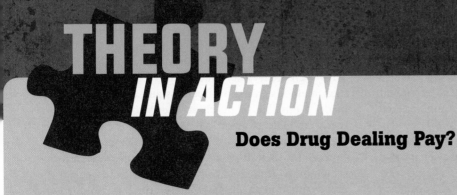

THEORY IN ACTION

Does Drug Dealing Pay?

The drug trade offers the potential to earn large sums of money, enhancing status and power in the underground community. Studies of drug traffickers have revealed how their world operates. One study tracked over 4,900 offenders enrolled in the National Supported Work Demonstration project over a 27 to 30 month period. The results showed that when offenders earned more from drug sales, they also profited from other forms of illegal activity. These forms of crime complemented each other in terms of profitability. Cocaine and heroin use contributed to an across the board increase in all forms of illegal earnings.

However, getting out of the trade is not easy. A study based on life-history interviews with 30 drug traffickers from the El Paso, Texas–Ciudad Juárez, Mexico drug corridor examined their feelings and perceptions about leaving the drug trade. They highlighted five reasons for getting out of the game: (1) punishment: fear of apprehension or death at the hands of cartel members; (2) self-identity and image: power and status were major factors that prevented their exit from drug trafficking; (3) social ties; (4) changes in the life course: family obligations (to protect them from harm) led many traffickers out of the drug trade; and (5) drug use/abuse: many of the traffickers were drug users and abstaining exacerbated the need to get out. Many of these former traffickers had dreams of book deals, movie and TV appearances, or documentaries based on their life experiences. Consider the following case study.

Max was an 18-year-old organizer and leader of a drug crew dealing in a major eastern city in the mid-1980s, before the advent of crack cocaine. Max's supplier "loaned" him 3–5 kilos of pure cocaine (the street value of which was between $180,000 and $360,000 at the time) for distribution. Max returned about $100,000 a week.

When the crew was formed in 1983, Max supplied each member with the amount of cocaine they needed. They handled sales to customers. After a designated time, they would return either money or unsold cocaine to Max and he would pay their supplier. Estimates in the mid-1980s were that Max

and his top dealer could easily make a tax-free income of $100,000 or more after expenses.

Thus, Max and his crew chose the benefits they could derive from their illegal activities and were selling their labor and sales skills in spite of the risk of receiving a substantial prison sentence on apprehension and conviction. By selling high-quality cocaine to middle-class buyers (who would seldom interact with them otherwise), Max and his crewmembers were taking advantage of the benefits of an illicit economy. The profits they could realize from the cocaine market were unlikely to present themselves elsewhere.

Max could enjoy the cocaine economy. He regularly sent a trusted relative back to Santo Domingo with $50,000 in cash, which they converted at a very favorable exchange rate to the national economy. Max's otherwise destitute relatives could thus purchase comfortable homes in their homeland. Upon their arrival in the United States, several of his relatives also benefited by purchasing grocery stores (bodegas) and other cash businesses with Max's drug profits.

By the end of the 1980s, Max retired from the cocaine business at the request of his wife. He is reported to be living comfortably in Florida.

Use Merton's theory of anomie and Messner and Rosenfeld's institutional anomie theory to analyze Max's involvement in the cocaine trade. Do these theories explain his involvement?

Sources: Campbell, H., & Hansen, T. (2012). Getting out of the game: Desistence from drug trafficking. *International Journal of Drug Policy*, *23*, 481–487; Johnson, B. D., Williams, T., Dei, K. A., & Sanabria, H. (1990). Drug abuse in the inner city: Impact upon hard-drug users and the community. In M. Tonry & N. Morris (Eds.), *Drugs and crime.* Chicago: University of Chicago Press, pp. 25–26; Thompson, M., & Uggen, C. (2012). Dealers, thieves, and the common determinants of drug and nondrug illegal earnings. *Criminology, 50*, 4, 1057–1087.

---

use and distribution. These crimes represent an outgrowth of the system of drug dealing (e.g., gang wars) or reflect disputes between dealers and consumers (e.g., poor-quality drugs, failure to make payment) within a black market, elimination of informers, and robberies of drug dealers followed by retaliation.

Collins and Lapsley have noted that a fourth model could be added—crimes that directly result from the drug trade, such as drug manufacturing and trafficking.[62]

Inciardi states that heroin use promotes psychopharmacological violence. For example, heroin-using prostitutes often engage in violence against their customers due to the irritability caused by withdrawal. This leads them to rob, rather than service, their clients.[63] He also believes that all three of the Goldstein models explain the impact of crack cocaine. First, the chronic use of crack leads to the "cocaine psychosis-paranoia that may lead to violent behavior against imagined persecutors." Cocaine-related violence may thus fit the psychopharmacological model. Second, crack addicts may commit robberies and muggings to support their drug habit (economic-compulsive model). Third, systemic violence between cocaine traffickers is a byproduct of the crack trade.[64] This violence is so common it has a street name: tweaking. Studies in New York City and Miami report that cocaine is the "most frequently identified illegal drug in the bodies of homicide victims."[65] TABLE 15-2 shows the norms that have sprung up in this criminal subculture. However, data from the FBI's Uniform Crime Reporting (UCR) program show that, nationwide, the percentage of drug-related homicides is declining and has leveled off since the peak year of 1989—declining to 3.9 percent by 2007 (see TABLE 15-3).

Bennett and Holloway considered the relevance of the Goldstein models to their analysis of interviews with drug offenders in the UK. They stated that Goldstein's models neglect the social context of drug crimes described by these offenders. Their beliefs about how money is obtained and spent, appropriate behavior after intoxication, and lifestyle factors determine their motives and actions. These offenders noted the need for "fast cash" to support their habit and avoid the pain of withdrawal. Drug use was a way to celebrate the successful completion of a crime and a hedonistic pleasure of its own. They expressed no interest in planning for the future and for the consequences of their actions. They were only interested in getting more drugs and their methods were both reckless and dangerous. Money made it possible to purchase showy, conspicuous items that would attract attention and envy on the street. Thus, the social and cultural setting of these drug offenders accounted for their drug use and crime. However, it must be remembered that Goldstein's purpose was to explain the link between drug use and violent crime, not all forms of drug-related crime.[66]

The Goldstein models helped explain the experiences of a treatment sample of 571 substance abuse clients in Ontario, Canada, who did not necessarily have issues with crime and delinquency. Nearly one-half of the clients were involved in at least one violent event in the past year. Most of them reported being under the influence of both drugs and alcohol at the time of the violent event. To obtain drugs, these clients hurt their friends or partners and/or were victimized themselves. They put themselves at risk to get drugs by associating with drug dealers and the dangerous places they inhabit. Thus, all elements of the Goldstein model were in play, illustrating the impact of risky situations sponsored by the attempt to get scarce and illegal substances.[67]

A study of juvenile offenders from the Toledo Adolescent Relationships Study (N = 1,148) examined whether drug dealing had an effect independent of drug use on involvement with delinquent peers, violence,

> **Drug use was a way to celebrate the successful completion of a crime and a hedonistic pleasure of its own.**

TABLE 15-2

Norms of the Criminal Underclass Subculture

The criminal underclass subculture appears to have several norms that facilitate the drug trade:

Illegal means are better than legal means for earning money. Legal money is "chump change." Hustlers are admired for their ability.

Other people are to be manipulated and their goods or money taken for the offender's benefit. For example, women are "hos" valued for sexual favors and the family is expected to provide basic necessities with no financial input from the criminal.

Violence should be used to gain funds and maintain one's reputation.

Illegal income should be spent on luxury items (e.g., gold jewelry, fancy clothes), drugs, and parties rather than basic necessities (e.g., food, shelter, and savings).

Criminals should remain unknown to public officials (police and tax authorities).

Data from Based on Johnson, B. D., Williams, T., Dei, K. A., & Sanabria, H. (1990). Drug abuse in the inner city: Impact upon hard-drug users and the community. In M. Tonry & J. Q. Wilson (Eds.), *Drugs and Crime: Crime and Justice* (13th ed.). Chicago: University of Chicago Press, pp. 26–28.

TABLE 15-3

Drug-Related Homicides by Year

Year	Number of Homicides	Drug Related (%)
1987	17,963	4.9
1988	17,971	5.6
1989	18,954	7.4
1990	20,273	6.7
1991	21,676	6.2
1992	22,716	5.7
1993	23,180	5.5
1994	22,084	5.6
1995	20,232	5.1
1996	16,967	5.0
1997	15,837	5.1
1998	14,276	4.8
1999	13,011	4.5
2000	13,230	4.5
2001	14,061	4.1
2002	14,263	4.7
2003	14,408	4.6
2004	14,210	3.9
2005	14,965	4.0
2006	14,990	5.3
2007	14,831	3.9

Data from Bureau of Justice Statistics. *Drug and crime facts: Drug use and crime*. Retrieved July 7, 2014, from http://www.bjs.gov/content/dcf/duc.cfm

weapons, and drug related conflicts. Drug dealing increased average levels of delinquency within the peer group of the dealer and had a stronger relationship with Goldstein's models than drug use did. The illegal nature of the drug trade sponsors violence and limits the protection of the law that legal markets naturally possess. However, drug dealers had a lower risk for violence and less contact with delinquent peers. As drug users, the drug dealers had more interest in promoting a party lifestyle than engaging in the violent activity that would be required to increase their share of the illegal drug marketplace.[68]

Interviews with 30 incarcerated carjackers who also engaged in drug trafficking found that drug use sponsored violence. They reported that the drugs caused them to act violently when they would not normally do so, and violence was normal behavior in the drug battleground.[69] Circumstances promoting violence are a result of drug prohibition that promotes "virtual anarchy" in the drug market. Fear of apprehension and punishment can lead drug dealers to assault informants and rush exchanges (resulting in fraud and then payback by customers) and violence used by the police.[70] These factors add to the Goldstein models to provide viable explanations for the violence associated with the illegal drug trade.

Women, Drug Abuse, and Crime

To what extent do males and females differ when it comes to substance abuse and crime? Drug use in the month before incarceration among women held in federal prisons increased by more than 11 percentage points in 2004, up from 37 percent in 1997.[71] Researchers studying women, crime, and drug abuse have focused on females as a separate group in treatment programs (e.g., methadone maintenance) and in jail or prison.

One study examined the results of drug testing on probationers and parolees and found that females had a more pronounced and persistent addiction problem than males, and that females were more likely to be cross-addicted to both drugs and alcohol. Women had higher long-term rates of substance abuse and were more likely to inject substances and engage in prostitution to acquire hard drugs. Both of these behaviors put them at greater risk for contracting HIV/AIDS. Females had more problems finding jobs due to their lack of training and experience and their need for childcare and referrals for Aid to Families with Dependent Children (AFDC).[72] Therefore, women face different treatment needs to overcome substance abuse and to return to society. Therapeutic communities for female offenders should include dealing with abusive relationships and domestic violence and anonymous HIV and TB testing.[73] Maybe prison is the best site to provide substance-abuse treatment for substance-abusing, criminally involved females.[74] Prison provides an opportunity to offer services to a group in need while they are incarcerated.

In California, Anglin and Hser studied 328 Anglo and Chicana female methadone-maintenance clients from 1976 to 1978. Although most of the women had committed property crimes before becoming addicted, their criminal activity increased with their level of substance abuse.[75] Sanchez and Johnson found a similar pattern among drug-abusing women at New York's Rikers Island prison. The women who were daily users of heroin and cocaine had higher crime rates (e.g., property and drug crimes, fraud, and prostitution) than those who limited their drug use to marijuana, depressants, stimulants, or illegal methadone.[76]

Research reveals no clear distinction between the level of substance abuse and the crimes committed by female substance abusers. Inciardi and Pottieger compared interview data from two Miami female cohorts. The first cohort used a variety of drugs heavily and committed a great number of property crimes, vice offenses, and drug sales. The second cohort was more likely to abuse heroin and cocaine daily and committed more vice and drug sale crimes but fewer property crimes than the first cohort.[77] Inciardi and his colleagues also found that black female heroin addicts had "productive" criminal careers. Sixty-three women reported that they committed over 32,000 offenses in the past year (median = 332), with prostitution, drug sales, and shoplifting accounting for most of the crimes.[78] Crack cocaine use caused street criminal women to engage in intense patterns of criminality and high-risk sexual behaviors.[79] These substance-abusing women lacked job skills and did not have funds from legal sources to get social and health services, making them more vulnerable to their street-addict lifestyle.[80]

The relationship between female juvenile prostitution and drug use was explored in the analysis of a sample of 128 girls from a large southeastern state in the U.S. About 60 percent of these prostitutes reported the use of drugs and/or alcohol, with most beginning their use 1 year prior to entering the sex trade. The profile of the drug users predominantly featured poor parental control, poor adjustment in school, and prior delinquency referrals. Overall, they presented a troubling set of attributes that are traditionally linked with delinquency that were exacerbated by drug use.[81]

A related question is how women form drug partnerships (for the possession and/or sale of illegal drugs) with men. Pettiway examined the effect of domestic arrangements, drug use, and criminal involvement on participation in crime partnerships by women. He found drug partnerships with men caused women to engage in a greater number of crimes. Also, these crimes were more likely to be vice and predatory crimes when women partnered with men.[82]

Several studies have examined the substance abuse histories of female inmates. A study of 60 female prisoners in a maximum security institution examined the relationship between adverse childhood events and their substance abuse. It found that these female inmates initially turned to drugs as a coping mechanism to deal with such traumas as the loss of a parent or parental abandonment and the effect of poverty, addiction, and violence in the home. Addiction among their family members led to a lack of supervision and the subsequent introduction of the girls to drugs and alcohol.[83]

A review of studies on substance abuse among prisoners (13 studies, 7,653 inmates) reveals substantial differences between male and female inmates. Rates of illegal drug use are higher in the prison than in the general population but the difference is even greater for female inmates. In addition, female inmates have a greater range of drug abuse and dependency than their male counterparts.[84] A comparison of the drug abuse problems of federal male (1,326) and female (318) inmates reached similar conclusions. Women used drugs more frequently, used harder drugs, and used for different reasons than men. They also confronted more difficulties than men in areas linked to substance abuse such as educational background, childhood family environment, adult social environment, mental health, and physical health. These findings underscore the need to establish drug treatment services that address the gender differences in the prison population.[85]

A study of 801 female inmates incarcerated in Minnesota reveal drug abuse differences within the population itself. Overall, these inmates exhibited problems of dependence for stimulants, marijuana, and heroin. Nearly half of the group depended on two or more substances. Over one-half of the female inmates dependent on alcohol also abused another substance. Differences in substance abuse disorder existed across ethnic groups of female inmates. Stimulant dependence was notable among Caucasian women. They were 10 times more likely to receive this diagnosis. African American female inmates were 2.83 times more likely to depend on cocaine. Native Americans were more likely to abuse alcohol and heroin than the other ethnic groups. Again, these findings show that female inmates may require treatment services that are tied to their individual substance abuse issues and that these differences may extend further across ethnic groups.[86]

Survey results from a nationally representative sample of female inmates (N = 2,930) examined the relationship between mental health issues, drug usage, and institutional misconduct. Serious misconduct offenses were higher for younger, African American, unmarried, female inmates and those convicted of violent offenses, a history of prior arrests, and who reported pre-incarceration victimization. However, female inmates with co-occurring disorders (COD; both mental illness and substance abuse) were the most likely to be charged with prison misconduct. These findings show that females suffering from COD are likely to have significant problems adjusting to the prison environment.[87] Problems with COD for female inmates (N = 655) existed in a sample from a large prison in the southeastern U.S. The study found that injection drug use (IDU) was highest for prisoners who: were white, had a prior history of substance abuse treatment, had a prior drug related charge, had a history of mental illness, had more than a high school education, and were problem drinkers. Since inmates who engaged in IDU are at higher risk for HIV/AIDS, these findings show the need to focus on the factors that identify this prison subpopulation.[88]

Overall, the research on women, drug abuse, and crime show that addicted women engage in higher rates of crime when they are abusing drugs. However, instead of violent crimes, they more often commit property and vice crimes. The studies also confirm that female offenders with drug problems have different treatment needs that should be addressed to protect the community from further victimization. Programs must address these differences and not treat males and females in the same fashion. Because the impact of addiction is so dissimilar for males and females, treatment

A female drug addict smoking heroin.
© CREATISTA/ShutterStock, Inc.

programs must consider the special problems that women, particularly mothers, face.

Delinquency and Drug Abuse

Drugs also appear to play a central role in delinquency. Chaiken and Johnson reported that adolescents who used multiple drugs were more likely to be seriously delinquent. Young men and women who drank alcohol and used marijuana were likely to be truant and to steal. Juveniles who distributed drugs committed 60 percent of all teenage felony thefts. In addition, they were more likely to continue their criminal careers as adults.[89]

In Florida, youths who tested positive for marijuana/hashish use had more juvenile court referrals for nondrug felony offenses[90,91] Interviews from New York City revealed that seriously delinquent youths were regular users of drugs and alcohol. The most delinquent youths had the most significant substance-abuse histories.[92] The National Youth Survey is an important source of information on substance-abuse rates among juveniles. An analysis of these data revealed that a very small proportion of drug-abusing delinquents (less that 5 percent of American youths) accounted for up to 60 percent of felony crimes committed by delinquents. However, these reported crimes were not the result of an attempt to get drug money.[93] Findings from the Pittsburgh Youth Study show that drug-abusing youths often commit violent crimes and offenses with others and are likely to be arrested.[94] The Youth Risk Behavior Survey determined that the availability of drugs raised the level of school violence and increased with the number of drugs used.[95]

Other studies on drug abuse and delinquency established no direct relationship between the two. In one study, there was some indication that alcohol played a role in sexual assault and that serious drug abuse led to prolonged involvement in serious delinquency.[96] Factors influencing drug abuse among juveniles included age (older) and peer group influence. Yet they did not relate to delinquency. A survey of male and female adolescents revealed that marijuana use was related to property offenses but was not associated with aggressive delinquency.[97]

A study of four waves of data on 449 Los Angeles county youths on probation examined the relationship between substance use and delinquency over four time periods. For all three types of delinquent behavior (interpersonal, drug related, and violent offenses), substance use predicted future delinquency. For interpersonal crime, delinquent behavior predicted future substance abuse in a reciprocal relationship. Both behaviors had an equal impact on the other. Therefore, if one is influenced or prevented, the other should also be reduced.[98]

The long-term influence of delinquency on drug use initiation was examined in a sample of African American youth among serious and non-serious delinquents who were residents of Woodlawn, an inner city community in Chicago. Serious delinquency increased the risk of drug initiation for marijuana and cocaine. Yet, the serious delinquents also presented problems that could influence drug initiation—evidence of conduct problems in school, weak family discipline, and early onset of marijuana use.[99] Additional analysis of this sample found that heavy marijuana users were more likely to engage in drug related and property crime but not violent crime. This activity led to a more extensive arrest record that increased their risk of incarceration. Preventing heavy marijuana use among juveniles may prove effective in reducing the juvenile incarcerated population.[100]

Studies also show that drug use is related to childhood physical and sexual abuse.[101] A study of juvenile drug abusers and their families revealed that juvenile self-esteem and perception of parental behavior, as well as parental attitudes toward child rearing, influenced levels of drug use. Juveniles who are physically and sexually abused and who are raised in a laissez-faire atmosphere about drugs without strict parental supervision were more likely to abuse illegal drugs.[102]

Gang involvement also plays an important role in the link between delinquency and drug abuse. In examining drug use and dealing among juvenile gang members in Los Angeles, San Diego, and Chicago, Fagan found that the level of gang-crime activity was related to the amount of drug use within the gang.[103] However, the link to violent crime was not directly related to substance abuse. Gangs closely involved in the sale of drugs were disorganized. Predominately male gangs who had, and were willing to use, guns were more likely to engage in drug trafficking.[104–107]

However, the nature of the drug used may play a role in this relationship. For example, Inciardi and Pottieger interviewed 254 Miami delinquents concerning their involvement with crack cocaine. The youths in the crack business used marijuana, depressants, or crack on an almost daily basis. These dealers also spent more money on crack than other delinquents and had a longer and more serious delinquent career at a younger age.[108]

In her review of the literature on delinquency and drug use, White concluded that these behaviors are not causally related, but rather are independent manifestations of the deviant behavior in which juveniles engage. She also found that the majority of adolescents, despite their level of substance abuse, have little or no involvement with delinquency. Peer-group influences appear to be the best predictors of both delinquency and drug abuse.[109]

Types of Illegal Drugs: Drug Abuse and Trends

Controlled substances are grouped by pharmacological and legal criteria, and they fall into several categories: anabolic steroids, cannabis, depressants, hallucinogens, inhalants, and stimulants. Drugs, substances, and certain chemicals used to make drugs are classified into five distinct categories or schedules depending on the drug's acceptable medical use and its abuse or dependency potential. The abuse rate is a determinate factor in the scheduling of the drug; for example, Schedule I drugs are considered the most dangerous class of drugs with a high potential for abuse and potentially severe psychological and/or physical dependence. As the drug schedule changes—Schedule II, Schedule III, etc., so does the abuse potential—Schedule V drugs represents the least potential for abuse. Here is a partial listing of drugs and their schedule under the Federal Controlled Substance Act:[110]

- *Schedule I*: The most dangerous drugs with potentially severe psychological or physical dependence: heroin, LSD, marijuana, ecstasy, methaqualone, and peyote
- *Schedule II*: Considered to have a high potential for abuse and considered dangerous: cocaine, methamphetamine, Dilaudid, Demerol, Oxycontin, fentanyl, Dexedrine, Adderall, and Ritalin
- *Schedule III*: Moderate to low potential for abuse and dependency: Tylenol with codeine, ketamine, anabolic steroids, and testosterone
- *Schedule IV*: Low potential for dependency: Xanax, Soma, Darvon, Darvocet, Valium, Ativan, Talwin, and Ambien
- *Schedule V*: Even lower potential for abuse: Robitussin AC, Lomotil, Motofen, Lyrica, and Parepectolin

Since 1970, the Controlled Substances Act places all substances regulated in some way under existing federal law into these categories.

Trends in Use

Since 1975, the annual Monitoring the Future (MTF) survey has studied the extent of drug abuse among high school 12th-graders. The survey was expanded in 1991 to include 8th- and 10th-graders. Funded by the National Institute on Drug Abuse, the survey is conducted by the University of Michigan's Institute for Social Research. The goal of the survey is to collect data (30-day, annual, and lifetime) for drug use among students. **TABLE 15-4** lists the key findings from the 2013 MTF.

The use of several drugs held steady in 2013. These include cocaine (both powder and "crack" forms), LSD, amphetamines, ecstasy, methamphetamine, crystal methamphetamine, heroin, Rohypnol, Ketamine, steroids, and sedatives. Also holding steady was the illegal use of the prescription drugs Adderall, Ritalin, Oxycontin, and any other prescription drug taken without medical supervision.

Alcohol was the substance most widely used by teenagers. Despite recent declining rates, seven out of every ten students (68%) have consumed alcohol (more than just a few sips) by the end of high school, and three out of ten (28%) have done so by 8th grade. In fact, about half (52%) of 12th graders and one eighth (12%) of 8th graders in 2013 reported having been drunk at least once in their life.

Data from the 2013 National Drug Assessment from the U.S. Drug Enforcement Administration estimated the flow and availability of illegal drugs. However, one of the greatest threats was the availability of controlled prescription drugs (CPDs). CPDs were the most common drug used illegally in 2012 and were the drug group most commonly involved in drug overdose deaths. In 2011, 6.1 million people (2.7% of the U.S. population) abused CPDs.[111]

Analysis of data from the ADAM program (10 sites) over the decade beginning in the year 2000 revealed that, although crack cocaine was declining in use, an older group of crack addicts still existed. Heroin use appeared to be strongly related to a small population of offenders that continues to attract new users. Powder cocaine was not nearly as popular as crack had once been, but a small group of active offenders appears to still use the drug. In addition, methamphetamine use appeared to be limited to a specific population of arrestees at certain locations. The current drug of choice among arrestees was marijuana—a drug that is presently being decriminalized and legalized.[112]

Patterns of prescription drug use in a survey of young New York City adults (N = 1,207) who frequented nightlife venues found that respondents had a lifetime misuse rate for prescription drugs of 44.1 percent and recent misuse of 29.2 percent. The misuse of prescription drugs declined as this group aged. Men had higher rates of prescription drug misuse but no other demographic differences emerged.[113] Again, these results showed that drug use in different populations must be studied before any conclusions are reached.

TABLE 15-4

Key Findings from the 2013 Monitoring the Future Survey

Any illicit drug	Annual prevalence of using any illicit drug increased in all three grades: by 1.5 percentage points in 8th grade, 1.6 percentage points in 10th, and 0.6 percentage points in 12th. For the three grades combined, the rate was up by 1.3 percentage points in 2013.
Synthetic marijuana	Use decreased by 3.4 percentage points in 2013 to 7.9% among 12th graders and declined over the three grades by a statistically significant rate of 1.6%.
Inhalants	The sharpest decline occurred among 8th graders, the grade with the highest prevalence; use dropped by 1.1 percentage points to 5.2%
Vicodin	Use for nonmedical purposes significantly declined among 12th graders; annual prevalence fell from 7.5% in 2012 to 5.3% in 2013. However, the lower grades showed virtually no change, though use has declined significantly in all grades since 2008.

Data from Johnston, L. D., O'Malley, P. M., Miech, R. A., Bachman, J. G., & Schulenberg, J. E. (2014). *Monitoring the future national results on drug use: 1975–2013: Overview, key findings on adolescent drug use.* Ann Arbor: Institute for Social Research, The University of Michigan.

The Threat of Methamphetamine

Methamphetamine (meth) proved to be the scourge of the early 21st century. Its use has a great and deleterious effect—increasing energy and alertness while decreasing appetite. It is a powerful central nervous system stimulant that produces a short, intense "rush" when used due to release of high levels of dopamine from the brain. Methamphetamine can be smoked (in its granulated, crystal form known as "ice"), snorted, ingested orally, or injected.[114,115]

Nationally, the 2012 National Survey on Drug Use and Health (NSDUH) noted that the number of recent new users of methamphetamine among people age 12 or older was 133,000 in 2012. This figure duplicated the 2011 estimate and was similar to the 2010 estimate for meth use. However, the number of initiates in 2012 was lower than those in previous years. The average age at first use among new methamphetamine users in 2012 was 19.7 years. This figure was similar to the corresponding estimates from 2002 to 2011 (ranging from 17.8 to 22.2 years).[116] In a 2004 survey, approximately 23.5 percent of state prisoners and 17.9 percent of federal inmates admitted using meth at some point in time. Between 1997 and 2007, the number of persons admitted to drug treatment primarily for meth use increased from 53,694 in 1997 to 137,154 in 2007—a 155 percent increase.[117] While national trends have registered a decline in meth use, variations are present across regions of the country. In the first half of 2012, individuals using meth registered first in drug related treatment admissions in Hawaii and San Diego, second in San Francisco, and third in Denver and Phoenix.[118]

The average age at first use among new methamphetamine users in 2012 was 19.7 years.

Self-reported meth use was studied in a survey of 8th and 11th grade Oregon residents and the Oregon Healthy Teens survey. The results determined that the rate of meth use was 6 percent for girls and 5.6 percent for boys in the 11th grade. Gender differences were also noted for variables associated with meth use. Females in both grades were much more likely than males to use meth if they had engaged in antisocial behavior. Female 8th graders were more likely to use meth if they also used marijuana. Substance abuse correlated for both 8th grade (alcohol) and 11th grade (marijuana) boys. Engagement in risky sexual behaviors were reported by females in both grades and for 11th grade males. Parental influence had little effect on meth use for these adolescents.[119]

A sample of Wyoming inmates screened for drug use in 2005–2006 as they entered prison found that whites and males were more likely to have used meth prior to incarceration. In terms of social disorganization theory (see Chapter 6), inmates with family-type living arrangements and more extensive friendship networks were less likely to use the drug. Those inmates from female-headed households and from racially and ethnically more homogenous and less densely populated areas were more likely to use meth. Therefore, meth use was common in socially disorganized areas where primary social relationships were weak. Rural areas that are less densely populated provide ideal conditions to produce meth and racial/ethnic homogeneity is more likely to promote social norms conducive to its use.[120] However, the location of over 14,000 seized meth labs were found to be unrelated to social disorganization measures. Counties with high rates of meth lab seizures were predominantly white,

English-speaking, racially segregated, and had a considerable presence of evangelical churches, manufacturing-based employment, greater farm population, more female-headed households, a higher than average property crime rate, a population that had recently moved into the area, and a higher rate of occupied housing. The policy that made meth precursors more difficult to obtain had a significant impact. Prior to the implementation of this mandate, meth lab seizures spiked but after its passage, they declined and maintained that lower level.[121]

One unique aspect of the drug is that the dreadful effects of its use hit both individuals and others. Chronic abuse of methamphetamine can lead to psychotic behavior—intense paranoia, visual and auditory hallucinations (including the delusion that "crank bugs" are crawling under the user's skin), and out of control violent rages. Physically, the drug can cause inflammation of the heart lining, rapid heart rate, irregular heartbeat, increased blood pressure, damage to the small blood vessels of the brain, and even acute lead poisoning (lead acetate is commonly used to produce this drug).[122]

Meth producers can sustain life-threatening injuries from the volatile chemicals used to make the drug and the explosions and fires that can result from its production. These threats also extend to the partners and children of producers and to their neighbors and first responders to the site of a meth lab. Because meth increases the libido while reducing inhibitions, users (both hetero- and homosexual) face an increased risk of acquiring STDs, including AIDS.[123] Another study of meth patients from a Level I trauma center, determined that meth patients were more likely to have injuries from assaults, including gunshot and stab wounds. They were also more likely to have attempted suicide, had an altercation with the police, or been the victim of domestic violence.[124] A RAND Corporation study estimated that the economic burden of methamphetamine in the United States in 2005 (drug treatment, health costs, addiction, premature death, lost productivity, crime and criminal justice costs, child endangerment, and harms resulting from production) was between $16.2 to $48.3 billion.[125]

Interviews with 350 California meth users in treatment found support for the Goldstein model of drug based violence. Meth related violence was strongest among youths, and

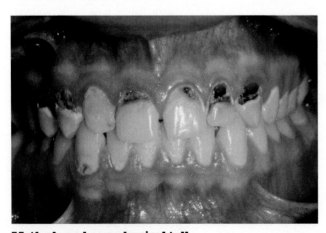

Meth abuse has a physical toll.
© Dr. Douglas Damm, University of Kentucky College of Dentistry/AP Photos

people with a history of psychiatric hospitalization, paranoia, and selling meth. Meth users said that they were more violent when under the numbing effect of the drug. Yet, more than one-half of the violent meth users stated that their behavior began before they used meth. Meth use thus may have aggravated violent tendencies that were already evident.[126]

Weisheit notes that meth labs pose a threat to citizens that other illegal drugs do not. First, production of the drug can be very close to the point of sale and can be located anywhere. It is not subject to a growing season like cocaine and heroin. Its production is elastic—the meth manufacturer can expand and contract operations as he or she sees fit. Its domestic, illicit manufacture poses several problems. Methamphetamine production "becomes a business run by people with no stake in the well-being of the local community."[127]

Meth laboratories contaminate surrounding property. One pound of meth produced in a lab yields 5–6 pounds of hazardous waste.[128] Meth labs contain hazardous and health-threatening levels of such chemicals as phosphine (a severe pulmonary irritant), iodine, anhydrous ammonia (exposure may cause chronic cough, bronchitis, asthma, vocal cord dysfunction, reactive airways, disease, and lung fibrosis), and hydrogen chloride (a strong irritant to the eyes, mucous membranes, and skin). Iodine persisted in the walls, carpeting, draperies, and furnishings of meth lab locations—a danger to children in such enclosures. On the basis of such evidence, one study concluded that the chemical concentrations present in meth labs present "an extremely dangerous environment for investigating officers, the criminals themselves, and especially for children."[129]

Overall, the toxic threat posed by meth labs makes methamphetamine an illegal drug unlike any other that challenges the United States today. Meth manufacturing creates a hazard to the community on the scale of environmental and violent crimes. No other drug presents such a danger to all who might encounter it. Meth precursor availability laws brought the hazards of meth production under control by making its manufacture more difficult.

As with other drugs, control of meth availability is more difficult to accomplish. The academic and professional literature on meth production revealed that shifts in local manufacturing were counterbalanced by changes in production and trafficking by Mexican drug cartels. Operatives in the illegal drug trade have been able to easily adapt to changes in meth availability. The violence that accompanies Mexican drug trafficking worsens the dangers of meth production.[130]

The effect of requiring prescriptions for ephedrine and pseudoephedrine products (meth precursors) on meth labs was examined over several states. These prescription precursors had no effect on meth lab seizure rates in Oregon but their seizure rate was low prior to implementation. Mississippi experienced a significant reduction in meth lab seizures—a decrease of 50.2 percent from the baseline preceding the regulation. Collective adoption by states was recommended to make manufacture of meth more difficult.[131]

The Impact of Treatment

Treatment for drug-abusing offenders can be effective. A research compendium of 41 treatment programs reported significant decreases in heroin and cocaine use among clients in treatment.[132] A review of the treatment literature by Gendreau and Ross found that "addicts who stay the course of treatment or re-enroll after initial failure can decrease their drug intake and reduce criminal offenses."[133] Reviewing drug-abuse treatment programs, Anglin and Hser conclude that the longer a client remains in treatment, the greater the probability of success.[134] Boyum and Kleiman note that drug treatment has supply-reduction and demand-reduction benefits that hold whether participation in treatment is voluntary or coerced.[135]

These findings underscore the value of effective offender treatment programs. For example, a New York City study of a methadone maintenance program discovered that clients who stayed with the treatment had less involvement in criminal activity.[136] Research on the Kentucky Substance Abuse Program (KSAP) found that parolees who completed the program had lower reincarceration rates during the first and second year of operations (3.6% and 9.7%) than those who did not complete treatment (35.2% and 36.6%). Other research tracked clients referred to KSAP because of a positive drug test. Clients who completed treatment had a 3 percent reincarceration rate compared with 17.5 percent of persons who were referred but did not complete treatment and 6 percent for members of a comparison group.[137] A longitudinal study of clients from the Treatment Outcome Perspective study revealed that the longer they were in treatment, the less likely clients were to use drugs, have drug-related problems, and engage in criminal behavior. Time in treatment was found to be more significant than employment and criminal activity in promoting the recovery and rehabilitation of clients.[138]

A meta-analysis of 243 studies of drug treatment programs applied the Andrews' risk principles to the effectiveness of these treatments. Andrews' risk principles are designed to guide the provision of services to offenders to prevent recidivism. This study considered what effect they had on drug use and recidivism. It found that Andrews' risk principles had a greater impact on recidivism than on drug use outcomes.[139]

Research on substance abuse treatment programs for offenders found that programs based on cognitive–behavioral therapy, therapeutic communities, and drug courts produced both lower recidivism rates and drug use. The most effective programs focused on high-risk offenders, provided strong inducements for treatment, included several types of simultaneous interventions (treatment plus drug testing), provided intensive treatment, and included an aftercare component.

Aftercare was important regarding prison-based programs (boot camps and therapeutic communities).[140]

Initiated in Miami in 1989, drug courts are another method for dealing with offenders convicted of drug offenses. A drug court is an intensive, community-based treatment and supervision program that is supervised by a judge, coupled with interaction between treatment, law enforcement, and court personnel.[141] Overall, studies have showed that drug courts can effectively reduce both substance abuse and recidivism.[142] Their use is continuing to expand across the country.

These findings underscore the need for effective offender treatment. Punitive sanctions should be coupled with treatment to prevent crime. For example, a therapeutic community (TC) can be combined with work release to treat offenders while helping the community. The impact of prison-based therapeutic communities in a study of five prisons with established comparison groups found some modest impact for them. TCs had a moderate impact on reincarceration over the 4-year follow-up period. However, its effect on drug relapse was negligible and on re-arrest was not significant. Older offenders were more likely to relapse into drug abuse. Inmates who had time remaining on their sentence and those who were employed on release had lower rates of reincarceration, drug relapse, and rearrest. The results confirmed the effectiveness of TCs as a drug treatment regimen for offenders.[143]

Diverting felons convicted of drug offenses to residential treatment is a demonstrated method of handling these crimes.[144] Evidence of the effectiveness of treatment for opioid-dependent offenders was found in the study of a nationally representative sample of over 1,100 patients. The average overall reduction in convictions was estimated at 10 percent for every 6 months in treatment.[145] A comparison of the recidivism rates of offenders referred to mandatory treatment under Kansas Bill 123 with offenders under community supervision found that the bill had no effect on reincarceration, decreased the likelihood of reconviction relative to court services and community corrections, and decreased the likelihood of revocation compared to those in community corrections but increased revocation compared to those inmates in court services. Due to the increased levels of supervision, offenders who served under the program had higher rates of revocation—a common finding among such initiatives.[146]

A report by the Justice Policy Institute argues that treatment is a much more productive and cost-effective method of dealing with substance abusing offenders. It reduces the societal costs of drug abuse more effectively than incarceration by decreasing illicit drug use and recidivism while building ties to the community.[147] In sum, drug treatment is a promising method to deal with drugs and crime.

> *Punitive sanctions should be coupled with treatment to prevent crime.*

The Economics of Drugs and Crime

Drug selling is a lucrative business. The United Nations Office for Drug Control and Crime estimated that transnational organized crime gained about $130 billion from the international illicit drug trade in 2009. Gross profits for cocaine sales were estimated at $84 billion in 2009. It was also estimated that the socioeconomic costs of the illegal drug trade were three times higher than the profits generated.[148] High profitability attracts sellers to the drug marketplace. According to a report to the Office of National Drug Control Policy, wholesale powder cocaine prices nationwide ranged from $125 to $145 per gram from 2003 to 2008. Crack cocaine prices ranged from $170 to $200 per gram. The price of heroin per gram ranged from $360 to $400. Retail methamphetamine prices ranged from $125 to $260 per gram.[149]

Several economic costs are associated with illicit drug use. From 2000–2010, drug users in the United States spent on the order of $100 billion annually on cocaine, heroin, marijuana, and meth.[150] In 2007, the overall societal cost of drug abuse (lost productivity, health, and others, including criminal justice costs) was estimated at $182 billion.[151] In 2010, over 1.6 million arrests were made for drug abuse violations.[152] However, new court commitments for drug offenders have decreased 22 percent between 2006 and 2011.[153]

The crimes that drug abusers commit also cost society dearly. In 2007, the total estimated cost of drug-related crime in the United States was over $61 million (includes criminal justice system costs, victim costs, and other related crime costs).[154]

The link between addiction and crimes committed as a result of drug use has been pursued in research on heroin users. One study estimated that the average heroin abuser committed about 100 crimes per year (especially robbery, burglary, larceny, and shoplifting). The average addict supplemented an annual legal income of $1,000 with an illegal income of $12,000 and contributed more than $20,000 annually to the underground economy. Addicts also increased their illegal income as their daily use of heroin and cocaine increased.[155]

Evidence concerning the link between employment, drug abuse, and levels of criminal activity is mixed. Interviews with 318 narcotic addicts revealed that they derived most of their income during periods of heavy use from illegal activities. When they were not engaged in heavy use, their illegal income plummeted to less than 30 percent of their total income.[156] Similarly, 544 heroin users from five U.S. cities reported that they had lower rates of criminality while they were employed. Employment did not impact the rate of property crimes committed by women, nor did it slow drug sale offenses.[157] A 3-year interview-based study of 615 Australian heroin addicts in treatment found that their criminal involvement declined. The reduction in recidivism led to lower rates of heroin use, severity of dependence, and depression. Gains were also noted with employment so occupational training should be a part of the treatment for heroin addict offenders.[158]

The profits associated with the cocaine trade show similar effect on the economies of developing nations. For example, it is estimated that cocaine dealing added between $2 and $4 billion to the Columbian economy in the 1980s and 1990s. It generated a real estate boom, revalued the Columbian peso, and encouraged contraband imports. However, it also became a source of income for left and right wing guerilla groups and contributed to corruption of the government.[159]

An anti-narcotics officer surveys cocaine seized from a lab in Colombia.
© Ricardo Mazalan/AP Photos

Legalization of Drugs

Some argue that the best way to deal with the drug problem is to legalize drugs. Morris and Hawkins, for example, propose that neither the acquisition nor the purchase, possession, or use of any drug should be a criminal offense as long as it is bought from a licensed druggist through a prescription.[160] Other drug policy analysts have markedly different viewpoints.

Arguments in Favor of Legalization

Proponents of legalization argue that today's drug laws contribute to the drug problem in the following ways:[161]

- In the illegal narcotic trade, the criminal law operates as a "crime tariff" (a tax or duty) that makes the supply of narcotics profitable for the dealers by driving up prices. Simultaneously, it discourages competition by keeping other vendors out of the market.
- Enhanced profits draw organized crime into the drug trade; these crime families grow, diversify, and promote other criminal activity.
- The high price caused by criminalization has a secondary criminogenic effect because it causes people to resort to crime to get the money for drugs.
- Harsh drug laws sponsor and enhance the growth of an extensive criminal subculture. They give drug addiction the romantic aura of rebellion against authority, whereby the addict is viewed as heroic. The rebellious image may have a particular appeal to juveniles and encourage experimentation with dangerous drugs.
- The attempts to enforce drug statutes consume disproportionate amounts of the time, energy, and resources of the criminal justice system, making it more difficult to deal with other types of crime.
- The drug trade promotes the corruption of the criminal justice system, particularly law enforcement officers. The availability of funds makes it possible to bribe officials.
- The drug trade promotes racial injustice. There are five times as many white drug users, yet black men are imprisoned at a rate that is 13.4 times greater than that of white men. In seven states, blacks constitute 80 percent to 90 percent of all drug offenders sentenced to prison.[162]

Current laws against drugs cause rather than deter crime. Therefore, according to these points, current illegal drugs should be legalized and addiction treated as a medical condition. This action would undercut the illicit traffic and largely eliminate the profit incentive supporting that traffic.

Weisheit challenges the "criminalizers" of drugs by attacking several basic assumptions. He makes the following points:[163]

- Criminalizers rely on deterrence theory to provide answers to the drug problem, but fail to identify the most effective level of punishment. Extreme penalties are morally offensive and probably ineffective.
- It is impossible to "take back the streets" and halt the flow of illegal drugs. If law enforcement cannot keep drugs out of prisons, how can interdiction be effective in the free world?
- Criminalizers have been "shamefully silent" on whether the supervised use of drugs for the treatment of some medical problems should be permitted.
- It is difficult to assess the effectiveness of the war on drugs.
- Legal drugs, particularly alcohol and tobacco, are harmful. If some drugs deserve criminal penalties to combat their use, why don't these?
- There are problems associated with drug testing. First, drug tests measure use in the recent past, not current impairment. Second, they violate basic legal principles by presuming guilt until subjects can prove their innocence.
- Increasing the legal stigma attached to drug abuse and trafficking makes it more difficult for offenders to enter legitimate occupations following arrest.
- Law enforcement consumes the bulk of resources available, to the neglect of alternatives such as treatment and prevention.
- Criminalizers assert that controlling the drug problem is the province of social institutions such as the family and the school systems. However, the use of classmates, teachers, and family members as informants may weaken, not strengthen, these institutions.

Criminalization works against society in a variety of other ways. First, it introduces the lower-class juvenile to the illegal drug market because of the vast profits available. Second, it leads to the corruption of law enforcement for the same reason. Third, it exposes police officers to increased risk of death and injury when battling organized crime and juvenile gangs involved in the drug trade. Fourth, drug investigations bend civil liberties in the name of crime control. Fifth, the war on drugs is waged primarily against the poor and thus obscures the rate and type of substance abuse in the middle and upper classes. It also ignores the money that legal enterprises like banks (money laundering) and real estate agencies (the purchase of real estate by drug dealers for cash) gain from the illegal drug trade. Criminalization promotes disrespect for the law and leaves the door open to extreme, totalitarian penalties such as work camps for drug offenders.[164]

Another proponent of legalization, Arnold Trebach, makes several "policy resolutions:"[165]

- The war on drugs should end everywhere. Experiments should be encouraged in various nations and localities that include different forms of decriminalization, legalization, and medicalization.
- Small dealers and simple users should be virtually ignored by the police unless they commit other crimes, such as robbery or burglary, or create public nuisances by interfering with the normal flow of street traffic in the drug dealing area.

- The federal government should provide leadership and funds for treatment.
- AIDS treatment should be a special priority, because it is a greater threat to survival than all drugs combined. Intravenous drug abuse is directly linked with the passage of the AIDS virus.
- Society should not forget alcohol and tobacco, because abusers of these legal drugs have the greatest need for affordable treatment.

Trebach calls for consideration of the Dutch approach to drug abuse. This approach features "flexible enforcement," which seeks to ensure that drug users are not caused more harm by prosecution and imprisonment than by using drugs. Addicts are viewed as patients who cannot be helped by being put in jail. In Holland, all drugs remain illegal but peaceful users and small-scale sellers are left alone. Arrest is reserved for blatant sellers and those who are violent or connected with organized crime. Trebach predicts that by following the Dutch model, the United Sates could reduce overcrowding in the criminal justice system.[166]

Arguments Against Legalization

The nation's first drug czar, William Bennett, viewed the legalization arguments as "a call to surrender" with social costs "too great to contemplate."[167] In a similar fashion, James Q. Wilson takes a moral stand against legalization:[168]

I believe that the moral and welfare costs of heavy drug use are so large that society should bear the heavy burden of law enforcement, and its associated corruption and criminality, for the sake of keeping the number of people regularly using heroin and crack as small as possible. I also believe that children should not be raised in communities in which heroin and cocaine are sold at the neighborhood drugstore.

Obviously, there is some point at which the law enforcement costs might become too great for the gains they produce, but I do not think we are at that point yet.

To the criminalizers, the costs of enforcement are worthwhile burdens to prevent the greater and graver evils that the legalization of drugs would create.

Miron offers a "positive analysis of prohibition"—describing its effects. Legalization would make illicit drugs subject to governmental tax and regulation, like other products. However, the demand for illicit drugs would continue. Rather than

eliminate this demand, the black market in illicit drugs would continue despite legalization. Prohibition might reduce demand if consumers exhibit respect for the law and are deterred by the punishment provided for purchase or possession of the drug. In addition, prohibition may have an effect on supply because it increases the cost of manufacturing, transporting, and distributing drugs. As a result, higher prices could lower consumption by drug users.[169]

Inciardi and McBride assert that the drug legalizers are offering a quick solution to a complex problem. Legalization is not a panacea and would require a great deal of thought. The policy questions surrounding legalization include the following:[170]

- What drugs should be legalized and according to what criteria? Who should determine the criteria?
- What potency level should be permitted?
- As with alcohol, should there be age limits on drug use?
- Should certain drugs be made available only to those already dependent on them?
- Where should drugs be sold?
- Will certain establishments be permitted to serve drugs (which ones) to their customers the way bars serve alcohol? Will there be separate drug-using sections in planes, restaurants, and public areas?
- Should it be necessary to get a prescription from a physician? How often should prescriptions be refillable?
- Where should the raw material for the drugs originate? Would cultivation be restricted to U.S. lands or would foreign sources be permitted?
- What kinds of advertising should be permitted?
- If drugs are to be legalized, what types of restrictions on their use should be enacted?
- Which government bureaucracy should be charged with the enforcement of the legalization statutes?

No evidence suggests that government regulation of illegal drugs would be more effective than current law enforcement efforts to reduce substance abuse. The civil lawsuits that would be filed against the government, similar to the suits now being filed against alcohol and tobacco companies by users, would be extremely costly. The government has been arguing for years that these drugs are dangerous. The costs necessary to cover these legal expenses would be passed on to the consumer, making a black market attractive.

Present societal norms are moving toward better health practices, improved diets, more exercise, and a restricted use of alcohol and tobacco. By making harmful substances more readily available, the government would violate these norms.

> **No evidence suggests that government regulation of illegal drugs would be more effective than current law enforcement efforts to reduce substance abuse.**

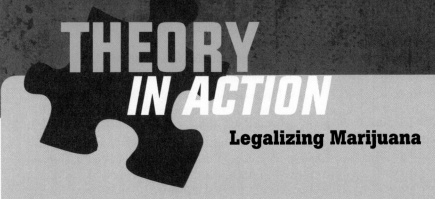

THEORY IN ACTION

Legalizing Marijuana

The drug that has and will continue to attract the most attention for legalization is marijuana. At this writing, marijuana is legal in Colorado and Washington and 18 states (CA, 1996; AK & OR, 1998; ME, 1999; NV, 2000; MT, 2004; RI, 2006; VT & NM, 2007; MI, 2008; NJ, 2010; DE, 2011; CT & MA, 2012; IL & NH, 2013; MD & MN, 2014) and one jurisdiction (Washington, DC; 2011) allow the use of marijuana for medical purposes. *The New York Times* editorial board has called for the legalization of marijuana, advocating that the federal government lift their criminal penalties and allow the states to determine policy on this matter.

A report by the ACLU determined that there were over 8 million marijuana arrests from 2001 to 2010—constituting over half of all drug arrests in the United States. Even though blacks and whites have similar rates of marijuana use, an African American was 3.73 times more likely to be arrested for a marijuana possession. The ACLU report recommended that "it is time to end marijuana possession arrests."

NSDUH estimates that the rate of marijuana use nationwide has increased from 5.8 to 7.3 percent of the population between 2007 and 2012, and that the number of users increased from 14.5 to 18.9 million. Drug testing results on arrestees in 2013 found that marijuana was the most commonly detected drug with results ranging from 34 (Atlanta) to 59 (Sacramento) percent. Marijuana use is higher among offenders, but it does not cause crime and delinquency. The two factors are correlated. Unlike other drugs, marijuana use does not induce violent behavior.

Legalization will increase the number of persons in need of treatment but will also reduce the workload of the criminal justice system and make it possible for law enforcement to focus on other serious problems (like terrorism). Taxes could be based on dollar value or potency of the drug. Taxes of $5/ounce could be easily collected. Tax revenue could reach several billion dollars per year nationwide. Legalization could also reduce the funding of Mexican drug cartels and the violence they promote. A study by the Mexican Institute of Competitiveness estimated that Mexican drug cartels would lose $1.425 billion from Colorado and $1.372 billion from Washington marijuana legalization. Survey results from the Pew Research Center in 2013 notes that 54 percent of Americans now favor marijuana legalization. Of the respondents, 72 percent also felt that government enforcement of marijuana laws was more trouble than it was worth.

Preliminary information from Colorado shows that sales of cannabis from January through May, 2014 brought the state about $23.6 million in revenue from taxes, licenses, and fees.

Across the state, marijuana prosecutions have declined by 77 percent while the number of burglaries and robberies are also down. The Colorado State Patrol reported that traffic fatalities are down 25.5 percent in the first quarter of 2014. However, emergency room visits have documented problems with edible marijuana products. They often contain enough THC to make several people high, so care must be exercised by the user when consuming these products.

In terms of potential tax revenue, Colorado levies a 15 percent tax on cultivators and a 10 percent sales tax on retail sales. Colorado estimates for marijuana tax revenue are $48 million for fiscal year 2014–2015. The state of Washington charges a 25 percent excise tax on marijuana businesses and projects a tax revenue and licensing fee income of $133.7 million in the fiscal 2015–2017 period.

The risks of marijuana legalization appear to be minimal but the consequences of prohibition are evident.

Sources: American Civil Liberties Union. (2014). *The war on marijuana in black and white.* New York: American Civil Liberties Union; Bajaj, V. (August 5, 2014). Rules for the marijuana market. *The New York Times* [Editorial section]. p. 10; Caulkins, J. P., Hawken, A., Kilmer, B., & Kleiman, M. A. R. (2012). *Marijuana legalization: What everyone needs to know.* New York: Oxford University Press; CBS News.com. (October 31, 2012). Study: US marijuana legalization would hurt Mexican cartels. Retrieved August 1, 2014, from http://www.cbsnews.com/news/study-us-marijuana-legalization-would-hurt-mexican-cartels/; Downes, L. The great Colorado weed experiment. (August 3, 2014). *The New York Times* [Editorial section]. p. 10; Let states decide on marijuana. (July 27, 2014). *The New York Times* [Editorial section]. p. 10; Office of National Drug Control Policy. (2014). *2013 Annual Report: Arrestee drug abuse monitoring program II.* Washington, DC: Executive Office of the President; Repeal prohibition, again. (July 27, 2014). *The New York Times, Sunday Review.* p. 1, 10; Substance Abuse and Mental Health Services Administration. (2013). *Results from the 2012 National survey on drug use and health: Summary of national findings*, NSDUH Series H-46, HHS Publication No. (SMA) 13-4795. Rockville, MD: Substance Abuse and Mental Health Services Administration; The National Center for Addiction and Substance Abuse at Columbia University. (2010). *Behind bars II: Substance abuse and America's prison population.* New York: Columbia University; The public lightens up about weed. (July 27, 2014). *The New York Times, Sunday Review.* p. 10.

Even marijuana, now legal for medical use in several states and completely legal in Colorado and Washington, has some very damaging side effects. Smoking marijuana delivers more carcinogens to the system than tobacco. THC (tetrahydrocannabinol) is stored in the parts of the body that have a high-fat content (e.g., brains, lungs, liver, reproductive organs) and thus is more difficult to "flush out."[171] In addition, there is no sign of what the long-term effects of such a buildup might be. The potency of marijuana has risen dramatically over the years. Inciardi notes that heavy use affects the behavior of users, such that they tolerate life's problems rather than confront them and thus problems magnify.[172]

Inciardi believes marijuana should also be classified as a dangerous drug. He points out that legalization would include cocaine (crack in particular)—the drug responsible for much of the drug-related violence (psychopharmacologic, economic, and systemic). It would thus add to and compound the present levels of violence associated with another legal, regulated drug: alcohol.[173]

Most dramatically, proponents of legalization ignore the impact it would have on the lower classes, especially minorities living in ghetto areas. Again, Inciardi notes that drug use is one mode of adaptation to ghetto life. The legalization of drugs would be a nightmare. Inciardi feels it is an "elitist and racist policy that supports the neocolonialist views of underclass population control" and "legalization would initiate a public health problem of unrestrained proportions."[174] Legalization would legitimize the chemical destruction of an urban generation and culture. In place of legalization, Inciardi argues that more attention should be paid to treatment and education of drug users, particularly to ghetto youth.

The War on Drugs

It is abundantly clear that there is no easy solution to this country's drug problems. Perhaps it is time to drop the call for war while continuing more restrained enforcement efforts. The combat analogy has several weaknesses:[175]

- The lack of a clear-cut enemy—the drug war assumes that there are two kinds of people: good and bad. Either one is a drug user or one is drug free, which dehumanizes drug offenders.
- The lack of a clear-cut front—if it is a civil war, this country is the front. If U.S. citizens are concerned with halting production, the front is in foreign countries.
- The lack of consensus on what type of warfare is acceptable—force can have some unintended effects. For example, New York's strict Rockefeller laws led to overcrowding of the courts and jails. It also introduced juveniles into the drug business (because they could avoid the penalties through the juvenile justice system).[176]
- The lack of education and treatment are difficult to successfully implement.
- The lack of total mobilization and unlimited resources.

- The lack of expendable personnel and a willingness to take casualties.
- The lack of strategic leadership by professionals.
- The lack of a national will for victory at any cost.

Beyond increased efforts at education and treatment, a peace policy (to use Trebach's phrase) could be pursued.[177] Drugs and crime are intertwined, but an emphasis on enforcement has damaging hidden costs. A balanced approach to these problems is in order. Enforcement efforts should be related to treatment, but the public should be protected from the harmful effects of illegal drugs. One attempt to deal differently with the drug-crime problem is California's Proposition 36 (see **TABLE 15-5**). It proposes dealing with drug offenders by treating them in the community, rather than putting them in prison.

Conclusion

Drug abuse has had a varied history in the United States. A review of drug policies reveals an equally diverse approach. Illicit drug use may be declining in the United States, but there is evidence that a strong population of users still exists. Strategies to reduce the flow or trafficking of illicit drugs into the United States have been supplemented with education and treatment, with crime reduction as the goal.

There appears to be a strong connection between adult criminality and substance abuse. Efforts that combat drug abuse have stressed deterrence and interdiction even though the research evidence suggests that treatment must be a strong component of any attempt to break the cycle of substance abuse and crime.

Females and juveniles who abuse drugs have different links to crime than adult males. Women are more likely to commit crimes to support their habit, while self-esteem and gang involvement appear to be key factors in juvenile involvement with drugs. Here, again, treatment seems to offer more promise than a hard-line approach.

As Musto suggests, drug use and abuse in the history of the United States is cyclical: "at the beginning phase of a drug epidemic, we are filled with hopeful fantasies about drugs; in the decline phase, we are caught up in anger, scapegoating, and excessive punishment."[178] In fact, the American public goes through a learning process on drug use. It ranges from seeking shortcuts through the use of a new drug to developing awareness by experiencing the unfortunate consequences of drug abuse.

Although the drug market is lucrative and interdiction appears to be ineffective in stopping the flow of drugs, legalization is no panacea to the drug problem. Weisheit notes that there seems to be an "80–20 rule" regarding illegal drugs, in that 20 percent of drug users consume 80 percent of the drugs. This hard-core group is also most likely to be involved in crime and least likely to respond to drug prevention or treatment programs. To Weisheit, the main issue to be faced is what happens to these hard-core users after they have been identified by the criminal justice system.[179]

TABLE 15-5

California's Proposition 36

In 1996, California led the nation in the incarceration of drug offenders—134 per 100,000 citizens—an increase of over 260% over the 1986 rate. In 1999, California spent over $1 million per year to imprison over 45,000 drug offenders. To reverse these trends, California voters passed Proposition 36—the Substance Abuse and Crime Prevention Act (SACPA)—in 2000. Based on an Arizona initiative, this act gives drug offenders the opportunity to take part in community drug treatment programs in place of incarceration or probation.

However, initial research on the impact of the law is mixed. Relative to other comparable groups of drug users, clients of SACPA were more likely to be rearrested for a drug crime, even after controlling for drug use severity and treatment modality. However, the demand for treatment among drug offenders under this act was inadequately met. There were more offenders than available placements. Treatment programs prescribed by California's Proposition 36 reported that high risk offenders had a greater number of rearrests than their low risk counterparts. In both groups, shorter time in treatment created a higher likelihood of recidivism. Therefore, longer treatment periods may prove beneficial for high risk offenders who also required mental health treatment. A study of the costs of the program determined that the additional cost of treatment was offset by savings in other domains.

The California method holds great promise and should be examined in the future. In fact, other states are looking for methods to handle the same problem.

Data from Anglin, M. D., Nosyk, B., Jaffe, A., Urada, D., & Evans, E. (April 18, 2013) Offender diversion into substance abuse disorder treatment: The economic impact of California's proposition 36. *American Journal of Public Health, 103*(6), 1096–1102; Appel, J., Backes, G., & Robbins, J. (2004). California's proposition 36: A success ripe for refinement and replication. *Criminology and Public Policy. 3*, 585–592; Baskin, D. (2004). Proposition 36: Editorial introduction. *Criminology and Public Policy, 3*, 561–562; Evans, E., Huang, D., & Hser, Y-I. (2011). High-risk offenders participating in court-supervised substance abuse treatment: Characteristics, treatment received, and factors associated with recidivism. *Journal of Behavioral Health Services & Research, 38*, 4, 510–525; Farabee, D., Hser, Y-I., Anglin, M. D., & Huang, D. (2004). Recidivism among an early cohort of California's proposition 36 offenders. *Criminology and Public Policy, 3*, 563–584; Inciardi, J. A. (2004). Proposition 36: What did you really expect? *Criminology and Public Policy, 3*, 593–598; Schiraldi, V., Holman, B., & Beatty, P. (2000). *Poor prescription: The costs of imprisoning drug offenders in the United States.* Washington, DC: Justice Policy Institute, pp. 7–9.

Kleiman, Caulkins, and Hawken offer a "consensus list" of drug policies that may have widespread support:[180]

1. Apply testing and sanctions to drug involved offenders.
2. Use behavioral triage to focus treatment on those with greatest need.
3. Expand opiate substitution therapy.
4. Push drug treatment providers toward the use of evidence-based treatment practices and management approaches.
5. Engage healthcare providers in finding problem drug use and interrupting it before it gets out of control.
6. Encourage spontaneous remission.
7. Don't expect the police to eliminate mature drug markets.
8. Use drug law enforcement to reduce violence and disorder.
9. De-emphasize international supply control.
10. Stop pretending that alternative development (i.e. crop substitution) is drug control.
11. Use prevention programs that work.

- The war on drugs is a well-publicized effort waged on several "fronts." Proposed solutions to the drug problem include education, interdiction, and treatment.
- There is a strong link between substance abuse and criminal behavior. Offenders with a substance abuse problem are involved in a high percentage of violent crimes. Drug addicts commit more crime when under the influence of drugs than when they are clean and sober. High levels of illicit drug use are related to greater rates of drug trafficking offenses and other serious crimes.
- Offenders with active drug problems are likely to continue their criminal activities. Prisoners with the most serious criminal records reported a substantial involvement in drug abuse. The crime rate among heroin addicts is higher during periods of active use than in periods of abstinence.
- There is debate whether drug use causes crime or crime causes drug use. The enslavement theory of addiction argues that drug abuse fuels crime because heroin addicts need money to purchase more drugs. Others argue (with the support of research) that although drug use intensifies and perpetuates criminal behavior, it rarely causes it. Others believe that among violent offenders, drug use enhances the continuation and seriousness of a criminal career.
- The Goldstein models explain how drug abuse sponsors violent behavior through the effect of the drug and the motivation for the violent crime. The psychopharmacological model asserts that violent crime results from the effect of the drug on the offender and/or the victim—that it supports irrational and violent behavior. The economic-compulsive model explains that the offender commits a violent crime during the course of a robbery; the addict commits crime to get money to support a drug habit. The systemic model maintains that some violent crimes are committed because of the drug use and distribution system.
- There are differences between males and females regarding substance abuse. Male inmates abuse drugs more often. Women prisoners are more likely to have used heroin, cocaine, PCP, LSD, or methadone. Women who were daily users of heroin and cocaine had higher crime rates than those who limited their drug use to marijuana, depressants, stimulants, or illegal methadone. Women form drug partnerships with men in a variety of ways. Addicted women engage in higher rates of crime when they are abusing drugs.
- Drugs appear to play a crucial role in delinquency. Adolescents who use multiple drugs are more likely to be seriously delinquent. Young men and women who drink alcohol and use marijuana are likely to be truant and to steal. They are more likely to continue their criminal careers as adults. Seriously delinquent youth are regular users of drugs and alcohol. Active delinquent youths had the most significant substance abuse histories.
- Treatment for drug abusing offenders can be effective. Addicts who stay the course of treatment or re-enroll after initial failure can decrease their drug intake and reduce criminal offenses. The longer a client remains in treatment, the greater the probability of success. Research findings emphasize the need for effective offender treatment coupled with punitive sanctions to prevent crime—as specified by the drug court model.
- Drug selling is a lucrative business that establishes an underground economy. High profitability attracts sellers to the drug marketplace. The crimes that drug abusers commit also cost society dearly. Evidence concerning the link between employment, drug abuse, and levels of criminal activity is mixed. The profits associated with the cocaine trade affect the economies of drug-producing countries such as Columbia.
- There appears to be a strong connection between adult criminality and substance abuse, and the efforts to combat drug abuse have stressed deterrence and interdiction. Research suggests that treatment must be a strong component of any attempt to break the cycle of substance abuse and crime.
- Females and juveniles who abuse drugs have different links to crime than adult males. Self-esteem and gang involvement appear to be key factors in juvenile involvement with drugs.

- Legalization is not an easy solution to the drug problem. Treatment is more effective in reducing drug abuse and crime than is generally believed. A more balanced approach toward solving the problems of substance abuse and crime appears to be in order.

PUTTING IT ALL TOGETHER

1. List the arguments for and against the legalization of drugs. Which arguments do you agree with and why?
2. Which approach has the most promise to combat drug abuse: enforcement or treatment? Explain.
3. How does substance abuse promote crime? Is it more accurate to say that crime promotes substance abuse? Compare and contrast these ideas.
4. Discuss the role of violence in drug trafficking.
5. Create a model for a program that will be implemented on campus to deal with substance abuse. What specific needs does your campus have? List the drug issues and outline how to approach each. Which elements would you include in your plan and why?

KEY TERMS

economic-compulsive model of drug crime The offender commits a violent crime (e.g., murder or assault) during the course of a robbery. The addict commits crime to obtain money to support a drug habit.

enslavement theory of addiction This theory assumes that addicts are "slaves" to their habit and are driven to crime by the high cost of drugs.

psychopharmacological model of drug crime Violent crime is a result of the effect of the drug on the offender and/or the victim. In short, the drug sponsors irrational and violent behavior.

systemic model of drug crime Some violent crimes are committed as a result of the pattern of drug use and distribution. These crimes represent an outgrowth of the system of drug dealing (e.g., gang wars) or reflect disputes between dealers and consumers (e.g., poor-quality drugs, failure to make payment) within a black market, elimination of informers, and robberies of drug dealers followed by retaliation.

tweaking The violence against each other in which cocaine dealers routinely engage, in an attempt to control the drug market.

Modern crime, like modern business, is tending toward centralization, organization, and commercialization. Ours is a business nation. Our criminals apply business methods. The men and women of evil have formed trusts.

—Colonel Henry Barrett Chamberlain, Director, Chicago Crime Commission (1919)[1]

Crimes >> of the Powerful: Organized and White-Collar Crime

Objectives

- Explain the similarities between organized crime and legitimate business enterprises.

- Describe the characteristics of organized crime groups in the United States.

- Recognize the difficulties in using current criminological theories to explain white-collar criminals.

- Understand the complexities in defining white-collar crimes.

- Identify different categories of white-collar crimes.

- Identify societal impacts of white-collar crimes.

- Explain white-collar crimes with historic and present examples.

- Describe factors that influence sentencing for white-collar criminals.

Introduction

"Crimes of the powerful" refer to offenses committed by influential persons or groups in society. These offenses are also characterized as "organized," "white-collar," and "enterprise" crime. Besides the fact that both organized crime groups and white-collar criminals have power, they also share other common characteristics. First, they strive for economic control of financial markets, both legal and illegal. They desire monopolistic control of a market so they can control prices. Second, they work to circumvent not only criminal law but also governmental regulations that are aimed at governing markets and protecting consumers. Third, the crimes they commit are costly to society in both human and financial terms. Their goal is to accumulate wealth and exercise power for the benefit of the organization and its members, regardless of the cost to others in society.

Up to this point, we have concentrated on "crimes of the street:" murder, rape, robbery, burglary, and theft. Thus, our focus has been on the less affluent, more disenfranchised people in society. Although members of the middle and upper classes also commit these kinds of street crimes, their position in society creates opportunities for them to commit other kinds of crimes. The crimes of the powerful are often committed by individuals, but large and small groups are just as capable of this type of criminal activity.

Criminologists have devoted a great deal of attention to these forms of crime. This chapter provides an introduction to crimes of the powerful and examines the methods, motives, patterns, and extent of organized and white-collar crime.

Organized crime attempts to gain monopolistic control over illegal markets.

Organized Crime

A considerable number of criminal groups, including street and prison gangs, exist in American society. Some of these groups are organized along racial and ethnic lines. Almost every group of immigrants to American society has developed some form of organized crime, including the Irish, Jews, African Americans, Puerto Ricans, Vietnamese, and Chinese. This chapter focuses on two organized crime groups. The first, the Sicilian Mafia, became a model for others to follow. The second, Russian organized crime, reveals how the Sicilian model has been altered to fit the expanding operations of new organized crime groups.

Similarities Between Organized Crime and Legitimate Business Enterprises

Some marked similarities exist between organized crime and legitimate businesses. Some common attributes are historical. Abadinsky points out that "robber barons" (e.g., John Jacob Astor, Cornelius Vanderbilt, and John D. Rockefeller) founded many of America's foremost businesses but made their fortunes in questionable ways.[2] They rose to the top of American society, enjoying not only great wealth but also legitimate status and power. Bell suggested that organized crime provides immigrant groups with a "queer ladder of social mobility"—a function similar to the opportunities for achievement in legitimate business.[3] These opportunities are otherwise denied to immigrants because of societal prejudice and bias.

In a classic example of Merton's theory of anomie (see Chapter 6), talented individuals gain access to commonly held societal goals of wealth, status, and power through illegitimate means because their access to them by legitimate methods is blocked. Merton believed that upper- and lower-class people adapt to societal goals (i.e., emphasizing money and materialism), whether legitimately or illegitimately, based on the opportunities available to them to achieve those goals. In a capitalist society, the opportunities to achieve goals are not equally distributed. If a person has access to numerous legitimate opportunities to achieve wealth, expectations rise as he or she becomes more successful. If these higher expectations become harder and more difficult to achieve, illegitimate means may become more enticing. Merton would also point out that the difficulties in prosecuting white-collar crimes might add to an environment of anomie for privileged persons.

Organized crime attempts to gain monopolistic control over illegal markets. As with legitimate businesses, the goal is to maximize profit, minimize risk, and meet the public demand for goods and services. Illegal markets follow the same market forces that legitimate businesses routinely deal with (e.g., supply and demand) with the exception they seek monopolistic control, eliminating competition to secure an absolute advantage in the marketplace[4] (see **TABLE 16-1**).

Jay Albanese also argues that corporations often use the same tactics as organized crime families. For example, the "captains of industry"—industry leaders throughout American history—have employed violent tactics to break strikes and maintain their control over a particular market or industry. In the early 1970s, Lockheed Corporation made payments to Japanese officials to get lucrative business contracts and gain a clear advantage over the competition.[5] To hide their financial operations and transactions, organized crime often attempts to enter legal markets. Albanese maintains that these "takeovers" can be predicted (see **TABLE 16-2**). Organized crime is most likely to enter a market in which businesses are small and weak, the markets are open and easy to enter, demand is inelastic, and the people in charge are not well trained.[6]

For example, criminological studies have documented organized crime involvement in the solid and toxic waste disposal industries.[7,8] Szasz reported that corporations and the government made it possible for organized crime families to become involved in these businesses. Lax implementation

TABLE 16-1

Elements of Organized and White-Collar Crime

Element	Organized Crime	White-Collar Crime
Goal	Money and power. Will attempt to fix elections to manipulate the political system. Bribery and corruption of public officials (i.e., police, judiciary) to control the criminal justice system.	Uses profits to amass economic and political power. Will make illegal campaign contributions to gain favor with politicians.
Product	Provides illegal goods and services (drugs, prostitution, gambling, etc.). Use of "muscle" to squeeze out competitors.	Provides legal goods and services but will engage in illegal methods to make a profit.
Monopoly	Aim is to dominate an industry or product (often in a limited geographic area). Will often attempt to enter and control legal markets to protect funds generated from illegal ventures.	Aim is to control an entire market (good or service) to fix prices and ensure profit.
Violence and harm	Violence is used and/or threatened, is a common element, and is direct (i.e., murder with firearms); however illegal services (like the drug trade) also produce great harm indirectly through the product sold. Economic harm is also produced through the manipulation of pension funds and creating a "crime tariff" on construction and other legal goods and services.	Violence is indirect and takes two forms—physical: providing unsafe products, pollution of the environment; and economic: the destruction of jobs and pensions, raising prices.
Organizational	Vertical and hierarchical with "positional power" structure—power resides in the position rather than the person who holds it. Specialization and a division of labor are present, as are rules and regulations to govern the organization. Organization lasts into the future (i.e., many crime families, like the Gambino family, outlive their namesake).	Dependent on the business involved but often bureaucratic and hierarchical. Specialization and a division of labor are present, as are rules and regulations to govern the organization. Organizations are designed to outlive their founders.
Membership	Limited based on expertise ("expert power") and often exclusive based on race or ethnic background.	Also based on expertise (specialized knowledge, advanced degrees), background, and ability.

Source: Bobellian, M. (July 14, 2005). Ebbers sentenced to 25 years for roll in WorldCom fraud. Law.com, available at http://www.law.com.

TABLE 16-2

Organized Crime Risk Assessment Tool

Risk Factors	Measurement Methods
Economic	
Local standard of living is low, encouraging illegal activity	Local economic indicators
High demand for product or service: specific drug, business protection, prostitution, etc.	Addiction levels, arrests, surveys
Affordable supply of product or service (i.e., availability)	Research estimates, seizures
Competitive market: Is it favorable for entry/low barriers for criminal groups?	Research and intelligence on the market

(Continued)

TABLE 16-2 (CONTINUED)

Organized Crime Risk Assessment Tool

Risk Factors	Measurement Methods
Government	
Local government weak in enforcing laws and contracts: the effectiveness of government and courts in enforcing the law	Comparative assessment of effectiveness
Corruption level among local government leaders and businesses: the extent to which local institutions abuse their authority or engage in misconduct	Reports and indicators of corruption
Laws that create or expand the illicit market (e.g., changes in drug laws and tax laws)	Analysis of new and existing laws
Law enforcement	
Level of training of local law enforcement in organized crime investigation (e.g., application of conspiracy laws, fraud and financial crime investigation, use of informants, undercover operations, multijurisdictional task force investigations, witness protection methods, conflict of interest, ethics training)	Comparative assessment of police training in these areas
Working conditions of local law enforcement (to encourage loyalty to profession: e.g., salary level, nature of work assignments, promotional opportunities based on merit)	Comparative assessment of conditions
Level of government interference in police agency(s): Do other government agencies interfere with police investigations or personnel?	Assess known past cases where this occurred
Social/technological change	
Social change? Do recent social changes create or expand illegal opportunity in the market (e.g., local immigration wave, major political upheaval, and cross-border travel)?	Research and intelligence on impact of social changes
New technology? Creates or expands illegal opportunities for a product or service (e.g., level of Internet access, cell phones, and availability of weapons)	Research on impact of current changes in technology
Criminal history and special skills	
Have criminals existed in this market in the past? (increasing the likelihood of future involvement)	Police records, victimization surveys
Have criminal groups existed in this market in the past? (increasing the likelihood of organized crime group involvement in the market)	Police records, victimization surveys
Are technical or language skills or other special access required to participate in the illicit activity (i.e., barriers to entry for new offenders)?	Comparative level of skills/access needed
Harm	
How serious is the potential harm? Estimate the financial and human costs of the activity on this jurisdiction	Projections of cost and social impact

Source: Albanese, J. S. (2001). *The prediction and control of organized crime: A risk assessment instrument for targeting law enforcement efforts,* Research Partnership with Ukraine: Teaming U.S. Researchers and Practitioners with Ukrainian Counterparts to Research High Priority Crime Topics, available at http://www.ojp.usdoj.gov/nij/international/programs/ukr_pred_text.html. Reproduced with permission from the U.S. Department of Justice.

and enforcement of government regulations opened the door to this market. Corporations sponsored further participation by claiming that they were ignorant of organized crime activity or powerless to take an active role against it.[9] When organized crime groups attempt to enter legal markets, it is typical that violence need only be threatened, not actually used.

James Jacobs documents the control that organized crime families had over New York City's legitimate businesses, including the garment district, the Fulton Fish Market, John F. Kennedy Airport, the Javits Convention Center, and the waste hauling and construction industries. He notes that the Italian Mafia had several assets that made it attractive to legitimate businesses. First, the threat of violence deterred would-be competitors and helped maintain control over union labor. Second, they were a reliable business partner who could protect business owners from other criminals or opportunists. The organized crime families had "an entrepreneurial world view and an aptitude for business." One of their prescribed methods was to take a cut of a business rather than take it over. This method is consistent with the Mafia norm "to wet its beak" (*fari vagnari u pizzu*) and also an attribute noted in a study of America's excellent companies—"sticking to the knitting"—concentrating on one's specialty and avoiding overextension.[10,11]

The methods of organized crime are undoubtedly entrepreneurial, opportunistic, and adaptable.[12] Organized crime activities have become diversified, moving beyond the traditional "rackets" (e.g., from prostitution to pornographic DVDs). Like corporations, organized crime has developed into a conglomerate, franchising markets and firms—"the McDonald's-ization of the Mafia."[13] Evidence shows that the Mafia crime families have become involved in white-collar crime scams in health insurance fraud, prepaid telephone cards, and victimization of small Wall Street brokerage houses with loans to stockbrokers who are in debt or need capital to expand their business. Thus, the Mafia has diversified into legal markets through the use of their traditional illegal methods.[14]

International organized crime groups have developed methods to infiltrate and influence financial institutions across the globe. This is accomplished by corrupting bank officials, attorneys, and accountants and through the use of "enemy insiders" to conduct money laundering and financial fraud. The result is billions of dollars in losses each year to consumers and the economy. For example, a case against the Bank of China revealed the existence of a laundering scheme that embezzled more than $485 billion over a 13-year period. A similar scheme run through the Bank of New York by enemy insiders transferred about $7 billion to third parties across the world. Wire transfers were used by Russian Mafia members to launder more than $130 billion through the Moscow-based Intellect Bank to accounts in Sandy, Utah. The stock of YBM Magnex International was used to defraud investors of over $150 million by creating an illusion of profitability.[15]

Theories of Organized Crime

The Alien Conspiracy Model

According to the **alien conspiracy model**, foreign criminals (e.g., Sicilians) import their crime values and family structures and secretly control crime activities. In terms of structure, organized crime is a business-like hierarchy based on a system of formally defined relationships, obligations, and duties.

FIGURE 16-1 outlines the organizational structure of a traditional Mafia (also known as LCN—"La Cosa Nostra"—literally "our thing") family. The *capo* (head or boss) is the unquestioned leader of the family. He settles disputes and tries to avoid making enemies because it is bad for business. In the movie, *The Godfather*, Don Corleone (Marlon Brando) was asked to provide financial and political support to establish drug dealing operations. When he refused, armed conflict broke out among the New York City families. There are three ways to become the boss:

1. When a boss dies of natural causes, the underboss (second in command) often moves up. In *The Godfather*, Don Corleone's son, Michael (Al Pacino) became the boss when Don Corleone died of a heart attack.
2. Forming alliances with other family leaders.
3. Succeeding a boss after he receives a long prison sentence and steps down.

The income, prestige, and power of the boss makes him a target for assassination by ambitious underlings and law enforcement officials. In 1930s New York, Charles "Lucky" Luciano became the head of a Family by arranging the death of Salvatore Maranzano. Later, New York Mayor Rudolph Guiliani built his political career on the reputation he established as a successful federal prosecutor of Mafia kingpins.

The *consigliere* (counselor) is a trusted advisor to the boss. Typically, he is a respected Mafia elder, devoid of ambition, and gives advice because it is the "right thing to do." Often a settler of disputes, the *consigliere* offers mediation between members of the Family and the boss and advises the boss on business matters. The boss selects an underboss based on loyalty, trust, and talent. He helps guide day-to-day operations. The *caporegimes* (captains) are appointed by the boss and run of a crew of soldiers that varies in size. The more money they produce, the more respect they gain in the eyes of the boss. The soldiers are the "made men" of the Family. They are expected to make money and kick up a portion to their captain and ultimately to the boss. Associates engage in regular criminal activity with the blessing of a made Mafia member, but they are not formal members of the organization. They are also expected to generate income. If they prove to be successful, they often become soldiers.

According to the Task Force on Organized Crime of the President's Commission on Law Enforcement and Administration of Justice, this organized crime structure is national in scope, with several families operating across the country.

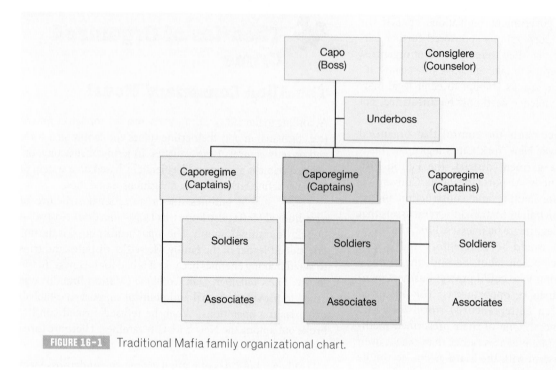

FIGURE 16-1 Traditional Mafia family organizational chart.

These bosses formed a commission to govern activities across the United States.[16] **TABLE 16-3** summarizes the key elements of the alien conspiracy model.

Central to the alien conspiracy model is the **Mafia code**, which is a list of secret oaths and norms that govern behavior within the family. This code includes the following elements:

- *Omerta*: Family members must maintain the secrecy of the organization, its operations, and membership.
- *Loyalty*: The organization comes before the individual and his family.
- *Respect*: Members must respect other members of the organization and never harm them in any way. In addition, members must be honest in all relationships with one another. Reputed Mafia head

Joseph Bonanno referred to Sicilians who follow "the tradition" as "men of honor" (*uomo di rispetto*) who arbitrate disputes with both diplomacy and violence.[17,18]

- *Discipline*: Orders are to be carried out and strictly obeyed. The "stand-up guy" who lives by the rules and will die for them is the hero of this social system.[19]

Although films and novels have popularized these norms, the alien conspiracy model is exaggerated. For example, Lombardo conducted a content analysis of 280 Chicago newspaper articles from 1892 to 1931 on the Black Hand—a supposed secret organization of extortionists who preyed on Italian immigrants. His analysis revealed that the Black Hand was a social construction, conceived by reporters, that

TABLE 16-3

Organized Crime: The Alien Conspiracy Model

Organized crime groups exhibit many structural features of legitimate corporate enterprises. For example, they are rationally and bureaucratically structured to maximize profits gained from illegal enterprise. They also feature feudal elements of a "Mafia code."

Like businesses, they seek to monopolize criminal enterprises by expanding in size and forming large cartels of national and international scope.

Ethnic or racial identity (especially Sicilian Italian) is the key to determining group membership in organized crime.

Organized crime groups undermine the foundations of democracy by corrupting public servants and professionals.

Data from Mastrofski, S., & Potter, G. (1987). Controlling organized crime: A critque of law enforcement policy. *Criminal Justice Policy Review, 2*. 270–272.

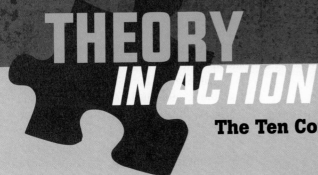
The Ten Commandments of the Mafia

When Italian police found and arrested Mafia leader Salvatore Lo Piccolo in Sicily, they made an unexpected finding. Lo Piccolo had typed out a list of "rights and duties" for Mafia members that was believed to be drafted as an effort to rein in the objectionable behavior of recent recruits.

1. No one can present himself directly to another of our friends. There must be a third person to do it. The phrase "*amico nostra*" is used, meaning "He is a friend of ours."

2. Never look at the wives of friends. This rule also extends to daughters and girlfriends (*comares*) of married Mafiosi.

3. Never be seen with cops.

4. Don't go to pubs and clubs.

5. Always being available for La Cosa Nostra is a duty—even if your wife's about to give birth. Mafia soldiers and associates are supposed to get their capo's permission before doing anything, including business dealings with other members or traveling.

6. Appointments must absolutely be respected.

7. Wives must be treated with respect.

8. When asked for any information, the answer must be the truth.

9. Money cannot be appropriated if it belongs to others or to other families.

10. People who can't be part of La Cosa Nostra: anyone who has a close relative in the police, anyone with a

Genovese crime family members indicted for attempting to control the trash hauling industry.
© Mike Derer/AP Photos

two-timing relative in the family, anyone who behaves badly and doesn't hold to moral values.

How does this list of norms compare to those of the "Mafia Code"?

Sources: BBC News. (November 9, 2007). Mafia's ten commandments found. Retrieved July 31, 2014, from http://news.bbc.co.uk/2/hi/world/europe/7086716.stm

---

resulted in a bias against Italians. The term Black Hand referred to extortion letter messages that featured a black hand, daggers, and the skull and crossbones. Such crimes were committed by small groups of offenders or individuals, not a purposeful criminal organization. Review of the newspaper articles found that 28 percent of the stories featured no evidence of extortion. There also was no evidence of Mafia involvement, victims and offenders were not always Italian and few people were killed for failing to honor Black Hand demands.[20]

Joseph Albini offers several reasons for the persistence of this traditional conspiracy view:[21]

- Belief in a secret society (especially Sicilians) allows Americans to ignore the fact they handle the great demand for illegal goods and services.
- It creates the image of an all-powerful menace that the government must take the necessary steps to destroy.
- The Mafia has provided entertainment and excitement for a public that does not fear its existence and wants to believe in it.

Such portrayals divert allegations of failure by law enforcement officials and sponsor discrimination against Italian Americans.

The Local, Ethnic Group Model

Several scholars disagree that organized crime represents a unified, national conspiracy.[22] Rather, they suggest that crime bodies are independent, local entities, often centered in major cities, with no formal national ties. Here, "organized criminality occurs in an informal, loosely structured, open system."[23] Function, not rational bureaucratic action, determines structure. Still, most families share some "cultural underpinnings," including:

> ... crime bodies are independent, local entities, often centered in major cities, with no formal national ties.

- Strong familial ties and obligations and a heritage of kinship, ethnicity, and clannishness.
- A distrust of outsiders and government.
- A proclivity for sanctioned violence and private revenge (e.g., the Sicilian vendetta or "blood feud").
- A capacity for effective organization, including a pragmatic recognition of the need for cooperation and coordination with competing crime groups.[24] Haller notes that Al Capone's gang was most effective in organizing and effectively using the talents of nonmembers.[25]
- The savvy to cultivate the goodwill of local residents and simultaneously exploit them for personal advantage. For example, the estate of the late New York City boss, Carlo Gambino, donated money to construct a new wing of a cancer hospital. Also in New York, reputed boss John Gotti regularly staged a Fourth of July celebration, complete with a fireworks display, in his neighborhood. When he was sentenced to life in prison for murder, a crowd of people protested.

Unlike the alien conspiracy model, the local, ethnic group model maintains that the locus of control is limited to certain cities or areas of the country. Here, the level of organization is rational but not bureaucratic. For example, Ianni noted that kinship played a significant role in the recruitment of crime family members but that expertise was also a factor.[26] Albini stressed the cohesive nature of the patron–client relationship as a central element in family formations.[27] An individual's connections—his social network—enable him to get things done.[28] These roles shift depending on the transaction and the ability of the individual to meet obligations.

Mark Haller maintains that organized crime families often function as organizations such as the Rotary Club. They can provide members with contacts, mutual assistance, and partnership opportunities.[29] Alan Block has argued that the conspiracy model must be abandoned. The term illegal enterprise should be used in place of organized crime.[30] Instead of following strict organizational lines, families are decentralized. The boss must be consulted, not only out of respect, but also because he can make schemes work and provide protection. For example, Donnie Brasco (an undercover FBI agent who infiltrates the Mafia in the 1997 movie by the same name) details the steps he had to take to start a vending machine operation in the territory of Milwaukee crime family boss Frank Balistrieri. Although the final deal never materialized, Brasco had to pay tribute money to Balistrieri before any plans could be put in place.[31] All members may engage in any moneymaking activity, as long as the boss receives tribute.[32] Small, fragmented enterprises, not large corporate syndicates, dominate illegal markets.[33]

These values may contradict one another and set up inconsistencies in Mafia behavior. For example, the traditional notion, promoted by the movie *The Godfather*, is that Mafia dons were disinterested in drug trafficking, regarding it as too dangerous and as intolerable to the public. This position allowed these gangsters to engage in moral posturing.

There is strong evidence of long and deep Mafia involvement in drug sales. Family leaders could not keep their associates out of this large, lucrative market. As Peter Lupsha noted, such organized crime luminaries as Charles "Lucky" Luciano and Vito Genovese had official criminal records for heroin trafficking. Luciano started the infamous "French connection" heroin route to the United States. Many dons who opposed drug sales tried to keep their people out of it through threats (Bonanno) or bribes (Accardo).[34] In fact, Capeci states that Joseph Bonanno used his legitimate businesses in the United States, Canada, and Haiti to smuggle heroin and make millions of dollars with his partner, Carmine Galante.[35] Others, such as Philadelphia's Angelo Bruno, franchised the drug trade to others, such as the Greeks and motorcycle gangs (the Outlaws). Lupsha contends that Mafia dominance of the drug market faded with the drop in demand for heroin.[36] Obviously, the Mafia would not simply abandon the drug trade for moral or any other reasons while consumer demand and vast profits remained.

The Mafia: La Cosa Nostra

The Mafia, also known as La Cosa Nostra, offers a powerful and recurring image of crime in America. La Cosa Nostra, which literally means "our thing" in Italian, is a shorthand term used by Mafia members. The federal government made further use of shorthand when it reduced this term to the acronym "LCN." Italian organized crime groups are also referred to as the Mob, the Outfit, and the Office.

Organized crime is a favorite Hollywood theme, as evidenced by films such as *The Godfather* series and *Goodfellas* and the television series *The Sopranos*. Both the President's Commission report (1967) and Donald Cressey's influential *Theft of*

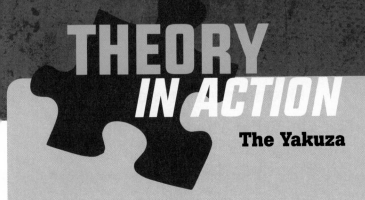

The Yakuza

The Yakuza of Japan are one of the world's most powerful organized crime groups. Their members trace their origins back to the 17th-century samurai warrior outsiders (*kabuki-mono*—the "crazy ones") or the underdog folk heroes (*machi-yokko*—"servants of the town") who stood up against marauders for the poor and defenseless, like Robin Hood. After the collapse of the Japanese government after World War II, another Yakuza precursor (the *Gurentai*) patterned themselves after America's Al Capone-like gangsters and used violence and threats to extort money. The term *yakuza* comes from a card game, the object of which was to draw three cards totaling as close as possible to 19 (similar to 21 in black jack). *Yakuza* is Japanese for 8, 9, 3—totaling 20 in the game. Thus, the term is synonymous with "good for nothing."

The Yakuza follow a typical pyramid power structure with the patriarch in charge and his followers below him in an *oyabun* (father-role) and *kobun* (child-role) relationship. After admittance to the Yakuza, the member must accept this role and pledge unquestioning loyalty and obedience to the boss. In return, the boss must provide protection and good counsel.

The formal organizational structure of the Yakuza is complex. The *kumicho* (supreme boss) is counseled by the *saiko komon* (senior advisor) and followed by the *so-honbucho* (headquarters chief). Immediately after them is the regional boss (*wakagashira* or "number two man"), who runs several local gangs and is assisted by the *fuku-honbucho* who also operates several local gangs. A Yakuza family comprises dozens of *shatei* (younger brothers) and *wakashu* (junior leaders).

Yakuza members have two prominent physical attributes. Often they are heavily tattooed over their entire torso, showing their proud status as "outsiders" and their ability to withstand pain. If they have committed an offense against the boss, parts of their little finger are often missing. This punishment (known as *yubizume*) is self-inflicted and is symbolic of the loss of their ability to wield a samurai sword skillfully.

The Yakuza are heavily ensconced in Japanese society. Through violence and intimidation, they established their presence in legitimate businesses. In terms of criminal enterprises, they are involved in gun, drug (heroin and methamphetamine), and human trafficking (foreign women as sex slaves and foreign workers), prostitution, gambling, and white-collar crime (investment fraud and money laundering) activity in both Japan and the United States. There is some evidence they contributed to rescue efforts following the tsunami that hit Japan in 2011 and the Kobe earthquake in 1995—efforts to secure support from the populace.

Regarding these attributes, do the Yakuza follow the alien conspiracy or the local, ethnic group model?

Sources: Adelstein, J. (2011). Yakuza to the rescue. *The Daily Beast*. Retrieved August 3, 2014, from http://www.thedailybeast.com/articles/2011/03/18/japanese-yakuza-aid-earthquake-relief-efforts.print.html; Abadinsky, H. (2010). *Organized crime*. Belmont, CA: Wadsworth, pp. 213–219; Bruno, A. (n.d.). The Yakuza, the Japanese Mafia. The Crime Library. Retrieved December 4, 2010, from http://www.crimelibrary.com/gangsters_outlaws/gang/yakuza/1.html?sect=25; Bosmia, A. N., Griessenauer, C. J., & Tubbs, R. S. (2014). Yubitsume: Ritualistic self-amputation of proximal digits among the Yakuza. *Injury & Violence, 6, 2*, 54–56; Kaplan, D. E., & Dubro, A. (2003). *Yakuza: Japan's criminal underworld*. Berkeley, CA: University of California Press; Lyman, M. D., & Potter, G. W. (2004). *Organized crime*. Upper Saddle River, NJ: Prentice-Hall, pp. 346–347.

a Nation cited the existence of an all-powerful secret organization that controlled crime.[37,38] This view was also perpetuated by events like the 1957 discovery of a meeting of organized crime leaders in Apalachin, New York, and the testimony of La Cosa Nostra member Joseph Valachi before the U.S. Senate in 1963.[39] These common threads formed a portrait of an omnipotent national crime syndicate known as the Mafia. Although the organization did exist, its all-powerful nature was often exaggerated.

La Cosa Nostra is the prototype for other organized crime models or it has the same critical features. Jacobs asserts that La Cosa Nostra "stands apart" for several reasons:[40]

No other organized-crime group has shown anything resembling the business sophistication and acumen of the Italian American organized-crime families. No other group has demonstrated the ability to control labor unions, much less play the roles of peacemaker, cartel enforcer, and "fixer" for entire industries. None has become a political force by underwriting campaigns and taking control of grassroots party organizations. Cosa Nostra is distinctive, even unique, because it has successfully penetrated labor unions to seize control of legitimate industries.

Thus, La Cosa Nostra is a unique example of organized crime.

Yet, there is some controversy over the proper definition of organized crime.[41] For example, to what extent and in what manner is crime "organized?" Elements of the definition consider the breadth of organized crime operations, the markets and products they deal in, and their typical methods of operation.

Organized crime families seek to establish and maintain monopolistic control over various profitable enterprises—both legal and illegal. **TABLE 16-4** lists the traditional and new forms of enterprises in which organized crime groups engage. They use violence as an instrument: first, to gain monopolistic control over an enterprise by eliminating or discouraging competitors, and second, as a means of internal discipline to maintain control over family members. They also attempt to elude the criminal justice system by bribing and corrupting government officials. The existence and survival of organized crime groups are based on societal demand for the illegal goods and services that they provide.[42] Profit motive drives organized crime families. They seek the same goals of any business enterprise. They provide goods and services for which there is a well-established public demand but that are not widely available because they are illegal (e.g., narcotics, gambling, and prostitution). **TABLE 16-5** gives a definition of organized crime—its attributes and elements.

Lupsha argues that organized crime in America reflects American values and offers a twist on rational choice theory—the supposedly easy money draws people to organized crime—only "suckers" work.[43]

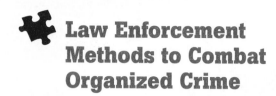

Law Enforcement Methods to Combat Organized Crime

Headhunting: The Racketeer Influenced and Corrupt Organizations Statute

Given their insistence that the Mafia is a nationwide conspiracy, law enforcement officials traditionally have sought to control organized crime by apprehending and prosecuting family members, especially the bosses. They engage in **headhunting**. Heads of criminal families are targeted, and a "scorched earth" policy is followed: "freezing or seizing the assets used in or obtained through criminal enterprise."[44]

Since 1970, several specific law enforcement strategies to combat organized crime have been designed. The central issue surrounding them is that they may pose a threat to civil liberties. Primarily, they are based on Packer's "crime control model," the idea that certain harsh methods are necessary to capture criminals and that if abuses occur they will be corrected later in the criminal justice process.[45] One example of this approach is the Organized Crime Control Act, passed by Congress and signed by President Nixon in 1970. A segment of this law is the Racketeer Influenced and Corrupt Organizations Act (RICO). It strengthened the ability of the federal government to combat and prosecute criminal

TABLE 16-4	
Organized Crime Activities	
Legitimate Industry Infiltration	**Criminal Activities**
Food products and restaurants	Gambling (numbers, policy, dice, bookmaking, and Internet)
Garbage disposal	Drug trafficking
Produce	Labor union corruption
Garment manufacturing	Prostitution (street and Internet)
Bars and taverns	Human trafficking
Securities	Extortion of local and larger businesses
Vending machines	Money laundering
	Forgery of CDs, DVDs, and software
	Business fraud (strategic commodities, credit, insurance, stocks, securities, and investments)
	Disposal of illegal waste (pollution)
	Loansharking
	Fencing stolen property
	Corruption and bribery of public officials
	Manufacture and sale of counterfeit products (clothing, handbags, etc.)
	Counterfeit Currency
	Cigarette Trafficking
	Tax evasion scams

Data from President's Commission on Law Enforcement and the Administration of Justice, The Challenge of Crime in a Free Society. (1967). Washington, DC: U.S. Government Printing Office, p. 164.

TABLE 16-5

Definition of Organized Crime

Organized crime is characterized by:

- Its great capacity for harm. Groups have greater potential for damage than individuals because they:
  - Are larger
  - Are more criminally sophisticated
  - Use planning, knowledge, and skill
  - Have organizational strength
  - Have a reputation—the ability to intimidate
- They use corruption as an insurance policy to protect themselves from law enforcement.
- They undermine the credibility and integrity of the political and judicial processes.
- They seek to gain monopolistic control over criminal enterprises to maximize profits and eliminate competition.

Organized refers to concerted and collective action and illicit profit generated via a criminal enterprise. Crime refers to serious and continuing criminal activity. Essential elements of organized crime include the elements of harm, threat, and risk:

- Harm: the exercise of control, significant profit or loss, serious violence, corruption, and/or having a significant impact on community safety.
- Threat: the ability of organized criminals to inflict harm via intimidation and menace that is grounded in their present danger. It represents the ability of these groups to grow and grip a community—the scale of their organization.
- Risk: how "evolved" is the organized crime group? Does it have the resources needed (both physical—money, people, communication routes; and the ideology—the willingness to use violence or to exploit others).

Organized crime is defined by three basic attributes:

- Organized crime is synonymous with the provision of illegal goods and services and predatory crimes (fraud, theft, robbery, trafficking in human beings and drugs, cybercrime, extortion, and smuggling).
- A "patchwork" character: indicated by the prevalence of types of illegal substances provided to customers. Illegal markets that are the product of a fairly complex interplay of diverse factors other than simple "supply and demand."
- Diverse areas of crime: trafficking in stolen motor vehicles, cigarette smuggling, serial burglary, product piracy, child pornography and prostitution, human and organ trafficking, trafficking in certain products (plundered antiquities, endangered plants and species), and illegal toxic waste disposal.

Data from Finckenauer, J. (2009). Organized crime. In M. Tonry (Ed.), *The Oxford handbook of crime and public policy.* New York: Oxford University Press, pp. 304–324; Gilmour, S. (2008). Understanding organized crime: A local perspective. *Policing, 2*, 18–27; von Lampe, K. (2008). Organized crime in Europe: Conceptions and realities. *Policing, 2*, 7–17.

organizations. It provided for special grand juries to investigate multi-jurisdictional organized crime and to produce reports on public corruption and organized crime conditions in their respective districts. RICO allows for the prosecution of anyone who takes part or conspires to take part in a criminal enterprise or organization through two acts of racketeering activity within a 10-year period of time.[46]

RICO has been criticized for being too inclusive of individuals and groups that would not be considered as a part of organized crime. Here, again, the problem lies in how to define organized crime. According to RICO, organized crime comprises the acquisition, operation, or income from an "enterprise" through a "pattern" of "racketeering activity." An enterprise is defined as any individual or group. A pattern is two or more offenses within a 10-year period, and racketeering activity is any offense punishable by a year or more in prison.[47]

There are some problems with the headhunting approach. Stephen Mastrofski and Gary Potter suggest that successful headhunting causes long-term problems for society because organized crime becomes more decentralized and less visible.[48] New tactics are needed to discover information about organized crime activities, such as following large bank transactions, real estate sales, and transfers of funds to foreign bank accounts. Pagano argues that organized crime control strategies must focus on systems because systems remain intact even when the bosses are removed. More attention must be paid to illicit markets and how they operate.[49–52]

Other strategies used to prosecute organized crime from 1980 to 1990 included the use of court-appointed trustees to oversee the operation of businesses (e.g., garment and construction industries) and unions that had been infiltrated by organized crime, and the use of regulatory strategies to monitor businesses and markets targeted by organized crime (e.g., New York City Trade Waste Commission).[53]

Since the passage of RICO, Congress has enacted legislation regarding asset forfeiture and money laundering, both of which have increased the federal government's ability to combat organized crime. They have provided a means

THEORY IN ACTION

The Business of Organized Crime

When Toto Riina was arrested by Italian police on January 15, 1993, Bernardo Provenzano became the head of the Sicilian Mafia. He was an infamous killer with many deaths on his hands. Eluding police for 43 years, The "Phantom of Corleone" was presumed dead, but he ran the Mafia's criminal enterprises in secret through typewritten notes providing orders to his associates that police found following his arrest in 2006. He is serving a lengthy prison term for more than a dozen murders, including those of anti-Mafia magistrates, Giovanni Falcone and Paolo Borsellino.

Provenzano is credited with using several businesslike tactics to guide the Mafia through the police crackdown that followed the magistrate assassinations. His seven reforms can be viewed as basic rules for running a successful business:

1. *Submersion*: When a company is failing, the first step is to take it below the radar. "Bury your mistakes and get on with it." His aim was to make Mafia enterprises invisible so they could recover and reorganize. Mafiosi were instructed to avoid any activity that would attract publicity and to use peaceful persuasion rather than violence. Provenzano warned that this system would take time. Members might have to wait between 5 and 7 years to make profits again. Rebuilding links with business and political leaders would be done out of the glare of publicity. The aim was to shake off their parasitic image and become part of industrial and political institutions.

2. *Mediation*: Provenzano sponsored the use of negotiation and dialogue. He adopted a dictatorial but kind style of leadership—consulting with competing groups within the organization and offering mediation rather than imposing his will.

3. *Building consensus*: Provenzano promoted the image of the Mafia as a positive force. The boss would provide advice and mediation outside the Mafia. They would use persuasion, not violence to promote themselves. "Let me know whatever the people need, they must expect nothing but good from us."

4. *"Keep God on your side"*: Provenzano adopted the style of the parish priest, quoting the Bible to give support to his organizational decisions to punish and reprimand. "May the Lord bless and keep you . . . know that where I can be of use to you, with the will of God, I am completely at your disposal."

5. *Be politically flexible*: He sought the support of politicians to obtain light sentences for convicted Mafiosi and the end of protection for informants against the Mafia.

6. *Reinvention*: In light of a public scandal or business failure, the boss must be able to distance himself from such disasters. This also fit the image of peacemaker he was trying to promote.

7. *Modesty*: Provenzano rose from thug and hit man to the top position in the Sicilian Mafia, running their businesses successfully while eluding capture from the authorities. He wrote that he would rather have someone else in charge of the organization: "They want me to tell them what to do, but who am I to tell them how to conduct themselves? I can't give orders to anyone; indeed I look for someone who can give orders to me."

Provenzano's modesty obscures the stranglehold that the Mafia has on the Italian economy. A report by the Italian business group, *Confesercenti*, documented that organized crime was the largest business in Italy with an annual income of $204 billion—a budget larger than that of the European Union. The association also noted that some Mafia clans were the largest banks in the country with $83 billion in liquidity, thus making it possible for the Mafia to make investments that were difficult for legitimate businesses to make in a dire Italian economy burdened by increased taxes. Small and medium businesses were Mafia targets for extortion (*pizzo*—regular payments to the local clan), loansharking, and robberies and netting large profits.

Organized crime scholars have recommended that businesses pay close attention to the tactics being used against them and take steps to protect their businesses against organized crime infiltration. Careful and accurate financial investigations must be conducted to reveal organized crime attempts to secure access to legal businesses.

How do these methods compare to those used by white-collar criminals?

Sources: Europol. (2013). *Threat assessment: Italian organised crime*. The Hague: Europole; Goodman, M. (2011). What business can learn from organized crime. *Harvard Business Review, 11*, 1–4; Longrigg, C. How to do business like the Mafia. (April 8, 2008). Retrieved August 1, 2014, from http://www.theguardian.com/world/2008/apr/09/internationalcrime.italy/print; Nathanson, P. (January 10, 2012). Mafia is Italy's largest business, biggest banker: Study finds that Italy's organized crime is worth $204 billion a year. Retrieved August 1, 2014, from http://abcnews.go.com/International/mafia-italy-biggest-business-biggest-banker/story?id=15329463&singlePage=true; Vintiadis, M. (2012–2013). Organized crime penetration in Italian and European businesses. *Kroll Global Fraud Report*, 50–51.

for the federal government to further attack the financial structure and assets of organized crime groups. The U.S. Department of Justice has developed a comprehensive strategy to combat international organized crime. Its four key elements are:[54]

1. Prioritize and target the most significant IOC threats.
2. Marshall information and intelligence.
3. Capitalize on foreign partnerships with law enforcement IOC task forces.
4. Employ non–law enforcement measures (i.e., economic sanctions) to combat IOC groups.

The Federal Witness Protection Program

Attorney General Robert F. Kennedy and U.S. Attorney Gerald Shur developed this program for the Organized Crime and Racketeering section of the U.S. Department of Justice. It was formally authorized by the Organized Crime Control Act of 1970 and again by the Comprehensive Crime Control Act of 1984. The 1970 act granted the attorney general the authority to provide witnesses protection for their testimony against alleged offenders who could retaliate against them. RICO also allowed for witnesses of organized crime to be granted immunity from prosecution for testimony under the witness security (WITSEC) program.

The WITSEC program allows for the protection and relocation of witnesses and their families, whose lives may be in danger because of their testimony in organized and other major crime cases. Thus, La Cosa Nostra members such as Joseph Valachi and Sammy "the Bull" Gravano were able to break their oath of silence (*omerta*) and testify in court against bosses like John Gotti.[55] The program provided not only protection for witnesses while testifying but also a new identity, housing, medical care, job training, employment, and subsistence funding until they became self-sufficient.[56]

Since its inception, more than 7,500 witnesses and 9,500 family members have entered WITSEC, where they were given new identities and protected by the U.S. Marshals Service. The testimonies of WITSEC witnesses have generated an 89 percent conviction rate. None of the witnesses who have followed program guidelines has been harmed while under the protection of the U.S. Marshals, and fewer than 17 percent of the participants have been arrested and charged with a new crime after joining the program.[57,58]

Impact of Law Enforcement Methods on Organized Crime

In 1986, *Fortune* magazine published an article on the top 50 Mafia bosses, similar to its famous list of the top 500 legitimate companies.[59] By the end of 2004, only six of these Mafia leaders were out of prison, and the extent of their illegal activities is doubtful. One of the leaders, Michael Franzese, has become an author and a motivational speaker based on

his experiences. Two of the leaders could not be located with Internet sources. In 2005, Capeci noted that 57 Mafia members (including some bosses) had been convicted and sent to prison.[60]

However, Finckenauer offers a critique of these law enforcement tactics. He notes the problems with current enforcement methods or operations:

- *Electronic surveillance techniques*: constitute an invasion of privacy.
- *Undercover operations*: may encourage entrapment and place law enforcement agents at substantial risk.
- *Informants*: may provide false information to implicate enemies and drive out competition.
- *Immunity packages*: are often too broad and thus cover up criminal activity.
- *Witness protection*: has unintended victims, individuals and organizations unable to recover debts from witnesses and their dependents, non-relocated parents denied access to their children, and the communities who unwittingly receive these criminals.
- *Forfeiture*: can punish innocent victims.
- *RICO*: widens the net and includes persons who would ordinarily not be charged. It threatens civil liberties and due process of law. Also, it has been applied injudiciously and indiscriminately.

In sum, Finckenauer notes that law enforcement policy regarding organized crime has placed too much emphasis on headhunting with little evidence of its effectiveness. In its place, Finckenauer recommends a more preventive approach—"cutting off the feet"—to remove or impair the public settings where organized crime criminals and their clients meet, with a focus on monitoring and thwarting opportunities for crime.[61]

John Gotti, nicknamed the "Teflon Don" because of his ability to elude prosecution. He was eventually convicted and died in prison of cancer.

© Mark Lennihan/AP Photos

Russian Organized Crime

Despite inroads against La Cosa Nostra, organized crime has arisen in other forms. For example, motorcycle gangs such as Hells Angels and the Outlaws have become involved in drug dealing, especially methamphetamine.[62–65] In addition, organized crime has become "transnational" in nature, crossing borders and continents to control illegal markets in many goods and services.[66,67] For example, Russian organized crime groups in the United States have become involved in such markets as drugs, arms trafficking, stolen automobiles, trafficking in women and children, and money laundering.[68]

Russian organized crime groups have similarities to and differences from La Cosa Nostra families. Although Russian groups are often lumped under the all-encompassing label of "Mafia," they look nothing like La Cosa Nostra. Their structure is highly flexible—groups come together to commit a crime for the financial gain and do not answer to a boss or head. Their loyalty is not based on shared ethnicity or culture. Their partnerships are more opportunistic, and they do not seek monopolization or the systematic use of corruption.[69] Both the Italian Mafia and Russian organized crime groups began by extorting their fellow immigrants but quickly moved on to major enterprise offenses in mainstream American society. In addition to using violence as a means to an end, both groups possess high-tech equipment, including military weapons.[70] The organizational characteristics of the Russian Mafia are related to the political and economic structure of the former Soviet Union. Because of the rigid class structure under the czars and later in the state-run Soviet economy, the Russian populace developed a "connive to survive" attitude in which stealing from the nobility (or the government) was not considered a crime, but "fit for the taking." Also, the black market was a normal vehicle to obtain the basic necessities of life. It was under the control of a professional criminal class (*vory v zakone*)—career criminals who were completely devoted to a life of crime. These elements combined to form a milieu of lawlessness that has aided the development of Russian organized crime.[71,72]

In the United States, Russian organized criminals are involved in long-established organized crime activities such as extortion, abduction, human smuggling, prostitution, drug trafficking, and theft; they are also involved in white-collar criminal activities including money laundering and fraud of various types. The fraud and scams in which Russian criminals take part extend across industries from health care and strategic commodities (e.g., precious metals)

Members of the Russian Mafia are escorted from FBI Headquarters.

© Monika Graff/AP Photos

fraud to credit card, insurance, securities, and investment fraud. They are also involved in scams in domains such as tax evasion and energy price rigging. Russian organized crime groups operate in New York, New Jersey, Boston, Philadelphia, Chicago, Los Angeles, San Francisco, and Miami, among other cities.[73]

Their members are also prone to extreme violence. Officials estimate that at least 65 murders in the New York–New Jersey area were because of the Russian Mafia. Their financial abilities are also evident. In 1999, a Russian organized crime case involved laundering more than $7 billion through legitimate channels.[74] Thus, Russian Mafia members have experience in complex areas of business and technology and may thus represent an even greater threat to society.[75]

 ## White-Collar Crime

As with organized crime, the desire for profit drives most white-collar crime, and individuals or groups who wield considerable power perpetrate the crimes. Unlike organized crime, however, well-respected members of society who enjoy high social status commit white-collar crime. In fact, it is precisely the offender's prominent status that provides the opportunity for the crime.

White-collar crime is a generic term that refers to a broad range of illegal acts committed by seemingly respectable people in business settings as a part of their occupational roles. They range from antitrust offenses to health-care fraud; impose enormous financial, physical, and social harms on individuals, communities, and society; and pose significant problems for law enforcement and

> *Unlike organized crime, however, well-respected members of society who enjoy high social status commit white-collar crime.*

regulatory agencies that attempt to control and prevent such offenses.[76]

The Sutherland Definition of White-Collar Crime

Building on the work of other criminologists and social commentators, Edwin H. Sutherland provided the breakthrough appraisal of white-collar crime; he defined a white-collar crime as "a crime committed by a person of respectability and high social status in his occupation."[77] Sutherland gave three reasons such actions are criminal. First, the law states that these crimes harm the public. For example, misrepresentation in advertising, unfair labor practices, financial fraud, violations of war regulations, and infringements of patents, trademarks, and copyrights are all crimes. Second, penalties for practices such as forming monopolies (combinations in restraint of trade) were already on the books. Third, these activities are willful and intentional, and the motive (profit, personal gain) is usually clear.

Sutherland called for a change in public values so that respectable white-collar offenders would be viewed as being equally criminal as their street-level counterparts. He claimed that white-collar crime is not treated as seriously as street crime because the upper classes have the power to influence the creation and administration of the law. He also questioned criminological theories that focused only on the lower classes. Specifically, he recommended the use of his theory of differential association to study white-collar crime. Like other criminals, Sutherland believed that white-collar offenders learned their methods, motives, and drives through interaction in small personal groups. Sutherland's definition focuses on the white-collar offender, a person of respectability and high social status who committed a crime during the course of an occupation.[78]

The Impact of White-Collar Crime

Unquestionably, white-collar offenses are as harmful to the public as street crimes. For example, estimates suggest that the bailout required by the savings and loan scandal will cost taxpayers as much as $500 billion by the year 2021.[79] As Bohm states, white-collar crimes are not always nonviolent:[80]

Conservative estimates show that each year at least 10,000 lives are lost due to unnecessary surgeries, 20,000 to errors in prescribing drugs, 20,000 to doctors spreading diseases in hospitals, 100,000 to industrial disease, 14,000 to industrial accidents, 200,000 to environmentally caused cancers, and an unknown number to lethal industrial products.

These deaths dwarf the number of murders recorded each year.

The impact of white-collar and economic crime on American society is considerable and alarming:

- In fiscal year 2011, the Department of Justice and the Department of Health and Human Services recovered about $4.1 billion in healthcare fraud—funds stolen or taken improperly from federal healthcare programs.[81]

- For the year 2004, illegal credit card purchases totaled $788 million in the United States alone, which represents 4.7 cents of every $100 of total purchases.[82]

- It is estimated that the credit card or personal information of over 229 million Americans has been compromised since 2005. This information could further perpetrate crimes that could total hundreds of millions of dollars.[83]

- The approximate annual cost of white-collar crime is between $300 and $660 billion.[84]

The American public understands that white-collar crimes represent severe threats to the community. In 2010, the National Public Survey on White Collar Crime was conducted by the National White Collar Crime Center to determine the public's experience with: victimization, reporting behaviors, and attitudes toward the seriousness of white-collar crime. Here are some selected findings from the survey:[85]

- Twenty-four percent of households and 17 percent of individuals reported experiencing at least one form of white-collar crime victimizations within the previous year.

- Respondents reported victimization at both household and individual levels most often because of credit card fraud, price misrepresentation, and unnecessary object repairs.

- Of these crimes, 54.7 percent were reported to at least one external recipient or agency (e.g., credit card company, business or person involved, law enforcement, consumer protection agency, personal attorney, etc.).

- Only 11.7 percent were reported to law enforcement or some other crime control agency.

In terms of their perceptions of white-collar crime seriousness, survey respondents were presented with 12 scenarios that included both white-collar and other crime descriptions. The responses showed that:[86]

- White-collar crime was viewed as slightly more serious than traditional crime types.

- White-collar offenses committed at the organizational level were viewed more harshly than those committed by individuals.

- Crimes committed by high-status offenders in a position of trust were seen as more troubling than those committed by lower status persons.

- A majority of the respondents believed that white-collar crime contributed to the current economic crisis.

- Nearly one-half of respondents said that government is not devoting enough resources to combat white-collar crime.

Traditional definitions of white-collar crime include the following offenses:[87]

1. *Consumer crimes*: false advertising, commercial misrepresentations, price manipulation, and related criminal and/or unethical behaviors

2. *Intellectual property crimes*: two basic types—criminal versions of trademark dilutions and criminal versions of copyright infringement
3. *Counterfeit merchandise*: copies of goods that are not manufactured by the company on the label
4. *Counterfeit pharmaceuticals*: unauthentic versions of medications
5. *Software, movie, and music piracy*: estimated losses from these crimes in 2011—$9.8 billion in the United States and $63.4 billion worldwide
6. *Business and financial crimes*: the Enron scandal and the crimes committed by Bernie Madoff
7. *Embezzlement*: crimes committed by people in a position of trust within an organization
8. *Financing of terrorism*
9. *Computer crimes*: as listed in Chapter 13

Official figures on white-collar crime victimization are difficult to estimate for several reasons. First, white-collar crime offenses fall under the jurisdiction of several different federal agencies (such as the Food and Drug Administration or the Internal Revenue Service). Second, the investigation of corporate crime is often left to regulatory and professional organizations (such as the American Medical Association or the American Bar Association) rather than law enforcement agencies. Therefore, corporate crime is usually handled by regulatory sanctions (such as "cease and desist" orders) or in civil law cases.[88] The National Incident-Based Reporting

> **White-collar crime differs from the street-level variety because it is more complex in method and impact.**

System (NIBRS), however, is attempting to compile and count white-collar offenses in the same manner that they do other crimes. An estimate of white-collar victimization for selected offenses and limited jurisdictions for 1997 to 1999 is presented in **TABLE 16-6**. According to these figures, individuals were most likely to be the victims of property and bribery offenses, whereas businesses were most likely to be victimized in crimes of fraud, counterfeiting, and embezzlement.

White-collar crime differs from the street-level variety because it is more complex in method and impact. In addition, the nature, degree, and volume of victimization are more substantial.[89] Sponsored by stated-income loans, the collapse of the housing market in 2007 led to a global financial crisis.[90] Ponzi schemes like those structured by Bernie Madoff and Allen Stanford cost their investors billions of dollars and debilitated their retirement funds.[91] Victims of white-collar crimes suffer greatly at the hands of their "assailants," even though the results of the crime may take years to become evident. For example, exposure to unsafe working conditions can cause long-term, progressively debilitating illnesses. Victims of crimes such as the savings and loan scandal may have a diminished faith in a free economy and business leaders, and a lower standard of living. The public may withhold financial support and economic investment. Such crimes also cause a loss of confidence in political

TABLE 16-6

Victims of White-Collar Crime Reported to NIBRS, 1997–1999

Victims	Property	Fraud	Bribery	Counterfeiting	Embezzlement	Total
Individual	2,621,843	47,826	143	45,270	3,006	2,718,088
Business	934,469	47,907	16	55,676	17,627	1,055,695
Financial institution	11,378	2,989	0	5,310	182	19,859
Government	73,623	3,844	36	2,949	260	80,712
Religious organization	10,794	70	0	104	35	11,003
Society or other	417,217	1,357	3	1,236	246	420,059
Totals	4,069,324	103,993	198	110,545	21,356	4,305,416

institutions, processes, and leaders, and an erosion of public morality.[92] White-collar offenses are financially based and committed by nonphysical means, such as by concealment or guile to obtain money or property, to avoid payment of money or property, or to get a business advantage. They often represent a physical danger to the public (violations of workplace safety, manufacture and distribution of unsafe products, violation of environmental laws and regulations).[93]

In terms of public policy, the boundaries between organized and white-collar crimes will continue to blur because of inconsistent definitions of these terms and the increasing number of new crimes that add to the complexities of enforcement. The public demands stricter enforcement of these crimes and punishment of these offenders, although allocated resources continue to be limited and focus more on street crimes.[94]

Research evidence shows that public attitudes toward white-collar crimes are becoming more punitive. A survey of a nationally representative sample that paired white-collar and street offenses found that white-collar crimes were considered more serious in four out of six pairings. Between 14 and 21 percent of the respondents felt that white-collar and street crimes were equally serious—especially older and college educated respondents. However, 65 percent of the sample believed that more resources should be devoted to combating white-collar crime.[95] A vignette survey of six crime scenarios examined the attitudes of respondents (N = 900) toward street and white-collar crime committed by male and female offenders. Ponzi and embezzlement schemes were viewed as more serious than street crimes like burglary, auto theft, and prostitution.

Bernie Madoff, possibly the most infamous white-collar criminal of all time.

© REUTERS/ Lucas Jackson/ Landov Media

With either type of crime, respondents held members of their own gender to account and felt that their crimes were more serious. They also considered white-collar offenders to be more remorseful about their crimes but more driven by greed than street criminals. However, male respondents were less likely to advocate for incarceration on two white-collar offenses—embezzlement and corporate crimes.[96] Coupled with the findings from the National White Collar Crime Survey, these results show that American citizens are becoming more aware of the damage wrought by white-collar crimes.

Expanded Definitions of White-Collar Crime

Sutherland's original definition of white-collar crime has been criticized. Criminologists have had some problems with accurately defining white-collar crime and in adequately capturing all of its nuances and describing its many forms. Although his sample included 70 of the largest manufacturing, mining, and mercantile corporations in 1929 and 1938, Sutherland's definition focused on the individual white-collar criminal and did not consider corporations or organizations acting as a whole. This creates a dichotomy in the definition of white-collar crime: crimes committed by (for) and against the organization.[97-100]

The earliest studies of white-collar criminality feature crimes committed by organizations. For example, Clinard's study of pricing and rationing violations during World War II found that businesses committed 338,029 violations during 1944 alone.[101,102] Although agreeing that differential association could explain some violations, Clinard argued that the personality of the violator also accounted for the crime.[103]

Hartung's investigation of the wholesale meat industry in Detroit,[104] Quinney's analysis of the violations of retail pharmacists,[105] and Geis' study of antitrust violations by manufacturers of heavy electrical equipment,[106] all examined crimes committed by organizations. Studies that followed dealt with this dichotomy directly by expanding the definition of white-collar crime to include corporate criminality.

Shapiro argues that white-collar crime should be viewed as an abuse of trust. From this perspective, white-collar criminals hold monopolies of information that cannot be verified by their clients. Clients are separated from the perpetrators both physically and socially. Often, the perpetrators act in a collective fashion as a bank, charity, or company. Usually, their activities are hidden and difficult to follow. Thus, lying, stealing, misappropriation, self-dealing, and corruption are violations of a relationship based on trust.[107]

In effect, the definition of white-collar crime has been split in two: **occupational crime** and **corporate crime**.

Occupational Crime

Shover defines occupational crime as "the violation of criminal statutes committed in pursuit of the goals of legitimate organizations, organizational subunits, or work groups."[108]

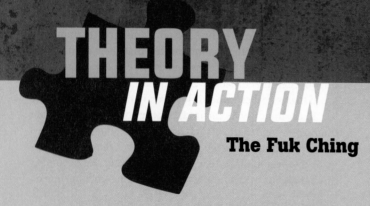

THEORY IN ACTION

The Fuk Ching

The Fuk Ching gang is an example of Chinese transnational organized crime. One of the most powerful Chinese gangs in the United States, the Fuk Ching gang operates in New York City, where it operates extortion and protection rackets that victimize businesses in Chinatown neighborhoods. It also engages in human (illegal movement of migrants) and drug (heroin and methamphetamine) trafficking and ownership of legitimate businesses.

In terms of organizational structure, one of the key features of the Fuk Ching is its relationship to Chinese adult organizations known as tongs. The Fuk Ching are affiliated with the Fukein American Association, giving them a physical hangout and also a legitimate reason to operate in the community served by the tong. Sometimes, the tong may protect the gang's gambling operations and supply them with necessities such as guns and money.

Their internal structure follows a family model. The grandfather (*ah kung*) or uncle (*shuk foo*) is the leader of the tong. The head of the gang is the *dai dai lo* (big, big brother)

who communicates with the head of the tong. In descending order, the gang leader is followed by *dai los* (big brothers), the *yee lo/sam lo* (clique leaders), and the *mai jai* (little horses) at the bottom of the organizational pyramid. Gang norms include respecting the ah kung, beating up members of other gangs on one's turf, not using drugs, following the orders of the dai lo, and not betraying the gang. Punishment for violators includes beating and death.

Regarding these attributes, do the Fuk Ching follow the alien conspiracy model or the local, ethnic group model?

Sources: Finckenauer, J. O. (n.d.) *Chinese transnational organized crime: The Fuk Ching*. National Institute of Justice International. Retrieved July 4, 2007, from http://www.ojp .usdoj.gov/nij/international/chinese.html; Kleinknecht, W. (1996). *The new ethnic mobs*. New York: The Free Press, pp. 166–174; Lyman, M. D., & Potter, G. W. (2004). *Organized crime*. Upper Saddle River, NJ: Prentice-Hall, p. 345.

These violations are fostered by the desire to maintain profitability and the promotion of an organizational culture that causes decision makers to stress profit regardless of the method used to achieve it.[109]

Occupational crime can be divided into four major types:[110]

1. *Crimes committed for the benefit of an employing organization.* Here, the employers, not the individuals, benefit directly from the offense. Insurance fraud in auto body repair is an example of this crime. Paul Tracy and James Fox conducted an experiment in which four drivers took their damaged autos to 96 repair shops in Massachusetts. Repair estimates were about one-third higher for drivers who said they were covered by insurance than for those who said they were not. This finding held despite the type of car, the extent of the damage, the sex of the driver, and the location of the shop.[111]

2. *Crimes committed as the result of state-based authority.* To commit this crime, the offender must be "legally vested with governmental powers to make or enforce laws or to command others."[112] Chambliss defines **state-organized crime** as, "acts defined by law as criminal and committed by state officials in the pursuit of their job as representatives of the state." For example,

CIA support of opium-growing feudal lords in the mountains of Vietnam, Laos, Cambodia, and Thailand during and after the Vietnam War represented occupational crime. Chambliss also includes arms smuggling (e.g., U.S. government arms sales to the Nicaraguan Contras) and state-organized assassinations (e.g., a CIA-sponsored coup in Chile that resulted in the assassination of socialist President Salvador Allende) in this category. The war on Iraq is also considered within this definition.[113]

3. *Crimes committed by professionals in their professional capacity.* These crimes directly result from the trust that others have vested in certain individuals, usually an elite group (e.g., physicians, attorneys, and psychologists). Several studies have detected high levels of fraud committed by physicians against the Medicare and Medicaid programs. For example, doctors have submitted bills for procedures (e.g., x-rays and blood and urine tests) that were unnecessary or never performed.[114] Psychiatrists have been sanctioned for charging the cost of individual therapy for patients treated in a group, billing for "therapy" that involved sexual contact between patient and physician, and inflating the cost of treatment.[115] In these offenses, the victim was not only the individual but also the taxpayer. It is difficult to detect and effectively

sanction crimes committed under the veil of professional confidentiality by autonomous practitioners.[116]

4. *Occupational crimes committed by individuals for personal gain.* These individuals have the same motives as armed robbers or muggers. Another study of auto repair shops revealed that they may misrepresent the need for a new car battery. Honesty was related to the presence of the owner, the economic health of the shop, incentive or commission payment procedures, and the longevity of the current management.[117] Interventions (e.g., public service announcements, filing of a suit against a major dealer, and a letter from the California Bureau of Automobile Repair) did not deter dishonest dealers.[118] The individual salesperson was attempting to gain through the sale of a new battery.

Corporate Crime

Kramer defines corporate crime as:[119]

> . . . *crimes committed by corporate organizations. They are the result of deliberate decision making by persons who occupy structural positions within the organization. The organization makes decisions intentionally to benefit itself.*

Two of the most infamous examples of corporate crime are the Ford Pinto case and the savings and loan scandal.

Ford Pinto Case

An article in *Mother Jones* magazine brought the Ford Pinto case to the attention of the public. Mark Dowie accused Ford Motor Company of ignoring a life-threatening defect in its profitable subcompact, the Pinto. Ford crash-tested the Pinto and discovered that in every test performed at over 25 miles per hour, the fuel tank ruptured. Although inexpensive modifications ($11 per car) would have prevented any threat of fire, Ford decided not to issue a recall. An internal cost–benefit analysis estimated that the recall would cost Ford approximately $137 million, although 180 burn deaths would cause a company loss of only $49.5 million.[120] In August 1978, three Indiana teenagers died when a rear-end collision caused their Pinto to burst into flames. In 1980, Ford Motor Company was indicted and brought to trial in Indiana under the reckless homicide provision of a state law. It was charged with building a dangerous vehicle and ignoring the company's duty to protect its customers from known dangers.[121] The trial resulted in a jury verdict of not guilty. The case established that a corporation could face criminal liability because of its actions.[122]

Savings and Loan Scandal

The savings and loan (S&L) crisis introduced a new form of corporate criminality: **collective embezzlement**—the siphoning of company funds for personal use by top management at the expense of the institution itself and with the implicit or explicit sanction of its management.[123] In effect, the S&L executives robbed their own banks.

During the 1970s, stagflation, high interest rates, and slow growth plagued the S&L industry. In addition, the development of money market mutual funds led to massive withdrawals from S&Ls. The Reagan administration pushed deregulation as the cure for the ills plaguing these institutions. The belief was that loosening restraints would make S&Ls more competitive under the "self-regulating mechanisms of the free market." Thus, restrictions on interest rates paid by S&Ls were phased out. Simultaneously, the federal protection offered by the Federal Savings and Loan Insurance Corporation was raised from a maximum of $40,000 to $100,000 per deposit.

The loosening of federal restrictions permitted such practices as linked financing ("daisy chains") to occur. Here, deposits were made and loans were made to the depositors. The brokers defaulted on the loans, essentially obtaining free cash ("drag loans"). Middlemen received a generous "finder's fee," and S&L operators recorded hefty deposits and inflated assets, which spelled extra bonuses and dividends for S&L executives.

These practices developed under the S&L-sponsored "casino economy." Speculative ventures led to windfall profits. "Junk" bonds transformed debt into wealth—one of the greatest fortunes in Wall Street history. This "fiddling with money," however, only produces capital gains—not jobs or products. The S&L corporate executives had little to lose by reckless behavior: The taxpayers would foot the bill for this casino extravaganza.

Thus, the S&L scandal is an example of a new form of corporate crime: crime by the corporation against the corporation with state complicity. Deregulation and the ideologies that fueled it gave birth to this fraud epidemic. Deregulation unleashed the temptation and the opportunity to commit fraud, and the systematic embezzlement of company funds became company policy.[124] Two distinguished scholars of occupational crime, Henry Pontell and Gil Geis are less than optimistic that regulation will prevent this type of financial fraud. Following a review of materials following the economic crisis of 2008, Pontell and Geis concluded that despite new legislation, the absence of adequate oversight virtually guarantees that fraud will again hit our economic system.[125]

The Criminal Careers of Corporations

In Chapter 9, we considered the idea of career criminality in which the focus was the individual criminal. Here, we shift our concern to the criminal careers of organizations. Again, the centerpiece of the analysis is how frequently the same corporations commit a crime. Is there a pattern to this level of offending? These questions go back to Sutherland's original study.

Sutherland found that every corporation in his sample had at least one judgment against it, but the maximum number was 50. A total of 980 decisions were levied. Specifically, 60 corporations had decisions for restraint of trade, 53 for infringement, 44 for unfair labor practices, 43 for miscellaneous offenses, 28 for misrepresentation in advertising, and 26 for rebates. From the beginning, apparently, there was a career-like pattern to corporate criminality.[126]

Clinard and Yeager conducted a large, sophisticated examination of the pattern of corporate criminality. Their study encompassed criminal actions initiated or completed during 1975 and 1976 by 25 federal agencies. It examined the 477 largest publicly owned manufacturing corporations and 105 of the largest wholesale, retail, and service corporations in the United States. The corporations in the sample account for 1,553 federal cases filed by government agencies, an average of 2.7 cases per corporation. Over 60 percent of these corporations had at least one federal case initiated against them. Almost half had multiple violations and multiple cases during 1975 to 1976. A few corporations (13%) accounted for a disproportionate number (52%) of offenses. Thus, "street" thugs are not the only type of career criminals. Clinard and Yeager speculated that these corporations had developed a subculture favorable to unethical and illegal behavior. Their executives and employees may have become socialized to violate the law.[127]

Certain businesses had higher rates of offending. For example, the motor vehicle industry accounted for one-half of the hazardous product violations. Oil corporations committed violations far in excess of their size. Together, they accounted for over 90 percent of the financial and over 70 percent of the water pollution violations.

Another possible predictor of corporate crime is the "financial strain thesis": corporations in depressed industries and those with poor performance records violated federal laws more frequently than those that performed well. The study also revealed that larger corporations, in terms of sales, were more likely to commit violations than were smaller ones.[128,129]

Using the Clinard and Yeager data, Wang and Holtfreter examined how corporation- and industry-level factors influenced illegal corporate behavior within a theoretical framework provided by strain and opportunity theories. There was no evidence of corporate-level strain on violations. Corporations in rapidly growing (but not decaying) industries had higher violation rates. Strain was less pronounced in corporations with a high level of diversification. Financially strained corporations had even higher rates of violation when their industries were experiencing financial decline. Corporations experiencing growth in their finances had higher violation rates when in rapidly growing industries. Financially strained corporations did not have higher violation rates, even when in industries where corporate illegality was the norm.[130]

The Enron Scandal

The now infamous Enron scandal was one of the greatest securities frauds in American history. Based in Houston, Texas, the Enron Corporation was created in 1985 when Houston Natural Gas merged with a company called InterNorth. It grew quickly and entered into the energy and commodities trading markets. It became one of the 10 largest companies in America and profited mightily from the 2001 energy crisis in California by selling electricity at inflated prices.

Enron became involved in several complicated deals and contracts that plunged the company into massive debt, which was subsequently hidden from its stockholders and lower-level employees. By October 2001, Enron was worth $1.2 billion less than publicly reported. An investigation by the U.S. Securities and Exchange Commission revealed illegal practices by high-ranking executives (such as CEO Kenneth Lay), investment banking partners, and even the company's accounting firm (Arthur Anderson).[131] The indictment and prosecution of Enron officials is well under way. The Enron experience represents "a corporation whose recklessness and dishonesty has devastated thousands of innocent victims and has hung a cloud of public distrust over American financial markets."[132] It is hoped that this example will lead to the promotion of ethical conduct and more socially responsible behavior by corporations and that they will place less emphasis on profitmaking and more stress on the establishment of economic democracy.[133]

Other Categories of White-Collar Crimes

White-collar crimes include a multitude of dimensions that continue to expand and complicate this area of study. Several crimes are still studied and classified as white-collar crimes even though some researchers question whether they should still be "housed under this umbrella." These crimes include environmental crimes and money laundering. Additionally, these crimes expand boundaries from the national to the international arena. These specific crimes may be broad concepts themselves that encompass a wide variety of crimes that extend beyond the focus of white-collar crimes. Although they fall into more than one area of criminology, to date, these illegal activities are still part of the discussion of white-collar crimes.

> *Strain was less pronounced in corporations with a high level of diversification.*

Environmental Crimes

Environmental crime refers to a broad range of illegal actions that endanger natural resources and the health of all living creatures. One of the first environmental problems to gain governmental attention in the 1970s was the issue of water pollution because of its relationship to public health and diseases.[134] Since then, political and public attention to violations of environmental standards allowed environmental crimes to be a staple within the study of white-collar crime.

Businesses and corporations were the first perpetrators to be investigated and prosecuted under the category of white-collar crimes. Although environmental crimes cause more damage and harm to greater numbers of people, this area is still limited in existing research regarding the causes and consequences of these actions. Consistent with other white-collar crimes, little attention is given to environmental crimes. Limited resources exist for investigations, and few cases are criminally prosecuted because of the status and power of those committing these illegal acts. Civil suits against corporations are more likely to occur than criminal prosecution. For example, from 1949–1952, the Bethlehem Steel plant in Lackawanna (near Buffalo, New York) produced plutonium rods for nuclear weapons under a U.S. government contract. Employees were never told that they were handling uranium and were not given proper instructions or equipment to handle it safely. These events resulted in several thousand injuries and over 100 fatalities among Bethlehem Steel employees and posed a danger to the entire Western New York environment.[135]

Kramer contends that the failure of the U.S. government to act to mitigate greenhouse gas emissions (GGEs) as well as failure to ratify of the Kyoto Protocol and denial of the resulting effects of climate change is state-corporate crime. Achieving reductions in GGEs would entail a reordering of the global political economy. Failing to act leads to the state-corporate crimes of climate change denial and failing to lessen global warming.[136]

Why do offenders engage in environmental crime? A vignette based, factorial survey of business leaders measured their intentions to take part in two types of environmental crimes. Findings showed that individuals were more willing to violate environmental law when they believed their participation would advance their career and when they perceived of this behavior as thrilling. If the informal costs associated with violating the law were believed to be certain and severe, individuals were significantly less likely to engage in crime. Similar effects were found if formal sanctions were likely and harsh. The results show that formal and informal sanctions could act as a deterrent to environmental crime. However, none of the interventions appeared to substantially lessen the powerful influence of the career benefits of committing such offenses. When such benefits appeared to be available, they overcame any expected loss of respect or future harm to job prospects that could be caused by the offense.[137]

In the United States, the Environmental Protection Agency protects the environment and public health by developing laws, supporting research, conducting environmental testing, and educating the public on these issues. This agency is not responsible for prosecuting violators (the U.S. Department of Justice has taken this position), which adds to the difficulty in securing adequate resources, enforcement, and sanctions for these activities. Today, the concept of environmental crime includes crimes related to dumping toxic waste, air pollution, dangerous consumer products, aquatic

pollution, environmental racism, selling hazardous chemicals, employee exposure to hazardous materials, and unsafe work areas.[138] The FBI prioritizes its work on environmental crimes to focus on hazards that place workers at risk, environmental catastrophes, chronic violators of federal environmental laws, and actions of organized crime groups in the waste industry.[139] Many of these crimes have transitioned into their own areas of study (e.g., employee safety) or found a place within other areas of study (e.g., organized crime and racism), but all of them still belong within the discussion of white-collar crimes.

Money Laundering

Money laundering involves concealing the nature, location, source, ownership, or control of proceeds from an illegal activity. These illegal funds are processed through a variety of methods to make them usable. Methods and routes for money laundering include the use of banks, check cashers, money transmitters, businesses, casinos, complex wire transfers, "shell companies," and currency smuggling. The complexity of money laundering does not counter the simplicity of the practice: converting monies obtained from illegal activities into the appearance of legitimate funds. Money laundering allows criminals to go undetected by law enforcement and other officials, and thus, they can spend and enjoy the profits they made by committing crimes. Although participants of organized crime commit a variety of acts, money laundering has been a classic practice within this criminal group. Today, money laundering is associated with drug-related crimes, computer hackers, and terrorist groups.

> *Money laundering allows criminals to go undetected by law enforcement and other officials, and thus, they can spend and enjoy the profits they made by committing crimes.*

Money laundering has been classified as a white-collar crime for a variety of reasons. Organized crime groups, such as the Russian Mafia have a history of laundering money. The groups use their privilege and status to hide illegally acquired funds from detection. Bankers have used their position and social trust to launder money in order to enhance their profitability.[140] Large investment corporations (e.g., J. P. Morgan Chase) have been investigated for their role in the financial devastation with the Enron Corporation.[141] In all of these situations, individuals, groups, and corporations used their privilege and status to process illegal funds into legitimate funds.

As with other white-collar crimes, few individuals or groups are prosecuted. Federal laws have been in place since the 1970s, with the Bank Secrecy Act requiring banks to produce reports to justify their money processes. Enforcing these acts requires collaboration and cooperation from various agencies at the local, state, and federal levels. Since September 11, 2001, terrorist activities and the funding of these activities have brought national and international attention to money laundering. The USA Patriot Act of 2001 has

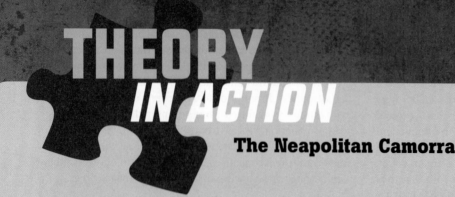

THEORY IN ACTION

The Neapolitan Camorra

The Neapolitan Camorra comprises a variety of independent criminal groups and gangs. They exercise a political power over a certain territory (the city of Naples, capital of the region Campania) by infiltrating local government. It is fragmented, comprising more than 100 gangs, with a boss at its center. To strengthen their legitimacy and cohesion, Camorra groups use symbols and rituals dating back to the 19th century. However, they also operate transnationally and collaborate with foreign criminal organizations—purchasing drugs directly from producing countries.

Despite law enforcement efforts in the 1990s, the most powerful Camorra clans control the local legitimate economy through illegal activities (extortion, fraud, drug trafficking and dealing, loansharking, counterfeiting, and exploitation of prostitution) and are more than willing to use violence to protect their businesses and turf.

The establishment of the Camorra criminal economy has devastating and irreversible effects on the local economy of the area under its control. It perverts traditional economic enterprise, such as the provision of credit, and promotes a black market and removes sums from the governmental tax system. It constructs a system of business profit sharing to launder criminal funds. It creates an air of legitimacy for this criminal economy due to its acceptance by a public that is starved for work of any type. The citizens come to regard the economic exploits of the Camorra as normal. Campania has had the highest rate of murders and violent crime in all of Italy for more than a decade. One of their major businesses, the disposal of toxic waste, has poisoned the Naples region, dumping and burning an estimated 10 million tons of such garbage since the early 1990s, giving the region such nicknames as the "Land of Fires" and the "Triangle of Death" (due to the emergence of clusters of cancer cases in the populace).

The Camorra also works internationally and collaborates with foreign criminal groups in such illicit markets as the drug and arms trade; smuggling of counterfeit goods; collecting, transporting, keeping, and recycling of toxic waste; and money laundering of illegal profits. They maintain full and complete control of their own territory and its economic activity with foreign organized crime groups assuming subordinate and cooperative roles only. Even robbers must get permission to conduct business in their fiefdoms and are often required to pay a portion of the swag for the ability to conduct criminal activities. They have proven adept at predicting the opening of new illegal markets for exploitation in Eastern Europe. They buy drugs directly from producing countries, cutting out the "middleman," and establishing investments that allow them to lower consumer prices and quadruple profits.

The Camorra has been an integral part of Naples for two centuries. Roberti states that to combat this organized crime it is necessary to make a decision that has never been made before—fighting the Camorra must become a top political priority across the Italian criminal justice system.

How are the Camorra different from or similar to the Russian Mafia, Yazuka, and Fuk Ching?

Sources: Abadinsky, H. (2010). *Organized crime.* Belmont, CA: Wadsworth, pp. 147–151; Paoli, L. (2007). Organised crime in Italy: Mafia and illegal markets—Exception and normality. In C. Fijnaut & L. Paoli (Eds.), *Organised crime in Europe* Vol. 4. Netherlands: Springer, pp. 277–278; Paoli, L. (2003). *Mafia brotherhoods: Organized crime, Italian style.* New York: Oxford University Press; Roberti, F. (2008). Organized crime in Italy: The Neapolitan Camorra today. *Policing, 2,* 43–49; Saviano, R. (2007). *Gomorrah: A personal journey into the violent empire of Naples' organized crime system.* New York: Farar, Strauss and Giroux; Yardley, J. (January 29, 2014). A Mafia legacy taints the earth in Southern Italy. *The New York Times.* Retrieved August 1, 2014, from http://www.nytimes.com/2014/01/30/world/europe/beneath-southern-italy-a-deadly-mob-legacy.html

provisions to combat terrorism and terrorist activities that impact the U.S. financial system.[142] Money laundering has traditionally been placed under the heading of white-collar crime, although increasing attention and globalization may allow these crimes to venture into their own category of crime or expand to include a multitude of other crimes that extend beyond the scope of traditional white-collar crime research.

The Careers and Motivations of Individual White-Collar Criminals

Some evidence suggests that white-collar offenders also have criminal careers. A study of white-collar criminals revealed that they began their criminal careers later and at a lower rate of offending than street criminals.[143,144] More than one-quarter of tax offenders had two or more prior arrests, and more than 10 percent of bank embezzlers and bribery offenders had multiple prior arrests. Many of these repeat white-collar offenders, ranging from 19 percent of bribery offenders to 46 percent of credit fraud offenders, had prior convictions. Among a subset of offenders who held elite positions or owned significant assets, over 25 percent had criminal records (10 percent had felony convictions; 6 percent had been previously incarcerated). White-collar criminals are often repeat offenders and are not much different from persistent street criminals.

A study comparing 39 white-collar offenders (WCOs), 88 white-collar versatile offenders (WCVs; committed white-collar plus other offenses) and 86 non–white-collar offenders (NWCs) in a federal prison found psychological differences between the three groups. WCOs had lower levels of criminal thinking and fewer behaviors that evidenced a criminal lifestyle. WCVs registered higher levels of self-centeredness and anxiety than NWCs. Both white-collar offender groups scored higher than NWCs on measures of perceived social influence and alcohol use. NWCs were more likely to abuse drugs and have more prior arrests.[145]

Heroic leaders are defined as persons who have received official recognition for their contributions to society. Arnulf and Gottschalk studied 179 white-collar criminals and found a subset of 28 offenders who could be considered as heroic leaders prior to their offense. The heroic leader white-collar criminals were determined to be older, richer, and more powerful than the rest of the group and were also more likely to assume the role of leader in the crime committed. They committed large scale opportunistic crimes late in their lives and seemed to use their social status to disguise their criminal intent.[146]

In their study of white-collar offenders, Stadler and Benson found that they used the same techniques of neutralization (see Chapter 7) commonly used by other types of criminals. Both groups were most likely to use "denial of injury/victim" as a justification for and were less likely to invoke "condemn the condemners" or "appeal to higher loyalties" to excuse their crimes. Yet, the white-collar offenders were much less likely to believe that they were criminals who deserved a prison sentence and to blame someone else for their crimes.[147]

Occupational white-collar offenders commit their offenses while in a position of fiduciary responsibility and trust within their company. Klenowski interviewed 40 occupational white-collar offenders and found that a new neutralization technique was at work with these offenders. They made "claims of obedience" ("I learned it from them," "I was just following orders," and "It is how it has always been done") acquired through workplace socialization as justifications for their crimes. In sum, they "learned to be bad at work."[148]

A survey of MBA students presented a vignette on the sale of Panalba (a hypothetical pharmaceutical drug known to be harmful) to determine if gender moderated the relationship between techniques of neutralization and corporate offending decisions. The analysis revealed that men were more likely than women to commit corporate crime by agreeing to continue to market and sell the dangerous drug in question. Both sexes were likely to rely on "denial of injury," while "appeal to higher loyalties" was greatest for men and women identified "denial of responsibility" as the justification for their felonious decision.[149]

Prosecution of White-Collar Criminals

Prosecutors are the gatekeepers of the sentencing process, and the prosecutorial process always involves selection, meaning that cases are chosen for prosecution because of their severity but also because of the strength of the evidence against the accused. Benson identifies several reasons white-collar offenders are difficult to prosecute. First, victims may be unaware they have been victimized and who is responsible for the crime. Second, it is difficult to assign responsibility for the offense because the crime may result from the collective efforts of several people within an organization. Third, white-collar offenders are defended by high-powered, strong defense counsel who try to control the prosecution's access to the evidence of the crime.[150] These problems show why so few white-collar crime cases are prosecuted. Gurney's study of economic crime cases (e.g., fraud, embezzlement) determined that roughly one-third of 1,000 incidents were prosecuted in one Midwestern city over a 6-year period.[151]

Several factors frame the decision to prosecute white-collar crimes. Individuals were more likely to be prosecuted than organizations, although the probability of prosecution increased when the victim was an organization. A survey of California prosecutors revealed that the primary obstacle to prosecution was the level of resources available to them.[152] Political influence was also evident: Prosecutors from small districts were less likely to take on a corporate prosecution that would have a major impact on the local economy.

Prosecutorial decisions also vary by the type of crime. Scott's study of corporate collusion between 1946 and 1970 determined that price fixing was the most common charge. On average, cases spanned 7 years and required 21 months to investigate and 23 months to litigate. There was no clear concentration of cases by industry. Most cases began with negotiations that started before charges were actually filed. Although the penalties levied were often weak, Scott believes they had a deterrent effect.[153]

Sentencing typically follows the traditional rationales for the punishment of crime: retribution, deterrence, and just deserts.[154] In terms of retribution, white-collar offenders are treated more leniently than street criminals, although they may inflict more harm and affect more people than other crimes. White-collar criminals use their position to violate public trust and should be punished as any criminal would be. Punishment in the criminal justice system is a way of getting back at them for violating the public trust of their position in society. General deterrence theory demands we punish these offenders severely to send a message that these crimes are intolerable. Just deserts theory stresses that the offender deserves to be punished because he or she has committed a crime.

Governmental regulatory agencies are also legally charged with the oversight of businesses that operate in their field.

Regulatory agencies, like the Food and Drug Administration and the Environmental Protection Agency, have several distinct advantages over criminal justice law enforcement agencies in the control of white-collar crime:[155]

- *Specialized expertise*: They know the subject of the business and what the problems are.
- *Greater investigative powers*: They have explicit authority to enter premises and gather information from businesses.
- *More flexibility and discretion*: They can work with businesses to create innovative solutions to problems.

However, they can also be co-opted by the businesses they regulate and act in their interests rather than in the interests of the general public.

Sentencing of White-Collar Criminals

White-collar criminals are not always sentenced severely. Some officials, including judges, believe that these offenders have "suffered enough."[156] The process of arrest and conviction causes them to lose their high place in society and "fall from grace."[157] They are also considered sensitive to imprisonment because of their lack of experience with the criminal justice system.[158] A survey of New York judges revealed their belief that prison was more severe punishment for a white, middle-class offender than was the same sentence for a black or Hispanic lower-class offender.[159]

However, an analysis of a sample of 366 federal prison inmates found that white-collar offenders have no more difficulty in adjusting to prison life than other types of offenders. They were less likely to fear for their safety or report problems with their cellmates. They were also more likely to report having friends in prison.[160]

Yet, sentencing of white-collar offenders appears to be affected by bias. In a study of offenders charged with the violation of federal security laws, Eitle discovered that offenders who had positions of authority and control in the workplace were less likely to receive a punitive sanction. The differences in outcome may not be entirely due to bias but instead to prosecutorial resources and expertise.[161] There is also some evidence that female white-collar offenders sanctioned under federal sentencing guidelines received more lenient sentences than males.[162] Holtfreter examined a white-collar crime data set compiled by the Association of Certified Fraud Examiners (N = 633). Her comparison of female and male white-collar offenders revealed that women committed their crimes alone and committed less serious crimes than males. Both sexes were likely to commit asset manipulation (theft of cash or other inventory) but women were not present in the higher level positions required to commit more serious levels of this crime. Both their legitimate and illegitimate opportunities were restricted. However, in terms of sentencing, both sexes were punished according to the blameworthiness of their crimes. Solo offending, criminal history, and crime seriousness (as measured by dollar loss) determined the likelihood of incarceration for this group of offenders.[163]

Van Slyke and Bales analyzed Florida sentencing guidelines data (1994–2004) to examine the factors leading to the incarceration of white-collar and street property offenders. They determined that white-collar offenders were treated more leniently than street property offenders despite the influence of the sentencing guidelines. This relationship varied by the type of white-collar crime committed, the social status of the offender, and whether the sentence was levied before or after the Enron scandal. White-collar offenders who defrauded the government were sentenced more leniently than credit card fraud offenders. White-collar criminals who defrauded businesses, committed credit card fraud, and committed bribery were punished more harshly than consumer fraud offenders. One factor that could account for these differences is the "dramatization" that certain white-collar crimes (i.e., credit card fraud) has received in the media. Upper-class white-collar offenders who committed crimes like Medicaid provider fraud were sentenced more leniently than those who committed similar crimes associated with lower class offenders, such as public assistance fraud. Overall, white-collar offenders sentenced after the Enron scandal were more likely to receive a prison sentence than those sentenced before this national corporate scandal. Thus, the Enron scandal has had a significant effect on white-collar sentencing that has raised punishment levels.[164]

Shaming

John Braithwaite has suggested that punishing organizational criminals should take the more constructive approach of shaming.[165] Shaming involves the attempt to reintegrate offenders by confronting them with the seriousness of their conduct while forgiving those who reform. Stigmatization is counterproductive:[166]

> Criminal subcultures are less likely to develop when potent shaming is mobilized against both guilty individuals and the organization itself by the general community, professional or industry peers, and government regulatory officials.

Shaming thus involves all aspects of the community acting together. It promotes self-regulation by the professional community in place of a subculture of organizational criminality and it fosters both crime prevention and improved public service.

Does shaming have an impact on white-collar offenders? What is the impact of conviction and sentencing on individuals convicted of white-collar crimes? Michael Benson determined that not all offenders suffer in the same fashion. He interviewed 70 white-collar offenders drawn from the Chicago Federal District Courts in 1979 and 1980. Professionals (e.g., lawyers, doctors) had different experiences than businesspeople because of their conviction—loss of or changes in their occupational status. Professionals and public sector employees were more likely to change their status and experience a greater loss than private business executives or employees. Large-scale offenders were most likely to lose their jobs.[167,168]

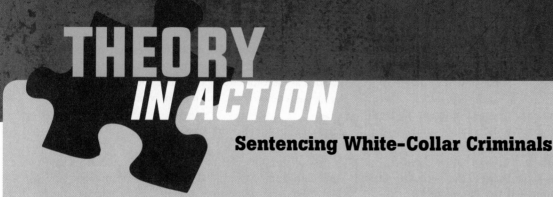

Sentencing White-Collar Criminals

Robert Waldrop is the founder of the Oscar Romero Catholic Worker House in Oklahoma City, Oklahoma. This institution helps people in need (i.e., the poor and the homeless). Waldrop drew up this list of "Necessary Measures for Curbing the Corporate Crime Wave."

1. The stockholders and management of corporations convicted of felonies should lose their right to vote and run for public office.

2. A registry should be maintained in each area of criminal corporations, and any corporations convicted of a felony should be required to register with the local police. A notice should be sent to all of the neighbors that a criminal corporation is taking up residence in their locality.

3. Criminal corporations should lose all corporate welfare benefits and government contracts.

4. Criminal corporations should be required to make weekly visits to parole officers, and their stockholders and management should be subject to random drug tests (either urine or hair).

5. Criminal corporations should not be allowed to operate within 500 yards of a school, church, or library.

6. Criminal corporations should be required to place the phrase "a criminal corporation" on all advertising, signs, and vehicles as a public warning.

7. If criminal corporations violate the terms of their parole, their stockholders and officers should go to jail.

8. Besides the fine on the corporation, the personal assets of stockholders should be forfeited for their criminal negligence and lack of oversight.

9. The increasing number of lawless corporations calls for stricter penalties. Bring back the death penalty for corporations. In this context, the "death penalty" is the closure of the corporation, the forfeiture of its assets to its victims and/or the government, and the winding up of its affairs by a court-appointed receiver.

10. Stockholders and management should be required to wear monitoring bracelets for the duration of their parole and may not travel outside of their jurisdiction without a written pass from their parole officer.

11. The stockholders and management of criminal corporations may not associate with stockholders and management of other corporate felons and are forbidden to keep and bear arms.

Do Waldrop's measures fit the aims of white-collar crime sentencing listed in this chapter? If so, how? If not, why not?

Source: Mokhiber, R., & Weissman, R. (2000, April 26). *Corporate focus: Taming corporate criminals in 11 easy steps.* Alter Net. Retrieved January 29, 2011, from http://www.alter-net.org/module/printversion/1056. Reproduced with permission from R. Waldrop.

These offenders held the media (the newspapers) responsible for holding them up for public ridicule. They felt that the media focused on their crime and ignored any good deeds in their life. They also blamed the criminal justice system for treating them "just like another criminal" and ignoring their status and public service record. Like Braithwaite, Benson condemns this process of stigmatization as counterproductive. Although it separates the offender and begins the process of punishment, it brands the offender and hinders repentance and reintegration.

Severity of Sentencing

There is some evidence that judges are following public sentiment when sentencing white-collar offenders. Some judges may apply harsher sentences on white-collar criminals that violate public trust.[169] Federal judges with heavy white-collar crime caseloads have been outraged by these crimes. They believed that upper-class persons should display a higher level of responsibility because of their status and the privileges it brings. Some white-collar criminals, because of their higher status, may receive a greater penalty levied by judges (e.g., prison time).[170–173]

Benson and Walker reconsidered the question of severity or leniency in white-collar sentencing. They examined the sentences given to 189 white-collar criminals in a Midwestern federal court between 1970 and 1980. They determined that higher status offenders were no more likely to be incarcerated or to receive a longer sentence than lower status ones. Neither status nor post-Watergate morality played a role in the type or length of sentence levied. The impact of a criminal case extends far beyond the sentence itself.[174] Conviction is damaging to white-collar offenders, often setting other punishments in motion (e.g., fines, restitution, disbarment, civil penalties, tort suits, and lost business/reputation).[175]

Punishing corporations, however, is a different matter. Arriving at a punitive sanction in a corporate criminal case requires a certain amount of creativity when the offender is an organization.[176] Schwartz and Ellison have offered several suggestions. First, fines could be set to the level of profit generated by the corporation. Second, the offending organization could be punished by putting it under the control of a state-appointed receiver. The corporation would pay the salaries of the individual taking over the company and the probation officer assigned to the case.[177]

When the white-collar offender is an individual, some punishments can be more severe than a prison sentence. These punishments strike at the heart of the motive: greed and the desire for greater profits. One example is corporate disqualification. This action blocks offenders for a limited time from conducting managerial functions comparable to those that led to the initial offense. Here, the punishment can fit both the crime and the criminal. Union officials, physicians, security dealers, and police officers who abused their position for personal gain have received this sanction.[178] During the probation period, they were forbidden to hold their former position. It may be the most severe punishment available, because the offender suffers the financial costs of lost work opportunities.

Shover advocates the use of corporate fines as a sanction because they offer several benefits. They can provide compensation to victims, prevent illegal gains, and lead to other penalties such as asset forfeiture. Therefore, they have the potential to serve as a deterrent to this form of white-collar crime.[179]

Conclusion

Crimes of the powerful have a massive impact on society: Their damage far exceeds that of street-level crime. The power yielded by organized crime families, white-collar criminals, and corporate offenders makes it more difficult to apprehend, prosecute, and punish these individuals.

Organized crime is an evolving entity taking different forms than originally perceived. However, as Abadinsky notes, these different perceptions have several common threads. Organized crime families follow a hierarchy and seek both profit and power.[180] They strive for monopolistic control of illegal markets and limit competition through bribery or the threat or use of violence. They have a restricted membership based on either kinship or skill. They attempt to keep their structure and operations secret. They are similar to legitimate business and they provide services (illegal) to meet public demand with the ultimate goal of wealth and power. As Albanese maintains, organized crime has less to do with ethnic conspiracies than with entrepreneurial activity.[181]

White-collar crimes are harmful and just as dangerous to society as street crimes. White-collar crimes, whether occupational or corporate, are willful and intentional.

WRAP-UP

CHAPTER SPOTLIGHT

Texture: © Malchev/Shutterstock; Police Tape: © SkillUp/Shutterstock

- "Crimes of the powerful" are those offenses committed by influential persons or groups in society. These offenses are also characterized as "organized," "white-collar," and "enterprise" crime.
- Organized crime groups and white-collar criminals share characteristics: They both strive for economic control of financial markets, both legal and illegal; they work to circumvent criminal law and governmental regulations aimed at governing the market and protecting consumers; the crimes they commit are costly to society in both human and financial terms; and their goal is to accumulate wealth and exercise power for the benefit of the organization and its members, regardless of the cost to others in society.

- The alien conspiracy model and the local, ethnic group model make up the major theories of organized crime. The alien conspiracy model contends that organized crime is a businesslike hierarchy based on a system of formally defined relationships, obligations, and duties. The local, ethnic group model maintains that the locus of control is limited to certain cities or areas of the country. In this model, the level of organization is rational but not bureaucratic.
- The Mafia code refers to a list of secret oaths and norms that govern behavior within an organized crime family. This code includes omerta (secrecy), loyalty, respect, and discipline.
- To control organized crime activities, law enforcement officials have used "headhunting,"

or targeting high-level crime family members for apprehension and prosecution. In addition, the Racketeer Influenced and Corrupt Organizations (RICO) Act was enacted as part of the Organized Crime Control Act of 1970 and enabled law enforcement to seek greater penalties for certain crimes; according to this act, organized crime comprises the acquisition, operation, or income from an "enterprise" through a "pattern" of "racketeering activity." An enterprise is any individual or group.

- White-collar crime can be classified as either occupational (a crime committed while doing business that is legal) or corporate crime (crimes committed by corporate organizations).
- White-collar crimes continue to expand and include crimes such as environmental crimes and money laundering. Although these illegal activities fall into more than one area of criminology, they are part of the discussion of white-collar crimes.

PUTTING IT ALL TOGETHER

1. The cliché "only in America" has been applied to organized crime. What elements or norms of American society allow organized crime to flourish?

2. What do organized and white-collar criminals have in common? How do they differ?

3. Is "shaming" a useful way to combat white-collar crime?

4. Use a current newspaper to find an example of organized crime. Use the material in this chapter to analyze your selected case.

5. Use a current newspaper to find an example of white-collar crime. Use the material in this chapter to analyze your selected case.

alien conspiracy model Assumes that foreign criminals (e.g., Sicilians) imported the crime values and family structures into the United States and secretly control crime activities in this country.

collective embezzlement Refers to company funds siphoned off for personal use by top management at the expense of the institution itself.

corporate crime Illegal acts by corporate officials to benefit the corporation.

headhunting Method of combating organized crime that focuses on the heads of criminal families and also seeks to freeze or seize the assets used in or obtained through organized crime.

local, ethnic group model Maintains that organized crime families have a decentralized structure and focus on operating businesses.

Mafia code Secret oaths and norms that govern behavior within organized crime families by maintaining secrecy and promoting loyalty, respect, and discipline.

occupational crime Illegal acts arising from opportunities created in the course of a legal occupation.

organized crime Criminal activity conducted by any group with some manner of formalized structure. The primary objective of organized crime groups is to obtain money through illegal activities.

shaming Punishment of white-collar criminals by confronting them with the seriousness of their conduct while forgiving and reintegrating those who reform.

state-organized crime Illegal acts committed by state officials in the course of their job as representatives of the state.

white-collar crime Deliberately harmful, illegal acts committed by persons of respectability and high social status in the course of their occupation.

Appendix

Chapter 1

1. Great-Quotes.com. Retrieved October 17, 2010, from http://www.great-quotes.com/quote/853703
2. Brainyquote.com. Retrieved January 2, 2006, from http://www.brainyquote.com/quotes/quotes/w/willrogers106272.html
3. Bureau of Justice Statistics. (n.d.). *Sourcebook of criminal justice statistics online.* Retrieved May 16, 2014, from http://www.albany.edu/sourcebook/pdf/t2402007.pdf
4. Kcykelhahn, T. (2013). *Local government corrections expenditures, FY 2005–2011.* Washington, DC: Bureau of Justice Statistics.
5. Pew Research Center. (April 2, 2013). *Feds may be rethinking the drug war, but states have been leading the way.* Retrieved May 16, 2014, from http://www.pewresearch.org/fact-tank/2014/04/02/feds-may-be-rethinking-the-drug-war-but-states-have-been-leading-the-way/
6. Note 5.
7. Sutherland, E., & Cressey, D. (1960). *Principles of criminology* (6th ed.). Philadelphia: J.B. Lippincott.
8. Sumner, G. W. (1906). *Folkways.* Boston: Ginn & Co.
9. Salvelsberg, J. J., & Sampson, R. J. (2002). Introduction: Mutual engagement: Criminology and sociology? *Crime, Law, and Social Change, 37,* 99–105.
10. Short, J. F., Jr. (2002). Criminology, the Chicago School, and Sociological Theory. *Crime, Law, and Social Change, 37,* 107–115.
11. Enriquez, R., & Barnes, J. C. (2009). Criminal law. In J. M. Miller (Ed.), *21st century criminology: A reference handbook,* Vol. 2. Thousand Oaks, CA: Sage, p. 646.
12. Note 11.
13. Pollock, J. M. (2009). *Criminal law* (9th ed.). Cincinnati, OH: Anderson, pp. 8–12.
14. Cornell University Law School. Legal Information Institute. Available at http://www.law.cornell.edu
15. Note 13, pp. 119–121.
16. Note 13, pp. 4, 21.
17. Note 11, p. 647.
18. U.S. Department of Justice. *Preserving life and liberty.* Retrieved January 2, 2010, from http://www.justice.gov/archive/ll/archive.htm
19. Electronic Freedom Foundation. *The USA Patriot Act.* Retrieved January 2, 2010, from http://www.eff.org/patriot
20. Note 19.
21. Farrell, M. B. (2010, March 1). Obama signs Patriot Act extension without reforms. *Christian Science Monitor.* Retrieved March 8, 2010, from http://www.csmonitor.com/USA/Politics/2010/0301/Obama-signs-Patriot-Act-extension-without-reforms.
22. Note 13, pp. 4–6.
23. Black, D. (2010). *The behavior of law.* Howard House, UK: Emerald, pp. 2–4.
24. Note 23, p. 21.
25. Note 23, p. 25.
26. Note 23, p. 27.
27. Note 23, p. 30.
28. Note 23, p. 44.
29. Smith, D. A. (1987). Police response to interpersonal violence: Defining the parameters of legal control. *Social Forces, 65*(3), 767–782.
30. Avakame, E. F., Fyfe, J. J., & McCoy, C. (1999). "Did you call the police? What did they do?" An

empirical assessment of Black's theory of mobilization of law. *Justice Quarterly, 16*(4), 765–792.

31. Chappell, A. T., & Maggard, S. R. (2007). Applying Black's theory of law to crack and cocaine dispositions. *International Journal of Offender Therapy and Comparative Criminology, 51*(3), 264–278.

32. Miller, J. M., Schreck, J. C., & Tewksbury, R. (2008). *Criminological theory: A brief introduction.* Boston: Allyn and Bacon, pp. 196–197.

33. Akers, R. L., & Sellers, C. (2004). *Criminological theories: Introduction, evaluation and application.* Los Angeles: Roxbury, pp. 5–6.

34. Note 7.

35. Barnes, H. E. (1972). *The story of punishment.* Montclair, NJ: Patterson-Smith.

36. Note 35.

37. Burns, W. E. (2003). *Witch hunts in Europe and America: An encyclopedia.* Westport, CT: Greenwood Press.

38. Lilly, J. R., Cullen, F. T., & Ball, R. A. (2010). *Criminological theory: Context and consequences.* Thousand Oaks, CA: Sage.

39. Newman, G. (1985). *The punishment response.* Philadelphia: Lippincott.

40. Pfohl, S. J. (1985). *Images of deviance and social control: A sociological history.* New York: McGraw-Hill, p. 25.

41. Note 38, pp. 13–15.

42. Note 38, p. 14.

43. Wellford, C. F. (2009). History and evolution of criminology. In J. M. Miller (Ed.), *21st century criminology: A reference handbook,* Vol. 1. Thousand Oaks, CA: Sage, p. 11.

44. Young, D. (1984). Let us content ourselves with praising the work while drawing a veil over its principles: Eighteenth century reactions to Beccaria's "On Crimes and Punishments." *Justice Quarterly, 1,* 155–170.

45. Note 38, pp. 14–15.

46. Vold, G. B. (1970). *Theoretical criminology.* New York: Oxford University Press, pp. 18–22.

47. Note 38, p. 15.

48. Rennie, Y. F. (1978). *The search for criminal man: A conceptual history of the dangerous offender.* Lexington, MA: Lexington Books, p. 18.

49. Monachesi, E. (1960). Cesare Beccaria. In H. Mannheim (Ed.), *Pioneers in criminology.* Montclair, NJ: Patterson-Smith.

50. Cullen, F. T., & Agnew, R. (2003). *Criminological theory: Past to present.* Los Angeles: Roxbury, p. 18.

51. Note 29, p. 32.

52. Rafter, N. (2004). The unrepentant horse-slasher: Moral insanity and the origins of criminological thought. *Criminology, 42,* 979–1008.

53. Fishman, G. (1981). Positivism and neo-Lombrosianism. In I. Barak-Glantz, & C. R. Huff (Eds.), *The mad, the bad, and the different: Essays in honor of Simon Dinitz.* Lexington, MA: Lexington Books, p. 17.

54. Jeffrey, C. R. (1960). The historical development of criminology. In H. Mannheim (Ed.), *Pioneers in criminology.* Montclair, NJ: Patterson-Smith, p. 468.

55. Cullen, F. T., & Gilbert, K. E. (2013). *Reaffirming rehabilitation.* Cincinnati, OH: Anderson.

56. Gibbs, J. P. (1987). The state of criminological theory. *Criminology, 25,* 821–840.

57. Canton, R., & Yates, J. (2008.) Applied criminology. In B. Stout, J. Yates, & B. Williams (Eds.), *Applied criminology.* London: Sage Publications Ltd, p. 6.

58. Note 57, p. 12.

59. Bennett, L. A. (1988). Practice in search of theory: The case of intensive supervision—An extension of an old practice or a new approach? *American Journal of Criminal Justice, 12,* p. 293.

60. Petersilia, J., & Turner, S. (1993). Evaluating intensive supervision probation/parole. *Research in Brief.* Washington, DC: National Institute of Justice.

61. Carter, R. M., Robison, J., & Wilkins, L. T. (1967). *The San Francisco project: A study of federal probation and parole.* Berkeley: University of California Press.

62. Latessa, E. J., & Vito, G. F. (1988). The effects of intensive supervision on shock probationers. *Journal of Criminal Justice, 16,* 319–330.

63. Byrne, J. M., Lurigio, A. J., & Baird, C. (1989). The effectiveness of the new intensive supervision programs. *Research in Corrections, 2,* 1–48.

64. Fulton, B., Latessa, E. J., Stichman, A., & Travis, L. F. (1997). The state of ISP: Research and policy implications. *Federal Probation, 61,* 65–76.

65. Henggeler, S. W., Cunningham, P. B., Pickrel, S. G., Schoenwald, S. K., & Brondino, M. J. (1996). Multisystemic therapy: An effective violence prevention approach for serious juvenile offenders. *Journal of Adolescence, 19,* 47–61; *see also* Henggeler, S. W., Clingempeel, W. G., Brondino, M. J., & Pickrel, S. G. (2002). Four-year follow-up of multisystemic therapy with substance-abusing and substance-dependent juvenile offenders. *Journal of the American Academy of Child & Adolescent Psychiatry, 41*(7), 868–874; Schaeffer, C. M., & Borduin, C. M. (2005). Long-term follow-up to a randomized clinical trial of multisystemic therapy with serious and violent juvenile offenders. *Journal of Consulting and Clinical Psychology, 73*(3), 445; Simmons-Mitchell, J., Bender, M. B., Kishna, M. A., & Mitchell, C. C. (2006). An independent effectiveness trial of multisystemic therapy with juvenile justice youth. *Journal of Clinical Child and Adolescent Psychology,*

35(2), 227–236; Borduin, C. M., Schaeffer, C. M., & Heiblum, N. (2009). A randomized clinical trial of multisystemic therapy with juvenile sexual offenders: Effects on youth social ecology and criminal activity. *Journal of Consulting and Clinical Psychology, 77*(1), 26; Letourneau, E. J., Henggeler, S. W., Borduin, C. M., Schewe, P. A., McCart, M. R., Chapman, J. E., & Saldana, L. (2009). Multisystemic therapy for juvenile sexual offenders: 1-year results from a randomized effectiveness trial. *Journal of Family Psychology, 23*(1), 89.

66. Cullen, F. T., & Gendreau, P. (2000). Assessing correctional rehabilitation: Policy, practice, and prospects. *Criminal Justice 2000.* Washington, DC: National Institute of Justice.

67. Martinson, R. M. (1974). What works? Questions and answers about prison reform. *The Public Interest, 55 (Spring),* 24.

68. Note 67, p. 10.

69. Vito, G. F., Kunselman, J., & Tewksbury, R. (2008). *Introduction to criminal justice research methods: An applied approach* (2nd ed.). Springfield, IL: Charles C. Thomas, p. 111.

70. Martinson, R. M., & Wilks, J. (1977). Save parole supervision. *Federal Probation, 41,* 23–27.

71. Martinson, R. M. (1979). New findings, new views: A note of caution regarding sentencing reform. *Hofstra Law Review, 7,* 242–258.

72. Sanchez, J. E. (1990). The use of Robert Martinson's "Writings on correctional treatment: An essay on the justification of correctional policy." *Journal of Contemporary Criminal Justice, 6,* 127–138.

73. Gendreau, P., & Ross, R. R. (1987). Revivication of rehabilitation: Evidence from the 1980s. *Justice Quarterly, 4,* 349–407.

74. Dowden, C., & Andrews, D. A. (2004). The importance of staff practice in delivering effective correctional treatment: A meta-analytic review of core correctional practice. *International Journal of Offender Therapy and Comparative Criminology, 48,* 204–214.

75. Dowden, C., & Andrews, D. A. (2000). Effective correctional treatment and violent reoffending: A meta-analysis. *Canadian Journal of Criminology, 42,* 449–467.

76. Latessa, E. J. (2004). The challenge of change: Correctional programs and evidence-based practices. *Criminology and Public Policy, 3,* 554–558; Lowenkamp, C. T., Latessa, E. J., & Holsinger, A. M. (2006). The risk principle in action: What have we learned from 13,676 offenders and 97 correctional programs? *Crime & Delinquency, 52*(1), 77–93.

77. Petersilia, J., Turner, S., Kahan, J., & Peterson, J. (1985). Executive summary of Rand's study: "Granting felons probation: Public risks and alternatives." *Crime and Delinquency, 31,* 379–392.

78. McGaha, J., Fichter, M., & Hirschburg, P. (1987). Felony probation: A re-examination of public risk. *American Journal of Criminal Justice, 11,* 1–9.

79. Vito, G. F. (1987). Felony probation and recidivism: Replication and response. *Federal Probation, 50,* 17–25.

80. Whitehead, J. (1991). The effectiveness of felony probation: Results from an eastern state. *Justice Quarterly, 9,* 525–543.

81. Langan, P. A., & Cunniff, M. A. (1992). *Recidivism of felons on probation, 1986–1989.* Washington, DC: Bureau of Justice Statistics.

82. Benedict, W. R., & Huff-Corzine, L. (1997). Return to the scene of the punishment: Recidivism of adult male property offenders on felony probation, 1986–1989. *Journal of Research in Crime and Delinquency, 34,* 237–252.

83. Sims, B., & Jones, M. (1997). Predicting success or failure on probation: Factors associated with felony probation outcomes. *Crime and Delinquency, 43,* 314–327.

84. Sherman, L. W., Smith, D. A., Schmidt, J. D., & Rogan, D. P. (1992). Crime, punishment, and stake in conformity: Legal and informal control of domestic violence. *American Sociological Review, 57,* 680–690.

85. Sherman, L. W., & Berk, R. A. (1984). The specific deterrent effects of arrest for domestic assault. *American Sociological Review, 49,* 261–272.

86. Berk, R. A., & Sherman, L. W. (1988). Police responses to domestic violence incidents: An analysis of an experimental design with incomplete randomization. *Journal of the American Statistical Association, 83,* 70–76.

87. Bailey, K. D. (2010). Lost in translation: Domestic violence, "the personal is political," and the criminal justice system. *Journal of Criminal Law & Criminology, 100*(4), 1292.

88. Zorza, J. (1995). Mandatory arrest for domestic violence: Why it may prove the best first step in curbing repeat abuse. *Criminal Justice, 10*(2), 8.

89. Sack, E. J. (2004). Battered women and the state: The struggle for the future of domestic violence policy. *Wisconsin Law Review,* 1658–1740.

90. Note 84, p. 680.

91. Dunford, F. W., Huizinga, D., & Elliott, D. S. (1990). The role of arrest in domestic assault: The Omaha police experiment. *Criminology, 28,* 183–206.

92. Hirschel, J. D., Hutchison, I. W., & Dean, C. W. (1992). The failure of arrest to deter spouse abuse. *Journal of Research in Crime and Delinquency, 29,* 7–33.

93. Sherman, L. W., Schmidt, J. D., Rogan, D. P., Gartin, P. R., Cohen, E. G., Collins, D. J., & Bacich, A. R. (1991). From initial deterrence to long-term escalation: Short term custody arrest for poverty ghetto domestic violence. *Criminology, 29*, 821–850.

94. Note 84.

95. Note 93, p. 846.

96. Binder, A., & Meeker, J. W. (1993). Implications of the failure to replicate the Minneapolis experimental findings. *American Sociological Review, 58*, 887.

97. Sherman, L. W. (1993). Implications of the failure to read the literature. *American Sociological Review, 58*, 888.

98. Berk, R. A. (1993). Policy correctness in the ASR. *American Sociological Review, 58*, 889.

99. Sherman, L. W., & Harris, H. M. (2013). Increased homicide victimization of suspects arrested for domestic assault: A 23-year follow-up of the Milwaukee Domestic Violence Experiment (MilDVE). *Journal of Experimental Criminology, 9*, 491–514.

100. Jeffery, C. R. (1977). *Crime prevention through environmental design.* Beverly Hills, CA: Sage, p. 331.

101. Carter, R. M. (1976). The police view of the justice system. In M. W. Klein (Ed.), *The juvenile justice system.* Beverly Hills, CA: Sage, p. 123.

102. Kirkham, G. L. (1974). From professor to patrolman: A fresh perspective on the police. *Journal of Police Science and Administration, 2*, 137.

103. Kirkham, G. L. (1976). *Signal zero: The professor who became a cop.* Philadelphia: Lippincott, p. 206.

104. Carter, R. M. (1972). Where have all the crime fighters gone? *Gunsmoke Gazette, 1*, 9.

105. Note 100, p. 124.

106. Wesley, W. A. (1970). *Violence and the police: A sociological study of law, custom, and morality.* Cambridge, MA: The MIT Press, pp. 65–66.

107. Allen, A., & Jacques, S. (2014). Police officers' theories of crime. *American Journal of Criminal Justice, 39*(2), 206–227.

108. Note 103, p. 213.

109. Note 103, pp. 214–245.

110. Tuck, M. (1989). Is criminology any use? *The Criminologist, 16*, 1.

111. Austin, J. (2003). Why criminology is irrelevant. *Criminology and Public Policy, 2*, 557.

112. Note 109, p. 6.

113. Petersilia, J. (1991). Policy relevance and the future of criminology. *Criminology, 29*, 1–16.

114. Gilsinan, J. F. (1991). Public policy and criminology: An historical and philosophical reassessment. *Justice Quarterly, 8*, 202, 204.

115. Tonry, M. (2013). Evidence, ideology and politics in the making of American criminal justice policy. *Crime & Justice, 42*(1), 1–13.

116. Note 114, p. 4.

117. Tonry, M., & Green, D. (2003). Criminology and public policy in the USA and UK. In L. Zedner & A. Ashworth, *The criminological foundations of public policy: Essays in honour of Roger Hood.* Oxford: Oxford University Press, pp. 485–526.

118. Note 112.

119. Note 56, p. 824.

120. Williams, F. (1984). The demise of criminological imagination: A critique of recent criminology. *Justice Quarterly, 1*, 91–106.

121. Note 119. *See also* Nelson, M. S., Wooditch, A., & Gabbidon, S. L. (2014). Is criminology out of date? A research note on the use of common types of data. *Journal of Criminal Justice Education, 25*, 1, 16–33.

122. Note 119.

123. Wells, L. E. (1995). Explaining crime in the year 2010. In J. Klofas & S. Stojkovic (Eds.), *Crime and justice in the year 2010.* Belmont, CA: Wadsworth, p. 45.

124. Note 122, p. 53.

125. Finckenauer, J. O. (1978). Crime as a national political issue, 1964–76. *Crime and Delinquency, 24*, 10–19.

126. Vito, G. F. (1983). The politics of crime control: Implications of Reagan administration pronouncements on crime. *Journal of Contemporary Criminal Justice, 2*, 1–7.

127. Miller, W. B. (1978). Ideology and criminal justice policy. In N. Johnson and L. D. Savitz (Eds.), *Justice and corrections.* New York: John Wiley, 7.

128. Note 126, pp. 8, 9.

129. Note 126, pp. 9, 10.

130. Kania, R. R. E. (1988). Conservative ideology in criminology and criminal justice. *American Journal of Criminal Justice, 13*, 80.

131. Wilson, J. Q. (1985). *Thinking about crime.* New York: Vintage Books, 46.

132. Note 130, p. 49.

133. Note 130, pp. 50–51.

134. Bohm, R. M. (1986). Crime, criminal and crime control policy myths. *Justice Quarterly, 3*, 194.

135. Walker, S. (2010). *Sense and nonsense about crime, drugs, and communities: A policy guide.* Belmont, CA: Cengage Learning.

136. Reiman, J., & Leighton, P. (2013). *The rich get richer and the poor get prison: Ideology, class and criminal justice.* Boston: Pearson.

137. Currie, E. (1989). Confronting crime: Looking toward the twenty-first century. *Justice Quarterly, 6*, 16.

138. Note 136, p. 21.

139. Currie, E. (1985). *Confronting crime: An American challenge.* New York: Pantheon.

140. Currie, E. (1998). *Crime and punishment in America.* New York: Henry Holt.

141. Travis, L. F., III, Latessa, E. J., & Vito, G. F. (1985). Agenda building in criminal justice: The case of determinate sentencing. *American Journal of Criminal Justice, 10,* 1–21.

142. Note 67, pp. 119–122.

143. Note 67.

144. Durkheim, E. (1971). Crime as normal phenomenon. In L. Radzinowicz & M. E. Wolfgang (Eds.), *The criminal in society: Crime and justice,* Vol 1. New York: Basic Books, pp. 391–392.

145. Cohen, A. K. (1966). *Deviance and control.* Englewood Cliffs, NJ: Prentice Hall, pp. 6–10.

146. Moynihan, D. P. (1996). Defining deviancy down. In R. C. Monk (Ed.), *Taking sides: Clashing views on controversial issues in crime and criminology.* Guilford, CT: Dushkin, p. 11.

147. Williams, F. P., & McShane, M. D. (1994). *Criminological theory.* Englewood Cliffs, NJ: Prentice Hall.

148. Finckenauer, J. O. (1999). *Scared straight! And the panacea phenomenon.* Prospect Heights, IL: Waveland Press, pp. 5–6.

Chapter 2

1. President's Commission on Law Enforcement and the Administration of Justice. (1967). *Task force report: Crime and its impact—an assessment.* Washington, DC: U.S. Department of Justice.

2. CQ Press. *2012 city crime rate rankings.* Retrieved May 20, 2013, from http://os.cqpress.com/citycrime/2012/CityCrime2013_CityCrimeRateRankings.pdf

3. Schwartz, A. E., Susin, S., & Voicu, I. (2003). Has falling crime driven New York City's real estate boom? *Journal of Housing Research, 14,* 101–136.

4. Lynch, A. K., & Rasmussen, D. W. (2001). Measuring the impact of crime on house prices. *Applied Economics, 33,* 1981–1989.

5. Nickerson D. B., & Feinberg, R. M. (1998, May 4). *The impact of crime rates on residential mortgage default.* Retrieved November 15, 2010, from http://ssrn.com/abstract=141593. *See also:* Tita, G. E., Petras, T. L., & Greenbaum, R. T. (2006). Crime and residential choice: A neighborhood level analysis of the impact of crime on housing prices. *Journal of Quantitative Criminology, 22*(4), 299–317.

6. Rand, M. R., & Rennison, C. M. (2002). True crime stories? Accounting for differences in our national crime indicators. *Chance, 15,* 47.

7. Note 6, p. 48.

8. Note 6.

9. Conklin, J. E. (2003). *Why crime rates fell.* Boston: Allyn and Bacon.

10. Blumstein, A., & Wallman, J. (Eds.) (2000). *The crime drop in America.* Cambridge, UK: Cambridge University Press.

11. Vito, G. F., Kunselman, J., & Tewksbury, R. (2008). *Introduction to criminal justice research methods: An applied approach* (2nd ed.). Springfield, IL: Charles C. Thomas, pp. 70–74.

12. Reaves, B. A. (1993). *Using NIBRS data to analyze violent crime.* Washington, DC: Bureau of Justice Statistics, pp. 1–2.

13. U.S. Department of Justice, Federal Bureau of Investigation, Criminal Justice Information Services Division. *2012 National Incident Based Reporting System.* Retrieved May 20, 2014, from http://www.fbi.gov/about-us/cjis/ucr/nibrs/2012

14. U.S. Department of Justice, Federal Bureau of Investigation, Criminal Justice Information Services Division. *Summary of NIBRS 2012.* Retrieved May 20, 2014, from http://www.fbi.gov/about-us/cjis/ucr/nibrs/2012

15. Note 14.

16. Sherman, L. W. (2009). Hot spots. In A. Wakefield & J. Fleming, *The Sage dictionary of policing.* London: Sage.

17. Truman, J., Langdon, L., & Planty, M. (2013). *Criminal victimization, 2012.* Washington, DC: Bureau of Justice Statistics.

18. Decker, S. H. (1977). Official crime rates and victim surveys: An empirical comparison. *Journal of Criminal Justice, 5,* pp. 47–54; Eck, J. E., & Riccio, L. J. (1979). Relationship between reported crime rates and victimization survey results. *Journal of Criminal Justice, 7,* 293–308.

19. Hindelang, M. J. (1974). The Uniform Crime Reports revisited. *Journal of Criminal Justice, 2,* 1–17.

20. Schneider, A. L. (1981). Differences between survey and police information about crime. In R. G. Lehnen & W. G. Skogan (Eds.), *The national crime survey: Working papers,* Vol. I. Washington, DC: U.S. Government Printing Office.

21. Note 6, p. 48.

22. Note 16.

23. Catalano, S. (2013). *Intimate partner violence, 1993-2010.* Washington, DC: Bureau of Justice Statistics.

24. Harrell, E., & Langton, L. (2013). *Victims of identity theft, 2012.* Washington, DC: Bureau of Justice Statistics.

25. Robers, S., Kemp, J., Truman, J., & Synder, T. D. (2013). *Indicators of school crime and safety: 2012.* Washington, DC: National Center for Education Statistics, U.S. Department of Education, and Bureau of Justice Statistics, Office of Justice Programs, U.S. Department of Justice.

26. Harrell, E. (2011). *Violence in the workplace, 1993-2009.* Washington, DC: Bureau of Justice Statistics.

27. Levine, J. P. (1974). The potential for crime overreporting in criminal victimization surveys. *Criminology, 14,* 307–330.

28. Schneider, A. L., & Sumi, D. (1981). Patterns of forgetting and telescoping: An analysis of LEAA survey victimization data. *Criminology, 19,* 400–410.

29. Eigenberg, H. M. (1990). The national crime survey and rape: The case of the missing question. *Justice Quarterly, 7,* 657.

30. Minton, T. D. (2013). *Jail inmates at midyear 2012–statistical tables.* Washington, DC: Bureau of Justice Statistics.

31. Carson, A. E., & Golinelli, D. (2013). *Prisoners in 2012—Trends in admissions and releases, 1991–2012.* Washington, DC: Bureau of Justice Statistics.

32. Maruschak, L. M., & Parks, E. (2012). *Probation and parole in the United States, 2011.* Washington, DC: Bureau of Justice Statistics.

Chapter 3

1. Finckenauer, J. O. (1978). Crime as a national political issue: 1963–1976—from law and order to domestic tranquility, *Crime and Delinquency, 23,* 23.

2. Cullen, F. T., & Gilbert, K. T. (1982). *Reaffirming rehabilitation.* Cincinnati, OH: Anderson, pp. 95–96.

3. Note 2, pp. 89–149.

4. Newman, G. (1985). *The punishment response.* Philadelphia: Lippincott.

5. van den Haag, E., & Conrad, J. P. (1983). *The death penalty: A debate.* New York: Plenum.

6. Griffin, M. L. (2001). *The use of force by detention officers.* New York: LFB Scholarly Publishing, pp. 38–40.

7. Maricopa County Sheriff's Office. (n.d.). Retrieved July 2014, from http://www.mcso.org/About/Sheriff.aspx

8. Grupp, S. E. (1971). *Theories of punishment.* Bloomington: Indiana University Press.

9. Young, D. (1983). Let us content ourselves with praising the work while drawing a veil over its principles: Eighteenth century reactions to Beccaria's "On Crimes and Punishments." *Justice Quarterly, 1,* 155–170.

10. van den Haag, E. (1975). *Punishing criminals.* New York: Basic Books, p. 15.

11. Note 10, p. 60.

12. Makinen, T., & Hannu, T. (1980). The 1976 police strike in Finland. *Scandinavian Studies in Criminology, 7,* 87–106.

13. Clark, G. (1969, November 16). What happens when the police go on strike. *New York Times Magazine,* 176–185, 187, 194–195.

14. Cochran, J. K., Chamlin, M. B., & Seth, M. (1993). Deterrence or brutalization? An impact assessment of Oklahoma's return to capital punishment. *Criminology, 32,* 107–133.

15. Note 14.

16. Sellin, T. (1980). *The penalty of death.* Beverly Hills, CA: Sage.

17. Yang, B., & Lester, D. (2008). The deterrent effect of executions: A meta-analysis thirty years after Ehrlich. *Journal of Criminal Justice, 36,* 453–460.

18. Kovandzic, T. V., Vieraitis, L. M., & Boots, D. P. (2009). Does the death penalty save lives? New evidence from state panel data, 1977 to 2006. *Criminology & Public Policy, 8,* 803–843.

19. Berk, R. (2009). Can't tell: Comments on 'Does the death penalty save lives?' *Criminology & Public Policy, 8,* 845–851.

20. McFarland, S. G. (1983). Is capital punishment a short-term deterrent to homicide? A study of the effects of four recent American executions. *Journal of Criminal Law and Criminology, 73,* 1013–1032.

21. Note 14.

22. Bailey, W. C. (1998). Deterrence, brutalization, and the death penalty: Another examination of Oklahoma's return to capital punishment. *Criminology, 36,* 711–733.

23. Bowers, W. J., & Pierce, G. L. (1975). The illusion of deterrence in Isaac Ehrlich's research on capital punishment. *Yale Law Journal, 85,* 187–208.

24. Cochran, J. K., & Chamlin, M. B. (2000). Deterrence and brutalization: The dual effects of executions. *Justice Quarterly, 17,* 685–706.

25. Land, K. C., Teske, R. H., & Zheng, H. (2012). The differential short-term impacts of executions on felony and non-felony homicides. *Criminology and Public Policy, 11,* 541–563.

26. Doob, A. N., & Webster, C. M. (2003). Sentence severity and crime: Accepting the null hypothesis. *Crime and Justice,* Vol. 30. Chicago: University of Chicago Press, 143–195.

27. Chamlin, M. B. (1991). A longitudinal analysis of the arrest-crime relationship: A further examination of the tipping effect. *Justice Quarterly, 8,* 187–199.

28. Tittle, C. R., & Rowe, A. R. (1973). Certainty of arrest and crime rates: A further test of the deterrence hypothesis. *Social Forces, 52,* 355–362.

29. Note 27, p. 196.

30. Kelling, G. L., Pate, T., Dieckman, D., & Brown, C. (1973). *The Kansas City preventive patrol experiment: A technical report.* Washington, DC: The Police Foundation.

31. Larson, R. C. (1973). What happened to patrol operations in Kansas City? A review of the Kansas City preventive patrol experiment. *Journal of Criminal Justice, 3,* 267–297.

32. Sherman, L. W. (1995). General deterrent effects of police patrol in crime 'hot spots': A randomized, controlled trial. *Justice Quarterly, 12,* 625–638.

33. Sorg, E. T. Haberman, C. P., Ratcliffe, J. H., & Groff, E. R. (2013). Foot patrol in violent crime hot spots: The longitudinal impact of deterrence and posttreatment effects of displacement. *Criminology, 51,* 65–102.

34. Caeti, T. (1999). *Houston's targeted beat program: A quasi-experimental test of police patrol strategies.* Unpublished doctoral dissertation, Sam Houston State University, Texas.

35. Wilson, J. Q., & Kelling, G. R. (1982, March). Broken windows: The police and neighborhood safety. *The Atlantic Monthly,* 29–38.

36. Rosenfeld, R., Fornango, R., & Rengifo, A. F. (2007). The impact of order-maintenance policing on New York City homicide and robbery rates: 1988–2001. *Criminology, 45,* 355–384.

37. Goodman, D. J., & Baker, A. (2014). Waves of protests after grand jury doesn't indict officer in Eric Garner case. *New York Times.* Retrieved April, 2014 from http://www.nytimes.com/2014/12/04/nyregion/grand-jury-said-to-bring-no-charges-in-staten-island-chokehold-death-of-eric-garner.html

38. Langan, P. A., & Levin, D. J. (2004). *Recidivism of prisoners released in 1994.* Washington, DC: Bureau of Justice Statistics.

39. Erwin, B. S. (1986). Turning up the heat on probationers in Georgia. *Federal Probation, 50,* 17–23.

40. Petersilia, J., & Turner, S. (1993). Evaluating intensive supervision probation and parole: Results of a nationwide experiment. *Research in Brief.* Washington, DC: U.S. National Institute of Justice.

41. Petersilia, J., & Turner, S. (1991). An evaluation of intensive probation in California. *Journal of Criminal Law and Criminology, 82,* 610–658.

42. Latessa, E. J., & Vito, G. F. (1988). The effects of intensive supervision on shock probationers. *Journal of Criminal Justice, 16,* 319–330.

43. Hawken, A., & Kleiman, M. (2009). Managing drug involved probationers with swift and certain sanctions: Evaluating Hawaii's HOPE. Washington D.C: U.S. National Institution of Justice.

44. MacKenzie, D. L., Wilson, D. B., & Kider, S. B. (2001). Effects of correctional boot camps on offending. *Annals of the American Academy of Political and Social Sciences, 578,* 126–143.

45. Cullen, F. T., Wright, J. P., & Applegate, B. K. (1996). Control in the community: The limits of reform? In A. T. Harland (Ed.), *Choosing correctional options that work: Defining the demand and evaluating the supply* (pp. 69–116). Thousand Oaks, CA: Sage.

46. Note 6, pp. 41–44.

47. Sherman, L. W., Schmidt, J. D., Rogan, D. P., Gartin, P. R., Cohen, E. G., Collins, D. J., & Bacich, A. R. (1991). From initial deterrence to long-term escalation: Short-term custody arrest for poverty ghetto domestic violence. *Criminology, 29,* 821–850.

48. Berk, R. A., & Sherman, L. W. (1988). Police responses to domestic violence incidents: An analysis of an experimental design with incomplete randomization. *Journal of the American Statistical Association, 83,* 70–76.

49. Sherman, L. W., & Berk, R. A. (1983). The specific deterrent effects of arrest for domestic assault. *American Sociological Review, 39,* 261–272.

50. Sherman, L. W., & Smith, D. A. (1992). Crime, punishment, and stake in conformity: Legal and informal control of domestic violence. *American Sociological Review, 57,* 680–690.

51. Note 47, p. 836.

52. Note 50, pp. 685–688.

53. Berk, R. A., Campbell, A., Klap, R., & Western, B. (1992). The deterrent effect of arrest: A Bayesian analysis of four field experiments. *American Sociological Review, 57,* 698–708.

54. Williams, K. R., & Hawkins, R. (1986). Perceptual research on general deterrence: A critical review. *Law and Society Review, 20,* 535–572.

55. Kennedy, D. M. (2009). *Deterrence and crime prevention: Reconsidering the prospect of sanction.* New York: Routledge.

56. Note 55, p. 157.

57. Seabrook, J. (2009, June 22). Don't shoot. *The New Yorker,* 32–42.

58. Braga, A. A., Kennedy, D. M., Waring, E., & Piehl, A. M. (2001). Problem-oriented policing, deterrence, and youth violence: An evaluation of Boston's Operation Ceasefire. *Journal of Research in Crime and Delinquency, 38,* 195–225.

59. Kennedy, D. M. (2009). Comment on 'Gangs and public policy': Constructing and deconstructing gang databases. *Criminology and Public Policy, 8,* 711–716.

60. Engel, R. S., Tillyer, M. S., & Corsaro, N. (2013). Reducing gang violence using focused deterrence: Evaluating the Cincinnati Initiative to Reduce Violence (CIRV). *Justice Quarterly, 30,* 403–439.

61. Goldstein, H. (1990). *Problem-oriented policing.* New York: McGraw-Hill.

62. Braga, A., & Weisburd, D. (2012). The effects of focused deterrence strategies on crime: A systematic review and meta-analysis of the empirical evidence. *Journal of Research in Crime and Delinquency, 49,* 323–358.

63. Note 57, p. 39.

64. Note 54, p. 535–572

65. Paternoster, R. (1985). Assessments of risk and behavioral experience: An exploratory study of change. *Criminology, 23,* 417–436.

66. Finckenauer, J. O. (1982). *Scared straight and the panacea phenomenon.* Englewood Cliffs, NJ: Prentice Hall.

67. Nagin, D. S., & Pogarsky, G. (2001). Integrating celerity, impulsivity, and extralegal sanction threats into a model of general deterrence: Theory and evidence. *Criminology, 39,* 865–892, 867.

68. Pratt, T. C., Cullen, F. C., Blevins, K. R., Daigle, L. E., & Madensen, T. D. (2006). The empirical status of deterrence theory: A meta-analysis. In J. P. Wright & K. R. Blevins (Eds.), *Taking stock: The status of criminological theory, advances in criminological theory.* Piscataway, NJ: Transaction Press, 367–396.

69. Akers, R. L., & Sellers, C. S. (2013). *Criminological theories: Introduction, evaluation, and application.* New York: Oxford University Press, p. 24.

70. Cornish, D. B., & Clarke, R. V. (1985). Crime as rational choice. In *The Reasoning Criminal.* New York: Springer-Verlag.

71. Piliavin, I., Thornton, C., Gartner, R., & Matsueda, R. L. (1986). Crime, deterrence, and rational choice. *American Sociological Review, 51,* 101–119.

72. Tunnel, K. D. (1992). *Choosing crime: The criminal calculus of property offenders.* Chicago: Nelson-Hall.

73. Decker, S. H., & Chapman, M. T. (2008) *Drug smugglers on drug smuggling: Lessons from the inside.* Philadelphia: Temple University Press, p. 134.

74. Cromwell, P. F., Olson, J. N., and Avary, D. W. (1991). *Breaking and entering: An ethnographic analysis of burglary.* Newbury Park, CA: Sage, p. 42.

75. Akers, R. A. (1990). Rational choice, deterrence, and social learning in criminology: The path not taken. *Journal of Research in Crime and Delinquency, 27,* 653–676.

76. Note 74.

77. Note 73, p. 44.

78. Cohen, L. E., & Felson, M. (1979). Social change and crime rate trends: A routine activity approach. *American Sociological Review, 33,* 588–608.

79. Felson, M., & Boba, R. (2010). *Crime and everyday life* (4th ed.). Thousand Oaks, CA: Sage.

80. Note 79, p. 28.

81. Felson, M. (1998). *Crime and everyday life* (2nd ed.). Thousand Oaks, CA: Pine Forge, pp. 53–60

82. Clarke, R. V. (1999). Hot products: Understanding, anticipating and reducing demand for stolen goods. *Paper No. 112, Police Research Series.* London: Home Office.

83. Note 78, pp. 591–593.

84. Pratt, T. C., Holtfreter, K., & Resig, M. D. (2010). Routine online activity and internet fraud targeting: Extending the generality of routine activity theory. *Journal of Research in Crime and Delinquency, 47,* 267–296.

85. Hindelang, M. J., Gottfredson, M. R., & Garofalo, J. (1978). *Victims of personal crime: An empirical foundation for a theory of personal victimization.* Cambridge, MA: Ballinger.

86. Sacco, V. F., & Kennedy, L. W. (2002). *The criminal event: Perspectives in time and space.* Belmont, CA: Wadsworth, p. 63.

87. Note 85, pp. 251–264.

88. Cohen, L. E., & Felson, M. (1979). Social change and crime rate trends: A routine activities approach. *American Sociological Review, 44,* 588–608.

89. Miethe, T. D., Meier, R. F., & Sloane, D. (1990). Lifestyle changes and risks of criminal victimization. *Journal of Quantitative Criminology, 6,* 357–376.

90. Kennedy, L. W., & Ford, D. R. (1990). Risky lifestyles and dangerous results: Routine activities and exposure to crime. *Sociology and Social Research 73,* 208–211.

91. Miethe, T. D., & McDowall, D. (1993). Contextual effects in models of criminal victimization. *Social Forces, 71,* 731–760.

92. Wilcox, P., Madensen, T. D., & Tillyer, M. S. (2007). Guardianship in context: Implications for burglary victimization risk and prevalence. *Criminology, 45,* 771–804.

93. Lauritsen, J. L., Sampson, R. J., & Laub, J. H. (1991). The link between offending and victimization among adolescents. *Criminology, 29,* 265–292.

94. Lauritsen, J. L., Sampson, R. J., & Laub, J. H. (1992). Conventional and delinquent activities: Implications for the prevention of violent victimization among adolescents. *Violence and Victims 7,* 91–108.

95. Spano, R., Freilich, J. D., & Bolland, J. (2008). Gang membership, gun carrying, and employment: Applying routine activities theory to explain violent victimization among inner city, minority youth living in extreme poverty. *Justice Quarterly, 25,* 381–410.

96. Taylor, T. J., Freng, A., & Esbensen, F. A. (2008). Youth gang membership and serious violent victimization: The importance of lifestyles and routine activities. *Journal of Interpersonal Violence, 23,* 1441–1464.

97. Wooldredge, J. D. (1998). Inmate lifestyles and opportunities for victimization. *Journal of Research in Crime and Delinquency, 35,* 380–502.

98. Weisburd, D. (1997). *Reorienting crime prevention research and policy: From the causes of criminality to the context of crime.* Washington, DC: U.S. National Institute of Justice.

99. Jeffery, C. R. (1978). *Crime prevention through environmental design.* Beverly Hills, CA: Sage.

100. Newman, O. (1972). *Defensible space.* New York: Macmillan.

101. Note 79, p. 154.
102. Welsh, B. C., & Farrington, D. P. (2008). Public area CCTV and crime prevention: An updated systematic review and meta-analysis. *Justice Quarterly, 26,* 716–745.
103. Note 79, p. 171.
104. Wallis, A., Ford, D., & Westinghouse Electric Corporation. (1980). *Crime prevention through environmental design: The commercial demonstration in Portland, Oregon.* Washington, DC: U.S. National Institute of Justice.
105. Kushmuk, J., & Whitmore, S. (1981). *A re-evaluation of the CPTED program in Portland, Oregon.* Washington, DC: U.S. National Institute of Justice.
106. Griswold, B. (1983). Crime prevention and commercial burglary: A time series analysis. *Journal of Criminal Justice, 12,* 393–501.
107. Painter, K. A., & Farrington, D. P. (2001). Evaluation of situational crime prevention using a young people's survey. *British Journal of Criminology, 31,* 266–283.
108. Painter, K. A., & Farrington, D. P. (1997). The crime reducing effect of improved street lighting: The Dudley project. In R. V. Clarke (Ed.), *Situational crime prevention: Successful case studies* (2nd ed.). New York: Harrow and Heston, pp. 209–226.
109. Ekblom, P., Law, H., & Sutton, M. (1996). Safer cities and domestic burglary. *Home Office Research Study 164.* London: Home Office.
110. Note 109, pp. 35–40.
111. Weisburd, D., Wyckoff, L., Ready, J., Eck, J., Hinkle, J. C., & Gajewski, F. (2006). Does crime just move around the corner? A controlled study of spatial displacement and diffusion of crime control benefits. *Criminology, 443,* 549–591.
112. Guerette, R. T., & Bowers, K. J. (2009). Assessing the extent of crime displacement and diffusion of benefits: A review of situational crime prevention evaluations. *Criminology, 47,* 1331–1368.
113. Ekblom, P., & Tilley, N. (2000). Going equipped: Criminology, situational crime prevention and the resourceful offender. *Journal of British Criminology, 40,* 367–389.
114. Durlauf, S. N., & Nagin, D. S. (2011). Imprisonment and crime. *Criminology and Public Policy, 10,* 13–54.

Chapter 4

1. Rafter, N. (2008). *The criminal brain: Understanding biological theories of crime.* New York: New York University Press, pp. 235–236.
2. Raine, A. (2013). *The anatomy of violence: The biological roots of crime.* New York: Pantheon, p. xiii.
3. Ellis, L., & Hoffman, H. (1990). Ideology: Views of contemporary criminologists on causes and theories of crime. In L. Ellis & H. Hoffman (Eds.), *Crime in biological, social, and moral contexts.* New York: Praeger.
4. Shah, S. A., & Roth, L. H. (1974). Biological and psychophysical factors in criminality. In D. Glaser (Ed.), *Handbook of criminology.* Chicago: Rand McNally.
5. Rafter, N. (2005). The murderous Dutch fiddler: Criminology, history and the problem of phrenology. *Theoretical Criminology, 9,* 65–96.
6. Allen, H. E., Friday, P. C., Roebuck, J. B., & Sagarin, E. (1981). *Crime and punishment: An introduction to criminology.* New York: The Free Press.
7. Note 1, pp. 65–88.
8. Martin, R., Mutchnick, R. J., & Austin, W. T. (1990). *Criminological thought: Pioneers past and present.* New York: Macmillan, p. 21.
9. Note 1, p. 84.
10. Lombroso, C., & Lombroso-Ferrero, G. (1895). *The female offender.* London: Fisher Urwin, pp. xiv–xv.
11. Lombroso, C. (1918). *Crime, its causes and remedies.* Boston: Little, Brown and Company.
12. Goring, C. (1972/1913). *The English convict: A statistical study.* Montclair, NJ: Patterson Smith.
13. Hooten, E. (1939). *Crime and the man.* Cambridge, MA: Harvard University Press.
14. Sheldon, W. (1954). *Atlas of men.* New York: Harper.
15. Sheldon, W. H. (1949). *Varieties of delinquent youth: An introduction to constitutional psychiatry.* New York: Harper and Brothers.
16. Glueck, S., & Glueck, E. (1950). *Unraveling juvenile delinquency.* New York: Commonwealth Fund.
17. Hartl, E. M., Monnelly, E. P., & Elderkin, R. D. (1982). *Physique and delinquent behavior: A thirty-year follow-up of William H. Sheldon's varieties of delinquent youth.* New York: Academic Press.
18. Sampson, R. J., & Laub, J. H. (1993). *Crime in the making: Pathways and turning points through life.* Cambridge, MA: Harvard University Press, p. 95.
19. Jacobs, P. (1965). Aggressive behavior, mental subnormality and the XYY male. *Nature, 208,* 1351–1352.
20. Katz, J., & Chambliss, W. J. (1991). Biology and crime. In J. F. Sheley (Ed.), *Criminology.* Belmont, CA: Wadsworth, pp. 257–258.
21. Mednick, S., & Volavka, J. (1980). Biology and crime. In N. Morris & M. Tonry (Eds.), *Crime and justice: An annual review of research* (Vol. 2). Chicago: University of Chicago Press, p. 93.
22. Note 13, p. 392.
23. Rowe, D. C. (2002). *Biology and crime.* Los Angeles: Roxbury.
24. Note 1, p. 163.
25. Gould, S. J. (1996). *The mismeasure of man.* New York: W. W. Norton.
26. Note 20, p. 257.

27. Jeffery, C. R. (1993, January/February). Genetics, crime and the canceled conference. *Criminologist, 18*, 1–8.

28. Dugdale, R. L. (1877). *The Jukes: A study in crime, pauperism, disease, and heredity.* New York: Putnam.

29. Goddard, H. H. (1912). *The Kallikak family: A study in the heredity of feeblemindedness.* New York: Macmillan.

30. Dugdale, R. (1994). The Jukes: A study in crime, pauperism, and heredity. In J. E. Jacoby (Ed.), *Classics of criminology* (2nd ed.). Prospect Heights, IL: Waveland, p. 134.

31. Christianson, S. (2003, February 8). Bad seed or bad science: The story of the notorious Jukes family. *The New York Times.*

32. Lipsey, M. W., & Derzon, J. H. (1998). Predictors of violent or serious delinquency in adolescence and early childhood: A synthesis of longitudinal research. In R. Loeber & D. Farrington (Eds.), *Serious and violent juvenile offenders: Risk factors and successful interventions.* Thousand Oaks, CA: Sage.

33. Note 18, p. 69.

34. Christiansen, K. O. (1977). Preliminary study of criminality among twins. In S. A. Mednick & K. O. Christiansen (Eds.), *Biosocial bases of criminal behavior.* New York: Gardner Press.

35. Rowe, D. C. (1985). Sibling interaction and self-reported delinquent behavior. *Criminology, 23*, 223–240.

36. Rhee, S. H., & Waldman, I. D. (2002). Genetic and environmental influences on antisocial behavior: A meta-analysis of twin and adoption studies. *Psychological Bulletin, 128*, 490–529.

37. Note 23, p. 21.

38. Carey, G. (1992). Twin imitation for antisocial behavior: Implications for genetic and family environment research. *Journal of Abnormal Psychology, 101*, 18–22.

39. Brennan, P. A., Mednick, S. A., & Volavka, J. (1995). Biomedical factors in crime. In J. Q. Wilson & J. Petersilia (Eds.), *Crime.* Lexington, MA: Lexington Books, p. 71.

40. Mednick, S. A., Gabrielli, W. F., & Hutchings, B. (1984). Genetic influences in criminal convictions. *Science, 224*, 891–894.

41. Note 39, p. 75.

42. Note 36, p. 496.

43. Moffitt, T. E. (2005). The new look of behavioral genetics in developmental psychopathology: Gene-environment interplay in antisocial behavior. *Psychological Bulletin, 131*, 533–554, 548.

44. Burt, C. H., & Simons, R. (2014). Pulling back the curtain on heritability studies: Biosocial criminology in the postgenomic era. *Criminology, 52*, 223–262.

45. Wright, J. P., Barnes, J. C., Boutwell, B. B., Schwartz, J. A., Connolly, E. J., Nedelec, et al. Mathematical proof is not minutiae and irreducible complexity is not a theory: A final response to Burt and Simons and a call to criminologists. *Criminology, 53*, 113–120.

46. Beaver, K. M. (2009). Molecular genetics and crime. In A. Walsh & K. M. Beaver (Eds.), *Biosocial Criminology.* New York: Routledge.

47. Note 46, p. 53.

48. Note 23, p. 100.

49. Brunner, H. G., Nelen, M. R., Breakefield, X. O., Ropers, H. H., & van Oost, B. A. (1993). Abnormal behavior associated with a point mutation in the structural gene for monoamine oxidase A. *Science, 262*, 578–580.

50. Note 23, pp. 101–102.

51. U.S. Department of Energy, National Institutes of Health. (2003). Human Genome Project information. Retrieved May 20, 2010, from http://www.ornl.gov/sci/techresources/Human_Genome/project/about.shtml

52. Note 46, pp. 62–68.

53. Note 23, p. 85.

54. Guo, G., Ou, X. M., Roettger, M., & Shih, J. C. (2008). The VNTR 2 repeat in MAOA and delinquent behavior in adolescence and young adulthood: Associations and MAOA promoter activity. *European Journal of Human Genetics, 16*, 626–634.

55. Caspi, A., McClay, J., Moffitt, T. E., Mill, J., Martin, J., Craig, I., et al. (2002). Role of genotype in the cycle of violence in maltreated children. *Science, 297*, 851–854.

56. Kim-Cohen, J., Caspi, A., Taylor, A., Williams, B., Newcombe, R., et al. (2006). MAOA, maltreatment, and gene-environment interactions predicting children's mental health: New evidence and a meta-analysis. *Molecular Psychiatry, 11*, 903–913.

57. Moffitt, T. E., Caspi, A., & Rutter, M. (2006). Measured gene–environment interactions in psychopathology: Concepts, research strategies, and implications for research, intervention, and public understanding of genetics. *Perspectives on Psychological Science, 1*, 5–27.

58. Beaver, K. M., Wright, J. P., DeLisi, M. A., Walsh, A., Vaughn, M. G., & Vaske, J. (2007). A gene x gene interaction between DRD2 and DRD4 is associated with conduct disorder and antisocial behavior in males. *Behavioral and Brain Functions, 3*, 30.

59. Note 1, pp. 230–236.

60. Note 23, pp. 81–82.

61. Raine, A., Buchsbaum, M. S., Stanley, J., Lottenberg, S., Abel, L., & Stoddard, J. (1993). Selective reductions in prefrontal glucose metabolism in murderers. *Biological Psychiatry, 36*, 365–373.

62. Note 1, p 79.

63. Raine, A., Lencz, T., Bihrle, S., LaCasse, L., & Colletti, P. (2000). Reduced prefrontal gray matter volume and reduced autonomic activity in antisocial personality disorder. *Archives of General Psychiatry, 57,* 119–127.

64. Note 39, p. 82.

65. Note 1, p. 57.

66. Note 23, p. 75.

67. Moffitt, T. E., Brammer, G. L., Caspi, A., Fawcett, J. P., Raleigh, M., Yuwiler, A., et al. (1998). Whole blood serotonin relates to violence in an epidemiological study. *Biological Psychiatry, 43,* 446–457.

68. Cherek, D., & Lane, S. (1999). Effects of d,1-fenfluramine on aggressive and impulsive responding in adult males with a history of conduct disorder. *Psychopharmacology, 146,* 473–481.

69. Moffit, T. E., Lynam, D. R., & Silva, P. A. (1994). Neuropsychological tests predicting persistent male delinquency. *Criminology, 32,* 277–300.

70. Raine, A. (1993). *The psychopathology of crime: Criminal behavior as a clinical disorder.* San Diego: Academic Press.

71. Note 1, pp. 103–106.

72. Raine, A. (1997). Antisocial behavior and psychophysiology: A biosocial perspective and a prefrontal dysfunction hypothesis. In D. M. Stoff, J. Breiling, & J. D. Master (Eds.), *Handbook of antisocial behavior.* New York: John Wiley & Sons.

73. Raine, A. (2002). The role of prefrontal deficits, low autonomic arousal, and early health factors in the development of antisocial and aggressive behavior in children. *Journal of Child Psychology and Psychiatry, 43,* 417–434.

74. Portnoy, J., Raine, A., Chen, R. R., Pardini, D., Loeber, R., & Jennings, J. R. (2014). Heart rate and antisocial behavior: The mediating role of sensation seeking. *Criminology, 52,* 292–311.

75. Fox, J. A., & Levin, J. (1985). *Mass murder: America's growing menace.* New York: Plenum, pp. 16–17.

76. Joseph, R. (n.d.). Charles Whitman: The amygdala and mass murder. Retrieved November 18, 2010, from http://brainmind.com/Case5.html

77. Note 76.

78. Kelly, S. J., Day, N., & Streissguth, A. P. (2000). Effects of prenatal alcohol exposure on social behavior in humans and other species. *Neurotoxicology and Teratology, 22,* 143–149.

79. Roebuck, T. M., Mattson, S. N., & Riley, E. P. (1999). Behavioral and psychosocial profiles of alcohol-exposed children. *Alcoholism: Clinical and Experimental Research, 23,* 1070–1076.

80. Brennan, P. E., Grekin, E. R., & Mednick, S. A. (1999). Maternal smoking during pregnancy and adult male criminal outcomes. *Archives of General Psychiatry, 56,* 215–219.

81. Goldschmidt, L., Day, N. L., & Richardson, G. A. (2000). Effects of prenatal marijuana exposure on child behavior problems at age 10. *Neurotoxicology and Teratology, 22,* 325–336.

82. Kandel, E., & Mednick, S. (1991). Perinatal complications predict violent offending. *Criminology, 29,* 519–530.

83. Brennan, P. E., Mednick, S. A., & Raine, A. (1997). Biosocial interactions and violence: A focus on perinatal factors. In A. Raine, P. Brennan, D. Farrington, & S. Mednick (Eds.), *Biosocial bases of violence.* New York: Plenum.

84. Tibbetts, S. G., & Piquero, A. R. (1999). The influence of gender, low birth weight, and disadvantaged environment in predicting early onset of offending: A test of Moffitt's interactional hypothesis. *Criminology, 37,* 843–878.

85. Neugebauer, R., Hoek, H. W., & Susser, E. (1999). Prenatal exposure to wartime famine and development of antisocial personality disorder in early adulthood. *Journal of the American Medical Association, 282,* 455–462.

86. U. S. Environmental Protection Agency. (n.d.). Sources of indoor air pollution—lead (Pb). Retrieved June 1, 2010, from http://www.epa.gov/iaq/lead.html

87. National Safety Council. (2009, April). Lead poisoning. Retrieved June 1, 2010, from http://www.nsc.org/news_resources/Resources/Documents/Lead_Poisoning.pdf

88. Stretesky, P. B., & Lynch, M. J. (2001). The relationship between lead exposure and homicide. *Archives of Pediatric Adolescent Medicine, 155,* 579–582.

89. Wolpaw Reyes, J. (2007). Environmental policy as social policy? The impact of childhood lead exposure on crime. *NBER Working Paper No. 13097.* Retrieved October 27, 2010, from http://www.nber.org/papers/w13097

90. Nevin, R. (2007). Understanding international crime trends: The legacy of preschool lead exposure. *Environmental Research, 104,* 315–336.

91. Denno, D. (1993). Considering lead poisoning as a criminal defense. *Fordham Urban Law Journal, 20,* 377–385.

92. Wright, J. P., Dietrich, K. N., Ris, M. D., Hornung, R. W., Wessel, S. D., Lanphear, B. P., et al. (2008). Association of prenatal and childhood blood lead concentrations with criminal arrests in early adulthood. *PLoS Medicine 5.* Retrieved October 26, 2010, from http://www.plosmedicine.org/

93. New York City Department of Health and Mental Hygiene. (n.d.). Lead poisoning prevention program. Retrieved June 3, 2010, from http://www.nyc.gov/html/doh/html/lead/lead.shtml

94. Kanarek, R. B. (1994). Nutrition and violent behavior. In A. J. Reiss, Jr., K. A. Mixzik, & J. A. Roth (Eds.), *Understanding and preventing violence: Biobehavioral influences* (Vol. 2). Washington, DC: National Academy Press, p. 521.

95. Note 94, p. 523.

96. Note 1, pp. 213–218.

97. Mazur, A. (2009). Testosterone and violence among young men. In A. Walsh & K. M. Beaver (Eds.), *Biosocial criminology.* New York: Routledge.

98. Olweus, D., Mattsson, A., Schalling, D., & Low, H. (1988). Testosterone, aggression, physical and personality dimensions in normal adolescent males. *Psychosomatic Medicine, 2,* 253–269.

99. Dabbs, J. M., Carr, T. S., Frady, R. L., & Raid, J. K. (1995, May). Testosterone, crime, and misbehavior among 692 male prison inmates. *Personality and Individual Differences, 18,* 627–633.

100. Booth, A., & Osgood, D. W. (1993). The influence of testosterone on deviance in adulthood: Assessing and explaining the relationship. *Criminology, 31,* 93–117.

101. Rowe, R., Maughan, B., Worthman, C. M., Costello, E. J., & Angold, A. (2004). Testosterone, antisocial behavior, and social dominance in boys: Pubertal development and biosocial interaction. *Biological Psychiatry, 55,* 546–552.

102. Dabbs, J. M., Jr., & Hargrove, M. F. (1997). Age, testosterone, and behavior among female prison inmates. *Psychosomatic Medicine, 59,* 477–480.

103. Thompson, S. R. (n.d.). Premenstrual syndrome. *Medline Plus Medical Encyclopedia.* Retrieved September 24, 2005, from http://www.nlm.nih.gov/medlineplus/ency/article/001505.htm

104. Cook, C. R. (1945). Presidential address: The differential psychology of the American woman. *American Journal of Obstetrics and Gynecology, 49,* 457–472.

105. Morton, L., Addison, H., Addison, R., Hunt, L., & Sullivan, J. (1953). A clinical study of premenstrual tension. *American Journal of Obstetrics and Gynecology, 65,* 1182–1191.

106. D'Orban, P. T., & Dalton, J. (1980). Violent crime and the menstrual cycle. *Psychological Medicine, 10,* 353–359.

107. Note 20, p. 256.

108. Fishbein, D. (1993). The psychobiology of female aggression. *Criminal Justice and Behavior, 19,* 99–126, 113.

109. Huang, C. (2002). It's a hormonal thing: Premenstrual syndrome and postpartum psychosis as criminal defense. *Southern California Review of Law and Women's Studies, 11,* 345–367.

110. Holtzman, E. (1984). Premenstrual syndrome: The indefensible defense. *Harvard Women's Law Journal, 7,* 1–3.

111. Note 109, p. 349.

112. Raine, A. (2002). Biosocial studies of antisocial and violent behavior in children and adults: A review. *Journal of Abnormal Child Psychology, 30,* 311–326.

113. Eysenck, H. J. (1977). *Crime and personality.* London: Paladin.

114. Moffitt, T. E. (1993). Adolescent-limited and life-course-persistent behavior: A developmental taxonomy. *Psychological Review, 100,* 674–701.

115. Note 114, p. 687.

116. Moffitt, T. E. (1990). Juvenile delinquency and attention deficit disorder: Boys' developmental trajectories from age 3 to age 15. *Child Development, 61,* 893–910.

117. Raine, A., Moffitt, T. E., Caspi, A., Loeber, R., Stouthamer-Loeber, M., & Lynam, D. (2005). Neurocognitive impairments in boys on the life-course persistent antisocial path. *Journal of Abnormal Psychology, 114,* 38–49.

118. Note 117.

119. Wright, J. P., & Beaver, K. (2005). Do parents matter in creating self-control in their children? A genetically informed test of Gottfredson and Hirschi's theory of low self-control. *Criminology, 43,* 1169–1202.

120. Beaver, K., DeLisi, M., Vaugh, M., Wright, J. P., & Boutwell, B. B. (2008). The relationship between self-control and language: Evidence of a shared etiological pathway. *Criminology, 46,* 939–969.

121. Beaver, K., Wright, J. P., & DeLisi, M. (2008). Genetic influences on the stability of low self-control: Results from a longitudinal sample of twins. *Journal of Criminal Justice, 36,* 478–485.

122. Beaver, K., Wright, J. P., & DeLisi, M. (2007). Self-control as an executive function: Reformulating Gottfredson and Hirschi's parental socialization thesis. *Criminal Justice and Behavior, 34,* 1345–1361.

123. Caspi, A., Lynam, D., Moffitt, T. E., & Silva, P. A. (1993). Unraveling girls' delinquency: Biological, dispositional, and contextual contributions to adolescent misbehavior. *Developmental Psychology, 29,* 19–30.

124. Wilson, E. O. (1975). *The new synthesis.* Cambridge, MA: Harvard University Press.

125. Dawkings, R. (1977). *The selfish gene.* New York: Oxford University Press.

126. Ellis, L., & Walsh, A. (1997). Gene-based evolutionary theories in criminology. *Criminology, 35,* 229–276.

127. Note 126, p. 245.

128. Note 126, pp. 246–249.

129. Note 23, p. 64.

130. Wilson, J. Q., & Herrnstein, R. J. (1985). *Crime and human nature.* New York: Simon & Schuster, 66.

131. Wright, R. A., & Miller, J. M. (1998). Taboo until today? The coverage of biological arguments in criminology textbooks, 1961 to 1970 and 1987 to 1996. *Journal of Criminal Justice, 26,* 1–19.

132. Walsh, A. (2002). *Biosocial criminology.* Cincinnati, OH: Anderson, 2002.

133. Beaver, K. M. (2009). *Biosocial criminology: A primer.* Dubuque, IA: Kendall/Hunt.

134. Wright, J. P., Tibbetts, S. G., & Daigle, L. E. (2008). *Criminals in the making: Criminality across the life course.* Thousand Oaks, CA: Sage.

135. Cullen, F. T. (2009). Preface. In A. Walsh & K. M. Beaver (Eds.), *Biosocial criminology.* New York: Routledge.

136. Rose, N. (2000). The biology of culpability: Pathological identity and crime control in a biological culture. *Theoretical Criminology, 4,* 5–34.

137. Note 39, pp. 88–89.

138. Olds, D. L., Kitzman, H. J., Cole, R. E., Hanks, C. A., Arcoleo, K. J., Anson, E. A., et al. (2010). Enduring effects of prenatal and infancy home visits on maternal home life and government spending: Follow up of a randomized trial among children at age 12 years. *Archives of Pediatrics and Adolescent Medicine, 164,* 419–424.

139. Note 23, p. 105.

Chapter 5

1. Glickman, J., & Ryan, L. (Executive Producers), & Armitage, G. (Director). (1997). *Grosse Pointe blank* [Motion Picture]. United States: Hollywood Pictures.

2. Bartol, C. R., & Bartol, A. M. (2008). *Introduction to forensic psychology* (2nd ed.). Thousand Oaks, CA: Sage, pp. 7–12.

3. Scott, P. (1960). Henry Maudsley. In H. Mannheim (Ed.), *Pioneers in criminology.* Montclair, NJ: Patterson Smith, pp. 208–231.

4. Note 3, p. 216.

5. Van Voorhis, P., & Salisbury, E. J. (2013). Psychoanalytic therapy. In *Correctional counseling and rehabilitation* (8th ed.). Cincinnati, OH: Elsevier/Anderson, pp. 47–66.

6. Note 5, p. 50.

7. Note 5, p. 51.

8. Redl, F., & Wineman, D. (1951). *Children who hate.* Glencoe, IL: Free Press.

9. Aichorn, A. (1979). Wayward youth. In J. E. Jacoby (Ed.), *Classics of criminology.* Prospect Heights, IL: Waveland, p. 124.

10. Warren, M. Q., & Hindelang, M. J. (1986). Current explanations of offender behavior. In H. Toch (Ed.), *Psychology of crime and criminal justice.* Prospect Heights, IL: Waveland, p. 172.

11. Akers, R. L., & Sellers, C. S. (2009). *Criminological theories: Introduction, evaluation, and application* (5th ed.). Los Angeles: Roxbury, pp. 71–74.

12. Finckenauer, J. O. (1984). *Juvenile delinquency and corrections: The gap between theory and practice.* Orlando, FL: Academic Press, p. 27.

13. Andrews, D. A., Zinger, I., Hoge, R. D., Bonta, J., Gendreau, P., & Cullen, F. T. (1990). Does correctional treatment work? A clinically relevant and psychologically informed meta-analysis. *Criminology, 28,* 369–404.

14. Note 5, p. 62.

15. Palmer, T. (1994). Issues in growth-centered intervention with serious juvenile offenders. *Legal Studies Forum, 18,* 236–298.

16. Listwan, S., Sperber, K., Spruance, L., & Van Voorhis, P. (2004). Anxiety in correctional settings: It's time for another look. *Federal Probation, 68,* 43–50.

17. Note 5, p. 63.

18. Van Voorhis, P., & Salisbury, E. J. (2013). Radical behavioral interventions. In *Correctional counseling and rehabilitation* (8th ed.). Cincinnati, OH: Elsevier/Anderson, pp. 67–89.

19. Bartol, C. R., & Bartol, A. M. (2004). *Criminal behavior: A psychosocial approach* (7th ed.). Englewood Cliffs, NJ: Prentice Hall.

20. Skinner, B. F. (1953). *Science and human behavior.* New York: Macmillan.

21. Pavlov, I. (1929). *Conditioned reflexes: An investigation of the physiological activity of the cerebral cortex.* London: Lawrence and Wishart.

22. Sampson, R. J., & Laub, J. H. (1993). *Crime in the making: Pathways and turning points through life.* Cambridge, MA: Harvard University Press, pp. 73–74.

23. Andrews, D., & Bonta, J. (2010). *The psychology of criminal conduct* (5th ed.). Cincinnati, OH: Anderson.

24. Akers, R. L. (1990). Rational choice, deterrence, and social learning theory: The path not taken. *Journal of Criminal Law and Criminology, 81,* 653–676.

25. McCord, W., & McCord, J. (1959). *Origins of crime: A new evaluation of the Cambridge-Somerville youth study.* New York: Columbia University.

26. Glueck, S., & Glueck, E. (1950). *Unraveling juvenile delinquency.* New York: Commonwealth Fund.

27. Loeber, R., & Dishion, T. (1983). Early predictors of male delinquency: A review. *Psychological Bulletin, 93,* 68–98.

28. Lipsey, M. W., & Derzon, J. H. (1998). Predictors of violent or serious offending in adolescence and early adulthood: A synthesis of longitudinal research. In R. Loeber & D. P. Farrington (Eds.), *Serious and violent juvenile offenders: Risk factors and successful treatments.* Thousand Oaks, CA: Sage, pp. 86–105.

29. Patterson, G., Reid, J., & Dishion, T. (1992). *Antisocial boys.* Eugene, OR: Castalia.
30. Patterson, G. (1980). Children who steal. In T. Hirschi & M. R. Gottfredson (Eds.), *Understanding crime.* Beverly Hills, CA: Sage, pp. 73–90.
31. Harris, J. R. (1998). *The nurture assumption: Why children turn out the way they do. Parents matter less than you think and peers matter more.* New York: The Free Press.
32. Wright, J. P., & Cullen, F. T. (2001). Parental efficacy and delinquent behavior: Do control and support matter? *Criminology, 39,* 677–706.
33. Harris, J. R. (1995). Where is the child's environment? A group socialization theory of development. *Psychological Review, 102,* 458–489.
34. Lundahl, B., Risser, H. J., & Lovejoy, M. C. (2006). A meta-analysis of parent training: Moderators and follow-up effects. *Clinical Psychology Review, 26,* 86–104.
35. Farrington, D. P. (2013). Longitudinal and experimental research in criminology. *Crime & Justice, 42,* 453–527.
36. Bandura, A. (1973). *Aggression: A social learning analysis.* Englewood Cliffs, NJ: Prentice Hall.
37. Bandura, A., Ross, D., & Ross, S. A. (1961). Imitation of film: Mediated aggressive models. *Journal of Abnormal and Social Psychology, 63,* 3–11.
38. Bandura, A. (1977). *Social learning theory.* Englewood Cliffs, NJ: Prentice Hall.
39. Note 38.
40. Warr, M. (2002). *Companions in crime: The social aspects of criminal conduct.* New York: Cambridge University Press.
41. Mazerolle, P., Maahs, J., & Bachman, R. (2000). Exposure to violence in the family: Unpacking the linkages to intimate partner violence. In G. L. Fox & M. L. Benson (Eds.), *Families, crime, and criminal justice.* New York: JAI, pp. 45–71.
42. American Psychological Association. (1993). *Summary report of the American Psychological Association commission on violence and youth.* Washington, DC: American Psychological Association.
43. The Nielson Company. (2015). Content is king, but viewing habits vary by demographic. Retrieved May 26, 2015, from http://www.nielsen.com/us/en/insights/news/2014/content-is-king-but-viewing-habits-vary-by-demographic.html
44. The Nielson Company. (2014). Multi-platform gaming: For the win! Retrieved May 26, 2015, from http://www.nielsen.com/us/en/insights/news/2014/multi-platform-gaming-for-the-win.html
45. Smith, S. L., Wilson, B. J., Kunkel, D., Linz, D., Potter, W. J., Colvin, C. M., & Donnerstein, E. (1998). *National television violence study.* Thousand Oaks, CA: Sage.
46. Surette, R. (2015). *Media, crime, and criminal justice* (5th ed.). Belmont, CA: Wadsworth, pp. 74–81.
47. Sourcebook. (2003). *Sourcebook of criminal justice statistics.* Retrieved January 15, 2005, from www.albany.edu/sourcebook/pdf/t239.pdf
48. Bacon, P., Jr. (2007, May 6). Romney reaches to the Christian right. *Washington Post.* Retrieved March 20, 2015, from http://www.washingtonpost.com/wp-dyn/content/article/2007/05/05/AR2007050501081.html
49. Bushman, B. J., & Gibson, B. (2010). Violent video games cause an increase in aggression long after the game has been turned off. *Social Psychological and Personality Science, 2,* 29–32.
50. Johnson, J. G., Cohen, P., Smailes, E. M., Kasen, S., & Brook, J. S. (2002). Television viewing and aggressive behavior during adolescence and adulthood. *Science, 295,* 2468–2471.
51. Huesmann, L. R., & Taylor, L. D. (2006). The role of media violence in violent behavior. *Annual Review of Public Health, 27,* 6–13.
52. Anderson, C. A., Ihori, N., Bushman, B. J., Rothstein, H. R., Shibuya, A., Swing, et al. (2010). Violent video game effects on aggression, empathy, and prosocial behavior in eastern and western countries: A meta-analytic review. *Psychological Bulletin, 136,* 151–173.
53. Savage, J., & Yancey, C. (2008) The effects of media violence exposure on criminal aggression: A meta-analysis. *Criminal Justice and Behavior, 35,* 1123–1136.
54. Hirschi, T. (1969). *Causes of delinquency.* Berkley: University of California Press.
55. Robinson, T. N., Wilde, M. L., Navracruz, L. C., Haydel, F., & Varady, A. (2001). Effects of reducing children's television and video game use on aggressive behavior: A randomized controlled trial. *Archives of Pediatrics & Adolescent Medicine, 155,* 17–23.
56. Note 18, p. 71.
57. Maletzky, B. (1991). *Treating the sexual offender.* Newbury Park, CA: Sage.
58. Stolz, S. B., Wienckowski, L. A., & Brown, B. S. (1978). Behavior modification. In N. Johnston & L. D. Savitz (Eds.), *Justice and corrections.* New York: Wiley.
59. Bippes, R., McLaughlin, T. F., & Williams, R. L. (1986). A classroom token system in a detention center. *Techniques, 2,* 126–132.
60. Janzen, W. B., & Love, W. (1977). Involving adolescents as active participants in their own treatment plans. *Psychological Reports, 41,* 931–934.
61. Reid, J., Patterson, G., & Snyder, J. (2003). *Antisocial behavior in children and adolescents: A*

developmental analysis and model for intervention. Washington, DC: American Psychological Association.

62. Note 34.

63. Kazdin, A. (1997). Parent management training: Evidence, outcomes, and issues. *Journal of the American Academy of Child and Adolescent Psychiatry, 36,* 1349–1357.

64. Pearson, F. S., Lipton, D. S., Cleland, C. M., & Yee, D. S. (2002). The effects of behavioral/cognitive programs on recidivism. *Crime and Delinquency, 48,* 476–496.

65. Note 64, pp. 489–490.

66. Van Voorhis, P., & Salisbury, E. J. (2013). Cognitive therapies. In *Correctional counseling and rehabilitation* (8th ed.). Cincinnati, OH: Elsevier/Anderson, pp. 183–209.

67. Note, 66, p. 186.

68. Gibbs, J. C., Potter, G. B., & Goldstein, A. P. (1995). *The EQUIP program: Teaching youth to think and act responsibly through a peer helping approach.* Champaign, IL: Research Press, pp. 45–48.

69. Note 68, pp. 43–65.

70. Ross, R. R., & Fabiano, E. A. (1989). *Reasoning and rehabilitation: A handbook for teaching cognitive skills.* Ottawa, Ontario: Flix Desktop Services.

71. Ross, R. R., & Fabiano, E. A. (1985). *Time to think: A cognitive model for delinquency prevention.* Johnson City, TN: Institute of Social Sciences and Arts.

72. Note 66, p. 194.

73. Yochelson, S., & Samenow, S. E. (1976). *The criminal personality,* Vol 1. New York: Jason Aronson.

74. Sykes, G., & Matza, D. (1958). Techniques of neutralization: A theory of delinquency. *American Sociological Review, 22,* 664–670.

75. Beech, A., & Mann, R. (2002). Recent developments in the assessment and treatment of sex offenders. In J. McGuire (Ed.), *Offender rehabilitation and treatment: Effective programmes and policies to reduce re-offending.* West Sussex, UK: John Wiley & Sons, pp. 259–288.

76. Note 66, p. 194.

77. National Institute of Corrections. (2012). *Thinking for a Change 3.1.* Retrieved May 24, 2015, from http://static.nicic.gov/Library/025057/default.html

78. Lipsey, M. W. (2009). The primary factors that characterize effective interventions with juvenile offenders: A meta-analytic overview. *Victims and Offenders, 4,* 124–147.

79. Note 64, p. 490.

80. Note 64, pp. 490–491.

81. Henggeler, S. W., Cunningham, P. B., Pickrel, S. G., Schoenwald, S. K., & Brondino, M. J. (1996). Multisystemic therapy: An effective violence prevention approach for serious juvenile offenders. *Journal of Adolescence, 19,* 55–56.

82. Miller, J. D., & Lynam, D. (2001). Structural models of personality and their relation to antisocial behavior: A meta-analytic review. *Criminology, 39,* 765–798.

83. McCrae, R. R., & Costa, P. T. (1990). *Personality in adulthood.* New York: Guilford Press.

84. Tellegen, A. (1985). Structures of mood and personality and their relevance to assessing anxiety with an emphasis on self-report. In A. H. Tuma & J. D. Maser (Eds.), *Anxiety and the anxiety disorders.* Hillsdale, NJ: Lawrence Earlbaum Associates, pp. 681–706.

85. Tenenbaum, D. J. (1977). Personality and criminality: A summary and implications of the literature. *Journal of Criminal Justice, 5,* 225–235.

86. Hosie, J., Gilbert, F., Simpson, K., & Daffern, M. (2015). An examination of the relationship between personality and aggression using the general aggression and five factor models. *Aggressive Behavior, 40,* 61–72.

87. Caspi, A., Moffitt, T. E., Silva, P. A., Stoughamer-Loeber, M., Krueger, R. F., & Schmutte, P. S. (1994). Are some people crime-prone? Replications of the personality–crime relationship across countries, genders, races, and methods. *Criminology, 32,* 163–195.

88. Note 82, p. 780.

89. Rafter, N. (2004). The unrepentant horse-slasher: Moral insanity and the origins of criminological thought. *Criminology, 42,* 979–1008.

90. Note 89, p. 994.

91. Cleckly, H. (1976). *The mask of sanity* (5th ed.). St. Louis, MO: Mosby.

92. Hare, R. D. (1996). Psychopathy: A clinical construct whose time has come. *Criminal Justice and Behavior, 23,* 25–54.

93. Note 92, pp. 45–46.

94. Blair, J. R., Mitchell, D. G., Richell, R. A., Kelly, S., Leonard, A., Newman, C., & Scott, S. K. (2002). Turning a deaf ear to fear: Impaired recognition of vocal affect in psychopathic individuals. *Journal of Abnormal Psychology, 111,* 682–686.

95. Note 92, pp. 45–46.

96. Wiebe, R. P. (2009). Psychopathy. In A. Walsh & K. M. Beaver (Eds.), *Biosocial criminology.* New York: Routledge, pp. 225–242.

97. Walsh, A., & Wu, H. H. (2008). Differentiating antisocial personality disorder, psychopathy, and sociopathy: Evolutionary, genetic, neurological, and sociological considerations. *Criminal Justice Studies, 21,* 135–152.

98. Skeem, J. L., & Cooke, D. J. (2010). Is criminal behavior a central component of psychopathy? Conceptual directions for resolving the debate. *Psychological Assessment, 22,* 433–445.

99. Polaschek, D. L. L., & Daly, T. E. (2013). Treatment and psychopathy in forensic settings. *Aggression and Violent Behavior, 18*, 592–603.

100. Raine, A. (2013). *The anatomy of violence: The biological roots of crime.* New York: Pantheon, pp. 120–128.

101. Bibiak, P., & Hare, R. D. (2006). *Snakes in suits: When psychopaths go to work.* New York: Harper Collins.

102. Rice, M. R., Harris, G. T., & Cormier, C. A. (1992). An evaluation of a maximum security therapeutic community for psychopaths and other mentally disordered offenders. *Law and Human Behavior, 16*, 399–412.

103. Note 99, pp. 595–600.

104. Eysenck, H. J. (1997). Personality and the biosocial model of antisocial and criminal behavior. In A. Raine, P. A. Brennan, D. P. Farrington, & S. A. Mednick (Eds.), *Biosocial bases of violence.* New York: Plenum, pp. 21–37.

105. Hare, R. D. (1999). *Without conscience: The disturbing world of psychopaths among us.* New York: The Guilford Press, p. 173.

106. Note 105, pp. 186–191.

107. Salekin, R. T., Worley, C., & Grimes, R. D. (2010). Treatment of psychopathy: A review and brief introduction to the mental model approach for psychopathy. *Behavioral Sciences & the Law, 28*, 235–266.

108. Gould, S. J. (1996). *The mismeasure of man.* New York: W. W. Norton, pp. 176–185.

109. Note 108, p. 185.

110. Note 108, p. 230.

111. Note 108, pp. 250–252.

112. Note 108, pp. 204–222.

113. Perkins, D. (1995). *Outsmarting IQ: The emerging science of learnable intelligence.* New York: The Free Press.

114. Goddard, H. H. (1972). *Feeblemindedness: Its causes and consequences.* New York: Arno.

115. Sutherland, E. H. (1931). Mental deficiency and crime. In K. Young (Ed.), *Social attitudes.* New York: Holt, pp. 357–375.

116. Hirschi, T., & Hindelang, M. J. (1977). Intelligence and delinquency. *American Sociological Review, 42*, 571–587.

117. Hernstein, R. J., & Murray, C. (1994). *The bell curve: Intelligence and class structure in American life.* New York: The Free Press.

118. Note 117, p. 544.

119. Cullen, F. T., Gendreau, P., Jarjoura, G. R., & Wright, J. P. (1997). Crime and the bell curve: Lessons from intelligent criminology. *Crime and Delinquency, 43*, 387–411.

120. Ward, D. A., & Tittle, C. R. (1994). IQ and delinquency: A test of two competing explanations. *Journal of Quantitative Criminology, 10*, 189–212.

121. McGloin, J. M., Pratt, T. C., & Maahs, J. Rethinking the IQ–delinquency relationship: A Longitudinal analysis of multiple theoretical models. *Justice Quarterly, 21*, 603–635.

122. Note 119, pp. 403–404.

123. Note 23, p. 7.

124. Cullen, F. T. (2005). The twelve people who saved rehabilitation: How the science of criminology made a difference. *Criminology, 43*, 1–42.

Chapter 6

1. Springsteen, B. (1984). My home town. On *Born in the U.S.A.* [CD]. New York: Columbia Records.

2. Lilly, J. R., Cullen, F. T., & Ball, R. A. (2007). *Criminological theory: Context and consequences* (4th ed.). Thousand Oaks, CA: Sage.

3. Note 2, p. 35.

4. Conklin, J. E. (2004). *Criminology* (8th ed.). New York: Macmillan.

5. Barkan, S. E. (2001). *Criminology: A sociological understanding* (2nd ed.). Upper Saddle River, NJ: Prentice Hall, pp. 145–146.

6. Chandler, C., Sigelman, L., & Tsai, Y. M. (1986). Division of Labor and social disorder: A cross-national test of a Durkheimian interpretation. *International Journal of Comparative Sociology, 27*, 161–171.

7. Durkheim, E. (1966, original manuscript published in 1897). *Suicide: A study in sociology.* New York: Macmillan, p. 253.

8. Park, R. (1952). *Human communities.* Glencoe, IL: Free Press.

9. Park, R. (1966). *The criminal area.* New York: Humanities Press.

10. Burgess, E. W. (1968, original work published in 1925). The growth of the city: An introduction to a research project. In R. E. Park & E. W. Burgess (Eds.), *The city.* Chicago: University of Chicago Press, pp. 85–97.

11. Note 2, pp. 33–34.

12. Shaw, C., & McKay, H. (1969). *Juvenile delinquency and urban areas: A study of rates of delinquency in relation to differential characteristics of local communities in American cities.* Chicago: University of Chicago Press.

13. Note 12, pp. 383–388.

14. Bursik Jr., R. J. (1988). Social disorganization and theories of crime and delinquency: Problems and prospects. *Criminology, 26*, 519–546.

15. Note 14, pp. 521–538.

16. Morenoff, J. D., Sampson, R. J., & Raudenbush, S. W. (2001). Neighborhood inequality, collective efficacy, and the spatial dynamics of urban violence. *Criminology, 39*, 517–560.

17. Silver, E., & Miller, L. L. (2004). Sources of informal social control in Chicago neighborhoods. *Criminology, 42,* 551–583.

18. Sampson, R. J., Raudenbush, S., & Earls, F. (1997). Neighborhoods and violent crime: A multilevel study of collective efficacy. *Science, 277,* 918–924.

19. Sampson, R. J., Morenoff, J. D., & Earls, F. (1999). Beyond social capital: Spatial dynamics of collective efficacy for children. *American Sociological Review, 64,* 633–660.

20. Morenoff, J. D., Sampson, R. J., & Raudenbush, S. W. (2001). Neighborhood inequality, collective efficacy, and the spatial dynamics of urban violence. *Criminology, 39,* 517–559.

21. Note 18, pp. 921–922.

22. Osgood, D. W., & Chambers, J. M. (2000). Social disorganization outside the metropolis: An analysis of rural youth violence. *Criminology, 38,* 81–116.

23. Triplett, R. A., Gainly, R. R., & Sun, I. Y. (2003). Institutional strength, social control, and neighborhood crime. *Theoretical Criminology, 7,* 439–467.

24. Bernburg, J. G., & Thorlindsson, T. (2007). Community structure and adolescent delinquency in Iceland: A contextual analysis. *Criminology, 45,* 415–444.

25. Maimon, D., & Browning, C. R. (2010). Unstructured socializing, collective efficacy, and violent behavior among urban youth. *Criminology, 48,* 443–474.

26. Peterson, R. D. (2012). The central place of race in crime and justice—The American Society of Criminology's 2011 Sutherland Address. *Criminology, 50,* 303–327.

27. Note 26, pp. 306–307.

28. Wilson, W. J. (1987). *The truly disadvantaged: The inner city, the underclass, and public policy.* Chicago: University of Chicago Press.

29. Wilson, W. J. (1996). *When work disappears: The world of the urban poor.* New York: Alfred Knopf.

30. Wilson, W. J., & Sampson, R. J. (1995). Toward a theory of race, crime, and urban inequality. In J. Hagan & R. D. Peterson (Eds.), *Crime and inequality.* Stanford, CA: Stanford University Press, pp. 37–54.

31. Note 30, pp. 40–45.

32. Lynch, J. P., & Sabol, W. J. (2004). Assessing the effects of mass incarceration on informal social control in communities. *Criminology and Public Policy, 3,* 267–294.

33. Clear, T. (2007). *Imprisoning communities.* New York: Oxford University Press.

34. Sampson, R. J. (2013). The place of context: A theory and a strategy for criminology's hard problems. *Criminology, 51,* 1–32.

35. Peterson, R. D., & Krivo, L. J. (2010). *Divergent social worlds: Neighborhood crime and the racial-spatial divide.* New York: Russell Sage Foundation.

36. Cullen, F. T., & Agnew, R. (2011). *Criminological theory: Past to present* (4th ed.). New York: Oxford, p. 105.

37. Note 34, p. 12.

38. Wilson, J. Q. (1975). *Thinking about crime.* New York: Vintage.

39. Stark, R. (1987). Deviant places: A theory of the ecology of crime. *Criminology, 25,* 893–909.

40. Sherman, L. W., Gartin, P., & Buerger, M. E. (1989). Hot spots of predatory crime: Routine activities and the criminology of place. *Criminology, 27,* 27–56.

41. Spelman, W. (1995). Criminal careers of public places. In J. Eck & D. Weisburd (Eds.), *Crime and place: Crime prevention studies,* Vol. 4. Monsey, NY: Criminal Justice Press, pp. 115–144.

42. Spelman, W. (1993). Abandoned buildings: Magnets for crime? *Journal of Criminal Justice, 21,* 481–495.

43. Sherman, L. W. (1995). Hot spots of crime and criminal careers of places. In J. E. Eck & D. Weisburd (Eds.), *Crime and place, crime prevention studies,* Vol. 4. Monsey, NY: Criminal Justice Press, pp. 115–144.

44. Weisburd, D. (2014). The law of crime concentration and the criminology of place. *Criminology, 53,* 133–157.

45. Note 43, p.149.

46. Lundman, R. J. (1993). *Prevention and control of delinquency* (2nd ed.). New York: Oxford University Press.

47. Akers, R. L., & Sellers, C. S. (2004). *Criminological theories: Introduction, evaluation, and application.* Los Angeles: Roxbury, pp. 183–184.

48. Kling, J. R., Ludwig, J., & Katz, L. D. (2005). Neighborhood effects on crime for female and male youth: Evidence from a randomized housing voucher experiment. Quarterly Journal of Economics, 120, 87–130.

49. Sharkey, P., & Sampson, R. J. (2010). Destination effects: Residential mobility and trajectories of adolescent violence in a stratified metropolis. *Criminology, 48,* 639–682.

50. Anderson, E. (1990). *Streetwise: Race, class, and change in an urban community.* Chicago: University of Chicago Press.

51. Trojanowicz, R., Kappeler, V. E., & Gaines, L. K. (2002). *Community policing: A contemporary perspective* (3rd ed.). Cincinnati, OH: Anderson.

52. Tonry, M. (1995). *Malign neglect: Race, crime, and punishment in America.* New York: Oxford University Press.

53. Merton, R. K. (1938). Social structure and anomie. *American Sociological Review, 3*, 672–682.

54. Note 52, p. 674.

55. Mitchell, R. G. (1984). Alienation and deviance: Strain theory reconsidered. *Sociological Inquiry, 54*, 330–345.

56. Violent Femmes. (1993). America is. On *Add It Up* [CD]. Burbank, CA: Reprise Records.

57. Merton, R. K. (1968). *Social theory and social structure.* Glencoe, IL: Free Press, p. 236.

58. Hirschi, T. (1969). *Causes of delinquency.* Berkeley: University of California Press.

59. Burton Jr., V. S., Cullen, F. T., Evans, T. D., & Dunaway, R. G. (1994). Reconsidering strain theory: Operationalization, rival theories, and adult criminality. *Journal of Quantitative Criminology, 3*, 213–238.

60. Burton Jr., V. S., & Cullen, F. T. (1992). The empirical status of strain theory. *Journal of Crime and Justice, 2*, 1–30.

61. Agnew, R., Cullen, F. T., Burton Jr., V. S., Evans, T. D., & Dunaway, G. (1996). A new test of classic strain theory. *Justice Quarterly, 4*, 681–704.

62. Messner, S. F., & Rosenfeld, R. (2007). *Crime and the American dream* (4th ed.). Belmont, CA: Wadsworth, pp. 108–109.

63. Tittle, C. R., Villemez, W. J., & Smith, D. A. (1978). The myth of social class and criminality: An empirical assessment of the empirical evidence. *American Sociological Review, 43*, 643–656.

64. Kornhauser, R. (1978). *Social sources of delinquency: An appraisal of analytical models.* Chicago: University of Chicago Press.

65. Agnew, R. (1992). Foundation for a general strain theory of crime and delinquency. *Criminology, 30*, 47–86.

66. Agnew, R. (2006). *Pressured into crime: An overview of general strain theory.* Los Angeles: Roxbury.

67. Paternoster, R., & Mazerolle, P. (1994). General strain theory and delinquency: A replication and extension. *Journal of Research on Crime and Delinquency, 31*, 235–263.

68. Hoffman, J. P., & Su, S. S. (1998). A latent variable analysis of strain theory. *Journal of Quantitative Criminology, 14*, 83–110

69. Mazerolle, P., & Maahs, J. (2000). General strain and delinquency: An alternative examination of conditioning influences. *Justice Quarterly, 17*, 751–778.

70. Agnew, R., Brezina, T., Wright, J. P., & Cullen, F. T. (2002). Strain, personality traits, and delinquency: Extending general strain theory. *Criminology, 40*, 43–72.

71. Baron, S. W. (2004). General strain, street youth and crime: A test of Agnew's revised theory. *Criminology, 42*, 457–484.

72. Botchkovar, E. V., Tittle, C. R., & Antonaccio, O. (2009). General strain theory: Additional evidence using cross-cultural data. *Criminology, 47*, 131–176.

73. Tittle, C. R., Broidy, L. M., & Gertz, M. C. (2008). Strain, crime, and contingencies. *Justice Quarterly, 25*, 283–312.

74. Messner, S. F. (1988). Merton's 'Social structure and anomie': The road not taken. *Deviant Behavior, 9*, 33–53.

75. Note 61, pp. 68–71.

76. Note 61, p. 69.

77. Note 61, pp. 76–84.

78. Baumer, E. P., & Gustafson, R. (2007). Social organization and instrumental crime: Assessing the empirical validity of classic and contemporary anomie theories. *Criminology, 45*, 617–664.

79. Chamlin, M. B., & Cochran, J. K. (1995). Assessing Messner and Rosenfeld's institutional anomie theory: A partial test. *Criminology, 33*, 411–429.

80. Messner, S. F., & Rosenfeld, R. (1997). Political restraint of the market and levels of criminal homicide: A cross-national application of institutional anomie theory. *Social Forces, 75*, 1393–1416

81. Pratt, T. C., & Godsey, T. W. (2003). Social support, inequality, and homicide: A cross-national test of an integrated theoretical model. *Criminology, 41*, 101–131.

82. Note 61, p. 112.

83. Note 61, p. 122.

84. Cohen, A. (1955). *Delinquent boys: The culture of the gang.* New York: Free Press.

85. Martin, R., Mutchnick, R. J., & Austin, W. T. (1990). *Criminological thought: Pioneers past and present.* New York: Macmillan.

86. Note 61, p. 119.

87. Jarjoura, G. R. (1993). Does dropping out of school enhance delinquent involvement? Results from a large-scale national probability sample. *Criminology, 31*, 149–171.

88. Cloward, R. A., & Ohlin, L. E. (1960). *Delinquency and opportunity: A theory of delinquent gangs.* New York: Free Press.

89. Bernard, T. J. (1984). Control criticisms of strain theories: An assessment of theoretical and empirical adequacy. *Journal of Research in Crime and Delinquency, 21*, 353–372.

90. Hagedorn, J. M. (1994). Homeboys, dope fiends, legits, and new jacks. *Criminology, 32*, 197–219.

91. Hagedorn, J. M. (1994). Neighborhoods, markets, and gang drug organization. *Journal of Research in Crime and Delinquency, 31*, 264–294.

92. Note 89, p. 214.

93. Hagedorn, J. M. (1991). Gangs, neighborhoods, and public policy. *Social Problems, 38*, 529–542.

94. Huff, C. R. (1990). *Gangs in America*. Newbury Park, CA: Sage.

95. Warr, M. (1996). Organization and instigation in delinquent groups. *Criminology, 34*, 11–38.

96. Miller, W. B. (1958). Lower class culture as a generating milieu of gang delinquency. *Journal of Social Issues, 15*, 5–19.

97. Weisfeld, G. E., & Feldman, R. (1982). A former street gang leader reinterviewed eight years later. *Crime and Delinquency, 28*, 567–581.

98. Note 30, pp. 38–40.

99. Anderson, E. (1999). *The code of the street: Decency, violence, and the moral life of the inner city*. New York: W. W. Norton.

100. Stewart, E. A., & Simons, R. (2010). Race, code of the street, and violent delinquency: A multilevel investigation of neighborhood street culture and individual norms of violence. *Criminology, 48*, 569–603.

101. Kirk, D. S., & Matsueda, M. (2011). Legal cynicism, collective efficacy, and the ecology of arrest. *Criminology, 49*, 443–472.

102. Yablonski, L. (1959). The delinquent gang as a near group. *Social Problems, 7*, 108–109.

103. Note 57, pp. 5–6.

104. Note 2, p. 68.

105. Note 2.

106. Rosenfeld, R. (2011). The big picture: 2010 Presidential Address to the American Society of Criminology. *Criminology, 49*, 1–26.

107. Note 31, pp. 50–52.

108. Note 57, pp. 6–7.

Chapter 7

1. Proverbia.net. (n.d.). Napoleon Bonaparte. Retrieved February 3, 2011, from http://en.proverbia.net/citastema.asp?tematica=278

2. Hirschi, T. (1969). *Causes of delinquency*. Berkeley, CA: University of California Press, p. 34.

3. Beirne, P. (1987). Between classicism and positivism: Crime and penalty in the writing of Gabriel Tarde. *Criminology, 25*, 785–819.

4. Martin, R., Mutchnick, R. J., & Austin, W. T. (1990). *Criminological thought: Pioneers past and present*. New York: Macmillan, p. 147.

5. Nettler, G. (1984). *Explaining crime*. New York: McGraw-Hill.

6. Borch-Jacobsen, M. (1991). *The Freudian subject*. Stanford, CA: Stanford University Press, p. 266.

7. Mannheim, H. (1972). *Pioneers in criminology*. Montclair, NJ: Patterson-Smith.

8. Note 7, p. 295.

9. Surette, R. (2015). *Media, crime, and criminal justice* (5th ed.). Belmont, CA: Wadsworth, pp. 74–96.

10. Dugan, L., LaFree, G., & Piquero, A. R. (2005). Testing a rational choice model of airline hijackings. *Criminology, 43*, 1031–1066.

11. Lilly, J. R., Cullen, F. T., & Ball, R. A. (2007). *Criminological theory: Context and consequences* (4th ed.). Thousand Oaks, CA: Sage, pp. 38–39.

12. Sutherland, E. H., & Cressy, D. R. (1955). *Principles of criminology* (5th ed.). Chicago: J.B. Lippincott, pp. 84–85.

13. Note 12, pp. 77–79.

14. Cullen, F. T., & Agnew, R. (2011). *Criminological theory: Past to present*. New York: Oxford University Press, pp. 118–119.

15. Gaylord, M. S., & Galliher, J. F. (1988). *The criminology of Edwin Sutherland*. New Brunswick, NJ: Transaction Books.

16. Laub, J. H. (2004). The lifecourse of criminology in the United States: The American Society of Criminology 2003 presidential address. *Criminology, 42*, 1–26.

17. Burgess, R. L., & Akers, R. L. (1966). A differential association reinforcement theory of criminal behavior. *Social Problems, 14*, 128–147.

18. Akers, R. L. (1985). *Deviant behavior: A social learning approach* (3rd ed.). Belmont, CA: Wadsworth.

19. Akers, R. L., & Sellers, C. S. (2009). *Criminological theories: Introduction, evaluation, and application* (5th ed.). New York: Oxford University Press, pp. 89–93.

20. Note 19, p. 90.

21. Note 19, pp. 93–96.

22. Pratt, T. C., Cullen, F. T., Sellers, C. S., Thomas Winfree Jr, L., Madensen, T. D., Daigle, L. E., et al. (2010). The empirical status of social learning theory: A meta-analysis. *Justice Quarterly, 27*, 6, 765–802.

23. Akers, R. L., Krohn, M. D., Lanza-Kaduce, L., & Radosevich, M. (1979). Social learning and deviant behavior: A specific test of a general theory. *American Sociological Review, 44*, 636–655.

24. Skinner, W. F., & Fream, A. M. (1997). A social learning analysis of computer crime among college students. *Journal of Research in Crime and Delinquency, 34*, 495–518.

25. Esbensen, F. A., & Deschenes, E. P. (1998). A multisite examination of youth gang membership: Does gender matter? *Criminology, 36*, 799–827.

26. Winfree, T. L., Vigil-Backstrom, T., & Mays, G. L. (1994). Social learning theory, self-reported delinquency, and youth gangs: A new twist on a general theory of crime and delinquency. *Youth and Society, 26*, 147–177.

27. Sykes, G., & Matza, D. (1958). Techniques of neutralization: A theory of delinquency. *American Sociological Review, 22*, 664–670.

28. Hollinger, R. C. (1991). Neutralizing in the workplace: An empirical analysis of property theft

and production deviance. *Deviant Behavior, 12,* 169–202.

29. Levi, K. (1981). Becoming a hit man: Neutralization in a very deviant career. *Urban Life, 10,* 47–63.

30. Hamlin, J. E. (1988). The misplaced role of rational choice in neutralization theory. *Criminology, 26,* 425–438.

31. Warr, M. (2002). *Companions in crime: The social aspects of criminal conduct.* Cambridge: Cambridge University Press, p. 40.

32. Haynie, D. L. (2002). Friendship networks and delinquency: The relative nature of peer delinquency. *Journal of Quantitative Criminology, 18,* 99–134.

33. Morselli, C., Tremblay, P., & McCarthy, B. (2006). Mentors and criminal achievement. *Criminology, 44,* 17–44.

34. Van de Rakt, M., Nieuwbeerta, P., & Apel, R. (2009). Association of criminal convictions between family members: Effects of siblings, fathers and mothers. *Criminal Behavior and Mental Health, 19,* 94–108.

35. Kornhauser, R. (1978). *Social sources of delinquency: An appraisal of analytical models.* Chicago: University of Chicago Press.

36. Elliott, D. S., & Menard, S. (1996). Delinquent friends and delinquent behavior: Temporal and development patterns. In J. D. Hawkins (Ed.), *Delinquency and crime: Current theories.* New York: Cambridge University Press, pp. 28–67.

37. McGloin, J. M. (2009). Delinquency balance: Revisiting peer influence. *Criminology, 47,* 439–478.

38. Weerman, F. M. (2011). Delinquent peers in context: A longitudinal network analysis of selection and influence effects. *Criminology, 49,* 253–286.

39. Akers, R. L. (1999). Social learning and social structure: Reply to Sampson, Moorish, and Krohn. *Theoretical Criminology, 3,* 477–493.

40. Wood, P. B., Cochran, J. K., & Pfefferbaum, B. (1995). Sensation-seeking and delinquent substance use: An extension of learning theory. *Journal of Drug Issues, 25,* 173–193.

41. Andrews, D. A. (1980). Some experimental investigations of the principles of differential association through deliberate manipulations of the structure of service systems. *American Sociological Review, 45,* 448–462.

42. Lipsey, M. W. (2009). The primary factors that characterize effective interventions with juvenile offenders: A meta-analytic overview. *Victims and Offenders, 4,* 124–147.

43. Pearson, F. S., Lipton, D. S., Cleland, C. M., & Yee, D. S. (2002). The effects of behavioral/cognitive programs on recidivism. *Crime and Delinquency, 48,* 476–496.

44. Nye, I. F. (1958). *Family relationships and delinquent behavior.* New York: Wiley.

45. Reckless, W. (1961). A new theory of delinquency and crime. *Federal Probation, 25,* 42–46.

46. Reckless, W. (1967). *The crime problem.* New York: Appleton Century Crofts.

47. Reckless, W., Dinitz, S., & Kay, B. (1957). The self component in potential delinquency and potential nondelinquency. *American Sociological Review, 25,* 566–570.

48. Reckless, W., Dinitz, S., & Murray, E. (1956). Self concept as an insulator against delinquency. *American Sociological Review, 21,* 744–756.

49. Dinitz, S., Scarpitti, F. R., & Reckless, W. C. (1962). Delinquency vulnerability: A cross group and longitudinal analysis. *American Sociological Review, 27,* 515–517.

50. Orcutt, J. D. (1980). Self-concept and insulation against delinquency: Some critical notes. *Sociological Quarterly, 2,* 381–390.

51. Reckless, W., & Dinitz, S. (1972). *The prevention of juvenile delinquency.* Columbus, OH: The Ohio State University Press.

52. Note 4, pp. 185–186.

53. Hirschi, T. (1969). *Causes of delinquency.* Berkeley: University of California Press.

54. Note 53, pp. 1–14.

55. Note 53.

56. Krohn, M. D., & Massey, J. L. (1980). Social control and delinquent behavior: An examination of the elements of the social bond. *The Sociological Quarterly, 21,* 529–543.

57. Agnew, R. (1985). Social control theory and delinquency: A longitudinal test. *Criminology, 23,* 47–61.

58. Agnew, R. (1991). A longitudinal test of social control theory and delinquency. *Journal of Research in Crime and Delinquency, 28,* 126–156.

59. Leonard, K. K., & Decker, S. (1994). The theory of social control: Does it apply to the very young? *Journal of Criminal Justice, 22,* 89–105.

60. Nagin, D. S., & Paternoster, R. (1994). Personal capital and social control: The deterrence implications of a theory of individual differences in criminal offending. *Criminology, 32,* 581–606.

61. Glueck, S., & Glueck, E. (1959). *Predicting delinquency and crime.* Cambridge, MA: Harvard University Press.

62. Wells, E., & Rankin, J. H. (1988). Direct parental controls and delinquency. *Criminology, 26,* 263–285.

63. Note 2, p. 141.

64. Giordano, P. C., Lonardo, R. A., Manning, W. D., & Longmore, M. A. (2010). Adolescent romance and delinquency: A further test of Hirschi's "cold and brittle" hypothesis. *Criminology, 48,* 919–946.

65. Kandel, D., & Davies, M. (1991). Friendship networks, intimacy, and illicit drug use in young adulthood: A comparison of two competing theories. *Criminology, 29,* 441–469.

66. Tas, J. J. (1992). An empirical test of social control theory. *Journal of Quantitative Criminology, 8,* 9–28.

67. Note 65.

68. Baier, C., & B. R. (2001). If you love me, keep my commandments: A meta-analysis of the effect of religion on crime. *Journal of Research in Crime and Delinquency, 38,* 3–21.

69. Johnson, B. R., Spencere, D. L., Larson, D. B., & McCullough, M. (2000). A systematic review of the religiosity and delinquency literature. *Journal of Contemporary Criminal Justice, 16,* 32–52.

70. Evans, T. D., Cullen, F. T., Dunaway, R. G., & Burton Jr., V. S. (2006). Religion and crime reexamined: The impact of religion, secular controls, and social ecology on adult criminality. *Criminology, 33,* 195–224.

71. Gottfredson, M., & Hirschi, T. (1990). *A general theory of crime.* Palo Alto, CA: Stanford University Press.

72. Note 71, pp. 97–100.

73. Note 71, p. 90.

74. Pratt, T. C., & Cullen, F. T. (2000). The empirical status of Gottfredson and Hirschi's general theory of crime: A meta-analysis. *Criminology, 38,* 931–964.

75. Gottfredson, M. R. (2006). The empirical status of control theory in criminology. In F. T. Cullen, J. P. Wright, & K. K. Blevins (Eds.), *Taking stock: The status of criminological theory—advances in criminological theory,* Vol. 15. New Brunswick, NJ: Transaction, pp. 77–100.

76. Goode, E. (Ed.). (2008). *Out of control: Assessing the general theory of crime.* Stanford, CA: Stanford University Press.

77. Unnever, J. D., Cullen, F. T., & Pratt, T. C. (2003). Parental management, ADHD, and delinquent involvement: Reassessing Gottfredson and Hirschi's general theory. *Justice Quarterly, 20,* 471–500.

78. Simons, R. L., Simons, L. G., Chen, Y. F., Brody, G. H., & Lin, K. H. (2007). Identifying the psychological factors that mediate the association between parenting practices and delinquency. *Criminology, 45,* 481–518.

79. Pratt, T. C. (2015). A reconceptualized model of self-control and crime: Specifying the role of self-control variability, *Criminal Justice and Behavior, 42,* 662–679.

80. Na, C., & Paternoster, R. (2012). Can self-control change substantially over time? Rethinking the relationship between self and social control. *Criminology, 50,* 427–462.

81. Sampson, R. J., & Laub, J. H. (1993). *Crime in the making: Pathways and turning points through life.* Cambridge, MA: Harvard University Press.

82. Note 81, pp. 145–156.

83. Sampson, R., Laub, J. H., & Wimer, C. (2006). Does marriage reduce crime? A counterfactual approach to within-individual causal effects. *Criminology, 44,* 465–508.

84. King, R. D., Massoglia, M., & MacMillan, R. (2007). The context of marriage and crime: Gender, the propensity to marry, and offending in early adulthood. *Criminology, 45,* 33–66.

85. Horney, J. D., Osgood, D. W., & Marshall, I. H. (1995). Criminal careers in the short-term: Intra-individual variability in crime and its relation to local life circumstances. *American Sociological Review, 60,* 655–673.

86. Cullen, F. T. (1994). Social support as an organizing concept for criminology: Presidential address to the Academy of Criminal Justice Sciences. *Justice Quarterly, 11,* 527–559.

87. Cullen, F. T., Wright, J. P., & Chamlin, M. B. (1999). Social support and social reform: A progressive crime control agenda. *Crime and Delinquency, 45,* 188–207.

88. Note 87, pp. 192–193.

89. Wright, J. P., & Cullen, F. T. (2001). Parental efficacy and delinquent behavior: Do control and support matter? *Criminology, 39,* 677–736.

90. Pratt, T. C., & Godsey, T. W. (2003). Social support, inequality, and homicide: A cross-national test of an integrated theoretical model. *Criminology, 41,* 611–643.

91. Chamlin, M. B., & Cochran, J. K. (1997). Social altruism and crime. *Criminology, 35,* 203–227.

92. Note 91.

93. Note 80, p. 505.

94. Worrall, J. (2005). Reconsidering the relationship between welfare spending and serious crime: A panel data analysis with implications for social support theory. *Justice Quarterly, 22,* 364–391.

95. Hirschi, T. (1990). Crime and family policy. In R. A. Weisheit & R. G. Culbertson (Eds.), *Juvenile delinquency: A justice perspective.* Prospect Heights, IL: Waveland Press, pp. 53–68.

96. SSDP homepage. (n.d.) Retrieved June 5, 2015, from http://ssdp-tip.org/SSDP/index.html

97. Hawkins, J. D., Catalano, R. F., Morrison, D. M., O'Donnell, J., Abbott, R. D., & Day, L. E. (1992). The Seattle social developmental project: Effects of the first four years on protection factors and problem behaviors. In J. McCord & R. E. Tremblay (Eds.), *Interventions from birth through adolescence.* New York: Guilford Press, pp. 139–161.

98. Hawkins, J. D., Catalano, R. F., Kosterman, R., Abbott, R., & Hill, K. G. (2005). Long-term effects from the Seattle social developmental project. *Archives of Pediatric & Adolescent Medicine, 159,* 25–31.

99. Hawkins, J., Kosterman, R., Catalano, R. F., Hill, K. G., & Abbott, R. D. (2008). Effects of social development intervention in childhood 15 years later. *Archives of Pediatric & Adolescent Medicine, 162*, 1133–1141.

100. Thornberry, T. P. (1987). Towards an interactional theory of delinquency. *Criminology, 25*, 863–891.

101. Note 11, pp. 134–135.

102. Becker, H. (1963). *The outsiders: Studies in the sociology of deviancy*. New York: Free Press.

103. Phol, S. (1985). *Images of deviance and social control: A sociological history*. New York: McGraw-Hill.

104. Note 102, p. 9.

105. Note 11, pp. 116–117.

106. Cooley, C. H. (1902). *Human nature and social order*. New York: Scribner.

107. Merton, R. K. (1957). *Social theory and social structure*. Glencoe, IL: Free Press.

108. Note 19, p. 155.

109. Lemert, E. M. (1967). *Human deviance, social problems, and social control*. Englewood Cliffs, NJ: Prentice Hall.

110. Tannenbaum, F. (1938). *Crime in the community*. Boston: Ginn.

111. Hartjen, C. A. (1978). *Crime and criminalization* (2nd ed.). New York: Praeger.

112. Note 102.

113. Note 102.

114. Farrington, D. P., Loeber, R., & Van Kammen, W. B. (1990). Long-term criminal outcomes of hyperactivity-impulsivity-attention deficit and conduct problems in childhood. In L. N. Robins & M. Rutter (Eds.), *Straight and devious pathways from childhood to adulthood*. New York: Cambridge University Press, pp. 62–81.

115. Sagarin, E. (1975). *Deviants and deviance*. New York: Praeger, pp. 129–142.

116. Keil, T. J., & Vito, G. F. (1990). Race and the death penalty in Kentucky murder trials: An analysis of post-Gregg outcomes. *Justice Quarterly, 7*, 189–207.

117. Pratt, T. C. (1998). Race and sentencing: A meta-analysis of conflicting empirical research results. *Journal of Criminal Justice, 26*, 513–523.

118. Walker, S., Spohn, C., & DeLone, M. (2000). *The color of justice: Race, ethnicity, and crime in America*. Belmont, CA: Wadsworth.

119. Hagan, J., & Palloni, A. (1990). The social reproduction of a criminal class in working class London, circa 1950–1980. *American Journal of Sociology, 96*, 265–299.

120. Chiricos, T., Barrick, K., Bales, W., & Bontrager, S. (2007). The labeling of convicted felons and its consequences for recidivism. *Criminology, 45*, 547–582.

121. Nagin, D. S., Cullen, F. T., & Jonson, C. L. (2009). Imprisonment and reoffending. In M. Tonry (Ed.), *Crime and justice: A review of the research*. Chicago: University of Chicago Press, pp. 115–200.

122. Pager, D. (2007). *Marked: Race, crime and finding work in an era of mass incarceration*. Chicago: University of Chicago Press.

123. Note 14, p. 242.

124. Becker, H. (1973). *Outsiders: Studies in the sociology of deviance* (2nd ed.). New York: Free Press.

125. Schur, E. M. (1973). *Radical nonintervention: Rethinking the delinquency problem*. Englewood Hills, NJ: Prentice Hall.

126. Note 125.

127. Snyder, H. N., & Sickmund, M. (1999). Juvenile justice: A century of change. *Juvenile Justice Bulletin*. Washington, DC: U.S. Department of Justice.

128. Matsueda, R. L. (1992). Reflected appraisals, parental labeling, and delinquency: Specifying a symbolic interactionist theory. *American Journal of Sociology, 97*, 1577–1611.

129. Braithwaite, J. (1989). *Crime, shame, and reintegration*. New York: Cambridge University Press.

130. Sherman, L. W. (1993). Defiance, deterrence, and irrelevance: A theory of the criminal sanction. *Journal of Research in Crime and Delinquency, 30*, 445–473.

131. Bazemore, G., & Umbreit, M. (1995). Rethinking the sanctioning function of the juvenile court: Retributive or restorative responses to juvenile crime. *Crime and Delinquency, 41*, 296–316.

Chapter 8

1. Reiman, J. (2007). *The rich get richer and the poor get prison: Ideology, class, and criminal justice* (8th ed.). Boston: Allyn and Bacon.

2. Lilly, J. R., Cullen, F. T., & Ball, R. A. (2007). *Criminological theory: Context and consequences* (4th ed.). Thousand Oaks, CA: Sage, pp. 134–135.

3. Note 2, p. 155.

4. Cullen, F. T., & Agnew, R. (2011). *Criminological theory: Past to present*. New York: Oxford, pp. 271–272.

5. Chambliss, W. J. (1984). The law of vagrancy. *Social Problems, 12*, 67–77.

6. Chambliss, W. J., & Seidman, R. T. (1982). *Law, order, and power*. Reading, MA: Addison-Wesley, pp. 33–38.

7. Note 6.

8. Vold, G. B. (1958). *Theoretical criminology*. New York: Oxford University Press, pp. 208–209.

9. Chambliss, W. J. (1975). *Criminal law in action*. Santa Barbara, CA: Hamilton, pp. i–ii.

10. Williams, F. P., III, & McShane, M. D. (2010). *Criminological theory* (5th ed.). Upper Saddle River, NJ: Prentice Hall, pp. 129–130.

11. Ritzer, G. (1992). *Sociological theory* (3rd ed.). New York: McGraw Hill, pp. 263–270.

12. Kennedy, M. C. (1970). Beyond incrimination: Some neglected facets of the theory of punishment. *Catalyst, 5,* 1–37.

13. Akers, R. L., & Sellers, C. S. (2009). *Criminological theories: Introduction, evaluation, and application* (5th ed.). New York: Oxford, pp. 218–221.

14. Wolfgang, M. E., Figlio, R. M., Tracy, P. E., & Singer, S. (1985). The *national survey of crime severity.* Washington, DC: Bureau of Justice Statistics.

15. Fang, L. (2014, March 10). Where have all the lobbyists gone? On paper, the influence-peddling business is drying up. But lobbying money is flooding into Washington, DC, like never before. What's going on? *The Nation.* Retrieved June 1, 2015, from http://www.thenation.com/article/178460/shadow-lobbying-complex

16. Note 13, p. 218.

17. Turk, A. T. (1969). *Criminality and legal order.* Chicago: Rand McNally.

18. Greenleaf, R. G., & Kaduce, L. L. (1995). Sophistication, organization, and authority subject conflict: Rediscovering and unraveling Turk's theory of norm resistance. *Criminology, 33,* 565–586.

19. Weidner, R. R., & Terrell, W. (2005). A test of Turk's theory of norm resistance using observational data on police–suspect encounters. *Journal of Research in Crime and Delinquency, 42,* 84–109.

20. Note 6, p. 31.

21. Note 6, p. 269.

22. Carson, E. A., & Golinelli, D. (2014). *Prisoners in 2012.* Washington, DC: U.S. Department of Justice.

23. Note 13, pp. 224–226.

24. Black, D. (1980). The social organization of arrest. In R. J. Lundman (Ed.), *Police behavior: A sociological perspective.* New York: Oxford University Press.

25. Walker, S., Spohn, C., & DeLone, M. (2007). *The color of justice: Race, ethnicity, and crime in America* (4th ed.). Belmont, CA: Wadsworth.

26. Lundman, R., & Kowalski, B. R. (2009). Speeding while black? Assessing the generalizabiltiy of Lange et al.'s (2001, 2005) New Jersey Turnpike speeding survey findings. *Justice Quarterly, 26,* 562–591.

27. Engel, R. S. (2008). A critique of the 'outcome test' in racial profiling research. *Justice Quarterly, 25,* 1–36, 11.

28. Warren, P., Tomaskovic-Devey, D., Smith, W., Zingraff, M., & Mason, M. (2006). Driving while black: Bias processes and racial disparity in police stops. *Criminology, 44,* 709–738.

29. Kochel, T. R., Wilson, D. B., & Mastrofski, S. D. (2011). Effect of suspect race on officers' arrest decisions. *Criminology, 49,* 473–512.

30. Blumstein, A. (1982). On the racial disproportionality of the United States' prison populations. *Journal of Criminal Law and Criminology, 73,* 1259–1281.

31. Blumstein, A. (1993). Racial disproportionality of U.S. prison populations revisited. *University of Colorado Law Review, 64,* 1259–1281.

32. Austin, R. L., & Allen, M. D. (2000). Racial disparity in arrest rates and an explanation of racial disparity in commitment to Pennsylvania's prisons. *Journal of Research in Crime and Delinquency, 37,* 200–220.

33. Petersilia, J. (1983). *Racial disparities in the criminal justice system.* Santa Monica, CA: Rand.

34. Klein, S., Petersilia, J., & Turner, S. (1990). Race and imprisonment decisions in California. *Science, 247,* 812–816.

35. Wilbanks, W. (1987). *The myth of a racist criminal justice system.* Belmont, CA: Wadsworth.

36. Cole, D. (1999). *No equal justice: Race and class in the American criminal justice system.* New York: The New Press, pp. 150–151.

37. Huebner, B., & Bynum, T. (2008). The role of race and ethnicity in parole decisions. *Criminology, 46,* 907–938.

38. Blalock, H. M., Jr. (1967). *Toward a theory of minority-group relations.* New York: John Wiley & Sons.

39. Eitle, D., & Monahan, S. (2009). Revisiting the racial threat thesis: The role of police organizational characteristics in predicting race-specific drug arrest rates. *Justice Quarterly, 26,* 528–561.

40. Eitle, D., D'Alessio, S. J., & Stolzenberg, L. (2002). Racial threat and social control: A test of the political, economic, and threat of black crime hypothesis. *Social Forces, 81,* 557–576.

41. McGarrell, E. F. (1993). Institutional theory and the stability of a conflict model of the incarceration rate. *Justice Quarterly, 10,* 7–28.

42. Johnson, B., Stewart, E. A., Pickett, J., & Gertz, M. (2011). Ethnic threat and social control: Examining public support for judicial use of ethnicity in punishment. *Criminology, 49,* 401–442.

43. Abadinsky, H. (2001). *Drugs: An introduction.* Belmont, CA: Wadsworth, pp. 19–42.

44. Note 36, p. 8.

45. Tonry, M. (1995). *Malign neglect: Race, crime, and punishment in America.* New York: Oxford University Press, pp. 104–112.

46. Note 45, p. 123.

47. Eckholm, E. (2010, July 28). Congress moves to narrow cocaine sentencing disparities. *New York Times.* Retrieved June 10, 2015, from http://www.nytimes.com/2010/07/29/us/politics/29crack.html

48. American Civil Liberties Union. (2013). *The war on marijuana in black and white.* Retrieved June 10, 2015, from https://www.aclu.org/sites/default/files/field_document/1114413-mj-report-rfs-rel1.pdf

49. *Furman v. Georgia,* 408 U.S. 238 (1972), 242.

50. Brearley, H. C. (1930). The negro and homicides. *Social Forces, 9,* 247–253.

51. Johnson, E. H. (1957). Selective forces in capital punishment. *Social Forces, 36,* 165–169.

52. Wolfgang, M. E., Kelly, A., & Nolde, H. C. (1962). Comparison of executed and commuted among admissions to death row. *Journal of Criminal Law and Criminology, 53,* 301–311.

53. Zimring, F. E., Eigen, J., & O'Malley, S. (1976). Punishing homicides in Philadelphia: Perspectives on the death penalty. *University of Chicago Law Review, 43,* 227–252.

54. Wolfgang, M. E., & Riedel, M. (1973). Race, judicial discretion, and the death penalty. *The Annals of the American Academy of Political and Social Science, 407,* 119–133.

55. Radelet, M. L., & Pierce, G. L. (1991). Choosing those who will die: Race and the death penalty in Florida. *Florida Law Review, 43,* 1–34.

56. Paternoster, R., & Brame, R. (2008). Reassessing race disparities in Maryland capital cases. *Criminology, 46,* 971–1008.

57. Ekland-Olson, S. (1988). Structured discretion, racial bias, and the death penalty: The first decade after Furman in Texas. *Social Science Quarterly, 69,* 853–873.

58. Keil, T., & Vito, G. F. (1989). Race, homicide severity, and application of the death penalty: A consideration of the Barnett scale. *Criminology, 27,* 511–531.

59. U.S. General Accounting Office. (1990). *Death penalty sentencing: Research indicates a pattern of racial disparities.* Washington, DC: U.S. General Accounting Office.

60. Note 59, pp. 5–6.

61. Jacobs, D., & Kent, S. (2007). The determinants of execution since 1951: How politics, protests, public opinion and social divisions shape capital punishment. *Social Problems, 54,* 297–318.

62. Baldus, D. C., & Woodworth, G. A. (2003). Race discrimination in the administration of the death penalty: An overview of empirical evidence with special emphasis on the post-1990 research. *Criminal Law Bulletin, 39,* 194–227.

63. Pew Research Center. (2015). Less support for death penalty, especially among democrats: Supporters, opponents see risk of executing the innocent. Retrieved June 6, 2015, from http://www.people-press .org/2015/04/16/less-support-for-death-penalty-especially-among-democrats

64. The Innocence Project. (2015, June 15). DNA exonerations nationwide. Retrieved June 17, 2015, from http://www.innocenceproject.org/free-innocent/improve-the-law/fact-sheets/dna-exonerations-nationwide

65. Thrasher, F. M. (1927). *The gang: A study of 1,313 gangs in Chicago.* Chicago: University of Chicago Press.

66. Sutherland, E. H. (1929). Crime and the conflict process. *Journal of Juvenile Research, 13,* 38–48.

67. Sellin, T. (1938). *Culture conflict and crime.* New York: Social Science Research Council.

68. Rennie, Y. (1978). *The search for criminal man.* Lexington, MA: Lexington Books, p. 132.

69. Gagaz, T. T. (2002, September). Meet the khatheads. *Newsweek, 140,* 35.

70. Kelson, G. A. (1998). Female circumcision in the modern age: Should female circumcision now be considered grounds for asylum in the United States? *Buffalo Human Rights Law Review, 4,* 185–209.

71. Vold, G. (1958). *Theoretical criminology.* New York: Oxford University Press.

72. Note 71, p. 219.

73. Chambliss, W. J. (1969). *Crime and the legal process.* New York: McGraw Hill, p. 10.

74. Lynch, M. J., & Groves, W. B. (1989). *A primer in radical criminology* (2nd ed.). New York: Harrow and Heston, p. 11.

75. Note 74, p. 10.

76. Note 74, p. 13.

77. Taylor, I., Walton, P., & Young, J. (1973). *The new criminology: For a social theory of deviance.* New York: Harper and Row.

78. Engels, F. (1981). Crime in communist society. In D. F. Greenberg (Ed.), *Crime and capitalism.* Palo Alto, CA: Mayfield, p. 51.

79. Note 68, p. 112.

80. Bonger, W. A. (1969). *Criminality and economic conditions.* Bloomington: Indiana University Press, p. 141.

81. Antonaccio, O., & Tittle, C. R. (2007). A cross-national test of Bonger's theory of criminality and economic conditions. *Criminology, 45,* 925–958.

82. Rusche, G., & Kirchheimer, O. (1975). Punishment and social structure. In W. J. Chambliss (Ed.), *Criminal law in action.* New York: John Wiley, p. 364.

83. Zimring, F. E., & Hawkins, G. (1991). *The scale of imprisonment.* Chicago: University of Chicago Press.

84. Inverarity, J., & McCarthy, D. (1988). Punishment and social structure revisited: Unemployment and imprisonment in the U.S., 1948–1984. *Sociological Quarterly, 29,* 263–279.

85. Gardner, G. (1987). The emergence of the New York state prison system: A critique of the Rusche-Kirchheimer model. *Crime and Social Justice, 29,* 88–109.

86. D'Alessio, S. J., & Stolzenberg, L. (1995). Unemployment and the incarceration of pretrial defendants. *American Sociological Review, 60,* 350–359.

87. Quinney, R. (1977). *Class, state, and crime.* New York: David McKay.

88. Note 13, pp. 239–240.

89. Note 13, p. 240
90. Note 1, pp. 111–155.
91. Note 1, pp. 149–150.
92. Eisinger, J. (2014, April 30). The rise of corporate impunity, *Pro Publica*. Retrieved June 6, 2015, from http://www.propublica.org/article/the-rise-of-corporate-impunity
93. Patel, S. S. (2014, December 2). The biggest banks have paid $180 billion in fines since the financial crisis, *Market Watch*. Retrieved June 5, 2015, from http://www.marketwatch.com/story/large-banks-have-paid-180-billion-in-fines-since-2007-2014-12-02
94. Note 5, p. 35.
95. Adler, J. S. (1989). A historical analysis of the law of vagrancy. *Criminology, 27*, 209–230.
96. Platt, A. (1969). *The child savers: The invention of delinquency*. Chicago: University of Chicago Press.
97. Note 96, p. 83.
98. Quinney, R. (1974). *Critique of legal order*. Boston: Little Brown, p. 27.
99. Gordon, D. M. (1981). Class and the economics of crime. In D. F. Greenberg (Ed.), *Crime and capitalism*. Palo Alto, CA: Mayfield, p. 90.
100. Barnett, C. (2000). *The measurement of white-collar crime using Uniform Crime Reporting (UCR) data*. NIBRS Publication Series. Washington, DC: U.S. Department of Justice, p. 1.
101. Note 100.
102. Sparks, R. F. (1980). A critique of Marxist criminology. In N. Morris & M. Tonry (Eds.), *Crime and Justice*, Vol. 2. Chicago: University of Chicago, pp. 173–175.
103. Meier, R. F. (1976). The new criminology: Continuity in criminological theory. *Journal of Criminal Law and Criminology, 67*, 461–469.
104. Note 102, p. 190.
105. Klockars, C. (1979). The contemporary crises of Marxist criminology. *Criminology, 16*, 477–515.
106. Toby, J. (1979). The new criminology is the old sentimentality. *Criminology, 16*, 516–526.
107. Greenberg, D. F. (1981). *Crime and capitalism*. New York: Mayfield, 484.
108. Lea, J., & Young, J. (1984). *What is to be done about law and order*. London: Penguin.
109. Kinsey, R., Lea, J., & Young, J. (1986). *Losing the fight against crime*. London: Blackwell.
110. DeKeseredy, W. (1988). The left realist approach to law and order. *Justice Quarterly, 5*, 635–640.
111. Matthews, R. (2009). Beyond 'so what' criminology: Rediscovering realism. *Theoretical Criminology, 13*, 341–362.
112. Currie, E. (1997). Market, crime and community: Toward a mid-range theory of post-industrial violence. *Theoretical Criminology, 1*, 147–172.
113. Note 110, pp. 151–152.
114. Note 4, pp. 274–275.
115. Pepinsky, H. E. (1991). Peacemaking in criminology and criminal justice. In H. E. Pepinsky & R. Quinney (Eds.), *Criminology as peacekeeping*. Bloomington: Indiana University Press, p. 304.
116. Cordella, P. J. (1991). Reconciliation and the mutualist model of community. In H. E. Pepinsky & R. Quinney (Eds.), *Criminology as peacekeeping*. Bloomington: Indiana University Press, pp. 30–46.
117. Immarigeon, R. (1991). Beyond the fear of crime: Reconciliation as the basis for criminal justice policy. In H. E. Pepinsky & R. Quinney (Eds.), *Criminology as peacekeeping*. Bloomington: Indiana University Press, pp. 69–80.
118. Quinney, R. (1991). The way of peace: On crime, suffering, and service. In H. E. Pepinsky & R. Quinney (Eds.), *Criminology as peacekeeping*. Bloomington: Indiana University Press, p. 4.
119. Note 118, p. 12.
120. Fuller, J. R. (1998). *Criminal justice: A peacemaking perspective*. Boston: Allyn and Bacon.
121. Note 4, pp. 276–277.
122. Fuller, J. R., & Wozniak, J. F. (2007). Peacemaking criminology: Past, present, and future. In F. T. Cullen, J. P. Wright, & K. R. Blevins (Eds.), *Taking stock: The status of criminological theory*, Vol. 15. New Brunswick, NJ: Transaction.
123. Belknap, J. (1996). *The invisible woman: Gender, crime, and justice*. Belmont, CA: Wadsworth.
124. Klein, D. (1973). The etiology of female offending: A review of the literature. *Issues in Criminology, 8*, 3–30.
125. Note 4, pp. 320–321.
126. Simpson, S. S. (1989). Feminist theory, crime, and justice. *Criminology, 27*, 605–632.
127. Note 4, pp. 321–326.
128. Daly, K., & Chesney-Lind, M. (1988). Feminism and criminology. *Justice Quarterly, 5*, 497–533.
129. Federal Bureau of Investigation. (2013). *Crime in the United States 2012*, Table 42. Retrieved June 8, 2015, from https://www.fbi.gov/about-us/cjis/ucr/crime-in-the.u.s/2012/crime-in-the-u.s.-2012/tables/42tabledatadecoverviewpdf
130. Lauritsen, J. L., Heimer, K., & Lynch, J. P. (2009). Trends in the gender gap in violent offending: New evidence from the national crime victimization survey. *Criminology, 47*, 361–400.
131. Greenfeld, L. A., & Snell, T. L. (1999). *Women offenders*. Washington, DC: U.S. Department of Justice, Bureau of Justice Statistics.
132. Note 4, 320–323.
133. Note 128, p. 510.
134. Steffensmeier, D., & Allan, E. (1998). The nature of female offending: Patterns and explanation. In R. T. Zaplin (Ed.), *Female offenders: Critical perspectives*

and effective interventions. Gaithersburg, MD: Aspen, pp. 5–30.

135. Note 130.

136. Daly, K. (1989). Gender and varieties of white-collar crime. *Criminology, 27*, 769–794.

137. Zahn, M. A. (Ed.). *The delinquent girl.* Philadelphia: Temple University Press.

138. Agnew, R. (2009). The contribution of 'mainstream theories' to the explanation of female delinquency. In M. A. Zahn (Ed.), *The delinquent girl.* Philadelphia: Temple University Press, pp. 7–29.

139. Jenson, G. F. (2003). Gender variation in delinquency: Self image, beliefs, and peers as mediating mechanisms. In R. L. Akers & G. F. Jensen (Eds.), *Social learning theory and the explanation of crime.* New Brunswick, NJ: Transaction, pp. 9–38.

140. Note 134, pp. 15–16.

141. Mazerolle, P. (1998). Gender, general strain, and delinquency: An empirical examination. *Justice Quarterly, 15*, 65–91.

142. Chesney-Lind, M., & Faith, K. (2001). What about feminism? Engendering theory-making in criminology. In R. Paternoster & R. Bachman (Eds.), *Explaining crime and criminals.* Los Angeles: Roxbury, pp. 278–302.

143. Belknap, J., & Holsinger, K. (1998). An overview of delinquent girls: How theory and practice have failed and the need for innovative changes. In R. T. Zaplin (Ed.), *Female offenders: Critical perspectives and effective interventions.* Gaithersburg, MD: Aspen, pp. 34–35.

144. Daly, K. (1994). *Gender, crime, and punishment.* New Haven, CT: Yale University Press.

145. Simpson, S., Yahner, J. L., Durgan, L. (2008). Understanding women's pathways to jail: Analyzing the lives of incarcerated women. *The Australian and New Zealand Journal of Criminology, 41*, 84–108.

146. Costello, B. J., & Mederer, H. J. (2003). A control theory of gender differences in crime and delinquency. In C. L. Brit & M. R. Gottfredson (Eds.), *Control theories of crime and delinquency.* New Brunswick, NJ: Transaction, pp. 77–108.

147. Heimer, K., & De Coster, S. (1999). The gendering of violent delinquency. *Criminology, 37*, 277–318.

148. Note 147.

149. Note 13, pp. 268–272.

150. Daly, K. (1989). Neither conflict nor labeling nor paternalism will suffice: Intersections of race, ethnicity, gender, and family in criminal court decisions. *Crime and Delinquency, 35*, 136–168.

151. Visher, C. (1983). Gender, police arrest decisions, and notions of chivalry. *Criminology, 21*, 5–28.

152. Figueira-McDonough, J. (1985). Gender differences in informal processing: A look at charge bargaining

and sentence reduction in Washington, DC. *Journal of Research in Crime and Delinquency, 22*, 101–133.

153. Note 13, p. 269.

154. Bishop, D. M., & Frazier, C. E. (1992). Gender bias in juvenile justice processing: Implications of the JJDP Act. *Journal of Criminal Law and Criminology, 82*, 1162–1186.

155. Note 4, pp. 320–321.

Chapter 9

1. Cullen, F. T. (2011). Beyond adolescent limited criminology: Choosing our future. The American Society of Criminology 2010 Sutherland Address. *Criminology, 49*, 287–330.

2. Moffitt, T. E. (1993). Adolescent limited and life-course-persistent antisocial behavior: A developmental taxonomy. *Psychological Review, 100*, 674–701.

3. Glueck, S., & Glueck, E. T. (1950). *Unraveling juvenile delinquency.* Cambridge, MA: Harvard University Press.

4. Note 1, pp. 291–297.

5. Note 1, p. 310.

6. Letkemann, P. (1973). *Crime as work.* Englewood Cliffs, NJ: Prentice Hall.

7. Sutherland, E. H. (1937). *The professional thief.* Chicago: University of Chicago Press.

8. Klockars, C. B. (1976). *The professional fence.* New York: Free Press.

9. Jackson, J. E. (1993). Fraud masters: Studying an illusory, non-violent, gang specializing in credit card crimes. *Gang Journal, 1*, 17–36.

10. Wolfgang, M. E., Figlio, R. M., & Sellin, T. (1972). *Delinquency in a birth cohort.* Chicago: University of Chicago Press.

11. Farrington, D. P. (1992). Criminal career research in the United Kingdom. *British Journal of Criminology, 32*, 521–536.

12. Piquero, A. R., Farrington, D., & Blumstein, A. (2007). *Key issues in criminal career research.* New York: Cambridge University Press.

13. Elliott, D. S. (1994). Serious violent offenders: Onset, developmental course, and termination. The American Society of Criminology 1993 presidential address. *Criminology, 32*, 1–21.

14. Hamparian, D. M., Davis, J. M., Jacobson, J. M., & McGraw, R. E. (1985). *The young criminal years of the violent few.* Washington, DC: U.S. Department of Justice.

15. Hamparian, D. M., Schuster, R., Dinitz, S., & Conrad, J. P. (1978). *The violent few: A study of violent juvenile offenders.* Lexington, MA: Heath.

16. Note 14, p. 4.

17. Kempf, K. L. (1990). Career criminals in the 1958 Philadelphia birth cohort: A follow-up of

the early adult years. *Criminal Justice Review, 15,* 161–162.

18. Tracy, P. E., & Kempf, K. L. (1996). *Continuity and discontinuity in criminal careers.* New York: Plenum Press.

19. Tracy, P. E., Wolfgang, M. E., & Figlio, R. M. (1990). *Delinquency careers in two birth cohorts.* New York: Plenum Press, 101–103.

20. Mazerolle, P., Brame, R., Paternoster, R., Piquero, A., & Dean, C. (2000). Onset age, persistence, and offense versatility: Comparisons across gender. *Criminology, 38,* 1143–1172.

21. DeLisi, M. (2002). Not just a boy's club: An empirical assessment of female career criminals. *Women and Criminal Justice, 13,* 27–45.

22. Lab, S. P., & Doerner, W. G. (1987). Changing female delinquency in three birth cohorts. *Journal of Crime and Justice, 10,* 101–116.

23. Gottfredson, M., & Hirschi, T. (1988). Science, public policy, and the career criminal. *Criminology, 26,* 37–55.

24. Kempf, K. L. (1988). Crime severity and career criminal progression. *Journal of Criminal Law and Criminology, 79,* 524–540.

25. Piper, E. S. (1985). Violent recidivism and chronicity in the 1958 Philadelphia cohort. *Journal of Quantitative Criminology, 1,* 319–344.

26. Gottfredson, M., & Hirschi, T. (1990). *A general theory of crime.* Palo Alto, CA: Stanford University Press.

27. Hirschi, T., & Gottfredson, M. (1983). Age and the explanation of crime. *American Journal of Sociology, 89,* 552–584.

28. Thornberry, T. (1996). Introduction: Some advantages of developmental and life-course perspectives for the study of crime and delinquency. In T. Thornberry (Ed.), *Advances in criminological theory: Developmental theories of crime and delinquency* (Vol. 7). New Brunswick, NJ: Transaction, pp. 1–10.

29. Hirschi, T. (1969). *Causes of delinquency.* Berkeley, CA: University of California Press.

30. Merton, R. K. (1938). Social structure and anomie. *American Sociological Review, 3,* 672–682.

31. Note 2.

32. Loeber, R. (1982). The stability of antisocial child behavior. *Child Development, 53,* 1431–1446.

33. Loeber, R., & Dishion, T. (1983). Early predictors of male delinquency: A review. *Psychological Bulletin, 94,* 68–99.

34. Owleus, D. (1979). Stability of aggressive reaction patterns in males: A review. *Psychological Bulletin, 8,* 852–875.

35. Robbins, L. (1966). *Deviant children grown up.* Baltimore: Williams and Wilkins.

36. Robbins, L. (1978). Sturdy childhood predictors of adult antisocial behavior: Replications from longitudinal studies. *Psychological Medicine, 8,* 611–622.

37. Note 32.

38. Smith, J. D., Dishion, T. J. Shaw, D. S., Wilson, M. N., Winter, C. C., & Patterson, G. R. (2014). Coercive family process and early-onset conduct problems from age 2 to school entry. *Developmental Psychopathology, 26,* 917–932.

39. Cullen, F. T., & Agnew, R. (2011). *Criminological theory: Past to present* (4th ed.). New York: Oxford, p. 453.

40. Loeber, R., & Stouthamer-Loeber, M. (1998). Development of juvenile aggression and violence: Some common misconceptions and controversies. *American Psychologist, 53,* 242–259.

41. Jennings, W. G., & Piquero, A. R. (2009). Life course criminology. In J. M. Miller (Ed.), *21st century criminology: A reference handbook* (Vol. 1). Thousand Oaks, CA: Sage.

42. Farrington, D. P. (2011). Developmental and life course criminology: Theories and policy implications. In M. DeLisi & K. Beaver (Eds.), *Criminological theory: A life-course approach.* Sudbury, MA: Jones & Bartlett.

43. Note 39, pp. 454–460.

44. Note 26.

45. Hirschi, T., & Gottfredson, M. (1995). Control theory and the life-course perspective. *Studies on Crime and Crime Prevention, 4,* 131–142.

46. Sampson, R., & Laub, J. (1995). Understanding variability in lives through time: Contributions of life-course criminology. *Studies on Crime and Crime Prevention, 4,* 143–158.

47. Note 2.

48. Patterson, G. (1993). Orderly change in a stable world: The antisocial trait as a chimera. *Journal of Consulting and Clinical Psychology, 61,* 911–919.

49. Sampson, R. J., & Laub, J. H. (1993). *Crime in the making: Pathways and turning points through life.* Cambridge, MA: Harvard University Press.

50. Note 49, pp. 64–123.

51. Sampson, R. J, & Laub, J. H. (1990). Crime and deviance over the life course: The salience of adult social bonds. *American Sociological Review, 55,* 609–627.

52. Laub, J., & Sampson, R. (2003). *Shared beginnings, divergent lives.* Cambridge, MA: Harvard University Press, pp. 148–149.

53. Sampson, R. J., & Laub, J. H. (2003). Life-course desisters? Trajectories of crime among delinquent boys followed to age 70. *Criminology, 41,* 301–335.

54. Note 52, pp. 145–150.

55. Kirk, D. S. (2012). Residential change as a turning point in the life course of crime: Desistance or temporary cessation? *Criminology, 50,* 329–358.

56. Maruna, S. (2001). *Making good: How ex-convicts reform and rebuild their lives.* Washington, DC: American Psychological Association.

57. Moffitt, T. E. (1993). The neuropsychology of conduct disorder. *Development and Psychopathology, 5,* 135–151.

58. Note 2, p. 681.

59. Note 2.

60. Note 2.

61. Moffitt, T. E. (2006). A review of research on the taxonomy of life-course persistent versus adolescent limited antisocial behavior. In F. T. Cullen, J. P. Wright, & K. K. Blevins (Eds.), *Taking stock: The status of criminological theory—Advances in criminological theory* (Vol. 17). New Brunswick, NJ: Transaction.

62. Fairchild, G., van Goozen, S. H. M., Calder, A. J., & Goodyer, I. M. (2013). Research review: Evaluating and reformulating the developmental taxonomic theory of antisocial behaviour. *Journal of Child Psychology and Psychiatry, 54,* 924–940.

63. Piquero, A. R., Farrington, D., & Blumstein, A. (2007). *Key issues in criminal career research.* New York: Cambridge University Press.

64. Note 62, pp. 936–937

65. Pratt, T. C. (2015). A self-control/life-course theory of criminal behavior. *European Journal of Criminology,* published online before print May 31, 2015, doi: 10.1177/1477370815587771

66. DeLisi, M., & Gatling, J. M. (2003). Who pays for a life of crime? An empirical assessment of the assorted victimization costs posed by career criminals. *Criminal Justice Studies, 16,* 283–293.

67. Wilson, J. Q. (1975). *Thinking about crime.* New York: Basic Books.

68. Clear, T. (2007). *Imprisoning communities.* New York: Oxford University Press.

69. Pratt, T. C. (2009). *Addicted to incarceration.* Thousand Oaks, CA: Sage.

70. National Institute of Justice. (2011). John Laub and Robert Sampson awarded Stockholm Prize. Retrieved June 22, 2015, from http://www.nij.gov/about/director/pages/stockholm-prize.aspx

71. Martin, S. E. (1986). Policing career criminals—An examination of an innovative crime control program. *Journal of Criminal Law and Criminology, 77,* 1159–1182.

72. Martin, S. E., & Sherman, L. W. (1986). Selective apprehension: A police strategy for repeat offenders. *Criminology, 24,* 155–156.

73. Note 72, p. 170.

74. Abrahamse, A. F., Ebener, P. A., Greenwood, P. W., Fitzgerald, N., & Kosin, T. E. (1991). An experimental evaluation of the Phoenix repeat offender program. *Justice Quarterly, 8,* 141–168.

75. Kennedy, D. M. (2008). *Deterrence and crime prevention: Reconsidering the prospect of sanction.* New York: Routlege.

76. Ratcliffe, J. (2008). *Intelligence-led policing.* Portland, OR: Willan Publishing.

77. Engel, R. S., Tillyer, M. S., & Corsaro, N. (2013). Reducing gang violence using focused deterrence: Evaluating the Cincinnati Initiative to Reduce Violence (CIRV). *Justice Quarterly, 30,* 403–439.

78. Shichor, D. K., & Sechrest, D. K. (Eds.) (1996). *Three strikes and you're out: Vengeance as public policy.* Thousand Oaks, CA: Sage.

79. Chen, E. (2000). *Impacts of three strikes and truth in sentencing on the volume and composition of correctional populations.* Washington, DC: National Institute of Justice, p. 4.

80. Greenwood, P. W., Everingham, S. S., Chen, E., Abrahamse, A. F., Merritt, N., & Chiesa, J. (1998). *Three strikes revisited: An early assessment of implementation and effects.* Santa Barbara, CA: Rand Corporation, p. i.

81. Note 79, p. 13.

82. Schiraldi, V., Colburn, J., & Locke, E. (2004). *Three strikes and you're out: An examination of the impact of 3 strike laws 10 years after their enactment.* Washington, DC: The Justice Policy Institute, p. 5.

83. Note 82, p. 4.

84. Note 83, pp. 7–8.

85. New York Times Editorial Board (2013, August 10). California's continuing prison crisis. *The New York Times.* Retrieved June 25, 2015, from http://www.nytimes.com/2013/08/11/opinion/sunday/californias-continuing-prison-crisis

86. Bureau of Alcohol, Tobacco & Firearms. (1991). *Protecting America: The effectiveness of federal armed career criminal statutes.* Washington, DC: Department of the Treasury, p. 14.

87. Johnson, J. L., & Saint-Germain, M. A. (2005). Officer down: Implications of three-strikes for public safety. *Criminal Justice Policy Review, 16,* 443–460.

88. Note 68.

89. Note 69.

90. Currie, E. (1998). *Confronting crime: An American challenge.* New York: Pantheon Books.

91. Lipsey, M. W. (2009). The primary factors that characterize effective interventions with juvenile offenders: A meta-analytic overview. *Victims and Offenders, 4,* 124–147.

92. Farrington, D. P., & Welsh, B. C. (2008). *Saving children from a life of crime: Early risk factors and effective interventions.* Oxford, UK: Oxford University Press.

93. Stolzfus, E., & Lynch, K. E. (2009). *Home visitation for families with young children.* Washington, DC: Congressional Research Service.

94. Olds, D. L., Kitzman, H. J., Cole, R. E., Hanks, C. A., Arcoleo, K. J., Anson, E. A., et al. (2010). Enduring effects of prenatal and infancy home visits

on maternal home life and government spending: Follow up of a randomized trial among children at age 12 years. *Archives of Pediatrics and Adolescent Medicine, 164*, 419–424.

95. Reid, J., Patterson, G., & Snyder, J. (2003). *Antisocial behavior in children and adolescents: A developmental analysis and model for intervention.* Washington, DC: American Psychological Association.

96. Lundahl, B., Risser, H. J., & Lovejoy, M. C. (2006). A meta-analysis of parent training: Moderators and follow-up effects. *Clinical Psychology Review, 26*, 86–104.

97. Tremblay, R. E., Vitaro, F., Bertrand, L., LeBlanc, M., Beauchesne, H., Boileau, H., & David, L. (2001). Parent and child training to prevent early onset of delinquency: The Montreal longitudinal-experiment study. In A. Piquero & P. Mazerolle (Eds.), *Life-course criminology: Contemporary and classic readings.* Belmont, CA: Wadsworth/Thomson, pp. 355–373.

98. Dishion, T. J., Connell, A., Weaver, C., Shaw, D., Gardner, F., & Wilson, M. (2008). The Family Check-Up with high-risk indigent families: Preventing problem behavior by increasing parents' positive behavior support in early childhood. *Child Development, 79*, 1395–1414.

99. National Institute of Justice. (n.d.). *Program profile: Family Check-Up (FCU) for Children.* Retrieved June 20, 2015, from http://www.crimesolutions.gov/ProgramDetails.aspx?ID=396

100. Schweinhart, L. J., Montie, J., Zongping, X. W. Barnett, S., Belfield, C. R., & Nores, M. (2005). *Lifetime effects: The High/Scope Perry Preschool Study through age 40.* Ypsilanti, MI: High/Scope Press, pp. 194–215.

101. Henggeler, S. W., Cunningham, P. B., Pickrel, S. G., Schoenwald, S. K., & Brondino, M. J. (1996). Multisystemic therapy: An effective violence prevention approach for serious juvenile offenders. *Journal of Adolescence, 19*, 55–56.

102. Ward, T., Mann, R. E., & Gannon, T. A. (2007). The good lives model of offender rehabilitation: Clinical implications. *Aggression and Violent Behavior, 12*, 87–107.

103. National Institute of Justice. (n.d.). *Evaluation of Second Chance Act demonstration projects.* Retrieved June 20, 2015, from http://www.nij.gov/topics/corrections/reentry/pages/evaluation-second-chance.aspx

104. Note 42, p. 181.

Chapter 10

1. Snoop Dogg. (1998). 20 dollars 2 my name. On *da game is to be sold, not to be told.* No Limit Records. Retrieved January 26, 2011, from http://www.mp3lyrics.org/s/snoop-dogg/20-dollars-to-my-name/

2. Surette, R. (1998). *Media, crime, and criminal justice: Images and realities.* Belmont, CA: Wadsworth; Lee, M. (2007). *Inventing fear of crime: Criminology and the politics of anxiety.* Cullompton, England: Willan Publishing.

3. Federal Bureau of Investigation. (2013). *Crime in the United States, 2012: Violent crime.* Retrieved May 23, 2014, from http://www.fbi.gov/about-us/cjis/ucr/crime-in-the-u.s/2012/crime-in-the-u.s.-2012/violent-crime/violent-crime

4. Ashworth, A., & Horder, J. (2013). *Principles of criminal law.* New York: Oxford University Press.

5. Federal Bureau of Investigation. (2013). *Crime in the United States, 2012: Murder.* Retrieved May 23, 2014, from http://www.fbi.gov/about-us/cjis/ucr/crime-in-the-u.s/2012/crime-in-the-u.s.-2012/violent-crime/murder

6. United Nations Office on Drugs and Crime. (2013). *Global study on homicide, executive summary 2013.* Retrieved May 23, 2014, from http://www.unodc.org/unodc/en/data-and-analysis/crime_survey_eleventh.html

7. United Nations Office on Drugs and Crime. (2013). *Intentional homicide count and rate per 100,000, by country/territory 2000–2012.* Retrieved May 24, 2014, from http://www.unodc.org/gsh/en/data.html

8. Ousey, G. C., & Lee, M. R. (2010). The Southern culture of violence and homicide-type differentiation: An analysis across cities and time points. *Homicide Studies, 14*, 3, 268–295.

9. Federal Bureau of Investigation. (2013). *Crime in the United States, 2012: Murder.* Retrieved May 23, 2014, from http://www.fbi.gov/about-us/cjis/ucr/crime-in-the-u.s/2012/crime-in-the-u.s.-2012/tables/4tabledatadecoverviewpdf/table_4_crime_in_the_united_states_by_region_geographic_division_and_state_2011-2012.xls

10. Federal Bureau of Investigation. (2013). *Crime in the United States, 2012: Murder.* Retrieved May 23, 2014, from http://www.fbi.gov/about-us/cjis/ucr/crime-in-the-u.s/2012/crime-in-the-u.s.-2012/tables/6tabledatadecpdf/table-6

11. Rosenfeld, R. (2009). Homicide and serious assaults. In M. Tonry (Ed.), *The Oxford handbook of crime and public policy.* New York: Oxford University Press, pp. 36–37.

12. Federal Bureau of Investigation. (2013). *Crime in the United States, 2012: Murder.* Retrieved May 23, 2014, from http://www.fbi.gov/about-us/cjis/ucr/crime-in-the-u.s/2012/crime-in-the-u.s.-2012/offenses-known-to-law-enforcement/expanded-homicide/expanded_homicide_data_table_7_murder_types_of_weapons_used_percent_distribution_by_region_2012.xls; http://www.fbi.gov/about-us/cjis/ucr/

crime-in-the-u.s/2012/crime-in-the-u.s.-2012/ offenses-known-to-law-enforcement/expanded-homicide/expanded_homicide_data_table_8_murder _victims_by_weapon_2008-2012.xls

13. Wolfgang, M. (1958). *Patterns in criminal homicide*. Philadelphia: University of Pennsylvania Press.

14. Felson, R. B., & Steadman, H. J. (1983). Situational factors in disputes leading to criminal violence. *Criminology, 21,* 59–74.

15. Federal Bureau of Investigation. (2013). *Crime in the United States, 2012: Murder*. Retrieved May 14, 2011, from http://www.fbi.gov/about-us/cjis/ucr/ crime-in-the-u.s/2012/crime-in-the-u.s.-2012/ offenses-known-to-law-enforcement/expanded-homicide/expanded_homicide_data_table_10_ murder_circumstances_by_relationship_2012.xls

16. McCall, P. L., Land, K. C., & Parker, K. F. (2010). An empirical assessment of what we know about structural covariates of homicide rates: A return to a classic 20 years later. *Homicide Studies, 14,* 3, 236–237.

17. Federal Bureau of Investigation. (2013). *Crime in the United States, 2012: Murder*. Retrieved May 23, 2014, from http://www.fbi.gov/about-us/cjis/ucr/ crime-in-the-u.s/2012/crime-in-the-u.s.-2012/ offenses-known-to-law-enforcement/expanded-homicide/expanded_homicide_data_table_3_ murder_offenders_by_age_sex_and_race_2012.xls

18. Federal Bureau of Investigation. (2013). *Crime in the United States, 2012: Murder*. Retrieved May 23, 2014, from http://www.fbi.gov/about-us/cjis/ucr/ crime-in-the-u.s/2012/crime-in-the-u.s.-2012/ offenses-known-to-law-enforcement/expand-ed-homicide/expanded_homicide_data_table_6_ murder_race_and_sex_of_vicitm_by_race_and_ sex_of_offender_2012.xls

19. Federal Bureau of Investigation. (2013). *Crime in the United States, 2012: Murder*. Retrieved May 23, 2014, from http://www.fbi.gov/about-us/cjis/ucr/ crime-in-the-u.s/2012/crime-in-the-u.s.-2012/ offenses-known-to-law-enforcement/expanded-homicide/expanded_homicide_data_table_5_ murder_age_of_victim_by_age_of_offender_2012.xls

20. Federal Bureau of Investigation. (2013). *Crime in the United States, 2012: Murder*. Retrieved May 23, 2014, from http://www.fbi.gov/about-us/ cjis/ucr/crime-in-the-u.s/2012/crime-in-the-u.s.-2012/offenses-known-to-law-enforcement/ expanded-homicide/expanded_homicide_data_ table_6_murder_race_and_sex_of_vicitm_by_ race_and_sex_of_offender_2012.xls

21. Federal Bureau of Investigation. (2013). *Crime in the United States, 2012: Murder*. Retrieved May 23, 2014, from http://www.fbi.gov/about-us/cjis/ucr/ crime-in-the-u.s/2012/crime-in-the-u.s.-2012/

offenses-known-to-law-enforcement/expanded-homicide/expanded_homicide_data_table_10_ murder_circumstances_by_relationship_2012.xls

22. Reckdenwald, A., & Parker, K. F. (2009). Homicide. In J. M. Miller (Ed.), *21st century criminology: A reference handbook* (Vol. 1). Thousand Oaks, CA: Sage, pp. 503–504.

23. Roberts, D. W. (2009). Intimate partner homicide: Relationships to alcohol and firearms. *Journal of Contemporary Criminal Justice, 25,* 67–88.

24. Browne, A. (1987). *Battered women who kill*. New York: Free Press.

25. Campbell, J. C. (1995). Prediction of homicide of and by battered women. In J. C. Campbell (Ed.), *Assessing dangerousness: Violence by sexual offenders, batterers, and child abusers*. Thousand Oaks, CA: Sage.

26. Goetting, A. (1991). Female victims of homicide: A portrait of their killers and the circumstances of their deaths. *Violence and Victims, 3,* 303–324.

27. Belknap, J., Larson, D., Abrams, M., Garcia, C., & Anderson-Block, K. (2012). Types of intimate part-ner homicide committed by women: Self-defense, proxy/retaliation, and sexual proprietariness. *Homicide Studies, 16,* 4, 359–379.

27. Jurik, N. C., & Winn, R. (1990). Gender and homi-cide: A comparison of men and women who kill. *Violence and Victims, 5,* 227–242.

28. McFarlane, J. M., Campbell, J., Wilt, S., Sachs, C. J. U. Y., & Xu, X. (1999). Stalking and intimate partner femicide. *Homicide Studies, 3,* 300–316.

29. Morton, E., Runyan, C. W., Moracco, K. E., & Butts, J. (1998). Partner homicide-suicide involving female homicide victims: A population based study in North Carolina, 1988–1992. *Violence and Victims 13,* 91–106.

30. Wilson, M. I., & Daly, M. (1992). Who kills whom in spouse killings? On the exceptional sex ratio of spousal homicides in the United States. *Criminol-ogy, 30,* 189–215.

31. Wilson, M., & Daly, M. (1993). Spousal homicide risk and estrangement. *Violence and Victims, 8,* 3–16.

32. Wilson, M., & Daly, M. (1993). An evolutionary psychology perspective on male sexual proprietari-ness, and violence against wives. *Violence & Victims, 8,* 271–294.

33. Wilson, M., & Daly, M. (1996). Male sexual propri-etariness and violence against wives. *Current Direc-tions in Psychological Science, 5,* 2–7.

34. Wilson, M., Johnson, H., & Daly, M. (1995). Lethal and nonlethal violence against wives. *Canadian Journal of Criminology, 37,* 331–361.

35. Erikkson, L., & Mazerolle, P. (2013). A general strain theory of intimate partner homicide. *Aggres-sion & Violent Behavior, 18,* 5, 462–470.

36. Note 11, pp. 40–41.

37. Zimring, F. E., & Hawkins, G. (1997). *Crime is not the problem: Lethal violence in America.* New York: Oxford University Press.

38. GunPolicy.org. Retrieved May 26, 2014, from http://www.gunpolicy.org/firearms/region/united-states

39. Note 38.

40. Kleck, G., Kovandzic, T., Saber, M., & Hauser, W. (2011). The effect of perceived risk and victimization on plans to purchase a gun for self-protection. *Journal of Criminal Justice, 39,* 312–319.

41. Melamed, Y., Bauer, A., Kalian, M., Rosca, P., & Mester, R. (2011). Assessing the risk of violent behavior before issuing a license to carry a handgun. *Journal of the American Academy of Psychiatry & Law, 39,* 542–548.

42. Cook, P. J., & Ludwig, J. (2009). Firearm violence. In M. Tonry (Ed.), *The Oxford handbook of crime and public policy.* New York: Oxford University Press, p. 70.

43. Hoskin, A. W. (2001). Armed Americans: The impact of firearm availability on national homicide rates. *Justice Quarterly, 18,* 569–592.

44. Ludwig, J., & Cook, P. (2000). Homicide and suicide rates associated with the implementation of the Brady violence prevention act. *Journal of the American Medical Association, 284,* 585–591; La Valle, J. M. (2010). Re-estimating gun policy effects according to a National Science Academy Report: Were previous reports of failure premature? *Journal of Crime and Justice, 33,* 1, 71–95.

45. Task Force on Community Preventive Services. (2005). Recommendations to reduce violence through early childhood home visitation, therapeutic foster care, and firearms laws. *American Journal of Preventive Medicine, 28,* 2, Suppl. 1, 6–10. *See also*: Hahn, R. A., Bilukha, O., Crosby, A., Fullilove, M. T., Liberman, A., Moscicki, E., et al. (2005). *American Journal of Preventive Medicine, 28,* 2, Suppl. 1, 40–71.

46. Jacobs, J. B. (2002). Crime control via federal dealer regulation. *Criminology and Public Policy, 2,* 183–186.

47. Loftin, C., McDowall, D., Wiersema, B., & Cottey, T. J. (1991). Effects of restrictive licensing of handguns on homicide and suicide in the District of Columbia. *New England Journal of Medicine, 325,* 1085–1101.

48. Kleck, G. (1997). *Targeting guns: Firearms and their control.* New York: Aldine de Gruyter, p. 94.

49. Kleck, G., & Patterson, E. B. (1993). The impact of gun control and gun ownership levels on violence rates. *Journal of Quantitative Criminology, 9(3),* 249–287.

50. Lott, J. R., Jr. (2013). *More guns, less crime: Understanding crime and gun control laws.* Chicago: University of Chicago Press.

51. Messner, S. F., & Rosenfeld, R. (2007). *Crime and the American dream.* Belmont, CA: Thomson/Wadsworth.

52. Currie, E. (1998). *Crime and punishment in America.* New York: Holt/Metropolitan.

53. Butchart, A., & Engstrom, K. (2002). Sex and age specific relations between economic inequality and homicide rates in people 0–24 years: A cross-sectional analysis. *Bulletin of the World Health Organization, 10.*

54. Jacobs, D., & Richardson, A. M. (2008). Economic inequality and homicide in the developed nations from 1975 to 1995. *Homicide Studies, 12,* 28–45.

55. Lim, F., Bond, M. H., & Bond, M. K. (2005). Linking societal and psychological factors to homicide rates across nations. *Journal of Cross Cultural Psychology, 36,* 515–536.

56. Pratt, T. C., & Lowenkamp, C. T. (2002). Conflict theory, economic conditions and homicide. *Homicide Studies, 6,* 61–83.

57. Like, T. Z. (2011). Urban inequality and racial differences in risk for violent victimization. *Crime & Delinquency, 57,* 3, 432–457.

58. Levin, J., & Madfis, E. (2009). Mass murder at school and cumulative strain: A sequential model. *American Behavioral Scientist, 52,* 9, 1227.

59. Mullen, P. E. (2004). The autogenic (self-generated) massacre. *Behavioral Sciences and the Law, 22,* 3, 312.

60. Bowers, T. G., Holmes, E. S., & Rhom, A. (2010). The nature of mass murder and autogenic massacre. *Journal of Police & Criminal Psychology, 25,* 59–66.

61. Fox, J. A., & DeLateur, M. J. (2014). Mass shootings in America: Moving beyond Newtown. *Homicide Studies, 18,* 1, 129.

62. Nagourney, A. (2014, May 26). Parents' nightmare: Failed race to stop killings. *The New York Times,* A1, A10.

63. Fox, J. A., & Levin, J. (1998). Multiple homicide: Patterns of serial and mass murder. *Crime and Justice, 23,* 444.

64. Note 61.

65. Note 60, Note 62.

66. Note 62.

67. Note 61, p. 126.

68. Note 62, A10.

69. Note 62, A10.

70. Note 61, p. 133.

71. Note 61, p. 133.

72. Note 63, p. 434.

73. Note 61, p. 127.

74. Fox, J. A., & Levin, J. (2003). Mass murder: An analysis of extreme violence. *Journal of Applied Psychoanalytic Studies, 5,* 47–64.

75. Note 63, p. 441.
76. Note 60, p. 64.
77. Note 58.
78. Note 58, p. 1239.
79. Note 58, pp. 1241–1242.
80. Note 61, p. 133.
81. Note 62.
82. Note 61, p. 135.
83. Medina, J. (2014, May 26). Even in a state with restrictive laws, amassing weapons and ammunition. *The New York Times*, A10.
84. Holmes, R. M., & Holmes, S. T. (2010). *Serial murder*. Thousand Oaks, CA: Sage.
85. Hicks, J. (1987, March 6). Score card killer? *The [Louisville] Courier Journal*, A1, A16.
86. Olson, J. (1990). *The misbegotten son*. New York: Delacourte.
87. Quinet, K. (2011). Prostitutes as victims of serial homicide: Trends and case characteristics, 1970–2009. *Homicide Studies*, 15, 1, 81.
88. Egger, S. A. (1984). A Working Definition of Serial Murder and the Reduction of Linkage Blindness. *Journal of Police Science and Administration*, 12, 348–357.
89. Note 87, p. 84.
90. Note 87, p. 93.
91. Note 87, p. 93.
92. Note 63, p. 424.
93. Kraemer, G. W., Lord, W. D., & Heilbrun, K. (2004). Comparing single and serial homicide offenses. *Behavioral Sciences & the Law*, 22, 338.
94. Hickey, E. W. (1997). *Serial murderers and their victims*. Belmont, CA: Wadsworth.
95. Snook, B., Cullen, R. M., Mokros, A., & Harbort, S. (2005). Serial murderers spatial decisions: Factors that influence crime location choice. *Journal of Investigative Psychology & Offender Profiling*, 2, 161.
96. American Civil Liberties Union and the American Friends Service Committee. (2004). *The forgotten population: A look at death row in the United States through the experiences of women*. New York: American Civil Liberties Union, p. 208.
97. Keeney, B. T., & Heide, K. M. (1994). Gender differences in serial murderers: A preliminary analysis. *Journal of Interpersonal Violence*, 9, 383–398.
98. Kelleher, M. D., & Kelleher, C. L. (1998). *Murder most rare: The female serial killer*. Westport: Dell Publishing.
99. Farrell, A. L., Keppel, R. D., & Titterington, V. B. (2013). Testing existing classifications of serial murder considering gender: An exploratory analysis of solo female serial killers. *Journal of Investigative Psychology & Offender Profiling*, 10, 279.
100. Note 99, pp. 279–283.

101. Branson, A. L. (2013). African American serial killers: Over-represented yet under acknowledged. *The Howard Journal of Criminal Justice*, 52, 1, 7–10.
102. Note 101, p. 15.
103. Note 63, p. 413.
104. Holmes, R. M., & DeBurger, J. (1988). *Serial murder*. Newbury Park, CA: Sage.
105. Schreiber, F. (1984). *The shoemaker*. New York: Signet Books.
106. Stack, A. (1983). *The lust killer*. New York: Signet Books.
107. Note 63, p. 413.
108. Note 63, pp. 415–419.
109. Note 63, pp. 419–423.
110. Delisi, M., & Scherer, A. M. (2006). Multiple homicide offenders: Offense characteristics, social correlates, and criminal careers. *Criminal Justice & Behavior*, 33, 3, 367–391.
111. Note 111, pp. 385–387.
112. Ireland, C. E., & Rush, G. E. (2010). *Dictionary of criminal justice* (7th ed.). Guilford, CT: Dushkin/McGraw-Hill.
113. Cohn, A. M., Zinzow, H. M., Resnick, H. S., & Kilpatrick, D. G. (2013). Correlates of reasons for not reporting rape to the police: Results from a national telephone household probability sample of women with forcible or drug-or-alcohol facilitated/incapacitated rape. *Journal of Interpersonal Violence*, 28, 3, 455–473.
114. Suarez, E., & Gadalla, T. M. (2010). Stop blaming the victim: A meta-analysis on rape myths. *Journal of Interpersonal Violence*, 25, 2024–2025.
115. Federal Bureau of Investigation. (2012). *Crime in the United States, 2012, Forcible rape*. Retrieved on May 30, 2014, from http://www.fbi.gov/about-us/cjis/ucr/crime-in-the-u.s/2012/crime-in-the-u.s.-2012/violent-crime/rape
116. Truman, J., Langdon, L., & Planty, M. (2013). *Criminal victimization, 2012*. Washington, DC: Bureau of Justice Statistics, p. 5.
117. Note 116, p. 2.
118. Note 116, p. 4.
119. Tjaden, P., & Thoennes, N. (2006). *Extent, nature and consequences of rape victimization: Findings from the National Violence Against Women survey*. Washington, DC: U.S. Department of Justice, National Institute of Justice, p. 7.
120. Fisher, B. S., Cullen, F. T., & Turner, M. G. (2000). *The sexual victimization of college women*. Washington, DC: U.S. Department of Justice, National Institute of Justice.
121. Note 119, p. 21.
122. Note 120.
123. Planty, M., Langton, L., Krebs, C., Berzofsky, M., & Smiley-McDonald, H. (2013). *Female victims*

of sexual violence, 1945–2010. Washington, DC: Bureau of Justice Statistics, p. 1.

124. Note 123, p. 3.
125. Note 119, p. 27.
126. Note 123, p. 6.
127. Note 119, p. 29.
128. Terry, K. J. (2006). *Sexual offenses and offenders: Theory, practice, and policy.* Belmont, CA: Wadsworth, p. 114.
129. Note 123.
130. Martin, P. Y. (2005). *Rape work: Victims, gender, and emotions in organizational and community context.* New York: Routledge, p. 52.
131. Note 94, pp. 73–93.
132. Note 87, p. 123.
133. Frohman, L. (1991). Discrediting victims' allegations of sexual assault: Prosecutorial accounts of case rejection. *Social Problems, 38,* 213–226.
134. Spohn, C., & Holleran, D. (2001). Prosecuting sexual assault: A comparison of charging decisions in sexual assault cases involving strangers, acquaintances, and intimate partners. *Justice Quarterly, 18,* 651–688.
135. Note 94, pp. 55–58.
136. Frohmann, L. (1995). Discrediting victims' allegations of sexual assault: Prosecutorial accounts of case rejections. In P. Searles & R. J. Berger (Eds.), *Rape and society.* Boulder, CO: Westview.
137. Note 94, pp. 128–129.
138. Note 130.
139. Note 119, p. 36.
140. Bryden, D. P., & Grier, M. M. (2011). The search for rapists' "real" motives. *Journal of Criminal Law and Criminology, 101,* 1, 171–278.
141. Brownmiller, S. (1975). *Against our will: Men, women and rape.* New York: Simon & Schuster, p. 15.
142. Note 90.
143. Note 140, pp. 230–246.
144. Note 140, p. 254.
145. Lester, D., & Hurst, G. (2004). Treating sexual offenders. In *Correctional counseling and rehabilitation.* Cincinnati, OH: Anderson, p. 245.
146. Pardue, A., & Arrigo, B. A. (2008). Power, anger and sadistic rapists: Toward a differentiated model of offender personality. *International Journal of Offender Therapy and Comparative Criminology, 52,* 4, 380–382.
147. Note 146, p. 397.
148. Felson, R. B., Messner, S. F., Hoskin, A. W., & Deane, G. (2002). Reasons for reporting and not reporting domestic violence to the police. *Criminology, 40,* 617–648.
149. United Nations Entity for Gender Equality and the Empowerment of Women. *Facts and figures: Ending violence against women.* Retrieved June 3, 2014, from http://www.unwomen.org/en/what-we-do/ending-violence-against-women/facts-and-figures
150. Catalano, S. (2013). *Intimate partner violence: Attributes of victimization, 1993–2011.* Washington, DC: Bureau of Justice Statistics, p. 1.
151. Belknap, J. (2001). *The invisible woman: Gender, crime, and justice.* Belmont, CA: Wadsworth.
152. Dobash, R. P., Dobash, R. E., Wilson, M., & Daly, M. (1992). The myth of sexual symmetry in marital violence. *Social Problems, 39,* 71–91.
153. Melon, H. C., & Belknap, J. (2003). He hits, she hits: Assessing gender differences and similarities in officially reported intimate partner violence. *Criminal Justice and Behavior, 30,* 328–348.
154. Gover, A. R. (2009). Domestic violence. In J. M. Miller (Ed.), *21st century criminology: A reference handbook* (Vol. 1). Thousand Oaks, CA: Sage, p. 473.
155. Note 150.
156. Hague, G., & Malos, E. (1998). *Domestic violence: Action for change.* Gretton, England: New Clarion Press.
157. Kakar, S. (1998). *Domestic abuse: Public policy/criminal justice approaches toward child, spousal, and elderly abuse.* San Francisco: Austin and Winfield Publishers.
158. Miller, S. L., & Wellford, C. F. (1997). Patterns and correlates of interpersonal violence. In A. P. Cardarelli (Ed.), *Violence between intimates: Patterns, causes, and effects.* Boston: Allyn & Bacon.
159. Sever, A. (1997). Recent or imminent separation and intimate violence against women. *Violence Against Women, 3,* 566–589.
160. O'Neill, D. (1998). A post-structural review of the theoretical literature surrounding wife abuse. *Violence Against Women, 4,* 457–490.
161. Yllo, K. (1993). Through a feminist lens: Gender, power, and violence. In R. J. Gelles & D. Loeske (Eds.), *Current controversies on family violence.* Newbury Park, CA: Sage, pp. 47–62.
162. Dobash, R. E., & Dobash, R. (1979). *Violence against wives: A case against the patriarchy.* New York: Free Press.
163. Note 118.
164. Note 154, p. 475.
165. Richards, T. N., Jennings, W. G., Tomisch, E. A., & Gover, A. R. (2013). A longitudinal analysis of offending and specialization among a sample of Massachusetts domestic violence offenders. *Journal of Interpersonal Violence, 28,* 3, 643–663.
166. Buzawa, E. (1990). *Domestic violence: The criminal justice response.* London: Sage, 27.
167. Gover, A. R., Welton-Mitchell, C., Belknap, J., & DePrince, A. P. (2013). When abuse happens again:

Women's reasons for *not* reporting new incidents of intimate partner abuse to law enforcement. *Women & Criminal Justice, 23*, 99–120.

168. DePrince, A. P., Belknap, J., Labus, J. S., Buckingham, S. E., & Gover, A. R. (2012). The impact of victim-focused outreach on criminal legal system outcomes following police-reported intimate partner abuse. *Violence Against Women, 18*, 8, 861–881.

169. Note 154, p. 474.

170. Black, M. C., Basile, K. C., Breiding, M. J., Smith, S. G., Walters, M. L., Merrick, M. T., Chen, J., & Stevens, M. R. (2011). *The national intimate partner and sexual violence survey (NISVS): 2010 summary report*. Atlanta, GA: National Center for Injury Prevention and Control, Centers for Disease Control and Prevention, 29.

171. Note 170, p. 2.

172. Coleman, F. (1997). Stalking behaviors and the cycle of domestic violence. *Journal of Interpersonal Violence, 12*, 420–432.

173. Burgess, A., Baker, T., Greening, D., Hartman, C. R., Burgess, A., Douglas, J. E., et al. (1997). Stalking behaviors within domestic violence. *Journal of Family Violence, 12*, 389–403.

174. Roberts, A., & Dziegielewski, S. (1996). Assessment typology and intervention with the survivors of stalking. *Aggression and Violent Behavior, 1*, 359–368.

175. Spitzberg, B. H., & Cupach, W. R. (2007). The state of the art of stalking: Taking stock of the emerging literature. *Aggression & Violent Behavior, 12*, 67–69.

176. Note 175, p. 77.

177. Note 175, pp. 78–79.

178. McEwan, T., Mullen, P. E., & Purcell, R. (2007). Identifying risk factors in stalking: A review of current research. *International Journal of Law & Society,* |*30*, 1–9; Norris, S. M., Huss, M. T., & Palarea, R. E. (2011). A pattern of violence: Analyzing the relationship between intimate partner violence and stalking. *Violence and Victims, 26*, 1, 103–115.

179. Mumm, S. S., & Cupach, W. R. (2010). Turning points in the progression of obsessive relational intrusion and stalking. *Violence and Victims, 25*, 6, 707–727.

180. Winkleman, A., & Winstead, B. A. (2011). Student pursuers: An investigation of pursuit and stalking in the student-faculty relationship. *Violence and Victims, 26*, 5, 543–559.

181. Patton, C. L., Nobles, M. R., & Fox, K. A. (2010). Look who's stalking: Obsessive pursuit and attachment theory. *Journal of Criminal Justice, 38*, 282–290.

182. Miller, L. (2012). Stalking: Patterns, motives, and intervention strategies. *Aggression and Violent Behavior, 17*, 495–506.

183. Zona, M., Sharma, K., & Lane, J. (1993). A comparative study of erotomanic and obsessional subjects in a forensic sample. *Journal of Forensic Sciences, 38*, 894–903.

184. Holmes, R. M. (1993). Stalking in America: Types and methods of criminal stalkers. *Journal of Contemporary Criminal Justice, 9*, 17–27.

185. Roberts, A., & Dziegielewski, S. (1996). Assessment typology and intervention with the survivors of stalking. *Aggression and Violent Behavior, 1*, 359–368.

186. Davis, K., Ace, A., & Andra, M. (2000). Stalking perpetrators and psychological maltreatment of partners: Anger-jealousy, attachment insecurity, need for control, and break-up context. *Violence and Victims, 15*, 473–487.

187. Monhandie, K., Meloy, J. R., McGowan, M. G., & Williams, J. (2006). The RECON typology of stalking: Reliability and validity based upon a large sample of North American stalkers. *Journal of Forensic Sciences, 51*, 1, 147–155.

188. Racine, C., & Billick, S. (2014). Classification systems for stalking behavior. *Journal of Forensic Sciences, 59*, 1, 250–254.

189. Mustaine, E. E., & Tewksbury, R. (1999). A routine activity explanation for women's stalking victimizations. *Violence Against Women, 5*, 1, 43–62.

190. Engelbrecht, C. M., & Reyns, B. W. (2011). Gender differences in acknowledgement of the stalking victimization: Results from the 2006 NCVS stalking supplement. *Violence and Victims, 26*, 5, 560–579.

191. Ngo, F. T., & Paternoster, R. (2013). Stalking strain, concurrent negative emotions, and legitimate coping strategies: A preliminary test of gendered strain theory. *American Journal of Criminal Justice, 38*, 369–391.

192. Malsch, M., deKeijer, J. W., & Debets, S. E. C. (2011). Are stalkers recidivists? Repeated offending by convicted stalkers. *Violence and Victims, 26*, 1, 3–15.

193. Tittle, C. R. (2004). Refining control balance theory. *Theoretical Criminology, 8*, 395–428.

194. Nobles, M. R., & Fox, K. A. (2013). Assessing stalking behaviors in a control balance theory framework. *Criminal Justice & Behavior, 40*, 7, 737–762.

195. Fox, K. A., Nobles, M. R., & Akers, R. L. (2011). Is stalking a learned phenomenon? An empirical test of social learning theory. *Journal of Criminal Justice, 39*, 39–47.

196. Note 195.

197. Fox, K. A., Nobles, M. R., & Fisher, B. S. (2014). A multi-theoretical framework to assess gendered stalking victimization: The utility of self-control, social learning, and control balance theories. *Justice Quarterly*, Published online, 1–29.

198. Mechanic, M. B., Weaver, T. L., & Resick, P. A., (2000). Intimate partner violence and stalking behaviors: Exploration of patterns and correlates in a sample of acutely battered women. *Violence and Victims, 15*, 55–72.

199. Mechanic, M. B., Uhlmansiek, M. H., Weaver, T. L., & Resick, P. A. (2000). The impact of severe stalking experienced by acutely battered women: An examination of violence, psychological symptoms, and strategic responses. *Violence and Victims, 15*, 443–458.

200. Weller, M., Hope, L., & Sheridan, L. (2013). Police and public perceptions of stalking: The role of prior victim-offender relationship. *Journal of Interpersonal Violence, 28*, 2, 320–339.

201. Scott, A. J., Rajakaruna, N., & Sleath, E. (2014). International perceptions of stalking and responsibility: The influence of prior relationship and severity of behavior. *Criminal Justice & Behavior, 41*, 2, 220–236.

202. Lambert, E. G., Smith, B., Geistman, J., Cluse-Tolar, T., & Jiang, S. (2013). Do men and women differ in their perceptions of stalking: An exploratory study of among college students. *Violence and Victims, 28*, 2, 195–209.

203. Finnegan, H. A., & Timmons Fritz, P. A. (2012). Differential effects of gender on perceptions of stalking and harassment behavior. *Violence and Victims, 27*, 6, 895–910.

204. Cupach, W. R., & Spitzberg, B. H. (2004). *The dark site of relational pursuit: From attraction to obsession to stalking.* Mahwah, NJ: Lawrence Ehlbaum.

205. Nguyen, L. K., Spitzberg, B. H., & Lee, C. M. (2012). Coping with obsessive relational intrusion and stalking: The role of social support and coping strategies. *Violence and Victims, 27*, 3, 414–433.

206. Dutton, L. B., & Winstead, D. A. (2011). Types, frequency, and effectiveness of responses to unwanted pursuit and stalking. *Journal of Interpersonal Violence, 26*, 6, 1129–1156.

207. Note 182, p. 503.

208. Guy, R. A. (1993). The nature and constitutionality of stalking laws. *Vanderbilt Law Review, 46*, 991–1029.

209. Reyns, B. W., & Engelbrecht, C. M. (2010). The stalking victim's decision to contact the police: A test of Gottfredson & Gottfredon's theory of criminal justice decision making. *Journal of Criminal Justice, 38*, 998–1005.

210. Reyns, B. W., & Engelbrecht, C. M. (2012). The fear factor: Exploring predictors of fear among stalking victims throughout the stalking encounter. *Crime & Delinquency, 59*, 5, 788–808.

211. Logan, T.K., & Walker, R. (2010). Toward a deeper understanding of the harms caused by partner stalking. *Violence and Victims, 25(4)*, 440-455.

212. Storey, J. E., & Hart, S. D. (2011). How do police respond to stalking? An examination of risk management strategies and tactics used in a specialized anti-stalking law enforcement unit. *Journal of Police & Criminal Psychology, 26*, 128–142.

213. Mustaine, E. E. (2009). Child abuse. In J. M. Miller (Ed.), *21st century criminology: A reference handbook* (Vol. 1). Thousand Oaks, CA: Sage, p. 457.

214. Childhelp. (2012). *National Child Abuse Statistics, 2012.* Retrieved June 9, 2014, from http://www.childhelp.org/pages/statistics. National Children's Alliance (2013). *Statistical fact sheet.* Washington, DC: National Children's Alliance.

215. Malley-Morrison, K., & Hines, D. A. (2009). Child abuse. In M. Tonry (Ed.), *The Oxford handbook of crime and public policy.* New York: Oxford University Press, pp. 141, 156.

216. Douglas, E. M., & Mohn, B. L. (2014). Fatal and non-fatal child maltreatment in the U.S.: An analysis of child, caregiver, and service utilization within the National Child Abuse and Neglect data set. *Child Abuse & Neglect, 38*, 42–51.

217. Damashek, A., McDiarmid Nelson, M., & Bonner, B. L. (2013). Fatal child maltreatment: Characteristics of deaths from physical abuse versus neglect. *Child Abuse & Neglect, 37*, 735–744.

218. Welch, G. L., & Bonner, B. L. (2013). Fatal child neglect: Characteristics, causation, and strategies for prevention. *Child Abuse & Neglect, 37*, 745–752.

219. Stith, S. M., Liu, T., Davies, C., Boykin, E. L., Adler, M. C., Harris, J. M., et al. (2009). Risk factors in child maltreatment: A meta-analytic review of the literature. *Aggression & Violent Behavior, 14*, 13–29.

220. Platt, A. M. (1969). *The child savers: The invention of delinquency.* Chicago: University of Chicago Press.

221. Federal Bureau of Investigation. (2013). *Crime in the United States, 2012: Robbery.* Retrieved May 23, 2014, from http://www.fbi.gov/about-us/cjis/ucr/crime-in-the-u.s/2012/crime-in-the-u.s.-2012/violent-crime/robbery

223. Note 116, p. 2.

224. Bureau of Justice Statistics, *NCVS Victimization Analysis Tool (NVAT).* Retrieved June 12, 2014, from http://www.bjs.gov/index.cfm?ty=nvat

225. Cook, P. J. (2009). Robbery. In M. Tonry (Ed.), *The Oxford handbook of crime and public policy.* New York: Oxford University Press, p. 103.

226. Katz, J. (1998). *Seductions of crime.* New York: Basic Books, pp. 164–194.

227. Wright, R., & Decker, S. (1997). *Armed robbers in action: Stickups and street culture.* Boston: Northeastern University Press.

228. Felson, R., Baumer, E., & Messner, S. Acquaintance robbery. *Journal of Research in Crime and Delinquency, 37*, 284–305.

229. Jacobs, B. A., & Wright, R. (1999). Stick-up, street culture, and offender motivation. *Criminology, 37,* 160–162.

230. Eck, J. (2006). Preventing crime at places. In *Preventing crime: What works, what doesn't, and what's promising.* Retrieved February 23, 2006, from http://www.ncjrs.gov/works/

231. Harper, D. W., Khey, D. N., & Nolan, G. M. (2013). Spatial patterns of robbery at tourism sites: A case study of the Vieux Carre' in New Orleans. *American Journal of Criminal Justice, 38,* 589–601.

232. McCluskey, J. D. (2009). Robbery. In J. M. Miller (Ed.), *21st century criminology: A reference handbook* (Vol. 1). Thousand Oaks, CA: Sage, p. 514.

233. Haberman, C. P., Groff, E. R., & Taylor, R. B. (2013). The variable impacts of public housing community proximity on nearby street robberies. *Journal of Research in Crime and Delinquency. 50,* 2, 163–188.

234. Federal Bureau of Investigation. (2013). *Crime in the United States, 2012: Aggravated assault.* Retrieved June 13, 2014, from http://www.fbi.gov/about-us/cjis/ucr/crime-in-the-u.s/2012/crime-in-the-u.s.-2012/violent-crime/aggravated-assault

235. Note 234.

236. Note 224.

237. Nielsen, A. L., Martinez, R., & Lee, M. T. (2005). Alcohol, ethnicity and violence: The role of alcohol availability for Latino and Black aggravated assaults and robberies. *The Sociological Quarterly. 46,* 479–502.

238. Pridemore, W. A., & Grubesic, T. H. (2013). Alcohol outlets and community levels of interpersonal violence: Spatial density, outlet type, and seriousness of the assault. *Journal of Research in Crime and Delinquency, 50,* 1, 132–159.

239. Pridemore, W. A., & Grubesic, T. H. (2012). Community organization moderates the effect of alcohol outlet density on violence. *British Journal of Sociology, 63,* 4, 680–703.

240. Holzman, H. R., Hyatt, R. A., & Dempster, J. M. (2001). Patterns of aggravated assault in public housing: Mapping the nexus of offense, place, gender, and race. *Violence Against Women, 7,* 6, 662–684.

241. Suresh, G., & Vito, G. F. (2007). The tragedy of public housing: Spatial analysis of hotspots of aggravated assaults in Louisville, KY (1989–1998). *American Journal of Criminal Justice, 32,* 99–115.

Chapter 11

1. Wright, R. T., & Decker, S. (1994). *Burglars on the job: Streetlife and residential burglary.* Boston: Northeastern University Press, p. 60.

2. Federal Bureau of Investigation. (2013). *Crime in the United States, 2012. Property crime.* Retrieved June 16, 2014, from http://www.fbi.gov/about-us/cjis/ucr/crime-in-the-u.s/2012/crime-in-the-u.s.-2012/property-crime/property-crime

3. Truman, J., Langton, L., & Planty, M. (2013). *Criminal victimization in 2012.* Washington, DC: Bureau of Justice Statistics, p. 4.

4. Note 2.

5. Note 2.

6. Note 2, http://www.fbi.gov/about-us/cjis/ucr/crime-in-the-u.s/2012/crime-in-the-u.s.-2012/tables/29tabledatadecpdf

7. Bureau of Justice Statistics, *NCVS Victimization Tool (NVAT).* Retrieved June 16, 2014, from http://www.bjs.gov/index.cfm?ty=nvat

8. Note 7.

9. Note 7.

10. Lauritsen, J. L., & White, N. (2014). *Seasonal patterns in criminal victimization trends.* Washington, DC: Bureau of Justice Statistics.

11. Federal Bureau of Investigation. (2013). *Crime in the United States, 2012. Burglary.* Retrieved June 16, 2014, from http://www.fbi.gov/about-us/cjis/ucr/crime-in-the-u.s/2012/crime-in-the-u.s.-2012/property-crime/burglary

12. Note X, pp. 3, 4.

13. Note X, p. 11.

14. Lai, Y-L., Zhao, J. S., & Longmire, D. R. (2012). Specific crime-fear linkage: The effect of actual burglary incidents reported to the police on residents' fear of burglary. *Journal of Crime & Justice, 35,* 1, 13–34.

15. Dabney, D. (2004). *Crime types.* Belmont, CA: Wadsworth, p. 174.

16. Bernasco, W. (2009). Burglary. In M. Tonry (Ed.), *The Oxford handbook of crime and public policy.* New York: Oxford University Press, p. 172.

17. Willits, D., Broidy, L., & Denman, K. (2013). Schools, neighborhood risk factors, and crime. *Crime & Delinquency, 59,* 2, 292–315.

18. Johnson, S. D., & Bowers, K. J. (2010). Permeability and burglary risk: Are cul-de-sacs safer? *Journal of Quantitative Criminology, 26,* 89–111.

19. Note 16, pp. 165–166.

20. Cromwell, P., Olson, J., & D'Avary, A. W. (1991). *Breaking and entering: An ethnographic analysis of burglary.* Beverly Hills, CA: Sage.

21. Cromwell, P., Olson, J., & D'Avary, A. W. (1999). Decision strategies of residential burglars. In P. Cromwell (Ed.), *In their own words: Criminals on crime* (2nd ed.). Los Angeles: Roxbury, pp. 50–56.

22. Yu, S. V., & Maxfield, M. (2014). Ordinary business: Impacts on commercial and residential burglary. *British Journal of Criminology, 54,* 298–320.

23. Rey, S. J., Mack, E. A., & Kochinsky, J. (2012). Exploratory space-time analysis of burglary patterns. *Journal of Quantitative Criminology, 28,* 509–531.

24. D'Alessio, S. J., Eitle, D., & Stolzenberg, L. (2012). Unemployment, guardianship, and weekday residential burglary. *Justice Quarterly, 29,* 6, 919–932.

25. Wright, R., & Logie, R. H. (1988). How young house burglars choose targets. *Howard Journal of Criminal Justice, 27,* 92–104; Wright, R., Decker, S. H., Redfern, A. K., & Smith, D. L. (1992). A snowball's chance in hell: Doing fieldwork with active residential burglars. *Journal of Research in Crime and Delinquency, 29,* 2, 148–161.

26. Coupe, T., & Blake, L. (2006). Daylight and darkness targeting strategies and the risks of being seen at residential burglaries. *Criminology, 44,* 2, 431–464.

27. Nee, C., & Meenaghan, A. (2006). Expert decision making in burglars. *British Journal of Criminology, 46,* 935–949.

28. Snook, B., Dhami, M. K., & Kavanaugh, J. K. (2011). Simply criminal: Predicting burglars' occupancy decisions. *Law & Human Behavior, 35,* 316–326.

29. Shover, N. (1972). The social organization of burglary. *Social Problems, 20,* 499–514.

30. Note 16, pp. 176–177.

31. Decker, S., Wright, R., Redfern, A., & Smith, D. (1993). A woman's place is in the home: Females and residential burglary. *Justice Quarterly, 10,* 143–162.

32. Mullins, C., & Wright, R. (2003). Gender, social networks, and residential burglary. *Criminology, 41,* 813–839.

33. Note 32.

34. Fox, B. H., & Farrington, D. P. (2012). Creating burglary profiles using latent class analysis: A new approach to offender profiling. *Criminal Justice & Behavior, 39,* 12, 1593–1594.

35. Note 34, pp. 1595–1597.

36. Vaughn, M. G., DeLisi, M., Beaver, K. M., & Howard, M. O. (2008). Toward a quantitative typology of burglars: Latent profile analysis of career offenders. *Journal of Forensic Sciences, 53,* 6, 1387–1392.

37. Uniform Crime Reports. (2013). *Crime in the United States, 2012: Clearance rates.* Retrieved June 17, 2014, from http://www.fbi.gov/about-us/cjis/ucr/crime-in-the-u.s/2012/crime-in-the-u.s.-2012/offenses-known-to-law-enforcement/clearances

38. Uniform Crime Reports. (2013). *Crime in the United States, 2012: Arson.* Retrieved June 22, 2014, from http://www.fbi.gov/about-us/cjis/ucr/crime-in-the-u.s/2012/crime-in-the-u.s.-2012/property-crime/arson

39. Note 38.

40. U.S. Fire Administration. (2012). Intentionally set fires in residential buildings (2008–2010). *Topical Fire Report Series, 13,* 10, 1.

41. Burton, P. R. S., McNiel, D. E., & Binder, R. L. (2012). Firesetting, arson, pyromania and the forensic mental health expert. *The Journal of the American Academy of Psychiatry and the Law, 40,* 356–357.

42. Curtis, A., McVilly, K., & Day, A. (2012). Arson treatment programmes for offenders with disability: A systematic review of the literature. *Journal of Learning Disabilities and Offending Behaviour, 3,* 4, 186–205.

43. Häkkänen, H., Puolakka, P., & Santtila, P. (2004). Crime scene actions and offender characteristics in arsons. *Legal & Criminal Psychology, 9,* 197–214.

44. Roe-Sepowicz, D., & Hickle, K. (2011). Comparing boy and girl arsonists: Crisis, family and crime scene characteristics. *Legal & Criminal Psychology, 16,* 277–288; Roe-Sepowicz, D., & Hickle, K. (2011). Female juvenile arsonists: An exploratory look at characteristics and solo and group arson offenses. *Legal & Criminal Psychology, 15,* 385–399.

45. Tyler, N., Gannon, T. A., Lockerbie, L., King, T., Dickens, G. L., & De Burca, C. (2014). A firesetting offense chain for mentally disordered offenders. *Criminal Justice & Behavior, 41,* 4, 512–530.

46. Kocsis, R. N., & Cooksey, R. W. (2002). Criminal psychological profiling of serial arson crimes. *International Journal of Offender Therapy & Comparative Criminology, 46,* 6, 631–656.

47. Andrews, R. (2011). Exploring the impact of arson-reduction strategies. *British Journal of Criminology, 51,* 839–855.

48. Uniform Crime Reports. (2013). *Crime in the United States, 2012: Larceny-theft.* Retrieved June 24, 2014, from http://www.fbi.gov/about-us/cjis/ucr/crime-in-the-u.s/2012/crime-in-the-u.s.-2012/property-crime/larceny-theft

49. Note X, pp. 4, 5.

50. Note 48.

51. Klemke, L. (1992). *The sociology of shoplifting: Boosters and snitches today.* Westport, CT: Praeger.

52. Farrington, D. (1999). Measuring, explaining and preventing shoplifting: A review of British research. *Security Journal, 12,* 9–27.

53. Dabney, D., Hollinger, R., & Dugan, L. (2004). Who actually steals? A study of covertly observed shoplifters. *Justice Quarterly, 21,* 693–728.

54. Note 51.

55. Note 51, p. 215.

56. Cromwell, P., Parker, L., & Mobley, S. (1999). The five-finger discount: An analysis of motivations for shoplifting. In P. Cromwell (Ed.), *In their own words: Criminals on crime* (2nd ed.). Los Angeles: Roxbury, pp. 57–70.

57. Caputo, G. A., & King, A. (2011). Shoplifting: Agency, work and gender. *Feminist Criminology, 6,* 3, 159–177.

58. Shigihara, A. M. (2013). It's only stealing a little a lot: Techniques of neutralization for theft among restaurant workers. *Deviant Behavior, 34,* 494–512.

59. Kraut, R. (1976). Deterrent and definitional influences on shoplifting. *Social Problems, 25,* 358–368.

60. Blankenburg, E. (1976). The selectivity of legal sanctions: An empirical investigation of shoplifting. *Law and Society Review, 11,* 109–129.

61. Hindelang, M. (1974). Decisions of shoplifting victims to invoke the criminal justice process. *Social Problems, 21,* 580–593.

62. Hayes, R., Downs, D. M., & Blackwood, R. (2012). Anti-theft procedures and fixtures: A randomized controlled trial of two situational crime prevention measures. *Journal of Experimental Criminology, 8,* 1, 1–15.

63. Caputo, G. (1998). Program of treatment for adult shoplifters. *Journal of Offender Rehabilitation, 27,* 123–137.

64. Note 3.

65. Uniform Crime Reports. (2013). *Crime in the United States, 2012: Motor vehicle theft.* Retrieved June 25, 2014, from http://www.fbi.gov/about-us/cjis/ucr/crime-in-the-u.s/2012/crime-in-the-u.s.-2012/property-crime/motor-vehicle-theft

66. Cherbonneau, M., & Wright, R. (2009). Auto theft. In M. Tonry (Ed.), *The Oxford handbook of crime and public policy.* New York: Oxford University Press, pp. 192–193.

67. Fleming, Z. (1999). The thrill of it all. In P. Cromwell (Ed.), *In their own words: Criminals on crime* (2nd ed.). Los Angeles: Roxbury, pp. 71–79.

68. Note 66, pp. 204–205.

69. Clark, R., & Harris, P. (1995). Auto theft and its prevention. In M. Tonry (Ed.), *Crime and justice: An annual review of research* (Vol. 16). Chicago: University of Chicago Press, pp. 1–54.

70. Roberts, A. (2012). Motor vehicle recovery: A multilevel event history analysis of NIBRS data. *Journal of Research in Crime & Delinquency, 49,* 3, 444–467.

71. Roberts, A., & Block, S. (2012). Explaining temporary and permanent motor vehicle theft rates in the United States: A crime specific approach. *Journal of Research in Crime & Delinquency, 50,* 3, 445–471.

72. Suresh, G., & Tewksbury, R. (2013). Locations of motor vehicle theft and recovery. *American Journal of Criminal Justice, 38,* 200–215.

73. Jacobs, B. A., & Cherbonneau, M. (2014). Auto theft and restrictive deterrence. *Justice Quarterly, 31,* 2, 344–367.

74. Cherrboneau, M., & Copes, H. (2006). 'Drive it like you stole it': Auto theft and the illusion of normalcy. *British Journal of Criminology, 46,* 193–211.

75. Mullins, C. W., & Cherbonneau, M. (2011). Establishing connections: Gender, motor vehicle theft, and disposal networks. *Justice Quarterly, 28,* 2, 278–302.

76. Copes, H., & Tewksbury, R. (2011). Criminal experience and perception of risk: What auto thieves fear when stealing cars. *Journal of Crime & Justice, 34,* 1, 62–79.

77. Copes, H., & Cherbonneau, M. (2006). The key to auto theft: Emerging methods of auto theft from the offender's perspective. *British Journal of Criminology, 46,* 917–934.

78. Note 66, p. 212.

Chapter 12

1. Morris, N., & Hawkins, G. (1970). *The honest politicians' guide to crime control.* Chicago: University of Chicago Press, p. 2.

2. Schur, E. M., & Bedau, H. A. (1974). *Victimless crimes: Two sides of a controversy.* Englewood Cliffs, NJ: Prentice Hall.

3. Meier, R. F., & Geis, G. (1997). *Victimless crime? Prostitution, drugs, homosexuality, abortion.* Los Angeles: Roxbury.

4. Note 1, pp. 5–6.

5. Note 1, pp. 2–4.

6. Newman, G. (1976). *Comparative deviance.* New York: Elsevier.

7. Poll: Far more Americans prefer legalized marijuana to online gambling. NORML. Retrieved June 26, 2014, from http://norml.org/news/2014/05/15/poll-far-more-americans-prefer-legalized-marijuana-to-online-gambling

8. About marijuana. NORML. Retrieved June 26, 2014, from http://norml.org/marijuana

9. Pollock, J. M. (2009). *Criminal law* (9th ed.). Cincinnati: Anderson, pp. 8–12.

10. Becker, H. (1963). *The outsiders.* New York: Macmillan.

11. Erikson, K. T. (1966). *The wayward puritans: A study in the sociology of deviance.* New York: John Wiley and Sons.

12. Chambliss, W. J. (1964). A sociological analysis of the law of vagrancy. *Social Problems, 12,* 67–77.

13. Connor, A. (2009). Is your bedroom a private place? Fornication and fundamental rights. *New Mexico Law Review, 39,* 520–522.

14. Turley, J. (April 25, 2010). Adultery, in many states, is still a crime. *USA Today.* Retrieved on June 25, 2014, from http://usatoday30.usatoday.com/news/opinion/forum/2010-04-26-column26_ST_N.htm

15. Note 9.

16. Twelve states still ban sodomy a decade after court ruling. *USA Today.* Retrieved June 25, 2014, from http://www.usatoday.com/story/news/

nation/2014/04/21/12-states-ban-sodomy-a-decade-after-court-ruling/7981025/

17. *Bowers v. Hardwick*, 478 U.S. 186 (1986).

18. *Lawrence v. Texas*, 539 U.S. 558 (2003).

19. Sloman, L. (1979). *Reefer madness: A history of marijuana in America*. Indianapolis, IN: Bobbs-Merrill, p. 26.

20. Inciardi, J. A. (2008). *The war on drugs IV*. Boston: Allyn & Bacon, pp. 34–35.

21. Gusfield, J. (1963). *Symbolic crusade*. Champaign, IL: University of Illinois Press.

22. Lender, M. E., & Martin, J. R. (1982). *Drinking in America: A history*. New York: Free Press, p. 107.

23. Musto, D. F. (1987). *The American disease*. New York: Oxford University Press, p. 68.

24. Sournia, J. C. (1990). *A history of alcoholism*. Cambridge, MA: Basil Blackwell, p. 122.

25. Note 24.

26. Note 20, pp. 21–22.

27. Note 20, pp. 26–28.

28. Note 20, p. 29.

29. Note 23, pp. 101–109.

30. Wilson, J. Q., & Kelling, G. L. (1982, March). Broken windows: Police and neighborhood safety. *Atlantic Monthly, 249*, 29–38.

31. Note 30, p. 32.

32. Moore, M. H., & Kelling, G. L. (1983). To serve and protect: Learning from police history. *Public Interest, 70*, 65.

33. Sykes, G. W. (1986). Street justice: A moral defense of order maintenance policing. *Justice Quarterly, 3*, 497–512.

34. Kelling, G. L., & Coles, C. M. (1996). *Fixing broken windows: Restoring order and reducing crime in our communities*. New York: The Free Press, pp. 106–107.

35. Note 34, p. 111.

36. Note 34, p. 145.

37. Bratton, W., & Knobler, P. (1998). *Turnaround: How America's top cop reversed the crime epidemic*. New York: Random House.

38. Taylor, R. B. (2005). "Broken windows" or incivilities thesis. In L. E. Sullivan & M. S. Rosen (Eds.), *Encyclopedia of law enforcement, state and local* (Vol. 1). Thousand Oaks, CA: Sage, p. 31.

39. Note 30.

40. Note 34.

41. Note 34, p. 141.

42. Kane, R. J., & Cronin, S. W. (2009). Associations between order maintenance policing and violent crime: Considering the mediating effects of residential context. *Crime & Delinquency, 59*, 6, 910–929.

43. Hinkle, J., & Weisburd, D. (2008). The irony of broken windows policing: A micro-place study of the relationship between disorder, focused police crackdowns and fear of crime. *Journal of Criminal Justice, 36*, 503–512.

44. Jang, H., Hoover, L. T., & Lawton, B. A. (2008). Effect of broken windows enforcement on clearance rates. *Journal of Criminal Justice, 36*, 529–538.

45. Worrall, J. L. (2006). Does targeting minor offenses reduce serious crime? A provisional, affirmative answer based on an analysis of county-level data. *Police Quarterly, 9*, 47–72.

46. Chappell, A. T., Monk-Turner, E., & Payne, B. K. (2011). Broken windows or window breakers: The influence of physical and social disorder on the quality of life. *Justice Quarterly, 28*, 3, 522–540.

47. Hinkle, J. C., & Yang, S-M. (2014). A new look into broken windows: What shapes individuals' perceptions of social disorder. *Journal of Criminal Justice, 42*, 26–35.

48. Gau, J. M., & Pratt, T. C. (2010). Revisiting broken windows theory: Examining the sources of the discriminant validity of perceived disorder and crime. *Journal of Criminal Justice, 38*, 758–766.

49. Kramer, R. (2012). Political elites, "broken windows", and the commodification of public space. *Critical Criminology, 20*, 229–248.

50. Champion, D. J. (2005). *The American dictionary of criminal justice*. Los Angeles: Roxbury, p. 108.

51. Dombrink, J. (2009). Gambling. In M. Tonry (Ed.), *The Oxford handbook of crime and public policy*. New York: Oxford University Press, p. 606.

52. Wellford, C. (2001, April). When it's no longer a game: Pathological gambling in the United States. *National Institute of Justice Journal, 15*.

53. UNLV Center for Gaming Research. (2014). *United States commercial casino revenues: States with commercial and racetrack casinos, 2001–2013*. Las Vegas, NV.

54. UNLV Center for Gaming Research. (2014). *United States online gaming: Monthly and statewide national gaming*. Las Vegas, NV.

55. Note 51, p. 610.

56. Note 52, p. 15.

57. Note 52, pp. 16–17.

58. Phillips, J. G., Ogeil, R., Chow, Y-W., & Blaszcynski, A. (2013). Gambling involvement and increased risk of gambling problems. *Journal of Gambling Studies, 29*, 601–611.

59. Gamblers Anonymous. Home Page. Retrieved on June 27, 2014, from http://www.gamblersanonymous.org/ga/node/1

60. The National Coalition Against Legalized Gambling. Home Page. Retrieved on June 27, 2014, from http://www.gamblingexposed.org/gamblingexposed_708-389-1127__008.htm

61. Williams, R. J., Wood, R. T., & Currie, S. R. (2010). Stacked Deck: An effective, school-based program

for the prevention of problem gambling. *Journal of Primary Prevention, 31,* 109–125.

62. Piscatelli, F., & Albanese, J. S. (2000). Do casinos attract criminals? A study at the Canadian–U.S. border. *Journal of Contemporary Criminal Justice, 16,* 445–456.

63. Gazel, R. C., Rickman, D. S., & Thompson, W. N. (2001). Casino gambling and crime: A panel study of Wisconsin counties. *Managerial and Decision Economics, 22,* 65–75.

64. Grinols, E. L., & Mustard, D. B. (2006). Casinos, crime, and community costs. *The Review of Economics and Statistics, 88,* 1, 28–45.

65. Barthe, E., & Stitt, B. G. (2007). Casinos as "Hot Spots" and the generation of crime. *Journal of Crime & Justice, 30,* 2, 115–140.

66. Montolio, D., & Plannells-Struse, S. (2013). Does tourism boost criminal activity? Evidence from a top touristic country. *Crime & Delinquency.* Retrieved from http://cad.sagepub.com/content/early/2013/10/25/0011128713505489

67. Stitt, B. G., Nichols, M., & Giacopassi, D. (2003). Does the presence of casinos increase crime? An examination of casino and control communities. *Crime and Delinquency, 49,* 253–284.

68. Stitt, B. G., Giacopassi, D., & Nichols, M. (2000). The effect of casino gambling on crime in new casino jurisdictions. *Journal of Crime and Justice, 23,* 1–23.

69. Wilson, J. M. (2001). Riverboat gambling and crime in Indiana: An empirical investigation. *Crime and Delinquency, 47,* 610–640.

70. Moufakkir, O. (2005). An assessment of crime volume following casino gaming development in the city of Detroit. *UNLV Gaming Research & Review Journal, 9,* 1, 22.

71. Reece, W. S. (2010). Casinos, hotels, and crime. *Contemporary Economic Policy, 28,* 2, 145–161.

72. Falls, G. A., & Thompson, P. B. (2014). Casinos, casino size, and crime: A panel data analysis of Michigan counties. *The Quarterly Review of Economics and Finance, 54,* 123–132.

73. Humphreys, B. R., & Soebbing, B. P. (2014). Access to legal gambling and the incidence of crime: Evidence from Alberta. *Growth and Change, 45,* 1, 98–120.

74. Barthe, E., & Stitt, B. G. (2009). Temporal distributions of crime and disorder in casino and non-casino zones. *Journal of Gambling Studies, 25,* 139–152.

75. Koo, J. (2007). Rolling the dice? Casinos, tax revenues, and the social costs of gaming. *Journal of Urban Affairs, 29,* 367–381.

76. Cotti, C. D., & Walker, D. M. (2010). The impact of casinos on fatal alcohol-related traffic accidents in the United States. *Journal of Health Economics, 29,* 788–796.

77. Note 62, p. 18.

78. Note 50, p. 208.

79. Reckless, W. C. (1973). *The crime problem.* New York: Appleton, Century, Crofts, p. 167.

80. Human trafficking statistics and facts, countries where prostitution is legal. Retrieved June 30, 2014, from http://www.mapsofworld.com/poll/should-prostitution-be-legalized-text.html

81. Dank, M., Khan, B., Downey, P. M., Kotanias, C., Mayer, D., Owens, C., Pacifici, L., & Yu, L. (2014). *Estimating the size and structure of the underground commercial sex economy in eight major US cities.* Washington, DC: The Urban Institute.

82. Miller, J. (2009). Prostitution. In M. Tonry (Ed.), *The Oxford handbook of crime and public policy.* New York: Oxford University Press, p. 549.

83. Weitzer, R. (2005). Flawed theory and method in studies of prostitution. *Violence Against Women, 11,* 934–949.

84. Weitzer, R. (2000). Why we need more research on sex work. In R. Weitzer (Ed.), *Sex for sale: Prostitution, pornography, and the sex industry.* New York: Routledge, pp. 1–16.

85. Flowers, R. B. (1998). *The prostitution of women and girls.* Jefferson, NC: McFarland.

86. Inciardi, J. A., Lockwood, D., & Pottieger, A. E. (1993). *Women and crack cocaine.* New York: Macmillan.

87. Farley, M., & Kelly, V. (2004). Prostitution: A critical review of the medical and social sciences literature. *Women and Criminal Justice, 11,* 29–64.

88. Narag, R. E., & Maxwell, S. R. (2009). Prostitution. In J. M. Miller (Ed.). *21st century criminology* (Vol. 2). Thousand Oaks, CA: Sage, pp. 575–577.

89. Hunter, S. K. (1994). Prostitution is cruelty and abuse to women and children. *Michigan Journal of Gender and Law, 1,* 1–14.

90. Potterat, J. J., Rothenberg, R. B., Muth, S. Q., Darrow, W. W., & Phillips-Plummer, L. (1998). Pathways to prostitution: The chronology of sexual and drug abuse milestones. *Journal of Sex Research, 35,* 333–340.

91. Pettiway, L. E. (1997). *Workin' it: Women living through drugs and crime.* Philadelphia: Temple University Press.

92. Cobbina, J. E., & Oselin, S. S. (2011). It's not only the money: An analysis of adolescent versus adult entry into street prostitution. *Sociological Inquiry, 81,* 3, 310–332; see also Roe-Sipowitz, D. E. (2012). Juvenile entry into prostitution: The role of emotional abuse. *Violence Against Women, 18,* 5, 562–579.

93. Marcus, A., Hornung, A., Curtis, R., Sanson, J., & Thompson, E. (2014). Conflict and agency among sex workers and pimps: A closer look at domestic minor sex trafficking. *The Annals of the American Academy of Political and Social Science, 653,* 225–246.

94. Miller, J., & Schwartz, M. D. (1995). Rape myths and violence against street prostitutes. *Deviant Behavior, 16*, 1–23.

95. Miller, J. (1993). Your life is on the line every night you're on the streets: Victimization and resistance among street prostitutes. *Humanity & Society, 17*, 422–446.

96. Coston, C., & Ross, L. E. (1998). Criminal victimization of prostitutes: Empirical support for the lifestyle/exposure model. *Journal of Crime and Justice, 21*, 53–70.

99. Monto, M. A. (2004). Female prostitution, customers, and violence. *Violence Against Women, 10*, 160–168.

100. Tewksbury, R., & Gagné, P. (2002). Lookin' for love in all the wrong places: Men who patronize prostitutes. In R. M. Holmes & S. T. Holmes (Eds.), *Current perspectives on sex crimes*. Thousand Oaks, CA: Sage, pp. 88–89.

101. Note 88.

102. Brents, B. G., & Hausbeck, K. (2005). Violence and legalized brothel prostitution in Nevada: Examining safety, risk and prostitution policy. *Journal of Interpersonal Violence, 20*, 3, 270–295.

103. Note 100, p. 89.

104. Romero-Daza, N., Weeks, M., & Singer, M. (2005). Conceptualizing the impact of indirect violence on HIV risk among women involved in street-level prostitution. *Aggression and Violent Behavior, 10*, 153–170.

105. McCoy, C. B., Metsch, L. R., & Anwyl, R. S. (1996). Dual epidemics: Crack cocaine and HIV/AIDS. In D. D. Chitwood, J. E. Rivers, & J. A. Inciardi (Eds.), *The American pipe dream: Crack cocaine and the inner city*. New York: Harcourt Brace, p. 95.

106. Note 87.

107. Weitzer, R. (2005, September/October). The growing moral panic over prostitution and sex trafficking. *The Criminologist, 30*, 3.

108. Note 102.

109. Coalition Against Trafficking in Women. Retrieved June 30, 2014, from http://www.catwinternational.org/WhoWeAre/Mission

110. Lucas, A. M. (2005). The work of sex work: Elite prostitutes' vocational orientations and life experiences. *Deviant Behavior, 26*, 513–546.

111. Hubbard, P., & Sanders, T. (2003). Making space for sex work: Female street prostitution and the production of urban space. *International Journal of Urban and Regional Research, 27*, 75–89.

112. Carter, S. P., Carter, S. L., & Dannenberg, A. L. (2003). Zoning out crime and improving community health in Sarasota, Florida: Crime prevention through environmental design. *American Journal of Public Health, 93*, 1442–1445.

113. Scott, M. S. (2006). *Street prostitution—Problem-oriented guides for police series, No. 2* (2nd ed.). Washington, DC: U.S. Department of Justice, Office of Community Oriented Policing Services, p. 4.

114. Note 113, pp. 20–30.

115. Note 82, pp. 550–552.

116. Halter, S. (2010). Factors that influence police conceptualization of girls involved in prostitution in six U.S. cities: Child sexual exploitation victims or delinquents? *Child Maltreatment, 15*(2), 152–160; *see also* Mitchell, K. J., Finkelhor, D., & Wolak, J. (2010). Conceptualizing juvenile prostitution as child maltreatment: Findings from the National Juvenile Prostitution Study. *Child Maltreatment, 15*, 1, 18–36.

117. Saunders, P., & Kirby, J. (2010–2011). Move along: Community-based research into the policing of sex work in Washington, DC, *Social Justice, 37*, 1, 107–127.

118. Shively, M., Kliorys, K., Wheeler, K., & Hunt, D. (2012). *A national overview of prostitution and sex trafficking demand reduction efforts, final report*. Cambridge, MA: Abt Associates.

119. Holt, T. J., Blevins, K. R., & Kuhns, J. B. (2014). Examining diffusion and arrest avoidance practices among johns. *Crime & Delinquency, 60*, 2, 261–283.

120. Shively, M., Jalbert, S. K., Kling, R., Rhoades, W., Finn, P., Flygare, C., et al. (2008). *Final report on the evaluation of the first offender prostitution program: Report summary*. Cambridge, MA: Abt Associates.

Chapter 13

1. Jenkins, B. M. (1980). *The study of terrorism: Definitional problems*. Santa Monica, CA: RAND Corporation.

2. Hoffman, B. (1998). *Inside terrorism*. New York: Columbia University Press.

3. Hacker, F. J. (1976). *Crusaders, criminals, crazies: Terror and terrorism in our time*. New York: W. W. Norton.

4. FBI re Malvo

5. Michel, L., & Herbeck, D. (2001). *American terrorist: Timothy McVeigh and the Oklahoma City bombing*. New York: ReganBooks.

6. Lindsay, H., & Carlson, C. C. (1970). *The late great planet Earth*. Grand Rapids, MI: Zondervan.

7. Beam, L. (1992, February). Leaderless resistance. Retrieved March 23, 2011, from http://www.louisbeam.com/leaderless.htm

8. Combs, C. C. (1997). *Terrorism in the twenty-first century*. Upper Saddle River, NJ: Prentice Hall.

9. Note 8 p. 26.

10. Bailly, N. (2010, March 23). State sponsors: Cuba, Council on Foreign Relations. Retrieved March 18, 2011 from http://www.cfr.org/publication/9359/state_sponsors.html

11. U.S. Department of the Treasury. (2002, November 19). Press room: Treasury designates Benevolence International Foundation and related entities as financiers of terrorism. Retrieved March 18, 2011 from http://www.ustreas.gov/press/releases/po3632.htm

12. Note 11.

13. White, J. R. (2009). *Terrorism and homeland security: An introduction* (6th ed.). Florence, KY: Cengage Learning.

14. Shelley, L. I., & Melzer, S. A. (2008). The nexus of organized crime and terrorism: Two case studies in cigarette smuggling. *International Journal of Comparative and Applied Criminal Justice, 32,* 1, 43–63.

15. Ehrenfeld, R. (1990). *Narco-terrorism.* New York: Basic Books.

16. Peters, G. (2009). *Seeds of terror: How heroin is bankrolling the Taliban and al Qaeda.* New York: Thomas Dunne Books.

17. Martin, G. (2011). *Essentials of terrorism: Concepts and controversies* (2nd ed.). Thousand Oaks, CA: Sage, p. 186.

18. Note 17.

19. Varon, J. (2004). *Bringing the war home: The Weather Underground, the Red Army Faction, and revolutionary violence in the sixties and seventies.* Berkeley, CA: The University of California Press.

20. Note 19.

21. Mayo, M. (2008). *American murder: Criminals, crimes, and the media.* Canton, MI: Visible Ink Press.

22. Note 5.

23. Schwartz, D. (1991). The terrorist threat. *The Police Chief, 63,* 36–37.

24. Putney, R. (1991). Enhancing anti-terrorism skills. *The Police Chief, 63,* 40–42.

25. U.S. Department of Homeland Security. DHS Organization—The DHS Strategic Plan—Securing Our Homeland. Retrieved December 24, 2005, from www.dhs.gov/dhspublic/interapp/editorial/editorial_0413.xml

NEW REFERENCES

Herschinger, E. (2013). A battlefield of meanings: The struggle for identity in the UN debates on a definition of international terrorism. *Terrorism and Political Violence, 25,* 183–201.

Wright, S. (1995). *Armageddon in Waco.* Chicago: The University of Chicago Press.

Chapter 14

1. Gopal, R., Sanders, G. L., Bhattacharjee, S., Agrawal, M., & Wagner, S. (2004). A behavioral model of digital music piracy. *Journal of Organizational Computing and Electronic Commerce, 14,* 89–105.

2. Higgins, G. E., Fell, B. D., & Wilson, A. L. (2006). Digital piracy: Assessing the contributions of an integrated self-control theory and social learning theory. *Criminal Justice Studies, 19,* 3–22.

3. Wall, D. S. (2005). The Internet as a conduit for criminal activity. In A. Pattavina (Ed.), *Information Technology and the Criminal Justice System.* Thousand Oaks, CA: Sage, p. 78–94.

4. Note 3.

5. Note 1.

6. Hinduja, S. Trends and patterns among online software pirates. (2003). *Ethics and Information Technology, 5,* 49–61.

7. Note 2.

8. International Federation of the Phonographic Industry (IFPI). (2006). *The recording industry 2006 piracy report: Protecting creativity in music.* Retrieved on December 7, 2006, from http://www.ifpi.org

9. Motion Picture Association of America (MPAA). (2005). U.S. piracy fact sheet. Retrieved December 10, 2006, from www.mpaa.org/USPiracyFactSheet.pdf

10. Motion Picture Association of America (MPAA). (2004). U.S. piracy fact sheet. Retrieved December 12, 2004, from www.mpaa.org/anti-piracy/content.htm

11. Hinduja, S. (2003). Trends and patterns among online software pirates. *Ethics and Information Technology, 5,* 49–61.

12. Business Software Alliance—Fact Sheet: Higher Education Unlicensed Software Experience—Student and Academics. (2007); see also http://www.bsa.org/country/Research%20and%20Statistics/~/media/F3F0E9C1C2AB4B308D5D6D0E3042A5A7.ashx

13. Note 2.

14. Koen, C. M., & Im, J. H. (1997). Software piracy and its legal implications. *Security Journal, 31,* 265–272.

15. Note 14.

16. Higgins, G. E. (2005). Can low self-control help with the understanding of the software piracy problem. *Deviant Behavior, 26,* 1–24.

17. Note 16.

18. Note 16.

19. Higgins, G. E., & Makin, D. A. (2004). Does social learning theory condition the effects of low self-control on college students' software piracy? *Journal of Economic Crime Management, 2,* 1–22. Retrieved March 5, 2007, from www.jecm.org

20. Note 2.

21. Skinner, W. F., & Fream, A. M. (1997). A social learning theory analysis of computer crime among college students. *Journal of Research in Crime and Delinquency, 34,* 495–518.

22. Note 19.

23. Note 2.

24. Burruss, G. W., Bossler, A. M., & Holt, T. J. (2012). Assessing the mediation of a fuller social learning model on low self-control's influence on software piracy. *Crime and Delinquency, 58,* 798–822.

25. Higgins, G. E., Wilson, A. L., & Fell, B. D. (2005). An application of deterrence theory to software piracy. *Journal of Criminal Justice and Popular Culture, 12,* 166–194.

26. Ybarra, M. L., & Mitchell, K. J. (2005). Exposure to Internet pornography among children and adolescents: A national survey. *Cyberpsychology & Behavior, 8,* 473–486.

27. Fallows, D. (2005). Part 5. Functions of the Internet: How men and women use it as a tool to communicate, transact, get information, and entertain themselves. Pew Research Center. Retrieved September 3, 2105, from http://webcache. googleusercontent.com/search?q=cache:gcAF-NCB9KoJ:www.pewinternet.org/2005/12/28/part-5-functions-of-the-internet-how-men-and-women-use-it-as-a-tool-to-communicate-transact-get-information-and-entertain-themselves/+&cd=2&hl=en&ct=clnk&gl=us

28. Stack, S., Wasserman, I., & Kern, R. (2004). Adult social bonds and use of Internet pornography. *Social Science Quarterly, 85,* 75–88.

29. Buzell, T. (2005). Demographic characteristics of persons using pornography in three technological contexts. *Sexuality and Culture, 9,* 28–48.

30. Cohen-Almagor, R. (2013). Online child sex offenders: Challenges and counter measures. *The Howard Journal of Criminal Justice, 52,* 190–215.

31. Marcum, C. D., Higgins, G. E., Frieburger, T., & Ricketts, M. L. (2010). Policing possession of child pornography online: Investigating the training and resources dedicated to the investigation of cyber crime. *International Journal of Police Science and Management, 12,* 516–525.

32. Bellah, J. (2001). Training: Identity theft. *Law & Order, 49,* 10, 222–226.

33. Identity theft. (2004, December 15). Confusion between fraud, identity theft frustrates Industry. *LRP Publications, 8,* 12.

34. http://www.consumer.ftc.gov/features/feature-0014-identity-theft

35. Higgins, G. E., Hughes, T., Ricketts, M. L., & Fell, B. D. (2005). Student perception and understanding identity theft: "We're just dancing in the dark." *Law Enforcement Executive Forum, 5,* 5, 163–178.

36. 18 U.S.C. § 1028A.

37. As enumerated in section 2332b(g)(5)(B).

38. The Fair Debt Collection Practices Act focuses on debt collectors' practices.

39. 15 U.S.C. § 1681 to 1681u.

40. 15 U.S.C. 1666i.

41. 15 U.S.C. 41, 1693.

42. Federal Trade Commission. (2007). *National and state trends in fraud & identity theft: January–December 2005.* Retrieved September 13, 2007, from http://www.consumer.gov/idtheft/stats.html

43. Krebs, B. (2007). TransUnion to offer credit freeze in all U.S. states. Washintonpost.com. Retrieved November 2, 2007, from http://blog.washingtonpost.com/securityfix/2007/09/transunion_to_offers_credit_fr.html

44. Schneier, B. (2006). The anti-ID-theft bill that isn't. Retrieved November 1, 2007, from http://www.wired.com/politics/security/commentary/securitymatters/2006/04/70690

45. Allison, S. F. H., Schuck, A. M., & Lersch, K. M. (2005). Exploring the crime of identity theft: Prevalence, clearance rates, and victim/offender characteristics. *Journal of Criminal Justice, 3,* 1, 19–29.

46. Weingart, J. (2003). *Identity theft* (Northeast ed.) Mountainside, NJ: The Metropolitan Corporate Counsel.

47. Federal Trade Commission. (2006). *National and state trends in fraud & identity theft: January–December 2005.* Retrieved June 6, 2007, from http://www.consumer.gov/idtheft/stats.html

48. Federal Trade Commission. (2007). *National and state trends in fraud & identity theft: January–December 2005.* Retrieved September 13, 2007, from http://www.consumer.gov/idtheft/stats.html

49. Higgins, G. E. (2010). *Cybercrime: An introduction to an emerging phenomenon.* New York: McGraw-Hill Companies.

50. Holt, T. J., & Bossler, A. M. (2014). An assessment of the current state of cybercrime scholarship. *Deviant Behavior, 35,* 20–40.

51. Holt, T. J. (2009). The attack dynamics of political and religiously motivated hackers. Proceedings of the Cyber Infrastrucutre Protection Conference, City University of New York.

52. Holt, T. J., & Kilger, M. (2008). Techcrafters and makecrafters: A comparison of two populations of hackers. *WOMBAT Workshop on Information Security Threats Data Collection and Sharing,* 67–78.

53. Note 47.

54. Holt, T. J., & Kilger, M. (2012). Examining willingness to attach critical infrastructure on and off-line. Crime and Delinquency, *58,* 798–822.

55. Marcum, C. D., Higgins, G. E., Ricketts, M. L., & Wolfe, S. (2014). Hacking in High School: Cybercrime Perpetration by Juveniles. Deviant Behavior: An Interdisciplinary Journal, *35,* 581–591.

56. Hinduja, S., & Patchin, J. (2008). Cyberbullying: An exploratory analysis of factors related to offending and victimization. *Deviant Behavior, 29,* 1–29.

57. Ajzen, I. (1991). The theory of planned behavior. *Organizational Behavior and Human Decision Processes, 50*, 179–211.

58. Note 56.

59. Wolak, J., Mitchell, K. J., & Finkelhor, D. (2007). Does online harassment constitute bullying? An exploration of online harassment by known peers and online only contacts. *Journal of Adolescent Health, 41* (6,Suppl), S51–S58. PMID: 18047945 [CV172].

60. Note 56.

Chapter 15

1. Boyum, D. A., & Kleiman, M. A. R. (2004). Substance abuse policy from a crime control perspective. In J. Q. Wilson & J. Petersilia (Eds.), *Crime: Public policies for crime control*. Oakland, CA: ICS Press, p. 331.

2. Dupont, R. L. (1997). *The selfish brain: Learning from addiction*. Hazelden Center City, MN: The American Psychiatric Press.

3. Kuhn, C., Swartzwelder, S., & Wilson, W. (2003). *Buzzed: The straight facts about the most used and abused drugs from alcohol to ecstasy*. New York: The Hadden Craftsmen.

4. Note 3.

5. Lowinson, J. H., Ruiz, P., Millman, R. P., & Langrod, J. G. (1997). *Substance abuse: A comprehensive textbook*. Philadelphia: Lippincott Williams & Wilkins.

6. Laing, R., & Siegal, J. (2003). *Hallucinogens: A forensic drug handbook*. San Diego, CA: Academic Press.

7. Foner, E., & Garraty, J. A. (1991). *The reader's companion to American history*. New York: Houghton Mifflin Books.

8. Inciardi, J. A. (2008). *The war on drugs IV*. Boston: Allyn & Bacon.

9. Gallup. Illegal Drugs. Retrieved July 5, 2014, from http://www.gallup.com/poll/1657/illegal-drugs.aspx

10. Substance Abuse and Mental Health Services Administration. (2013). *Results from the 2012 national survey on drug use and health: Summary of national findings*, NSDUH Series H-46, HHS Publication No. (SMA) 13-4795. Rockville, MD: Substance Abuse and Mental Health Services Administration.

11. Jager, J., Schulenberg, J. E., O'Malley, P. M., & Bachman, J. G. (2013). Historical associations across drug use trajectories across the transition to adulthood: The trend toward lower intercepts and steeper, ascending slopes. *Development and Psychopathology, 25*, 527–543.

12. Johnston, L. D., O'Malley, P. M., Miech, R. A., Bachman, J. G., & Schulenberg, J. E. (2014). *Monitoring the future—national results on drug use: 1975–2013: Overview, key findings on adolescent drug use*. Ann Arbor, MI: Institute for Social Research, The University of Michigan.

13. Oesterle, S., Hawkins, J. D., Steketee, M., Jonkman, H., Brown, E. C., Moll, M., & Haggerty, K. P. (2012). A cross-national comparison of risk and protective factors for adolescent drug use and delinquency in the United States and Netherlands. *Journal of Drug Issues, 42*, 4, 337–357.

14. Fagan, A. A., VanHorn, M. L., Hawkins, J. D., & Jaki, T. (2013). Differential effects of parental controls on adolescent substance abuse: For whom is family most important? *Journal of Quantitative Criminology, 29*, 347–368.

15. Howard, M. O. (2011). Characteristics of abstainers from substance abuse and anti-social behavior in the United States. *Journal of Criminal Justice, 39*, 212–217.

16. Van Dorn, R., Volavka, J., & Johnson, N. (2012). Mental disorder and violence: Is there a relationship beyond substance abuse? *Social Psychiatry & Psychiatric Epidemiology, 47*, 487–503.

17. Kandall, S. R. (2010). Women and drug addiction: A historical perspective. *Journal of Addictive Diseases. 29*, 2, 117–126.

18. Vaughn, M. G., Salas-Wright, C. P., DeLisi, M., & Piquero, A. R. (2014). Health associations of drug-involved and criminal-justice involved adults in the United States. *Criminal Justice & Behavior, 41*, 3, 318–336.

19. Note 8, p. 303.

20. Bureau of Justice and Statistics. (1992). *Crime and the Justice System*. Washington, DC: U.S. Department of Justice, Office of Justice Programs.

21. MacCourt, R. J., & Martin, K. D. (2009). Drugs. In M. Tonry (Ed.), *The Oxford handbook of crime and public policy*. New York: Oxford University Press, p. 504.

22. NORML. States that have decriminalized. Retrieved July 5, 2014, from http://norml.org/aboutmarijuana/item/states-that-have-decriminalized

23. Mazerolle, P. (2000). Understanding illicit drug use: Lessons from developmental theory. In S. Simpson (Ed.), *Of crime and criminality*. Thousand Oaks, CA: Pine Forge Press, p. 186.

24. Note 23, p. 188.

25. Gentry, C. S. (1991). Drugs and crime. In J. F. Sheley (Ed.), *Criminology: A contemporary handbook*. Belmont, CA: Wadsworth, pp. 423–440.

26. White, H. R. (1990). The drug-use delinquency connection in adolescence. In R. Weisheit (Ed.), *Drugs, crime and the criminal justice system*. Cincinnati, OH: Anderson, pp. 215–256.

27. Note 1, p. 336.

28. McBride, D. C., & McCoy, C. B. (2003). The drugs-crime relationship: An analytical framework. In L. K. Gaines & P. B. Kraska (Eds.), *Drugs, crime &*

justice. Prospect Heights, IL: Waveland Press, pp. 109–110.

29. Deitch, D., Koutsenok, I., & Ruiz, A. (2000). The relationship between crime and drugs: What we have learned in recent decades. *Journal of Psychoactive Drugs, 32*, 391–397.

30. Gropper, B. A. (1985). *Probing the link between drugs and crime*. Washington, DC: National Institute of Justice.

31. Nurco, D. N., Hanlon, T. E., Balter, M. B., Kinlock, T. W., & Slaght, E. (1991). A classification of narcotic addicts based on the type, amount and severity of crime. *Journal of Drug Issues, 21*, 440.

32. Note 8, pp. 202–205.

33. Speckhart, G., & Anglin, M. D. (1985). Narcotics and crime: An analysis of existing evidence for a causal relationship. *Behavioral Science and the Law, 3*, 259–282.

34. The National Center on Addiction and Substance Abuse at Columbia University. (2010). *Behind bars II: Substance abuse and America's prison population*. New York: Columbia University, p. iii.

35. Wish, E. D., & Johnson, B. D. (1986). Impact of substance abuse on criminal careers. In A. Blumstein, J. Cohen, J. A. Cohen, & C. A. Visher (Eds.), *Criminal careers and career criminals* (Vol. 2). Washington, DC: National Academy Press, pp. 52–88.

36. Collins, J. J. (1986). Relationship of problem drinking to individual offending sequences. In A. Blumstein, J. Cohen, J. A. Cohen, & C. A. Visher (Eds.), *Criminal careers and career criminals* (Vol. 2). Washington, DC: National Academy Press, pp. 89–120.

37. Anglin, M. D., & Speckart, G. (1988). Narcotics use and crime: A multisample, multimethod analysis. *Criminology, 26*, 197–231.

38. Note 1, p. 334.

39. Farabee, D., Joshi, V., & Anglin, M. D. (2001). Addiction careers and criminal specialization. *Crime and Delinquency, 47*, 196–220.

40. Kacanek, D., & Hemenway, D. (2006). Gun carrying and drug selling among young incarcerated men and women. *Journal of Urban Health, 83*, 266–274.

41. Vaughn, M. G., DeLisi, M., Gunter, T., Fu, Q., Beaver, K. M., Perron, B. E., et al. (2011). The severe 5%: A latent class analysis of the externalizing behavior spectrum in the United States. *Journal of Criminal Justice, 39*, 75–80.

42. Nurco, D. N., Ball, J. C., Shaffer, J. W., & Hanlon, T. E. (1985). The criminality of narcotic addicts. *Journal of Nervous and Mental Disease, 173*, 94–102.

43. Shaffer, J. W., Nurco, D. N., Ball, J. C., & Kinlock, T. W. (1985). The frequency of nonnarcotic drug use and its relationship to criminal activity among narcotic addicts. *Comprehensive Psychiatry, 26*, 558–566.

44. Speckart, G., & Anglin, M. D. (1986). Narcotic use and crime: An overview of recent research evidence. *Contemporary Drug Problems, 13*, 741–769.

45. Ball, J. C., Rosen, L., Flueck, J. A., & Nurco, D. N. (1982). Lifetime criminality of heroin addicts in the United States. *Journal of Drug Issues, 21*, 225–239.

46. Ball, J. C. (1991). The similarity of crime rates among male heroin addicts in New York City, Philadelphia, and Baltimore. *Journal of Drug Issues, 21*, 413–427.

47. Hser, Y-I., Huang, D., Brecht, M-L., Li, L., & Evans, E. (2008). Contrasting trajectories of heroin, cocaine, and methamphetamine use. *Journal of Addictive Diseases, 27, 3*, 13–21.

48. Gordon, M. S., Kinlock, T. W., Schwartz, R. P., Couvillon, K. A., & O'Grady, K. E. (2013). The severity, frequency, and variety of crime in heroin-dependent prisoners enrolled in a buprenorphine clinical trial. *The Prison Journal, 93, 4*, 390–410.

49. Faupel, C. E. (1987). Heroin use and criminal careers. *Qualitative Sociology, 10*, 115–131.

50. Faupel, C. E., & Klockars, C. B. (1987). Drugs–crime connections: Elaborations from the life histories of hard-core heroin addicts. *Social Problems, 34*, 54–68.

51. Johnson, B., Wish, E. D., & Anderson, K. (1988). A day in the life of 105 drug addicts and abusers: Crime committed and how the money was spent. *Sociology and Social Research, 72*, 185–191.

52. Note 8, p. 292.

53. Note 8, pp. 293–294.

54. Chaiken, J. M., & Chaiken, M. R. (1990). Drugs and predatory crime. In M. Tonry & N. Morris (Eds.), *Drugs and crime*. Chicago: University of Chicago Press, pp. 203–240.

55. Office of National Drug Control Policy. (2013). *ADAM II: 2012 annual report—Arrestee drug abuse monitoring program*. Washington, DC: Executive Office of the President, p. viii.

56. National Institutes of Health. (2010). *Fact sheet: Addiction and the criminal justice system*. Washington, DC.

57. Bennett, T., Holloway, K., & Farrington, D. (2008). The statistical association between drug misuse and crime: A meta-analysis. *Aggression & Violent Behavior, 13*, 107–118.

58. French, M. T., McGerry, K. A., Chitwood, D. D., McCoy, C. B., Inciardi, J. A., & McBride, D. (2000). Chronic drug use and crime. *Substance Abuse, 21*, 95–109.

59. Goldstein, P. J. (1985). The drugs/violence nexus: A tripartite conceptual framework. *Journal of Drug Issues, 15*, 493–506.

60. Goldstein, P. J., Bellucci, P. A., Spunt, B. J., & Miller, T. (1991). Volume of cocaine use and violence: A comparison between men and women. *Journal of Drug Issues, 21*, 345–367.

61. Brownstein, H. H., & Goldstein, P. J. (1990). A typology of drug-related homicides. In R. Weisheit

(Ed.), *Drugs, crime and the criminal justice system.* Cincinnati, OH: Anderson, pp. 171–192.

62. Collins, D. J., & Lapsley, H. M. (2008). *The costs of tobacco, alcohol, and illicit drug abuse to Australian society in 2004/05.* Commonwealth of Australia, p. 41.

63. Note 8, pp. 203–204.

64. Note 8, p. 209.

65. McBride, D. C., & Swartz, J. A. (1990). Drugs and violence in the age of crack cocaine. In R. Weisheit (Ed.), *Drugs, crime and the criminal justice system.* Cincinnati, OH: Anderson, p. 153.

66. Bennett, T., & Holloway, K. (2009). The causal connection between drug misuse and crime. *British Journal of Criminology, 49,* 513–531.

67. Erickson, P. G., Macdonald, S., & Hathaway, A. D. (2009). Profiling violent incidents in a drug treatment sample: A tripartite model approach. *Journal of Drug Issues, 39,* 741–758.

68. Seffrin, P. M., & Domahidi, B. I. (2014). The drug-violence nexus: A systematic comparison of adolescent drug dealers and drug users. *Journal of Drug Issues,* 1–20. Retrieved July 7, 2014, from http://jod.sagepub.com/content/early/2014/03/18/0022042614526994

69. Copes, H., Hochstetler, A., & Sandberg, S. (2015). Using a narrative framework to understand the drugs and violence nexus. *Criminal Justice Review, 40,* 32–46.

70. Jacques, S., & Allen, A. (2015). Drug market violence: Virtual anarchy, police pressure, predation, and retaliation. *Criminal Justice Review, 40,* 87–99.

71. Mumola, C. J., & Karberg, J. C. (2006). *Drug use and dependence, state and federal prisoners, 2004.* Washington, DC: Bureau of Justice Statistics, p. 3.

72. Vito, G. F., & Tewksbury, R. (2000). Gender comparisons in drug testing probationers and parolees. *Corrections Compendium, 25,* 5.

73. Lockwood, D., McCorkel, J., & Inciardi, J. A. (1998). Developing comprehensive prison-based therapeutic community treatment for women. *Drugs and Society, 13,* 193–212.

74. Marquart, J. W., Brewer, V. E., Mullings, J., et al. (1999). The implications of crime control policy on HIV/AIDS-related risk among women prisoners. *Crime and Delinquency, 45,* 82–98.

75. Anglin, M. D., & Hser, Y-I. (1987). Addicted women and crime. *Criminology, 25,* 359–397.

76. Sanchez, J. E., & Johnson, B. D. (1987). Women and the drugs–crime connection: Crime rates among drug-abusing women at Rikers Island. *Journal of Psychoactive Drugs, 1,* 205–214.

77. Inciardi, J. A., & Pottieger, A. E. (1991). Kids, crack, and crime. *Journal of Drug Issues, 21,* 257–270.

78. Inciardi, J. A., Pottieger, A. E., & Faupel, C. E. (1982). Black women, heroin and crime: Some empirical notes. *Journal of Drug Issues, 12,* 241–250.

79. Inciardi, J. A., & Surratt, H. L. (2001). Drug use, street crime, and sex-trading among cocaine dependent women: Implications for public health and criminal justice policy. *Journal of Psychoactive Drugs, 33,* 379–388.

80. McCoy, H. V., Inciardi, J. A., Metsch, L. R., et al. (1995). Women, crack, and crime: Gender comparisons of criminal activity among "crack" cocaine users. *Contemporary Drug Problems, 22,* 435–451.

81. Braun, K. M., & Roe-Sepowitz, D. (2008). Female juvenile prostitutes: Exploring the relationship to substance abuse. *Children and Youth Services Review, 30,* 1395–1402.

82. Pettiway, L. E. (1987). Participation in crime partnerships by female drug users: The effects of domestic arrangements, drug use, and criminal involvement. *Criminology, 25,* 741–766.

83. Bowles, M. A., DeHart, D., & Webb, J. R. (2012). Family influences on female offender's substance abuse: The role of adverse childhood events among incarcerated women. *Journal of Family Violence, 27,* 681–686.

84. Fazel, S., Bains, P., & Doll, H. (2006). Substance abuse and dependence in prisoners: A systematic review. *Addiction, 101,* 2, 181–191.

85. Langan, N. P., & Pelissier, B. M. (2001). Gender differences among prisoners in drug treatment. *Journal of Substance Abuse, 13,* 3, 291–301.

86. Proctor, S. L. (2012). Substance use disorder prevalence among female state prison inmates. *The American Journal of Drug and Alcohol Abuse, 38,* 4, 278–285.

87. Houser, K. A., Belenko, S., & Brennan, P. K. (2012). The effects of mental health and substance abuse disorders on institutional misconduct among female inmates. *Justice Quarterly, 29,* 6, 799–828.

88. Jackson, D. O., Cropsey, K. L., Weaver, M. F., Villalobos, G. C., Eldridge, G., & Stitzer, M. L. (2010). Factors related to injection drug use among female prisoners. *Substance use & misuse, 45,* 3, 368–383.

89. Chaiken, M. R., & Johnson, B. D. (1988). *Characteristics of different types of drug-involved offenders.* Washington, DC: National Institute of Justice.

90. Dembo, R. Washburn, M., Wish, E., et al. (1987). Heavy marijuana use and crime among youths entering a juvenile detention center. *Journal of Psychoactive Drugs, 19,* 47–56.

91. Dembo, R., Washburn, M., Wish, E., et al. (1987). Further examination of the association between heavy marijuana use and crime among youths entering a juvenile detention center. *Journal of Psychoactive Drugs, 19,* 361–373.

92. Johnson, B. D., Wish, E. D., Schmeidler, J., & Huzinga, D. (1991). Concentration of delinquent

offending: Serious drug involvement and high delinquency rates. *Journal of Drug Issues, 21,* 229.

93. White, H. R., Tice, P. C., Loeber, R., et al. (2002). Illegal acts committed by adolescents under the influence of alcohol and drugs. *Journal of Research in Crime and Delinquency, 39,* 131–152.

94. Lowry, R., Cohen, L. R., Modzeleski, W., et al. (1999). School violence, substance use, and the availability of illegal drugs on school property among U.S. high school students. *Journal of School Health, 69,* 347–355.

95. Huizinga, D. H., Menard, S., & Elliott, D. S. (1988). Delinquency and drug use: Temporal and developmental patterns. *Justice Quarterly, 6,* 419–455.

96. White, H., Johnson, V., & Garrison, C. (1985). The drug–crime nexus among adolescents and their peers. *Deviant Behavior, 6,* 183–204.

97. Thornton, W. E. (1981). Marijuana use and delinquency: A reexamination. *Youth and Society, 13,* 23–37.

98. D'Amico, E. J., Edelen, M. O., Miles, J. N. V., & Morral, A. R. (2008). The longitudinal association between substance use and delinquency among high-risk youth. *Drug and Alcohol Dependence, 93,* 85–92.

99. Doherty, E. E., Green, K. M., & Ensminger, M. E. (2008). Investigating the long-term influence of adolescent delinquency on drug use initiation. *Drug and Alcohol Dependence, 93,* 72–84.

100. Green, K. M., Doherty, E. E., Stuart, E. A., & Ensminger, M. E. (2010). Does heavy marijuana use lead to criminal involvement in adulthood? Evidence from a multiwave longitudinal study of urban African Americans. *Drug and Alcohol Dependence, 112,* 117–125.

101. Dembo, R., Williams, L., LaVoie, L., et al. (1989). Physical abuse, sexual victimization, and illicit drug use. *Violence and Victims, 4,* 121–138.

102. Rees, C. D., & Wilborn, B. L. (1983). Correlates of drug abuse in adolescents: A comparison of families of drug abusers with families of nondrug abusers. *Journal of Youth and Adolescence, 12,* 55–63.

103. Fagan, J. (1989). The social organization of drug use and drug dealing among urban gangs. *Criminology, 27,* 633–669.

104. Decker, S. H., & Van Winkle, B. (1994). "Slinging dope": The role of gangs and gang members in drug sales. *Justice Quarterly, 11,* 583–604.

105. Esbensen, F. A., & Huizinga, D. (1993). Gangs, drugs, and delinquency in a survey of urban youth. *Criminology, 31,* 565–589.

106. Valdez, A., & Sifaneck, S. J. (2004). Getting high and getting by: Dimensions of drug selling behavior among Mexican gang members in Southern Texas. *Journal of Research in Crime and Delinquency, 41,* 82–105.

107. Turley, A. C. (2003). Female gangs and patterns of female delinquency in Texas. *Journal of Gang Research, 10,* 1–12.

108. Note 78.

109. Note 26, p. 240.

110. U.S. Drug Enforcement Administration. *Drug schedules.* Retrieved July 10, 2014, from http://www.justice.gov/dea/druginfo/ds.shtml

111. Drug Enforcement Administration. (2013). *2013 national drug threat assessment summary.* Washington, DC: U.S. Department of Justice.

112. Golub, A., & Brownstein, H. H. (2013). Drug generations in the 2000s: An analysis of arrestee data. *Journal of Drug Issues, 43,* 3, 335–356.

113. Kelley, B. C., Wells, B. E., LeClair, A., Tracy, D., Parsons, J. T., & Golub, S. A. (2013). Prevalence and correlates of prescription drug misuse among socially active young adults. *Journal of Drug Issues, 24,* 297–303.

114. ONDCP drug policy clearinghouse fact sheet. (2003). *Methamphetamine.* Washington, DC: Executive Office of the President, Office on National Drug Control Policy, p. 1.

115. Office of National Drug Control Policy. (2005, July 6). Drug facts—*Methamphetamine.* Retrieved July 6, 2005, from http://www.whitehousedrugpolicy.gov/drugfact/methamphetamine/index.html

116. Note 10, p. 59.

117. Note 71.

118. National Institute of Drug Abuse, *Methamphetamine.* Retrieved July 16, 2014, from http://www.drugabuse.gov/publications/research-reports/methamphetamine/what-scope-methamphetamine-abuse-in-united-states

119. Embry, D., Hankins, M., Biglan, A., & Boles, S. (2009). Behavioral and social correlates of methamphetamine use in a population-based sample of early and later adolescents. *Addictive Behaviors, 34,* 343–351.

120. Roussell, A., Holmes, M. D., & Anderson-Sprecher, R. (2009). Community characteristics and methamphetamine use in a rural state: Preincarceration usage by prison inmates. *Crime & Delinquency, 59,* 7, 1036–1063.

121. Weisheit, R. A., & Wells, L. E. (2010). Methamphetamine laboratories: The geography of drug production. *Western Criminology Review, 11,* 2, 9–26.

122. Note 118.

123. Lineberry, T. W., & Bostwick, J. M. (2006). Methamphetamine abuse: A perfect storm of complications. *Mayo Clinic Proceedings, 81,* 77.

124. Swanson, S. M., Sise, C. B., Sise, M. J., Sack, D. I., Holbrook, T. L., & Paci, G. M. (2007). The scourge of methamphetamine: Impact on a level I trauma

center. *Journal of Trauma-Injury Infection & Critical Care, 63,* 3, 531–537.

125. Nicosia, P., Pacula, R. L., Kilmer, B., Lundberg, R., & Chiesa, J. (2009). *The economic cost of methamphetamine use in the United States, 2005.* Santa Monica, CA: Rand Corporation.

126. Brecht, M-L., & Herbeck, D. M. (2013). Methamphetamine use and violent behavior: User perceptions and behaviors. *Journal of Drug Issues, 43,* 4, 468–482.

127. Weisheit, R. A. (2008). Making methamphetamine. *Southern Rural Sociology, 23,* 88.

128. Hunt, D. E. (2006). Methamphetamine abuse: Challenges for law enforcement and communities. *NIJ Journal, 254,* 1–5.

129. Martyny, J. W., Arbuckle, S. L., McCammon, Jr., C. S., Esswein, E. J., Erb, N., & Van Dyke, M. (2007, July/August). Chemical concentrations and contamination associated with clandestine methamphetamine laboratories. *Journal of Chemical Health & Safety,* 40–52.

130. Shukla, R. K., Crump, J. L., & Chrisco, E. S. (2012). An evolving problem: Methamphetamine production and trafficking in the United States. *International Journal of Drug Policy, 23,* 426–435.

131. Cunningham, J. K., Callaghan, R. C., Tong, D., Liu, L-M., & Li, Y-L. (2012). Changing over-the-counter ephedrine and pseudoephedrine products to prescription only: Impacts on methamphetamine clandestine laboratory seizures. *Drug and Alcohol Dependence, 126,* 55–64.

132. Hubbard, R. L., Marsden, M. E., Valley Rachal, J., Hartwood, H. J., Cavanaugh, E. R., & Ginzburg, H. (1989). *Drug abuse treatment: A national study of effectiveness.* Chapel Hill: University of North Carolina Press.

133. Gendreau, P., & Ross, R. R. (1987). Revivification of rehabilitation: Evidence from the 1980s. *Justice Quarterly, 4,* 385.

134. Anglin, M. D., & Hser, Y-I. (1990). Treatment of drug abuse. In M. Tonry & N. Morris (Eds.), *Drugs and crime.* Chicago: University of Chicago Press, p. 439.

135. Note 1, p. 368.

136. Hunt, D. E., Lipton, D. S., & Spunt, B. (1984). Patterns of criminal activity among methadone clients and current narcotics users not in treatment. *Journal of Drug Issues, 14,* 687–702.

137. Vito, G. F. (1989). The Kentucky substance abuse program: A private program to treat probationers and parolees. *Federal Probation, 53,* 65–72.

138. French, M. T., Hubbard, R. L., & Valley Rachal, J. (1993). The effects of time in drug abuse treatment and employment on post-treatment drug use and criminal activity. *American Journal of Drug and Alcohol Abuse, 19,* 19–33.

139. Prendergast, M. L., Pearson, F. S., Podus, D., Hamilton, Z. K., & Greenwell, L. (2013). The Andrews' principle of risk, needs, responsivity as applied in drug treatment programs: Meta-analysis of crime and drug use outcomes. *Journal of Quantitative Criminology, 9,* 275–300.

140. Bahr, S. J., Masters, A. L., & Taylor, B. M. (2012). What works in substance abuse treatment programs for offenders? *The Prison Journal,* http://tpj.sagepub.com/content/early/2012/03/05/0032885512438836

141. Vito, G. F., & Tewksbury, R. (1998). The impact of treatment: The Jefferson County (Kentucky) substance abuse program. *Federal Probation, 62,* 46–51; Sanford, J. S., & Arrigo, B. A. (2005). Lifting the cover on drug courts: Evaluation findings and policy concerns. *International Journal of Offender Therapy and Comparative Criminology, 49,* 239–259; Shaffer, D. K. (2011). Looking inside the black box of drug courts: A meta-analytic review. *Justice Quarterly, 28,* 3, 493–521.

142. Taxman, F. S. (1999). Unraveling "what works" for offenders in substance abuse services. *National Drug Court Institute Review, 2,* 93–134.

143. Nielsen, A. L., Scarpitti, F. R., Inciardi, J. A. et al. (1996). Integrating the therapeutic community and work release for drug-involved offenders. *Journal of Substance Abuse Treatment, 13,* 349–358.

144. Dynia, P., & Sung, H. E. (2000). The safety and effectiveness of diverting felony drug offenders to residential treatment as measured by recidivism. *Criminal Justice Policy Review, 11,* 299–311.

145. Welch, W. N., & Zajac, G. (2013). A multi-site evaluation of prison-based drug treatment: Four-year follow-up results. *The Prison Journal, 93,* 3, 251–271.

146. Renfiglio, A. F., & Stemen, D. (2009). The impact of drug treatment on recidivism: Do mandatory programs make a difference? Evidence from Kansas bill 123. *Crime & Delinquency, 59,* 6, 930–950.

147. McVay, D., Schiraldi, V., & Ziedenberg, J. (2004). *Treatment or incarceration? National and state findings on the efficacy and cost savings of drug treatment versus imprisonment.* Washington, DC: Justice Policy Institute; McCollister, K. E., French, M. T., Inciardi, J. A., et al. (2003). Post-release substance abuse treatment for criminal offenders: A cost-effectiveness analysis. *Journal of Quantitative Criminology, 19,* 389–407.

148. United Nations Office for Drug Control and Crime Prevention. (2011). *Estimating illicit financial flows resulting from drug trafficking and other transnational organized crimes.* Vienna: UNODCCP, p. 7.

149. Fries, A., Anthony, R. W., Cseko, A., Gaither, C. G., & Schulman, E. (2008). *The price and purity of illegal drugs, 1981–2007.* Washington, DC: Office of

National Drug Control Policy & Institute for Defense Analysis, pp. 9–11.

150. Kilmer, B., Everingham, S., Caulkins, J., Midgette, G., Pacula, R., Reuter, P., et al. (2014). *What America's users spend on illegal drugs: 2000–2010.* Santa Monica, CA: The Rand Corporation, p. 3.

151. Office of National Drug Control Policy. *How illicit drug use affects business and the economy.* Retrieved July 17, 2014, from http://www.whitehouse.gov/ondcp/ondcp-fact-sheets/how-illicit-drug-use-affects-business-and-the-economy

152. Federal Bureau of Investigation. *Crime in the United States—2012.* Washington, DC: U.S. Department of Justice. Retrieved July 17, 2014, from http://www.fbi.gov/about-us/cjis/ucr/crime-in-the-u.s/2010/crime-in-the-u.s.-2010/persons-arrested

153. Carson, A. E., & Golinelli, D. (2013). *Prisoners in 2012: Trends in admissions and releases, 1991–2012.* Washington, DC: Bureau of Justice Statistics, p. 2.

154. National Drug Intelligence Center. (2011). *The economic impact of illicit drug use on American society.* Washington DC: United States Department of Justice, p. ix.

155. Collins, J. J., Hubbard, R. L., & Valley Rachal, J. (1985). Expensive drug use and illegal income for narcotic addicts. *Criminology, 23,* 743–764.

156. Nurco, D. N., Cisin, I. H., & Ball, J. C. (1985). Crime as a source of income for narcotic addicts. *Journal of Substance Abuse Treatment, 2,* 113–114.

157. Faupel, C. E. (1988). Heroin use, crime, and employment status. *Journal of Drug Issues, 18,* 467–479.

158. Marel, C., Mills, K. L., Darke, S., Ross, J., Slade, T., Burns, L., et al. (2013). Static and dynamic predictors of criminal involvement among people with heroin dependence: Findings from a 3-year study. *Drug and Alcohol Dependence, 133,* 600–606.

159. Thoumi, F. E. (2002). Illegal drugs in Columbia: From illegal economic boom to social crisis. *The Annals of the American Academy of Political and Social Science, 582,* 102–114.

160. Morris, N., & Hawkins, G. (1969). *The honest politician's guide to crime control.* Chicago: University of Chicago Press, pp. 5–6.

161. Note 160.

162. Schiraldi, V., Holman, B., & Beatty, P. (2000). *Poor prescription: The costs of imprisoning drug offenders in the United States.* Washington, DC: Justice Policy Institute, p. 4.

163. Weisheit, R. (1990). Challenging the criminalizers. *The Criminologist, 15,* 1, 3–5.

164. Kraska, P. B. (1990). The unmentionable alternative: The need for, and the argument against, the decriminalization of drug laws. In R. Weisheit (Ed.), *Drugs, crime and the criminal justice system.* Cincinnati, OH: Anderson, pp. 118–126.

165. Trebach, A. S. (1989). Tough choices: The practical politics of drug policy reform. *American Behavioral Scientist, 32,* 249–258.

166. Note 165, p. 257.

167. Bennett, W. (1990, March). Should drugs be legalized? *Reader's Digest,* 90–96.

168. Wilson, J. Q. (1990). Drugs and crime. In M. Tonry & J. Q. Wilson (Eds.), *Drugs and crime: Crime and justice* (Vol. 13). Chicago: University of Chicago Press, p. 527.

169. Miron, J. A. (2001). The economics of drug prohibition and drug legalization. *Social Research, 68,* 835–855.

170. Inciardi, J. A., & McBride, D. C. (1989). Legalization: A high-risk alternative in the war of drugs. *American Behavioral Scientist, 32,* 261–262.

171. Liska, K. (2000). *Drugs and the human body with implications for society.* Upper Saddle River, NJ: Prentice Hall, p. 49.

172. Note 8, pp. 279–281.

173. Note 8, p. 288.

174. Note 8, p. 289.

175. Weisheit, R. (1990). Declaring a "civil" war on drugs. In R. Weisheit (Ed.), *Drugs, crime and the criminal justice system.* Cincinnati, OH: Anderson, pp. 1–10.

176. Note 164, p. 126.

177. Trebach, A. (2005). *The great drug war: And rational proposals to turn the tide.* Bloomington, IN: Unlimited Publishing.

178. Musto, D. F. (2003). The American experience with stimulants and opiates. In L. K. Gaines & P. B. Kraska (Eds.), *Drugs, crime and justice.* Prospect Heights, IL: Waveland Press, pp. 43–44.

179. Weisheit, R. A. (2009). Drugs and the criminal justice system. In J. M. Miller (Ed.), *21st century criminology: A reference handbook* (Vol. 2). Thousand Oaks, CA: Sage, p. 673.

180. Kleiman, M. A. R., Caulkins, J. P., & Hawken, A. (2011). *Drugs and drug policy: What everyone needs to know.* Oxford: Oxford University Press, pp. 198–201.

Chapter 16

1. Bergreen, L. (1994). *Capone: The man and the era.* New York: Touchstone, p. 86.

2. Abadinsky, H. (2010). *Organized crime.* Belmont, CA: Wadsworth.

3. Bell, D. (1964). *The end of ideology.* Glencoe, IL: The Free Press.

4. Smith, D. C. (1975). *The Mafia mystique.* New York: Basic Books.

5. Albanese, J. S. (1982). What Lockheed and La Cosa Nostra have in common. *Crime and Delinquency, 28,* 211–232.

6. Albanese, J. S. (2001). *The prediction and control of organized crime: A risk assessment instrument for targeting law enforcement efforts.* Research Partnership with Ukraine: Teaming U.S. Researchers and Practitioners with Ukrainian Counterparts to Research High Priority Crime Topics. Retrieved July 31, 2014, from http://www.ncjrs.gov/pdffiles1/nij/grants/199047.pdf

7. Reuter, P. (1987). *Racketeering in legitimate industries: A study in the economics of intimidation.* Santa Monica, CA: Rand Corporation.

8. Scarpitti, F. R., & Block, A. (1987). America's toxic waste racket: Dimensions of the environmental crisis. In T. S. Bynum (Ed.), *Organized crime in America: Concepts and controversies.* Monsey, NY: Willow Tree Press, 115–128; Block, A. A., & Scarpitti, F. R. (1985). *Poisoning for profit: The mafia and toxic waste in America.* New York: W. Morrow.

9. Szasz, A. (1986). Corporations, organized crime, and the disposal of hazardous waste: An examination of the making of a criminogenic regulatory structure. *Criminology, 2,* 1–28; Liddick, D. (2010). The traffic in garbage and hazardous wastes: an overview. *Trends in Organized Crime, 13,* 2/3, 134–146.

10. Jacobs, J. B., Friel, C., & Radick, R. (1999). *Gotham unbound: How New York City was liberated from the grip of organized crime.* New York: New York University Press, pp. 116–118.

11. Peters, T., & Waterman, R. (1982). *In search of excellence.* New York: Harper and Row.

12. Note 4.

13. Abadinsky, H. (1987). The McDonald's-ization of the Mafia. In T. S. Bynum (Ed.), *Organized crime in America: Concepts and controversies.* Monsey, NY: Willow Tree Press, pp. 43–54.

14. Finckenauer, J. O. (n.d.). La Cosa Nostra in the United States. United Nations Activities: Participating in the U.N.'s Crime Prevention Program. Retrieved October 5, 2005, from http://www.ncjrs.gov/pdffiles1/nij/218555.pdf

15. Ott, T. P. (2010). US law enforcement strategies to combat organized crime threats to financial institutions. *Journal of Financial Crime, 17,* 4, 375–386.

16. President's Commission on Law Enforcement and the Administration of Justice. (1967). *Task force report: Organized crime.* Washington, DC: U.S. Government Printing Office, p. 33.

17. Bonanno, J., & Lalli, S. (1983). *A man of honor: The autobiography of Joseph Bonanno.* New York: Simon and Schuster, pp. 40–41.

18. Gambetta, D. (1993). *The Sicilian Mafia: The business of private protection.* Boston: Harvard University Press, p. 139.

19. Maas, P. (1968). *The Valachi papers.* New York: G. P. Putnam's Sons, pp. 94–98.

20. Lombardo, R. M. (2010). The hegemonic narrative and the social construction of deviance: The case of the Black Hand. *Trends in Organized Crime, 13,* 263–282.

21. Albini, J. L. (1981). Reactions to the questioning of the Mafia myth. In I. L. Barak-Glantz & C. R. Huff (Eds.), *The mad, the bad and the different.* Lexington, MA: Lexington Books, pp. 125–134.

22. Note 5, p. 210.

23. Mastrofski, S., & Potter, G. (1987). Controlling organized crime: A critique of law enforcement policy. *Criminal Justice Policy Review, 2,* 275.

24. Pennsylvania Crime Commission. (1991). *Organized crime in Pennsylvania: A decade of change—1990 report.* Conshohocken: Commonwealth of Pennsylvania, pp. 103–104.

25. Haller, M. H. (1971). Organized crime in urban society: Chicago in the twentieth century. *Journal of Social History, 5,* 210–234.

26. Ianni, F. A. (1972). *A family business: Kinship and social control in organized crime.* New York: Russell Sage Foundation.

27. Albini, J. L. (1971). *The American Mafia: Genesis of a legend.* New York: Appleton-Century-Crofts.

28. McIllwain, J. S. (1999). Organized crime: A social network approach. *Crime, Law and Social Change, 32,* 301–323.

29. Haller, M. H. (1992). Bureaucracy and the Mafia: An alternative view. *Journal of Contemporary Criminal Justice, 8,* 1–10.

30. Block, A. (1978). History and the study of organized crime. *Urban Life, 6,* 455–474.

31. Pistone, J. D., & Woodley, R. (1987). *My undercover life in the Mafia: Donnie Brasco: A true story of an FBI agent.* New York: New American Library, pp. 202–225.

32. Note 24, p. 105.

33. Note 23, p. 276.

34. Lupsha, P. (1987). La Cosa Nostra in drug trafficking. In T. S. Bynum (Ed.), *Organized crime in America: Concepts and controversies.* Monsey, NY: Willow Tree Press, pp. 31–42.

35. Capeci, J. (2002). *The complete idiot's guide to the Mafia.* Indianapolis, IN: Alpha Press, p. 310.

36. Note 34, pp. 31–42.

37. President's Crime Commission on Law Enforcement and the Administration of Justice. (1967). *The challenge of crime in a free society.* Washington, DC: U.S. Government Printing Office.

38. Cressey, D. R. (1969). *The theft of a nation.* New York: Harper and Row.

39. Albanese, J. S. (1991). Organized crime: The Mafia mystique. In J. F. Sheley (Ed.), *Criminology: A*

contemporary handbook. Belmont, CA: Wadsworth, pp. 204–205.

40. Note 10, p. 128.
41. Bynum, T. S. (1987). Controversies in the study of organized crime. In T. S. Bynum (Ed.), *Organized crime in America: Concepts and controversies*. Monsey, NY: Willow Tree Press, pp. 3–12.
42. Note 14.
43. Lupsha, P. A. (1981). Individual choice, material culture, and organized crime. *Criminology, 19*, 3–24.
44. Note 23, pp. 280–281.
45. Packer, H. L. (1968). *The limits of the criminal sanction*. Palo Alto, CA: Stanford University Press.
46. Finklea, K. M. (2010). *Organized crime in the United States: Trends and issues for Congress*. Washington, DC: Congressional Research Service, p. 6.
47. Note 39, p. 213.
48. Note 23, p. 285.
49. Pagano, C. L. (1981). Organized crime control efforts: A critical assessment of the past decade. *The Police Chief, 48*, 20–25.
50. Dombrink, J., & Meeker, J. W. (1985). Racketeering prosecution: The use and abuse of RICO. *Rutgers Law Journal, 16*, 633–654.
51. Calder, J. D. (2000). RICO's troubled transition: Organized crime, strategic institutional factors, and implementation today. *Criminal Justice Review, 25*, 31–76.
52. Geary, W. R. (2002). The legislative recreation of RICO: Reinforcing the "myth" of organized crime. *Crime, Law and Social Change, 38*, 311–356; Blakely, G. R. (2006). RICO: The genesis of an idea. *Trends in Organized Crime, 9*, 4, 8–34.
53. Note 10, pp. 223–233.
54. Picarelli, J. (2011). Responding to transnational organized crime—Supporting research, improving practice. *NIJ Journal, 268*, 4–9.
55. Early, P., & Shur, G. (2003). *WITSEC: Inside the federal witness protection program*. New York: Bantam Books.
56. United States Marshals Service. *Witness security program*. Retrieved August 3, 2014, from http://www.usmarshals.gov/witsec/
57. Note 56.
58. Slate, R. N. (1997). The federal witness protection program: Its evolution and continuing growing pains. *Criminal Justice Ethics, 16*, 20–35.
59. Rowan, R. (1986, November 10). The 50 biggest Mafia bosses. *Fortune*, 25–28.
60. Capeci, J. (2005, January 17). What's left of the Mob. *New York Magazine*, 1–4.
61. Finckenauer, J. (2009). Organized crime. In M. Tonry (Ed.), *The Oxford handbook of crime and public policy*. New York: Oxford University Press, pp. 304–324.
62. Quinn, J. F. (2001). Angels, bandidos, outlaws, and pagans: The evolution of organized crime among the big four 1% motorcycle clubs. *Deviant Behavior, 22*, 379–399.
63. Quinn, J., & Koch, D. S. (2003). The nature of criminality within one-percent motorcycle clubs. *Deviant Behavior, 24*, 281–305.
64. Barker, T. (2004). Exporting American organized crime: Outlaw motorcycle gangs. *Journal of Gang Research, 11*, 37–50.
65. Barker, T. (2007). *Biker gangs and organized crime*. Cincinnati: Lexus Nexus.
66. Edwards, A., & Gill, P. (2002). Crime as enterprise? The case of transnational organized crime. *Crime, Law and Social Change, 37*, 203–223.
67. Zhang, S., & Chin, K. L. (2002). Enter the dragon: Inside Chinese human smuggling organizations. *Criminology, 40*, 737–768.
68. Finckenauer, J. O., & Voronin, Y. A. (2001). *The threat of Russian organized crime*. Washington, DC: U.S. Department of Justice, p. 1.
69. Finckenauer, J. O., & Waring, E. (2001, April). Challenging the Russian Mafia mystique. *National Institute of Justice Journal*, 6–7.
70. Rush, R. J., & Scarpitti, F. R. (2001). Russian organized crime: The continuation of an American tradition. *Deviant Behavior, 22*, 516–540.
71. Note 68, p. 5.
72. Note 69, pp. 4–5.
73. Note 46, p. 17.
74. Note 68, p. 27.
75. Serio, J. D. (2008). *Investigating the Russian Mafia*. Durham, NC: Carolina Academic Press.
76. Benson, M. L. (2009). White collar crime. In J. M. Miller (Ed.), *21st century criminology: A reference handbook*. Sage: Thousand Oaks, CA, p. 549.
77. Sutherland, E. H. (1949). *White collar crime*. New York: Dryden, p. 9.
78. Note 76.
79. Calavita, K., & Pontell, H. N. (1991). "Other people's money" revisited: Collective embezzlement in the savings and loan insurance industries. *Social Problems, 38*, 94.
80. Bohm, R. M. (1986). Crime, criminal and crime control policy myths. *Justice Quarterly, 3*, 195.
81. National White Collar Crime Center. (January 2013). *Health care fraud*. Fairmont, WV: National White Collar Crime Center, p. 3.
82. National White Collar Crime Center. (June 2008). *Credit card fraud*. Fairmont, WV: National White Collar Crime Center, p. 2.
83. Note 82.
84. Huff, R., Desilets, C., & Kane, J. (2010). *The 2010 national public survey on white collar crime*. Fairmont, WV: National White Collar Crime Center, p. 12.

85. Note 84, p. 8.

86. Note 84, pp. 8–9.

87. Cliff, G., & Desilets, C. (2014). White collar crime: What it is and where it's going. *Notre Dame Journal of Law, Ethics & Public Policy, 481*, 493–503.

88. Barnett, C. (2005). *The measurement of white-collar crime using Uniform Crime Reporting (UCR) data.* NIBRS Publication Series. Washington, DC: U.S. Department of Justice, Federal Bureau of Investigation, p. 6.

89. Wheeler, S., Weisburd, D., Bode, N., & Waring, E. (1988). White collar crime and criminals. *American Criminal Law Review, 25*, 331–357.

90. Nguyen, T. H., & Pontell, H. N. (2010). Mortgage origination fraud and the global economic crisis. *Criminology & Public Policy, 9*, 3, 591–612.

91. Note 84.

92. Moore, E., & Mills, M. (1990). The neglected victims and unexamined costs of white collar crime. *Crime and Delinquency, 36*, 408–418.

93. Note 76, pp. 549–550.

94. Meeker, J. W., Dombrink, J., & Pontell, H. N. (1987). White collar and organized crimes: Questions of seriousness and policy. *Justice Quarterly, 4*, 73–98.

95. Piquero, N. L., Carmichael, S., & Piquero, A. R. (2008). Research note: Assessing the perceived seriousness of white-collar and street crimes. *Crime and Delinquency, 54*, 2, 291–312.

96. Dodge, M., Bosick, S. J., & Van Antwerp, V. (2013). Do men and women perceive white-collar and street crime differently? Exploring gender differences in the perception of seriousness, motives and punishment. *Journal of Contemporary Criminal Justice, 29*, 3, 399–415.

97. Clinard, M. B., & Yeager, P. C. (1980). *Corporate crime.* New York: The Free Press.

98. Geis, G., & Goff, C. (1986). Edwin H. Sutherland's white collar crime in America: An essay in historical criminology. In L. A. Knafla, J. Cockburn, & E. Dwyer (Eds.), *Criminal justice history: An international annual.* Westport, CT: Meckler, pp. 1–31.

99. Kramer, R. C. (1984). Corporate criminality: The development of an idea. In E. Hochstedler (Ed.), *Corporations as criminals.* Beverly Hills, CA: Sage, pp. 13–38.

100. Rosoff, S. M., Pontell, H. N., & Tillman, R. H. (2013). *Profit without honor: White collar crime and the looting of America.* Upper Saddle River, NJ: Pearson-Prentice Hall.

101. Clinard, M. B. (1946). Criminological theories of violations of wartime regulations. *American Sociological Review, 11*, 258–270.

102. Clinard, M. B., & Quinney, R. (1973). *Criminal behavior systems: A typology.* New York: Holt, Rinehart and Winston.

103. Edelhertz, H. (1980). White collar and professional crime: The challenge for the 1980s. *American Behavioral Scientist, 27*, 109–128.

104. Hartung, F. E. (1950). White-collar offenses in the wholesale meat industry in Detroit. *American Journal of Sociology, 56*, 25–34.

105. Quinney, R. (1968). Occupational structure and animal behavior: Prescriptions violations by retail pharmacists. In G. Geis (Ed.), *White collar criminals.* New York: Atherton Press, pp. 190–221.

106. Geis, G. (1973). The heavy equipment antitrust cases of 1961. In M. B. Clinard & R. Quinney (Eds.), *Criminal behavior systems: A typology.* New York: Holt, Rinehart and Winston, pp. 139–150.

107. Shapiro, S. P. (1990). Collaring the crime, not the criminal: Reconsidering the concept of white collar crime. *American Sociological Review, 55*, 1346–1365.

108. Shover, N. (2009). Organizational crime and illegalities. In J. M. Miller (Ed.), *21st century criminology: A reference handbook.* Sage: Thousand Oaks, CA, p. 590.

109. Note 108, p. 593.

110. Green, G. (1996). *Occupational crime.* Belmont, CA: Wadsworth, pp. 15–16.

111. Tracy, P. E., & Fox, J. A. (1989). A field experiment on insurance fraud in auto body repair. *Criminology, 27*, 589–603.

112. Chambliss, W. J. (1989). State-organized crime. *Criminology, 27*, 184.

113. Kramer, R. C., & Michalowski, R. J. (2005). War, aggression and state crime: A criminological analysis of the invasion and occupation of Iraq. *British Journal of Criminology, 45*, 446–469.

114. Pontell, H. N., Jesilow, P. D., & Geis, G. (1982). Policing physicians: Practitioner fraud and abuse in a government medical program. *Social Problems, 30*, 116–125.

115. Geis, G., Jesilow, P., Pontell, H., & O'Brien, M. J. (1985). Fraud and abuse by psychiatrists against government medical benefit programs. *American Journal of Psychiatry, 142*, 231–234.

116. Jesilow, P. D., Pontell, H. N., & Geis, G. (1985). Medical criminals: Physicians and white collar offenses. *Justice Quarterly, 2*, 149–158.

117. Jesilow, P., Geis, G., & O'Brien, M. J. (1985). Is my battery any good? A field test of fraud in the auto repair business. *Journal of Crime and Justice, 8*, 1–20.

118. Jesilow, P., Geis, G., & O'Brien, M. J. (1986). Experimental evidence that publicity has no effect in suppressing auto repair fraud. *Sociology and Social Research, 70*, 222–233.

119. Note 99, p. 31.

120. Dowie, M. (1977). Pinto madness. *Mother Jones, 2*, 24.

121. Cullen, F. T., Maakestad, W. J., & Cavender, G. (1984). The Ford Pinto case and beyond: Corporate crime under attack. In E. Hochstedler (Ed.), *Corporations as criminals*. Thousand Oaks, CA: Sage, p. 120.

122. Cullen, F. T., Maakestad, W. J., & Cavender, G. (1987). *Corporate crime under attack: The Ford Pinto case and beyond*. Cincinnati: Anderson.

123. Note 79, p. 94.

124. Calavita, K., & Pontell, H. N. (1990). Heads I win, tails you lose: Deregulation, crime and crisis in the savings and loan industry. *Crime and Delinquency, 36*, 309–341.

125. Pontell, H. N., & Geis, G. (2014). The trajectory of white collar crime following the great economic meltdown. *Journal of Contemporary Criminal Justice, v30*, 1, 70–82.

126. Note 77.

127. Note 97.

128. Note 97.

129. Clinard, M. B., Yeager, P. C., Brissette, J. M., Petrashek, D., & Harries, E. (1979). *Illegal corporate behavior*. Washington, DC: U.S. Government Printing Office.

130. Wang, X., & Holtfreter, K. (2012). The effects of corporation and industry-level strain and opportunity on corporate crime. *Journal of Research in Crime and Delinquency, 49*, 2, 151–185.

131. Securities FraudFYI.com. (2005). How did Enron defraud shareholders? Retrieved January 4, 2005, from http://www.securitiesfraudfyi.com/enron_fraud.html

132. Note 100, p. 292.

133. Michalowski, R., & Kramer, R. (2003). Beyond Enron: Toward economic democracy and a new ethic of inclusion. *Risk Management: An International Journal, 5*, 37–47.

134. Coleman, J. W. (1985). *The criminal elite: The sociology of white collar crime*. New York: St. Martin's Press.

135. Barrett, K. L. (2013). Bethlehem Steel at Lackawanna: The state-corporate crimes that continue to victimize the residents and environment of Western New York. *Journal of Crime & Justice, 36*, 2, 263–282.

136. Kramer, R. C. (2013). Carbon in the atmosphere and power in America: Climate change as state-corporate crime. *Journal of Crime & Justice, 36*, 2, 153–170.

137. Simpson, S. S., Gibbs, C., Rorie, M., Slocum, L. E., Cohen, M. A., & Vandenbergh, M. (2013). An empirical assessment of corporate environmental crime-control strategies. *Journal of Criminal Law & Criminology, 103*, 1, 231–278.

138. Environmental Protection Agency. *What is environmental crime?* Retrieved August 6, 2014, from http://www2.epa.gov/enforcement/criminal-enforcement-what-environmental-crime

139. Federal Bureau of Investigation. *Dirty deeds— Enforcing environmental laws*. Retrieved August 6, 2014, from http://www.fbi.gov/news/stories/2006/july/envcrime072806

140. Villa, J. K. (1998). *Banking crimes*. New York: Clark Boardman.

141. Urban, R. (2002, December 10). 2 banks slammed for Enron activities. *Philadelphia Inquirer*, D1.

142. Office of the Comptroller of the Currency. (2002). *Money laundering: A banker's guide to avoiding problems*. Washington, DC: Author.

143. Weisburd, D., Chayet, E., & Waring, E. (1990). White-collar crime and criminal careers: Some preliminary findings. *Crime and Delinquency, 36*, 342–355.

144. Weisburd, D., Chayet, E., & Waring, E. (2001). *White-collar crime and criminal careers*. Cambridge, UK: Cambridge University Press.

145. Ragatz, L. L., Fremouw, W., & Baker, E. (2012). The psychological profile of white collar offenders: Demographics, criminal thinking, psychopathic traits, and psychopathology. *Criminal Justice & Behavior, 39*, 7, 978–977.

146. Arnulf, J. K., & Gottschalk, P. (2013). Heroic leaders as white-collar criminals: An empirical study. *Journal of Investigative Psychology and Offender Profiling, 10*, 96–113.

147. Stadler, W. A., & Benson, M. L. (2012). Revisiting the guilty mind: The neutralization of white-collar crime. *Criminal Justice Review, 37*, 4, 494–511.

148. Klenowski, G. (2012). Learning the good with the bad: Are occupational white-collar offenders taught to neutralize their crimes? *Criminal Justice Review, 37*, 4, 461–477.

149. Vieraitis, L. M., Piquero, N. L., Piquero, A. R., Tibbetts, S. G., & Blankenship, M. (2012). Do women and men differ in their neutralizations of corporate crime. *Criminal Justice Review, 37*, 4, 478–493.

150. Note 76, p. 551.

151. Gurney, J. N. (1985). Factors influencing the decision to prosecute economic crime. *Criminology, 23*, 609–628.

152. Benson, M. L., Maakestad, W. J., Cullen, F. T., & Geis, G. (1988). District attorneys and corporate crime: Surveying the prosecutorial gatekeepers. *Criminology, 26*, 505–518.

153. Scott, D. W. (1989). Policing corporate collusion. *Criminology, 27*, 559–587.

154. Schlegel, K. (1988). Desert, retribution, and corporate criminality. *Justice Quarterly, 5*, 615–634.

155. Note 76, p. 552.

156. Leaf, C. (2002, March 18). Enough is enough. *Fortune*, 61–76.

157. Benson, M. L. (1984). The fall from grace. *Criminology, 22*, 573–594.

158. Benson, M. L., & Cullen, F. T. (1988). The special sensitivity of white-collar offenders to prison: A critique and a research agenda. *Journal of Criminal Justice, 16,* 207–215.

159. Pollack, H. S., & Smith, A. B. (1983). White collar v. street crime sentencing disparity: How judges see the problem. *Judicature, 67,* 164–182.

160. Stadler, W. A., Benson, M. L., & Cullen, F. T. (2012). Revisiting the special sensitivity hypothesis: The prison experience of white-collar inmates. *Justice Quarterly, 30,* 6, 1090–1114.

161. Eitle, D. (2000). Regulatory justice: A re-examination of the influence of class position on the punishment of white-collar crime. *Justice Quarterly, 16,* 809–839.

162. Albonetti, C. A. (1998). The role of gender and departures in the sentencing of defendants convicted of white collar offenses under the federal sentencing guidelines. In J. T. Ulmer (Ed.), *Sociology of crime, law and deviance* (Vol. 1). Stamford, CT: Jai Press, pp. 3–48.

163. Holtfreter, K. (2013). Gender and "other people's money": An analysis of white-collar offender sentencing. *Women & Criminal Justice, 23,* 4, 326–344.

164. Van Slyke, S., & Bales, W. D. (2012). A contemporary study of the decision to incarcerate white-collar and street property offenders. *Punishment & Society, 14,* 2, 217–246.

165. Braithwaite, J. (1989). *Crime, shame and reintegration.* Oxford, UK: Cambridge University Press.

166. Braithwaite, J. (1989). Criminological theory and organizational crime. *Justice Quarterly, 6,* 346.

167. Benson, M. L. (1989). The influence of class position on the formal and informal sanctioning of white-collar offenders. *Sociological Quarterly, 30,* 465–479.

168. Benson, M. L. (1990). Emotions and adjudication: Status degradation ceremonies among white collar criminals. *Justice Quarterly, 7,* 515–528.

169. Croall, H. (2001). *Understanding white collar crime.* Buckingham, UK: Open University Press.

170. Wheeler, S., Mann, K., & Sarat, A. (1988). *Sitting in judgment: Sentencing the white-collar offender.* New Haven, CT: Yale University Press.

171. Wheeler, S., Weisburd, D., & Bode, N. (1982). Sentencing the white-collar offender: Rhetoric and reality. *American Sociological Review, 47,* 641–659.

172. Glater, D. (2002, July 28). Mad as Hell: Hard time for white collar criminals. *The New York Times,* wk 5.

173. Hagan, J., & Parker, P. (1985). White-collar crime and punishment: The class structure and legal sanctioning of securities violations. *American Sociological Review, 50,* 302–316.

174. Benson, M. L., & Walker, E. (1988). Sentencing the white collar offender. *American Sociological Review, 53,* 294–302.

175. Cohen, M. A. (1989). Corporate crime and punishment: A study of social harm and sentencing practice in the federal courts. *American Criminal Law Review, 26,* 605–660.

176. Bernard, T. J. (1984). The historical development of corporate criminal liability. *Criminology, 22,* 3–15.

177. Schwartz, M., & Ellison, C. (1982). Criminal sanctions for corporate misbehavior: A call for capitalist punishment. *Humanity and Society, 6,* 267–292.

178. McDermott, M. F. (1982). Occupational disqualification of corporate executives: An innovative condition of probation. *Journal of Criminal Law and Criminology, 73,* 628.

179. Note 100, pp. 595–597.

180. Note 2.

181. Note 5.

Glossary

adolescent-limited (AL) offenders In Moffitt's taxonomy of offenders, this group starts their deviance in their mid-teens, and desists from crime quickly.

adult social bonds An extension of Hirschi's social control theory from adolescence to adulthood. Adult social bonds include quality marriage and quality employment. They are a form of indirect control (something risked in order to engage in crime).

aggravated assault The "unlawful attack by one person upon another for the purpose of inflicting severe or aggravated bodily injury."

Al Qaeda A terrorist group with Islamic leanings that supports terror operations globally. Osama bin Laden, held to be the titular leader of Al Qaeda, is believed to have been involved in the planning of the 9/11 attacks on the United States.

alien conspiracy model Assumes that foreign criminals (e.g., Sicilians) imported the crime values and family structures into the United States and secretly control crime activities in this country.

altruism According to Bonger, altruism was a characteristic of primitive societies. In these societies, social solidarity was high, and individuals were more selfless and looked after one another's needs.

altruistic criminal Defined by Durkheim as a person somehow offended by the rules of society who wishes to change those rules for the better. This "criminal" is motivated by a sense of duty to improve society.

anomie Term coined by Durkheim to describe a state of affairs in which the norms and values of society weaken and are no longer able to control behaviors.

arson Any willful or malicious burning or attempting to burn, with or without intent to defraud, a dwelling house, public building, motor vehicle, aircraft, or personal property. The UCR categorizes the types of structures that are damaged by arson as structural, mobile, and other.

atavism Term used by Lombroso to describe people whom he believed were "evolutionary throwbacks" to a more primitive line of human beings.

aversion therapy The use of classical conditioning to reverse an unwanted relationship between a stimulus (e.g., alcohol) and a response (pleasure).

behavioral genetics The scientific study of how genes and heredity affect particular behaviors.

bourgeoisie Within Marxist theory, those who hold salaried and management positions.

brutalization effect A term used to illustrate the research finding that executions actually increase some forms of homicide.

burglary Defined under the UCR as the unlawful entry (whether or not force was used) of a structure (apartment, barn, house, house trailer, houseboat, office, railroad car, vessel) to commit a felony or theft. Burglary differs from robbery in that no interaction between the victim and offender may occur during the burglary, and thus there may be no violence against the victim during the crime.

capitalists Within Marxist theory, the owners of the means of production.

case law Law that is created when judges interpret constitutional provisions, statutes, or regulations created by administrative agencies.

Chicago Area Project (CAP) A large-scale delinquency prevention program developed by Shaw and McKay. The projects targeted high crime neighborhoods and created "community committees" to promote community organization; assigned "detached" local adults to neighborhood gangs; and made efforts to improve sanitation, traffic control, and physical decay.

child abuse Includes non-accidental physical injury; sexual abuse or exploitation; emotional or psychological injury; and neglect or maltreatment to a person under the age of 18 years (or the age specified by the law of the state).

chivalry hypothesis The idea that females are treated leniently by the criminal justice system because police, prosecutors, and judges are predominately male and have a gracious attitude toward women.

chronic offenders Persons who habitually engage in crime; in both Philadelphia birth cohorts (all persons born in 1945 and then 1958), the small group of offenders who were responsible for the bulk of serious crimes committed by the entire array.

classical conditioning By pairing an unconditioned stimulus (e.g., meat) with a conditioned stimulus (e.g., a bell), a conditioned response (e.g., salivation) is reproduced over time using only the conditioned stimulus.

code of the streets A set of informal rules that governs public behavior in some inner city neighborhoods. Caused in part by pervasive racism, joblessness, and alienation, the code emphasizes the importance of not being disrespected, or "dissed."

cognitive restructuring A rehabilitation technique in which criminal-thinking errors (cognitive distortions) are identified and contested.

cognitive skills programs Rehabilitation programs that attempt to build thinking skills, such as moral reasoning, empathy, and anger management.

cohort A group of individuals who share the same experience in time. Birth cohorts are often tracked to determine the groups that have the highest rates of offending.

collective efficacy The combination of social cohesion and informal social control within a neighborhood.

collective embezzlement Refers to company funds siphoned off for personal use by top management at the expense of the institution itself.

common criminal Defined by Durkheim as a person who rejects all laws and discipline and purposely violates the law without concern for the rightness of the acts.

concentrated disadvantage The idea that poverty and unemployment have become concentrated within certain neighborhoods, leaving isolated pockets of "truly disadvantaged" citizens.

concordance rate Focus of twin studies. The outcome (e.g., criminal behavior) is concordant if both twins exhibit the same behavior.

conflict model The belief that the law is the result of a battle between people or groups that have different levels of power. Control over the state (including the law and the criminal justice system) is the principal prize in the perpetual conflict of society.

conflict perspective View that criminal law is the result of constant clashes between groups with different levels of power. Those groups that win the clashes define the legal code in a manner consistent with their values.

conflict theory Theory that emphasizes a pluralistic perspective: Multiple groups within a society wield different levels of power.

consensus Widespread agreement in society that laws against crimes such as murder should be strictly enforced.

consensus model The belief that the law reflects common agreement over the fundamental values held by society.

consensus perspective View that criminal law is the result of widespread agreement among members of society as to what should be legal and illegal.

constitutional law The law as expressed in the U.S. Constitution, as well as the constitutions of individual states. Constitutions are the supreme law of the land.

contingency contract A tool to promote parental use of operant conditioning. Parents and children sign a contract that lays out expected behaviors, reinforcements, and consequences.

corporate crime Illegal acts by corporate officials to benefit the corporation.

correctional boot camps Like their military counterparts, these programs emphasize physical training and military drills. Research suggests that most of these programs have little effect on criminal behavior.

countertransference A term from psychoanalysis; when the client "pushes the buttons" of the counselor so that the resulting anger and hostility interferes with treatment.

CRAVED (concealable, removable, available, valuable, enjoyable, and disposable) The desirable attributes of stolen property.

crime displacement The idea that when crime is suppressed in one geographical area, it may simply shift to a new location.

crime prevention through environmental design (CPTED) A policy implication of routine activities theory. The way an environment is designed can promote or prevent crime.

criminal career perspective An area of criminology that characterized crime as a profession, like law or medicine, in that it involves the acquisition of specialized knowledge and skills. The focus on how crime develops over time now falls under the umbrella of life-course criminology.

criminal event In rational choice theory, decisions about how, when, and where of a particular crime.

criminal involvement In rational choice theory, decisions about whether to engage in crime in general, as opposed to satisfying needs and wants with noncriminal alternatives.

cumulative continuity An explanation for stability whereby initial deviant acts affect a person's environment in a negative way (e.g., job loss, peer rejection). These social outcomes then make desistence from deviance less likely.

cyberbullying Intentional, aggressive behavior that involves an imbalance of power that is performed through electronic means (i.e., high-tech devices).

cybercrime A criminal act that is committed using a computer that occurs over the Internet.

cyberpornography Promotion and the distribution of pornography using the computer or Internet.

defense mechanisms Psychological ploys that individuals use (often unconsciously) to reduce or eliminate anxieties.

delinquent ego Application of Freudian principles to describe an ego that effectively blocks any potential restraint from the conscience (superego) and permits the delinquent to rationalize criminal behavior.

delinquent superego Application of Freudian principles to describe a superego that is guided by a delinquent code of behavior rather than appropriate values.

deoxyribonucleic acid (DNA) Found on each chromosome, it contains the molecular code for all living organisms. DNA is made up of four chemicals, called bases, that bind together in different sequences on a sugar phosphate backbone.

desistence The cessation of offending and/or other antisocial behavior by individuals.

diffusion effect A process whereby the benefits of crime prevention efforts in one area may seep into adjoining areas. This is the reverse of the notion of crime displacement.

digital piracy The illegal act of copying digital goods, software, digital documents, digital audio (including music and voice), and digital video for a reason other than to back up without explicit permission from and compensation to the copyright holder.

distributive justice Campaign theme of liberal Democrats that contends that increased economic opportunity is the best defense against crime.

diversion programs Programs designed to divert juveniles away from official juvenile justice processing. A policy derived largely from labeling theory.

dizygotic (DZ) twins Fraternal twins who share the same amount of genetic similarity as non-twin siblings.

dramatization of evil Phrase coined by Frank Tannenbaum to characterize the process whereby the primary deviance of certain people is singled out and labeled as "bad."

economic-compulsive model of drug crime The offender commits a violent crime (e.g., murder or assault) during the course of a robbery. The addict commits crime to obtain money to support a drug habit.

ego The conscious part of the Freudian personality; the "psychological thermostat" that regulates the savage wishes and demands of the id and the social restrictions of the superego.

egoism A lack of consideration for others. According to Bonger, capitalism encourages selfishness, greed, and insensitivity to others.

enslavement theory of addiction This theory assumes that addicts are "slaves" to their habit and are driven to crime by the high cos t of drugs.

eugenics The goal of improving the human race through selective breeding. In the 20th century, eugenics led to limitations on the immigration of southern and eastern Europeans to the United States and the institutionalization or forced sterilization of the poor, deviant, and disabled.

extra-legal factors Characteristics such as race, class, and gender that can affect criminal justice decision making.

fearlessness theory An explanation of the relationship between low levels of arousal and antisocial behavior. This theory suggests that persons with low arousal are more likely to commit crime because punishment does not stimulate anxiety and fear.

felony murder Homicides committed while the offender is engaged in a separate felony offense (e.g., rape, robbery, arson).

fetal alcohol syndrome (FAS) A well-documented condition caused when pregnant women ingest high levels of alcohol. FAS is defined by a host of characteristics, including central nervous system dysfunction, growth retardation, and organ anomalies.

five-factor model A personality structure that includes five main personality dimensions: neuroticism, extraversion, openness to experience, agreeableness, and conscientiousness.

focused deterrence A strategy that narrowly tailors sanctions to specific individuals and/or specific criminal behaviors (e.g., handgun violence among gang members). This model also involves directly notifying offenders that they will be heavily sanctioned if they engage in the specified behavior.

free association A technique used in psychoanalysis in which the patient verbalizes uncensored—anything that comes to mind.

gender-ratio problem A key issue for criminologists is to explain the empirical observation that males account for the vast majority of delinquent and criminal offending.

gene A specific sequence of bases within a DNA molecule that works together to carry out a particular task.

general deterrence Punishing criminals so that the general public will get the message that crime doesn't pay.

generalizability problem Because most criminology theorists are male, mainstream criminological theories may not be applicable (i.e., may not generalize) to female offending.

genome The term used to describe an organism's complete set of DNA.

grand larceny Theft of property worth more than a certain amount of money, usually $300; considered a felony.

grand theories Sweeping theories that attempt to explain all types of criminal behavior.

hacking The activity of an individual or organization that attempts to access a computer system, network, or data source that does not have expressed consent from the system owner or operator.

headhunting Method of combating organized crime that focuses on the heads of criminal families and also seeks to freeze or seize the assets used in or obtained through organized crime.

hedonistic calculus Jeremy Bentham used this term to describe human nature—humans seek pleasure (hedonism) in a rational, calculating manner.

homicide The unlawful taking of life by another human.

Human Genome Project (HGP) Begun formally in 1990 and completed in 2006, the HGP was a coordinated effort by the U.S. Department of Energy and the National Institutes of Health to map the entire human genome.

hypotheses Testable statements about the relationship between variables in a scientific study.

id The unconscious, instinctual aspect of the Freudian personality. Id wishes often include the immediate gratification of basic drives (e.g., sex, aggression).

identity theft When someone uses your personally identifying information, such as your name, social security number, or credit card number, without permission, in order to commit fraud or other crimes.

incapacitation The use of prison and the death penalty to prevent crime by removing offenders from society.

index offenses The most serious crimes in the Uniform Crime Report: murder, rape, assault, burglary, larceny-theft, motor vehicle theft, and arson.

informal social control The perspective that inadequate or incomplete socialization leads to criminal behavior.

inner containment A form of internal control (good self-concept) from Walter Reckless' containment theory.

instrumental Marxism This type of Marxist theory argues that the law and criminal justice system are always instruments to be used by the capitalist class.

intensive supervision Practice based on the assumption that probation/parole officers with reduced caseloads can more effectively monitor and supervise high-risk offenders. This practice also has been touted as a potential solution to jail- and prisoncrowding problems.

intensive supervision probation (ISP) Offenders are supervised in the community under strict conditions, including frequent drug testing, curfews, and contacts with a probation officer. These programs were designed to increase the punishing aspect of probation. Research suggests that ISP programs do not reduce criminal behavior any more than traditional probation.

intimate partner homicide (IPH) A type of homicide in which the offender and victim are current or former intimate partners.

intimate partner violence Encompasses both spousal abuse and violence that occurs between couples who are not living together. It includes rape or sexual assault, robbery, aggravated assault, and simple assault committed by the victim's current or former spouse, boyfriend, or girlfriend.

just deserts A justification for punishment (e.g., prison) that emphasizes the pain caused and thus earned by the criminal. Punishment serves as a collective expression of society's disapproval for criminal acts.

Kansas City Preventive Patrol Study An experimental study of police patrols. The main conclusion from this experiment was that increased police presence has little effect on crime. Later research suggests that more dramatic increases in police presence can suppress crime.

labeling The perspective that a change in a person's self-concept, caused by criminal justice actions, may increase criminal behavior.

larceny-theft The unlawful taking or attempted taking of property from another person.

law and order Campaign theme of conservative Republicans that a "hard line" is the best defense.

laws of imitation An early form of social learning theory. Gabriel Tarde identified three laws to explain how criminals learned to engage in crime.

leaderless resistance Articulated by Louis Beam, this model of organizational structure is designed to avoid infiltration.

legal cynicism A set of cultural values that arise in communities with concentrated disadvantage and coercive policing. The law and the police come to be viewed as ineffective and illegitimate.

legal factors Factors such as offense seriousness and prior record that play a role in criminal justice decision making.

legitimacy of the law The belief in the rightness of and public support for a law.

life-course criminology An area of criminology that seeks to understand crime and its precursor behavior from childhood through adulthood. Central to this area is explaining the onset and persistence of criminal or antisocial behavior and desistence from offending. Some scholars refer to this as developmental criminology.

life-course-persistent (LCP) offenders A developmental pathway within Moffitt's theory of offending. LCP offenders exhibit deviance throughout their lives. This pathway is hypothesized by a biosocial interaction between biology (neurological deficits) and environment (social class, parenting, etc.). They are akin to the "chronic offenders" described in cohort studies.

limbic system A region of the brain located beneath the outer cortex that includes the hippocampus, amygdala, and thalamus. This more primitive area of the brain houses emotional life.

local, ethnic group model Maintains that organized crime families have a decentralized structure and focus on operating businesses.

looking-glass self The idea that self-concept is formed based on how other people respond to and react toward a person.

low self-control The key form of internal control in Gottfredson and Hirschi's general theory of crime. The authors believe that effective parenting produces self-control in children.

lumpenproletariat Within Marxist theory, the dispossessed, unorganized workers.

Mafia code Secret oaths and norms that govern behavior within organized crime families by maintaining secrecy and promoting loyalty, respect, and discipline.

mala in se Crimes that are considered as "evil in themselves" (e.g., homicide).

mala prohibita Crimes that are forbidden by laws that attempt to regulate behavior (e.g., drug abuse, gambling, prostitution).

marginal deterrence The idea that incremental increases in the certainty or severity of punishment should produce decreases in criminal behavior.

market society A country (such as the United States) where the capitalist economy dominates all other spheres of life. This is a sink-or-swim society that does not provide a strong safety net for citizens.

mass murder The intentional antisocial and non–state-sponsored killing of multiple victims during a single episode at one or more closely related locations. It has also been termed *autogenic (self-generated) massacre* because it involves individuals who kill in pursuit of personal goals—the killing is generated from the offender's problems, attitudes, and psychopathology.

mechanical solidarity Term used by Durkheim to describe rural societies that are homogeneous, cohesive, and self-sufficient.

middle-class measuring rod Term used by Cohen to describe a school system that favored middle-class dress, mannerisms, and etiquette. Cohen argued that lower-class boys were often unable to meet these standards, and therefore experienced strain, or "status frustration."

Mobilization for Youth Program (MFY) A program that Cloward and Ohlin actively supported. MFY attempted to attack the root causes of crime in New York City's Lower East Side by securing social services and establishing political structures in lower-class neighborhoods. The program became embroiled in political struggles with city officials, was investigated by the FBI (but exonerated of any wrongdoing), and ultimately disappeared.

molecular genetics The study of the expression of genes accomplished by identifying the DNA sequences of chromosomes.

monoamine oxidase A (MAOA) An enzyme that breaks down neurotransmitters so that they can be removed from the body. The genes for MAOA and direct measures of this enzyme have been linked to crime.

monozygotic (MZ) twins Identical twins who are products of a single egg and sperm, and thus are exactly the same genetically.

moral entrepreneurs Describes individuals (in the context of labeling theory) who seek to pass laws that prohibit particular behaviors.

motor vehicle theft Theft or attempted theft of a motor vehicle.

National Crime Victimization Survey (NCVS) A survey conducted since 1972 by the U.S. Bureau of Justice Statistics that attempts to uncover unreported crime by surveying victims. The NCVS is a representative sample drawn of about 60,000 U.S. households that is renewed every year.

National Incident-Based Reporting System (NIBRS) A system designed to collect a greater number of details than the UCR about crimes reported to the police. The NIBRS will contain information on both reported crime and arrests. It will eventually replace the UCR as the official source of crime information from police departments as reported to the FBI. NIBRS will contain information on 46 Group A offenses that represent 22 categories, rather than concentrate on the eight index offenses from the UCR. Unlike the UCR, NIBRS will make a distinction between attempted and completed crimes, provide more inclusive definitions of crime (i.e., the definition of rape has been expanded to include male victims), and will count all offenses that occur during an incident rather than concentrating on only the most serious crime.

negative reinforcement The removal of a noxious stimulus (e.g., bad smell) to increase a target behavior.

observational learning Learning behavior by observing and modeling the behavior of others.

occupational crime Illegal acts arising from opportunities created in the course of a legal occupation.

operant conditioning The use of reinforcement and punishment to shape behavior.

overdeveloped superego Application of Freudian principles to describe a superego that causes a person to seek out punishment.

organic solidarity Term used by Durkheim to describe industrial societies, which are more complex and based on exchanges of goods and services.

organized crime Criminal activity conducted by any group with some manner of formalized structure. The primary objective of organized crime groups is to obtain money through illegal activities.

outer containment A form of indirect control (supervision) from Walter Reckless' containment theory.

overgeneralization Jumping to sweeping conclusions based on the results of a single study.

overreach of the criminal law Norval Morris and Gordon Hawkins contend that the attempt to govern public order offenses like prostitution causes a number of secondary problems that aggravate the crime problem.

panaceas Cure-alls. Applied to criminology, the term refers to the search for simple solutions to the crime problem.

patriot and militia movement Active in the 1990s, this movement was characterized by paramilitary training and a deep-rooted fear of tyranny at the hands of the federal government. It lost considerable support after the sense of panic that Y2K caused waned.

people with serious mental illness (PSMI) Individuals who have a mental illness, such as schizophrenia, bipolar disorder, or major depression, that is defined by the law as serious.

personality The sum of personality traits that defines a person.

personality trait A characteristic of an individual that is stable over time and across different social circumstances.

petit larceny Theft of property worth less than $300; considered a misdemeanor.

primary conflict A concept from Thorsten Sellin's culture conflict theory. Primary conflict may arise between an established culture and a less powerful culture. For example, recent immigrants may conduct themselves based on codes from the old country that may be criminal in the dominant culture.

primary deviance Deviant behavior that occurs prior to any official reaction. Labeling theorists portray primary deviance as sporadic and relatively unimportant.

positive reinforcement The use of rewards (e.g., praise, money, tokens) to increase a target behavior.

policy analysis Focuses on the condition the government wishes to create rather than on the root causes of crime.

prefrontal cortex The part of the brain responsible for "executive functions" (i.e., abstract reasoning, the ability to sustain attention, self-monitoring, and the inhibition of impulsive behavior). Biological studies suggest that deficiencies in this region of the brain may lead to a criminal disposition.

procedural law The portion of the criminal law that dictates the type of behaviors in which criminal justice actors can legally engage.

Project on Human Development in Chicago Neighborhoods (PHDCN) A program where researchers interviewed almost 9,000 residents within 343 Chicago neighborhoods. Research results have largely supported the theory of collective efficacy.

proletariat Within Marxist theory, the working class.

psychopharmacological model of drug crime Violent crime is a result of the effect of the drug on the offender and/or the victim. In short, the drug sponsors irrational and violent behavior.

pulling levers An approach to policing where police use all available legal mechanisms to sanction those offenders who fail to heed explicit warnings against continuing specific crimes. This approach has been employed in focused deterrence strategies.

punishment The presentation of a noxious stimulus (e.g., spanking, scolding) to decrease a target behavior.

racial invariance hypothesis The idea that race differences in crime are due to differences in where people live. Because nonwhites are more apt to live in areas of concentrated disadvantage, they experience higher rates of crime.

racial profiling Racially biased law enforcement; targeting individuals for law enforcement based primarily on their race.

racial threat hypothesis The idea that as minority populations increase relative to the white population, they will be viewed as a threat and punitive measures against them will increase.

radical theory Theoretical perspective that emphasizes conflict between the wealthy elite and the rest of society.

rape Unlawful sexual intercourse by force or without legal or factual consent.

recidivism Repeat offending.

relational goal pursuit theory People tend to seek and possess relationships with others that they view as both desirable and feasible. Under this theory, stalkers continue to pursue relationships that the other person does not desire.

repeat offender program (ROP) Projects that selectively focus police resources on career criminals and take a proactive approach. Police target offenders and try to catch them in the act.

restorative justice A general philosophy that the proper role of the criminal justice system is to repair the harm caused by an offense. Victim–offender mediation is a central program in this perspective.

retribution Similar to just deserts, retribution is a justification for punishment that suggests that criminals deserve punishment because they have violated the legal code from which everyone benefits.

robbery The taking or attempting to take anything of value from the care, custody, or control of a person or persons by force, threat of force or violence, and/or by putting the victim in fear.

Seattle Social Developmental Project (SSDP) A project that implements many of the policy implications from the social control theory in an attempt to prevent childhood aggression and delinquency. The project attempts to increase direct control over youth, as well as to build attachment to parents and teachers and a commitment to education.

secondary conflict Concept from Thorsten Sellin's culture conflict theory. Secondary conflict occurs within a single culture that has different subcultures, each with its own conduct norms.

secondary deviance Deviance that is caused by the adoption of a delinquent self-concept. Without an official reaction to crime, secondary deviance would not be possible.

selective incapacitation Strategies that seek to identify and incarcerate chronic offenders for long periods of time in order to reduce crime.

sensation seeking theory An explanation of the relationship between low levels of arousal and antisocial behavior. This theory suggests that low arousal is an unpleasant state, and therefore causes people to seek out stimulating behaviors.

serial murder The killing of a number of people, usually three or more, over the course of more than a month.

serotonin A neurotransmitter that helps conduct the electrical impulses in the brain; low levels of serotonin hinder communication between cells. Research links low levels of serotonin with criminal behavior.

shaming Punishment of white-collar criminals by confronting them with the seriousness of their conduct while forgiving and reintegrating those who reform.

shoplifting Unlawful attempted or accomplished concealing, taking, and carrying away of goods from a commercial establishment.

skin conductance A method for measuring how an individual's fingers sweat. Although research is mixed, some studies find that criminals have lower skin conductance than noncriminals.

social bond From Hirschi's control theory. The social bond ties individuals to society so that they are not free to engage in crime. Elements of the bond include attachment, commitment, involvement, and belief.

social ecology The study of how human relationships are affected by a particular environment (the Chicago School is based on social ecology).

socialization The gradual process whereby a person learns the "proper" way to live, including the norms and values that guide human behavior.

social learning The perspective that socialization toward the wrong norms and values produces criminal behavior.

somatotype The classification of human body types into three categories. Sheldon argued that body type relates to a person's personality or disposition. Endomorphs are fat, soft, and round, and they tend to be extroverts. Ectomorphs are thin and wiry, and they are easily worried, sensitive, and introverted. Mesomorphs are muscular, gregarious, aggressive, assertive, and action oriented. Some research suggests that the mesomorph is the dominant body type among delinquents.

specific deterrence Punishing criminals so that they will be less likely to commit crimes in the future.

stalking A pattern of harassing or threatening tactics used by a perpetrator that is both unwanted and causes fear or safety concerns in the victim.

state-organized crime Illegal acts committed by state officials in the course of their job as representatives of the state.

statutory law Criminal code created by legislatures and governing bodies.

structural Marxism This type of Marxist analysis grants the government (at least in the short term) a degree of political autonomy. Some laws may run counter to the desires of the capitalists.

superego The conscience of the Freudian personality—the keeper of prohibitions ("Stealing is wrong") and wishes about what one wants to be ("I am going to be just like my father when I grow up").

superstructure The system of social institutions (e.g., law, education, and politics) that lend legitimacy to capitalist arrangements.

swift-certain-fair (SCF) model Programs that emphasize swift and certain sanctions. In the HOPE program, those who fail drug tests are immediately arrested and jailed for short periods.

symbolic interactionism A general perspective within sociology that emphasizes communication through symbolic labels and gestures.

systemic model of drug crime Some violent crimes are committed as a result of the pattern of drug use and distribution. These crimes represent an outgrowth of the system of drug dealing (e.g., gang wars) or reflect disputes between dealers and consumers (e.g., poor-quality drugs, failure to make payment) within a black market, elimination of informers, and robberies of drug dealers followed by retaliation.

techniques of neutralization Common excuses for delinquency identified by Sykes and Matza. These excuses neutralize the guilt associated with criminal behavior. This represents one of the first attempts to measure Sutherland's concept of "definitions favorable to law violation."

terrorism The use or implied use of force, violence, and/or coercion to influence the political, social, and/or religious attitudes and behaviors of individuals or groups in a desired manner.

testosterone For the embryo carrying a Y sex chromosome, the hormone responsible for development into a male fetus. Testosterone influences secondary sex characteristics (e.g., body hair, muscle mass). Research consistently demonstrates a relationship between levels of testosterone and aggression.

theory of differential association Edwin Sutherland's influential learning theory. He proposed that crime is learned in intimate groups through communication.

Timothy McVeigh A U.S. Army veteran, who, along with Terry Nichols, perpetrated the bombing of the Murrah Federal Building. McVeigh received the death penalty for his crimes.

token economy Application of operant conditioning to corrections. Individuals are reinforced and punished using "tokens" that can be exchanged for privileges.

transference A term from psychoanalysis to describe when the client uses the counselor as a "stand in" from the past.

tweaking The violence against each other in which cocaine dealers routinely engage, in an attempt to control the drug market.

typology A framework and theoretical construct that is used to describe and compare different forms of criminal behavior.

Uniform Crime Report (UCR) An annual report, published by the FBI since 1930, consisting of crimes reported to and uncovered by the police. Currently, the UCR is the major source of nationwide crime data, containing information from most U.S. jurisdictions.

value free The belief that researchers should keep their personal views out of their study and the interpretation of its findings. Objectivity is the goal.

victimless crimes Crimes that affect only the person committing them. Because of the absence of a complaining victim, some people question whether it is appropriate to label activities such as gambling and prostitution as crimes.

weed-and-seed strategy A federal initiative designed to reduce violent crime, drug abuse, and gang activity in targeted high crime neighborhoods across the country. The "weeding out" involves targeting chronic violent offenders for incapacitation. The "seeding" consists of programs designed to bring human services to the area and promote economic and physical revitalization to neighborhoods.

white-collar crime Deliberately harmful, illegal acts committed by persons of respectability and high social status in the course of their occupation.

XYY A rare chromosome abnormality in which a male (typically XY) has an extra Y chromosome. Early research suggested that these individuals were unusually aggressive ("supermales"). Later research indicated that they are no more violent than others, but they are perhaps slightly more crime prone.

zone in transition In Burgess' concentric zone theory, this is the geographical area just outside the business district. Research by Shaw and McKay confirmed that the zone in transition had consistently high crime rates from 1900–1930.

Index

feminist criminology, 187–188

fetal alcohol syndrome (FAS), 82, 91

"fetishism" of money, 130

financial crimes, 346

firearms, homicides and availability of, 217–218

fireplay, 252

first-degree murder, 214–215, 214*t*

first offender prostitution program (FOPP), 277

fish consumption, 84

five-factor model, 106, 114

focused deterrence, 64

    theory, 52–54

folkways, 4

FOPP. *See* first offender prostitution program

forcible rape, 30*t*

Ford Motor Co., Pinto scandal, 349

Ford Pinto case, 349

forensic psychology, 94

fornication, 265

fraud masters, 197

free association, 96, 114

Freud, Sigmund, 96

Freudian elements of personality, 96

Freudian theory, 97–98

Fuk Ching gang, 348

Furman v. Georgia, 48, 49, 176

G

gambling, 269–272

gangs, 132, 318

gender issues

    bias and conflict theory, 170

    criminal justice system and, 190

    feminist criminology, 187–188

    gender-ratio problem, 188–189

    generalizability problem, 188, 189–190

gender-ratio problem, 188–189

gene, 75, 91

gene-linkage analysis, 75

gene–environment interactions, 78

General Accounting Office (GAO), 177

general deterrence, 45–49, 64

General Social Survey (GSS), 299

general strain theory (GST), 129, 130*f*, 137*t*

General Theory of Crime, A (Gottfredson and Hirschi), 154–156, 155*f*

generalizability problem, 189–190

"Genetic Factors and Crime", 72

genetics

    behavioral, 72–79

    language of, 76–77

    molecular, 75–79

genome, 77, 91

gentlemen rapists. *See* power-reassurance rapists

geocoding, 125

geographical information systems (GIS), 125

"get-tough" movement, 44

GIS. *See* geographical information systems

GLM. *See* Good Lives Model

Goldstein models, 312–315, 320

Good Lives Model (GLM), 204

grand larceny, 253, 259

Grand Theft Auto (GTA), 101

grand theories, 10, 24

Gregg v. Georgia, 177

GST. *See* general strain theory

GTA. *See* Grand Theft Auto

gun control debate, 217–220

gun ownership, 217

H

hacking, 301–302, 305

Hagedorn, John, 133

Hamas, 285, 286

Harrison Narcotics Act (1914), 267, 308

Hawaii's Opportunity Probation Enforcement (HOPE) program, 51

Hawala, 286

headhunting, 340–343, 357

hedonistic calculus, 13, 24

heroin, 267, 321

    addicts, 311

Hezbollah, 282, 286, 287

HGP. *See* Human Genome Project

high rate offenders, 250

high-rise public housing projects, 118

    demolition of, 126

Hirschi's social bond theory, 152–154, 153*f*

hit stalker, 231

home visitation programs, 209

Homeland Security Act (2002), 291

homicide, 214–220, 243

    circumstances leading to, 216

    drug-related, 312, 314, 315*t*

    examples of different forms of, 214*t*

    explaining America's homicide rate, 217–220

    murder levels and trends, 215–216

    offender and victim characteristics, 216–217

methamphetamine (meth), 319–320

MFY. *See* Mobilization for Youth Program

micro-level theory, 11

middle-class measuring rod, 132, 140

MIECHV. *See* Maternal, Infant and Early Childhood Home Visiting

millenarianism, 285

Minnesota Multiphasic Personality Inventory (MMPI), 106

misdemeanors (petty crimes), 5

MMPI. *See* Minnesota Multiphasic Personality Inventory

Mobilization for Youth Program (MFY), 134, 136, 140–141

modeling theory, 100–101, 102

Moffitt's theory, 86–87, 203, 203t

molecular genetics, 73t, 75–79, 91

money laundering, 351, 352

Monitoring the Future (MTF), 319t

monoamine oxidase A (MAOA), 77, 78, 91

monozygotic (MZ) twins, 73, 74, 91

moral entrepreneurs, 159, 166, 263–266, 266–267

moral insanity, 107

More Guns, Less Crime: Understanding Crime and Gun Control Laws, 219–220

mores, 4

Morphine, 308

Mosaic Code of the Israelites, 5

Mothers Against Drunk Driving (MADD), 264, 265

motor vehicle theft (MVT), 30t, 255–257, 259
    patterns of, 255–256

Moving to Opportunity (MTO) program, 125

MPQ. *See* Multidimensional Personality Questionnaire

MRI. *See* magnetic resonance imaging

MST. *See* multisystemic therapy

MTF. *See* Monitoring the Future

MTO program. *See* Moving to Opportunity program

multicide, 220–224
    mass murder, 220–222
    serial murder, 222–224

Multidimensional Personality Questionnaire (MPQ), 106, 106t, 109

multiple homicide offenders, 224

multisystemic therapy (MST), 15, 104, 105, 210

murder, 30t, 214–216
    levels and trends, 215–216

Murrah Federal Building, Oklahoma City, 284–285, 291–292

MVT. *See* motor vehicle theft

MZ twins. *See* monozygotic twins

N

narco-terrorism, 287, 288

National Coalition Against Legalized Gambling (NCALG), 271

National Crime Victimization Survey (NCVS), 29, 41, 225, 246
    compared with UCR, 31t, 33t
    description of, 33–34, 33t
    limitations of, 36

National Incident-Based Reporting System (NIBRS), 32–33, 41, 346, 346t
    compared with UCR, 32t

National Institute on Alcohol Abuse and Alcoholism, 84

National Institute on Drug Abuse, 318

National Institutes of Health (NIH), 72, 77

National Insurance Crime Bureau (NICB), 257

National Longitudinal Study of Adolescent Health (Add Health), 77

National Violence Against Women Survey (NVAWS), 225

National Youth Survey (NYS), 59, 150, 198, 317

Nazi, 286

NCALG. *See* National Coalition Against Legalized Gambling

NCVS. *See* National Crime Victimization Survey

Neapolitan Camorra, 352

negative reinforcement, 98, 99, 114

neighborhood watch programs, 125, 127

neoclassical theory, 14
    deterrence theory, 45–55
        absolute, 45
        celerity, 55
        elements of, 45, 46t
        empirical tests of, 45, 46t
        focused, 52–54
        general, 45–49
        marginal, 45
        perceptual, 54
        specific, 45, 51–52
        summary of, 55
    lifestyle approach, 58–59
    rational choice theory, 55–57
    rise of, 44–45
    routine activities theory, 57–58, 57f

personality trait, 104, 115
  and crime, 106–107
personality–crime research, 107
PET scans. *See* positron emission tomography
  scans
petit larceny, 253, 259
PFLP. *See* Popular Front for the Liberation of
  Palestine
PHDCN. *See* Project on Human Development in
  Chicago Neighborhoods
phrenology, 68–69
physical deficiencies, 69–70
PIB. *See* Public Integrity Bureau
PIJ. *See* Palestine Islamic Jihad
Piracy and Counterfeiting Amendments
  Act of 1982, 297
PMS. *See* premenstrual syndrome
police presence, deterrence and, 50
policing street prostitution, 276–277
policy analysis, 20, 25
political stalker, 231
politics, influence on criminal justice policy,
  19–20
Popular Front for the Liberation of Palestine
  (PFLP), 286
pornography, cyber, 299
positive reinforcement, 98, 99, 115
positivism, 14
positivist school of crime, 12*t*, 14
positron emission tomography (PET) scans, 80
poverty, 123
power-assertive rapists, 227
power rapists, 227
power-reassurance rapists, 227
prefrontal cortex, 80, 91
premeditation, 215
premenstrual syndrome (PMS), 85
prevention, 208–210
primary conflict, 178, 192
primary deviance, 160, 166
Principles of Criminology (Sutherland), 145
principles of learning, 98–102
prison population, statistics on, 38
private stranger stalkers, 231
probation, statistics on, 39
problem-oriented policing, 54, 125
procedural law, 6, 25
professional burglars, 249
professional fence, 197
Professional Thief, The (Sutherland), 197

prohibition, 266–267, 277, 309
Project on Human Development in Chicago
  Neighborhoods (PHDCN), 122
projection, Freudian defense mechanisms, 97*t*
proletariat, 179, 192
property crime
  arson, 251–253
  burglary, 246–251
  estimation rate of, 246*t*
  larceny-theft, 253–255
  MVT, 255–257
  trends, 246
  victimization, 246, 247*t*
proposition, 58, 205, 206*t*
prostitutes, types of, 272–273
prostitution, 272–274, 276–277
  and commercialized vice, 1995–2012,
    arrest for, 272*t*
  dangers of, 273–274, 276
  entry into profession, 273
  streetwalkers, 272–273
  types of prostitutes, 272–273
  views of, 273
"pseudo-commando" style massacre, 221
PSMI. *See* people with serious mental illness
psychoanalytic/psychodynamic theory, 94–98
psychodynamic theory, 111*t*
psychological abuse, 228
psychological theories
  behaviorism
    policy implications of, 102–103
    principles of learning, 98–102
  cognitive, 103–104
  intelligence and crime, 109–111
  personality and crime, 104–109
  psychoanalytic/psychodynamic theory, 94–98
  summary of, 111, 112*t*
psychological thermostat, 96
psychopath, 107–109
Psychopathy Checklist (PCL), 107, 108
psychopharmacological model of drug crime,
  313, 329
psychoticism, 109
public figure stalkers. *See* celebrity stalker
public housing projects, 118
Public Integrity Bureau (PIB), 37
public order crimes, 262–263, 262*t*, 278
  drugs, alcohol, moral entrepreneurs, and
    interest groups, 266–267
  gambling, 269–272

S

sadistic rapists, 227
Safe Cities Program, 60, 61
Sampson age graded theory of social control,
    201–202, 201f
savings and loan (S&L) scandal, 349
Scared Straight!, 53–54
SCF model. *See* swift-certain-fair model
school violence, statistics on, 35
scientific method, 14
scientific theory, 8
scope, 10
scripts of violence, 223
search warrants, sneak-and-peak, 6
Seattle Social Developmental Project (SSDP),
    157, 166
second-degree murder, 214t, 215
secondary conflict, 178, 193
secondary deviance, 161, 166
selective incapacitation, 207, 211
self-control, 234
    theory, 205, 206t
self-generated massacre. *See* autogenic massacre
self-protection, 217
Selfish Gene, The (Dawkins), 87
semiprofessional shoplifters, 254
sensation seeking theory, 81, 91
September 11, 2001 attacks, 282
serial arsonists, 252–253
serial murder, 222–224, 243
    characteristics of, 222–223
    typology of, 223–224
serotonin, 80, 91
sex trafficking, 275
sex work, 274, 276
sexual assault
    defined, 224
    evolutionary perspective on, 87–88
shaming, 354, 355, 357
Shanghai Opium Commission, 308
shining path, 287–288
shock incarceration. *See* correctional
    boot camps
shoplifting, 253, 259
    criminal justice system response to, 254–255
    focus on, 254
short-term deterrent effect, 52
single homicide offenders, 224
Sisters in Crime (Adler), 188
situational crime prevention techniques, 60, 61t
situational prevention, 59–62

skin conductance, 81, 91
S&L scandal. *See* savings and loan scandal
SLA. *See* Symbionese Liberation Army
Snakes in Suits: When Psychopaths Go to Work
    (Bibiak), 109
social bond theory, 152–154, 153f, 156, 164t, 166
social control, informal, 144, 151–158, 166
social disorganization theory, 121–127,
    122f, 137t
   policy implications, 125–127
social ecology, 120–127, 141
    concentric zone theory, 120, 120f
    policy implications, 125–127
social institutions, 121
social interactional theory, 100, 100f
social learning theories, 102, 144, 150–151, 158,
    166, 232, 299
   from differential association to, 146–150
   policy implications, 150–151
social process theories, 144–165
   age-graded, 156
   containment, 151–152, 152t
   differential association, 145–151, 167
   informal social control theories, 144,
    151–158, 166
   labeling, 145, 158–161, 163, 166
   laws of imitation, 145
   low self-control, 154, 155, 155f, 164t, 166
   relationship between Chicago School and,
    144, 144f
   restorative justice, 162, 163, 166
   social bond theory, 152–154, 153f, 156,
    164t, 166
   social learning theories, 144, 145–151, 166
   summary of, 163, 164t
social revolution, 180
social structural theories, 137t–138t
   deviant places, 123–124, 124t
   differential opportunity, 132–133, 133t, 138t
   focal concerns of lower class, 133–134,
    133t, 138t
   general strain, 129, 130f, 137t
   hot spots of criminal behavior, 124–125
   institutional anomie, 129–131, 131f, 137t
   race, place, and crime, 122–123
   relationships among, 136, 136f
   social disorganization theory, 121–127, 122f
   social ecology, 120–127
   status frustration, 132, 137t
   strain/anomie, 127–131
   underclass, concerns of, 123